Merry Christmas!
To Dad
with Love,
Tiffany 1986

CHRISTMAS 1986

ATLAS of CALIFORNIA

MICHAEL W. DONLEY

STUART ALLAN

PATRICIA CARO

CLYDE P. PATTON

ACKNOWLEDGEMENTS

Many people have assisted in the compilation and production of this atlas. Our principal thanks go to the members of the atlas staff, whose able devotion made it possible to do the job in a remarkably short and pleasant time. Elizabeth Suwijn's abilities as a designer and producer of maps were invaluable; her skill and administrative responsibility made her the mainstay of the production staff and considerably lightened our load. Barbara Bulas, cartographer and researcher, and Houghton C. Knight, scriber and graphic artist, were an indispensable team whose precision and imagination enhanced every page. To these three, who shared our concerns almost from the beginning, our very special thanks. Equally heartfelt is our gratitude to the many others who also helped. Deborah Balaam was chiefly responsible for the Index and Gazetteer, and lent her cheer and ability to other aspects of compilation and production. Brian Coffey, Mary Lee Donley, Peter Teensma and Caren Tracy devoted their energies to a wide range of tasks. Linda Siskind, Gail Schraeger, Karen Thomas and Peg Falconer provided essential research and production assistance. Special thanks go to Sally Sharrard for generous help on page design, to Charles Bigelow for valuable advice on typography, to Jay Baker of McKenzie River Graphics for photographic services provided with professional competence and helpful interest, and to Patti Morris and Martin White of Irish Setter for accurate, timely and discriminating typesetting. The dust jacket photograph was taken by William A. Garnett. The photographs for the four divider pages were taken and separated by Timothy Nuckolls.

A great many people provided information, maps and advice on individual pages. We would particularly like to thank the many federal and state government workers whose interest in, and knowledge of, their many special fields contributed enormously to the atlas. Particular thanks are due the California Departments of Health Services, Corrections, Environmental Quality, Forestry, Water Resources and the Highway Division, all in Sacramento; the Department of Fish and Wildlife, Commercial Fisheries Division in Long Beach; the USDA Forest Service in Nevada City and King City; the Soil Conservation Service in Davis; and the Civil Aeronautics Board in Washington, D.C. The U.S. Geological Survey in Menlo Park was most cooperative in providing materials.

In addition to current public documents and maps, this volume relies heavily on the collections of a number of libraries. We would like to thank the librarians and staff at the Bancroft Library of the University of California, the State Library in Sacramento, California State Universities at Chico and at Northridge, Southern Oregon State College, the University of Oregon Rare Books Collection, and the Wells Fargo Bank History Room in San Francisco.

We would particularly like to express our appreciation to our friends and colleagues in geography, who gave us their advice, support, and expert knowledge throughout the compilation and production of this book. First mention must go to Dr. William G. Loy, editor of the *Atlas of Oregon*. Dr. Loy's encouragement and assistance in solving problems of atlas production made the present volume a practical possibility. Special thanks are also due Dr. Conrad Bahre, University of California at Davis; Dr. William Bowen, California State University at Northridge; Susan Trevitt Clark, and Dr. Deirdre Malarkey, University of Oregon; Dr. Gene E. Martin, and Charles Nelson, California State University at Chico; Harold Otness, Southern Oregon State College; Dr. William Preston, California State University at Sacramento, and Edward P. Thatcher, University of Oregon.

Our thanks to Dr. Edwin Hammond, University of Tennessee; Dr. A. W. Kuchler, University of Kansas; Dr. Donald Holtgrieve, California State University at Hayward; Dr. David Hornbeck, California State University at Northridge; Mrs. Erwin Raisz; Arnold Small of Los Angeles Harbor College, and to the Association of Petroleum Geologists, the University of Oklahoma Press, and *Scientific American* for permission to use their materials in this volume. We deeply appreciate the generosity of these and many other specialists. Much of the material presented here is based directly on their work; errors are, of course, our own.

Our heartfelt thanks are extended to all these people, and to Mary Lee Donley, who managed to carry on her own professional activities despite the conversion of her home into atlas office, production workshop, and cafeteria.

Finally, we would like to gratefully acknowledge Mr. Keith Barker, whose confidence in the value of this work led him to finance it. The book would not exist without his support.

Published 1979 by Pacific Book Center,
Culver City, California

Typographical Consultant: Charles Bigelow
Typesetting: Irish Setter, Portland, Oregon
Printing: Graphic Arts Center, Inc., Portland, Oregon
Binding: Lincoln and Allen, Portland, Oregon
Text is set in Sabon, display in Sabon and Syntax

Dust Jacket Photograph by William A. Garnett

LC: 79-84439
ISBN 0-9602544-0-4

INTRODUCTION

California's physical grandeur and productivity have evoked extravagant description since the earliest days of European settlement. The state's present pre-eminence in American life owes a good deal to the region's natural resources, but more to the character of its twenty-two million people, who have built a phenomenally wealthy, productive and diverse community. It is the aim of this atlas to record the many sides of this richness through maps which display the distributions and concentrations of the physical, human and economic elements which make up the state.

Each of the maps tells a story about California; the maps are the message of this book. We have included small text blocks which sketch out historical backgrounds and trends, or note points of interest which appear in the maps. Neither the maps nor the texts pretend to completeness. There is scarcely a topic in the book which does not warrant a short atlas in itself. The interested reader will have little difficulty filling a bookshelf with reference material on any subject. Our concern has not been to inform the reader fully about any topic, but rather, to introduce the reader to the spatial arrangement of things and places.

The table of contents includes some unconventional subjects. Some, like Prisons, were included because of their obvious social importance. Others, like Professional Sports, were chosen not only because they were socially and economically important, but also because they seemed particularly appropriate and were fun to do. Our choices were greatly influenced by availability of mapable information. Labor unions, for instance, about which good geographical information is difficult to assemble, are not treated, and private land holdings are covered superficially for the same reason. We feel, however, that the topics covered comprise a standard geographic reference as well as a graphic sketch of events and objects particularly meaningful to Californians. We hope that our most difficult decision, to use metric rather than English measurements, will not distract many readers from the pleasure of discovering California's grandeur on maps.

CONTENTS

THE HUMAN IMPRINT

ECONOMIC PATTERNS

THE PHYSICAL ENVIRONMENT

REFERENCE

THE HUMAN IMPRINT

AN EQUIDISTANT VIEW
of the WORLD

Distances along any line
through the center of
the projection are
true to scale.

Center of the
map at 37°
N., 120°
W.

SCALE OF DISTANCES

(along lines passing through center)

Scale of Kilometers

0   2000   4000   6000

Scale of Miles

0   1000   2000   3000

Azimuthal
Equidistant
Projection
$[f(\delta) = R\delta]$

Nominal Scale
1:175,000,000

Neither physical location nor history begins to suggest California's astonishing reputation all over the world. It has become a center of attention only after a long period of insignificance and obscurity. California's late geologic emergence as a product of the westward thrust of continental blocks against the more stable Pacific floor was matched by its late and peripheral settlement history. The Indian migrants from Asia avoided the area, and it became a Spanish colony in the dying days and at the far edge of the Spanish Empire. It was gold and Manifest Destiny that set California on a course of unprecedented growth in the mid-nineteenth century. Since then, its natural and human resources have made it increasingly significant in the economic, cultural, and political history of the United States. Indeed, for many people the most meaningful social developments of the second half of the twentieth century were conceived or elaborated in California. But it is a relatively isolated center of activity, bounded on the west by thousands of kilometers of ocean, and on the east by the empty lands of the western cordilleras and their intermountain plateaus. As a result, California is by far the most important focus of activity within a

radius of 2,000 kilometers. One must travel 4,000 kilometers to reach New York or Honolulu, and more than 8,000 kilometers to reach Europe or Japan. On the other hand, not much of the world's population lies more than 12,000 kilometers away, and the antipodes, 20,000 kilometers from the center of the map, lie in an isolated part of the Indian Ocean, more than 1,500 kilometers southeast of Madagascar.

The maps on the opposite page give a more egocentric view which emphasizes California at the expense of distant places. The views from San Francisco and Los Angeles show how differently the state appears depending on the vantage point of the observer. The small northern counties appear quite insignificant when seen from Los Angeles, and Los Angeles County shrinks when viewed from San Francisco.

The projections employed in the rest of the atlas reproduce the areal characteristics of the state more faithfully. Most of the maps are shown on the Lambert Conformal Conic Projection, which portrays directions correctly without much distortion of area, unlike these introductory maps with their obvious biases in favor of equidistance and egocentricity.

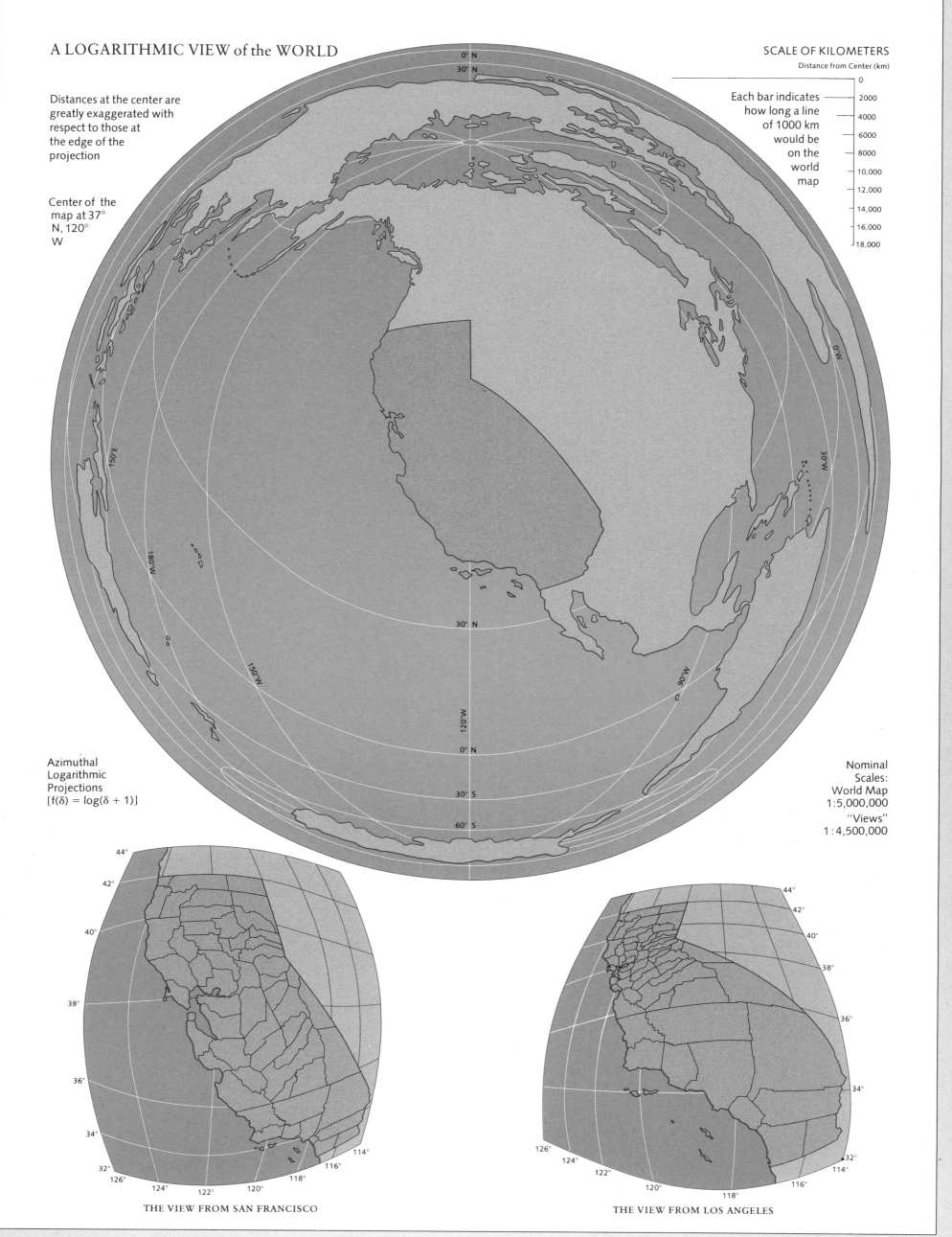

A LOGARITHMIC VIEW of the WORLD

Distances at the center are greatly exaggerated with respect to those at the edge of the projection

Center of the map at 37° N, 120° W

Azimuthal Logarithmic Projections [f(δ) = log(δ + 1)]

SCALE OF KILOMETERS

Distance from Center (km)

Each bar indicates how long a line of 1000 km would be on the world map

Nominal Scales: World Map 1:5,000,000 "Views" 1:4,500,000

THE VIEW FROM SAN FRANCISCO

THE VIEW FROM LOS ANGELES

THE VIEW FROM CALIFORNIA

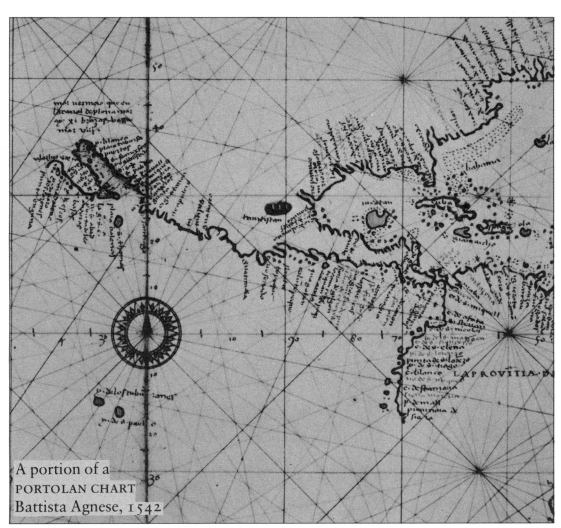

A portion of a
PORTOLAN CHART
Battista Agnese, 1542

Geographic knowledge of California unfolded slowly as Europeans gradually began to map the New World. Spanish expeditions fanned out from the Valley of Mexico soon after Cortes' conquest in 1523, and reached the peninsula of Lower California, among other places. National and individual interests spurred further exploration of the coast and eventual settlement of what is now the State of California. An expedition led by Francisco de Ulloa in 1539-40 discovered the mouth of the Colorado River and proved that Baja California was not an island. This knowledge found its way into Italy, where it was included in the *Portolan Atlases* of Battiste Agnese in 1544 (see left). Sebastian Cabot copied the maps in the Spanish colonial archives and transferred them to northern Europe where they were used by cartographers and explorers such as Abraham Ortelius and Richard Hakluyt (see below).

The Spanish, however, discouraged any interest in their possessions on the part of foreigners. Fact was replaced by myth as in the legend of California as "a golden island, peopled by black, golden-armed ladies, and not far from the Garden of Eden." Henry Briggs, for example, published a map in 1625 which was widely circulated (see page 5). It portrayed California as an island and was copied by English, French and Dutch cartographers in the 17th century. Only after the travels of Father Eusabio Kino in 1704-5 did fairly accurate maps begin to circulate in northern Europe. Diderot's *Encyclopédie* summarized this mapping problem which was resolved by the work of cartographers such as Delisle (see page 5).

By the middle of the 18th century most maps showed the coast correctly. Russian cartographers, either availing themselves of Kino's material or perhaps never having been fooled, showed the area correctly in 1737 (see page 6). The Spanish continued to refine their earlier charts and worked out the intricacies of form and location as far north as Cape Mendocino, as illustrated in Miguel Costanzo's map of 1771 (see page 6).

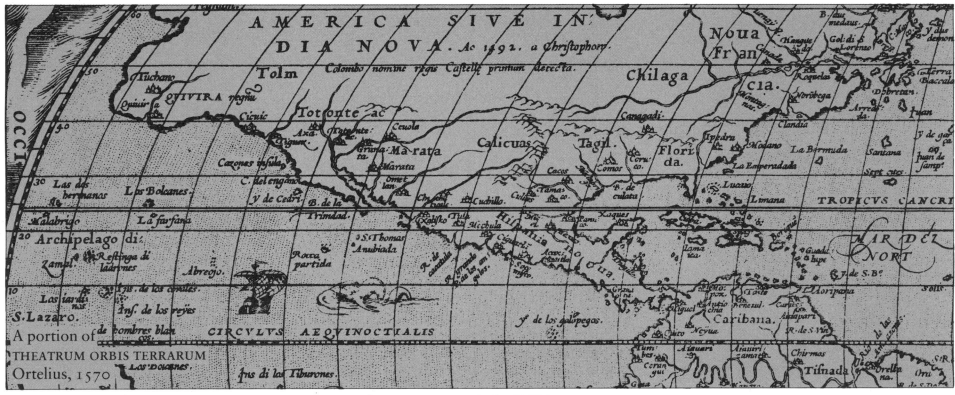

A portion of
THEATRUM ORBIS TERRARUM
Ortelius, 1570

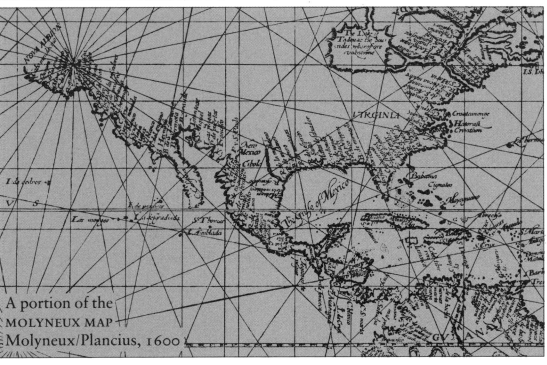

A portion of the
MOLYNEUX MAP
Molyneux/Plancius, 1600

From 1800 to 1850, the major task was that of filling in the interior. American expeditions began to map the recently acquired continental empire, and Gallatin's map of 1836 was largely based on the accounts of Lewis and Clark (see page 6). Later, and in California, Fremont's surveyors fleshed out the map of the Central Valley and the Sierra Nevada just on the eve of the Gold Rush (see page 6).

In southern California little mapping was done before 1849, when Lt. Edward Ord of the U.S. Army was hired to make a survey of the town of Los Angeles. Ord prepared a map of the general vicinity and a detailed survey of the town (see page 7). They were still the primary source when Bancroft, Thayer and Brooks produced their map of the area in 1875 (see page 7).

Gold and statehood had their effect on mapping. Many maps of the "Gold Fields" and "How to get to them" soon appeared; William Jackson's map of 1850 is one example (see page 7). The rapid rise of San Francisco resulted in surveys of the city and harbor by the U.S. Coast Survey in 1853, marking the beginning of a modern mapping program (see page 7).

HISTORICAL MAPS

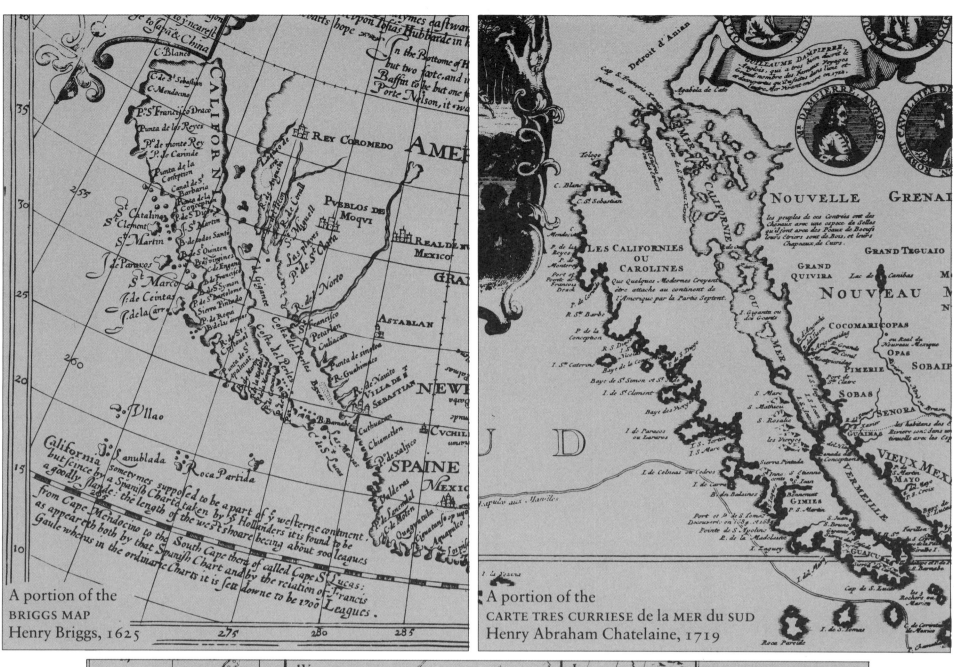

A portion of the
BRIGGS MAP
Henry Briggs, 1625

A portion of the
CARTE TRES CURRIESE de la MER du SUD
Henry Abraham Chatelaine, 1719

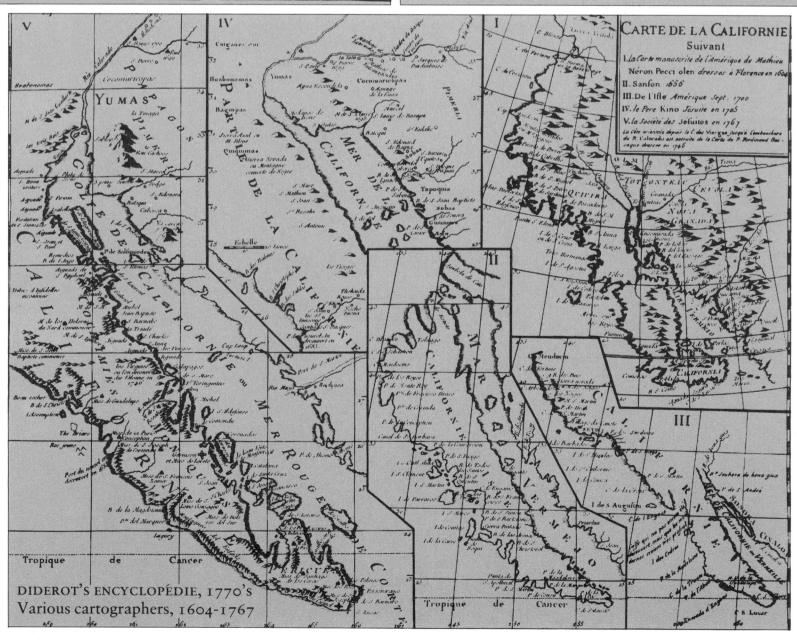

DIDEROT'S ENCYCLOPÉDIE, 1770's
Various cartographers, 1604-1767

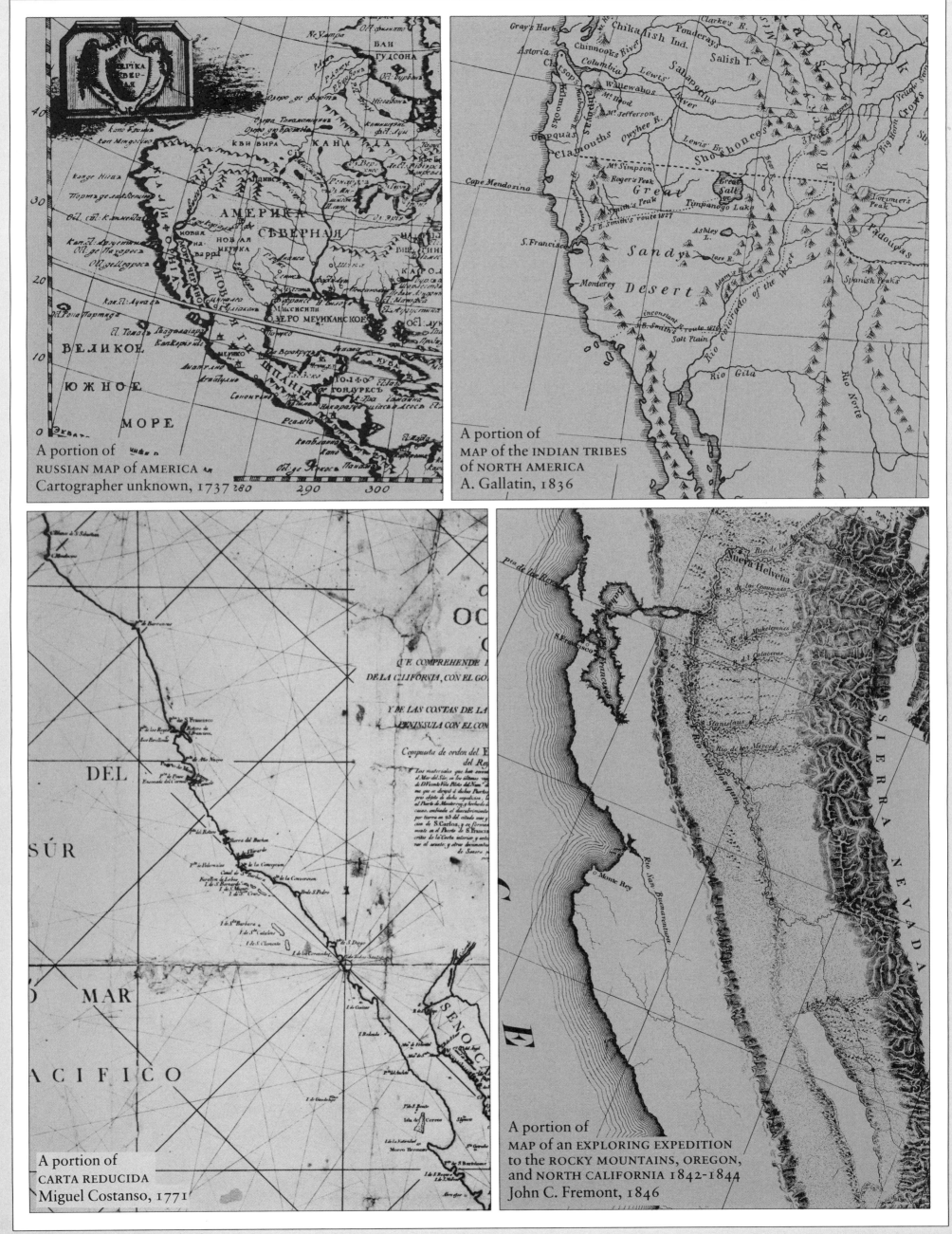

A portion of
RUSSIAN MAP of AMERICA
Cartographer unknown, 1737

A portion of
MAP of the INDIAN TRIBES
of NORTH AMERICA
A. Gallatin, 1836

A portion of
CARTA REDUCIDA
Miguel Costanso, 1771

A portion of
MAP of an EXPLORING EXPEDITION
to the ROCKY MOUNTAINS, OREGON,
and NORTH CALIFORNIA 1842-1844
John C. Fremont, 1846

HISTORICAL MAPS

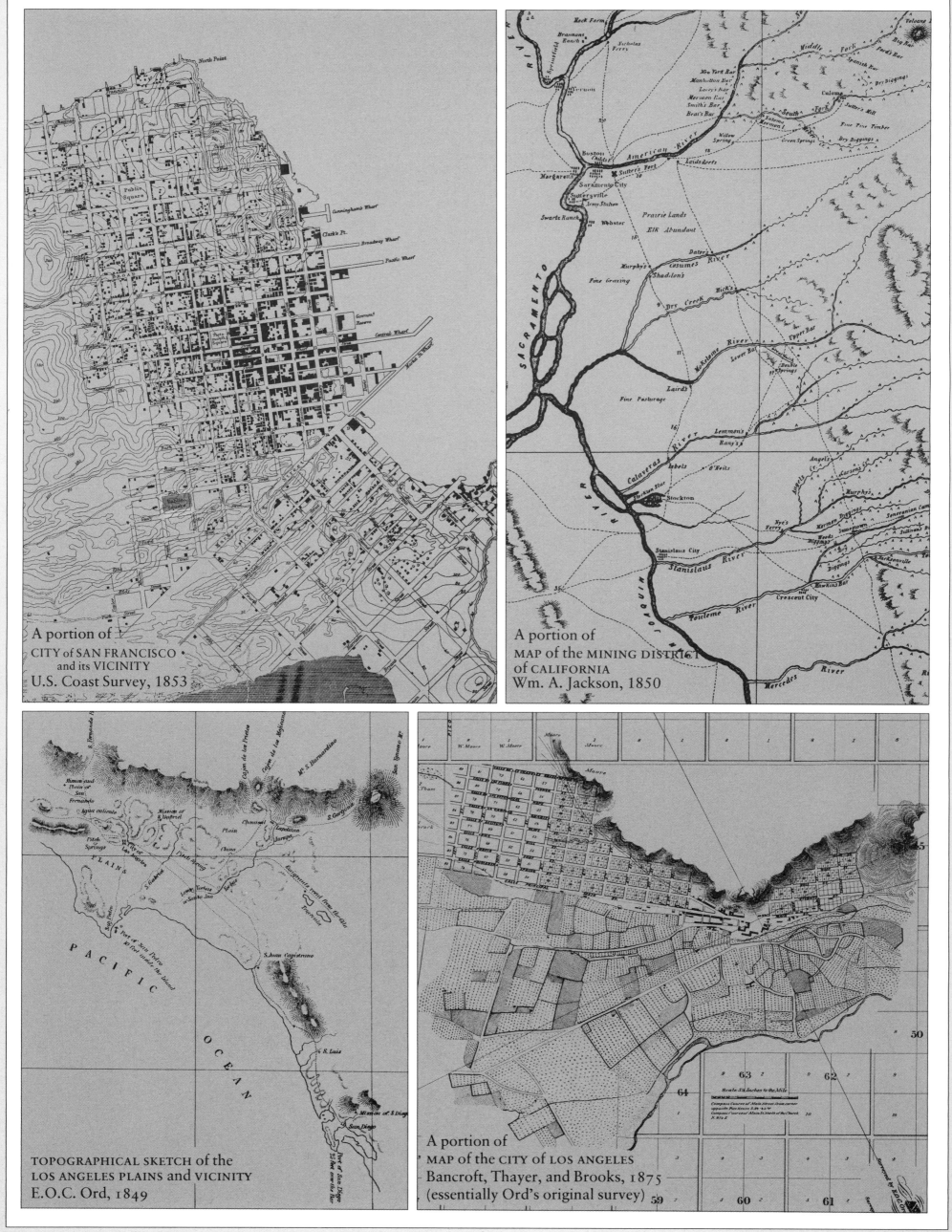

A portion of
CITY of SAN FRANCISCO
and its VICINITY
U.S. Coast Survey, 1853

A portion of
MAP of the MINING DISTRICT
of CALIFORNIA
Wm. A. Jackson, 1850

TOPOGRAPHICAL SKETCH of the
LOS ANGELES PLAINS and VICINITY
E.O.C. Ord, 1849

A portion of
MAP of the CITY of LOS ANGELES
Bancroft, Thayer, and Brooks, 1875
(essentially Ord's original survey)

HISTORICAL MAPS

8

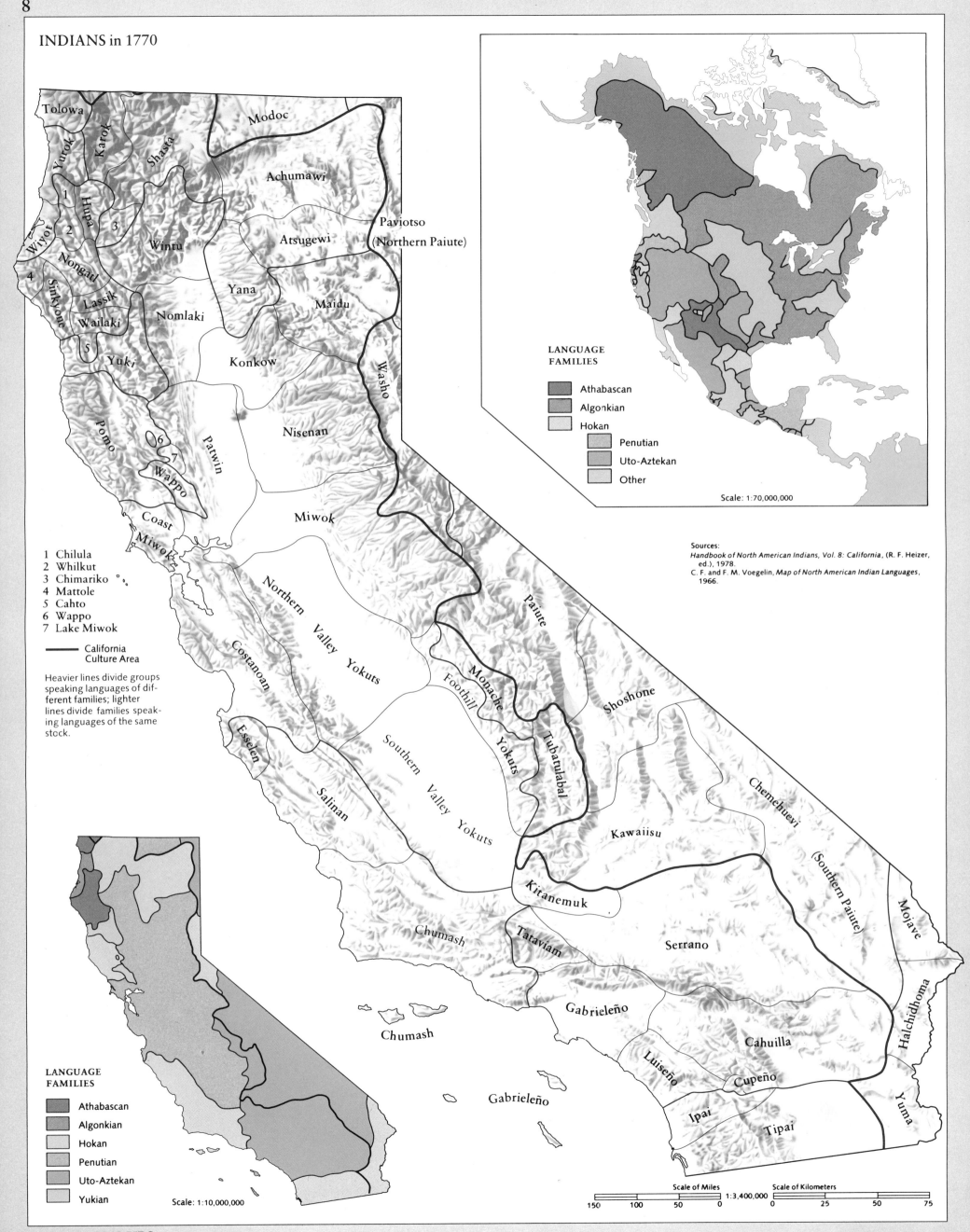

INDIANS in 1770

1 Chilula
2 Whilkut
3 Chimariko
4 Mattole
5 Cahto
6 Wappo
7 Lake Miwok

—— California Culture Area

Heavier lines divide groups speaking languages of different families; lighter lines divide families speaking languages of the same stock.

Tolowa
Modoc
Yurok
Karok
Shasta
Achumawi
Hupa
Wiyot
Nongatl
Wintu
Atsugewi
Paviotso (Northern Paiute)
Sinkyone
Lassik
Yana
Maidu
Wailaki
Nomlaki
Yuki
Konkow
Pomo
Patwin
Washo
Wappo
Nisenan
Coast Miwok
Miwok
Northern Valley Yokuts
Costanoan
Esselen
Southern Valley Yokuts
Salinan
Paiute
Monache
Foothill Yokuts
Shoshone
Tubatulabal
Kawaiisu
Chemehuevi
Kitanemuk
(Southern Paiute)
Chumash
Tataviam
Serrano
Mojave
Chumash
Gabrieleño
Luiseño
Cahuilla
Halchidhoma
Cupeño
Gabrieleño
Ipai
Tipai
Yuma

LANGUAGE FAMILIES

Athabascan
Algonkian
Hokan
Penutian
Uto-Aztekan
Other

Scale: 1:70,000,000

Sources:
Handbook of North American Indians, Vol. 8: California, (R. F. Heizer, ed.), 1978.
C. F. and F. M. Voegelin, Map of North American Indian Languages, 1966.

LANGUAGE FAMILIES

Athabascan
Algonkian
Hokan
Penutian
Uto-Aztekan
Yukian

Scale: 1:10,000,000

Scale of Miles
150   100   50   0

1:3,400,000

Scale of Kilometers
0   25   50   75

INDIAN GROUPS

Indians have lived in California for at least 10,000 years, and perhaps much longer, though evidence for human habitation before the last glacial retreat is not generally accepted. The Hokan language stock is thought once to have predominated over much of the state. It was displaced by Penutian and, still later, by Uto-Aztekan. Algonkian and, most recently, Athabaskan entered the northwestern part of the state but did not expand beyond that area.

Linguistic affinities do not determine cultural ones. The Hokan-speaking Colorado River tribes were culturally related to the farming societies of the Southwest, but they spoke unrelated languages. Both Algonkian- and Athabascan-speaking groups in the Northwest represent an extension of a single cultural tradition centered in British Columbia. All the groups along the eastern borders of the state, speaking diverse languages, belong to the Great Basin cultures which dominated much of the arid Intermountain West. The balance of the state is considered distinctly Californian, very much isolated from other cultural centers.

About 300,000 people were living in the state when the Spanish-Mexican occupation forces arrived. There was some armed resistance to missionization and some raiding between Spanish settlements and interior tribes, but it was epidemic disease that was mainly responsible for the population decline of some 50,000 by the end of the Mission period in the 1830's. Distribution of former Mission (originally Indian) lands to private ranchers reduced Missionized Indians to destitution, and epidemics continued: by 1845, the Indian population stood at about 125,000. The Gold Rush of 1849 brought greater devastation as it sent unprecedented numbers of well-armed and intolerant whites into previously remote regions. By 1855, only about 55,000 Indians survived, living in remote areas or scattered in very small groups.

The 1900 Census recorded only 15,000 Indians, but their numbers have risen steadily since then, to 90,000 in 1970. The registered increase has come, in part, from migration into California cities by Indians from other states and by a growing tendency to take pride in Indian ancestry.

INDIAN TRADE ROUTES

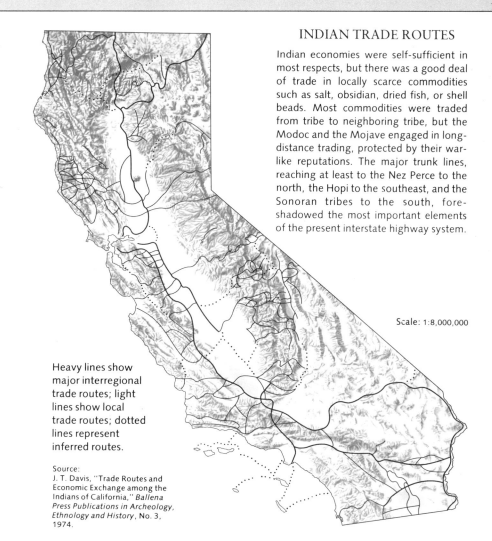

Indian economies were self-sufficient in most respects, but there was a good deal of trade in locally scarce commodities such as salt, obsidian, dried fish, or shell beads. Most commodities were traded from tribe to neighboring tribe, but the Modoc and the Mojave engaged in long-distance trading, protected by their warlike reputations. The major trunk lines, reaching at least to the Nez Perce to the north, the Hopi to the southeast, and the Sonoran tribes to the south, foreshadowed the most important elements of the present interstate highway system.

Scale: 1:8,000,000

Heavy lines show major interregional trade routes; light lines show local trade routes; dotted lines represent inferred routes.

Source:
J. T. Davis, "Trade Routes and Economic Exchange among the Indians of California," *Ballena Press Publications in Archeology, Ethnology and History*, No. 3, 1974.

INDIAN POPULATION DENSITY IN 1770

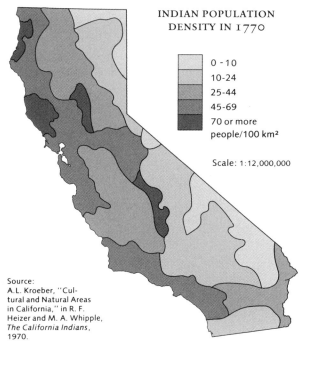

- 0 - 10
- 10-24
- 25-44
- 45-69
- 70 or more people/100 km²

Scale: 1:12,000,000

Source:
A.L. Kroeber, "Cultural and Natural Areas in California," in R. F. Heizer and M. A. Whipple, *The California Indians*, 1970.

INDIAN POPULATION DECLINE, 1770-1910

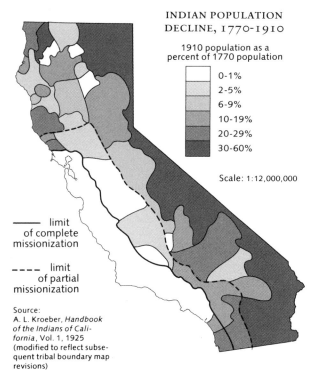

1910 population as a percent of 1770 population

- 0-1%
- 2-5%
- 6-9%
- 10-19%
- 20-29%
- 30-60%

Scale: 1:12,000,000

—— limit of complete missionization

- - - - limit of partial missionization

Source:
A. L. Kroeber, *Handbook of the Indians of California*, Vol. 1, 1925 (modified to reflect subsequent tribal boundary map revisions)

INDIAN LANDS in the 1970's

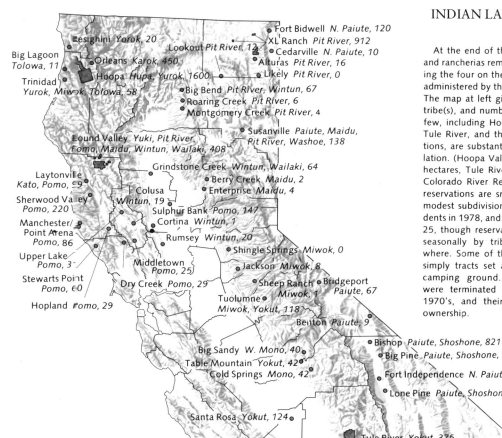

Fort Bidwell *N. Paiute*, 120
Tesighini *Yurok*, 20
Lookout *Pit River*, 12
XL Ranch *Pit River*, 912
Big Lagoon *Tolowa*, 11
Orleans *Karok*, 450
Cedarville *N. Paiute*, 10
Alturas *Pit River*, 16
Trinidad *Yurok, Miwok, Tolowa*, 58
Hoopa *Hupa, Yurok*, 1600
Likely *Pit River*, 0
Big Bend *Pit River*, 67
Roaring Creek *Pit River*, 6
Montgomery Creek *Pit River*, 4
Susanville *Paiute, Maidu, Pit River, Washoe*, 138
Round Valley *Yuki, Pit River, Pomo, Maidu, Wintun, Wailaki*, 408
Grindstone Creek *Wintun, Wailaki*, 64
Laytonville *Kato, Pomo*, 59
Berry Creek *Maidu*, 2
Enterprise *Maidu*, 4
Sherwood Valley *Pomo*, 220
Colusa *Wintun*, 19
Sulphur Bank *Pomo*, 147
Manchester/ Point Arena *Pomo*, 86
Cortina *Wintun*, 1
Rumsey *Wintun*, 20
Upper Lake *Pomo*, 3
Shingle Springs *Miwok*, 0
Middletown *Pomo*, 25
Jackson *Miwok*, 8
Stewarts Point *Pomo*, 60
Dry Creek *Pomo*, 29
Sheep Ranch *Miwok*, 1
Bridgeport *Paiute*, 67
Hopland *Pomo*, 29
Tuolumne *Miwok, Yokut*, 118
Benton *Paiute*, 9
Big Sandy *W. Mono*, 40
Table Mountain *Yokut*, 42
Cold Springs *Mono*, 42
Bishop *Paiute, Shoshone*, 821
Big Pine *Paiute, Shoshone*, 198
Fort Independence *N. Paiute*, 45
Lone Pine *Paiute, Shoshone*, 166
Santa Rosa *Yokut*, 124
Tule River *Yokut*, 375

Scale: 1:6,000,000

At the end of the 1970's, 82 reservations and rancherias remained in California, including the four on the Colorado River which are administered by the BIA Phoenix Area Office. The map at left gives the reservation name, tribe(s), and number of residents in 1978. A few, including Hoopa Valley, Round Valley, Tule River, and the Colorado River reservations, are substantial both in size and population. (Hoopa Valley includes nearly 35,000 hectares, Tule River nearly 22,000, and the Colorado River Reservation 109,000.) Most reservations are small, many no larger than modest subdivision tracts. Eight had no residents in 1978, and another 17 had fewer than 25, though reservation lands are often used seasonally by tribal members living elsewhere. Some of the smallest rancherias are simply tracts set aside for a cemetery and camping ground. Thirty-seven rancherias were terminated in the 1960's and early 1970's, and their lands sold into private ownership.

Fort Mojave *Mojave*, 412
Santa Ynez *Chumash*, 69
Chemehuevi *Chemehuevi*, 46
San Manuel *Serrano*, 28
Colorado River *Colorado River*, 1745
Twentynine Palms *Luiseno*, 0
Morongo *Cahuilla*, 283
Agua Caliente *Cahuilla*, 120
Soboba *Luiseno*, 277
Cabazon *Cahuilla*, 13
Ramona *Cahuilla*, 0
Augustine *Cahuilla*, 0
Cahuilla *Cahuilla*, 27
Torres Martinez *Cahuilla*, 63
Pechanga *Luiseno*, 89
Pala *Luiseno*, 322
Los Coyotes *Cahuilla*, 70
Rincon *Luiseno*, 268
San Pascual *Diegueno*, 63
Santa Ysabel *Diegueno*, 135
Mesa Grande *Diegueno*, 24
Inaja & Cosmit *Diegueno*, 0
Barona Ranch *Diegueno*, 166
Capitan Grande *Diegueno*, 0
Cuyapaipe *Diegueno*, 5
Sycuan *Diegueno*, 63
Manzanita *Diegueno*, 22
Campo *Diegueno*, 168
San Diego Co. reservations shown at left
Fort Yuma *Cocopah, Quechan*, 1225

1. Santa Rosa *Cahuilla*, 25
2. Pauma & Yuima *Luiseno*, 85
3. La Jolla *Luiseno*, 90
4. Viejas *Dieguena*, 148
5. La Posta *Diegueno*, 0

Scale: 1:3,400,000

Source:
Tribal Information and Directory, Bureau of Indian Affairs, Sacramento Area Office, 1978

USGS *California: South Half* (Map) 1:500,000 1970

INDIANS ON THE LAND

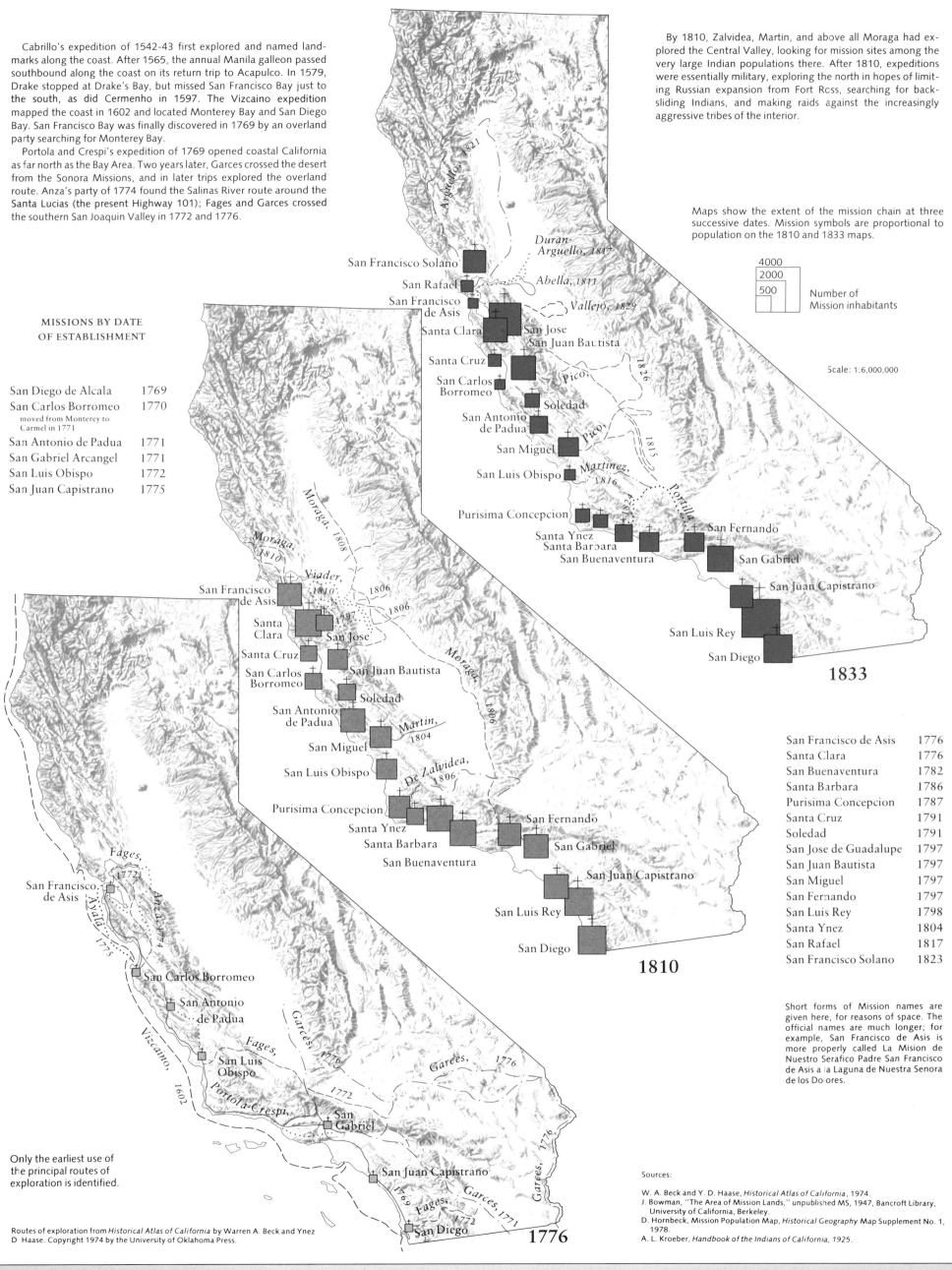

Cabrillo's expedition of 1542-43 first explored and named land-marks along the coast. After 1565, the annual Manila galleon passed southbound along the coast on its return trip to Acapulco. In 1579, Drake stopped at Drake's Bay, but missed San Francisco Bay just to the south, as did Cermenho in 1597. The Vizcaino expedition mapped the coast in 1602 and located Monterey Bay and San Diego Bay. San Francisco Bay was finally discovered in 1769 by an overland party searching for Monterey Bay.

Portola and Crespi's expedition of 1769 opened coastal California as far north as the Bay Area. Two years later, Garces crossed the desert from the Sonora Missions, and in later trips explored the overland route. Anza's party of 1774 found the Salinas River route around the Santa Lucias (the present Highway 101); Fages and Garces crossed the southern San Joaquin Valley in 1772 and 1776.

By 1810, Zalvidea, Martin, and above all Moraga had explored the Central Valley, looking for mission sites among the very large Indian populations there. After 1810, expeditions were essentially military, exploring the north in hopes of limiting Russian expansion from Fort Ross, searching for backsliding Indians, and making raids against the increasingly aggressive tribes of the interior.

Maps show the extent of the mission chain at three successive dates. Mission symbols are proportional to population on the 1810 and 1833 maps.

4000
2000
500
Number of
Mission inhabitants

Scale: 1:6,000,000

MISSIONS BY DATE OF ESTABLISHMENT

San Diego de Alcala	1769
San Carlos Borromeo	1770
moved from Monterey to Carmel in 1771	
San Antonio de Padua	1771
San Gabriel Arcangel	1771
San Luis Obispo	1772
San Juan Capistrano	1775

San Francisco de Asis	1776
Santa Clara	1776
San Buenaventura	1782
Santa Barbara	1786
Purisima Concepcion	1787
Santa Cruz	1791
Soledad	1791
San Jose de Guadalupe	1797
San Juan Bautista	1797
San Miguel	1797
San Fernando	1797
San Luis Rey	1798
Santa Ynez	1804
San Rafael	1817
San Francisco Solano	1823

Short forms of Mission names are given here, for reasons of space. The official names are much longer; for example, San Francisco de Asis is more properly called La Mision de Nuestro Serafico Padre San Francisco de Asis a la Laguna de Nuestra Senora de los Dolores.

Only the earliest use of the principal routes of exploration is identified.

1833

1810

1776

Routes of exploration from *Historical Atlas of California* by Warren A. Beck and Ynez D. Haase. Copyright 1974 by the University of Oklahoma Press.

Sources:

W. A. Beck and Y. D. Haase, *Historical Atlas of California*, 1974.
J. Bowman, "The Area of Mission Lands," unpublished MS, 1947, Bancroft Library, University of California, Berkeley.
D. Hornbeck, Mission Population Map, *Historical Geography* Map Supplement No. 1, 1978.
A. L. Kroeber, *Handbook of the Indians of California*, 1925.

MISSIONS AND EXPLORATION

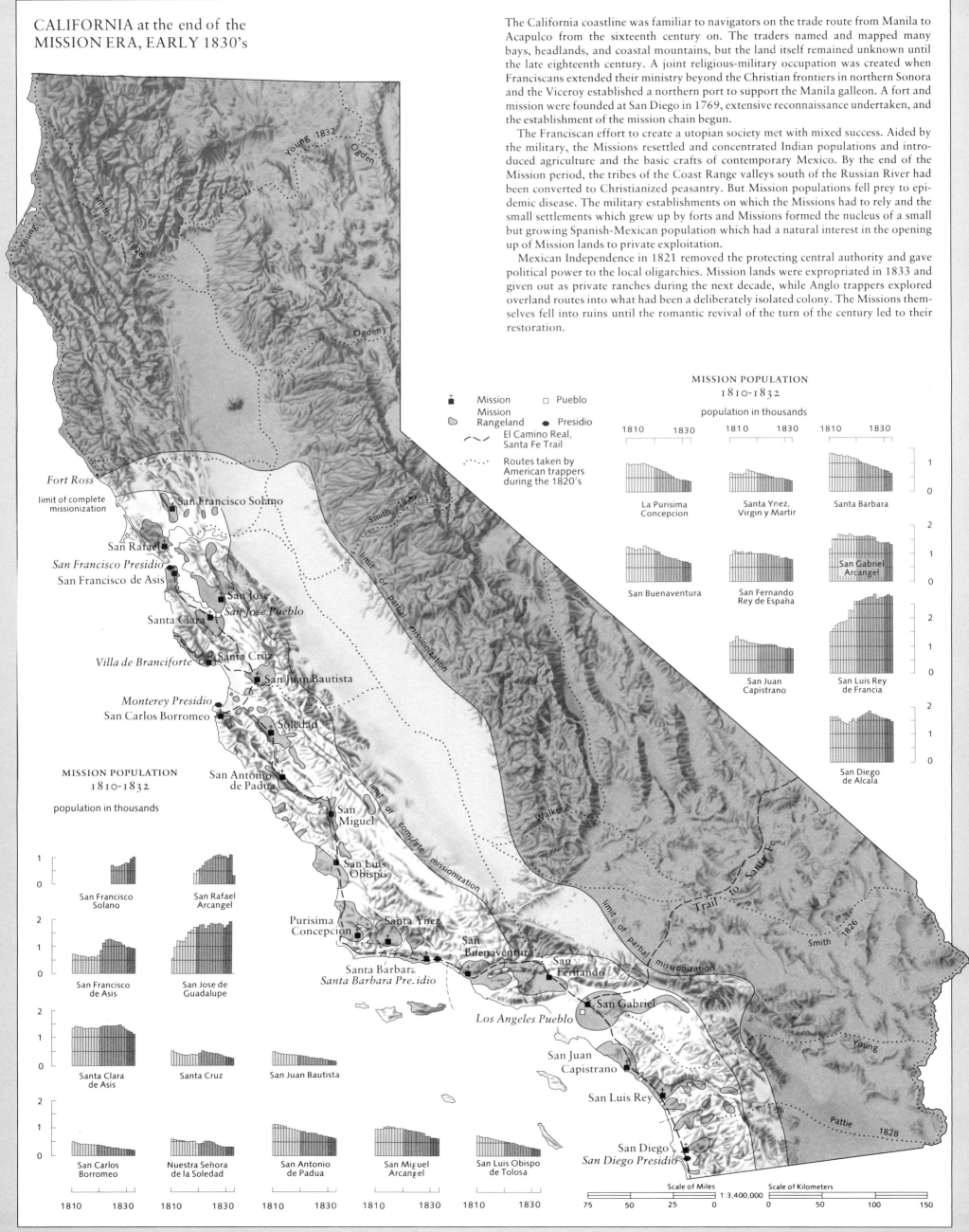

CALIFORNIA at the end of the MISSION ERA, EARLY 1830's

The California coastline was familiar to navigators on the trade route from Manila to Acapulco from the sixteenth century on. The traders named and mapped many bays, headlands, and coastal mountains, but the land itself remained unknown until the late eighteenth century. A joint religious-military occupation was created when Franciscans extended their ministry beyond the Christian frontiers in northern Sonora and the Viceroy established a northern port to support the Manila galleon. A fort and mission were founded at San Diego in 1769, extensive reconnaissance undertaken, and the establishment of the mission chain begun.

The Franciscan effort to create a utopian society met with mixed success. Aided by the military, the Missions resettled and concentrated Indian populations and introduced agriculture and the basic crafts of contemporary Mexico. By the end of the Mission period, the tribes of the Coast Range valleys south of the Russian River had been converted to Christianized peasantry. But Mission populations fell prey to epidemic disease. The military establishments on which the Missions had to rely and the small settlements which grew up by forts and Missions formed the nucleus of a small but growing Spanish-Mexican population which had a natural interest in the opening up of Mission lands to private exploitation.

Mexican Independence in 1821 removed the protecting central authority and gave political power to the local oligarchies. Mission lands were expropriated in 1833 and given out as private ranches during the next decade, while Anglo trappers explored overland routes into what had been a deliberately isolated colony. The Missions themselves fell into ruins until the romantic revival of the turn of the century led to their restoration.

MISSION LANDS

MEXICAN LAND GRANTS

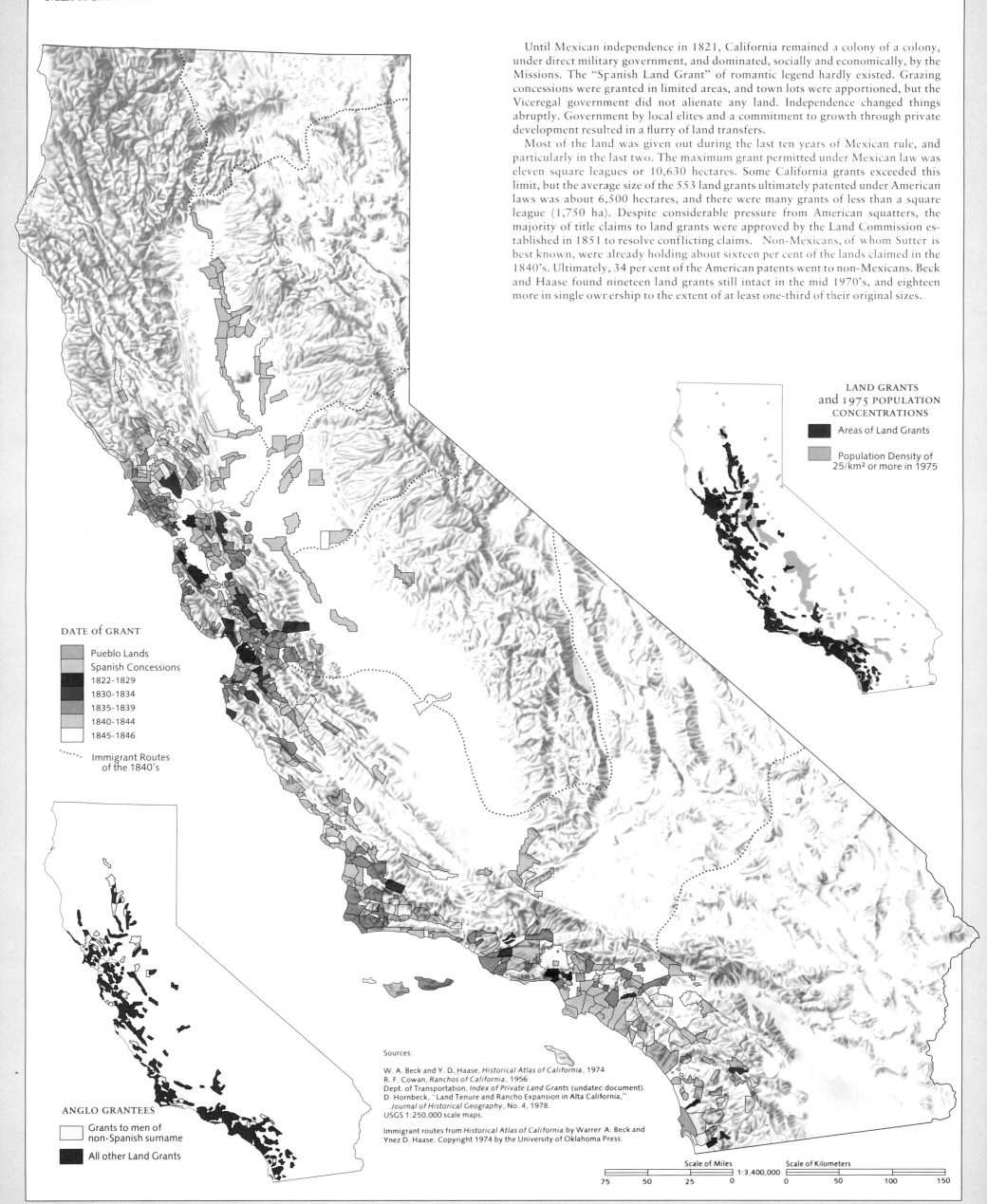

Until Mexican independence in 1821, California remained a colony of a colony, under direct military government, and dominated, socially and economically, by the Missions. The "Spanish Land Grant" of romantic legend hardly existed. Grazing concessions were granted in limited areas, and town lots were apportioned, but the Viceregal government did not alienate any land. Independence changed things abruptly. Government by local elites and a commitment to growth through private development resulted in a flurry of land transfers.

Most of the land was given out during the last ten years of Mexican rule, and particularly in the last two. The maximum grant permitted under Mexican law was eleven square leagues or 10,630 hectares. Some California grants exceeded this limit, but the average size of the 553 land grants ultimately patented under American laws was about 6,500 hectares, and there were many grants of less than a square league (1,750 ha). Despite considerable pressure from American squatters, the majority of title claims to land grants were approved by the Land Commission established in 1851 to resolve conflicting claims. Non-Mexicans, of whom Sutter is best known, were already holding about sixteen per cent of the lands claimed in the 1840's. Ultimately, 34 per cent of the American patents went to non-Mexicans. Beck and Haase found nineteen land grants still intact in the mid 1970's, and eighteen more in single ownership to the extent of at least one-third of their original sizes.

LAND GRANTS
and 1975 POPULATION
CONCENTRATIONS

■ Areas of Land Grants

■ Population Density of
25/km² or more in 1975

DATE of GRANT

Pueblo Lands
Spanish Concessions
1822-1829
1830-1834
1835-1839
1840-1844
1845-1846

······· Immigrant Routes
of the 1840's

ANGLO GRANTEES

☐ Grants to men of
non-Spanish surname

■ All other Land Grants

Sources:

W. A. Beck and Y. D. Haase, *Historical Atlas of California*, 1974
R. F. Cowan, *Ranchos of California*, 1956
Dept. of Transportation, *Index of Private Land Grants* (undated document).
D. Hornbeck, "Land Tenure and Rancho Expansion in Alta California,"
  Journal of Historical Geography, No. 4, 1978.
USGS 1:250,000 scale maps.

Immigrant routes from *Historical Atlas of California* by Warren A. Beck and
Ynez D. Haase. Copyright 1974 by the University of Oklahoma Press.

Scale of Miles   Scale of Kilometers
75 50 25 0   1:3,400,000   0   50   100   150

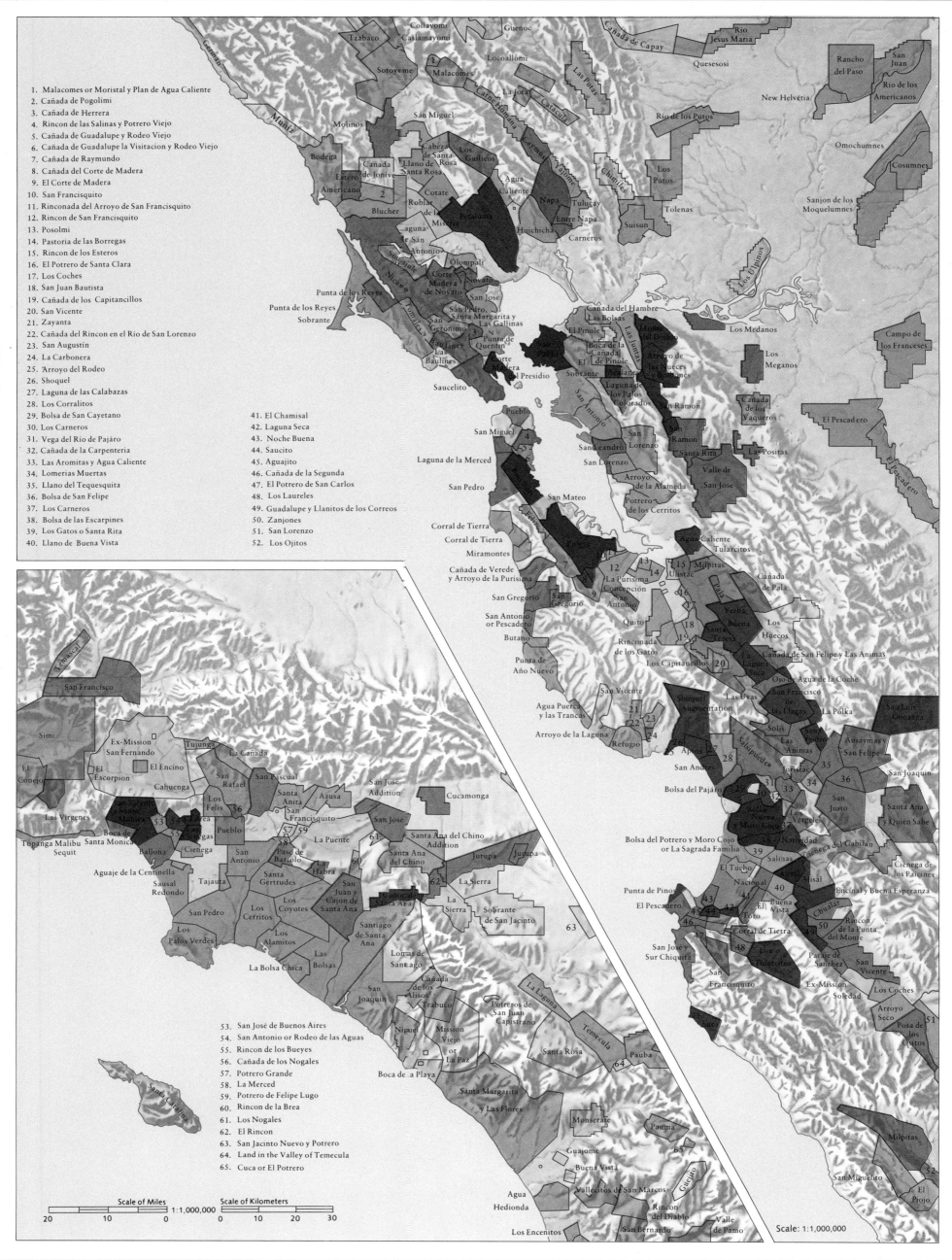

1. Malacomes or Moristal y Plan de Agua Caliente
2. Cañada de Pogolimi
3. Cañada de Herrera
4. Rincon de las Salinas y Potrero Viejo
5. Cañada de Guadalupe y Rodeo Viejo
6. Cañada de Guadalupe la Visitacion y Rodeo Viejo
7. Cañada de Raymundo
8. Cañada del Corte de Madera
9. El Corte de Madera
10. San Francisquito
11. Rinconada del Arroyo de San Francisquito
12. Rincon de San Francisquito
13. Posolmi
14. Pastoria de las Borregas
15. Rincon de los Esteros
16. El Potrero de Santa Clara
17. Los Coches
18. San Juan Bautista
19. Cañada de los Capitancillos
20. San Vicente
21. Zayanta
22. Cañada del Rincon en el Río de San Lorenzo
23. San Augustin
24. La Carbonera
25. Arroyo del Rodeo
26. Shoquel
27. Laguna de las Calabazas
28. Los Corralitos
29. Bolsa de San Cayetano
30. Los Carneros
31. Vega del Rio de Pajáro
32. Cañada de la Carpenteria
33. Las Aromitas y Agua Caliente
34. Lomerias Muertas
35. Llano del Tequesquita
36. Bolsa de San Felipe
37. Los Carneros
38. Bolsa de las Escarpines
39. Los Gatos o Santa Rita
40. Llano de Buena Vista

41. El Chamisal
42. Laguna Seca
43. Noche Buena
44. Saucito
45. Aguajito
46. Cañada de la Segunda
47. El Potrero de San Carlos
48. Los Laureles
49. Guadalupe y Llanitos de los Correos
50. Zanjones
51. San Lorenzo
52. Los Ojitos

53. San José de Buenos Aires
54. San Antonio or Rodeo de las Aguas
55. Rincon de los Bueyes
56. Cañada de los Nogales
57. Potrero Grande
58. La Merced
59. Potrero de Felipe Lugo
60. Rincon de la Brea
61. Los Nogales
62. El Rincon
63. San Jacinto Nuevo y Potrero
64. Land in the Valley of Temecula
65. Cuca or El Potrero

Scale of Miles Scale of Kilometers
1:1,000,000

LAND GRANTS IN THE BAY AREA AND LOS ANGELES

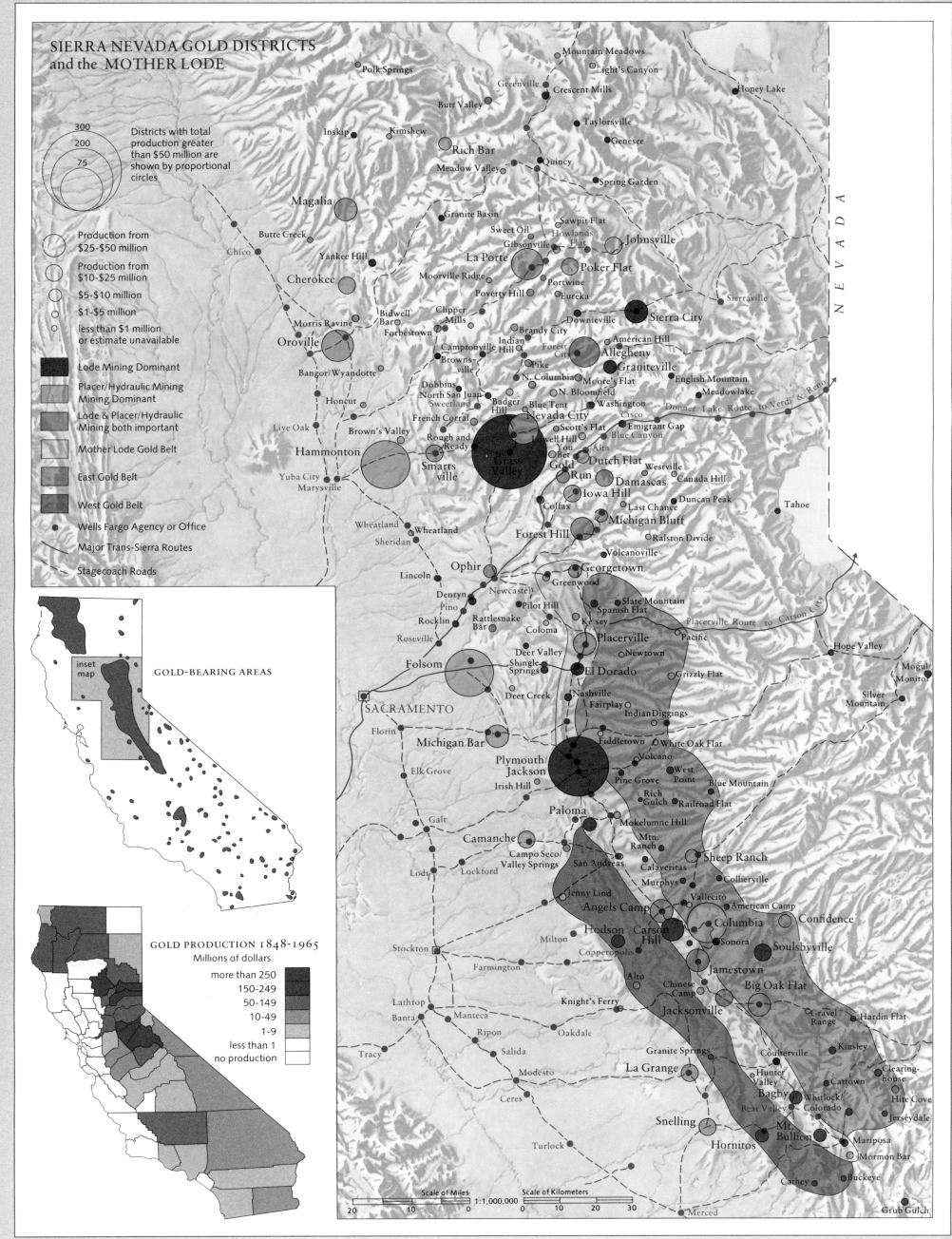

SIERRA NEVADA GOLD DISTRICTS and the MOTHER LODE

Districts with total production greater than $50 million are shown by proportional circles

300
200
75

Production from $25-$50 million

Production from $10-$25 million

$5-$10 million

$1-$5 million

less than $1 million or estimate unavailable

Lode Mining Dominant

Placer/Hydraulic Mining Mining Dominant

Lode & Placer/Hydraulic Mining both important

Mother Lode Gold Belt

East Gold Belt

West Gold Belt

Wells Fargo Agency or Office

Major Trans-Sierra Routes

Stagecoach Roads

GOLD-BEARING AREAS

inset map

GOLD PRODUCTION 1848-1965
Millions of dollars

more than 250
150-249
50-149
10-49
1-9
less than 1
no production

NEVADA

Scale of Miles   Scale of Kilometers
1:1,000,000
20 10 0   0 10 20 30

GOLD RUSH MINING DISTRICTS

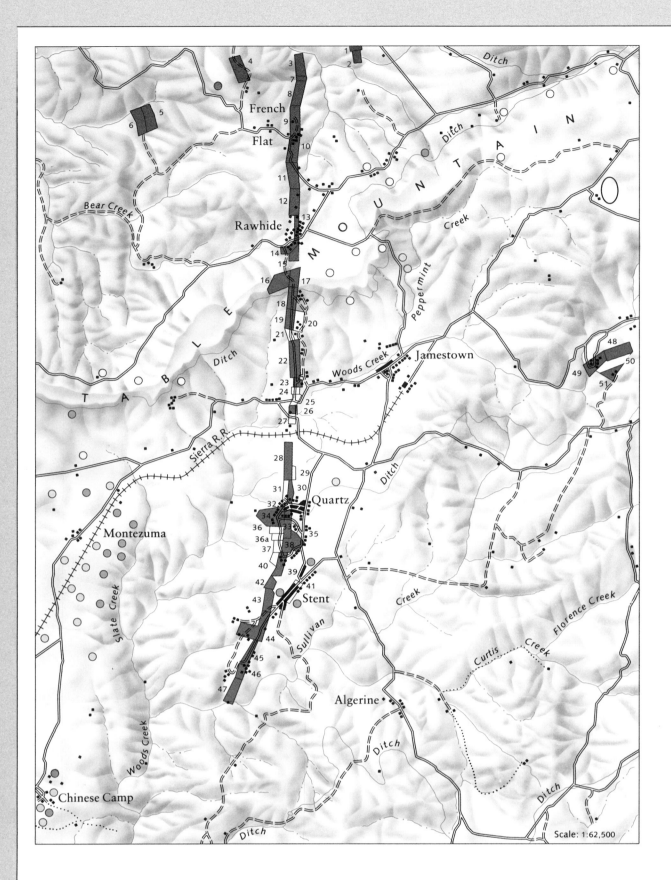

THE JAMESTOWN DISTRICT

TUOLUMNE COUNTY—MOTHER LODE

1899

- ● Gold Prospect or Pocket
- ○ Drift Mine in Auriferous Gravel
- ◉ Hydraulic Mine in Auriferous Gravel
- ○ Shallow Placer in Auriferous Gravel

▮ Claim with Developed Prospect or Quartz Lode Mine on Site

▯ Claim without Prospect or Lode Mine on Site

MINING CLAIMS

1 Gagnere Extension	27 Pacific
2 Gagnere	28 Sweeny
3 O.K. Extension	29 Sweeny Millsite
4 Prospect	30 Dutch Millsite
5 Pena Blanca	31 Dutch
6 Sara Francis	32 Dutch Millsite
7 Combination	33 Heslep
8 O.K.	34 App
9 Tarantula	35 Heslep Millsite
10 Alameda	36 Hitchcock
11 Isabella and Gem Consolidated	36a Gray Eagle
12 Rappahannock	37 Gray Eagle
13 Rawhide	38 Knox & Boyle
14 Rawhide Millsite	39 Miller & Holmes
15 Rawhide No. 2	40 Miller & Holmes
16 Table Omega	41 No. 1
17 Alabama Consolidated	42 Cloudman
18 Alabama Consolidated	43 Erin-go-bragh
19 Crystalline	44 Golden Rule
20 Shore	45 New Era
21 Ophir	46 Jumper
22 Trio	47 Mazeppa
23 Mooney	48 Golden Gate
24 McCann	49 Golden Sulphuret
25 Vulture	50 Gerrymander
26 Vulture	51 Gerrymander

MOTHER LODE MINE PRODUCTION—JAMESTOWN

App-Heslep	$6.5 million
Rawhide	$6.0 million
Jumper	$5.0 million
Dutch-Sweeney	$3.0 million
Harvard	$2-3 million

Only gold could have stamped the early history of the state of California in such a way as to pervade every aspect of life. Settlement was accelerated by decades; over 200,000 came to the Golden State between 1850 and 1860. Gold made San Francisco into a city, the only one west of St. Louis until the turn of the century. It opened up a controversy between conservationists and hydraulic miners, and it changed notions and rules regarding water rights. Mining operations have also left their trace in the landscape, particularly in the gravel deposits of hydraulic mines and, more incidentally, in the museums which house parts of stamp mills and other lode mining paraphernalia.

The earliest activity was placer mining in the Sierra Nevada streams, from the Feather River to the Tuolumne. The simple techniques of panning and rockers often yielded fantastic returns, and many settlements, now ghost towns, owe their start to this activity. By 1855, however, easy mining from surface placers was over. Lode mining in gold-bearing quartzes and hydraulic mining became the leading activities, maintaining a steady production until the Sawyer Decision of 1884 crippled hydraulic mining by prohibiting the dumping of debris into the rivers of the Central Valley. Thereafter, dredging and lode mining kept California production between half a million and a million ounces annually until 1933.

The major long-term producers are shown on page 14. Despite the glamorous reputation of the Mother Lode, the greatest production came from the rich mines in Nevada and Sierra counties and the later large scale dredge operations along the break in slope at the edge of the Valley. On the map, the lode mining districts of Grass Valley and Plymouth-Jackson stand out; next in importance are the dredge fields at Hammonton (on the Tuolumne) and Folsom; third are the placer activities near Columbia in Tuolumne County and La Porte in Plumas County. Each produced more than $60,000,000 worth of ore between 1850 and 1970.

The changes that affected gold mining in California are illustrated in the relict landscape of the Jamestown district in the Mother Lode. The shallow placers around

Montezuma and Chinese Camp were the first claims to be worked. Later, ditches were dug to supply water to the more sophisticated hydraulic and drift mines tapping the auriferous gravels beneath the lava cap of Table Mountain. The introduction of hard-rock lode mining prompted the claims which so clearly outline the gold vein of the Mother Lode. A string of mining towns and the railroad leading to the main mill at Jamestown complete this picture of past activity.

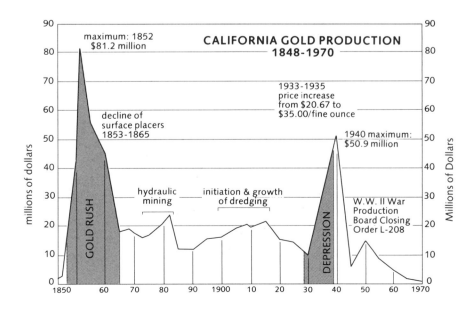

CALIFORNIA GOLD PRODUCTION 1848-1970

maximum: 1852 $81.2 million

decline of surface placers 1853-1865

1933-1935 price increase from $20.67 to $35.00/fine ounce

1940 maximum: $50.9 million

hydraulic mining

initiation & growth of dredging

W.W. II War Production Board Closing Order L-208

GOLD RUSH

DEPRESSION

THE JAMESTOWN DISTRICT AND THE MOTHER LODE

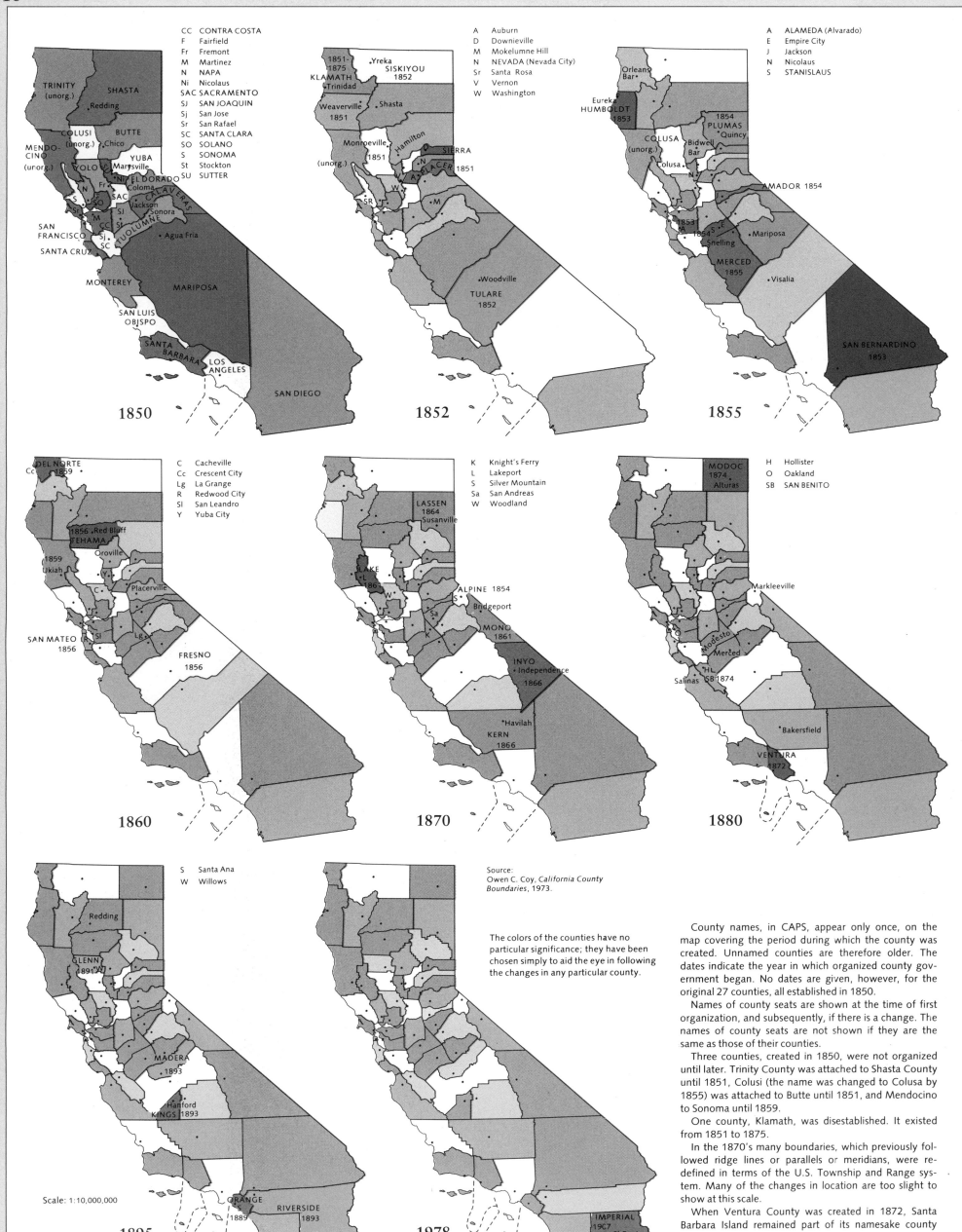

1850

CC CONTRA COSTA
F Fairfield
Fr Fremont
M Martinez
N NAPA
Ni Nicolaus
SAC SACRAMENTO
SJ SAN JOAQUIN
Sj San Jose
Sr San Rafael
SC SANTA CLARA
SO SOLANO
S SONOMA
St Stockton
SU SUTTER

TRINITY (unorg.)
SHASTA
Redding
COLUSI (unorg.)
MENDO-CINO (unorg.)
Chico
BUTTE
YUBA
Marysville
YOLO
EL DORADO
Coloma
SAC
CALAVERAS
Jackson
Sonora
TUOLUMNE
•Agua Fria
SAN FRANCISCO
SANTA CRUZ
MONTEREY
SAN LUIS OBISPO
SANTA BARBARA
LOS ANGELES
MARIPOSA
SAN DIEGO

1852

A Auburn
D Downieville
M Mokelumne Hill
N NEVADA (Nevada City)
Sr Santa Rosa
V Vernon
W Washington

•Yreka
SISKIYOU 1852
1851-1875 KLAMATH
•Trinidad
Weaverville 1851
•Shasta
Monroeville 1851
Hamilton
SIERRA
PLACER 1851
(unorg.)
W
SR
•M
•Woodville
TULARE 1852

1855

A ALAMEDA (Alvarado)
E Empire City
J Jackson
N Nicolaus
S STANISLAUS

Orleans Bar•
Eureka HUMBOLDT 1853
COLUSA (unorg.)
1854 PLUMAS Quincy
Bidwell Bar•
•Colusa
N
AMADOR 1854
1853
1854 S E
•Mariposa
Snelling
MERCED 1855
•Visalia
SAN BERNARDINO 1853

1860

C Cacheville
Cc Crescent City
Lg La Grange
R Redwood City
Sl San Leandro
Y Yuba City

DEL NORTE
Cc 1859
1856•Red Bluff
TEHAMA
Oroville
1859 Ukiah
•Y
C
•Placerville
SAN MATEO 1856
R Sl
Lg
FRESNO 1856

1870

K Knight's Ferry
L Lakeport
S Silver Mountain
Sa San Andreas
W Woodland

LASSEN 1864
•Susanville
LAKE 1861
W
N
ALPINE 1854
S•
•Bridgeport
Sa
K
MONO 1861
L
INYO •Independence 1866
•Havilah
KERN 1866

1880

H Hollister
O Oakland
SB SAN BENITO

MODOC 1874
Alturas
•Markleeville
•Modesto
•Merced
H•
Salinas SB 1874
•Bakersfield
VENTURA 1872

1895

S Santa Ana
W Willows

•Redding
GLENN 1891
MADERA 1893
Hanford KINGS 1893
ORANGE 1889
RIVERSIDE 1893

1978

Source:
Owen C. Coy, *California County Boundaries*, 1973.

The colors of the counties have no particular significance; they have been chosen simply to aid the eye in following the changes in any particular county.

Scale: 1:10,000,000

IMPERIAL 1907
El Centro

County names, in CAPS, appear only once, on the map covering the period during which the county was created. Unnamed counties are therefore older. The dates indicate the year in which organized county government began. No dates are given, however, for the original 27 counties, all established in 1850.

Names of county seats are shown at the time of first organization, and subsequently, if there is a change. The names of county seats are not shown if they are the same as those of their counties.

Three counties, created in 1850, were not organized until later. Trinity County was attached to Shasta County until 1851, Colusi (the name was changed to Colusa by 1855) was attached to Butte until 1851, and Mendocino to Sonoma until 1859.

One county, Klamath, was disestablished. It existed from 1851 to 1875.

In the 1870's many boundaries, which previously followed ridge lines or parallels or meridians, were redefined in terms of the U.S. Township and Range system. Many of the changes in location are too slight to show at this scale.

When Ventura County was created in 1872, Santa Barbara Island remained part of its namesake county despite its proximity to Ventura County.

EVOLUTION OF COUNTY BOUNDARIES

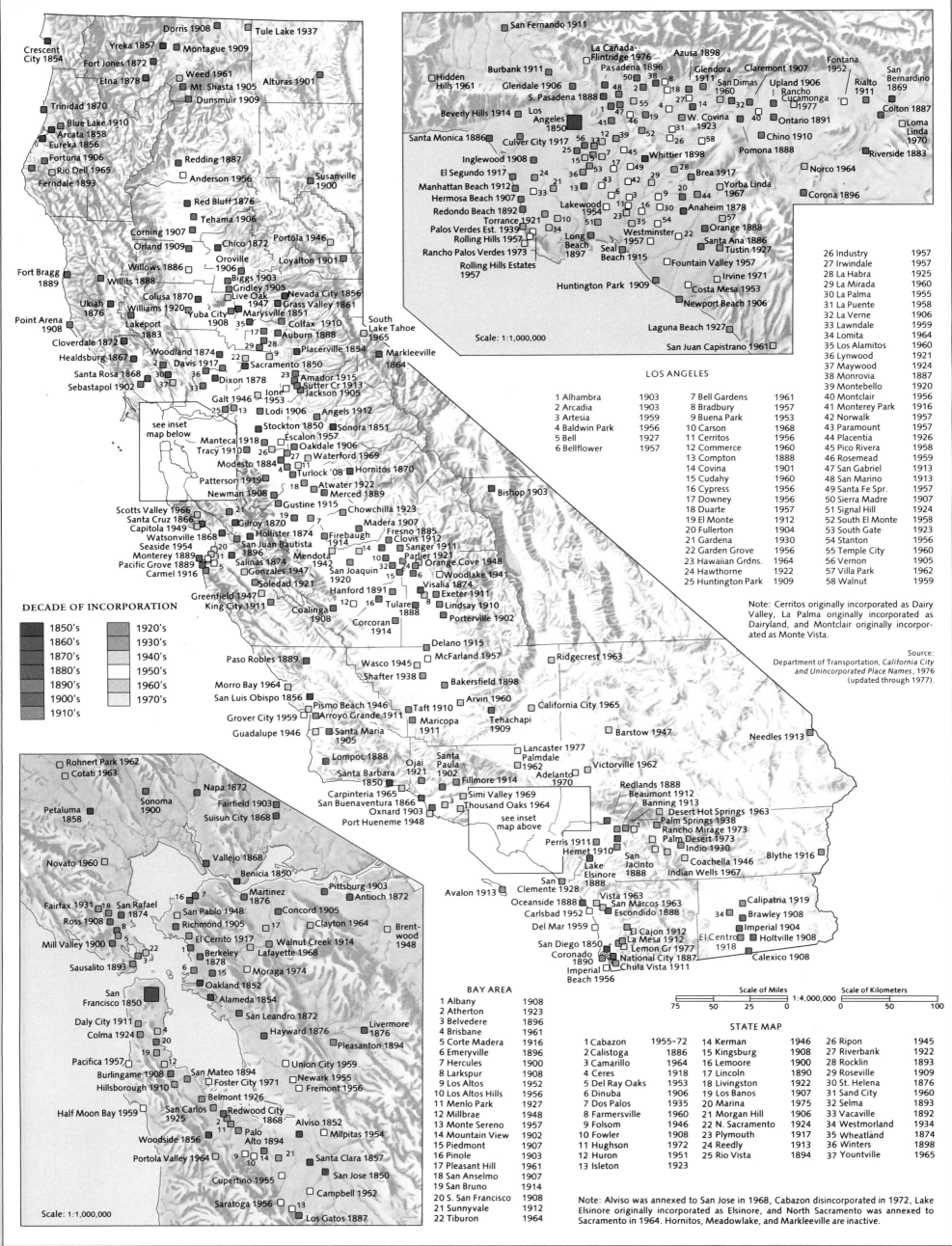

INCORPORATED TOWNS, 1850-1978

The maps of urban growth on this page and on page 20 show built-up areas at approximately twenty-five year intervals since 1900. They are based on USGS topographic maps, and are highly generalized because complete topographic coverage is not available for any single year and the representation of urbanized zones on the topographic maps is not based on single or consistent criteria. Furthermore, 1925 topographic coverage was available only for the Los Angeles area; road maps and other sources were used to fill in the gaps. Although subjective and generalized, the resulting maps clearly demonstrate the expansion of California's four leading urban areas. The smaller maps which show built-up areas at each of the four dates give a more quantitative aspect by indicating with proportional symbols the population of the individual cities, towns, and municipalities within each urban zone. In order to avoid overcrowding of symbols, every succeeding map deletes one or two of the population categories used on the earlier map. Therefore, some places which show up in 1900, such as Benicia, never appear again because of their lack of growth relative to other places on the maps. In contrast, other places, such as Fremont and El Cajon, appear only on more recent maps because of their very slow start as urban centers.

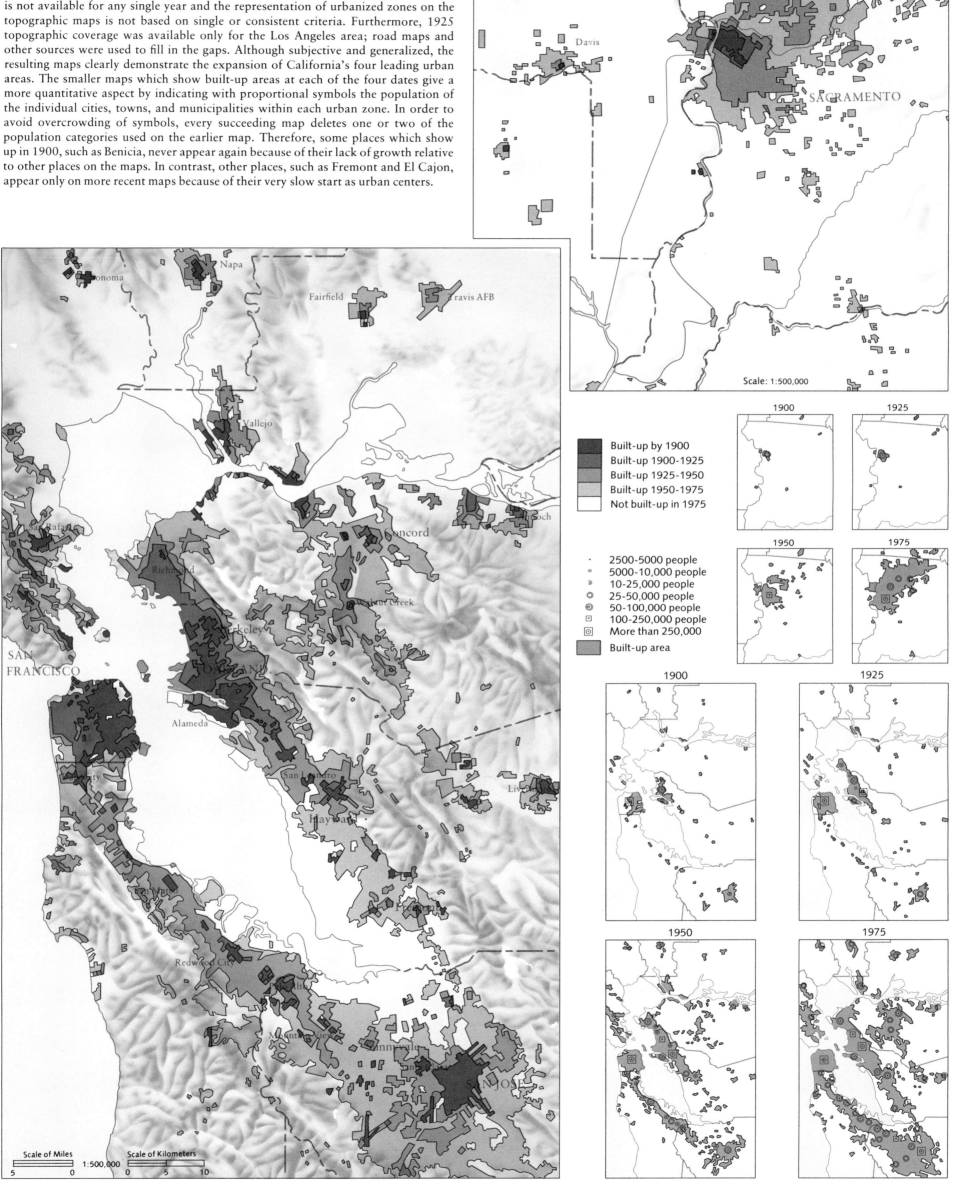

Scale: 1:500,000

Built-up by 1900
Built-up 1900-1925
Built-up 1925-1950
Built-up 1950-1975
Not built-up in 1975

- 2500-5000 people
- 5000-10,000 people
- 10-25,000 people
- 25-50,000 people
- 50-100,000 people
- 100-250,000 people
- More than 250,000
- Built-up area

1900   1925
1950   1975

1900   1925
1950   1975

Scale of Miles   Scale of Kilometers
5   0   1:500,000   0   5   10

EXPANSION OF BAY AREA CITIES AND SACRAMENTO

The form of the bay and the scarcity of level land have strongly shaped the pattern of land use in the Bay Area. Nevertheless, a generally concentric arrangement of decreasing land use intensity was centered on the ports of San Francisco and Oakland. Industry was concentrated along narrow bayside strips and along arterials on both sides of the bay and along the Contra Costa shore. The commercial and administrative centers of San Francisco and Oakland were located very close to their respective ports. Residential density decreased away from these centers: from 40,000 people per square kilometer in parts of Chinatown to less than 4,000 per square kilometer on land built up since 1950. Residential use of extremely low density had begun to move into former rangeland on the hilly outer margins of settlement.

A smaller and essentially independent center was based on the commercial core of downtown San Jose, whose residential growth had already filled the flat croplands and was beginning to climb into the hills. In Sacramento the historic pattern of development was shaped by the Sacramento and American River floodplains, but by the mid-1970's settlement had bypassed these natural hazards by extending onto higher, but still flat, terrain.

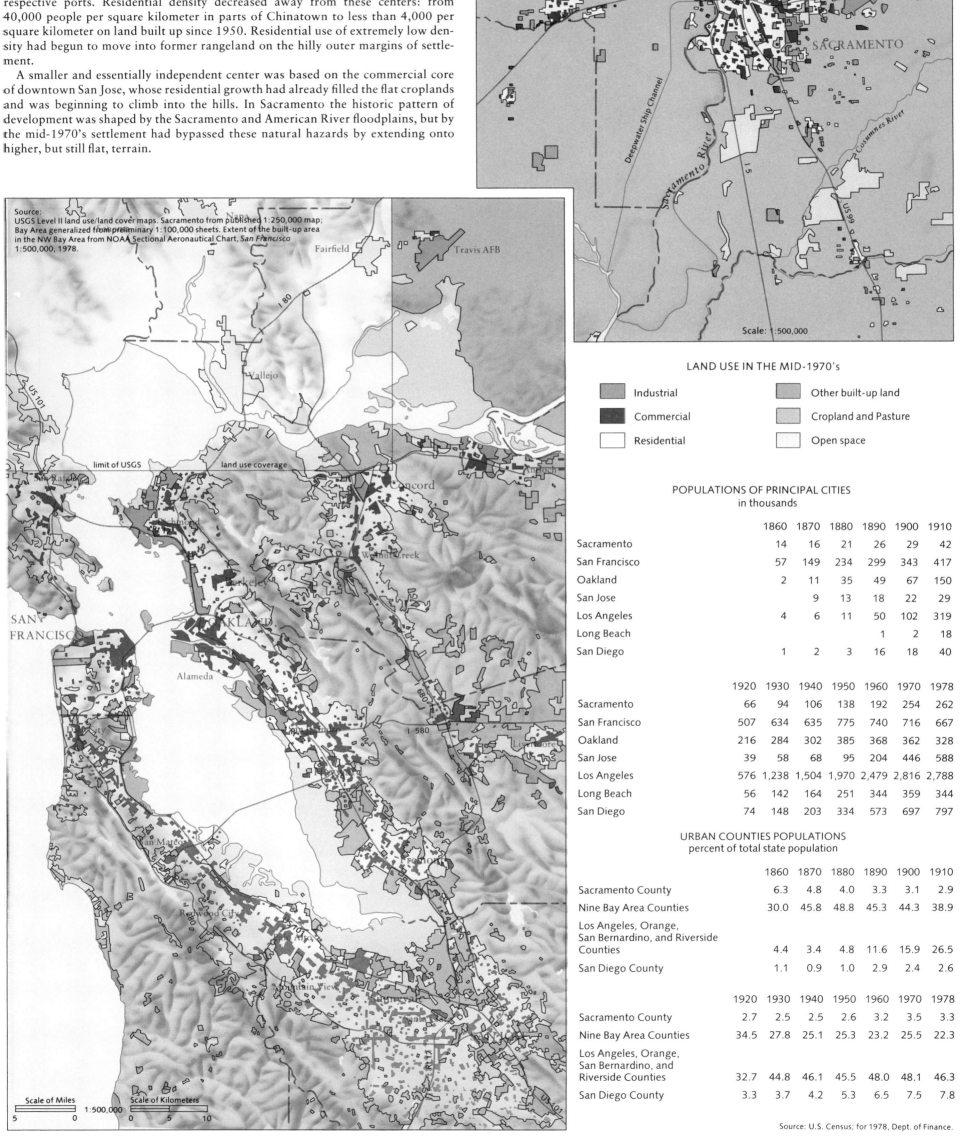

Scale 1:500,000

LAND USE IN THE MID-1970's

- Industrial
- Commercial
- Residential
- Other built-up land
- Cropland and Pasture
- Open space

POPULATIONS OF PRINCIPAL CITIES
in thousands

	1860	1870	1880	1890	1900	1910
Sacramento	14	16	21	26	29	42
San Francisco	57	149	234	299	343	417
Oakland	2	11	35	49	67	150
San Jose		9	13	18	22	29
Los Angeles	4	6	11	50	102	319
Long Beach				1	2	18
San Diego	1	2	3	16	18	40

	1920	1930	1940	1950	1960	1970	1978
Sacramento	66	94	106	138	192	254	262
San Francisco	507	634	635	775	740	716	667
Oakland	216	284	302	385	368	362	328
San Jose	39	58	68	95	204	446	588
Los Angeles	576	1,238	1,504	1,970	2,479	2,816	2,788
Long Beach	56	142	164	251	344	359	344
San Diego	74	148	203	334	573	697	797

URBAN COUNTIES POPULATIONS
percent of total state population

	1860	1870	1880	1890	1900	1910
Sacramento County	6.3	4.8	4.0	3.3	3.1	2.9
Nine Bay Area Counties	30.0	45.8	48.8	45.3	44.3	38.9
Los Angeles, Orange, San Bernardino, and Riverside Counties	4.4	3.4	4.8	11.6	15.9	26.5
San Diego County	1.1	0.9	1.0	2.9	2.4	2.6

	1920	1930	1940	1950	1960	1970	1978
Sacramento County	2.7	2.5	2.5	2.6	3.2	3.5	3.3
Nine Bay Area Counties	34.5	27.8	25.1	25.3	23.2	25.5	22.3
Los Angeles, Orange, San Bernardino, and Riverside Counties	32.7	44.8	46.1	45.5	48.0	48.1	46.3
San Diego County	3.3	3.7	4.2	5.3	6.5	7.5	7.8

Source: U.S. Census; for 1978, Dept. of Finance.

Source:
USGS Level II land use/land cover maps. Sacramento from published 1:250,000 map; Bay Area generalized from preliminary 1:100,000 sheets. Extent of the built-up area in the NW Bay Area from NOAA Sectional Aeronautical Chart, *San Francisco* 1:500,000, 1978.

LAND USE IN THE BAY AREA AND SACRAMENTO

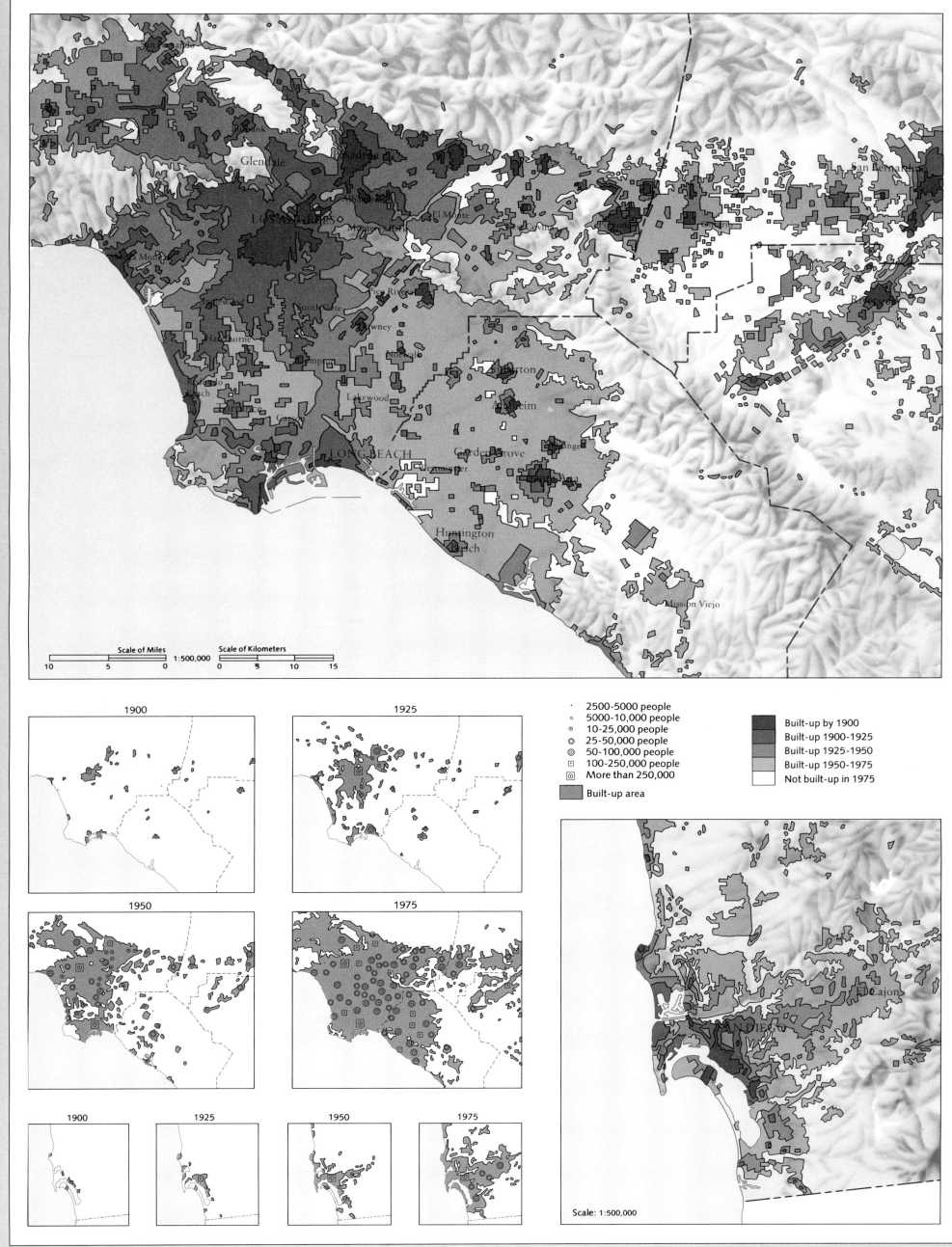

1900

1925

2500-5000 people
5000-10,000 people
10-25,000 people
25-50,000 people
50-100,000 people
100-250,000 people
More than 250,000

Built-up area

Built-up by 1900
Built-up 1900-1925
Built-up 1925-1950
Built-up 1950-1975
Not built-up in 1975

1950

1975

1900

1925

1950

1975

Scale: 1:500,000

Scale of Miles

Scale of Kilometers

1:500,000

EXPANSION OF LOS ANGELES AND SAN DIEGO

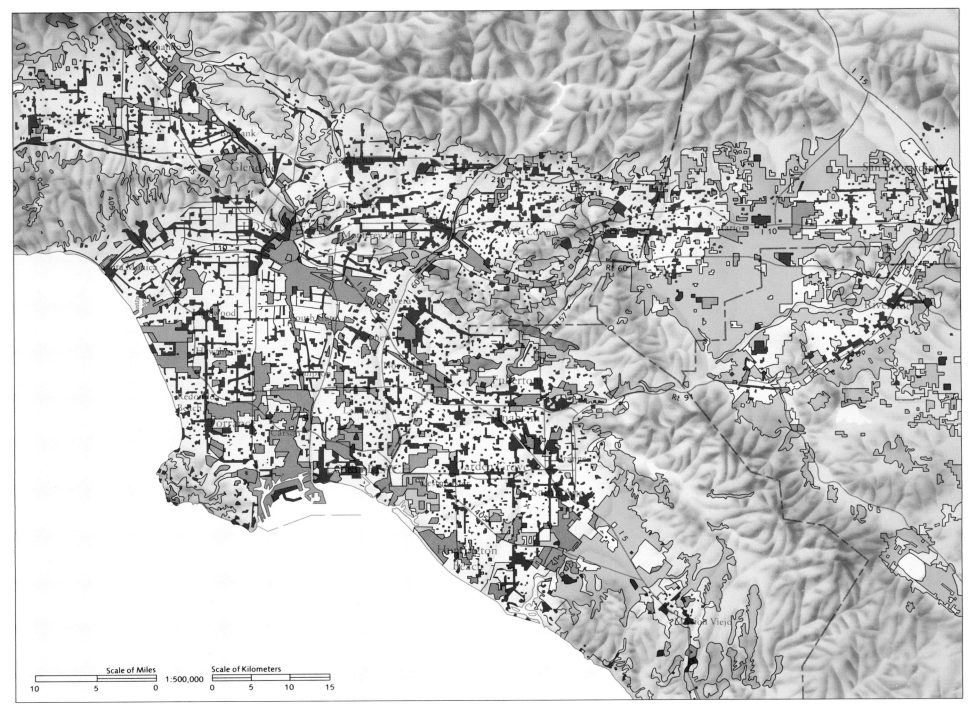

LAND USE IN THE MID-1970's

Industrial	Other Built-up Land
Commercial	Cropland and Pasture
Residential	Open Space

The arrangement of land uses in the Los Angeles area reflected the merging of many once-separate towns into a single continuously urbanized zone and, at the same time, the displacement of the growing residential fringe from the edges of the individual centers to the periphery of the whole agglomeration. The principal industrial area stretched south and east from downtown Los Angeles; narrow industrial belts radiated outward from this district, along the railroads; a second group of industrial zones followed the stretch of oil fields and refineries from Culver City southeastward into Orange County. This extensive complex, although largely devoid of heavy industry, ranked second only to the Chicago SMSA in 1970 in value added by manufacturing.

One of the conspicuous features of urban land use in Los Angeles was the absence of any single preeminent business and commercial center. Prosperity and the automobile liberated Los Angeles from the constraints which have traditionally shaped more compact settlements. They have allowed the simultaneous growth of many commercial centers and a well-developed grid of commercial strips. Consequently the downtown commercial center stayed relatively small. Los Angeles had the third-largest volume of retail sales in the country (1972), but commercial functions were amazingly decentralized.

By 1975, nearly all level land had been occupied, and residential growth was pushing further up the canyons in the hills and mountains surrounding the Los Angeles Basin. Residential land use has been extensive compared to that of older cities in the Northeast; but densities were about the same as in the San Francisco Bay Area. The older sections, built up by 1925, supported 4,000 to 10,000 people on every square kilometer in 1975. Most of the remaining built-up area had about half that density and much lower values were found in the hills and at the margin of the agglomeration.

The pattern in San Diego was much simpler, with built-up land radiating outward from the port. The city had spread across coastal lowlands and onto the adjoining terraces. Not much had been built on the slopes of the steep canyons, however, with the result that fingers of open land extended nearly to the heart of the urban area.

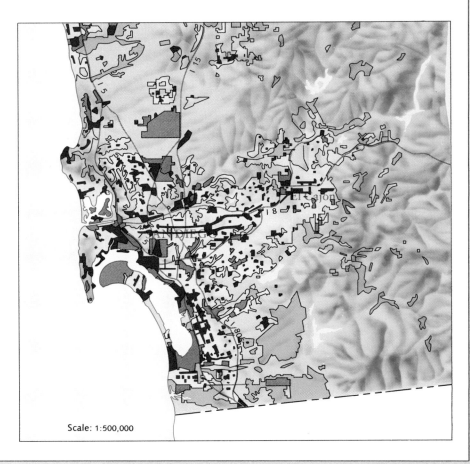

Scale: 1:500,000

Source:
USGS Level II land use/land cover maps, 1:250,000.
Maps are based on aerial photographs taken at various dates, all in the mid-1970's.

LAND USE IN LOS ANGELES AND SAN DIEGO

COMMERCIAL

- Retail
- Offices
- Finance/Insurance
- Wholesale
- Services
- Saloon/Bar
- Restaurant
- Hotel
- Manufacturing and Printing
- Utility & Substation

C Chinese establishment
(data lacking for 1913, 1950)

RESIDENTIAL

- Single Family
- Apartments & Flats
- Rooming/Boarding House
- Tenement

ENTERTAINMENT

- Brothel
- Theater
- Other: includes Social Clubs, Athletic Clubs, Shooting Galleries, Opium Dens.

PUBLIC/GOVERNMENTAL

- Government/Municipal
- Religious Institutions

- School
- Park

OTHER

- Parking Lot
- Parking Garage
- Vacant
- Miscellaneous outbuildings: stables, sheds, garages, privies
- Building entrance
- Special-purpose schools: dance, art, etc.
- Miscellaneous other uses: foundations, art galleries, civic organizations

Source:
Sanborn Map Co., Atlases for 1888, 1923, 1953. 1978 uses mapped by field survey.

1887

1913

Scale of Meters
0   50   100   150   200   250

HISTORICAL SAN FRANCISCO: 1887, 1913

The Sanborn Insurance Company has kept accurate atlases of urban land use for more than a century, and six of their maps are shown on these four pages to depict the changes that parts of San Francisco and Los Angeles have undergone since the 1880's. Maps for 1978 have been added on the basis of field surveys. Twenty blocks are shown in San Francisco and ten blocks in Los Angeles, but blocks are larger in Los Angeles, so that the area covered is about two-thirds of that in San Francisco.

The San Francisco section is shown with west at the top. Union Square is two blocks off to the left, and the map extends from Chinatown on the east and Sutter Street on the south to Nob Hill in the northwest corner. The famous Powell Street Cable Car rises from left to right across the map.

In 1887, San Francisco still retained much of the bawdy character and contrasts in wealth of the gold mining days, although it had 290,000 inhabitants. Nob Hill was occupied by the splendid mansions of the railroad and mining magnates, and the slopes were covered by densely packed single-family homes which gradually gave way, eastward, to boarding houses and tenements occupied by the Chinese, in what was already a recognizable ghetto. Beyond, on either side of Dupont Street, was a red-light district of considerable proportions, and a rim of retail stores bordered Sutter, Kearney and Sacramento Streets. In the twenty blocks there were but one school and three churches, including a synagogue and St. Mary's Catholic Church, one of the few buildings which has remained, even though its function as a cathedral was lost in 1894.

The earthquake and fire changed this scene radically and permanently. By 1913, seven years after the catastrophe, rebuilding had only begun. Multi-story apartment buildings were slowly replacing the single-family homes in the west. The commercial section had been rebuilt, but the whorehouses had moved elsewhere, and the Chinese tenements were gone. Few mansions survived the quake; none retained its old function. The Flood Mansion, for example, was converted into the Pacific Union Club.

1950

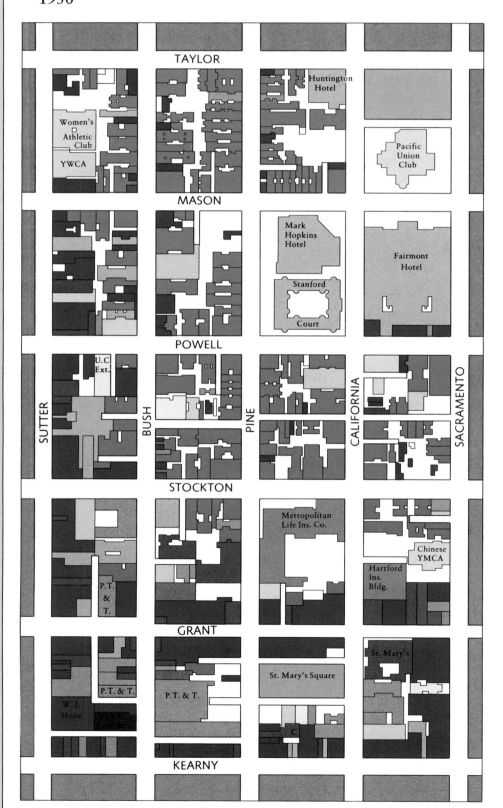

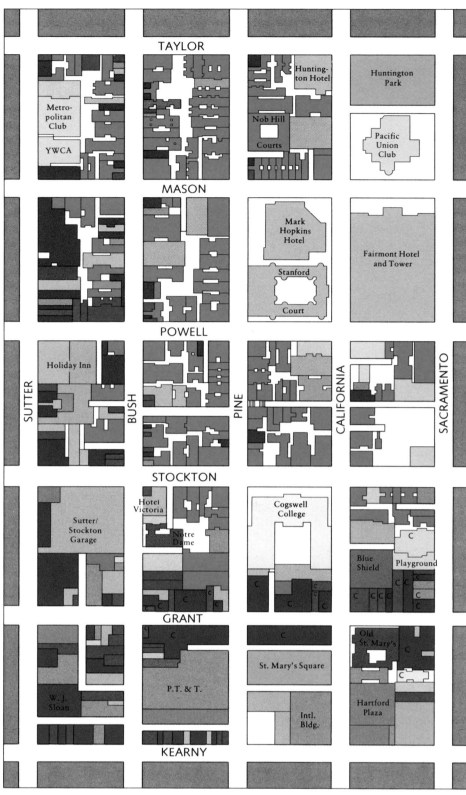

1978

HISTORICAL SAN FRANCISCO: 1950, 1978

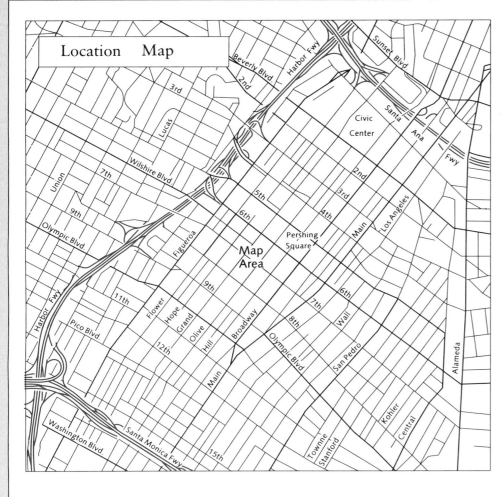

Location Map

1888

FLOWER

6th Street
Baseball Park

HOPE

GRAND

8TH

7TH

6TH

OLIVE

Horse
Sale
Yard

HILL

U.S. Military
Headquarters

FORT

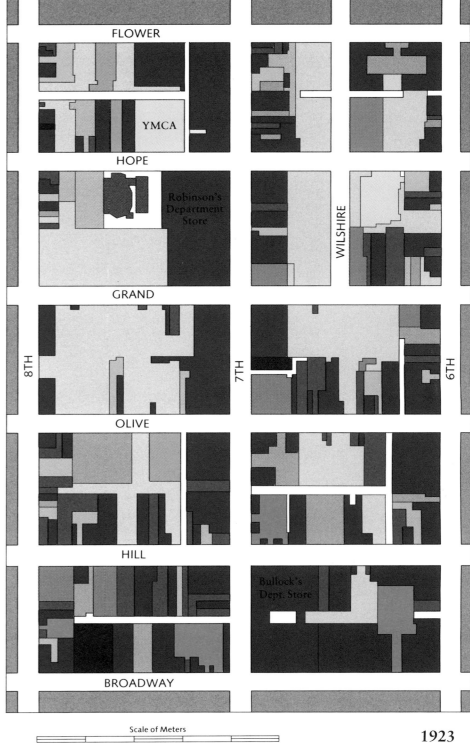

FLOWER

YMCA

HOPE

Robinson's
Department
Store

WILSHIRE

GRAND

8TH

7TH

6TH

OLIVE

HILL

Bullock's
Dept. Store

BROADWAY

Scale of Meters

0   50   100   150   200   250

1923

Elsewhere on Nob Hill the elegant traditions were partly reconstituted in the restored Fairmont Hotel, gutted on opening night by the fires of 1906, or in plush apartments such as Stanford Court. Much vacant land remained, however, as San Francisco rose slowly from its ashes.

By 1950, much had happened to San Francisco, but the land use pattern of 1913 had persisted. Famous hotels such as the Fairmont, the Mark Hopkins and the Huntington surrounded the Pacific Union Club and were, in turn, bounded by a solid phalanx of substantial apartment houses. The commercial zone had expanded westward along most of Sutter Street, but the major change was the appearance of office buildings. In this solidly residential and commercial part of town, there were few schools, churches and parks, but neither, surprisingly, was much space devoted to parking lots, garages, or service stations.

The main change after 1950 was the intrusion of corporate skyscrapers on the eastern edge of the area; the Hartford, International, and Pacific Telephone Buildings are all over 100 meters tall. A slight increase in the number and kinds of hotels, and a very slight increment of parking lots, represent the only significant differences on Nob Hill and its residential crown. Chinatown, however, continued to grow, harboring a denser population and becoming increasingly commercial along Grant Street, a tourist thoroughfare lined by restaurants and curio shops.

The Los Angeles blocks are located in downtown Los Angeles just southeast of the Harbor Freeway, halfway between its intersection with the Santa Monica and Santa Ana freeways. Northwest is at the top of the map, with Pershing Square immediately to the right, and Civic Center five blocks further northeast. Wilshire Boulevard extends two blocks into the area between 6th and 7th streets.

HISTORICAL LOS ANGELES: 1888, 1923

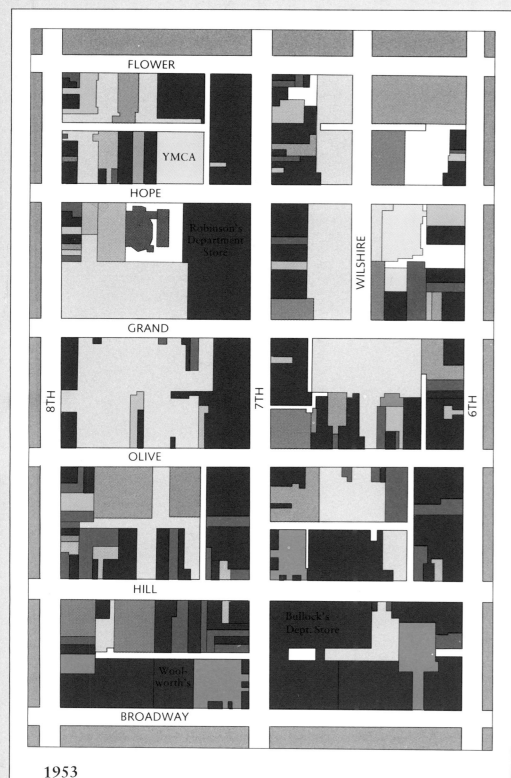

1953

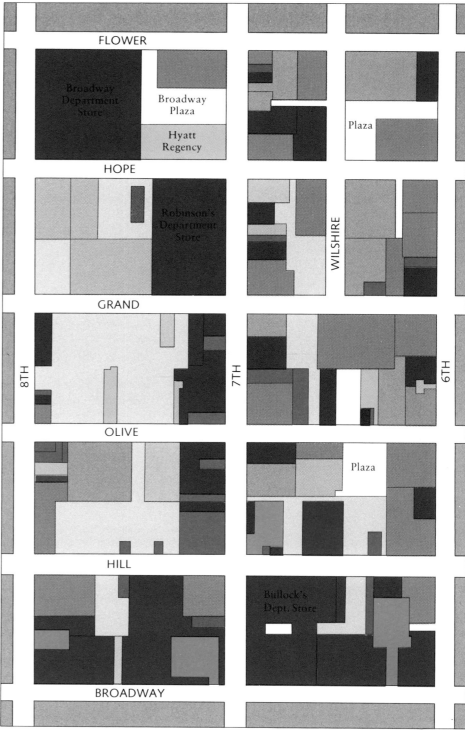

1978

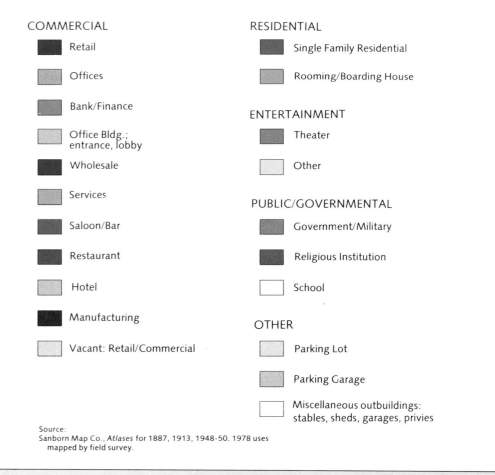

In 1888, Los Angeles was still a small but fast-growing city with a population of between 40,000 and 50,000. The ten-block area mapped, though very close to the center of town, was still almost completely residential. Apart from a church and two schools, there were only single-family homes and their outbuildings on relatively narrow but long lots. The streets were wide and tree-lined, probably by palms. The Baseball Park and the United States Military Headquarters added a touch of open greenery to an already diffuse residential landscape that set the tone for much of Los Angeles in subsequent years.

This section did not remain residential, however. It was soon overtaken by the spreading central business district as part of the phenomenal growth of Southern California and its metropolis. Between 1888 and 1923, the entire area had been given over to offices and retail stores, including two major department stores, and many small restaurants complemented the plethora of stores and offices. The early significance of automobiles in Southern California was already apparent: nearly 30 per cent of the total area was being used to park cars.

Relatively few changes occurred after 1923. By 1953, a small amount of consolidation of operations had taken place in one block, but otherwise the retail, office, and parking proportions of thirty years earlier were retained. By 1978, some parking lots and retail stores had made way for banks and offices, and some structures had been demolished in order to find room for cars. But, except for a slight increase in car parks and a change from retail to financial activities, the functions were very much as they had been in 1953, and even in 1923.

The only similarity between the San Francisco and Los Angeles tracts, other than their grid plans, is that both changed enormously at a relatively early date. The change in San Francisco was related to a disaster that crippled the city for a long time, whereas the change in Los Angeles came about from a continuing boom. San Francisco kept its dense but wealthy residential quarter near the center, while a prophetically low density of residential population in Los Angeles gave way entirely to other functions and was transferred outward to the limits of the existing transportation facilities.

COMMERCIAL

- Retail
- Offices
- Bank/Finance
- Office Bldg.; entrance, lobby
- Wholesale
- Services
- Saloon/Bar
- Restaurant
- Hotel
- Manufacturing
- Vacant: Retail/Commercial

RESIDENTIAL

- Single Family Residential
- Rooming/Boarding House

ENTERTAINMENT

- Theater
- Other

PUBLIC/GOVERNMENTAL

- Government/Military
- Religious Institution
- School

OTHER

- Parking Lot
- Parking Garage
- Miscellaneous outbuildings: stables, sheds, garages, privies

Source:
Sanborn Map Co., *Atlases* for 1887, 1913, 1948-50. 1978 uses mapped by field survey.

HISTORICAL LOS ANGELES: 1953, 1978

PATTERNS OF POPULATION CHANGE

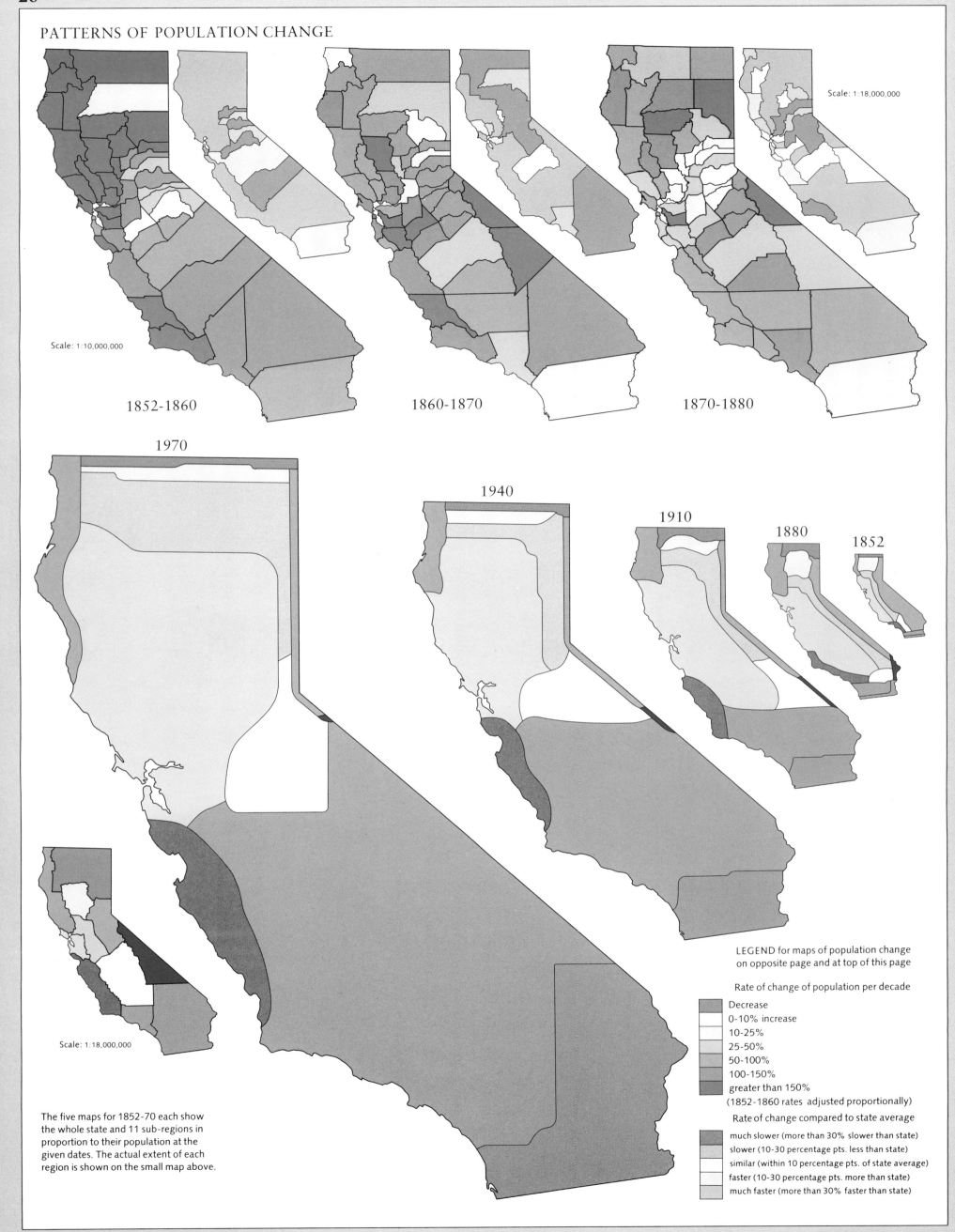

Scale: 1:18,000,000

Scale: 1:10,000,000

1852-1860

1860-1870

1870-1880

1970

1940

1910

1880

1852

Scale: 1:18,000,000

The five maps for 1852-70 each show the whole state and 11 sub-regions in proportion to their population at the given dates. The actual extent of each region is shown on the small map above.

LEGEND for maps of population change on opposite page and at top of this page

Rate of change of population per decade

Decrease
0-10% increase
10-25%
25-50%
50-100%
100-150%
greater than 150%
(1852-1860 rates adjusted proportionally)

Rate of change compared to state average

much slower (more than 30% slower than state)
slower (10-30 percentage pts. less than state)
similar (within 10 percentage pts. of state average)
faster (10-30 percentage pts. more than state)
much faster (more than 30% faster than state)

POPULATION GROWTH, 1852-1880

1880-1890

1890-1900

1900-1910

1910-1920

1920-1930

1930-1940

Scale: 1:18,000,000

Scale: 1:10,000,000

1940-1950

1950-1960

1960-1970

POPULATION GROWTH, 1880-1970

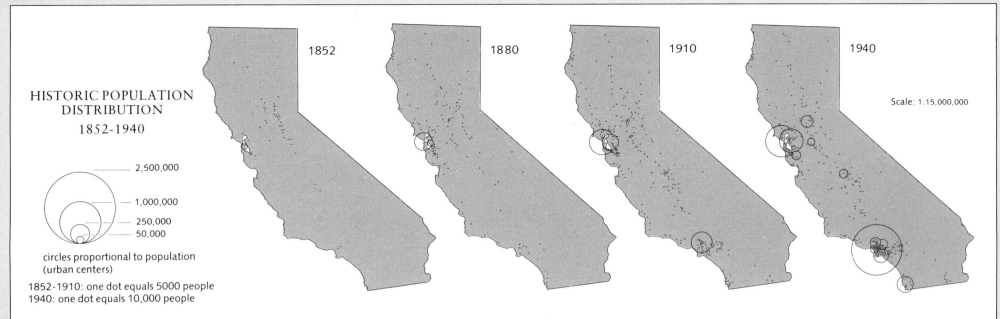

HISTORIC POPULATION
DISTRIBUTION
1852-1940

2,500,000
1,000,000
250,000
50,000

circles proportional to population
(urban centers)

1852-1910: one dot equals 5000 people
1940: one dot equals 10,000 people

1852   1880   1910   1940

Scale: 1:15,000,000

California is the only state that has grown faster than the rest of the Union during each decade since 1850. The population increases in the last decade of this century, in the '20's and again in the '40's, were particularly rapid both in absolute terms and in comparison to the rest of the country. The maps on pages 26 and 27 show the remarkable general increase in population since 1850; smaller inset maps indicate where population growth has been faster than the state average and where it has lagged. In the early decades, the Bay Area and Northern California grew more rapidly than the average. From 1900 to 1930, the San Joaquin Valley did the same. Southern California has had dramatic increases, well above the state average, particularly since 1880. Even the mountain counties, which experienced drastic declines after their first mushroom growth, ranked high in the 1890's and 1930's when hard times made mining relatively profitable. They were also among the fastest-growing areas in the 1970's when urban growth began to slow down.

One of the most striking features of the population distribution in 1978 was the large amount of empty terrain. Nearly two-thirds of the land had fewer than 2 persons per square kilometer, and only 15 per cent of the land supported densities greater than 10 per square kilometer. The rural population has only slowly filled in a few coastal areas and coast range valleys. Most of it is in the Central Valley, but even there, large numbers are found on the periphery of the urban areas. There are also a few "rural" extensions of urban living, such as the shores of Lake Tahoe or the desert around Palm Springs.

Most of California's population was, of course, urban. Almost 91 per cent lived in cities of more than 2,500, another 8 per cent was classed as rural non-farm leaving only a quarter of a million rural farm people in the whole state.

The urban places of California stretch out along major highways. The coastal string along US 101 is very sparse north of San Francisco, and indeed has very few beads except the three enormous clusters around San Francisco, Los Angeles, and San Diego. An inland string along US 99 is more evenly but less spectacularly strung from Bakersfield to Yreka with a small extension from San Bernardino to Calexico found along State 86. The linear pattern is internally evident along both shores of San Francisco Bay, but in Los Angeles, the urban centers, although limited to the lowland, form a more amorphous cluster.

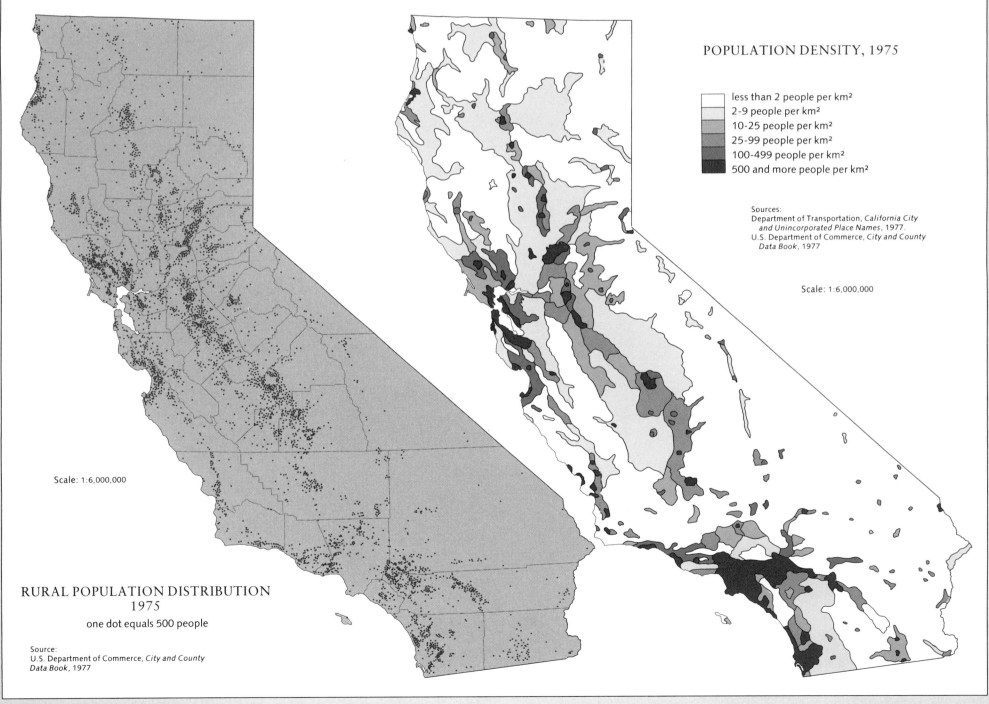

POPULATION DENSITY, 1975

less than 2 people per km²
2-9 people per km²
10-25 people per km²
25-99 people per km²
100-499 people per km²
500 and more people per km²

Sources:
Department of Transportation, *California City
and Unincorporated Place Names*, 1977.
U.S. Department of Commerce, *City and County
Data Book*, 1977

Scale: 1:6,000,000

RURAL POPULATION DISTRIBUTION
1975
one dot equals 500 people

Scale: 1:6,000,000

Source:
U.S. Department of Commerce, *City and County
Data Book*, 1977

POPULATION DENSITY

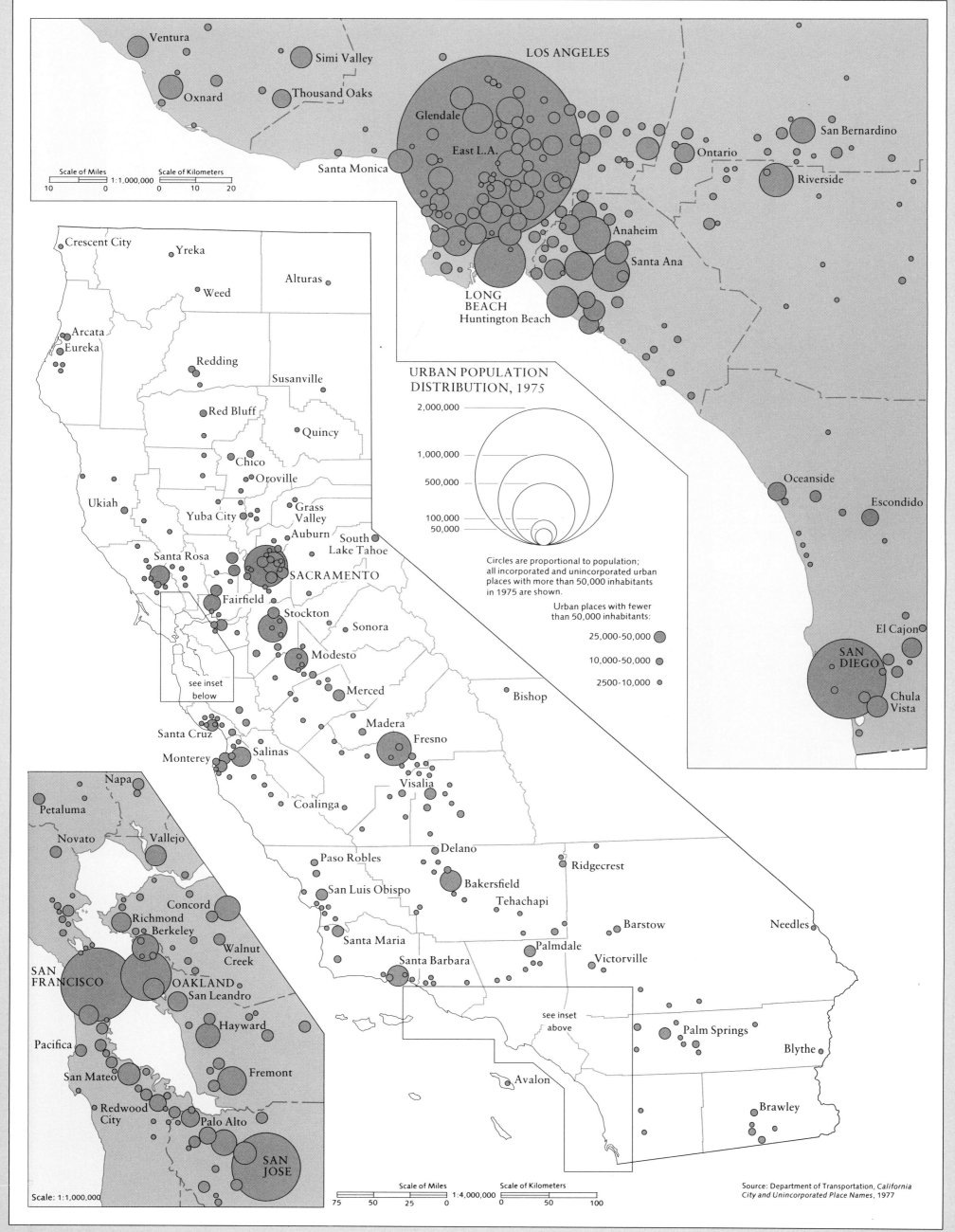

Ventura
Simi Valley
Oxnard
Thousand Oaks
Santa Monica

LOS ANGELES
Glendale
East L.A.

San Bernardino
Ontario
Riverside

Anaheim
Santa Ana

LONG
BEACH
Huntington Beach

Crescent City
Yreka
Weed
Alturas

Arcata
Eureka
Redding
Susanville
Red Bluff
Quincy
Chico
Oroville
Ukiah
Grass Valley
Yuba City
Auburn
South Lake Tahoe
Santa Rosa
SACRAMENTO
Fairfield
Stockton
Sonora
see inset below
Modesto
Santa Cruz
Merced
Monterey
Salinas
Madera
Fresno
Coalinga
Visalia
Bishop

Oceanside

Escondido

URBAN POPULATION
DISTRIBUTION, 1975

2,000,000

1,000,000

500,000

100,000
50,000

Circles are proportional to population;
all incorporated and unincorporated urban
places with more than 50,000 inhabitants
in 1975 are shown.

Urban places with fewer
than 50,000 inhabitants:

25,000-50,000

10,000-50,000

2500-10,000

El Cajon

SAN
DIEGO

Chula
Vista

Napa
Petaluma
Novato
Vallejo
Concord
Richmond
Berkeley
Walnut
Creek
SAN
FRANCISCO
OAKLAND
San Leandro
Hayward
Pacifica
San Mateo
Fremont
Redwood City
Palo Alto
SAN
JOSE

Delano
Paso Robles
Ridgecrest
San Luis Obispo
Bakersfield
Tehachapi
Santa Maria
Barstow
Needles
Palmdale
Victorville
Santa Barbara

see inset
above

Palm Springs

Blythe

Avalon

Brawley

Scale: 1:1,000,000

Scale of Miles   Scale of Kilometers
75   50   25   0   1:4,000,000   0   50   100

Source: Department of Transportation, *California
City and Unincorporated Place Names, 1977*

Scale of Miles   Scale of Kilometers
10   0   1:1,000,000   0   10   20

URBAN POPULATION

AGE-SEX PYRAMIDS, 1970

California, with its 22 million people, now models the age-sex structure of the United States. Until 1940, however, the state had a male surplus, particularly among the working-age groups. With the pioneering period over, women, children, and the elderly have balanced the state pyramid. In 1970, the counties exhibited some demographic variability: large percentages of children in the agricultural counties of the Central Valley, large cohorts in the working-age populations of the suburban counties, and over-representation of the elderly in resort counties such as Lake and Nevada. Male surpluses existed in the military and agricultural counties. More striking deviations existed at the neighborhood level, as the university tract in Berkeley and the naval tract in San Diego reveal.

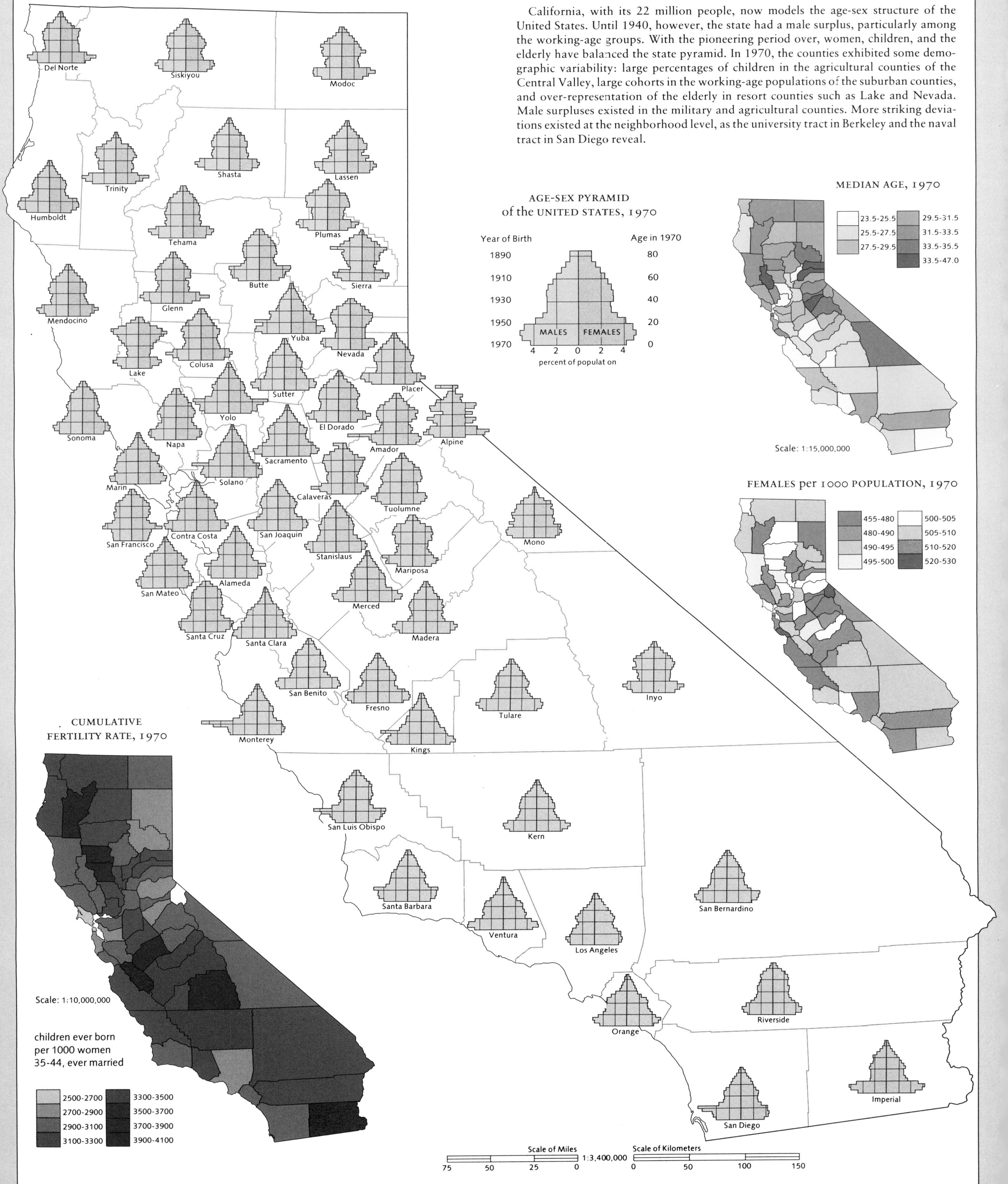

Del Norte
Siskiyou
Modoc
Shasta
Lassen
Trinity
Humboldt
Tehama
Plumas
Butte
Sierra
Glenn
Mendocino
Yuba
Nevada
Colusa
Lake
Sutter
Placer
Yolo
El Dorado
Sonoma
Napa
Amador
Alpine
Sacramento
Marin
Solano
Calaveras
Tuolumne
Contra Costa
San Joaquin
Mono
San Francisco
Stanislaus
Mariposa
Alameda
Merced
San Mateo
Madera
Santa Cruz
Santa Clara
Inyo
San Benito
Fresno
Tulare
Monterey
Kings
San Luis Obispo
Kern
Santa Barbara
San Bernardino
Ventura
Los Angeles
Orange
Riverside
San Diego
Imperial

AGE-SEX PYRAMID
of the UNITED STATES, 1970

Year of Birth		Age in 1970
1890		80
1910		60
1930		40
1950		20
1970	MALES FEMALES	0

4 2 0 2 4
percent of population

MEDIAN AGE, 1970

23.5-25.5   29.5-31.5
25.5-27.5   31.5-33.5
27.5-29.5   33.5-35.5
             35.5-47.0

Scale: 1:15,000,000

FEMALES per 1000 POPULATION, 1970

455-480   500-505
480-490   505-510
490-495   510-520
495-500   520-530

CUMULATIVE FERTILITY RATE, 1970

Scale: 1:10,000,000

children ever born
per 1000 women
35-44, ever married

2500-2700   3300-3500
2700-2900   3500-3700
2900-3100   3700-3900
3100-3300   3900-4100

Scale of Miles   Scale of Kilometers
75 50 25 0   1:3,400,000   0   50   100   150

DEMOGRAPHY

HISTORIC AGE-SEX PYRAMIDS of the STATE

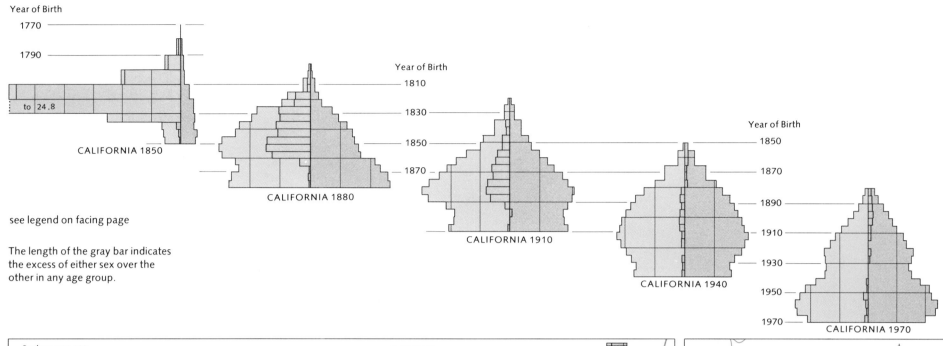

Year of Birth
1770
1790
to 24.8
CALIFORNIA 1850

see legend on facing page

The length of the gray bar indicates
the excess of either sex over the
other in any age group.

Year of Birth
1810
1830
1850
1870
CALIFORNIA 1880

Year of Birth
1850
1870
CALIFORNIA 1910

1890
1910
1930
CALIFORNIA 1940

Year of Birth
1850
1870
1890
1910
1930
1950
1970
CALIFORNIA 1970

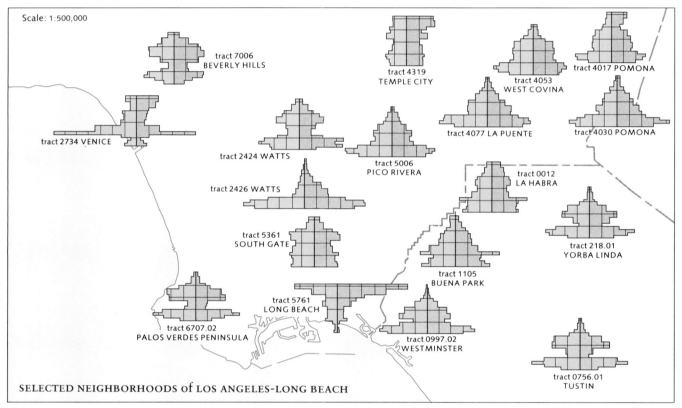

Scale: 1:500,000

tract 7006 BEVERLY HILLS
tract 4319 TEMPLE CITY
tract 4017 POMONA
tract 4053 WEST COVINA
tract 2734 VENICE
tract 2424 WATTS
tract 5006 PICO RIVERA
tract 4077 LA PUENTE
tract 4030 POMONA
tract 2426 WATTS
tract 0012 LA HABRA
tract 5361 SOUTH GATE
tract 218.01 YORBA LINDA
tract 1105 BUENA PARK
tract 5761 LONG BEACH
tract 6707.02 PALOS VERDES PENINSULA
tract 0997.02 WESTMINSTER
tract 0756.01 TUSTIN

SELECTED NEIGHBORHOODS of LOS ANGELES-LONG BEACH

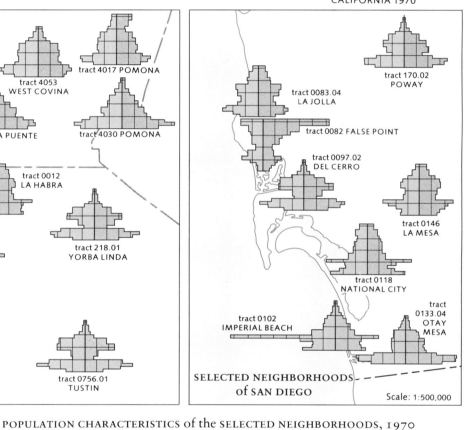

tract 170.02 POWAY
tract 0083.04 LA JOLLA
tract 0082 FALSE POINT
tract 0097.02 DEL CERRO
tract 0146 LA MESA
tract 0118 NATIONAL CITY
tract 0102 IMPERIAL BEACH
tract 0133.04 OTAY MESA

SELECTED NEIGHBORHOODS of SAN DIEGO

Scale: 1:500,000

SELECTED NEIGHBORHOODS of the SAN FRANCISCO BAY AREA

tract 3760 RICHMOND
tract 3373 WALNUT CREEK
tract 1230 BELVEDERE
tract 0114 SAN FRANCISCO (Chinatown)
tract 4229 BERKELEY (downtown)
tract 0307 SAN FRANCISCO (St. Francis Woods)
tract 4053 OAKLAND (Lake Merritt)
tract 0158 SAN FRANCISCO (Fillmore)
tract 4335 SAN LEANDRO
tract 4301 CASTRO VALLEY
tract 6002 DALY CITY
tract 4402 UNION CITY
tract 6033 PACIFICA
tract 6081 FOSTER CITY

Scale: 1:500,000

POPULATION CHARACTERISTICS of the SELECTED NEIGHBORHOODS, 1970

Tract	Popu-lation	Births/1000 Women, 35-44, ever married	Ethnic Composition	% Native of Native Parentage	Median Family Income	Median Years of Education
Watts 2424	1,147	3,444	98% Black	97%	$ 9,152	10.8
Watts 2426	5,175	5,897	99% Black	98	3,592	10.7
Venice 2734	3,193	2,106	97% Anglo	65	6,500	12.5
Pomona 4017	5,731	3,120	95% Anglo, 3% Black	82	11,739	12.5
Pomona 4030	4,750	3,800	43% Black, 30% Anglo, 20% Mexican	84	8,487	11.7
W. Covina 4053	7,462	3,009	88% Anglo, 10% Mexican	80	11,441	12.4
La Puente 4077	8,099	4,373	47% Mexican, 46% Anglo, 5% Black	67	9,298	12.0
Temple C. 4319	3,105	2,693	99% Anglo	72	6,771	12.3
Pico Riv. 5006	5,452	4,097	86% Mexican	48	7,345	9.7
South Gate 5361	7,759	2,243	90% Anglo	78	11,064	12.2
Long Beach 5761	2,673	—	98% Anglo	59	8,167	12.0
Palos Verd. 6707.02	5,561	2,722	98% Anglo	75	23,683	14.6
Bev. Hills 7006	6,285	2,591	96% Anglo	50	48,370	14.1
La Habra 0012	5,183	3,331	79% Anglo, 19% Mexican	75	8,014	12.0
Yorba Lin. 0218.01	6,865	5,500	92% Anglo, 7% Mexican	81	15,870	13.4
Tustin 0756	5,886	2,670	99% Anglo	81	22,174	15.0
Westminster 0997.02	3,515	3,587	96% Anglo	80	10,988	12.3
Buena Park 1105	5,022	2,618	85% Anglo, 13% Mexican	84	8,514	12.0
False Pt. 0082	3,253	2,645	96% Anglo	61	11,667	13.7
La Jolla 0083.04	4,949	2,347	99% Anglo	75	18,284	16.0
Del Cerro 0097.02	11,193	2,651	94% Anglo, 6% Mexican	77	19,713	15.0
Imperial B. 0102	6,442	3,438	86% Anglo, 9% Mexican	85	8,014	12.0
Natl. City 0118	6,309	2,613	60% Anglo, 30% Mexican	70	6,187	11.4
Otay Mesa 0133.04	1,056	5,459	50% Mexican, 35% Anglo, 15% Black	75	9,146	9.5
La Mesa 0146	6,065	2,737	98% Anglo	80	8,996	12.7
Poway 0170.02	5,186	3,672	98% Anglo	91	11,265	12.6
Chinatown 0114	3,697	2,608	99% Chinese	8	5,597	19.2
Fillmore 0158	7,464	2,533	80% Black	91	6,353	12.1
St. Fr. Wd. 0307	7,152	1,932	83% Anglo, 10% Mexican, 7% Black	63	15,454	12.7
Belvedere 1230	2,599	2,510	over 95% Anglo	74	24,213	15.7
Walnut Cr. 3373	4,800	2,844	93% Anglo	81	18,968	14.9
Richmond 3760	5,254	4,004	74% Black, 13% Mexican	87	6,434	9.6
Oakland 4053	4,098	1,477	over 90% Anglo, 8% Mexican	68	10,600	12.3
Berkeley 4229	6,663	1,630	over 90% Anglo, 4% Black	84	6,779	15.6
Castro V. 4301	1,355	2,400	95% Anglo, 3% Black	68	17,107	12.9
S. Leandro 4335	5,102	2,750	80% Anglo, 15% Mexican	75	13,120	12.4
Union City 4402	4,689	4,654	81% Mexican	54	8,396	8.7
Daly City 6002	3,308	2,741	80% Anglo, 12% Mexican, 9% Black	64	7,753	12.0
Pacifica 6033	7,814	3,057	over 85% Anglo, 11% Mexican	75	13,198	12.5
Foster City 6081	3,331	2,289	95% Anglo	79	16,743	14.1

Source:
Census of Population, 1970

DEMOGRAPHY

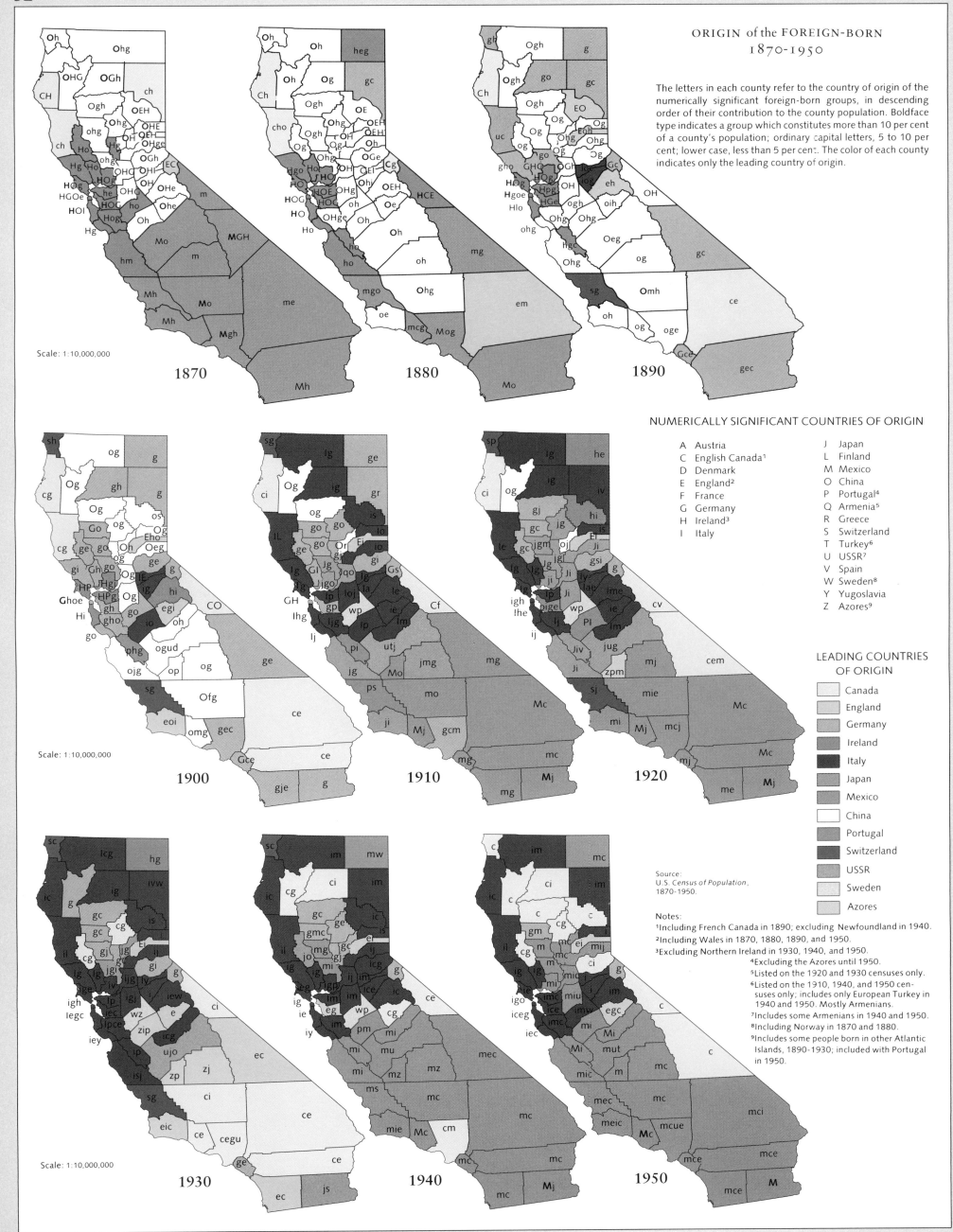

ORIGIN of the FOREIGN-BORN
1870-1950

The letters in each county refer to the country of origin of the numerically significant foreign-born groups, in descending order of their contribution to the county population. Boldface type indicates a group which constitutes more than 10 per cent of a county's population; ordinary capital letters, 5 to 10 per cent; lower case, less than 5 per cent. The color of each county indicates only the leading country of origin.

NUMERICALLY SIGNIFICANT COUNTRIES OF ORIGIN

A	Austria	J	Japan
C	English Canada[1]	L	Finland
D	Denmark	M	Mexico
E	England[2]	O	China
F	France	P	Portugal[4]
G	Germany	Q	Armenia[5]
H	Ireland[3]	R	Greece
I	Italy	S	Switzerland
		T	Turkey[6]
		U	USSR[7]
		V	Spain
		W	Sweden[8]
		Y	Yugoslavia
		Z	Azores[9]

LEADING COUNTRIES OF ORIGIN

- Canada
- England
- Germany
- Ireland
- Italy
- Japan
- Mexico
- China
- Portugal
- Switzerland
- USSR
- Sweden
- Azores

Source:
U.S. Census of Population, 1870-1950.

Notes:
[1] Including French Canada in 1890; excluding Newfoundland in 1940.
[2] Including Wales in 1870, 1880, 1890, and 1950.
[3] Excluding Northern Ireland in 1930, 1940, and 1950.
[4] Excluding the Azores until 1950.
[5] Listed on the 1920 and 1930 censuses only.
[6] Listed on the 1910, 1940, and 1950 censuses only; includes only European Turkey in 1940 and 1950. Mostly Armenians.
[7] Includes some Armenians in 1940 and 1950.
[8] Including Norway in 1870 and 1880.
[9] Includes some people born in other Atlantic Islands, 1890-1930; included with Portugal in 1950.

Scale: 1:10,000,000

1870   1880   1890

1900   1910   1920

1930   1940   1950

IMMIGRATION

Since statehood in 1850, California has been attractive to foreign and domestic migrants. In the nineteenth century, Germans, Irish, and Chinese joined the American pioneers. They were succeeded, early in the twentieth century, by large numbers of Italians. The diverse European immigration began to decline after 1920, however, with only Russia and the United Kingdom as significant source areas. Since then, Canada and particularly Mexico have supplied the greatest numbers of immigrants, augmented by lesser immigration from Southeast Asia. Within the United States, the Midwest and the South are the principal contributors to the population which is not native to the state.

All data is from U.S. Census. Graphs show only those countries or regions listed in continuous census years. The line from 1950 to 1970 is dotted or dashed, however, because the figures for foreign-born whites in 1960 are unpublished.

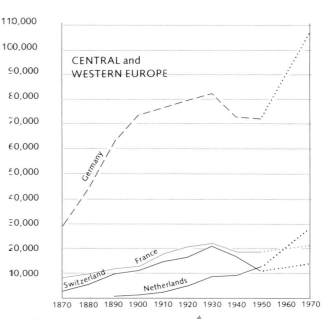

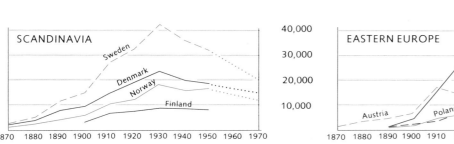

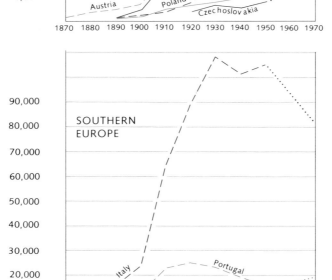

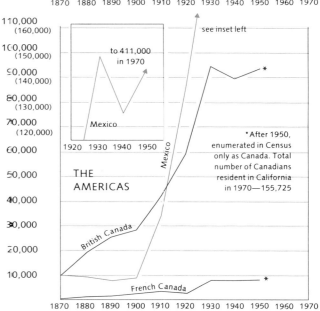

SCANDINAVIA

EASTERN EUROPE

CENTRAL and WESTERN EUROPE

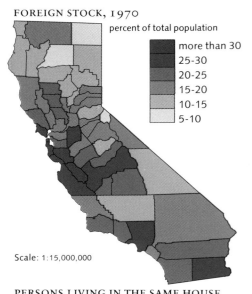

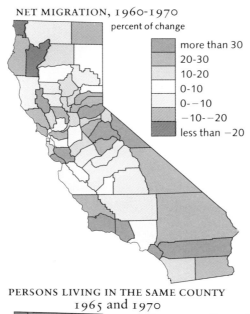

BRITISH ISLES

*After 1950, enumerated in Census only as United Kingdom. Total number in California in 1970—129,957

SOUTHERN EUROPE

THE AMERICAS

*After 1950, enumerated in Census only as Canada. Total number of Canadians resident in California in 1970—155,725

to 411,000 in 1970

Mexico

see inset left

FOREIGN-BORN WHITES in CALIFORNIA, 1870-1970
by country of origin

FOREIGN STOCK, 1970
percent of total population

| more than 30 |
| 25-30 |
| 20-25 |
| 15-20 |
| 10-15 |
| 5-10 |

Scale: 1:15,000,000

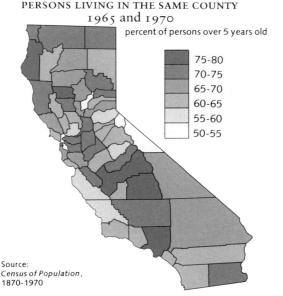

NET MIGRATION, 1960-1970
percent of change

| more than 30 |
| 20-30 |
| 10-20 |
| 0-10 |
| 0- -10 |
| -10- -20 |
| less than -20 |

MIGRANTS TO CALIFORNIA

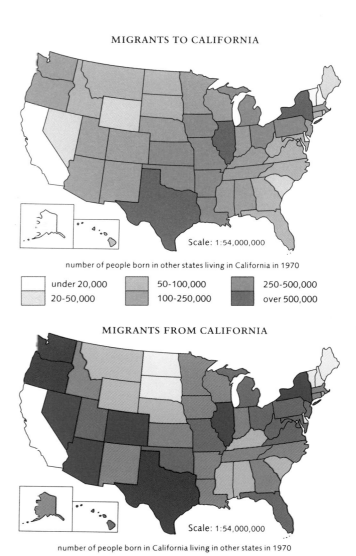

number of people born in other states living in California in 1970

| under 20,000 | 50-100,000 | 250-500,000 |
| 20-50,000 | 100-250,000 | over 500,000 |

Scale: 1:54,000,000

PERSONS LIVING IN THE SAME HOUSE
1965 and 1970
percent of persons over 5 years old

| 55-60 |
| 50-55 |
| 45-50 |
| 40-45 |
| 35-40 |

PERSONS LIVING IN THE SAME COUNTY
1965 and 1970
percent of persons over 5 years old

| 75-80 |
| 70-75 |
| 65-70 |
| 60-65 |
| 55-60 |
| 50-55 |

Source:
Census of Population,
1870-1970

MIGRANTS FROM CALIFORNIA

number of people born in California living in other states in 1970

| under 5,000 | 15-25,000 | 50-100,000 |
| 5-15,000 | 25-50,000 | over 100,000 |

Scale: 1:54,000,000

MIGRATION AND MOBILITY

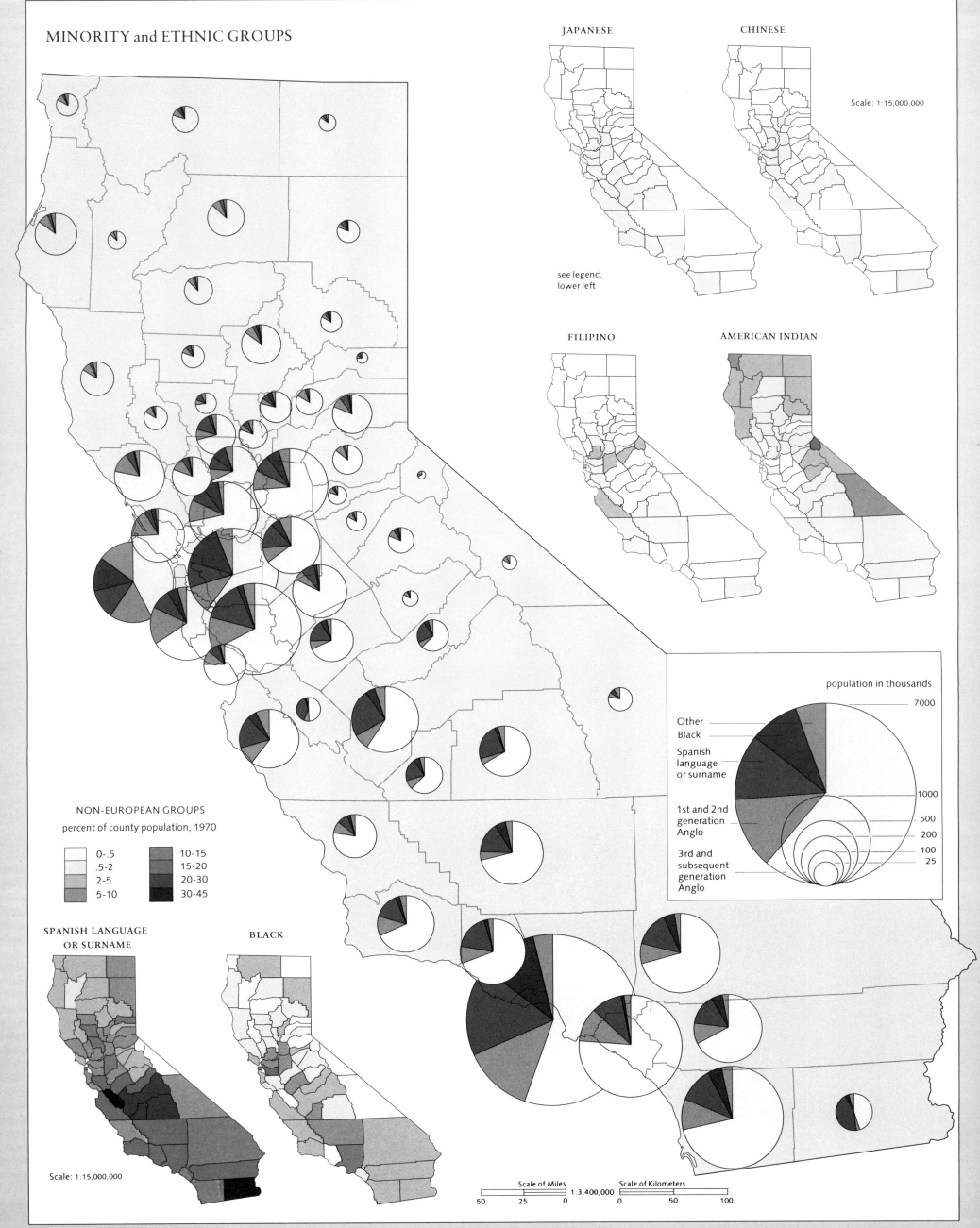

MINORITY and ETHNIC GROUPS

JAPANESE

CHINESE

Scale: 1:15,000,000

see legend,
lower left

FILIPINO

AMERICAN INDIAN

population in thousands

7000

Other
Black

Spanish
language
or surname

1000

1st and 2nd
generation
Anglo

500
200

3rd and
subsequent
generation
Anglo

100
25

NON-EUROPEAN GROUPS

percent of county population, 1970

0-.5
.5-2
2-5
5-10

10-15
15-20
20-30
30-45

SPANISH LANGUAGE
OR SURNAME

BLACK

Scale: 1:15,000,000

Scale of Miles
50   25   0

1:3,400,000

Scale of Kilometers
0   50   100

ETHNIC GROUPS

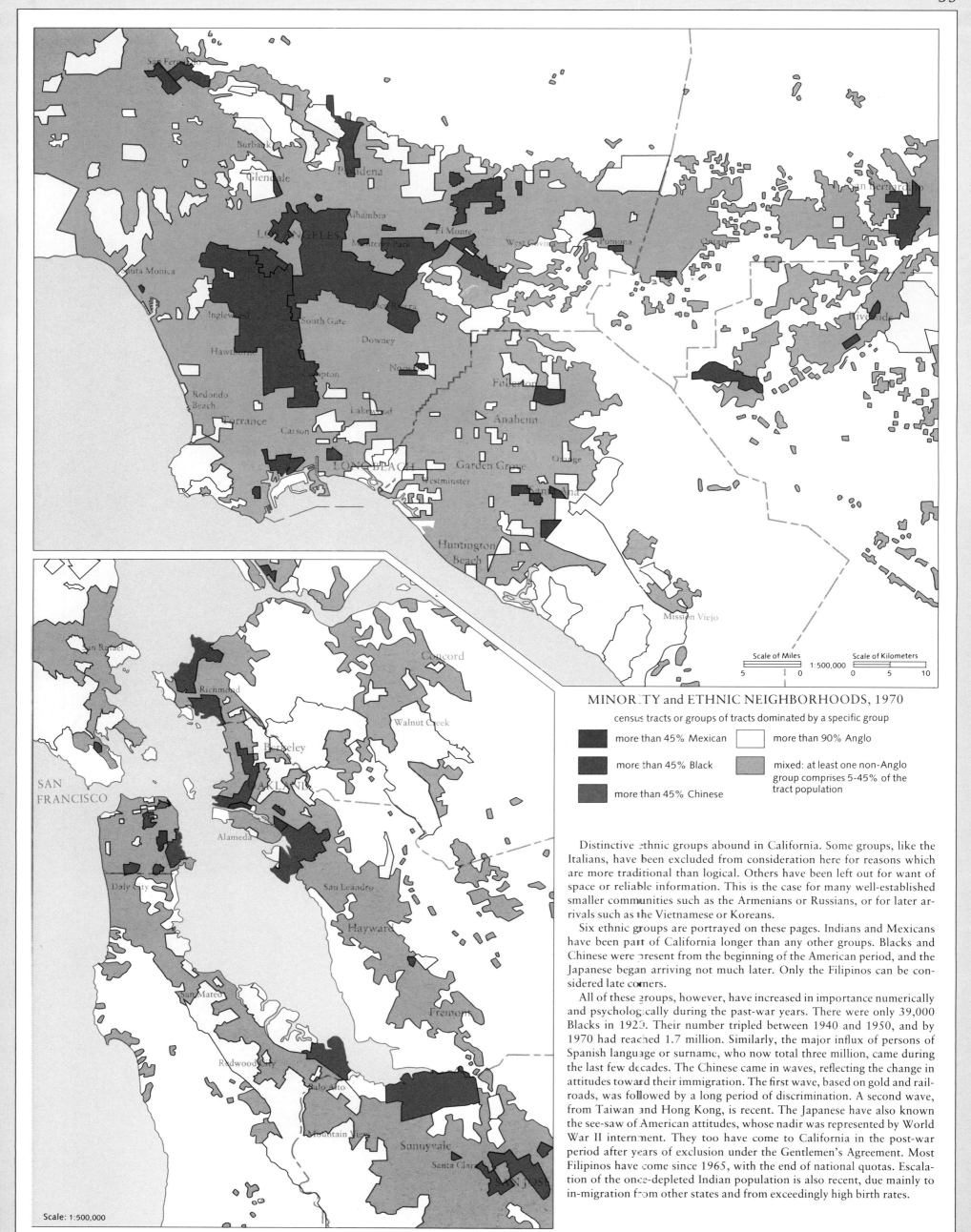

MINORITY and ETHNIC NEIGHBORHOODS, 1970

census tracts or groups of tracts dominated by a specific group

■ more than 45% Mexican	□ more than 90% Anglo
■ more than 45% Black	▨ mixed: at least one non-Anglo group comprises 5-45% of the tract population
■ more than 45% Chinese	

Scale of Miles   Scale of Kilometers
5   0   1:500,000   0   5   10

Scale: 1:500,000

   Distinctive ethnic groups abound in California. Some groups, like the Italians, have been excluded from consideration here for reasons which are more traditional than logical. Others have been left out for want of space or reliable information. This is the case for many well-established smaller communities such as the Armenians or Russians, or for later arrivals such as the Vietnamese or Koreans.
   Six ethnic groups are portrayed on these pages. Indians and Mexicans have been part of California longer than any other groups. Blacks and Chinese were present from the beginning of the American period, and the Japanese began arriving not much later. Only the Filipinos can be considered late comers.
   All of these groups, however, have increased in importance numerically and psychologically during the past-war years. There were only 39,000 Blacks in 1920. Their number tripled between 1940 and 1950, and by 1970 had reached 1.7 million. Similarly, the major influx of persons of Spanish language or surname, who now total three million, came during the last few decades. The Chinese came in waves, reflecting the change in attitudes toward their immigration. The first wave, based on gold and railroads, was followed by a long period of discrimination. A second wave, from Taiwan and Hong Kong, is recent. The Japanese have also known the see-saw of American attitudes, whose nadir was represented by World War II internment. They too have come to California in the post-war period after years of exclusion under the Gentlemen's Agreement. Most Filipinos have come since 1965, with the end of national quotas. Escalation of the once-depleted Indian population is also recent, due mainly to in-migration from other states and from exceedingly high birth rates.

ETHNIC NEIGHBORHOODS

EMPLOYMENT OF MEXICANS, BY ECONOMIC SECTOR (in places employing more than 5,000 Mexicans, 1970)

MEDIAN FAMILY INCOME

STATEWIDE

other industries*
professional & related services
personal services
wholesale & retail trade
transportation communications & public utilities
agriculture forestry & fishing
construction
manufacturing

25,000 or more
10-25,000
5-10,000

NUMBER OF EMPLOYEES

Scale: 1:1,000,000

Sacramento
Stockton
see inset at right
Fresno
Salinas
Santa Barbara
Oxnard
see inset at left

Scale: 1:10,000,000

Scale: 1:1,000,000

San Francisco
Daly City
Oakland
San Leandro
Hayward
Fremont
Santa Clara
San Jose

San Bernardino
Riverside
San Diego

Glendale
Pasadena
El Monte
East L.A.
Pico Rivera
Montebello
Norwalk
Long Beach
Anaheim
Santa Ana

Scale: 1:1,000,000

Note: "Mexican" refers to the 1970 census category, "persons of Spanish language or Spanish surname."

MEXICAN

BLACK

Scale: 1:15,000,000

JAPANESE

CHINESE

EMPLOYMENT OF OTHER ETHNIC GROUPS
(statewide, 1970)

JAPANESE   CHINESE   FILIPINO   AM. INDIAN

Median Family Income in SMSA's having more than 3000 residents of a minority group, 1970

$13,500-15,000
$12,000-13,500
$10,500-12,000
$9,000-10,500
$7,500-9,000
$6,000-7,500
$4,500-6,000

FILIPINO

EMPLOYMENT OF BLACKS, BY ECONOMIC SECTOR (in places employing more than 3,000 Blacks, 1970)

STATEWIDE

other industries*
professional & related services
personal services
wholesale & retail trade
agriculture forestry & fishing
construction
manufacturing
transportation communications & public utilities

25,000 or more
10-25,000
5-10,000

NUMBER OF EMPLOYEES

Scale: 1:1,000,000

Sacramento
see inset at right
Fresno

Scale: 1:1,000,000

Vallejo
Richmond
Berkeley
San Francisco
Oakland
East Palo Alto
San Jose

San Bernardino
see inset at left
San Diego

Scale: 1:10,000,000

Pasadena
Los Angeles
Florence-Graham
Inglewood
Compton
Carson
Long Beach

Scale: 1:1,000,000

*other industries: mining; finance, insurance, real estate; business & repair services; entertainment & recreation; and public administration.

Scale: 1:15,000,000

AM. INDIAN

Sources:
Census of Population, 1970, PC(1) cb, Report PC (92) 1F and PC(2) 1G.

ETHNIC GROUPS: EMPLOYMENT AND INCOME

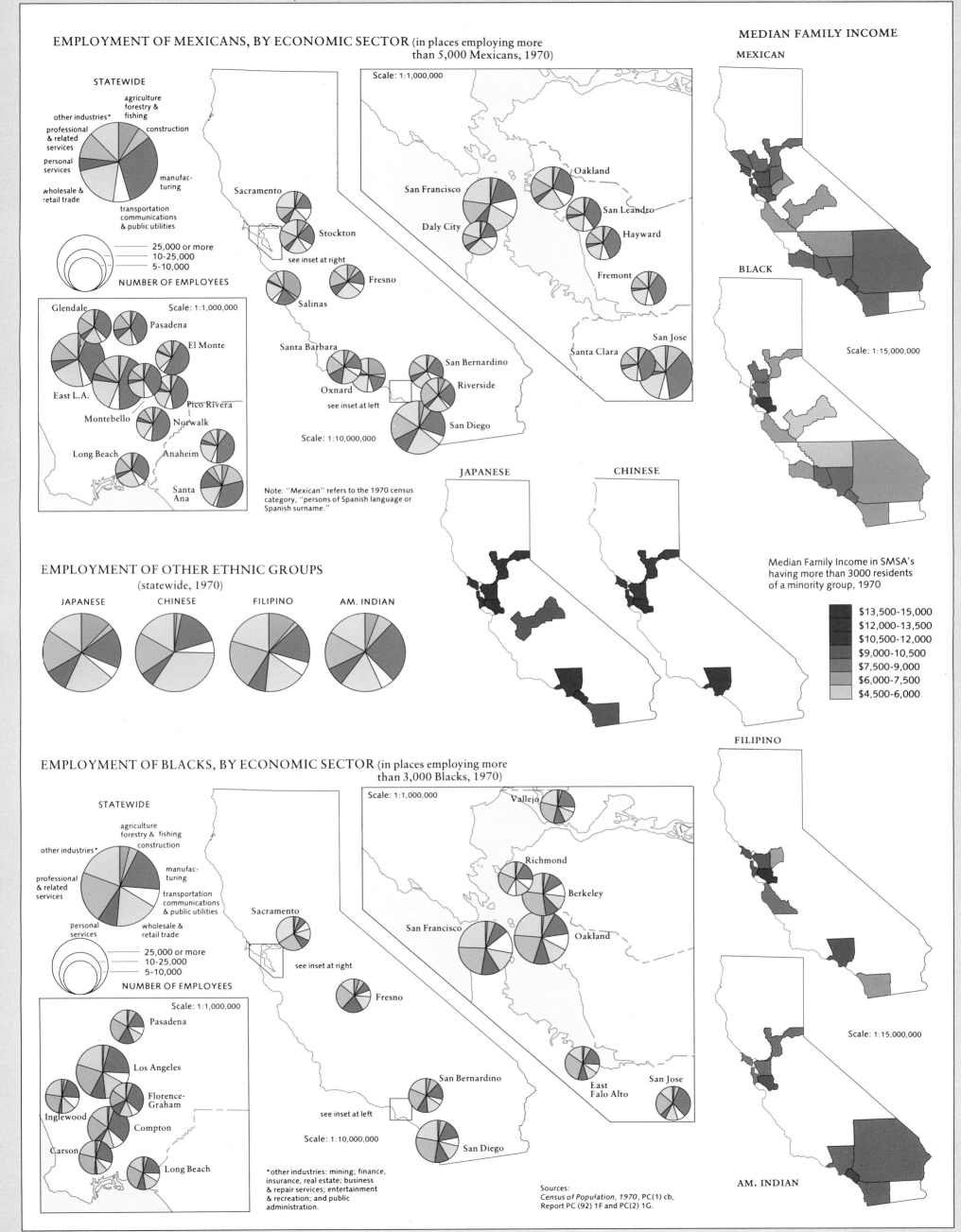

The social and historic developments of six ethnic groups are mirrored by the age-sex pyramids below. The Japanese and Chinese have large proportions of adults who are well paid and well educated. The other groups, with youthful pyramids, are handicapped by low educational levels and corresponding low incomes. The surplus of aged Filipino men reflects the immigration of agricultural workers before 1930; the surplus of middle-aged Japanese females represents the war brides of World War II; and the consistent surplus of Chinese males at all age levels reflects their continuing immigration into California.

Maps on the opposite page show the type of employment of Mexicans and Blacks in places where those groups are numerous. Almost one-third of the employed Mexicans work in manufacturing (higher in the cities of the East Bay and in Los Angeles), and nearly a quarter in wholesale and retail trade. Manufacturing, professional and related services, and "other" industries each employ about one-fifth of the Blacks, whose employment characteristics tend to be uniform throughout the state.

Except among Japanese and Chinese, income of all the ethnic groups is much lower than that of Anglos. It is highest for all ethnic groups in the Bay Area, particularly in the San Jose SMSA, but it is not much lower, except among the Blacks, even in the agricultural SMSA's of the Valley and Southern California.

MEDIAN AGE, 1970

AGE-SEX PYRAMIDS, STATEWIDE, 1970

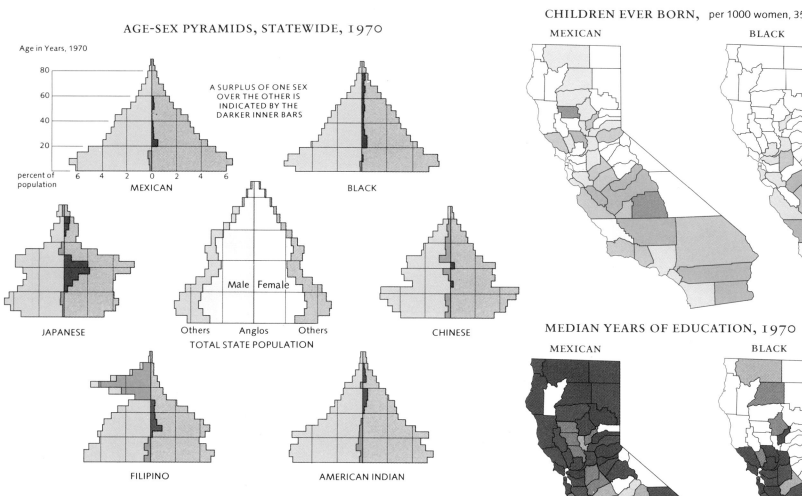

CHILDREN EVER BORN, per 1000 women, 35-44, ever married, 1970

MEDIAN YEARS OF EDUCATION, 1970

SELECTED SOCIOECONOMIC DATA, STATEWIDE, 1970

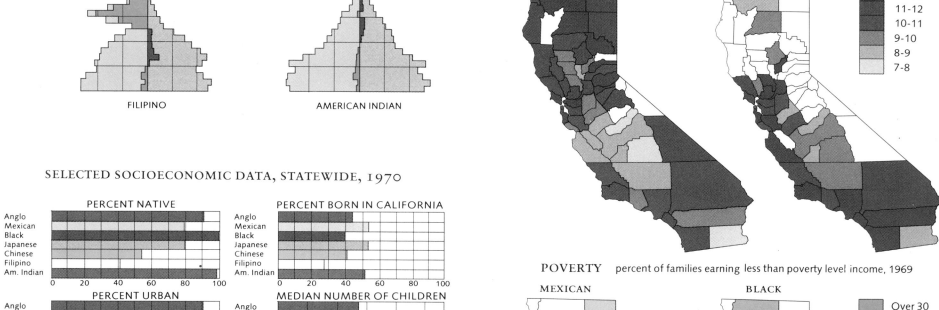
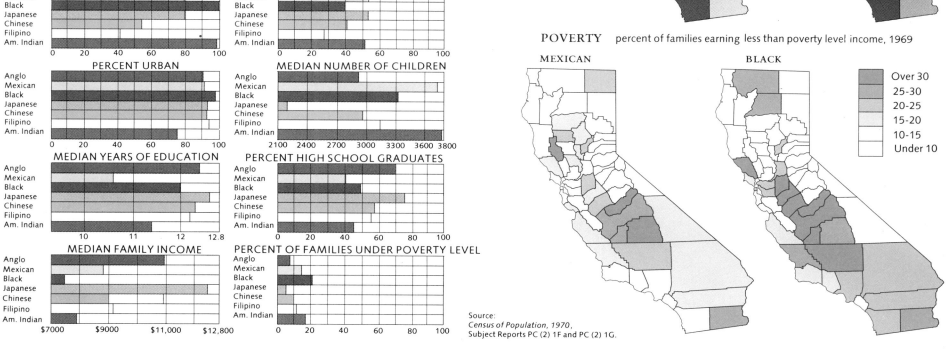

POVERTY percent of families earning less than poverty level income, 1969

Source:
Census of Population, 1970,
Subject Reports PC (2) 1F and PC (2) 1G.

ETHNIC GROUPS: SOCIAL CHARACTERISTICS

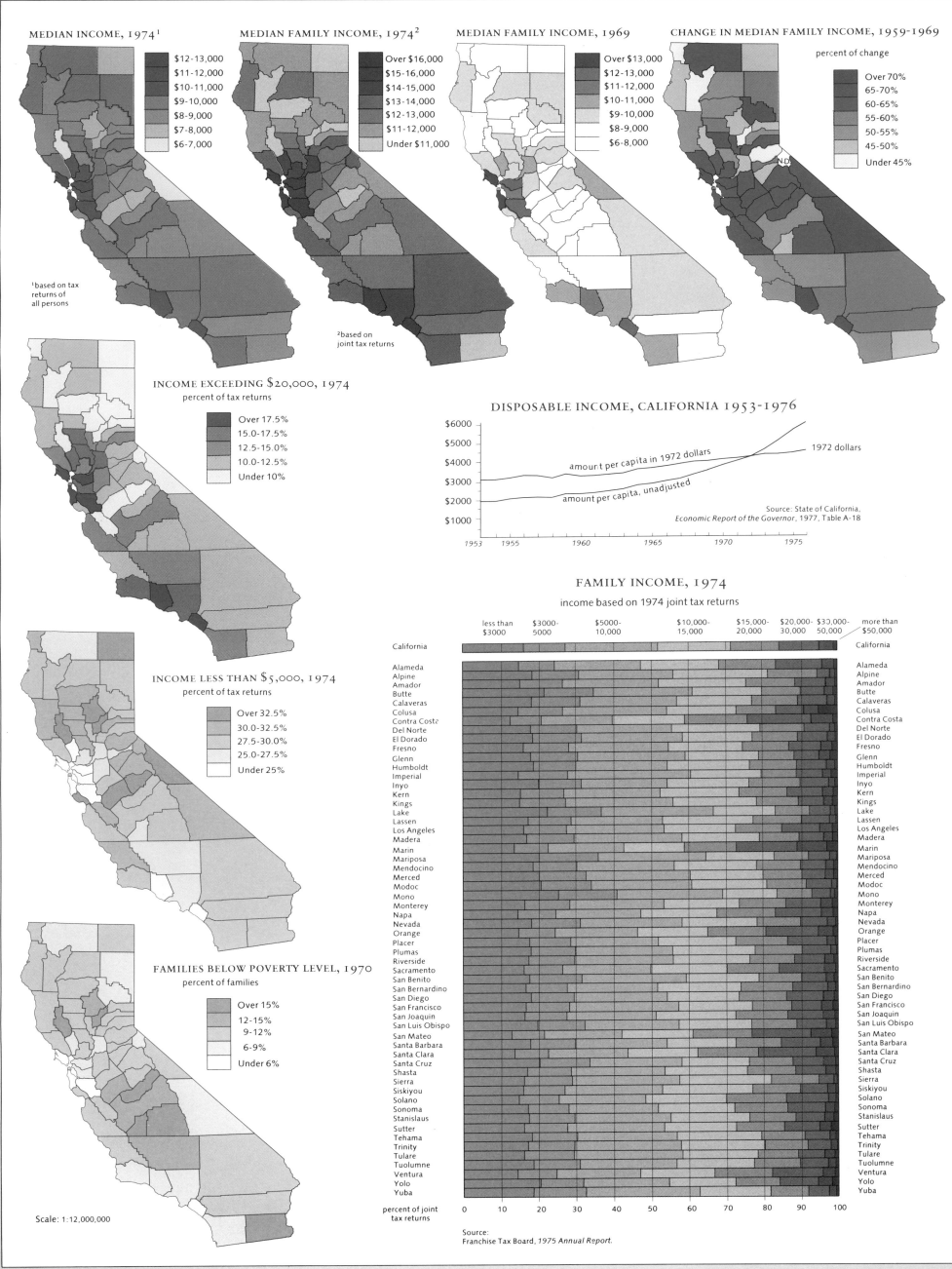

MEDIAN INCOME, 1974[1]

$12-13,000
$11-12,000
$10-11,000
$9-10,000
$8-9,000
$7-8,000
$6-7,000

[1] based on tax returns of all persons

MEDIAN FAMILY INCOME, 1974[2]

Over $16,000
$15-16,000
$14-15,000
$13-14,000
$12-13,000
$11-12,000
Under $11,000

[2] based on joint tax returns

MEDIAN FAMILY INCOME, 1969

Over $13,000
$12-13,000
$11-12,000
$10-11,000
$9-10,000
$8-9,000
$6-8,000

CHANGE IN MEDIAN FAMILY INCOME, 1959-1969

percent of change

Over 70%
65-70%
60-65%
55-60%
50-55%
45-50%
Under 45%

INCOME EXCEEDING $20,000, 1974

percent of tax returns

Over 17.5%
15.0-17.5%
12.5-15.0%
10.0-12.5%
Under 10%

INCOME LESS THAN $5,000, 1974

percent of tax returns

Over 32.5%
30.0-32.5%
27.5-30.0%
25.0-27.5%
Under 25%

FAMILIES BELOW POVERTY LEVEL, 1970

percent of families

Over 15%
12-15%
9-12%
6-9%
Under 6%

Scale: 1:12,000,000

DISPOSABLE INCOME, CALIFORNIA 1953-1976

$6000
$5000
$4000
$3000
$2000
$1000

amount per capita in 1972 dollars

1972 dollars

amount per capita, unadjusted

Source: State of California, *Economic Report of the Governor*, 1977, Table A-18

1953 1955 1960 1965 1970 1975

FAMILY INCOME, 1974

income based on 1974 joint tax returns

less than $3000 | $3000-5000 | $5000-10,000 | $10,000-15,000 | $15,000-20,000 | $20,000-30,000 | $30,000-50,000 | more than $50,000

California

Alameda
Alpine
Amador
Butte
Calaveras
Colusa
Contra Costa
Del Norte
El Dorado
Fresno
Glenn
Humboldt
Imperial
Inyo
Kern
Kings
Lake
Lassen
Los Angeles
Madera
Marin
Mariposa
Mendocino
Merced
Modoc
Mono
Monterey
Napa
Nevada
Orange
Placer
Plumas
Riverside
Sacramento
San Benito
San Bernardino
San Diego
San Francisco
San Joaquin
San Luis Obispo
San Mateo
Santa Barbara
Santa Clara
Santa Cruz
Shasta
Sierra
Siskiyou
Solano
Sonoma
Stanislaus
Sutter
Tehama
Trinity
Tulare
Tuolumne
Ventura
Yolo
Yuba

percent of joint tax returns

0 10 20 30 40 50 60 70 80 90 100

Source: Franchise Tax Board, *1975 Annual Report.*

INCOME

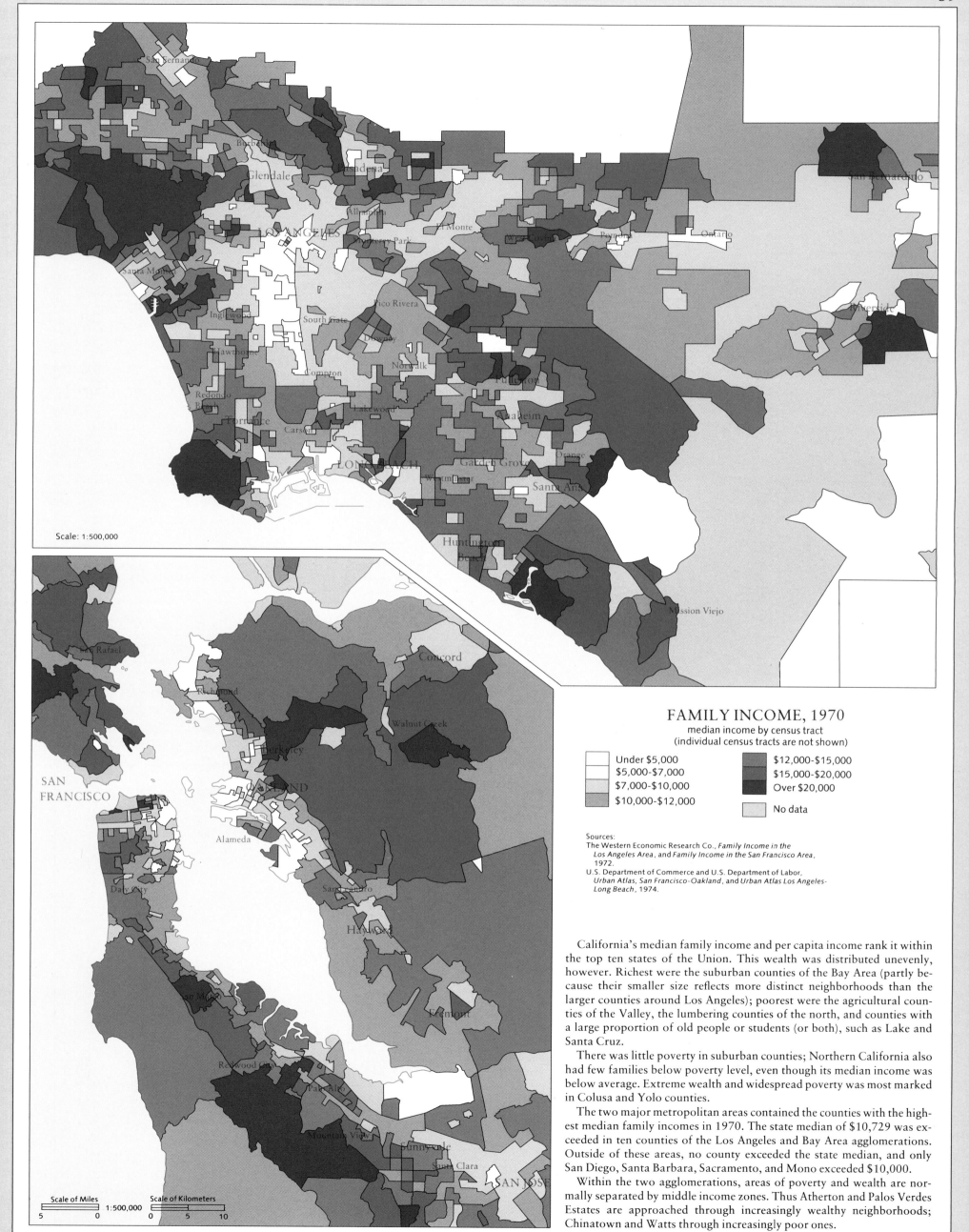

FAMILY INCOME, 1970
median income by census tract
(individual census tracts are not shown)

Under $5,000	$12,000-$15,000
$5,000-$7,000	$15,000-$20,000
$7,000-$10,000	Over $20,000
$10,000-$12,000	No data

Sources:
The Western Economic Research Co., *Family Income in the
Los Angeles Area*, and *Family Income in the San Francisco Area*,
1972.
U.S. Department of Commerce and U.S. Department of Labor,
Urban Atlas, San Francisco-Oakland, and *Urban Atlas Los Angeles-
Long Beach*, 1974.

Scale: 1:500,000

Scale of Miles   Scale of Kilometers
1:500,000
5   0   0   5   10

California's median family income and per capita income rank it within
the top ten states of the Union. This wealth was distributed unevenly,
however. Richest were the suburban counties of the Bay Area (partly because their smaller size reflects more distinct neighborhoods than the
larger counties around Los Angeles); poorest were the agricultural counties of the Valley, the lumbering counties of the north, and counties with
a large proportion of old people or students (or both), such as Lake and
Santa Cruz.

There was little poverty in suburban counties; Northern California also
had few families below poverty level, even though its median income was
below average. Extreme wealth and widespread poverty was most marked
in Colusa and Yolo counties.

The two major metropolitan areas contained the counties with the highest median family incomes in 1970. The state median of $10,729 was ex-
ceeded in ten counties of the Los Angeles and Bay Area agglomerations.
Outside of these areas, no county exceeded the state median, and only
San Diego, Santa Barbara, Sacramento, and Mono exceeded $10,000.

Within the two agglomerations, areas of poverty and wealth are nor-
mally separated by middle income zones. Thus Atherton and Palos Verdes
Estates are approached through increasingly wealthy neighborhoods;
Chinatown and Watts through increasingly poor ones.

INCOME IN THE BAY AREA AND LOS ANGELES

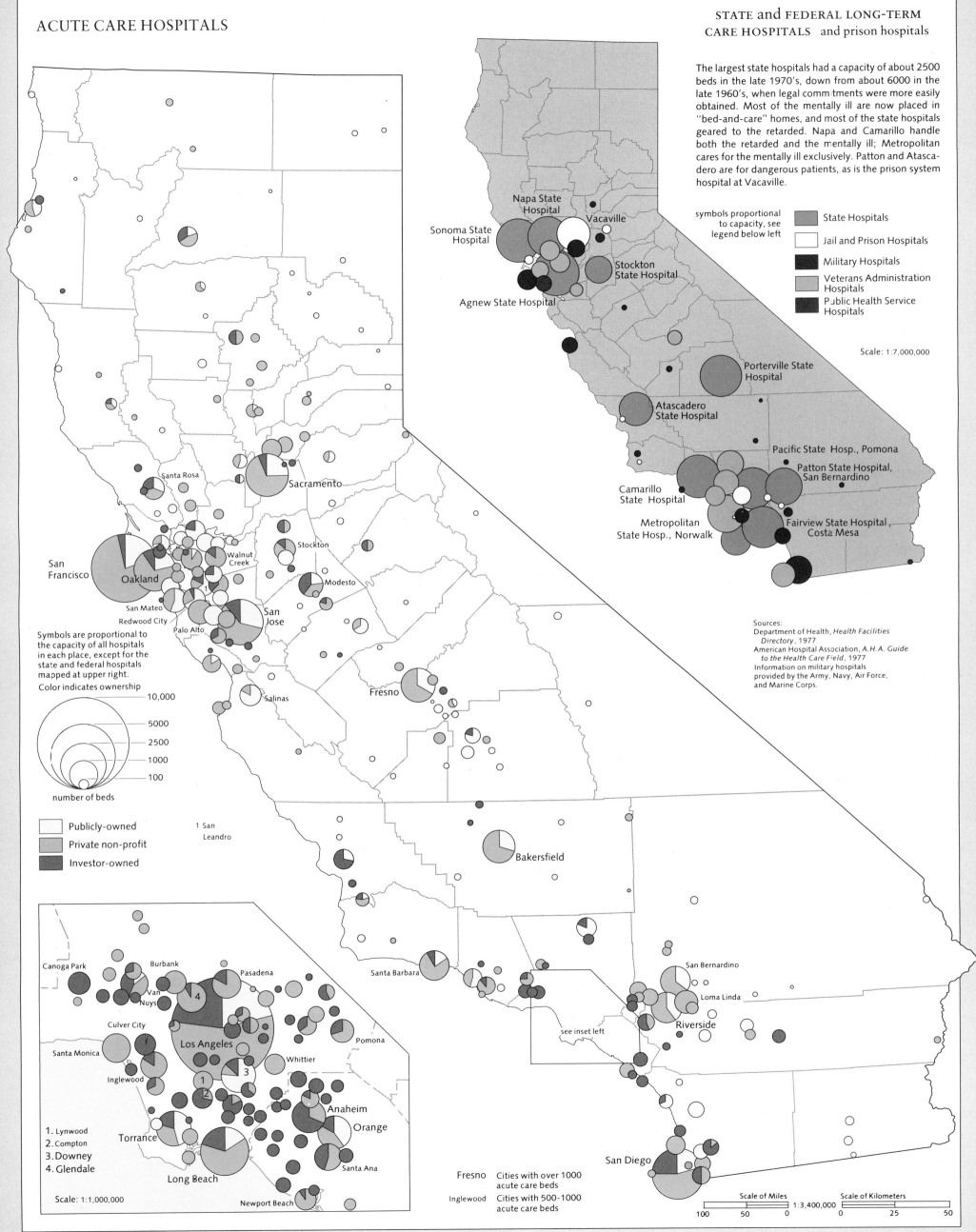

ACUTE CARE HOSPITALS

STATE and FEDERAL LONG-TERM CARE HOSPITALS and prison hospitals

The largest state hospitals had a capacity of about 2500 beds in the late 1970's, down from about 6000 in the late 1960's, when legal commitments were more easily obtained. Most of the mentally ill are now placed in "bed-and-care" homes, and most of the state hospitals geared to the retarded. Napa and Camarillo handle both the retarded and the mentally ill; Metropolitan cares for the mentally ill exclusively. Patton and Atascadero are for dangerous patients, as is the prison system hospital at Vacaville.

symbols proportional to capacity, see legend below left

- State Hospitals
- Jail and Prison Hospitals
- Military Hospitals
- Veterans Administration Hospitals
- Public Health Service Hospitals

Scale: 1:7,000,000

Napa State Hospital
Vacaville
Sonoma State Hospital
Stockton State Hospital
Agnew State Hospital
Porterville State Hospital
Atascadero State Hospital
Pacific State Hosp., Pomona
Patton State Hospital, San Bernardino
Camarillo State Hospital
Fairview State Hospital, Costa Mesa
Metropolitan State Hosp., Norwalk

Sources:
Department of Health, *Health Facilities Directory*, 1977
American Hospital Association, *A.H.A. Guide to the Health Care Field*, 1977
Information on military hospitals provided by the Army, Navy, Air Force, and Marine Corps.

Symbols are proportional to the capacity of all hospitals in each place, except for the state and federal hospitals mapped at upper right.

Color indicates ownership

10,000
5,000
2,500
1,000
100

number of beds

- Publicly-owned
- Private non-profit
- Investor-owned

1 San Leandro

Santa Rosa
Sacramento
Stockton
Walnut Creek
San Francisco
Oakland
Modesto
San Mateo
Redwood City
Palo Alto
San Jose
Salinas
Fresno
Bakersfield
Santa Barbara
San Bernardino
Loma Linda
Riverside
see inset left
San Diego

Canoga Park
Burbank
Pasadena
Van Nuys
Culver City
Pomona
Santa Monica
Los Angeles
Whittier
Inglewood
Anaheim
Orange
Torrance
Santa Ana
Long Beach
Newport Beach

1. Lynwood
2. Compton
3. Downey
4. Glendale

Scale: 1:1,000,000

Fresno — Cities with over 1000 acute care beds
Inglewood — Cities with 500-1000 acute care beds

Scale of Miles   Scale of Kilometers
100   50   0   1:3,400,000   50   25   0   50

HOSPITALS

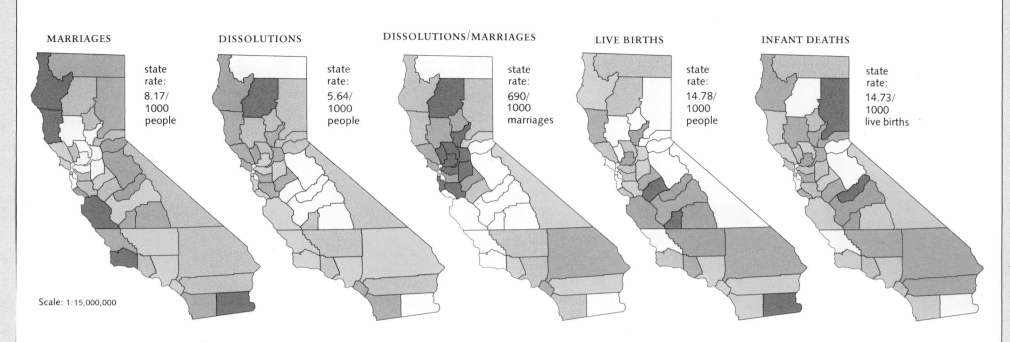

MARRIAGES
state rate: 8.17/ 1000 people

DISSOLUTIONS
state rate: 5.64/ 1000 people

DISSOLUTIONS/MARRIAGES
state rate: 690/ 1000 marriages

LIVE BIRTHS
state rate: 14.78/ 1000 people

INFANT DEATHS
state rate: 14.73/ 1000 live births

Scale: 1:15,000,000

In the late 1970's, California had 630 hospitals, of which the 95 largest contained half of the 121,000 hospital beds in the state. Nearly all of the very large hospitals were state-operated facilities caring for the mentally ill or severely retarded. These facilities, which had between 1,200 and 2,800 beds, are mapped separately on the facing page. Only two acute-care hospitals were as large, and both were in Los Angeles: Cedars-Sinai Medical Center with 1,100 beds and Los Angeles County-USC Medical Center with 2,100. Most acute-care hospitals were much smaller; half had fewer than 100 beds.

Hospital ownership varied regionally. In small towns of remote areas, most facilities were supported by taxes levied in hospital districts. District, city, and county-owned hospitals accounted for a fifth of the facilities and of the bed capacity. Most small hospitals in urban areas were privately owned, non-profit corporations; investor-owned hospitals were concentrated in Los Angeles and Orange counties. Whatever the ownership, most hospitals had to rely on federal and state funds for both construction and operation revenue.

Many factors affect the interpretation of the maps of health and vital statistics. Marriage, dissolution, and death rates, which were not adjusted for age, tended to reflect the age structure of the population. In addition, regional differences were obscured by the great mobility of the California population.

Sources:
Dept. of Health, *Vital Statistics of California, 1972-1973-1974*, 1976.
California Medical Association, "Physicians in California, December 1976," *Socioeconomic Report*,
    Vol. XVIII, No. 7, December 1977.
American Dental Association, *Distribution of Dentists in the United States*, 1976.

ABORTIONS/LIVE BIRTHS
state rate: 43.0/ 100 live births

DEATHS: ALL CAUSES
state rate: 8.29/ 1000 people

Under 75%
75-84%
85-94%
95-104%
105-114%
115-124%
125% or more

County rates are shown in relation to the statewide rate for each condition mapped. Counties with small populations aggregated.

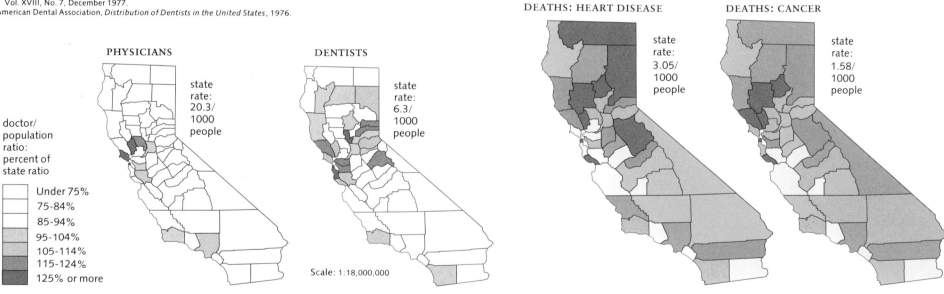

DEATHS: HEART DISEASE
state rate: 3.05/ 1000 people

DEATHS: CANCER
state rate: 1.58/ 1000 people

PHYSICIANS
state rate: 20.3/ 1000 people

DENTISTS
state rate: 6.3/ 1000 people

doctor/ population ratio: percent of state ratio

Under 75%
75-84%
85-94%
95-104%
105-114%
115-124%
125% or more

Scale: 1:18,000,000

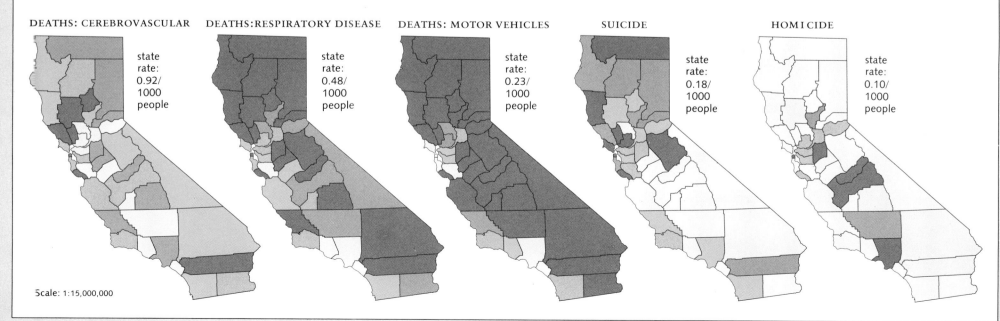

DEATHS: CEREBROVASCULAR
state rate: 0.92/ 1000 people

DEATHS: RESPIRATORY DISEASE
state rate: 0.48/ 1000 people

DEATHS: MOTOR VEHICLES
state rate: 0.23/ 1000 people

SUICIDE
state rate: 0.18/ 1000 people

HOMICIDE
state rate: 0.10/ 1000 people

Scale: 1:15,000,000

VITAL STATISTICS

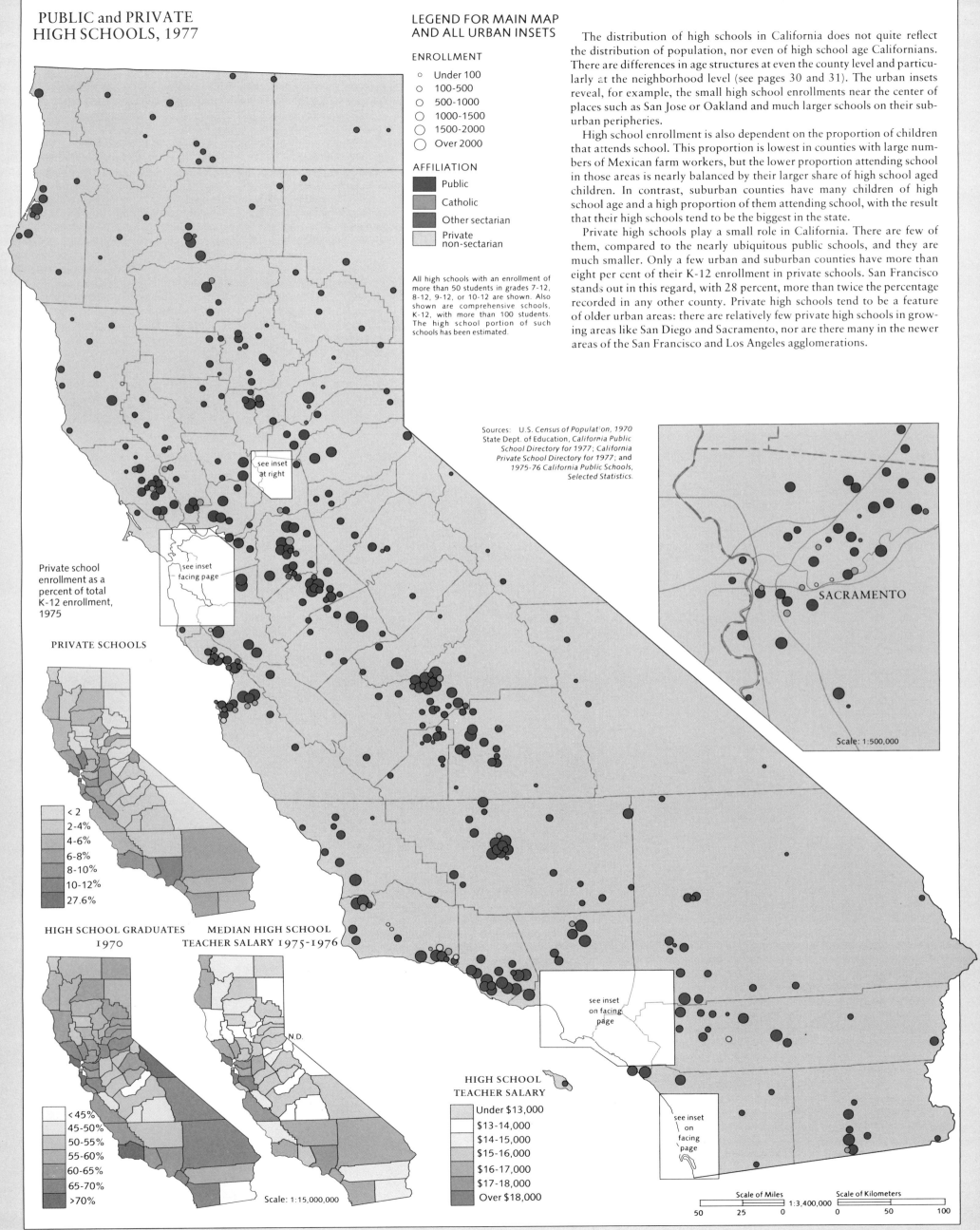

PUBLIC and PRIVATE HIGH SCHOOLS, 1977

LEGEND FOR MAIN MAP AND ALL URBAN INSETS

ENROLLMENT

○ Under 100
○ 100-500
○ 500-1000
○ 1000-1500
○ 1500-2000
○ Over 2000

AFFILIATION

Public
Catholic
Other sectarian
Private non-sectarian

All high schools with an enrollment of more than 50 students in grades 7-12, 8-12, 9-12, or 10-12 are shown. Also shown are comprehensive schools, K-12, with more than 100 students. The high school portion of such schools has been estimated.

The distribution of high schools in California does not quite reflect the distribution of population, nor even of high school age Californians. There are differences in age structures at even the county level and particularly at the neighborhood level (see pages 30 and 31). The urban insets reveal, for example, the small high school enrollments near the center of places such as San Jose or Oakland and much larger schools on their suburban peripheries.

High school enrollment is also dependent on the proportion of children that attends school. This proportion is lowest in counties with large numbers of Mexican farm workers, but the lower proportion attending school in those areas is nearly balanced by their larger share of high school aged children. In contrast, suburban counties have many children of high school age and a high proportion of them attending school, with the result that their high schools tend to be the biggest in the state.

Private high schools play a small role in California. There are few of them, compared to the nearly ubiquitous public schools, and they are much smaller. Only a few urban and suburban counties have more than eight per cent of their K-12 enrollment in private schools. San Francisco stands out in this regard, with 28 percent, more than twice the percentage recorded in any other county. Private high schools tend to be a feature of older urban areas: there are relatively few private high schools in growing areas like San Diego and Sacramento, nor are there many in the newer areas of the San Francisco and Los Angeles agglomerations.

Sources: U.S. Census of Population, 1970
State Dept. of Education, California Public School Directory for 1977; California Private School Directory for 1977; and 1975-76 California Public Schools, Selected Statistics.

SACRAMENTO

Scale: 1:500,000

see inset at right

see inset facing page

Private school enrollment as a percent of total K-12 enrollment, 1975

PRIVATE SCHOOLS

< 2
2-4%
4-6%
6-8%
8-10%
10-12%
27.6%

HIGH SCHOOL GRADUATES 1970

<45%
45-50%
50-55%
55-60%
60-65%
65-70%
>70%

MEDIAN HIGH SCHOOL TEACHER SALARY 1975-1976

N.D.

HIGH SCHOOL TEACHER SALARY

Under $13,000
$13-14,000
$14-15,000
$15-16,000
$16-17,000
$17-18,000
Over $18,000

see inset on facing page

see inset on facing page

Scale: 1:15,000,000

Scale of Miles
50   25   0
1:3,400,000
Scale of Kilometers
0   50   100

HIGH SCHOOLS

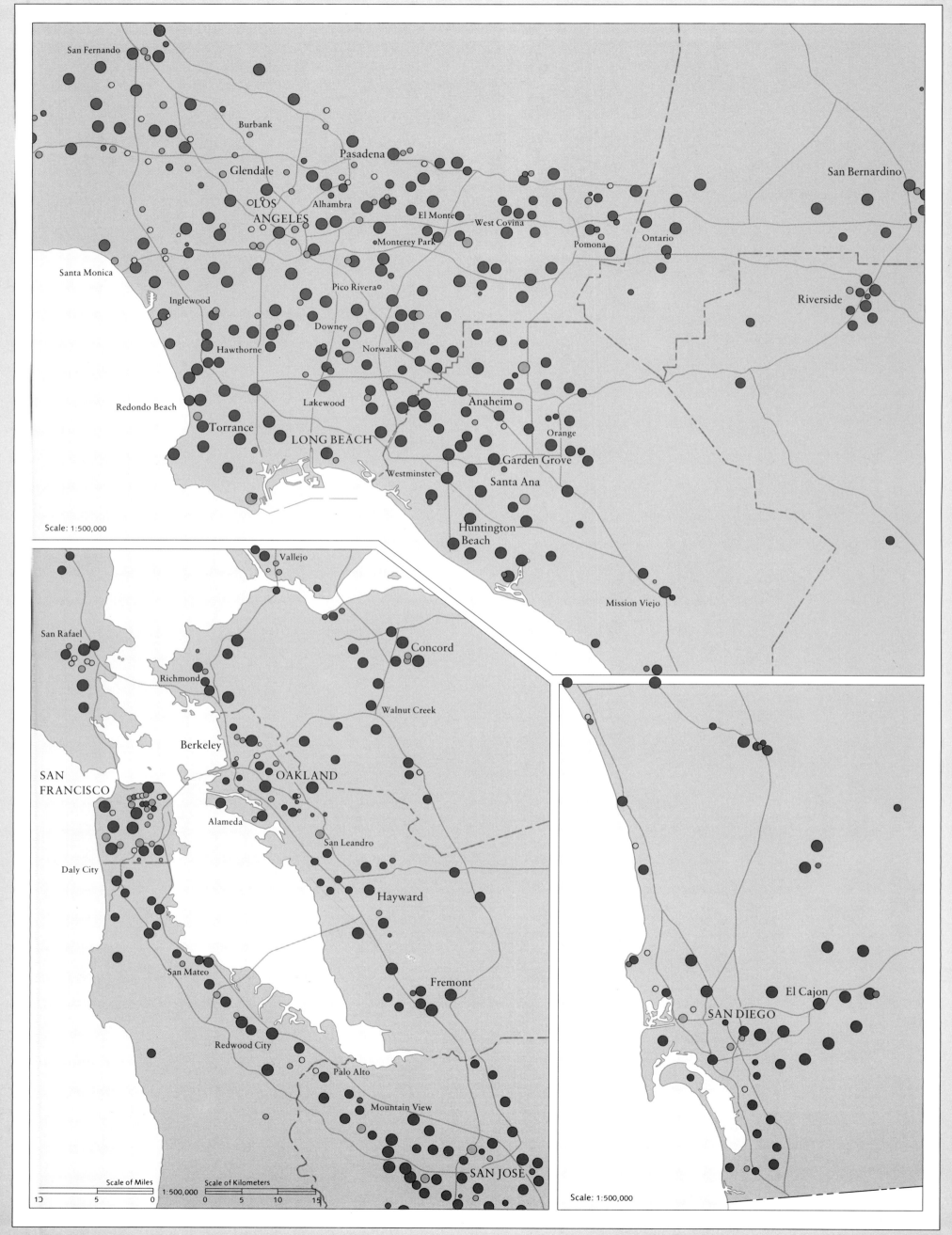

Scale: 1:500,000

Scale of Miles

10   5   0

1:500,000

Scale of Kilometers

0   5   10   15

Scale: 1:500,000

HIGH SCHOOLS

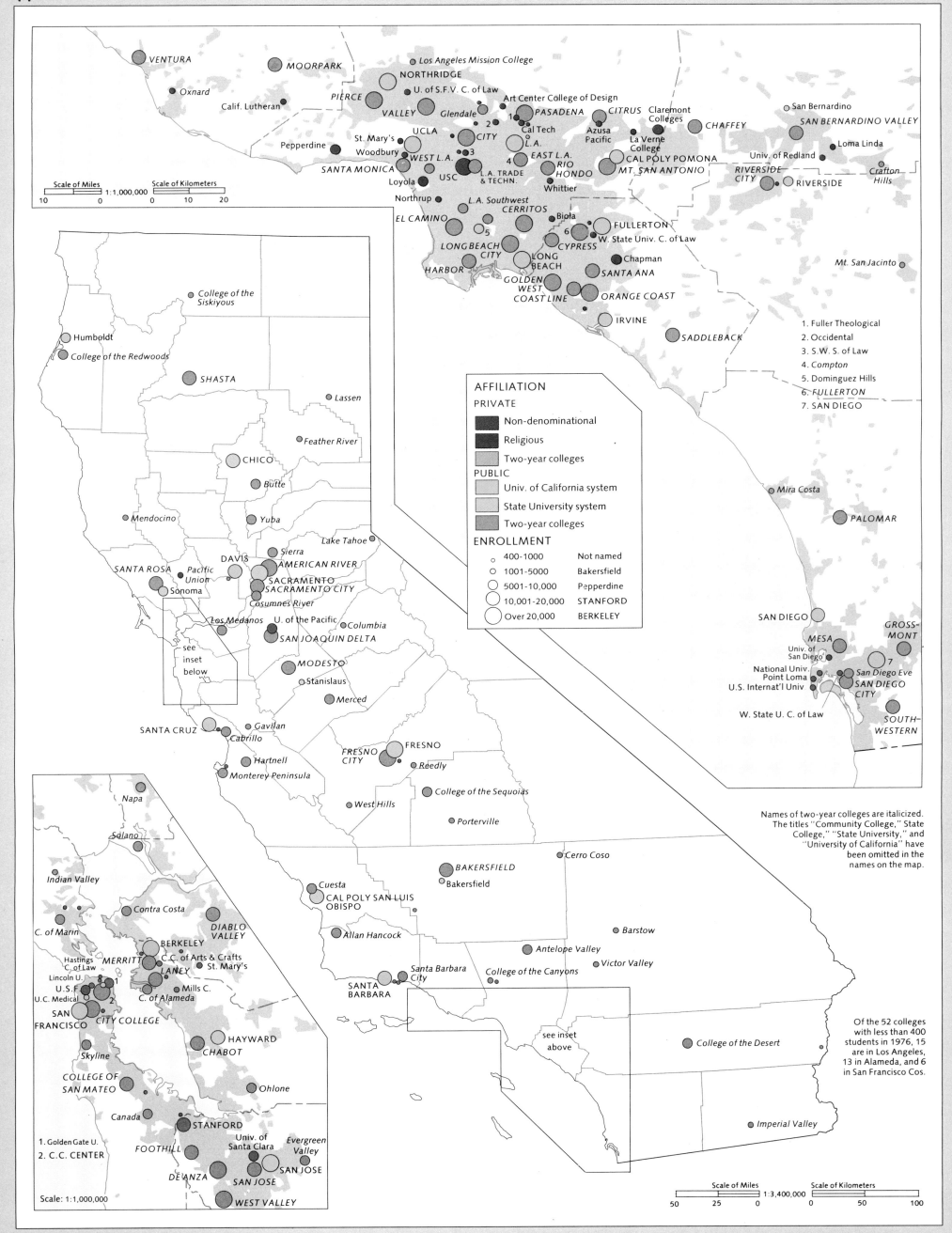

VENTURA
MOORPARK
Oxnard
Calif. Lutheran
Pepperdine
St. Mary's
Woodbury
SANTA MONICA
Loyola
Northrup
Los Angeles Mission College
NORTHRIDGE
PIERCE
U. of S.F.V. C. of Law
VALLEY
Glendale
UCLA
CITY
WEST L.A.
USC
2
1
Art Center College of Design
PASADENA
Cal Tech
L.A.
EAST L.A.
RIO HONDO
L.A. TRADE & TECHN.
Whittier
CITRUS
Claremont Colleges
Azusa Pacific
La Verne College
CAL POLY POMONA
MT. SAN ANTONIO
CHAFFEY
Univ. of Redland
RIVERSIDE CITY
San Bernardino
SAN BERNARDINO VALLEY
Loma Linda
RIVERSIDE
Crafton Hills

L.A. Southwest
EL CAMINO
LONG BEACH CITY
HARBOR
CERRITOS
Biola
5
6
CYPRESS
W. State Univ. C. of Law
FULLERTON
Chapman
LONG BEACH
SANTA ANA
GOLDEN WEST
COAST LINE
ORANGE COAST
IRVINE
SADDLEBACK

Mt. San Jacinto

1. Fuller Theological
2. Occidental
3. S.W. S. of Law
4. Compton
5. Dominguez Hills
6. FULLERTON
7. SAN DIEGO

Mira Costa

PALOMAR

San Diego
MESA
Univ. of San Diego
National Univ.
Point Loma
U.S. Internat'l Univ
W. State U. C. of Law
San Diego Eve
SAN DIEGO CITY
GROSS-MONT
7
SOUTH-WESTERN

Scale of Miles
1:1,000,000
10   0
Scale of Kilometers
0   10   20

AFFILIATION
PRIVATE
  Non-denominational
  Religious
  Two-year colleges
PUBLIC
  Univ. of California system
  State University system
  Two-year colleges
ENROLLMENT
  400-1000   Not named
  1001-5000   Bakersfield
  5001-10,000   Pepperdine
  10,001-20,000 STANFORD
  Over 20,000   BERKELEY

College of the Siskiyous
Humboldt
College of the Redwoods
SHASTA
Lassen
Feather River
CHICO
Butte
Mendocino
Yuba
Lake Tahoe
SANTA ROSA
Pacific Union
DAVIS
Sierra
AMERICAN RIVER
SACRAMENTO
SACRAMENTO CITY
Sonoma
Cosumnes River
Los Medanos
U. of the Pacific
Columbia
SAN JOAQUIN DELTA
see inset below
MODESTO
Stanislaus
Merced
SANTA CRUZ
Gavilan
Cabrillo
Hartnell
Monterey Peninsula
FRESNO CITY
FRESNO
Reedly
College of the Sequoias
West Hills
Porterville

Cerro Coso
BAKERSFIELD
Bakersfield

Napa
Solano
Indian Valley
C. of Marin
Contra Costa
DIABLO VALLEY
BERKELEY
Hastings C. of Law
MERRITT
C.C. of Arts & Crafts
St. Mary's
LANEY
Lincoln U.
1
U.S.F.
U.C. Medical
2
C. of Alameda
Mills C.
SAN FRANCISCO
CITY COLLEGE
HAYWARD
CHABOT
Skyline
COLLEGE OF SAN MATEO
Ohlone
Canada
STANFORD
FOOTHILL
Univ. of Santa Clara
Evergreen Valley
DE ANZA
SAN JOSE
WEST VALLEY

1. Golden Gate U.
2. C.C. CENTER
Scale: 1:1,000,000

Cuesta
CAL POLY SAN LUIS OBISPO
Allan Hancock
SANTA BARBARA
Santa Barbara City
College of the Canyons
Barstow
Antelope Valley
Victor Valley
College of the Desert
Imperial Valley

see inset above

Names of two-year colleges are italicized. The titles "Community College," State College," "State University," and "University of California" have been omitted in the names on the map.

Of the 52 colleges with less than 400 students in 1976, 15 are in Los Angeles, 13 in Alameda, and 6 in San Francisco Cos.

Scale of Miles
50   25   0
1:3,400,000
Scale of Kilometers
0   50   100

COLLEGES AND UNIVERSITIES

ENROLLMENT IN HIGHER EDUCATION

DATES OF FOUNDING OF COLLEGES AND UNIVERSITIES

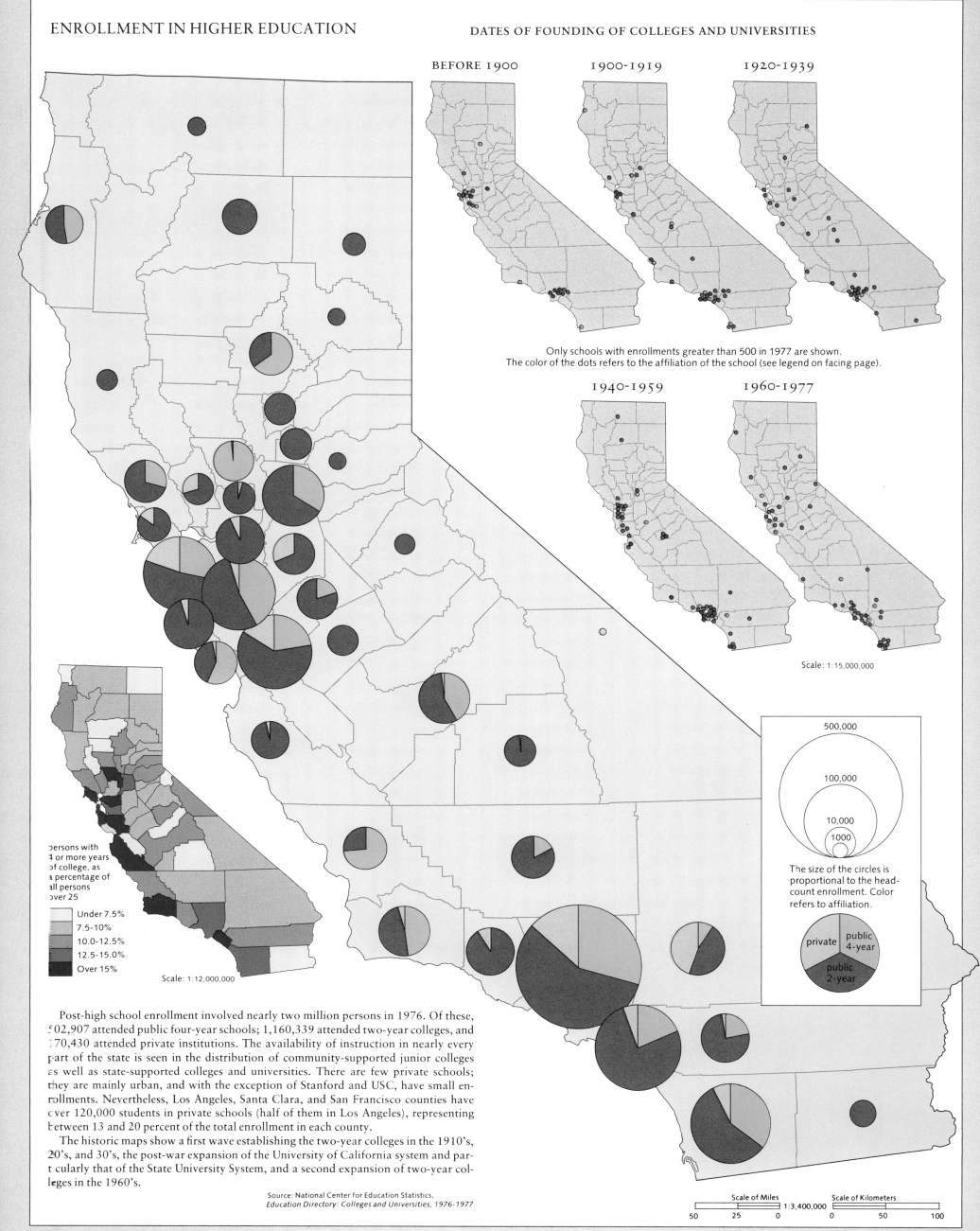

BEFORE 1900   1900-1919   1920-1939

Only schools with enrollments greater than 500 in 1977 are shown.
The color of the dots refers to the affiliation of the school (see legend on facing page).

1940-1959   1960-1977

Scale: 1:15,000,000

persons with 4 or more years of college, as a percentage of all persons over 25

Under 7.5%
7.5-10%
10.0-12.5%
12.5-15.0%
Over 15%

Scale: 1:12,000,000

500,000
100,000
10,000
1000

The size of the circles is proportional to the head-count enrollment. Color refers to affiliation.

private | public 4-year | public 2-year

Post-high school enrollment involved nearly two million persons in 1976. Of these, 502,907 attended public four-year schools; 1,160,339 attended two-year colleges, and 170,430 attended private institutions. The availability of instruction in nearly every part of the state is seen in the distribution of community-supported junior colleges as well as state-supported colleges and universities. There are few private schools; they are mainly urban, and with the exception of Stanford and USC, have small enrollments. Nevertheless, Los Angeles, Santa Clara, and San Francisco counties have over 120,000 students in private schools (half of them in Los Angeles), representing between 13 and 20 percent of the total enrollment in each county.

The historic maps show a first wave establishing the two-year colleges in the 1910's, 20's, and 30's, the post-war expansion of the University of California system and particularly that of the State University System, and a second expansion of two-year colleges in the 1960's.

Source: National Center for Education Statistics,
Education Directory: Colleges and Universities, 1976-1977

Scale of Miles   Scale of Kilometers
1:3,400,000

COLLEGES AND UNIVERSITIES

Although the military is found nearly everywhere outside of Northern California, its presence is nevertheless remarkably segregated.

Air Force bases are almost exclusively located in the Central Valley and desert hinterlands, with a major cluster around Sacramento. Sixth Army headquarters are at the Presidio in San Francisco, but the largest Army complex is in Monterey, where about 17,000 men were stationed at Fort Ord (1974). The Marine Corps is concentrated in Orange and San Diego counties, but also has a desert base at Twentynine Palms. The Navy dominates San Diego, with a complex of facilities around the 11th Naval District headquarters there. In addition, the Navy operates bases, shipyards, air stations and weapons testing ranges scattered throughout the state. There is little direct military presence in Los Angeles or San Jose, but their involvement is obvious from the maps at right: Los Angeles and Santa Clara counties are by far the leading recipients of Department of Defense expenditures for prime contracts.

MILITARY INSTALLATIONS

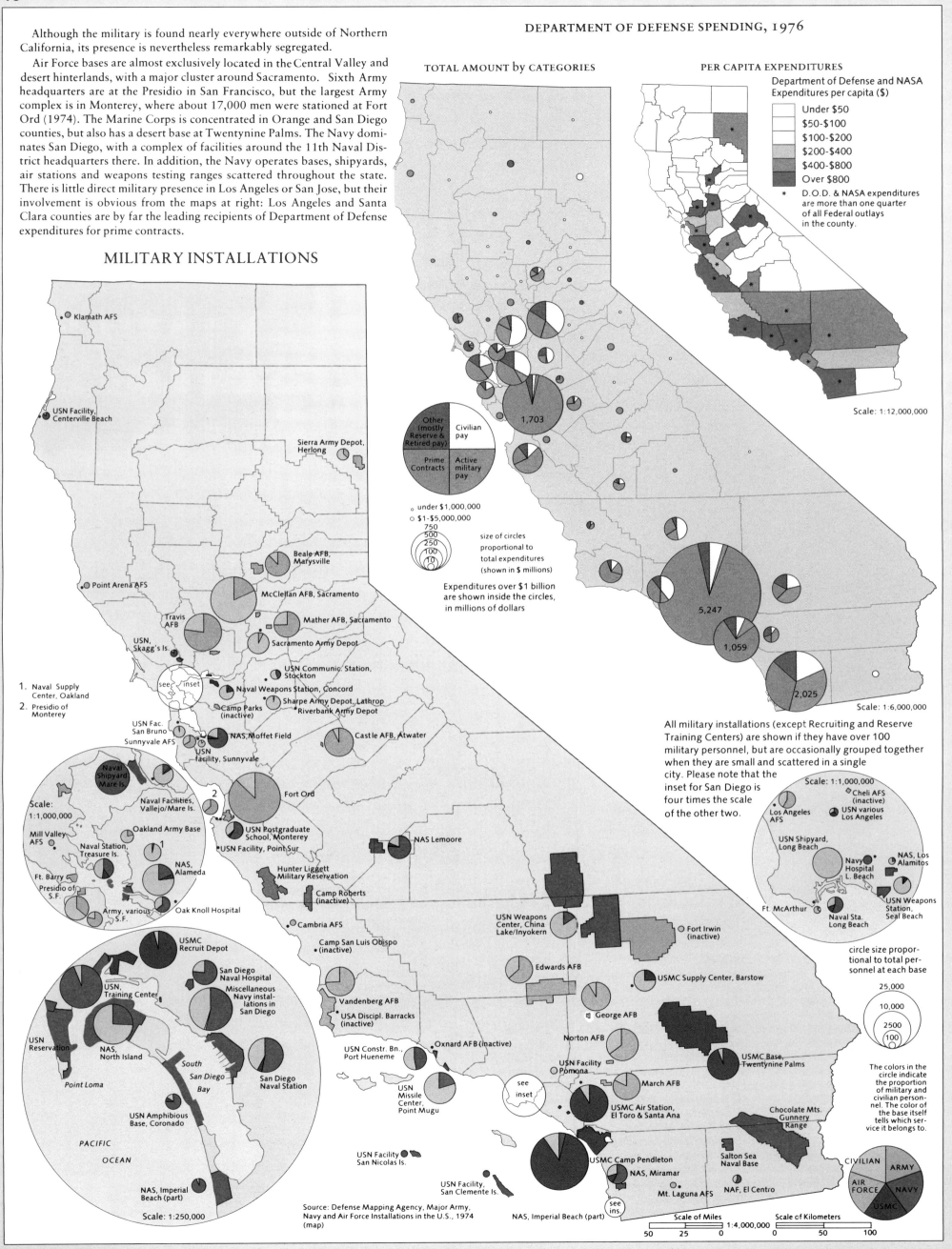

DEPARTMENT OF DEFENSE SPENDING, 1976

TOTAL AMOUNT by CATEGORIES

PER CAPITA EXPENDITURES

Department of Defense and NASA Expenditures per capita ($)

- Under $50
- $50-$100
- $100-$200
- $200-$400
- $400-$800
- Over $800

* D.O.D. & NASA expenditures are more than one quarter of all Federal outlays in the county.

Scale: 1:12,000,000

○ under $1,000,000
○ $1-$5,000,000

size of circles proportional to total expenditures (shown in $ millions)

Expenditures over $1 billion are shown inside the circles, in millions of dollars

Scale: 1:6,000,000

All military installations (except Recruiting and Reserve Training Centers) are shown if they have over 100 military personnel, but are occasionally grouped together when they are small and scattered in a single city. Please note that the inset for San Diego is four times the scale of the other two.

Scale: 1:1,000,000

circle size proportional to total personnel at each base

25,000
10,000
2500
100

The colors in the circle indicate the proportion of military and civilian personnel. The color of the base itself tells which service it belongs to.

CIVILIAN
ARMY
NAVY
USMC
AIR FORCE

1. Naval Supply Center, Oakland
2. Presidio of Monterey

Source: Defense Mapping Agency, Major Army, Navy and Air Force Installations in the U.S., 1974 (map)

Scale of Miles 1:4,000,000 Scale of Kilometers

THE MILITARY

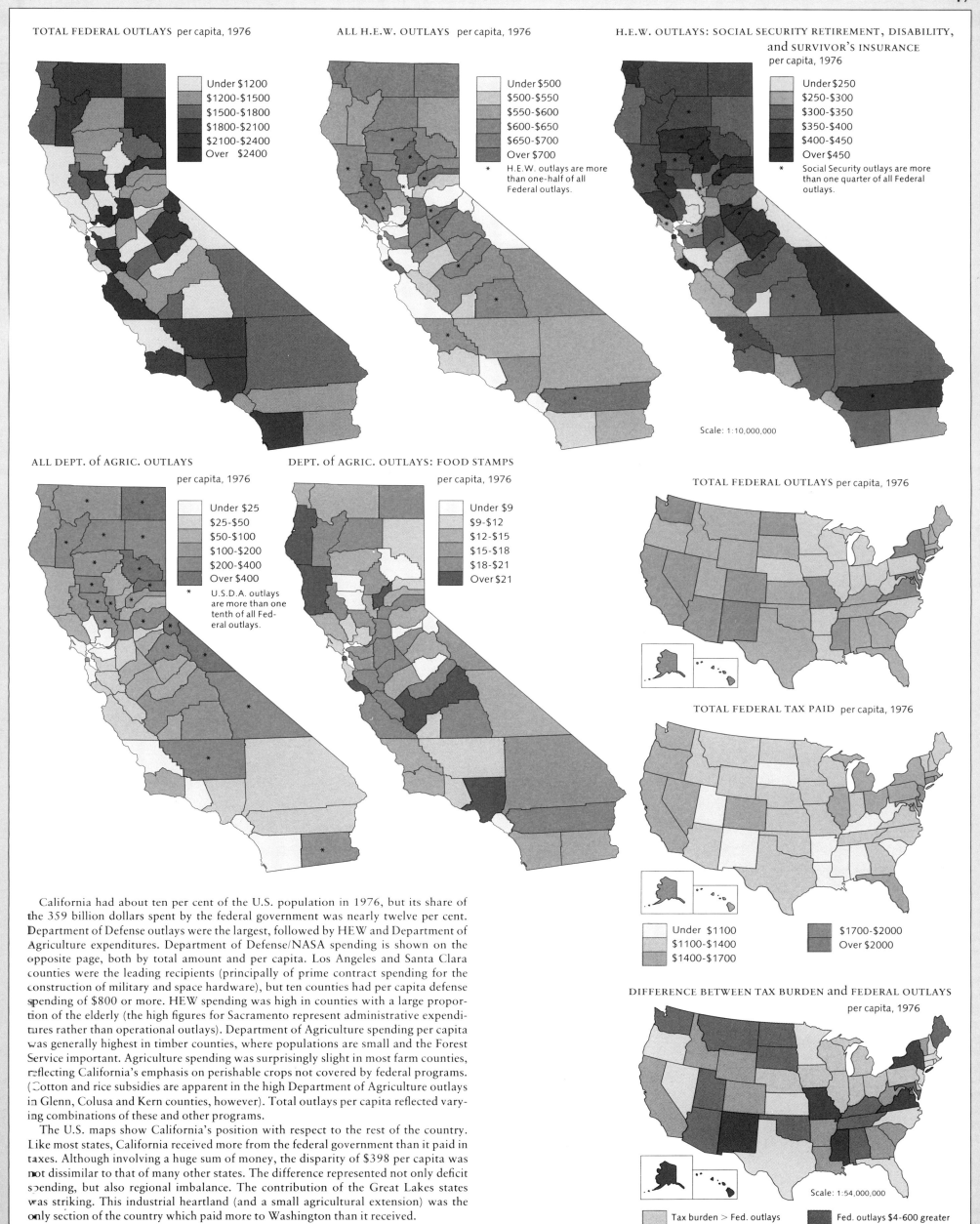

TOTAL FEDERAL OUTLAYS per capita, 1976

Under $1200
$1200-$1500
$1500-$1800
$1800-$2100
$2100-$2400
Over $2400

ALL H.E.W. OUTLAYS per capita, 1976

Under $500
$500-$550
$550-$600
$600-$650
$650-$700
Over $700

* H.E.W. outlays are more than one-half of all Federal outlays.

H.E.W. OUTLAYS: SOCIAL SECURITY RETIREMENT, DISABILITY, and SURVIVOR'S INSURANCE per capita, 1976

Under $250
$250-$300
$300-$350
$350-$400
$400-$450
Over $450

* Social Security outlays are more than one quarter of all Federal outlays.

Scale: 1:10,000,000

ALL DEPT. OF AGRIC. OUTLAYS per capita, 1976

Under $25
$25-$50
$50-$100
$100-$200
$200-$400
Over $400

* U.S.D.A. outlays are more than one tenth of all Federal outlays.

DEPT. of AGRIC. OUTLAYS: FOOD STAMPS per capita, 1976

Under $9
$9-$12
$12-$15
$15-$18
$18-$21
Over $21

TOTAL FEDERAL OUTLAYS per capita, 1976

TOTAL FEDERAL TAX PAID per capita, 1976

Under $1100
$1100-$1400
$1400-$1700
$1700-$2000
Over $2000

DIFFERENCE BETWEEN TAX BURDEN and FEDERAL OUTLAYS per capita, 1976

Tax burden > Fed. outlays
Fed. outlays $0-200 greater
Fed. outlays $2-400 greater
Fed. outlays $4-600 greater
Fed. outlays $6-800 greater
Fed. outlays > $800 greater

Scale: 1:54,000,000

California had about ten per cent of the U.S. population in 1976, but its share of the 359 billion dollars spent by the federal government was nearly twelve per cent. Department of Defense outlays were the largest, followed by HEW and Department of Agriculture expenditures. Department of Defense/NASA spending is shown on the opposite page, both by total amount and per capita. Los Angeles and Santa Clara counties were the leading recipients (principally of prime contract spending for the construction of military and space hardware), but ten counties had per capita defense spending of $800 or more. HEW spending was high in counties with a large proportion of the elderly (the high figures for Sacramento represent administrative expenditures rather than operational outlays). Department of Agriculture spending per capita was generally highest in timber counties, where populations are small and the Forest Service important. Agriculture spending was surprisingly slight in most farm counties, reflecting California's emphasis on perishable crops not covered by federal programs. (Cotton and rice subsidies are apparent in the high Department of Agriculture outlays in Glenn, Colusa and Kern counties, however). Total outlays per capita reflected varying combinations of these and other programs.

The U.S. maps show California's position with respect to the rest of the country. Like most states, California received more from the federal government than it paid in taxes. Although involving a huge sum of money, the disparity of $398 per capita was not dissimilar to that of many other states. The difference represented not only deficit spending, but also regional imbalance. The contribution of the Great Lakes states was striking. This industrial heartland (and a small agricultural extension) was the only section of the country which paid more to Washington than it received.

Source:
Office of Economic Opportunity, Federal Outlays 1976

FEDERAL SPENDING

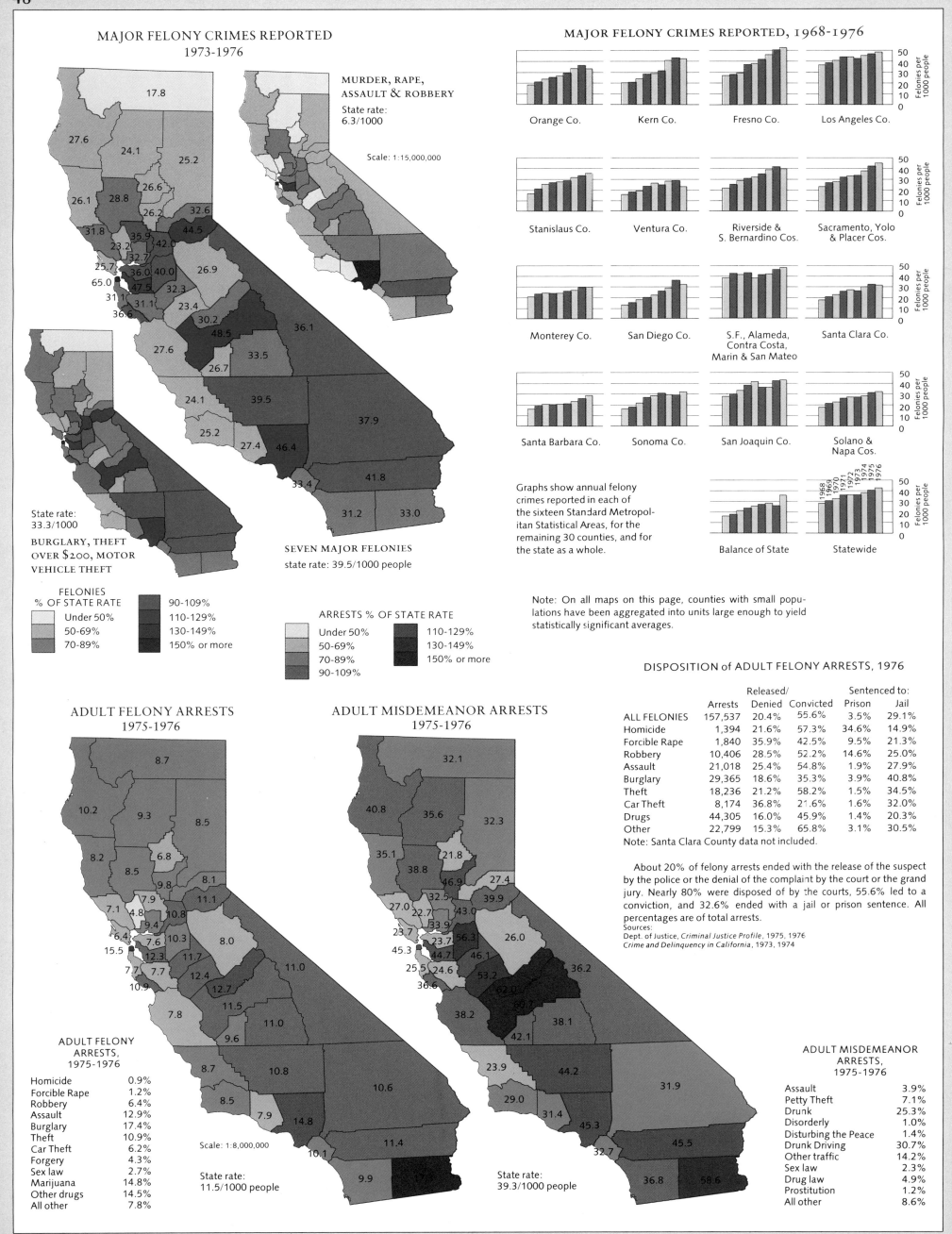

MAJOR FELONY CRIMES REPORTED
1973-1976

MURDER, RAPE, ASSAULT & ROBBERY
State rate: 6.3/1000

Scale: 1:15,000,000

BURGLARY, THEFT OVER $200, MOTOR VEHICLE THEFT
State rate: 33.3/1000

SEVEN MAJOR FELONIES
state rate: 39.5/1000 people

FELONIES % OF STATE RATE
- Under 50%
- 50-69%
- 70-89%
- 90-109%
- 110-129%
- 130-149%
- 150% or more

ARRESTS % OF STATE RATE
- Under 50%
- 50-69%
- 70-89%
- 90-109%
- 110-129%
- 130-149%
- 150% or more

MAJOR FELONY CRIMES REPORTED, 1968-1976

Orange Co. | Kern Co. | Fresno Co. | Los Angeles Co.
Stanislaus Co. | Ventura Co. | Riverside & S. Bernardino Cos. | Sacramento, Yolo & Placer Cos.
Monterey Co. | San Diego Co. | S.F., Alameda, Contra Costa, Marin & San Mateo | Santa Clara Co.
Santa Barbara Co. | Sonoma Co. | San Joaquin Co. | Solano & Napa Cos.
Balance of State | Statewide

Felonies per 1000 people: 50 40 30 20 10 0

1968 1969 1970 1971 1972 1973 1974 1975 1976

Graphs show annual felony crimes reported in each of the sixteen Standard Metropolitan Statistical Areas, for the remaining 30 counties, and for the state as a whole.

Note: On all maps on this page, counties with small populations have been aggregated into units large enough to yield statistically significant averages.

DISPOSITION of ADULT FELONY ARRESTS, 1976

	Arrests	Released/ Denied	Convicted	Sentenced to: Prison	Jail
ALL FELONIES	157,537	20.4%	55.6%	3.5%	29.1%
Homicide	1,394	21.6%	57.3%	34.6%	14.9%
Forcible Rape	1,840	35.9%	42.5%	9.5%	21.3%
Robbery	10,406	28.5%	52.2%	14.6%	25.0%
Assault	21,018	25.4%	54.8%	1.9%	27.9%
Burglary	29,365	18.6%	35.3%	3.9%	40.8%
Theft	18,236	21.2%	58.2%	1.5%	34.5%
Car Theft	8,174	36.8%	21.6%	1.6%	32.0%
Drugs	44,305	16.0%	45.9%	1.4%	20.3%
Other	22,799	15.3%	65.8%	3.1%	30.5%

Note: Santa Clara County data not included.

About 20% of felony arrests ended with the release of the suspect by the police or the denial of the complaint by the court or the grand jury. Nearly 80% were disposed of by the courts, 55.6% led to a conviction, and 32.6% ended with a jail or prison sentence. All percentages are of total arrests.
Sources:
Dept. of Justice, *Criminal Justice Profile*, 1975, 1976
Crime and Delinquency in California, 1973, 1974

ADULT FELONY ARRESTS
1975-1976

Scale: 1:8,000,000

State rate: 11.5/1000 people

ADULT FELONY ARRESTS, 1975-1976
Homicide	0.9%
Forcible Rape	1.2%
Robbery	6.4%
Assault	12.9%
Burglary	17.4%
Theft	10.9%
Car Theft	6.2%
Forgery	4.3%
Sex law	2.7%
Marijuana	14.8%
Other drugs	14.5%
All other	7.8%

ADULT MISDEMEANOR ARRESTS
1975-1976

State rate: 39.3/1000 people

ADULT MISDEMEANOR ARRESTS, 1975-1976
Assault	3.9%
Petty Theft	7.1%
Drunk	25.3%
Disorderly	1.0%
Disturbing the Peace	1.4%
Drunk Driving	30.7%
Other traffic	14.2%
Sex law	2.3%
Drug law	4.9%
Prostitution	1.2%
All other	8.6%

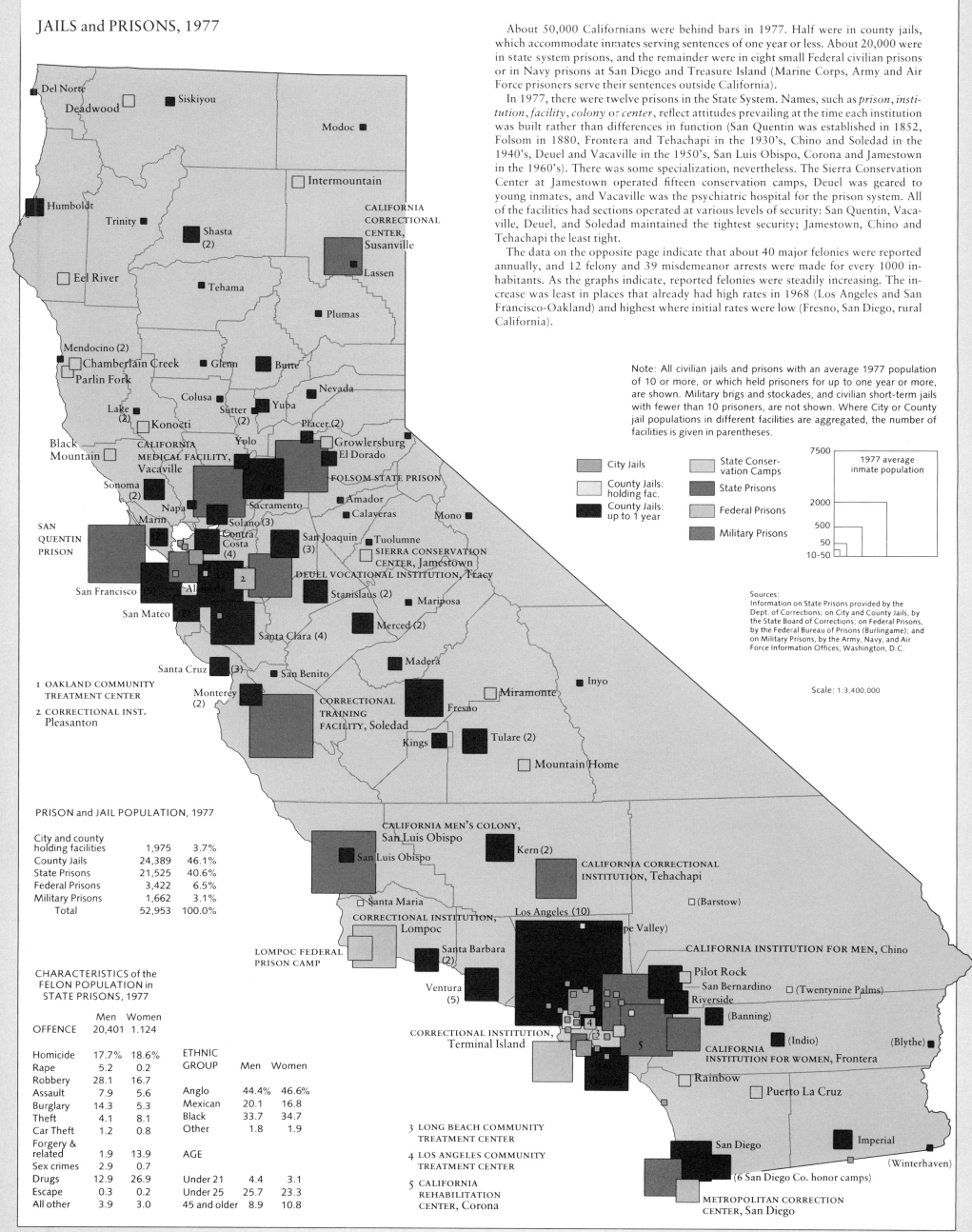

JAILS and PRISONS, 1977

About 50,000 Californians were behind bars in 1977. Half were in county jails, which accommodate inmates serving sentences of one year or less. About 20,000 were in state system prisons, and the remainder were in eight small Federal civilian prisons or in Navy prisons at San Diego and Treasure Island (Marine Corps, Army and Air Force prisoners serve their sentences outside California).

In 1977, there were twelve prisons in the State System. Names, such as *prison, institution, facility, colony or center*, reflect attitudes prevailing at the time each institution was built rather than differences in function (San Quentin was established in 1852, Folsom in 1880, Frontera and Tehachapi in the 1930's, Chino and Soledad in the 1940's, Deuel and Vacaville in the 1950's, San Luis Obispo, Corona and Jamestown in the 1960's). There was some specialization, nevertheless. The Sierra Conservation Center at Jamestown operated fifteen conservation camps, Deuel was geared to young inmates, and Vacaville was the psychiatric hospital for the prison system. All of the facilities had sections operated at various levels of security: San Quentin, Vacaville, Deuel, and Soledad maintained the tightest security; Jamestown, Chino and Tehachapi the least tight.

The data on the opposite page indicate that about 40 major felonies were reported annually, and 12 felony and 39 misdemeanor arrests were made for every 1000 inhabitants. As the graphs indicate, reported felonies were steadily increasing. The increase was least in places that already had high rates in 1968 (Los Angeles and San Francisco-Oakland) and highest where initial rates were low (Fresno, San Diego, rural California).

Note: All civilian jails and prisons with an average 1977 population of 10 or more, or which held prisoners for up to one year or more, are shown. Military brigs and stockades, and civilian short-term jails with fewer than 10 prisoners, are not shown. Where City or County jail populations in different facilities are aggregated, the number of facilities is given in parentheses.

City Jails
County Jails: holding fac.
County Jails: up to 1 year
State Conservation Camps
State Prisons
Federal Prisons
Military Prisons

1977 average inmate population

Sources:
Information on State Prisons provided by the Dept. of Corrections; on City and County Jails, by the State Board of Corrections; on Federal Prisons, by the Federal Bureau of Prisons (Burlingame); and on Military Prisons, by the Army, Navy, and Air Force Information Offices, Washington, D.C.

Scale: 1:3,400,000

PRISON and JAIL POPULATION, 1977

City and county holding facilities	1,975	3.7%
County Jails	24,389	46.1%
State Prisons	21,525	40.6%
Federal Prisons	3,422	6.5%
Military Prisons	1,662	3.1%
Total	52,953	100.0%

CHARACTERISTICS of the FELON POPULATION in STATE PRISONS, 1977

	Men	Women
OFFENCE	20,401	1,124
Homicide	17.7%	18.6%
Rape	5.2	0.2
Robbery	28.1	16.7
Assault	7.9	5.6
Burglary	14.3	5.3
Theft	4.1	8.1
Car Theft	1.2	0.8
Forgery & related	1.9	13.9
Sex crimes	2.9	0.7
Drugs	12.9	26.9
Escape	0.3	0.2
All other	3.9	3.0

ETHNIC GROUP	Men	Women
Anglo	44.4%	46.6%
Mexican	20.1	16.8
Black	33.7	34.7
Other	1.8	1.9

AGE		
Under 21	4.4	3.1
Under 25	25.7	23.3
45 and older	8.9	10.8

1 OAKLAND COMMUNITY TREATMENT CENTER
2 CORRECTIONAL INST. Pleasanton
3 LONG BEACH COMMUNITY TREATMENT CENTER
4 LOS ANGELES COMMUNITY TREATMENT CENTER
5 CALIFORNIA REHABILITATION CENTER, Corona

CALIFORNIA CORRECTIONAL CENTER, Susanville
CALIFORNIA MEDICAL FACILITY, Vacaville
SAN QUENTIN PRISON
FOLSOM STATE PRISON
SIERRA CONSERVATION CENTER, Jamestown
DEUEL VOCATIONAL INSTITUTION, Tracy
CORRECTIONAL TRAINING FACILITY, Soledad
CALIFORNIA MEN'S COLONY, San Luis Obispo
CALIFORNIA CORRECTIONAL INSTITUTION, Tehachapi
CORRECTIONAL INSTITUTION, Lompoc
LOMPOC FEDERAL PRISON CAMP
CALIFORNIA INSTITUTION FOR MEN, Chino
CALIFORNIA INSTITUTION FOR WOMEN, Frontera
CORRECTIONAL INSTITUTION, Terminal Island
METROPOLITAN CORRECTION CENTER, San Diego

(6 San Diego Co. honor camps)

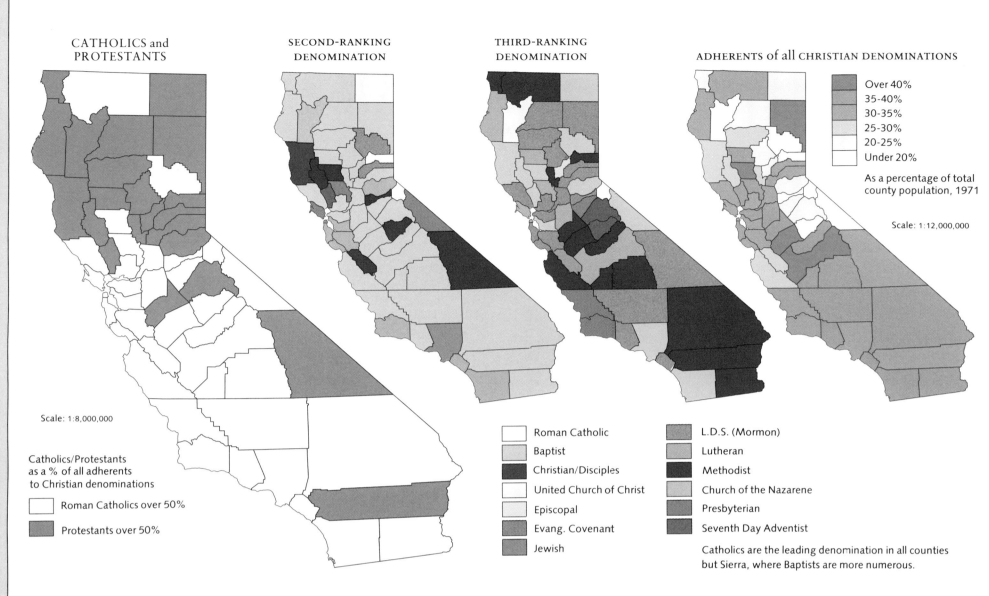

CATHOLICS and PROTESTANTS

Scale: 1:8,000,000

Catholics/Protestants
as a % of all adherents
to Christian denominations

Roman Catholics over 50%

Protestants over 50%

SECOND-RANKING DENOMINATION

THIRD-RANKING DENOMINATION

ADHERENTS of all CHRISTIAN DENOMINATIONS

Over 40%
35-40%
30-35%
25-30%
20-25%
Under 20%

As a percentage of total
county population, 1971

Scale: 1:12,000,000

Roman Catholic
Baptist
Christian/Disciples
United Church of Christ
Episcopal
Evang. Covenant
Jewish

L.D.S. (Mormon)
Lutheran
Methodist
Church of the Nazarene
Presbyterian
Seventh Day Adventist

Catholics are the leading denomination in all counties
but Sierra, where Baptists are more numerous.

THE EIGHT LEADING CHRISTIAN DENOMINATIONS
Adherents as a percent of the total county population, 1971

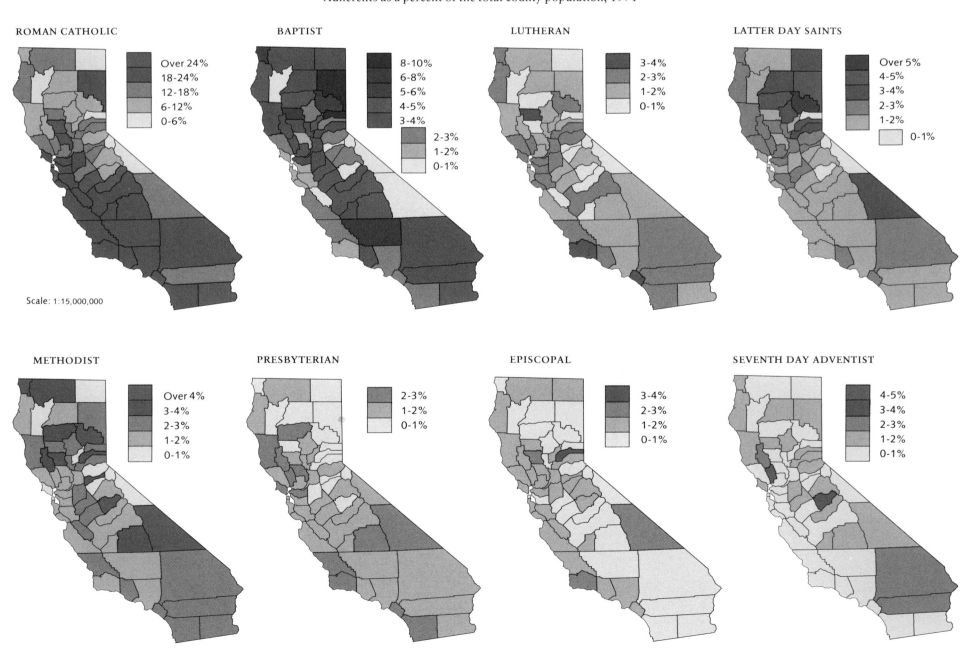

ROMAN CATHOLIC

Over 24%
18-24%
12-18%
6-12%
0-6%

Scale: 1:15,000,000

BAPTIST

8-10%
6-8%
5-6%
4-5%
3-4%
2-3%
1-2%
0-1%

LUTHERAN

3-4%
2-3%
1-2%
0-1%

LATTER DAY SAINTS

Over 5%
4-5%
3-4%
2-3%
1-2%
0-1%

METHODIST

Over 4%
3-4%
2-3%
1-2%
0-1%

PRESBYTERIAN

2-3%
1-2%
0-1%

EPISCOPAL

3-4%
2-3%
1-2%
0-1%

SEVENTH DAY ADVENTIST

4-5%
3-4%
2-3%
1-2%
0-1%

In 1971, 30 per cent of California's residents were adherents of one religion or another, and as in much of the American Northeast and Southwest, Roman Catholicism predominated. Catholics accounted for 59 per cent of the state's 6,187,071 churchgoers. They outnumbered adherents of all the Protestant denominations combined, and were the leading group in every county except Sierra. Catholic churches were well distributed, their location reflecting the presence of towns more than the density of the Catholic population itself.

California's 650,000 Jews constituted the second largest religious group in the state. Although not all were registered members of a synagogue, the total Jewish population is cited here because of the group's cohesion as a socio-religious body. Jews were highly concentrated in urban areas; seventy-five per cent lived in the Los Angeles agglomeration alone, with a notable clustering in and near Hollywood and Beverly Hills.

The number of church-going members of other denominations was remarkably small. The various Baptist bodies, who totaled 526,767 adherents in 1971 were relatively prominent in rural areas throughout the state and in the Black neighborhoods of the Bay Area and Los Angeles. The Baptist tradition of splintering has resulted in a very large number of churches. Lutherans, the next leading group with about 419,321 adherents, were found mainly in suburban areas. Latter Day Saints (Mormons), with 367,521 members, were concentrated in the northeastern part of the state. Adherents of the remaining denominations appeared numerous only in thinly peopled counties because of the dominance of Catholics in the larger counties.

RANKING CHRISTIAN DENOMINATIONS in the UNITED STATES

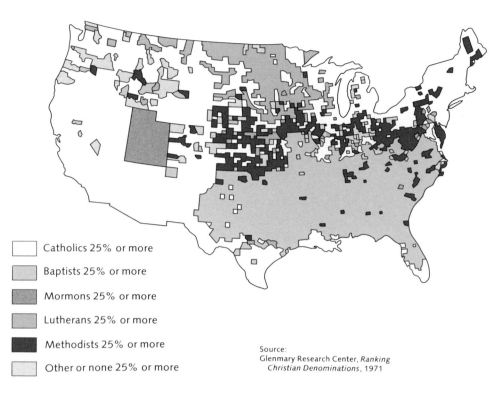

☐ Catholics 25% or more

☐ Baptists 25% or more

☐ Mormons 25% or more

☐ Lutherans 25% or more

■ Methodists 25% or more

☐ Other or none 25% or more

Source:
Glenmary Research Center, *Ranking Christian Denominations*, 1971

CATHOLIC and BAPTIST CHURCHES,
and SYNAGOGUES

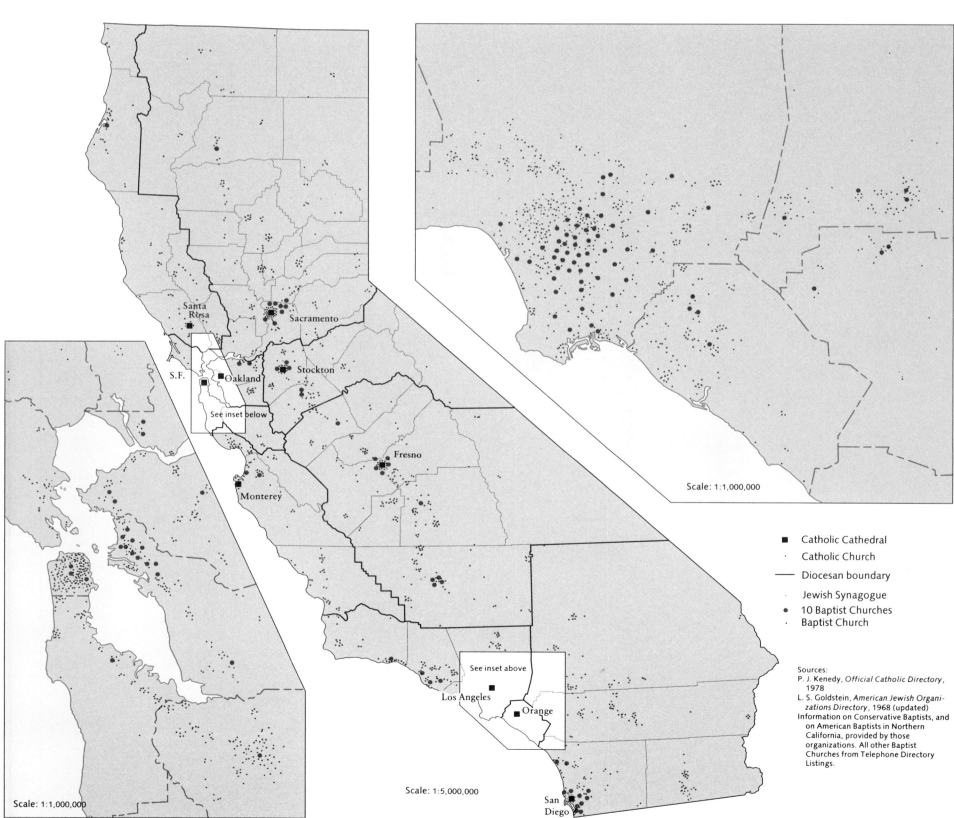

Santa Rosa
Sacramento
S.F.
Oakland
Stockton
See inset below
Fresno
Monterey
See inset above
Los Angeles
Orange
San Diego

Scale: 1:1,000,000

Scale: 1:1,000,000

Scale: 1:5,000,000

■ Catholic Cathedral

· Catholic Church

— Diocesan boundary

· Jewish Synagogue

● 10 Baptist Churches

· Baptist Church

Sources:
P. J. Kenedy, *Official Catholic Directory*, 1978
L. S. Goldstein, *American Jewish Organizations Directory*, 1968 (updated)
Information on Conservative Baptists, and on American Baptists in Northern California, provided by those organizations. All other Baptist Churches from Telephone Directory Listings.

RELIGION

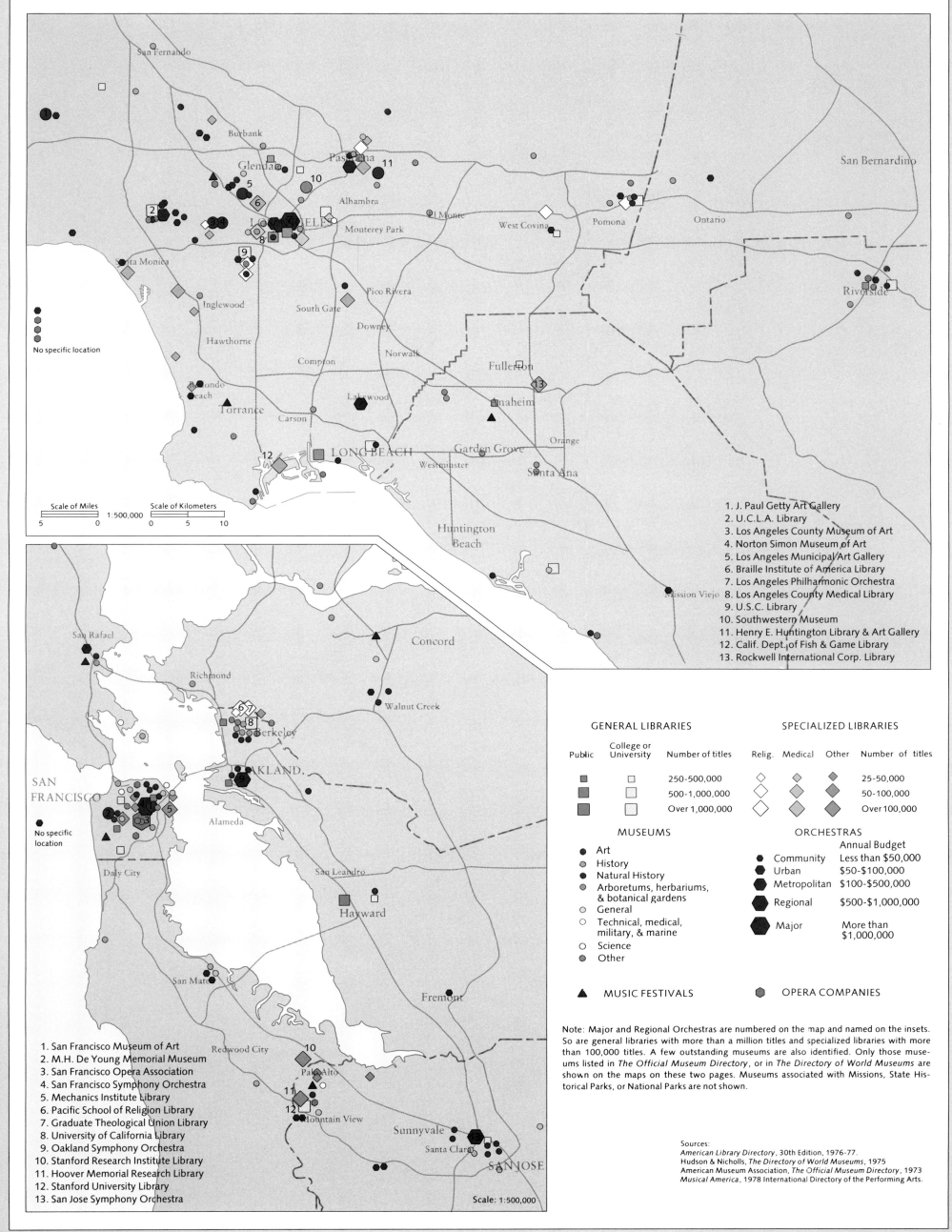

No specific location

Scale of Miles
5   0
1:500,000
Scale of Kilometers
0   5   10

1. J. Paul Getty Art Gallery
2. U.C.L.A. Library
3. Los Angeles County Museum of Art
4. Norton Simon Museum of Art
5. Los Angeles Municipal Art Gallery
6. Braille Institute of America Library
7. Los Angeles Philharmonic Orchestra
8. Los Angeles County Medical Library
9. U.S.C. Library
10. Southwestern Museum
11. Henry E. Huntington Library & Art Gallery
12. Calif. Dept. of Fish & Game Library
13. Rockwell International Corp. Library

No specific location

1. San Francisco Museum of Art
2. M.H. De Young Memorial Museum
3. San Francisco Opera Association
4. San Francisco Symphony Orchestra
5. Mechanics Institute Library
6. Pacific School of Religion Library
7. Graduate Theological Union Library
8. University of California Library
9. Oakland Symphony Orchestra
10. Stanford Research Institute Library
11. Hoover Memorial Research Library
12. Stanford University Library
13. San Jose Symphony Orchestra

Scale: 1:500,000

GENERAL LIBRARIES			SPECIALIZED LIBRARIES			
Public	College or University	Number of titles	Relig.	Medical	Other	Number of titles
■	□	250-500,000	◇	◇	◇	25-50,000
■	□	500-1,000,000	◇	◇	◇	50-100,000
■	□	Over 1,000,000	◇	◇	◇	Over 100,000

MUSEUMS
● Art
● History
● Natural History
● Arboretums, herbariums, & botanical gardens
○ General
○ Technical, medical, military, & marine
○ Science
● Other

ORCHESTRAS
Annual Budget
● Community   Less than $50,000
⬡ Urban $50-$100,000
⬡ Metropolitan $100-$500,000
⬡ Regional $500-$1,000,000
⬡ Major   More than $1,000,000

▲ MUSIC FESTIVALS   ⬡ OPERA COMPANIES

Note: Major and Regional Orchestras are numbered on the map and named on the insets. So are general libraries with more than a million titles and specialized libraries with more than 100,000 titles. A few outstanding museums are also identified. Only those museums listed in *The Official Museum Directory*, or in *The Directory of World Museums* are shown on the maps on these two pages. Museums associated with Missions, State Historical Parks, or National Parks are not shown.

Sources:
American Library Directory, 30th Edition, 1976-77.
Hudson & Nicholls, *The Directory of World Museums*, 1975
American Museum Association, *The Official Museum Directory*, 1973
Musical America, 1978 International Directory of the Performing Arts.

CULTURAL RESOURCES

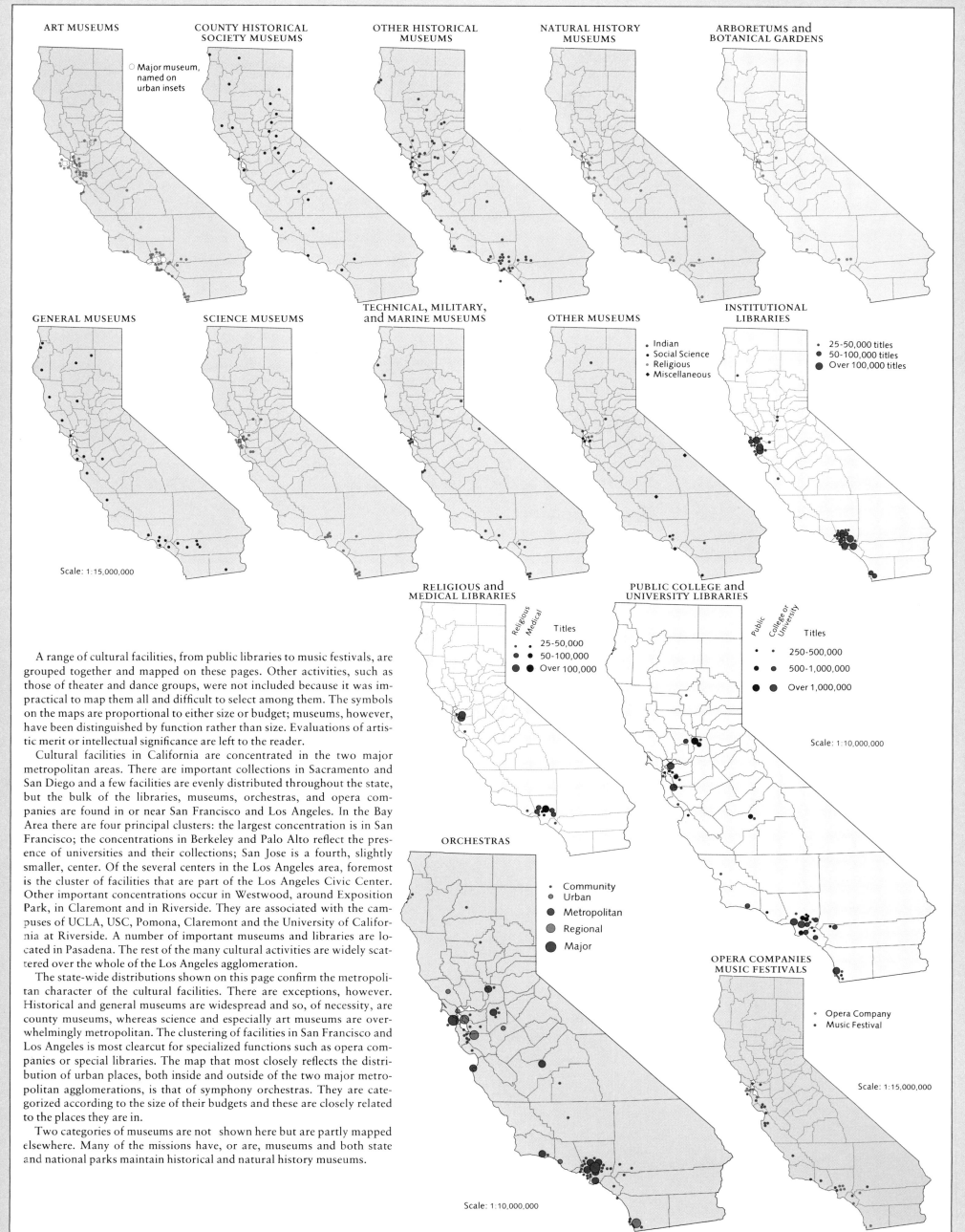

ART MUSEUMS

○ Major museum, named on urban insets

COUNTY HISTORICAL SOCIETY MUSEUMS

OTHER HISTORICAL MUSEUMS

NATURAL HISTORY MUSEUMS

ARBORETUMS and BOTANICAL GARDENS

GENERAL MUSEUMS

Scale: 1:15,000,000

SCIENCE MUSEUMS

TECHNICAL, MILITARY, and MARINE MUSEUMS

OTHER MUSEUMS

• Indian
• Social Science
• Religious
◆ Miscellaneous

INSTITUTIONAL LIBRARIES

• 25-50,000 titles
● 50-100,000 titles
● Over 100,000 titles

RELIGIOUS and MEDICAL LIBRARIES

Religious
Medical

Titles
• 25-50,000
● 50-100,000
● Over 100,000

PUBLIC COLLEGE and UNIVERSITY LIBRARIES

Public
College or University

Titles
• 250-500,000
● 500-1,000,000
● Over 1,000,000

Scale: 1:10,000,000

ORCHESTRAS

• Community
○ Urban
● Metropolitan
● Regional
● Major

OPERA COMPANIES MUSIC FESTIVALS

• Opera Company
• Music Festival

Scale: 1:15,000,000

A range of cultural facilities, from public libraries to music festivals, are grouped together and mapped on these pages. Other activities, such as those of theater and dance groups, were not included because it was impractical to map them all and difficult to select among them. The symbols on the maps are proportional to either size or budget; museums, however, have been distinguished by function rather than size. Evaluations of artistic merit or intellectual significance are left to the reader.

Cultural facilities in California are concentrated in the two major metropolitan areas. There are important collections in Sacramento and San Diego and a few facilities are evenly distributed throughout the state, but the bulk of the libraries, museums, orchestras, and opera companies are found in or near San Francisco and Los Angeles. In the Bay Area there are four principal clusters: the largest concentration is in San Francisco; the concentrations in Berkeley and Palo Alto reflect the presence of universities and their collections; San Jose is a fourth, slightly smaller, center. Of the several centers in the Los Angeles area, foremost is the cluster of facilities that are part of the Los Angeles Civic Center. Other important concentrations occur in Westwood, around Exposition Park, in Claremont and in Riverside. They are associated with the campuses of UCLA, USC, Pomona, Claremont and the University of California at Riverside. A number of important museums and libraries are located in Pasadena. The rest of the many cultural activities are widely scattered over the whole of the Los Angeles agglomeration.

The state-wide distributions shown on this page confirm the metropolitan character of the cultural facilities. There are exceptions, however. Historical and general museums are widespread and so, of necessity, are county museums, whereas science and especially art museums are overwhelmingly metropolitan. The clustering of facilities in San Francisco and Los Angeles is most clearcut for specialized functions such as opera companies or special libraries. The map that most closely reflects the distribution of urban places, both inside and outside of the two major metropolitan agglomerations, is that of symphony orchestras. They are categorized according to the size of their budgets and these are closely related to the places they are in.

Two categories of museums are not shown here but are partly mapped elsewhere. Many of the missions have, or are, museums and both state and national parks maintain historical and natural history museums.

Scale: 1:10,000,000

CULTURAL RESOURCES

The political history of California began by mirroring the national scene fairly closely. In the 1850's it voted for Democrats, intent on intra-party mayhem, then shifted to Lincoln by a close vote, and gradually became a Republican stronghold. Until 1932 it seldom gave its electoral votes to a Democrat, though Wilson is one notable exception. Nor have minor parties done well, except for the remarkable showing of the Progressives under Teddy Roosevelt and LaFollette.

As California's population increased, its registration became more Democratic. In 1920, when California had thirteen electoral votes and registration was about 1.5 million, Democrats made up less than a quarter of the total. By 1934 the two parties were even, and soon thereafter the Democrats achieved and maintained a 3 to 2 superiority, with only minor fluctuations. In 1972, about 10 million voters were registered and Democrats outnumbered Republicans by more than 2 million. This superiority was not reflected in the voting booths, however. Between 1952 and 1976, only Johnson was able to carry the state for the Democrats, and the disparity between party preference and voting habits was striking. Democratic registration in San Diego County, for example, was 53 per cent of the two-party total, yet Carter ob-

tained only 40 per cent of the vote; in Tulare County, the corresponding figures were 60 and 45 per cent.

The presidential vote since 1912 is shown in its regional variation on the facing page. All of the maps show Republican and Democratic percentages of the two-party total, except for 1912 which shows the Democratic-Progressive split and 1924 which indicates the Republican-Progressive division. Landslide victories of both parties are obvious. In closer elections, the maps show Democratic strength in mountain counties, from Placer to Trinity, in the San Joaquin Valley, and in Sacramento, Solano and San Francisco Counties. Republican votes came from Southern California, from east of the Sierras, and from coastal counties. This pattern has not changed much, as a comparison of the close elections of 1916 and 1976 with each other and with the map of aggregate voting record makes clear. A few shifts have taken place, nevertheless. Some agricultural counties, traditionally Democratic, have become Republican: Butte, Tehama, Glenn, Sutter, Tulare and Imperial. Some urbanized counties, once Republican, have become more Democratic: Alameda, Santa Clara and Los Angeles. The Democratic trends in Yolo and Santa Cruz can be associated with the growing university communities in those counties.

POLITICAL TRENDS in PRESIDENTIAL ELECTIONS, 1972-1976

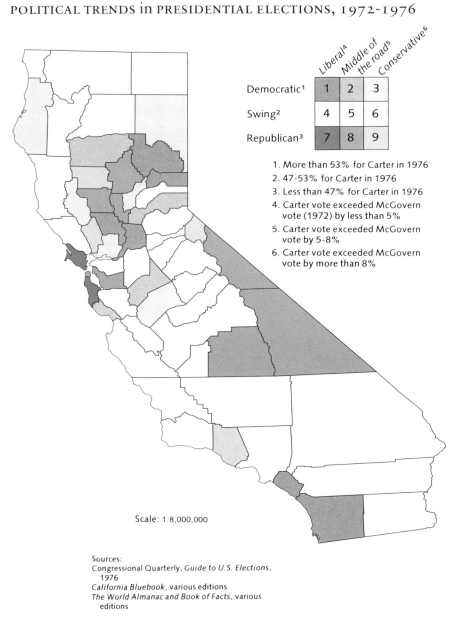

Scale: 1:8,000,000

Sources:
Congressional Quarterly, *Guide to U.S. Elections*, 1976
California Bluebook, various editions
The World Almanac and Book of Facts, various editions

PRESIDENTIAL VOTE 1912-1976 per cent of total votes cast

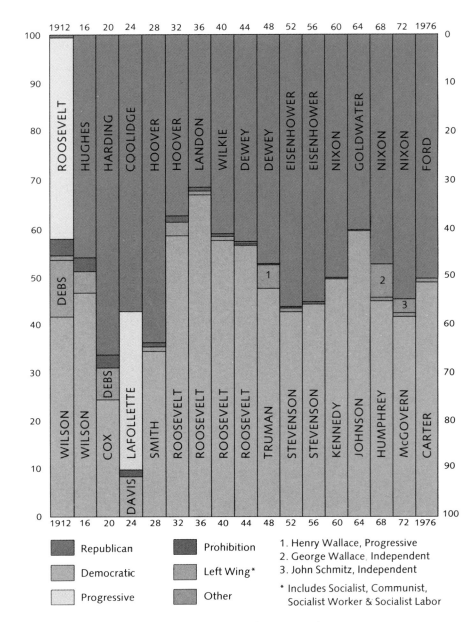

Republican
Democratic
Progressive
Prohibition
Left Wing*
Other

1. Henry Wallace, Progressive
2. George Wallace, Independent
3. John Schmitz, Independent

* Includes Socialist, Communist, Socialist Worker & Socialist Labor

PARTY DIVISION OF CALIFORNIA'S REPRESENTATIVES IN CONGRESS 1850-1976

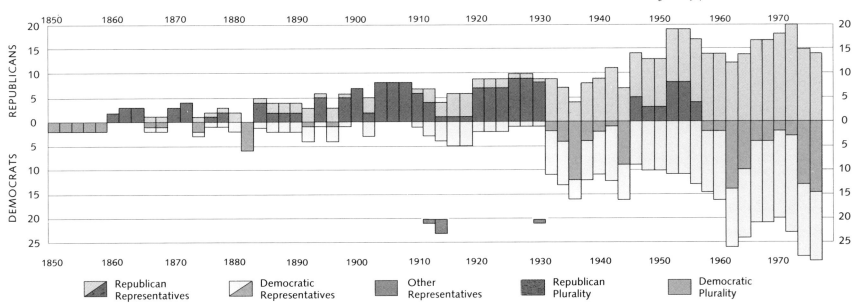

Republican Representatives
Democratic Representatives
Other Representatives
Republican Plurality
Democratic Plurality

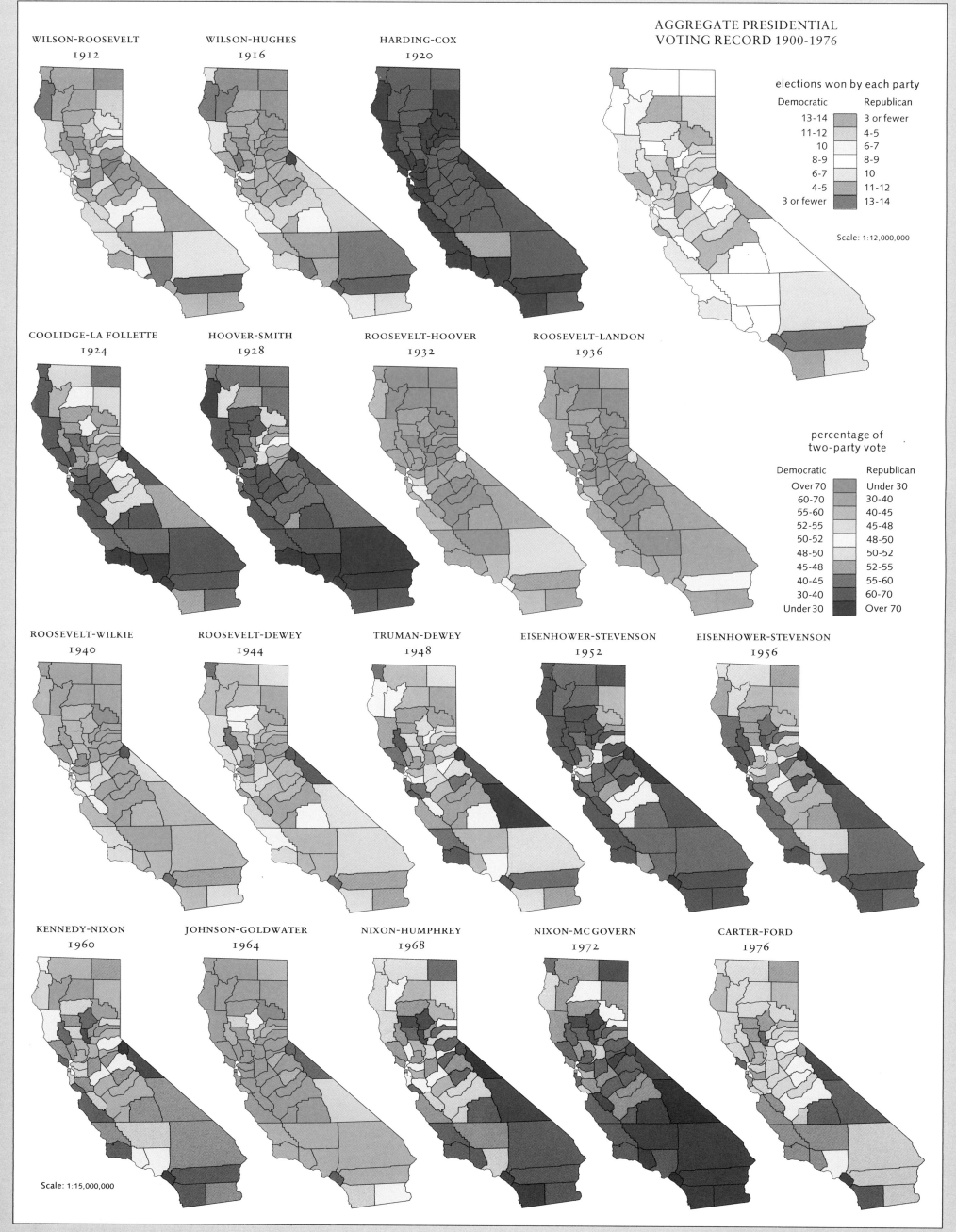

WILSON-ROOSEVELT
1912

WILSON-HUGHES
1916

HARDING-COX
1920

AGGREGATE PRESIDENTIAL
VOTING RECORD 1900-1976

elections won by each party

Democratic	Republican
13-14	3 or fewer
11-12	4-5
10	6-7
8-9	8-9
6-7	10
4-5	11-12
3 or fewer	13-14

Scale: 1:12,000,000

COOLIDGE-LA FOLLETTE
1924

HOOVER-SMITH
1928

ROOSEVELT-HOOVER
1932

ROOSEVELT-LANDON
1936

percentage of
two-party vote

Democratic	Republican
Over 70	Under 30
60-70	30-40
55-60	40-45
52-55	45-48
50-52	48-50
48-50	50-52
45-48	52-55
40-45	55-60
30-40	60-70
Under 30	Over 70

ROOSEVELT-WILKIE
1940

ROOSEVELT-DEWEY
1944

TRUMAN-DEWEY
1948

EISENHOWER-STEVENSON
1952

EISENHOWER-STEVENSON
1956

KENNEDY-NIXON
1960

JOHNSON-GOLDWATER
1964

NIXON-HUMPHREY
1968

NIXON-MCGOVERN
1972

CARTER-FORD
1976

Scale: 1:15,000,000

PRESIDENTIAL ELECTIONS

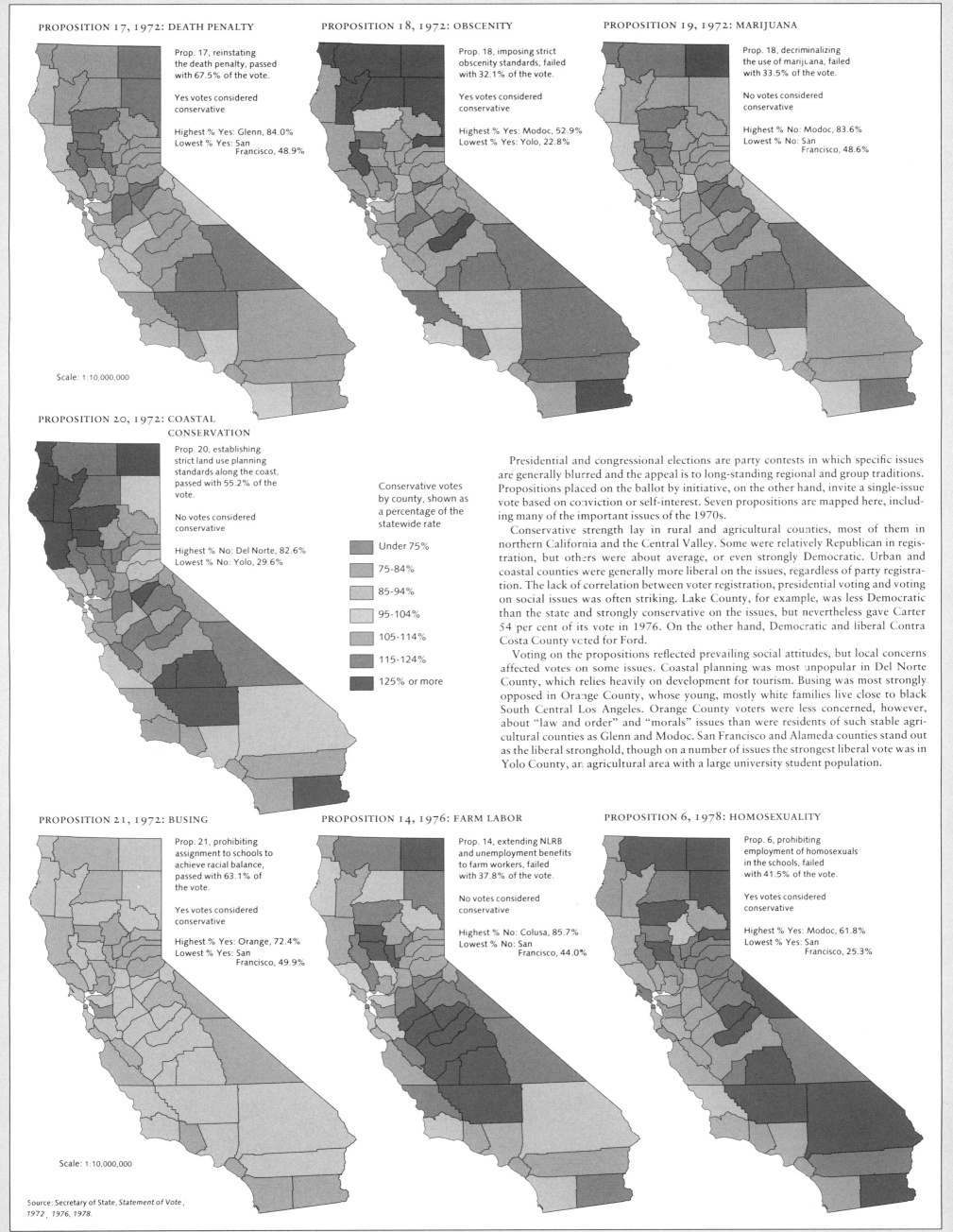

PROPOSITION 17, 1972: DEATH PENALTY

Prop. 17, reinstating the death penalty, passed with 67.5% of the vote.

Yes votes considered conservative

Highest % Yes: Glenn, 84.0%
Lowest % Yes: San Francisco, 48.9%

Scale: 1:10,000,000

PROPOSITION 18, 1972: OBSCENITY

Prop. 18, imposing strict obscenity standards, failed with 32.1% of the vote.

Yes votes considered conservative

Highest % Yes: Modoc, 52.9%
Lowest % Yes: Yolo, 22.8%

PROPOSITION 19, 1972: MARIJUANA

Prop. 18, decriminalizing the use of marijuana, failed with 33.5% of the vote.

No votes considered conservative

Highest % No: Modoc, 83.6%
Lowest % No: San Francisco, 48.6%

PROPOSITION 20, 1972: COASTAL CONSERVATION

Prop. 20, establishing strict land use planning standards along the coast, passed with 55.2% of the vote.

No votes considered conservative

Highest % No: Del Norte, 82.6%
Lowest % No: Yolo, 29.6%

Conservative votes by county, shown as a percentage of the statewide rate

- Under 75%
- 75-84%
- 85-94%
- 95-104%
- 105-114%
- 115-124%
- 125% or more

Presidential and congressional elections are party contests in which specific issues are generally blurred and the appeal is to long-standing regional and group traditions. Propositions placed on the ballot by initiative, on the other hand, invite a single-issue vote based on conviction or self-interest. Seven propositions are mapped here, including many of the important issues of the 1970s.

Conservative strength lay in rural and agricultural counties, most of them in northern California and the Central Valley. Some were relatively Republican in registration, but others were about average, or even strongly Democratic. Urban and coastal counties were generally more liberal on the issues, regardless of party registration. The lack of correlation between voter registration, presidential voting and voting on social issues was often striking. Lake County, for example, was less Democratic than the state and strongly conservative on the issues, but nevertheless gave Carter 54 per cent of its vote in 1976. On the other hand, Democratic and liberal Contra Costa County voted for Ford.

Voting on the propositions reflected prevailing social attitudes, but local concerns affected votes on some issues. Coastal planning was most unpopular in Del Norte County, which relies heavily on development for tourism. Busing was most strongly opposed in Orange County, whose young, mostly white families live close to black South Central Los Angeles. Orange County voters were less concerned, however, about "law and order" and "morals" issues than were residents of such stable agricultural counties as Glenn and Modoc. San Francisco and Alameda counties stand out as the liberal stronghold, though on a number of issues the strongest liberal vote was in Yolo County, an agricultural area with a large university student population.

PROPOSITION 21, 1972: BUSING

Prop. 21, prohibiting assignment to schools to achieve racial balance, passed with 63.1% of the vote.

Yes votes considered conservative

Highest % Yes: Orange, 72.4%
Lowest % Yes: San Francisco, 49.9%

Scale: 1:10,000,000

Source: Secretary of State, *Statement of Vote*, 1972, 1976, 1978.

PROPOSITION 14, 1976: FARM LABOR

Prop. 14, extending NLRB and unemployment benefits to farm workers, failed with 37.8% of the vote.

No votes considered conservative

Highest % No: Colusa, 85.7%
Lowest % No: San Francisco, 44.0%

PROPOSITION 6, 1978: HOMOSEXUALITY

Prop. 6, prohibiting employment of homosexuals in the schools, failed with 41.5% of the vote.

Yes votes considered conservative

Highest % Yes: Modoc, 61.8%
Lowest % Yes: San Francisco, 25.3%

POLITICAL ISSUES, 1972-1978

Proposition 13's announced goal of curbing "needless government spending" echoed Republican objections to Democratic social programs, and there was a modest correlation between areas of Democratic party strength and opposition to Proposition 13. Low-income areas in cities, with a high proportion of renters and social service recipients, generally voted against it. Outside the major urban areas, support for Proposition 13 was almost uniformly lower in towns and cities than outside their incorporated limits. The measure failed or barely passed in many places which appear as conservative bastions in the maps on the facing page.

Proposition 13's strongest support came from the new suburban areas. The San Fernando Valley and southern Alameda County stand out as particularly enthusiastic. While wealthy areas generally voted for the measure, support was markedly weaker in many of the well-established wealthy communities than in areas of new and expensive subdivisions.

Cities not named on map:
1. Alameda
2. Alhambra
3. Antioch
4. Arcadia
5. Atwater
6. Azusa
7. Baldwin Park
8. Bellflower
9. Buena Park
10. Burlingame
11. Carson
12. Cerritos
13. Claremont
14. Colton
15. Compton
16. Covina
17. Culver City
18. Cypress
19. Downey
20. El Monte
21. Fairfield
22. Foster City
23. Fountain Valley
24. Fullerton
25. Garden Grove
26. Gardena
27. Huntington Park
28. La Mirada
29. La Verne
30. Lafayette
31. Lakewood
32. Larkspur
33. Lynwood
34. Manteca
35. Martinez
36. Menlo Park
37. Mill Valley
38. Montebello
39. Mountain View
40. Napa
41. Norwalk
42. Novato
43. Oakdale
44. Paramount
45. Pico Rivera
46. Pomona
47. Redlands
48. Roseville
49. San Anselmo
50. San Bernardino
51. San Gabriel
52. Simi Valley
53. Sonoma
54. South Gate
55. Temple City
56. Torrance
57. Tracy
58. Turlock
59. Vacaville
60. West Covina
61. Westminster
62. Woodland

PROPOSITION 13, 1978: PROPERTY TAX LIMITATION

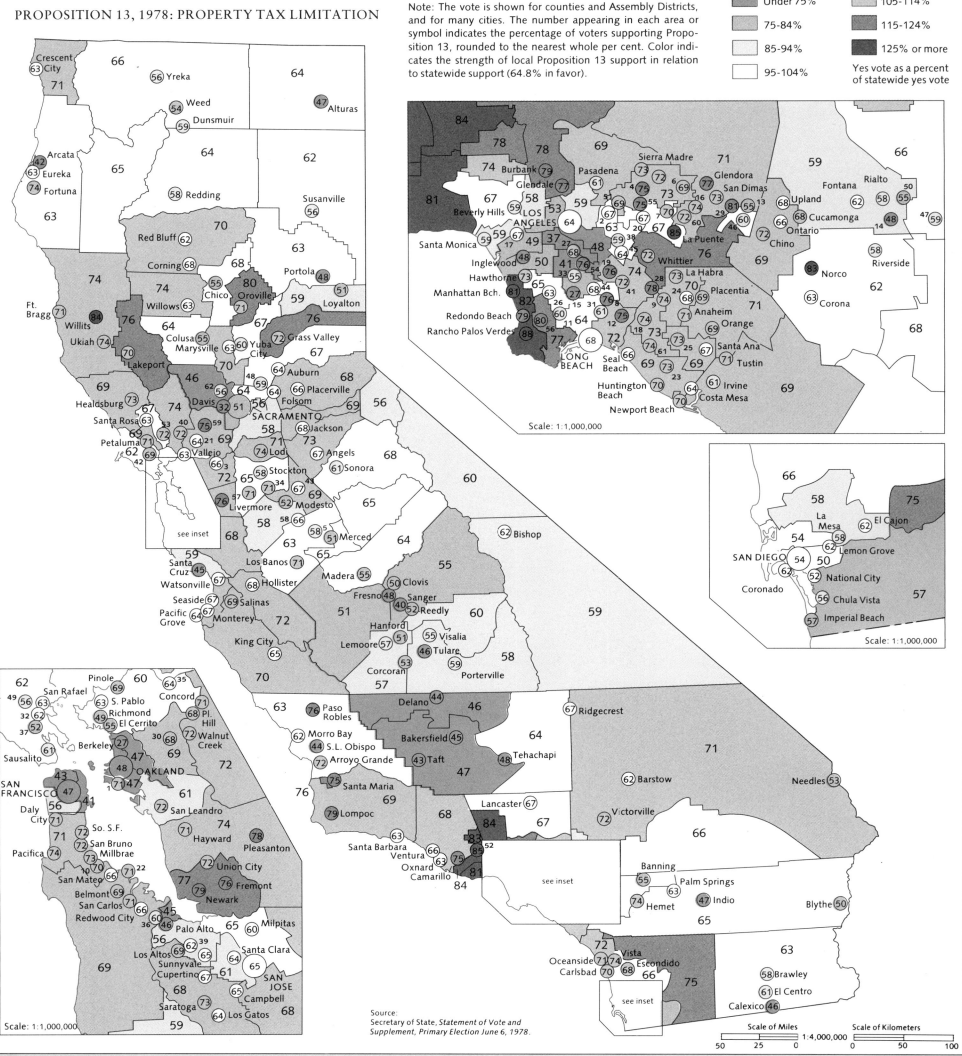

Source: Secretary of State, *Statement of Vote and Supplement, Primary Election June 6, 1978.*

The constitutions of 1850 and 1879 had stipulated that representation in both houses of the legislature should be based on population. Redistricting after a new census had thus been a normal, if often bitter, political tradition. But the growing urban population led to rural fear of political denomination. Even the House of Representatives was not reapportioned in 1920, and by 1926 the smaller counties in California had agitated successfully for a "federal" plan that kept the lower house representative, but created Senatorial districts of one, two or three counties. For 38 years, until the U.S. Supreme Court decided in favor of "one man-one vote" in 1964, the California Senate was full of rotten boroughs, and disparities of population were allowed to develop in Assembly and Congressional districts. Los Angeles County was particularly disadvantaged: in 1962, its more than six million residents were represented by one senator, just as were the 14,000 people of the Alpine-Mono-Inyo district.

After the 1970 census, a deadlock arose when the Republican governor vetoed the reapportionment proposal of the Democratic legislature. The State Supreme Court ruled that the election of 1972 be based on the legislative plan as far as Congressional Districts were concerned, but that a new scheme be drawn up by a special Master Committee. The committee used "apolitical" criteria, sacrificing traditional boundaries in favor of contiguity and strictly equal population as required by the court decision. The reapportionment plan of 1973 maintained county lines in most of the state outside of the urban areas, but Sacramento, Stanislaus, Fresno, Tulare and San Luis Obispo counties were divided, and county lines almost completely disregarded in the Bay Area and around Los Angeles.

The reapportionment plan of 1973 rearranged state legislative districts as well; these are mapped on the facing page. Some of the 40 state senate districts correspond roughly to Congressional Districts, but many bear no resemblance at all.

CONGRESSIONAL DISTRICTS

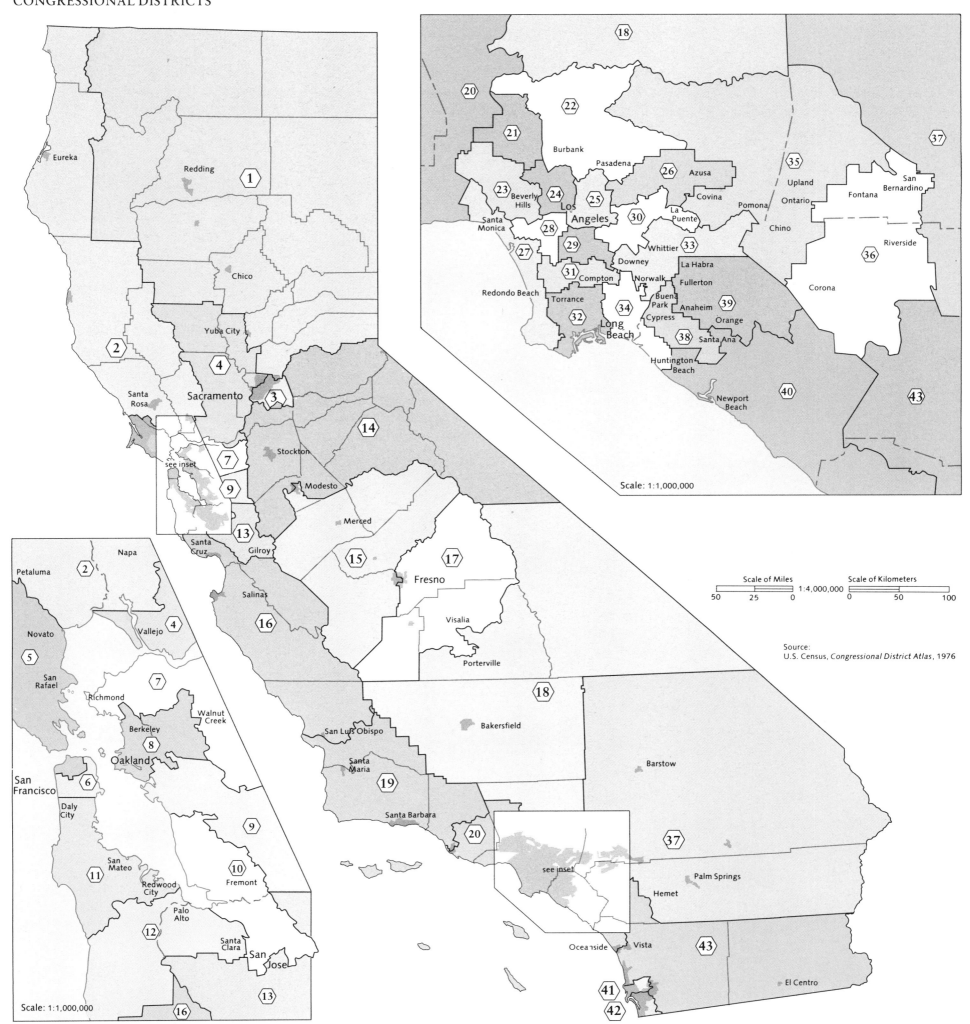

Scale: 1:1,000,000

1:4,000,000

Source:
U.S. Census, *Congressional District Atlas,* 1976

Scale: 1:1,000,000

CONGRESSIONAL DISTRICTS

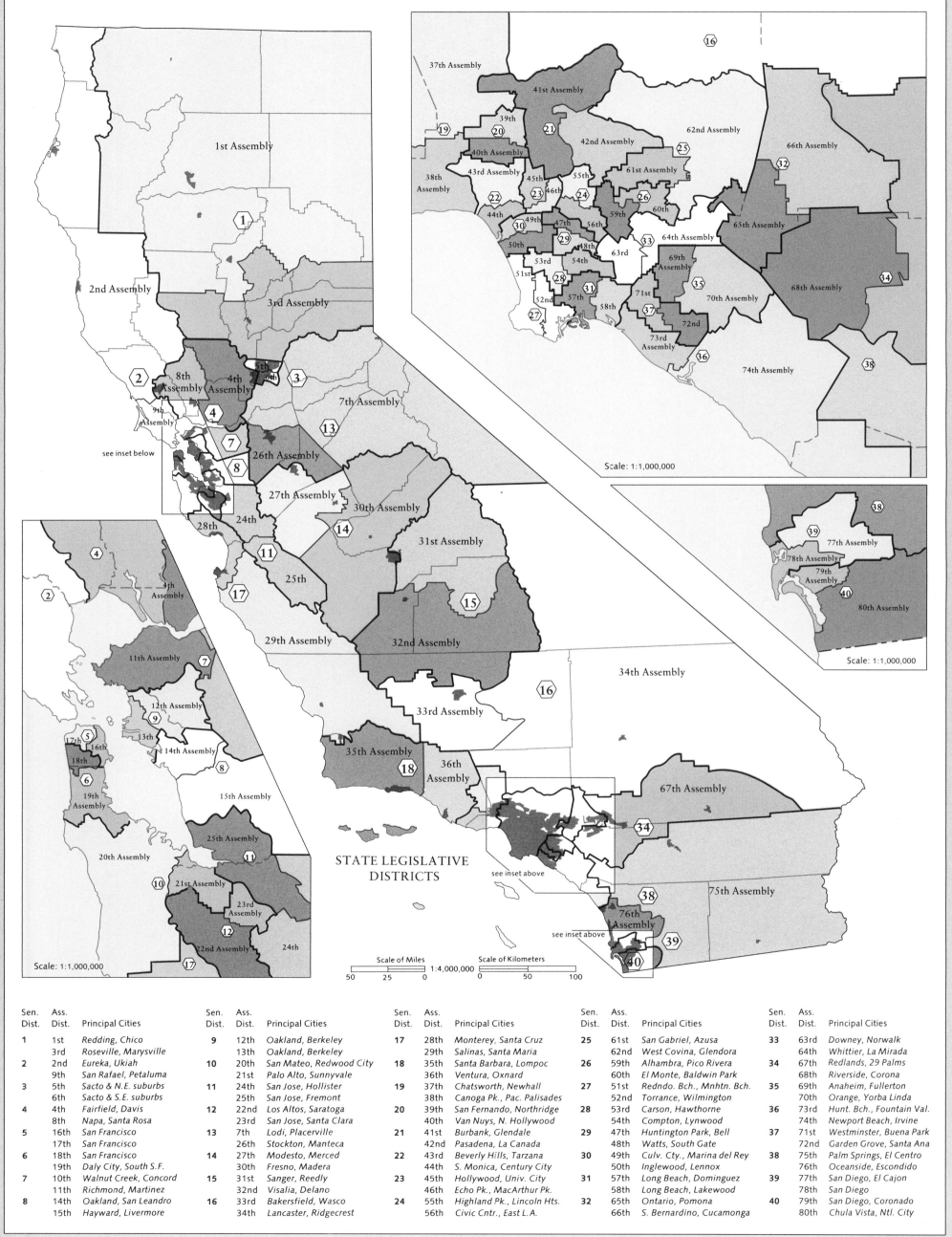

STATE LEGISLATIVE
DISTRICTS

Scale of Miles   Scale of Kilometers
50 25 0   1:4,000,000   0   50   100

STATE LEGISLATIVE DISTRICTS

Sen. Dist.	Ass. Dist.	Principal Cities	Sen. Dist.	Ass. Dist.	Principal Cities	Sen. Dist.	Ass. Dist.	Principal Cities	Sen. Dist.	Ass. Dist.	Principal Cities	Sen. Dist.	Ass. Dist.	Principal Cities
1	1st	Redding, Chico	9	12th	Oakland, Berkeley	17	28th	Monterey, Santa Cruz	25	61st	San Gabriel, Azusa	33	63rd	Downey, Norwalk
	3rd	Roseville, Marysville		13th	Oakland, Berkeley		29th	Salinas, Santa Maria		62nd	West Covina, Glendora		64th	Whittier, La Mirada
2	2nd	Eureka, Ukiah	10	20th	San Mateo, Redwood City	18	35th	Santa Barbara, Lompoc	26	59th	Alhambra, Pico Rivera	34	67th	Redlands, 29 Palms
	9th	San Rafael, Petaluma		21st	Palo Alto, Sunnyvale		36th	Ventura, Oxnard		60th	El Monte, Baldwin Park		68th	Riverside, Corona
3	5th	Sacto & N.E. suburbs	11	24th	San Jose, Hollister	19	37th	Chatsworth, Newhall	27	51st	Redndo. Bch., Mnhtn. Bch.	35	69th	Anaheim, Fullerton
	6th	Sacto & S.E. suburbs		25th	San Jose, Fremont		38th	Canoga Pk., Pac. Palisades		52nd	Torrance, Wilmington		70th	Orange, Yorba Linda
4	4th	Fairfield, Davis	12	22nd	Los Altos, Saratoga	20	39th	San Fernando, Northridge	28	53rd	Carson, Hawthorne	36	73rd	Hunt. Bch., Fountain Val.
	8th	Napa, Santa Rosa		23rd	San Jose, Santa Clara		40th	Van Nuys, N. Hollywood		54th	Compton, Lynwood		74th	Newport Beach, Irvine
5	16th	San Francisco	13	7th	Lodi, Placerville	21	41st	Burbank, Glendale	29	47th	Huntington Park, Bell	37	71st	Westminster, Buena Park
	17th	San Francisco		26th	Stockton, Manteca		42nd	Pasadena, La Canada		48th	Watts, South Gate		72nd	Garden Grove, Santa Ana
6	18th	San Francisco	14	27th	Modesto, Merced	22	43rd	Beverly Hills, Tarzana	30	49th	Culv. Cty., Marina del Rey	38	75th	Palm Springs, El Centro
	19th	Daly City, South S.F.		30th	Fresno, Madera		44th	S. Monica, Century City		50th	Inglewood, Lennox		76th	Oceanside, Escondido
7	10th	Walnut Creek, Concord	15	31st	Sanger, Reedly	23	45th	Hollywood, Univ. City	31	57th	Long Beach, Dominguez	39	77th	San Diego, El Cajon
	11th	Richmond, Martinez		32nd	Visalia, Delano		46th	Echo Pk., MacArthur Pk.		58th	Long Beach, Lakewood		78th	San Diego
8	14th	Oakland, San Leandro	16	33rd	Bakersfield, Wasco	24	55th	Highland Pk., Lincoln Hts.	32	65th	Ontario, Pomona	40	79th	San Diego, Coronado
	15th	Hayward, Livermore		34th	Lancaster, Ridgecrest		56th	Civic Cntr., East L.A.		66th	S. Bernardino, Cucamonga		80th	Chula Vista, Ntl. City

ECONOMIC PATTERNS

EMPLOYMENT in ALL SECTORS of the ECONOMY

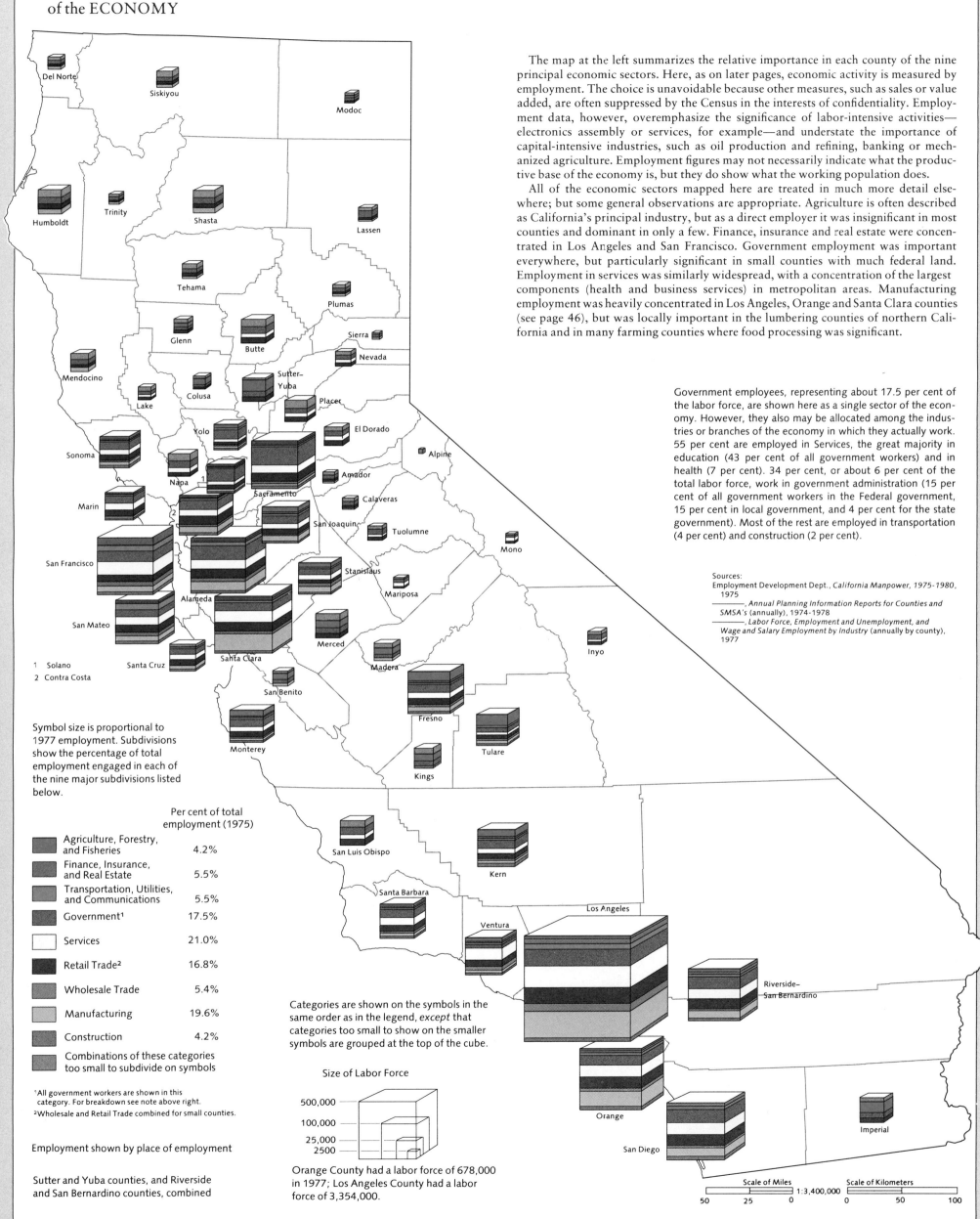

The map at the left summarizes the relative importance in each county of the nine principal economic sectors. Here, as on later pages, economic activity is measured by employment. The choice is unavoidable because other measures, such as sales or value added, are often suppressed by the Census in the interests of confidentiality. Employment data, however, overemphasize the significance of labor-intensive activities—electronics assembly or services, for example—and understate the importance of capital-intensive industries, such as oil production and refining, banking or mechanized agriculture. Employment figures may not necessarily indicate what the productive base of the economy is, but they do show what the working population does.

All of the economic sectors mapped here are treated in much more detail elsewhere; but some general observations are appropriate. Agriculture is often described as California's principal industry, but as a direct employer it was insignificant in most counties and dominant in only a few. Finance, insurance and real estate were concentrated in Los Angeles and San Francisco. Government employment was important everywhere, but particularly significant in small counties with much federal land. Employment in services was similarly widespread, with a concentration of the largest components (health and business services) in metropolitan areas. Manufacturing employment was heavily concentrated in Los Angeles, Orange and Santa Clara counties (see page 46), but was locally important in the lumbering counties of northern California and in many farming counties where food processing was significant.

Government employees, representing about 17.5 per cent of the labor force, are shown here as a single sector of the economy. However, they also may be allocated among the industries or branches of the economy in which they actually work. 55 per cent are employed in Services, the great majority in education (43 per cent of all government workers) and in health (7 per cent). 34 per cent, or about 6 per cent of the total labor force, work in government administration (15 per cent of all government workers in the Federal government, 15 per cent in local government, and 4 per cent for the state government). Most of the rest are employed in transportation (4 per cent) and construction (2 per cent).

Sources:
Employment Development Dept., *California Manpower, 1975-1980*, 1975
———, *Annual Planning Information Reports for Counties and SMSA's* (annually), 1974-1978
———, *Labor Force, Employment and Unemployment, and Wage and Salary Employment by Industry* (annually by county), 1977

1 Solano
2 Contra Costa

Symbol size is proportional to 1977 employment. Subdivisions show the percentage of total employment engaged in each of the nine major subdivisions listed below.

	Per cent of total employment (1975)
Agriculture, Forestry, and Fisheries	4.2%
Finance, Insurance, and Real Estate	5.5%
Transportation, Utilities, and Communications	5.5%
Government[1]	17.5%
Services	21.0%
Retail Trade[2]	16.8%
Wholesale Trade	5.4%
Manufacturing	19.6%
Construction	4.2%
Combinations of these categories too small to subdivide on symbols	

[1] All government workers are shown in this category. For breakdown see note above right.
[2] Wholesale and Retail Trade combined for small counties.

Employment shown by place of employment

Sutter and Yuba counties, and Riverside and San Bernardino counties, combined

Categories are shown on the symbols in the same order as in the legend, *except* that categories too small to show on the smaller symbols are grouped at the top of the cube.

Size of Labor Force

500,000
100,000
25,000
2500

Orange County had a labor force of 678,000 in 1977; Los Angeles County had a labor force of 3,354,000.

Scale of Miles   Scale of Kilometers
1:3,400,000
50 25 0   0 50 100

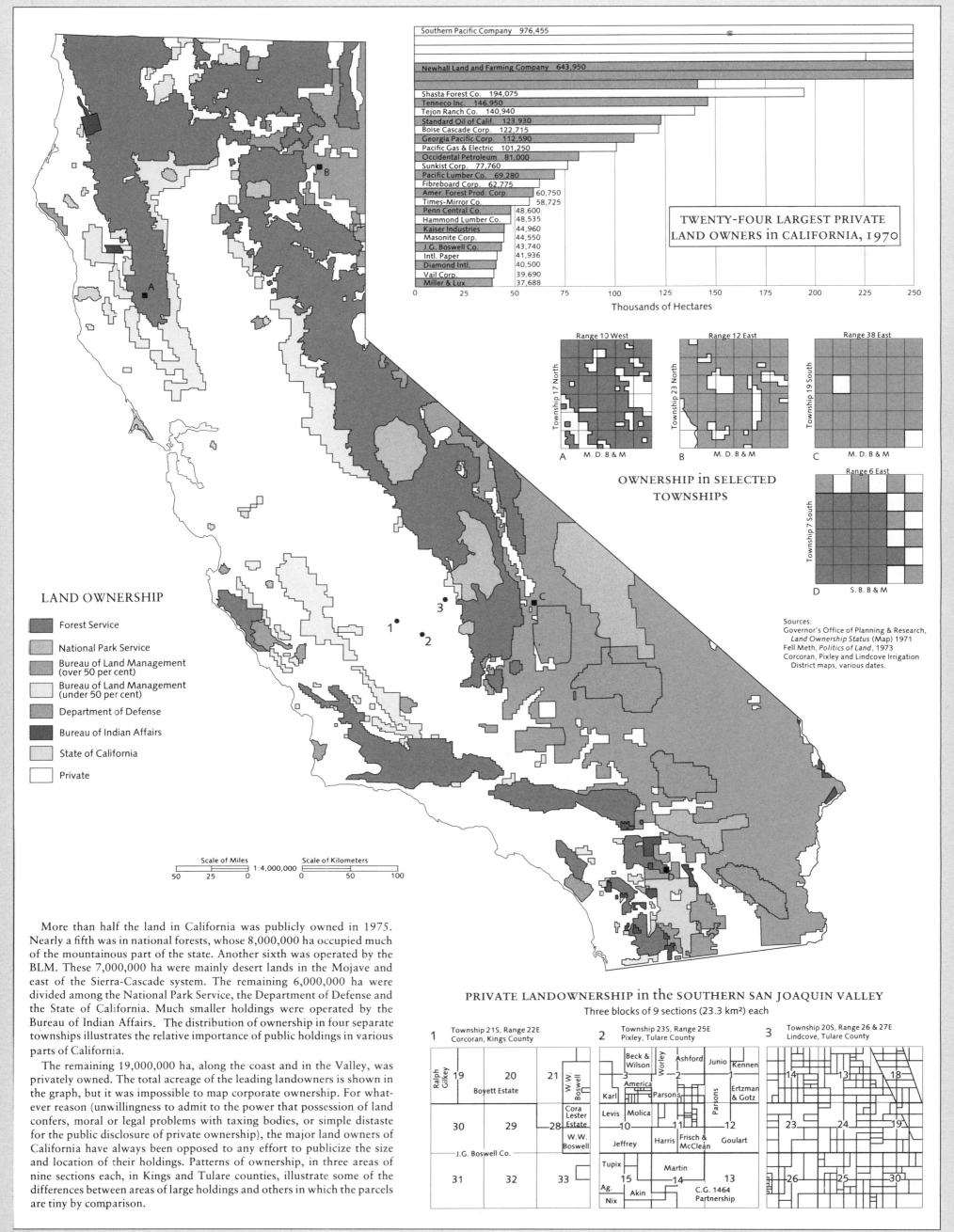

TWENTY-FOUR LARGEST PRIVATE LAND OWNERS in CALIFORNIA, 1970

Southern Pacific Company	976,455
Newhall Land and Farming Company	643,950
Shasta Forest Co.	194,075
Tenneco Inc.	146,950
Tejon Ranch Co.	140,940
Standard Oil of Calif.	123,930
Boise Cascade Corp.	122,715
Georgia Pacific Corp.	112,590
Pacific Gas & Electric	101,250
Occidental Petroleum	81,000
Sunkist Corp.	77,760
Pacific Lumber Co.	69,280
Fibreboard Corp.	62,775
Amer. Forest Prod. Corp.	60,750
Times-Mirror Co.	58,725
Penn Central Co.	48,600
Hammond Lumber Co.	48,535
Kaiser Industries	44,960
Masonite Corp.	44,550
J.G. Boswell Co.	43,740
Intl. Paper	41,936
Diamond Intl.	40,500
Vail Corp.	39,690
Miller & Lux	37,688

Thousands of Hectares

OWNERSHIP in SELECTED TOWNSHIPS

Range 10 West — Township 17 North — A — M. D. B & M
Range 12 East — Township 23 North — B — M. D. B & M
Range 38 East — Township 19 South — C — M. D. B & M
Range 6 East — Township 7 South — D — S. B. B & M

Sources:
Governor's Office of Planning & Research,
Land Ownership Status (Map) 1971
Fell Meth, *Politics of Land*, 1973
Corcoran, Pixley and Lindcove Irrigation
District maps, various dates.

LAND OWNERSHIP

- Forest Service
- National Park Service
- Bureau of Land Management (over 50 per cent)
- Bureau of Land Management (under 50 per cent)
- Department of Defense
- Bureau of Indian Affairs
- State of California
- Private

Scale of Miles — 50 25 0 — 1:4,000,000 — Scale of Kilometers — 0 50 100

More than half the land in California was publicly owned in 1975. Nearly a fifth was in national forests, whose 8,000,000 ha occupied much of the mountainous part of the state. Another sixth was operated by the BLM. These 7,000,000 ha were mainly desert lands in the Mojave and east of the Sierra-Cascade system. The remaining 6,000,000 ha were divided among the National Park Service, the Department of Defense and the State of California. Much smaller holdings were operated by the Bureau of Indian Affairs. The distribution of ownership in four separate townships illustrates the relative importance of public holdings in various parts of California.

The remaining 19,000,000 ha, along the coast and in the Valley, was privately owned. The total acreage of the leading landowners is shown in the graph, but it was impossible to map corporate ownership. For whatever reason (unwillingness to admit to the power that possession of land confers, moral or legal problems with taxing bodies, or simple distaste for the public disclosure of private ownership), the major land owners of California have always been opposed to any effort to publicize the size and location of their holdings. Patterns of ownership, in three areas of nine sections each, in Kings and Tulare counties, illustrate some of the differences between areas of large holdings and others in which the parcels are tiny by comparison.

PRIVATE LANDOWNERSHIP in the SOUTHERN SAN JOAQUIN VALLEY
Three blocks of 9 sections (23.3 km²) each

1 Township 21S, Range 22E — Corcoran, Kings County

Ralph Gilkey — 19 — 20 — 21 — W.W. Boswell
Boyett Estate
Cora Lester Estate — W.W. Boswell
30 — 29 — 28
J.G. Boswell Co.
31 — 32 — 33

2 Township 23S, Range 25E — Pixley, Tulare County

Beck & Wilson — Ashford — Junio — Kennen
Worley — America
Karl — Parsons — Ertzman & Gotz
Levis — Molica — 11 — 12 — Parsons
10 — Goulart
Jeffrey — Harris — Frisch & McClean
Tupix — Martin
15 — 14 — 13
Ag. — Akin — C.G. 1464 Partnership
Nix

3 Township 20S, Range 26 & 27E — Lindcove, Tulare County

14 — 13 — 18
23 — 24 — 19
26 — 25 — 30

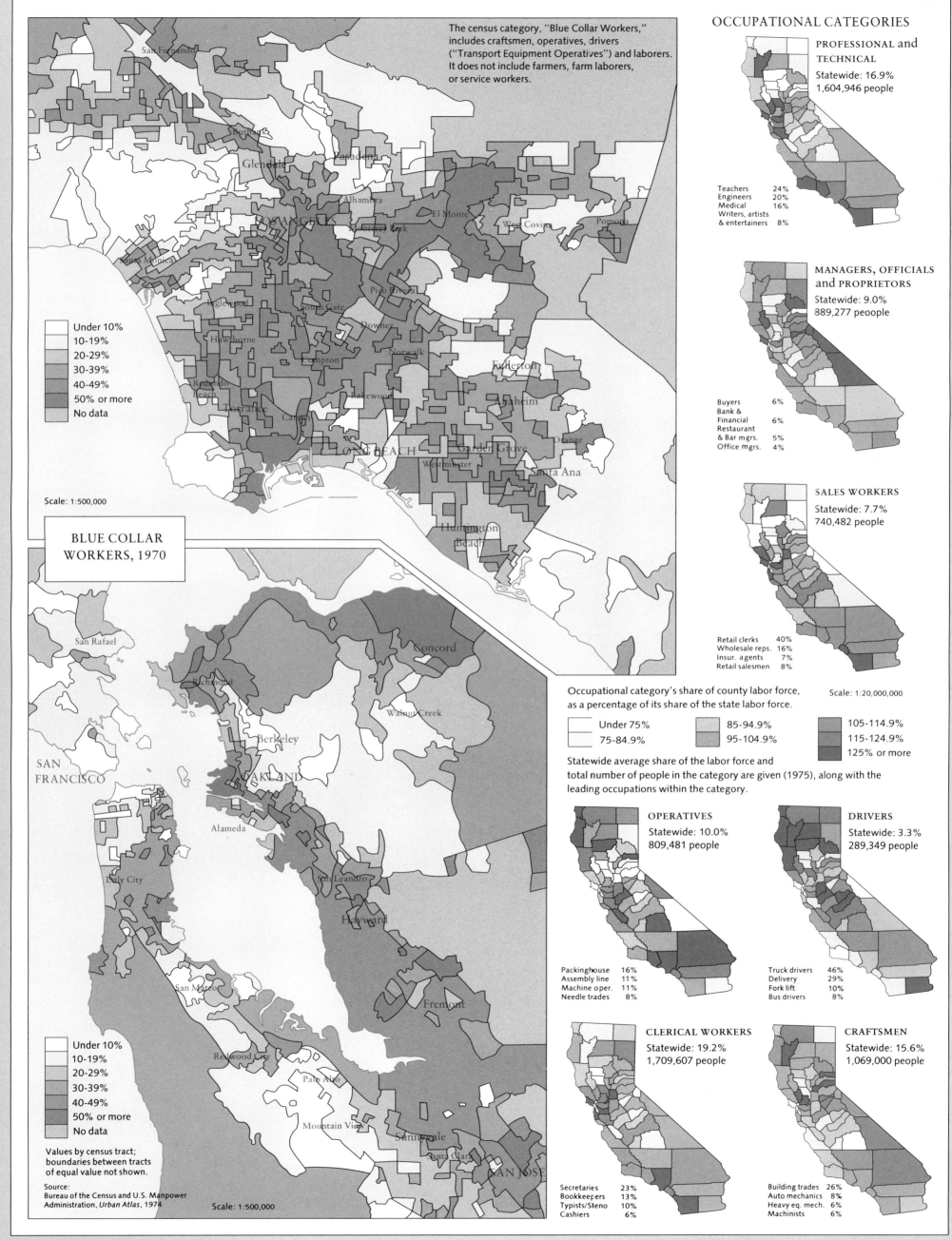

The census category, "Blue Collar Workers,"
includes craftsmen, operatives, drivers
("Transport Equipment Operatives") and laborers.
It does not include farmers, farm laborers,
or service workers.

Under 10%
10-19%
20-29%
30-39%
40-49%
50% or more
No data

Scale: 1:500,000

BLUE COLLAR
WORKERS, 1970

Under 10%
10-19%
20-29%
30-39%
40-49%
50% or more
No data

Values by census tract;
boundaries between tracts
of equal value not shown.

Source:
Bureau of the Census and U.S. Manpower
Administration, Urban Atlas, 1974

Scale: 1:500,000

OCCUPATIONAL CATEGORIES

PROFESSIONAL and TECHNICAL
Statewide: 16.9%
1,604,946 people

Teachers	24%
Engineers	20%
Medical	16%
Writers, artists & entertainers	8%

MANAGERS, OFFICIALS and PROPRIETORS
Statewide: 9.0%
889,277 peoople

Buyers	6%
Bank & Financial	6%
Restaurant & Bar mgrs.	5%
Office mgrs.	4%

SALES WORKERS
Statewide: 7.7%
740,482 people

Retail clerks	40%
Wholesale reps.	16%
Insur. agents	7%
Retail salesmen	8%

Occupational category's share of county labor force,
as a percentage of its share of the state labor force.

Scale: 1:20,000,000

Under 75%	85-94.9%	105-114.9%
75-84.9%	95-104.9%	115-124.9%
		125% or more

Statewide average share of the labor force and
total number of people in the category are given (1975), along with the
leading occupations within the category.

OPERATIVES
Statewide: 10.0%
809,481 people

Packinghouse	16%
Assembly line	11%
Machine oper.	11%
Needle trades	8%

DRIVERS
Statewide: 3.3%
289,349 people

Truck drivers	46%
Delivery	29%
Fork lift	10%
Bus drivers	8%

CLERICAL WORKERS
Statewide: 19.2%
1,709,607 people

Secretaries	23%
Bookkeepers	13%
Typists/Steno	10%
Cashiers	6%

CRAFTSMEN
Statewide: 15.6%
1,069,000 people

Building trades	26%
Auto mechanics	8%
Heavy eq. mech.	6%
Machinists	6%

THE LABOR FORCE

MONTHLY UNEMPLOYMENT, 1975-1977

Regional economic differences are reflected in unemployment trends and in the composition of the labor force. Northern and mountain counties, with small labor forces and a high proportion of seasonal jobs, routinely had 15 per cent unemployment in winter (1975-77), and often much more. Similar patterns appeared in farming counties which relied heavily on hand labor (in Imperial County, unemployment peaked in summer and dropped during the winter growing season). Unemployment was consistently lower in urban areas, and seasonal differences were less sharp. The counties of Alameda, San Francisco and Los Angeles, however, had higher unemployment rates than their suburban neighbors.

The composition of the urban labor force reflected the concentration of trade and administrative functions in the metropolitan area. Professionals, managers and sales workers tended to live outside the cities; clerical workers lived in them. The outstanding proportion of professionals in otherwise agricultural Yolo County was due to the presence of a large university and to the county's suburban role with respect to Sacramento. Operatives were concentrated in Los Angeles (as was the manufacturing which employed them), and in Alameda and Santa Clara counties. Drivers, laborers and farm workers were heavily represented in agricultural counties heavily dependent on manual labor; service workers (and managers) were particularly important in counties where seasonal tourism was significant. The relative importance of craftsmen in a county varied with the amount of construction being done at the time, particularly in counties with small population.

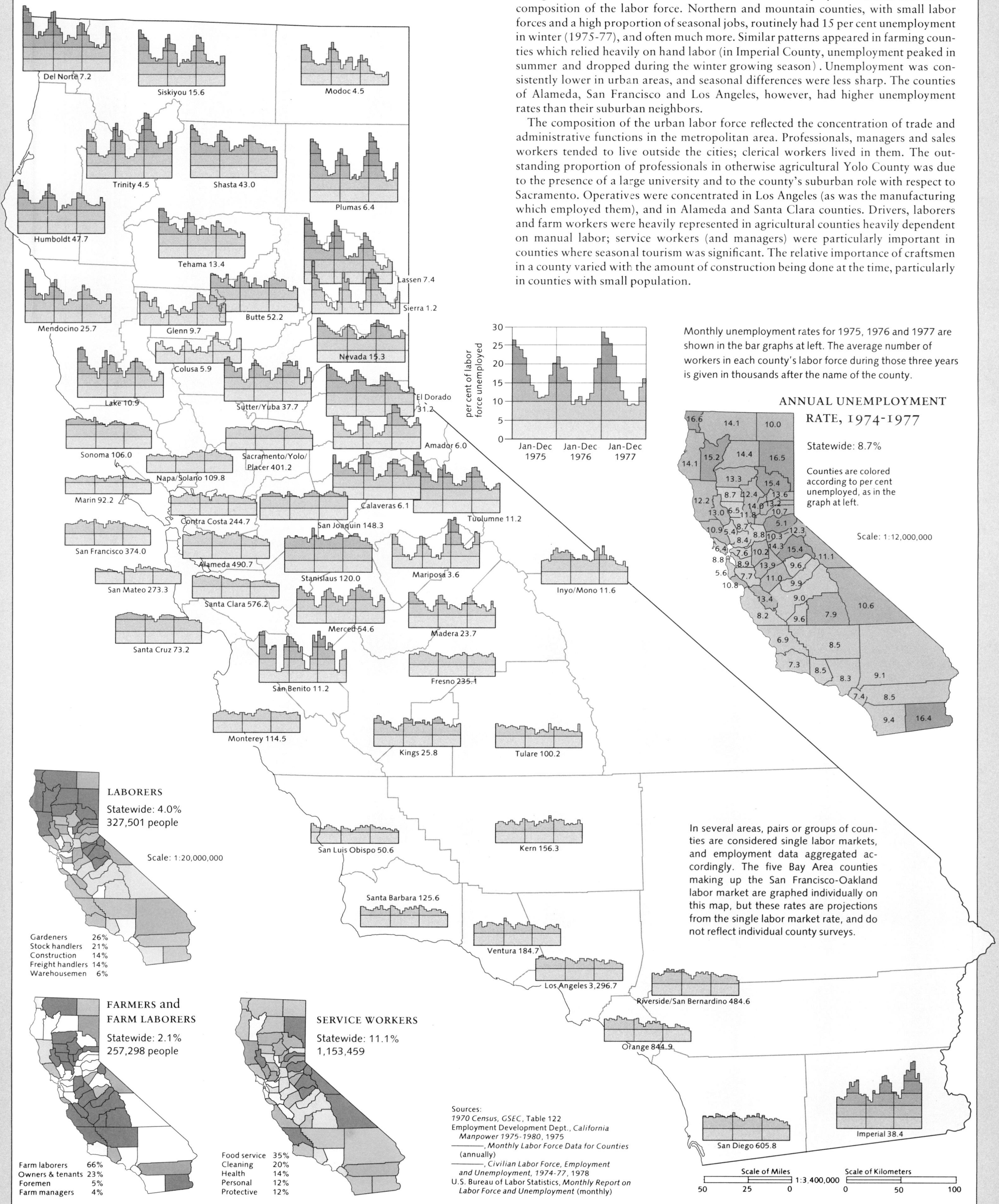

Del Norte 7.2
Siskiyou 15.6
Modoc 4.5
Trinity 4.5
Shasta 43.0
Plumas 6.4
Humboldt 47.7
Tehama 13.4
Lassen 7.4
Sierra 1.2
Mendocino 25.7
Glenn 9.7
Butte 52.2
Nevada 15.3
Colusa 5.9
Lake 10.9
Sutter/Yuba 37.7
El Dorado 31.2
Sonoma 106.0
Sacramento/Yolo/Placer 401.2
Amador 6.0
Napa/Solano 109.8
Marin 92.2
Calaveras 6.1
Contra Costa 244.7
Tuolumne 11.2
San Francisco 374.0
San Joaquin 148.3
Alameda 490.7
Mariposa 3.6
San Mateo 273.3
Stanislaus 120.0
Santa Clara 576.2
Inyo/Mono 11.6
Santa Cruz 73.2
Merced 54.6
Madera 23.7
San Benito 11.2
Fresno 235.1
Monterey 114.5
Kings 25.8
Tulare 100.2
San Luis Obispo 50.6
Kern 156.3
Santa Barbara 125.6
Ventura 184.7
Los Angeles 3,296.7
Riverside/San Bernardino 484.6
Orange 844.9
San Diego 605.8
Imperial 38.4

per cent of labor force unemployed

Jan-Dec 1975   Jan-Dec 1976   Jan-Dec 1977

Monthly unemployment rates for 1975, 1976 and 1977 are shown in the bar graphs at left. The average number of workers in each county's labor force during those three years is given in thousands after the name of the county.

ANNUAL UNEMPLOYMENT RATE, 1974-1977

Statewide: 8.7%

Counties are colored according to per cent unemployed, as in the graph at left.

Scale: 1:12,000,000

16.6 14.1 10.0
14.1 15.2 14.4 16.5
13.3 15.4
12.2 8.7 12.4 13.6
13.0 6.5 14.0 13.2
5.1 11.8 10.7
10.9 5.4 8.8 12.3
8.4 10.3
6.4 7.6 10.2 15.4 11.1
8.8 8.9 13.9 9.6
5.6 7.7 11.0 9.9
10.8
13.4 9.0
8.2 9.6 7.9 10.6
6.9 8.5
7.3 8.5 8.3 9.1
7.4 8.5
9.4 16.4

LABORERS

Statewide: 4.0%
327,501 people

Scale: 1:20,000,000

Gardeners   26%
Stock handlers   21%
Construction   14%
Freight handlers 14%
Warehousemen   6%

FARMERS and FARM LABORERS

Statewide: 2.1%
257,298 people

Farm laborers   66%
Owners & tenants 23%
Foremen   5%
Farm managers   4%

SERVICE WORKERS

Statewide: 11.1%
1,153,459

Food service 35%
Cleaning   20%
Health   14%
Personal   12%
Protective   12%

In several areas, pairs or groups of counties are considered single labor markets, and employment data aggregated accordingly. The five Bay Area counties making up the San Francisco-Oakland labor market are graphed individually on this map, but these rates are projections from the single labor market rate, and do not reflect individual county surveys.

Sources:
1970 Census, GSEC, Table 122
Employment Development Dept., California Manpower 1975-1980, 1975
———, Monthly Labor Force Data for Counties (annually)
———, Civilian Labor Force, Employment and Unemployment, 1974-77, 1978
U.S. Bureau of Labor Statistics, Monthly Report on Labor Force and Unemployment (monthly)

Scale of Miles   Scale of Kilometers
50 25 0   1:3,400,000   0 50 100

IRRIGATED, IRRIGABLE and BUILT-UP LAND, 1974

About one-third of the state was in farms and ranches in 1974, but most of this land was pasture and rangeland. Harvested cropland occupied only about 8 per cent of California's area. Dryland grain farming was significant in a few areas, but most farming was oasis farming, dependent on distant water supplies brought to arid and semi-arid regions. By the mid-1970's, almost all of the Central Valley, most of the large coastal valleys, and the Imperial-Coachella Valley were under irrigation.

There were nearly 68,000 farms in the state in 1974. One-quarter of these had annual sales of less than $2500 and are not mapped. Characteristics of the 51,000 "commercial farms," with sales greater than $2500, are shown on the facing page. Nearly half of these had annual sales of less than $20,000, accounting for less than 3 per cent of the value of farm products sold; 11,400 farms had sales of over $100,000, accounting for 87 per cent of sales. The number of small farms has been steadily declining. The number of commercial farms was reduced by about 6 per cent between 1969 and 1974, and the total number of farms in 1974 was less than half the 1950 figure.

Corporations owned just over 5 per cent of all commercial farms in 1974, but these accounted for almost 18 per cent of commercial farm land. The total value of corporation farm sales was unavailable, but 27 per cent of the farm corporations reported sales of over $500,000 in 1969. Corporate farming is important in sugar beet, rice, and cotton production, but it is especially prominent in high-value capital intensive crops such as lettuce and melons. The seasonal migration of corporate lettuce operations between the Imperial Valley and the Salinas Valley parallels the seasonal travels of the Mexican and Mexican-American migrant labor force on which the state's fruit and vegetable harvests depend.

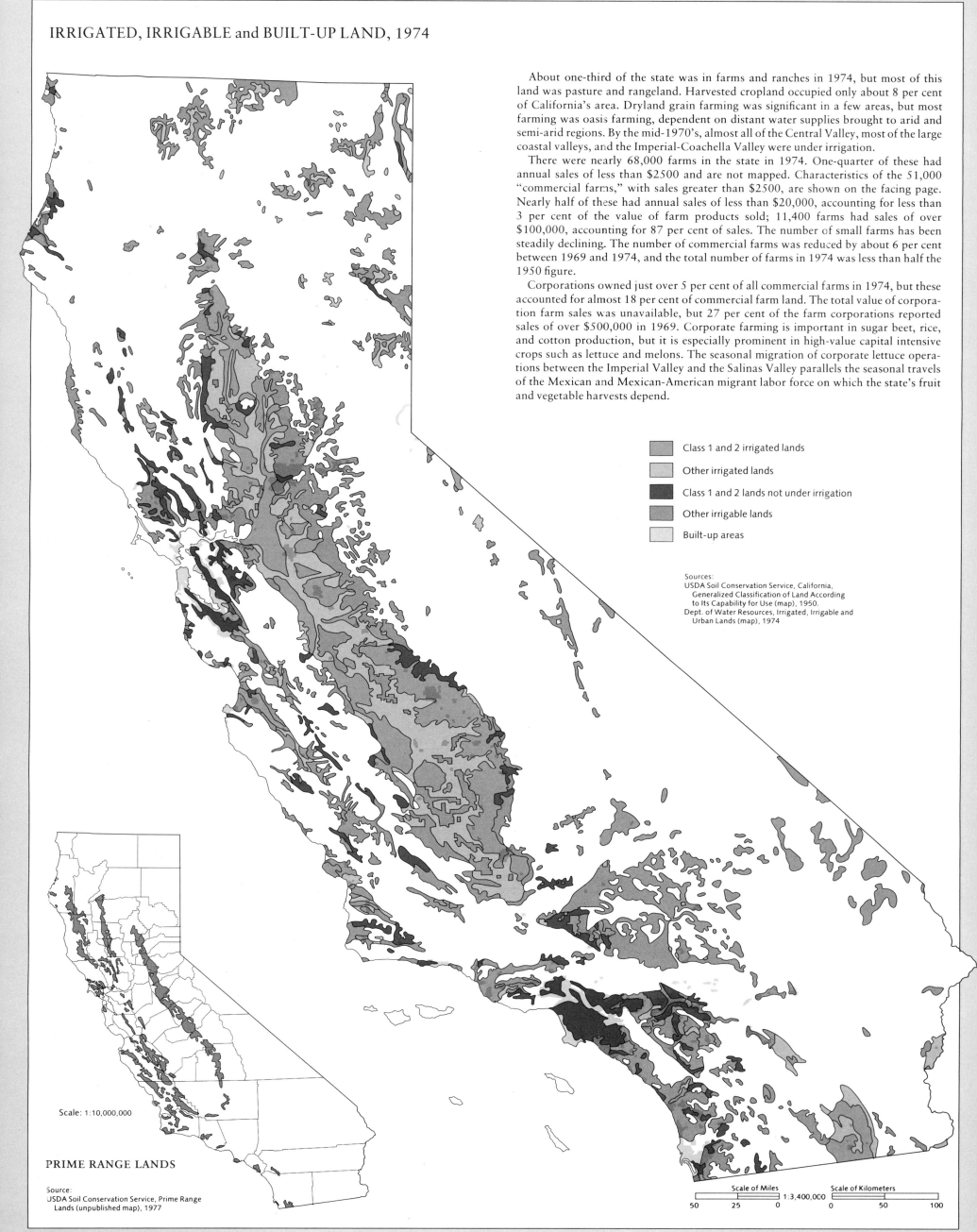

Class 1 and 2 irrigated lands
Other irrigated lands
Class 1 and 2 lands not under irrigation
Other irrigable lands
Built-up areas

Sources:
USDA Soil Conservation Service, California, Generalized Classification of Land According to Its Capability for Use (map), 1950.
Dept. of Water Resources, Irrigated, Irrigable and Urban Lands (map), 1974

Scale: 1:10,000,000

PRIME RANGE LANDS

Source:
USDA Soil Conservation Service, Prime Range Lands (unpublished map), 1977

Scale of Miles 1:3,400,000 Scale of Kilometers
50 25 0   0 50 100

PRIME AGRICULTURAL LAND

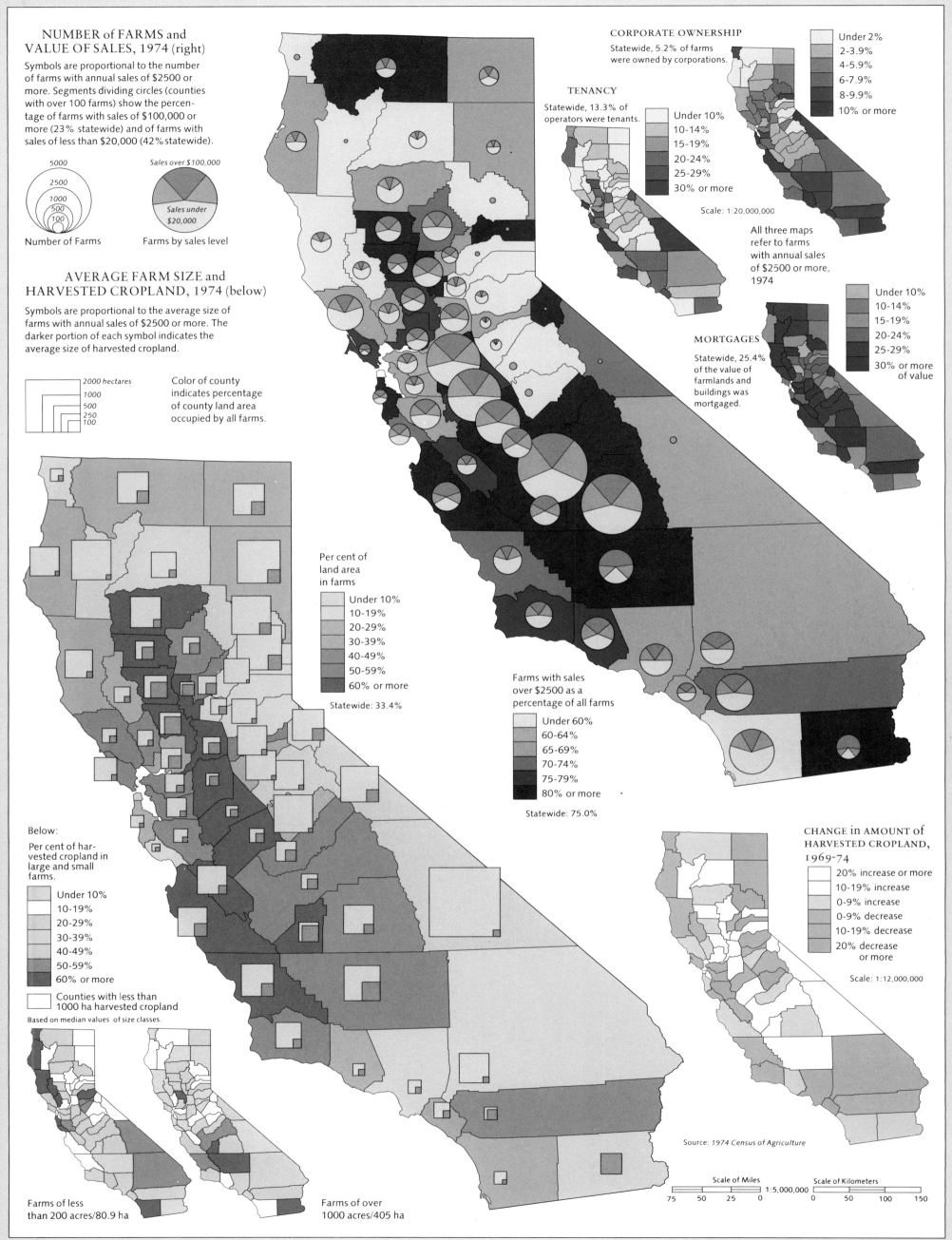

NUMBER of FARMS and VALUE OF SALES, 1974 (right)

Symbols are proportional to the number of farms with annual sales of $2500 or more. Segments dividing circles (counties with over 100 farms) show the percentage of farms with sales of $100,000 or more (23% statewide) and of farms with sales of less than $20,000 (42% statewide).

5000
2500
1000
500
100
Number of Farms

Sales over $100,000
Sales under $20,000
Farms by sales level

AVERAGE FARM SIZE and HARVESTED CROPLAND, 1974 (below)

Symbols are proportional to the average size of farms with annual sales of $2500 or more. The darker portion of each symbol indicates the average size of harvested cropland.

2000 hectares
1000
500
250
100

Color of county indicates percentage of county land area occupied by all farms.

Below:
Per cent of harvested cropland in large and small farms.

Under 10%
10-19%
20-29%
30-39%
40-49%
50-59%
60% or more

Counties with less than 1000 ha harvested cropland

Based on median values of size classes.

Farms of less than 200 acres/80.9 ha

Farms of over 1000 acres/405 ha

Per cent of land area in farms

Under 10%
10-19%
20-29%
30-39%
40-49%
50-59%
60% or more

Statewide: 33.4%

Farms with sales over $2500 as a percentage of all farms

Under 60%
60-64%
65-69%
70-74%
75-79%
80% or more

Statewide: 75.0%

CORPORATE OWNERSHIP

Statewide, 5.2% of farms were owned by corporations.

Under 2%
2-3.9%
4-5.9%
6-7.9%
8-9.9%
10% or more

TENANCY

Statewide, 13.3% of operators were tenants.

Under 10%
10-14%
15-19%
20-24%
25-29%
30% or more

Scale: 1:20,000,000

All three maps refer to farms with annual sales of $2500 or more, 1974

MORTGAGES

Statewide, 25.4% of the value of farmlands and buildings was mortgaged.

Under 10%
10-14%
15-19%
20-24%
25-29%
30% or more of value

CHANGE in AMOUNT of HARVESTED CROPLAND, 1969-74

20% increase or more
10-19% increase
0-9% increase
0-9% decrease
10-19% decrease
20% decrease or more

Scale: 1:12,000,000

Source: 1974 Census of Agriculture

Scale of Miles
75 50 25 0
1:5,000,000
Scale of Kilometers
0 50 100 150

FARMS AND FARMERS

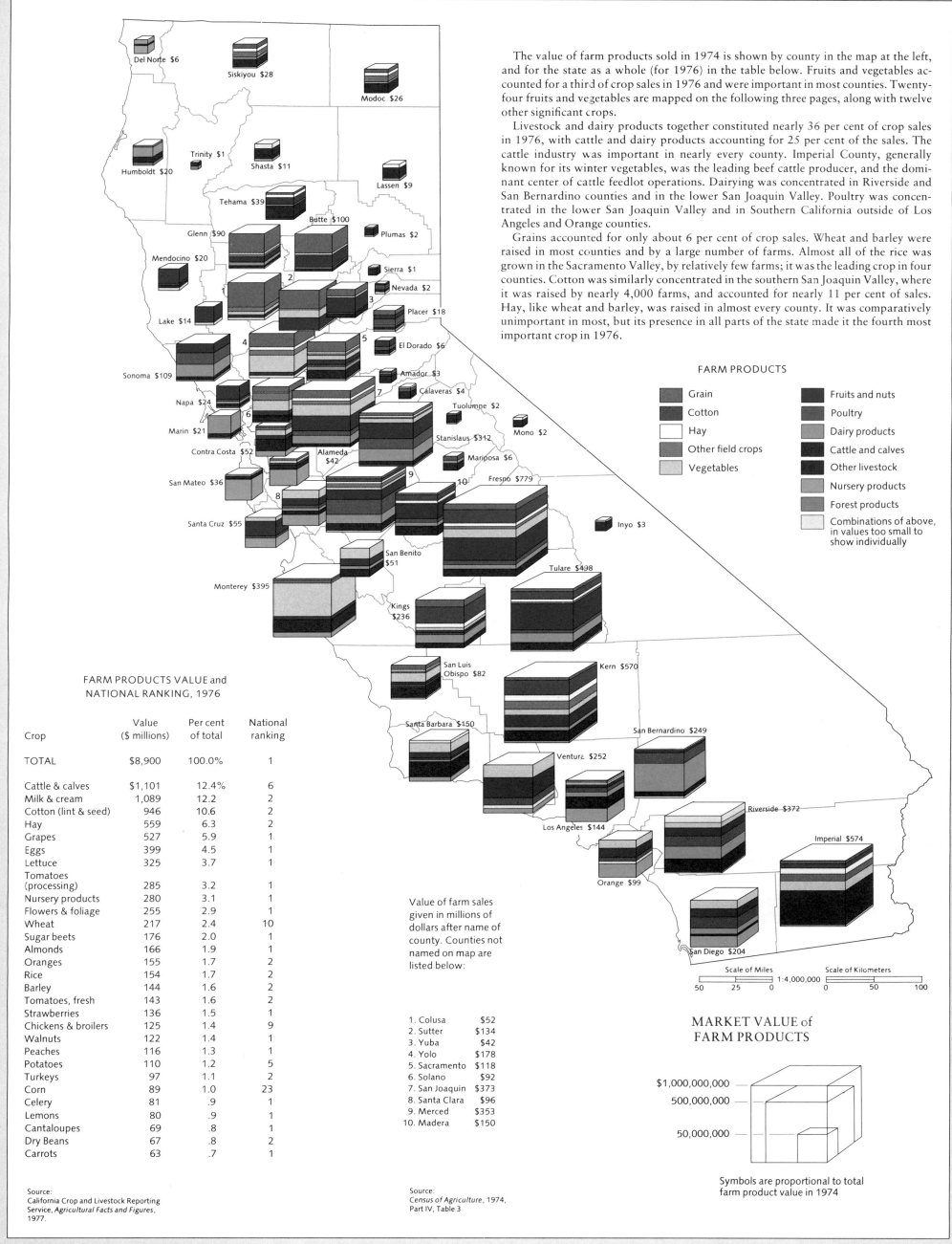

The value of farm products sold in 1974 is shown by county in the map at the left, and for the state as a whole (for 1976) in the table below. Fruits and vegetables accounted for a third of crop sales in 1976 and were important in most counties. Twenty-four fruits and vegetables are mapped on the following three pages, along with twelve other significant crops.

Livestock and dairy products together constituted nearly 36 per cent of crop sales in 1976, with cattle and dairy products accounting for 25 per cent of the sales. The cattle industry was important in nearly every county. Imperial County, generally known for its winter vegetables, was the leading beef cattle producer, and the dominant center of cattle feedlot operations. Dairying was concentrated in Riverside and San Bernardino counties and in the lower San Joaquin Valley. Poultry was concentrated in the lower San Joaquin Valley and in Southern California outside of Los Angeles and Orange counties.

Grains accounted for only about 6 per cent of crop sales. Wheat and barley were raised in most counties and by a large number of farms. Almost all of the rice was grown in the Sacramento Valley, by relatively few farms; it was the leading crop in four counties. Cotton was similarly concentrated in the southern San Joaquin Valley, where it was raised by nearly 4,000 farms, and accounted for nearly 11 per cent of sales. Hay, like wheat and barley, was raised in almost every county. It was comparatively unimportant in most, but its presence in all parts of the state made it the fourth most important crop in 1976.

FARM PRODUCTS

- Grain
- Cotton
- Hay
- Other field crops
- Vegetables
- Fruits and nuts
- Poultry
- Dairy products
- Cattle and calves
- Other livestock
- Nursery products
- Forest products
- Combinations of above, in values too small to show individually

FARM PRODUCTS VALUE and NATIONAL RANKING, 1976

Crop	Value ($ millions)	Per cent of total	National ranking
TOTAL	$8,900	100.0%	1
Cattle & calves	$1,101	12.4%	6
Milk & cream	1,089	12.2	2
Cotton (lint & seed)	946	10.6	2
Hay	559	6.3	2
Grapes	527	5.9	1
Eggs	399	4.5	1
Lettuce	325	3.7	1
Tomatoes (processing)	285	3.2	1
Nursery products	280	3.1	1
Flowers & foliage	255	2.9	1
Wheat	217	2.4	10
Sugar beets	176	2.0	1
Almonds	166	1.9	1
Oranges	155	1.7	2
Rice	154	1.7	2
Barley	144	1.6	2
Tomatoes, fresh	143	1.6	2
Strawberries	136	1.5	1
Chickens & broilers	125	1.4	9
Walnuts	122	1.4	1
Peaches	116	1.3	1
Potatoes	110	1.2	5
Turkeys	97	1.1	2
Corn	89	1.0	23
Celery	81	.9	1
Lemons	80	.9	1
Cantaloupes	69	.8	1
Dry Beans	67	.8	2
Carrots	63	.7	1

Source: California Crop and Livestock Reporting Service, *Agricultural Facts and Figures*, 1977.

Value of farm sales given in millions of dollars after name of county. Counties not named on map are listed below:

1. Colusa $52
2. Sutter $134
3. Yuba $42
4. Yolo $178
5. Sacramento $118
6. Solano $92
7. San Joaquin $373
8. Santa Clara $96
9. Merced $353
10. Madera $150

Source: *Census of Agriculture*, 1974, Part IV, Table 3

MARKET VALUE of FARM PRODUCTS

$1,000,000,000
500,000,000
50,000,000

Symbols are proportional to total farm product value in 1974

AGRICULTURAL PRODUCTION

GRAIN

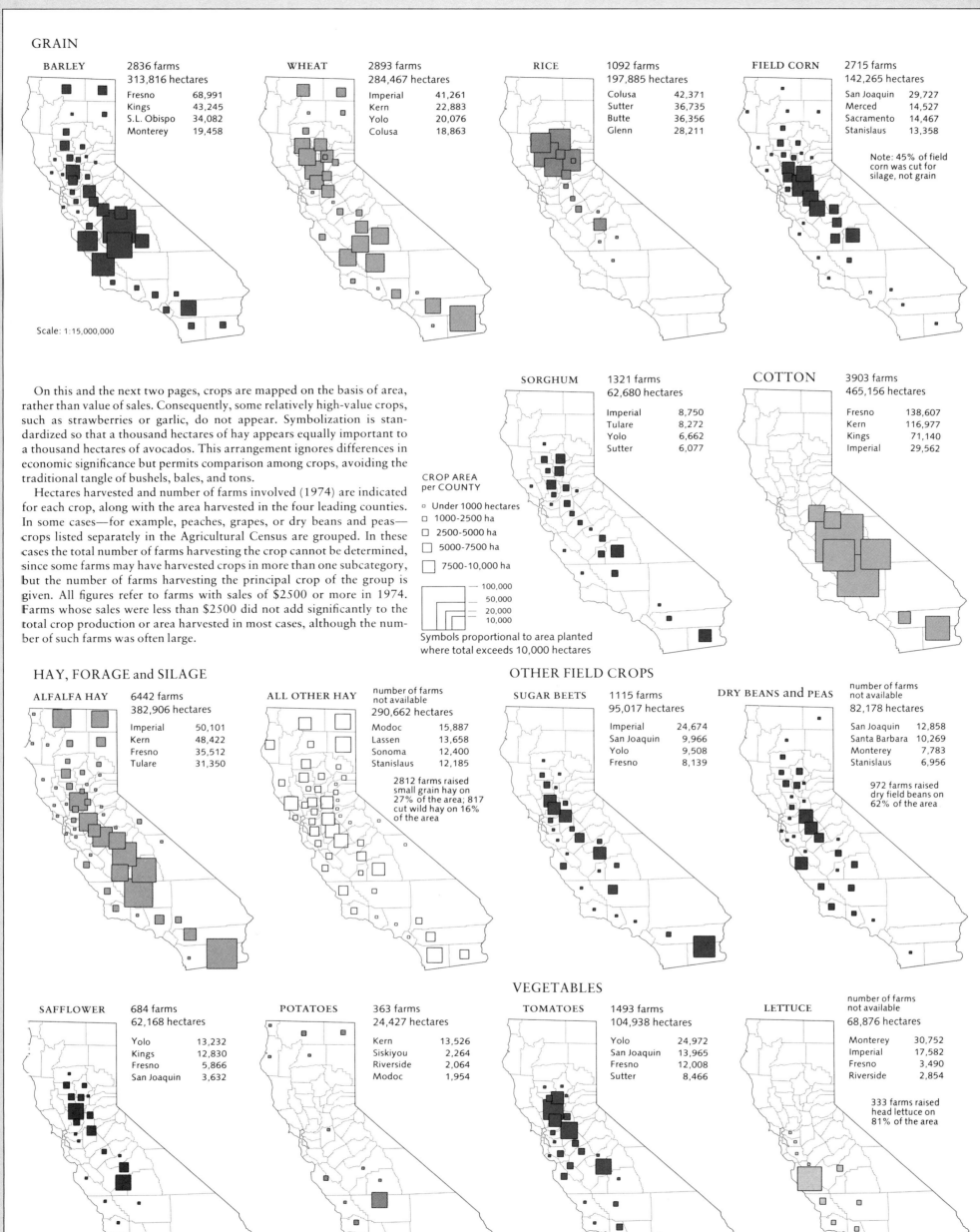

BARLEY — 2836 farms, 313,816 hectares
- Fresno 68,991
- Kings 43,245
- S.L. Obispo 34,082
- Monterey 19,458

Scale: 1:15,000,000

WHEAT — 2893 farms, 284,467 hectares
- Imperial 41,261
- Kern 22,883
- Yolo 20,076
- Colusa 18,863

RICE — 1092 farms, 197,885 hectares
- Colusa 42,371
- Sutter 36,735
- Butte 36,356
- Glenn 28,211

FIELD CORN — 2715 farms, 142,265 hectares
- San Joaquin 29,727
- Merced 14,527
- Sacramento 14,467
- Stanislaus 13,358

Note: 45% of field corn was cut for silage, not grain

On this and the next two pages, crops are mapped on the basis of area, rather than value of sales. Consequently, some relatively high-value crops, such as strawberries or garlic, do not appear. Symbolization is standardized so that a thousand hectares of hay appears equally important to a thousand hectares of avocados. This arrangement ignores differences in economic significance but permits comparison among crops, avoiding the traditional tangle of bushels, bales, and tons.

Hectares harvested and number of farms involved (1974) are indicated for each crop, along with the area harvested in the four leading counties. In some cases—for example, peaches, grapes, or dry beans and peas—crops listed separately in the Agricultural Census are grouped. In these cases the total number of farms harvesting the crop cannot be determined, since some farms may have harvested crops in more than one subcategory, but the number of farms harvesting the principal crop of the group is given. All figures refer to farms with sales of $2500 or more in 1974. Farms whose sales were less than $2500 did not add significantly to the total crop production or area harvested in most cases, although the number of such farms was often large.

SORGHUM — 1321 farms, 62,680 hectares
- Imperial 8,750
- Tulare 8,272
- Yolo 6,662
- Sutter 6,077

COTTON — 3903 farms, 465,156 hectares
- Fresno 138,607
- Kern 116,977
- Kings 71,140
- Imperial 29,562

CROP AREA per COUNTY
- □ Under 1000 hectares
- □ 1000-2500 ha
- □ 2500-5000 ha
- □ 5000-7500 ha
- □ 7500-10,000 ha
- 100,000
- 50,000
- 20,000
- 10,000

Symbols proportional to area planted where total exceeds 10,000 hectares

HAY, FORAGE and SILAGE

ALFALFA HAY — 6442 farms, 382,906 hectares
- Imperial 50,101
- Kern 48,422
- Fresno 35,512
- Tulare 31,350

ALL OTHER HAY — number of farms not available, 290,662 hectares
- Modoc 15,887
- Lassen 13,658
- Sonoma 12,400
- Stanislaus 12,185

2812 farms raised small grain hay on 27% of the area; 817 cut wild hay on 16% of the area

OTHER FIELD CROPS

SUGAR BEETS — 1115 farms, 95,017 hectares
- Imperial 24,674
- San Joaquin 9,966
- Yolo 9,508
- Fresno 8,139

DRY BEANS and PEAS — number of farms not available, 82,178 hectares
- San Joaquin 12,858
- Santa Barbara 10,269
- Monterey 7,783
- Stanislaus 6,956

972 farms raised dry field beans on 62% of the area

SAFFLOWER — 684 farms, 62,168 hectares
- Yolo 13,232
- Kings 12,830
- Fresno 5,866
- San Joaquin 3,632

Scale: 1:15,000,000

POTATOES — 363 farms, 24,427 hectares
- Kern 13,526
- Siskiyou 2,264
- Riverside 2,064
- Modoc 1,954

VEGETABLES

TOMATOES — 1493 farms, 104,938 hectares
- Yolo 24,972
- San Joaquin 13,965
- Fresno 12,008
- Sutter 8,466

LETTUCE — number of farms not available, 68,876 hectares
- Monterey 30,752
- Imperial 17,582
- Fresno 3,490
- Riverside 2,854

333 farms raised head lettuce on 81% of the area

FIELD CROPS

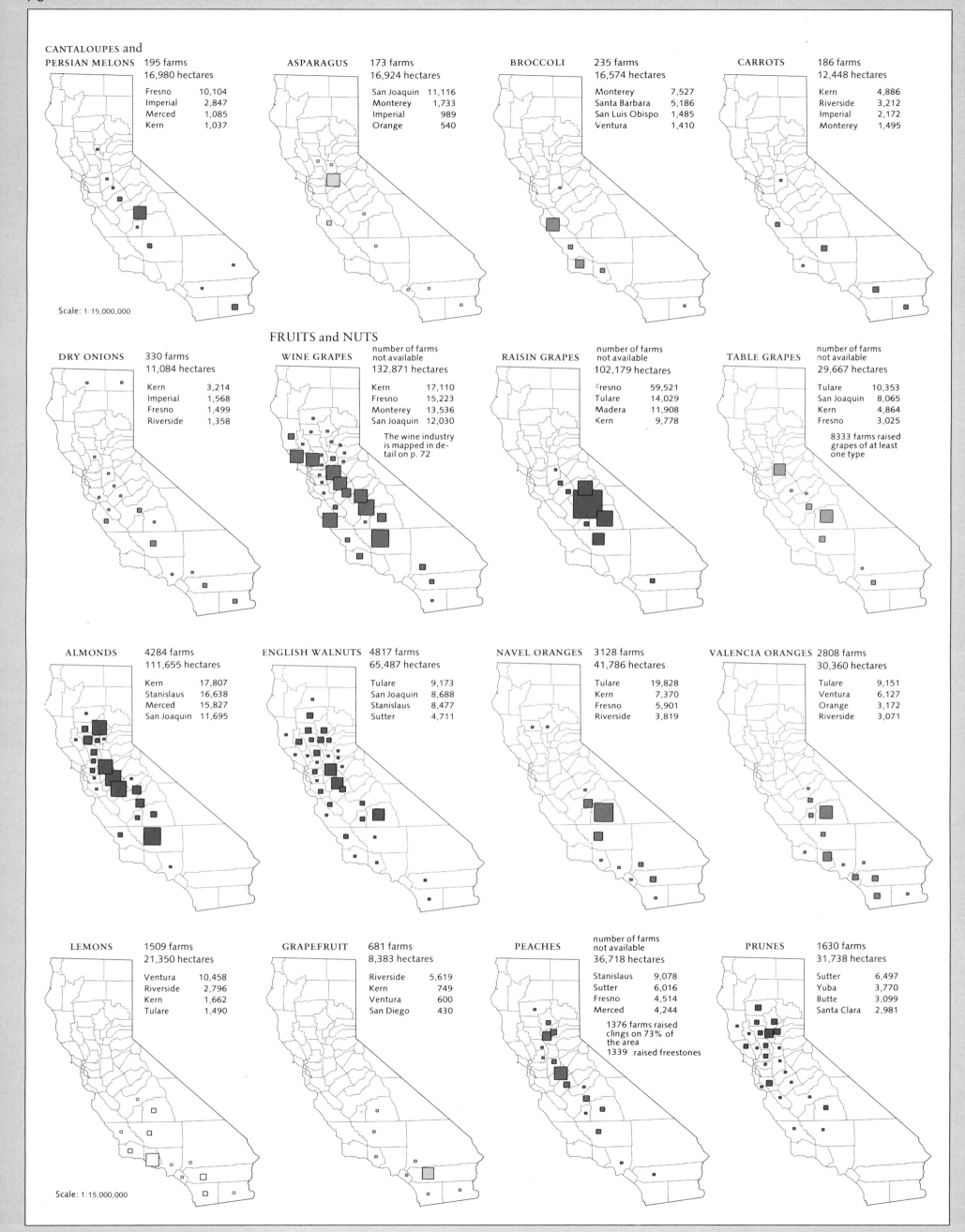

CANTALOUPES and
PERSIAN MELONS   195 farms
16,980 hectares

Fresno	10,104
Imperial	2,847
Merced	1,085
Kern	1,037

ASPARAGUS   173 farms
16,924 hectares

San Joaquin	11,116
Monterey	1,733
Imperial	989
Orange	540

BROCCOLI   235 farms
16,574 hectares

Monterey	7,527
Santa Barbara	5,186
San Luis Obispo	1,485
Ventura	1,410

CARROTS   186 farms
12,448 hectares

Kern	4,886
Riverside	3,212
Imperial	2,172
Monterey	1,495

Scale: 1:15,000,000

FRUITS and NUTS

DRY ONIONS   330 farms
11,084 hectares

Kern	3,214
Imperial	1,568
Fresno	1,499
Riverside	1,358

WINE GRAPES   number of farms
not available
132,871 hectares

Kern	17,110
Fresno	15,223
Monterey	13,536
San Joaquin	12,030

The wine industry
is mapped in de-
tail on p. 72

The wine industry is mapped in detail on p. 72

RAISIN GRAPES   number of farms
not available
102,179 hectares

Fresno	59,521
Tulare	14,029
Madera	11,908
Kern	9,778

TABLE GRAPES   number of farms
not available
29,667 hectares

Tulare	10,353
San Joaquin	8,065
Kern	4,864
Fresno	3,025

8333 farms raised
grapes of at least
one type

ALMONDS   4284 farms
111,655 hectares

Kern	17,807
Stanislaus	16,638
Merced	15,827
San Joaquin	11,695

ENGLISH WALNUTS   4817 farms
65,487 hectares

Tulare	9,173
San Joaquin	8,688
Stanislaus	8,477
Sutter	4,711

NAVEL ORANGES   3128 farms
41,786 hectares

Tulare	19,828
Kern	7,370
Fresno	5,901
Riverside	3,819

VALENCIA ORANGES   2808 farms
30,360 hectares

Tulare	9,151
Ventura	6,127
Orange	3,172
Riverside	3,071

LEMONS   1509 farms
21,350 hectares

Ventura	10,458
Riverside	2,796
Kern	1,662
Tulare	1,490

GRAPEFRUIT   681 farms
8,383 hectares

Riverside	5,619
Kern	749
Ventura	600
San Diego	430

PEACHES   number of farms
not available
36,718 hectares

Stanislaus	9,078
Sutter	6,016
Fresno	4,514
Merced	4,244

1376 farms raised
clings on 73% of
the area
1339   raised freestones

PRUNES   1630 farms
31,738 hectares

Sutter	6,497
Yuba	3,770
Butte	3,099
Santa Clara	2,981

Scale: 1:15,000,000

FRUITS, NUTS, AND VEGETABLES

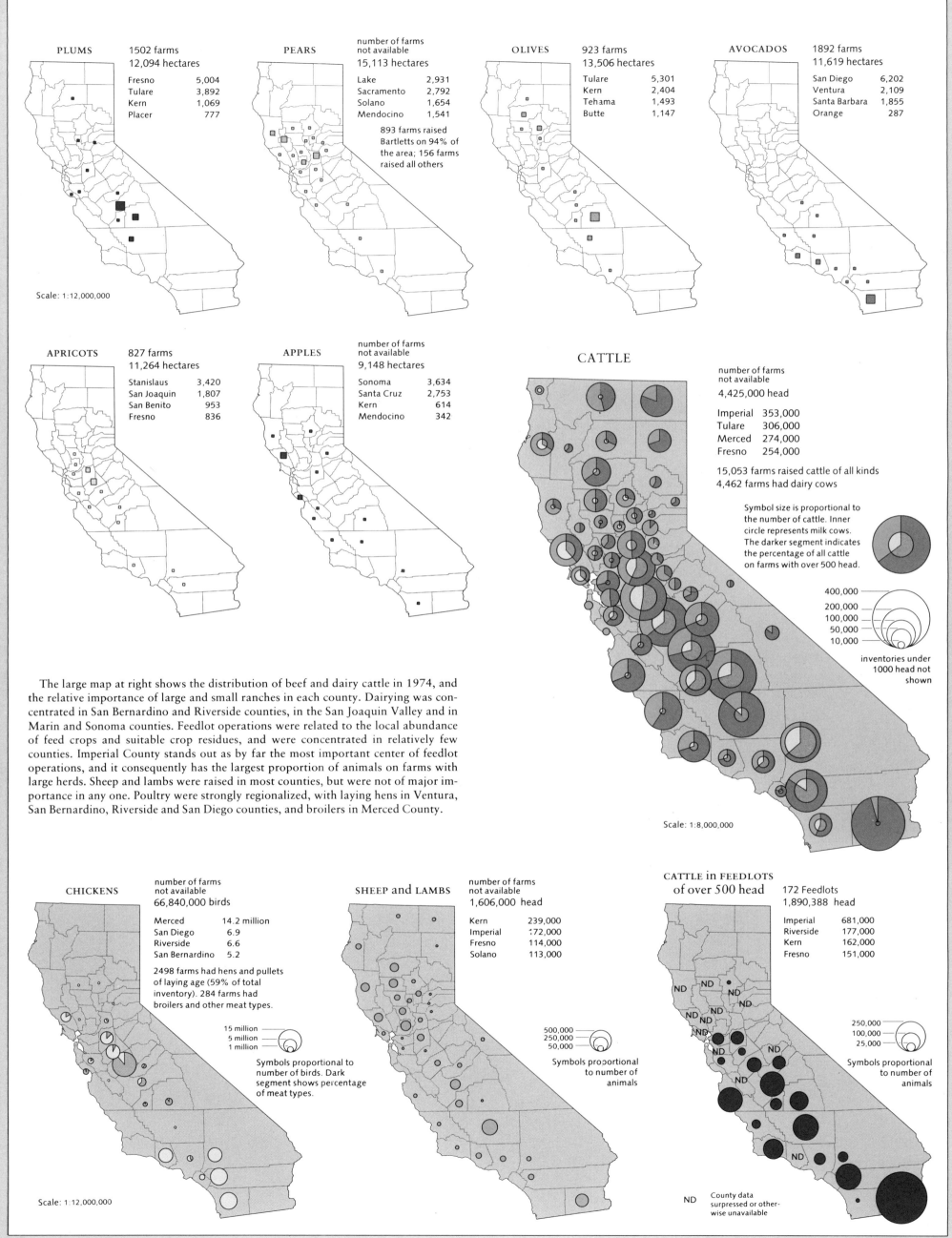

PLUMS — 1502 farms — 12,094 hectares
Fresno 5,004
Tulare 3,892
Kern 1,069
Placer 777
Scale: 1:12,000,000

PEARS — number of farms not available — 15,113 hectares
Lake 2,931
Sacramento 2,792
Solano 1,654
Mendocino 1,541
893 farms raised Bartletts on 94% of the area; 156 farms raised all others

OLIVES — 923 farms — 13,506 hectares
Tulare 5,301
Kern 2,404
Tehama 1,493
Butte 1,147

AVOCADOS — 1892 farms — 11,619 hectares
San Diego 6,202
Ventura 2,109
Santa Barbara 1,855
Orange 287

APRICOTS — 827 farms — 11,264 hectares
Stanislaus 3,420
San Joaquin 1,807
San Benito 953
Fresno 836

APPLES — number of farms not available — 9,148 hectares
Sonoma 3,634
Santa Cruz 2,753
Kern 614
Mendocino 342

CATTLE — number of farms not available — 4,425,000 head
Imperial 353,000
Tulare 306,000
Merced 274,000
Fresno 254,000
15,053 farms raised cattle of all kinds
4,462 farms had dairy cows

Symbol size is proportional to the number of cattle. Inner circle represents milk cows. The darker segment indicates the percentage of all cattle on farms with over 500 head.
400,000 / 200,000 / 100,000 / 50,000 / 10,000
inventories under 1000 head not shown
Scale: 1:8,000,000

The large map at right shows the distribution of beef and dairy cattle in 1974, and the relative importance of large and small ranches in each county. Dairying was concentrated in San Bernardino and Riverside counties, in the San Joaquin Valley and in Marin and Sonoma counties. Feedlot operations were related to the local abundance of feed crops and suitable crop residues, and were concentrated in relatively few counties. Imperial County stands out as by far the most important center of feedlot operations, and it consequently has the largest proportion of animals on farms with large herds. Sheep and lambs were raised in most counties, but were not of major importance in any one. Poultry were strongly regionalized, with laying hens in Ventura, San Bernardino, Riverside and San Diego counties, and broilers in Merced County.

CHICKENS — number of farms not available — 66,840,000 birds
Merced 14.2 million
San Diego 6.9
Riverside 6.6
San Bernardino 5.2
2498 farms had hens and pullets of laying age (59% of total inventory). 284 farms had broilers and other meat types.
15 million / 5 million / 1 million
Symbols proportional to number of birds. Dark segment shows percentage of meat types.
Scale: 1:12,000,000

SHEEP and LAMBS — number of farms not available — 1,606,000 head
Kern 239,000
Imperial 172,000
Fresno 114,000
Solano 113,000
500,000 / 250,000 / 50,000
Symbols proportional to number of animals

CATTLE in FEEDLOTS of over 500 head — 172 Feedlots — 1,890,388 head
Imperial 681,000
Riverside 177,000
Kern 162,000
Fresno 151,000
250,000 / 100,000 / 25,000
Symbols proportional to number of animals
ND County data surpressed or otherwise unavailable

CROPS AND LIVESTOCK

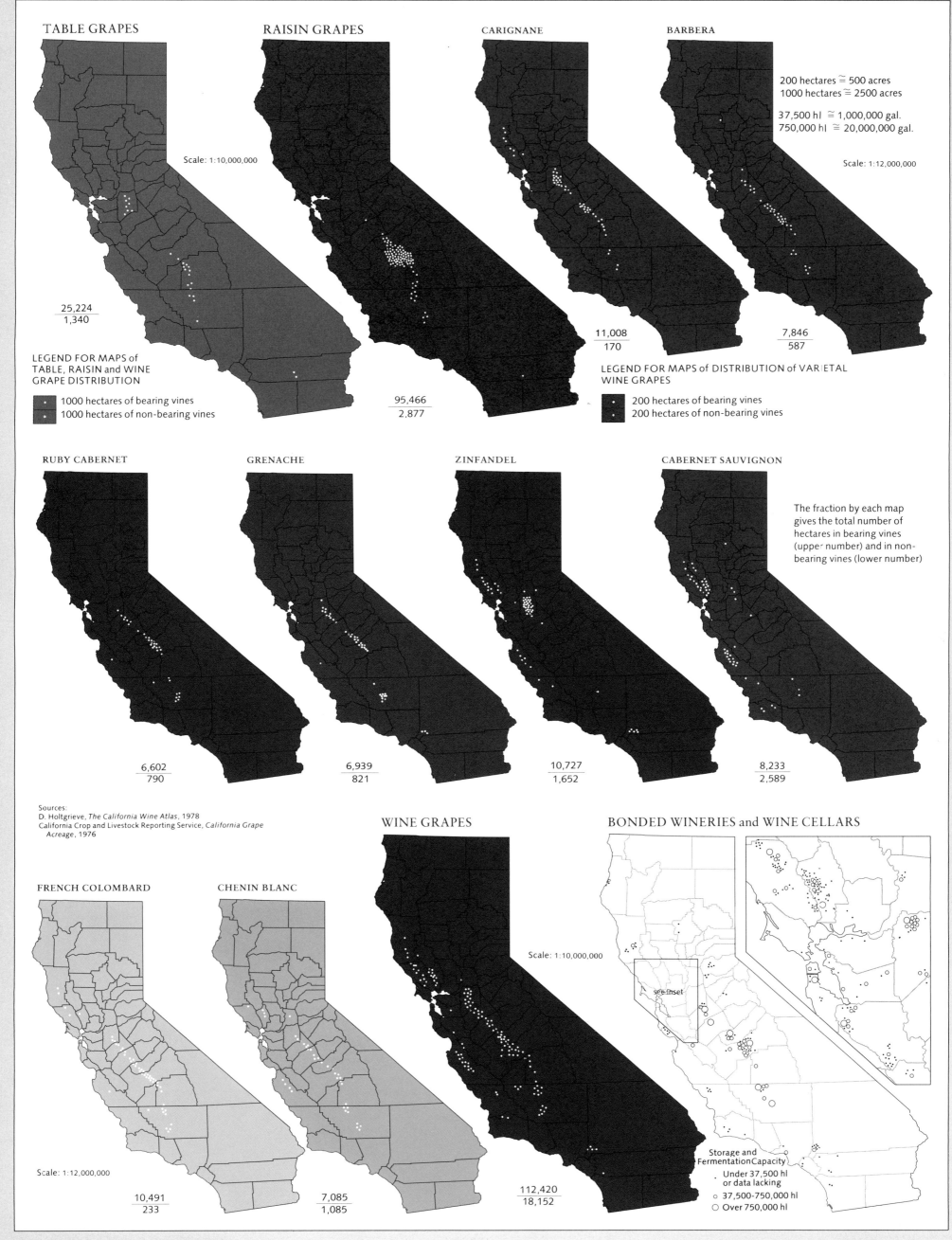

TABLE GRAPES

Scale: 1:10,000,000

$\frac{25,224}{1,340}$

LEGEND FOR MAPS of
TABLE, RAISIN and WINE
GRAPE DISTRIBUTION

· 1000 hectares of bearing vines
· 1000 hectares of non-bearing vines

RAISIN GRAPES

$\frac{95,466}{2,877}$

CARIGNANE

$\frac{11,008}{170}$

BARBERA

200 hectares ≅ 500 acres
1000 hectares ≅ 2500 acres

37,500 hl ≅ 1,000,000 gal.
750,000 hl ≅ 20,000,000 gal.

Scale: 1:12,000,000

$\frac{7,846}{587}$

LEGEND FOR MAPS of DISTRIBUTION of VARIETAL
WINE GRAPES

· 200 hectares of bearing vines
· 200 hectares of non-bearing vines

RUBY CABERNET

$\frac{6,602}{790}$

GRENACHE

$\frac{6,939}{821}$

ZINFANDEL

$\frac{10,727}{1,652}$

CABERNET SAUVIGNON

The fraction by each map
gives the total number of
hectares in bearing vines
(upper number) and in non-
bearing vines (lower number)

$\frac{8,233}{2,589}$

Sources:
D. Holtgrieve, *The California Wine Atlas*, 1978
California Crop and Livestock Reporting Service, *California Grape
    Acreage*, 1976

FRENCH COLOMBARD

Scale: 1:12,000,000

$\frac{10,491}{233}$

CHENIN BLANC

$\frac{7,085}{1,085}$

WINE GRAPES

Scale: 1:10,000,000

$\frac{112,420}{18,152}$

BONDED WINERIES and WINE CELLARS

see inset

Storage and
Fermentation Capacity

· Under 37,500 hl
  or data lacking
○ 37,500-750,000 hl
◯ Over 750,000 hl

VINEYARDS AND WINERIES

LAND CAPABILITY and URBANIZATION

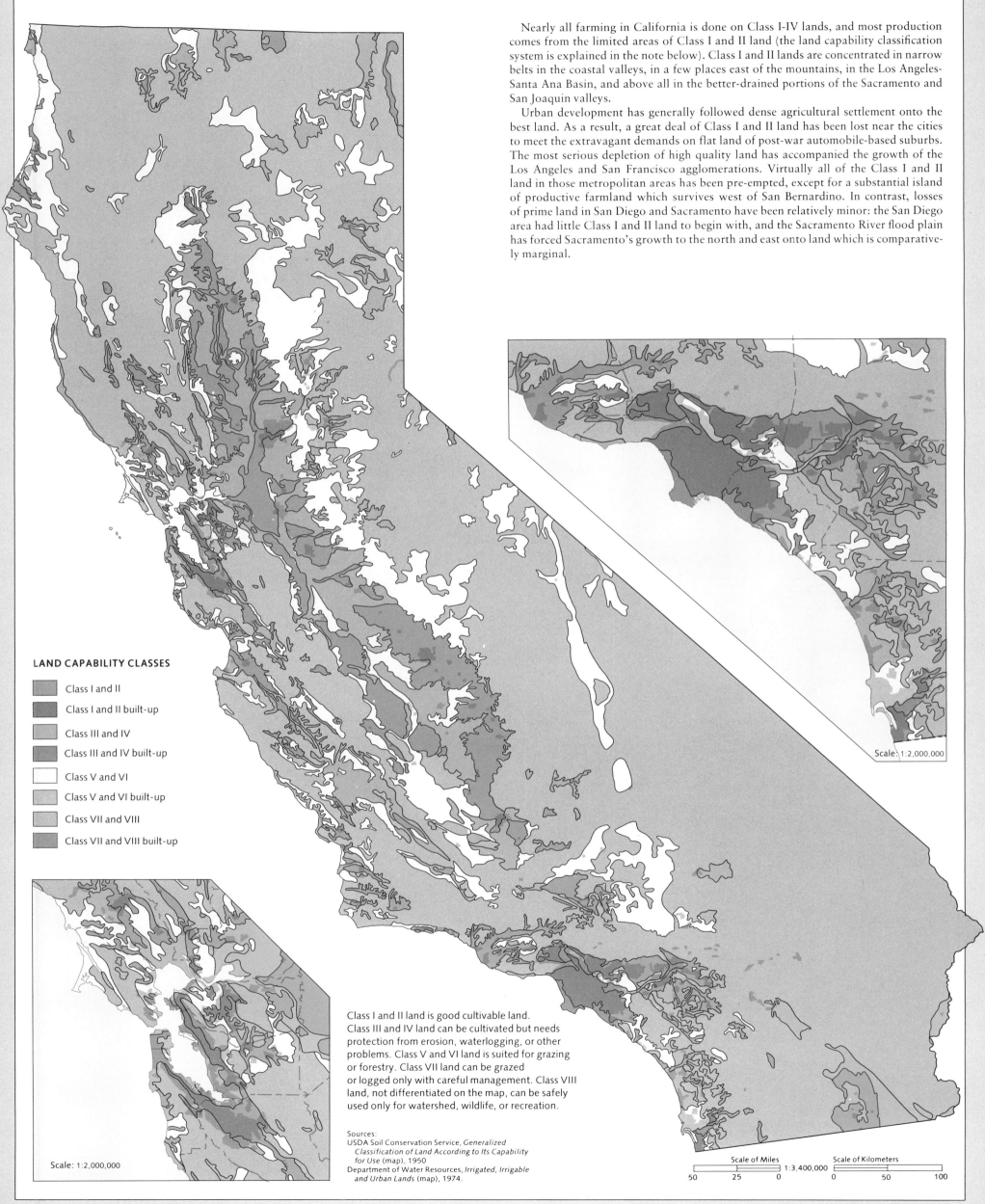

Nearly all farming in California is done on Class I-IV lands, and most production comes from the limited areas of Class I and II land (the land capability classification system is explained in the note below). Class I and II lands are concentrated in narrow belts in the coastal valleys, in a few places east of the mountains, in the Los Angeles-Santa Ana Basin, and above all in the better-drained portions of the Sacramento and San Joaquin valleys.

Urban development has generally followed dense agricultural settlement onto the best land. As a result, a great deal of Class I and II land has been lost near the cities to meet the extravagant demands on flat land of post-war automobile-based suburbs. The most serious depletion of high quality land has accompanied the growth of the Los Angeles and San Francisco agglomerations. Virtually all of the Class I and II land in those metropolitan areas has been pre-empted, except for a substantial island of productive farmland which survives west of San Bernardino. In contrast, losses of prime land in San Diego and Sacramento have been relatively minor: the San Diego area had little Class I and II land to begin with, and the Sacramento River flood plain has forced Sacramento's growth to the north and east onto land which is comparatively marginal.

LAND CAPABILITY CLASSES

- Class I and II
- Class I and II built-up
- Class III and IV
- Class III and IV built-up
- Class V and VI
- Class V and VI built-up
- Class VII and VIII
- Class VII and VIII built-up

Scale: 1:2,000,000

Scale: 1:2,000,000

Class I and II land is good cultivable land. Class III and IV land can be cultivated but needs protection from erosion, waterlogging, or other problems. Class V and VI land is suited for grazing or forestry. Class VII land can be grazed or logged only with careful management. Class VIII land, not differentiated on the map, can be safely used only for watershed, wildlife, or recreation.

Sources:
USDA Soil Conservation Service, *Generalized Classification of Land According to Its Capability for Use* (map), 1950
Department of Water Resources, *Irrigated, Irrigable and Urban Lands* (map), 1974.

Scale of Miles
Scale of Kilometers
1:3,400,000
50   25   0   0   50   100

LAND CAPABILITY

MANUFACTURING PLANTS, 1976

Manufacturing employed 1.6 million Californians in 1975, accounting for about 27 per cent of the state's employment and about 32 per cent of the payroll. (These numbers refer only to employment covered by social security; excluded are government and railroad employees, farm and domestic workers, and military personnel). Los Angeles County, alone, had over half of the manufacturing employment, and together with Orange County accounted for nearly three-fifths of the state's total. Another fifth were employed in the five metropolitan counties of the Bay Area, nearly half of them in Santa Clara County. San Diego employed about five per cent, and the remainder were scattered around the state, mostly in the Central Valley.

Many categories of manufacturing were represented in California in about the same proportion as in the rest of the country, but some specialization existed nevertheless. There was a relatively strong emphasis on certain industries, such as the production of aircraft and missiles, instruments and electric and electronic equipment; and relatively little productivity in other industries, such as textiles, chemicals and primary metals.

Specialization also took place within the state. Aircraft and missiles, the largest employer (16 per cent of the labor force), was primarily located in Los Angeles, Orange and San Diego counties, but had an important secondary center in Santa Clara County. Electric and electronic equipment (11 per cent of the labor force) employed relatively more people in San Mateo, Santa Clara, Orange, and San Diego counties than in the older urban cores. Employment in food processing (10 percent) was widely scattered, but relatively more significant in the Bay Area than in Southern California.

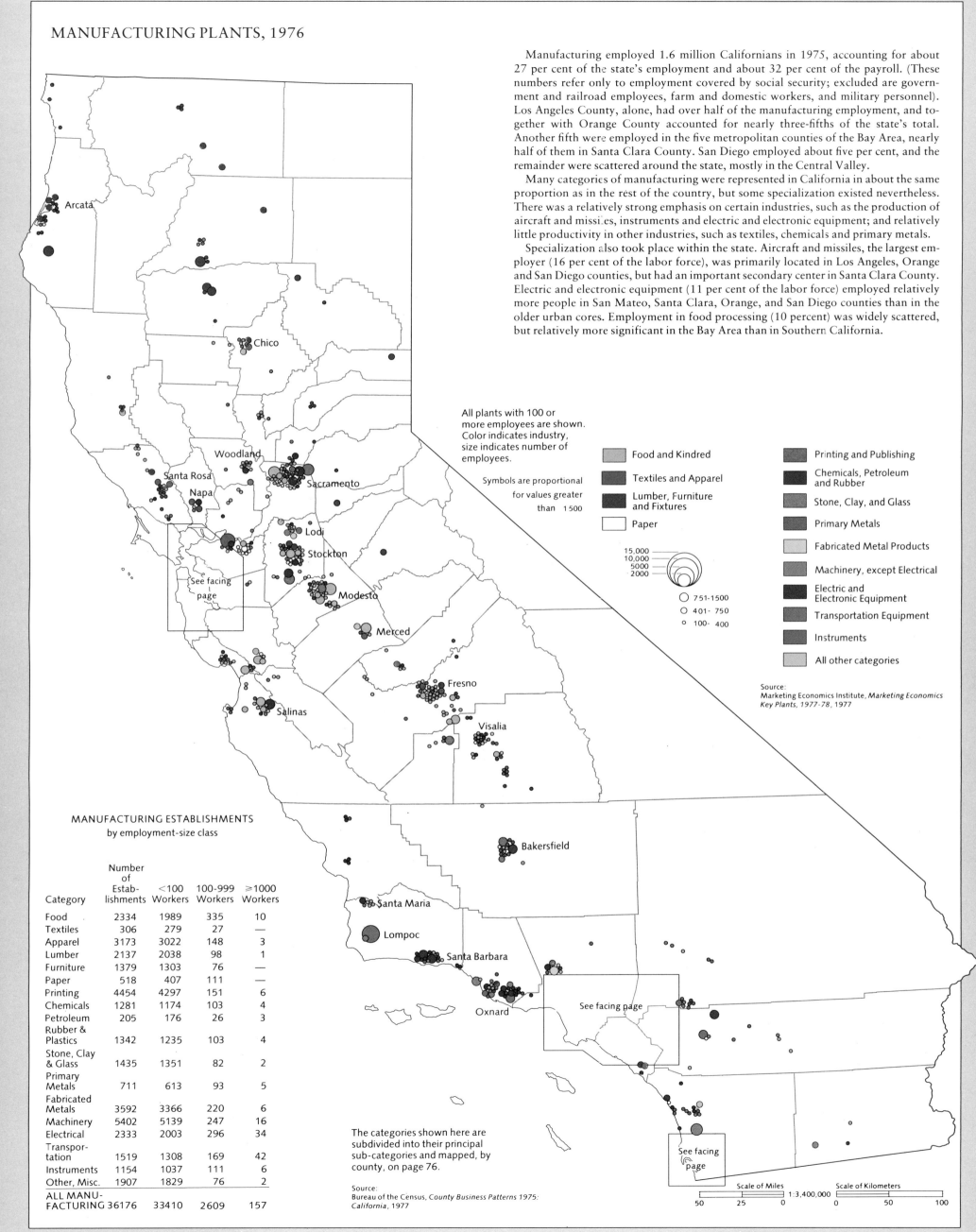

All plants with 100 or more employees are shown. Color indicates industry, size indicates number of employees.

Symbols are proportional for values greater than 1500

15,000
10,000
5,000
2,000

○ 751-1500
○ 401- 750
○ 100- 400

Food and Kindred	Printing and Publishing
Textiles and Apparel	Chemicals, Petroleum and Rubber
Lumber, Furniture and Fixtures	Stone, Clay, and Glass
Paper	Primary Metals
	Fabricated Metal Products
	Machinery, except Electrical
	Electric and Electronic Equipment
	Transportation Equipment
	Instruments
	All other categories

Source:
Marketing Economics Institute, *Marketing Economics Key Plants, 1977-78,* 1977

MANUFACTURING ESTABLISHMENTS
by employment-size class

Category	Number of Establishments	<100 Workers	100-999 Workers	≥1000 Workers
Food	2334	1989	335	10
Textiles	306	279	27	—
Apparel	3173	3022	148	3
Lumber	2137	2038	98	1
Furniture	1379	1303	76	—
Paper	518	407	111	—
Printing	4454	4297	151	6
Chemicals	1281	1174	103	4
Petroleum	205	176	26	3
Rubber & Plastics	1342	1235	103	4
Stone, Clay & Glass	1435	1351	82	2
Primary Metals	711	613	93	5
Fabricated Metals	3592	3366	220	6
Machinery	5402	5139	247	16
Electrical	2333	2003	296	34
Transportation	1519	1308	169	42
Instruments	1154	1037	111	6
Other, Misc.	1907	1829	76	2
ALL MANUFACTURING	36176	33410	2609	157

The categories shown here are subdivided into their principal sub-categories and mapped, by county, on page 76.

Source:
Bureau of the Census, *County Business Patterns 1975: California,* 1977

Scale of Miles
Scale of Kilometers
1:3,400,000
50   25   0   0   50   100

MANUFACTURING PLANTS

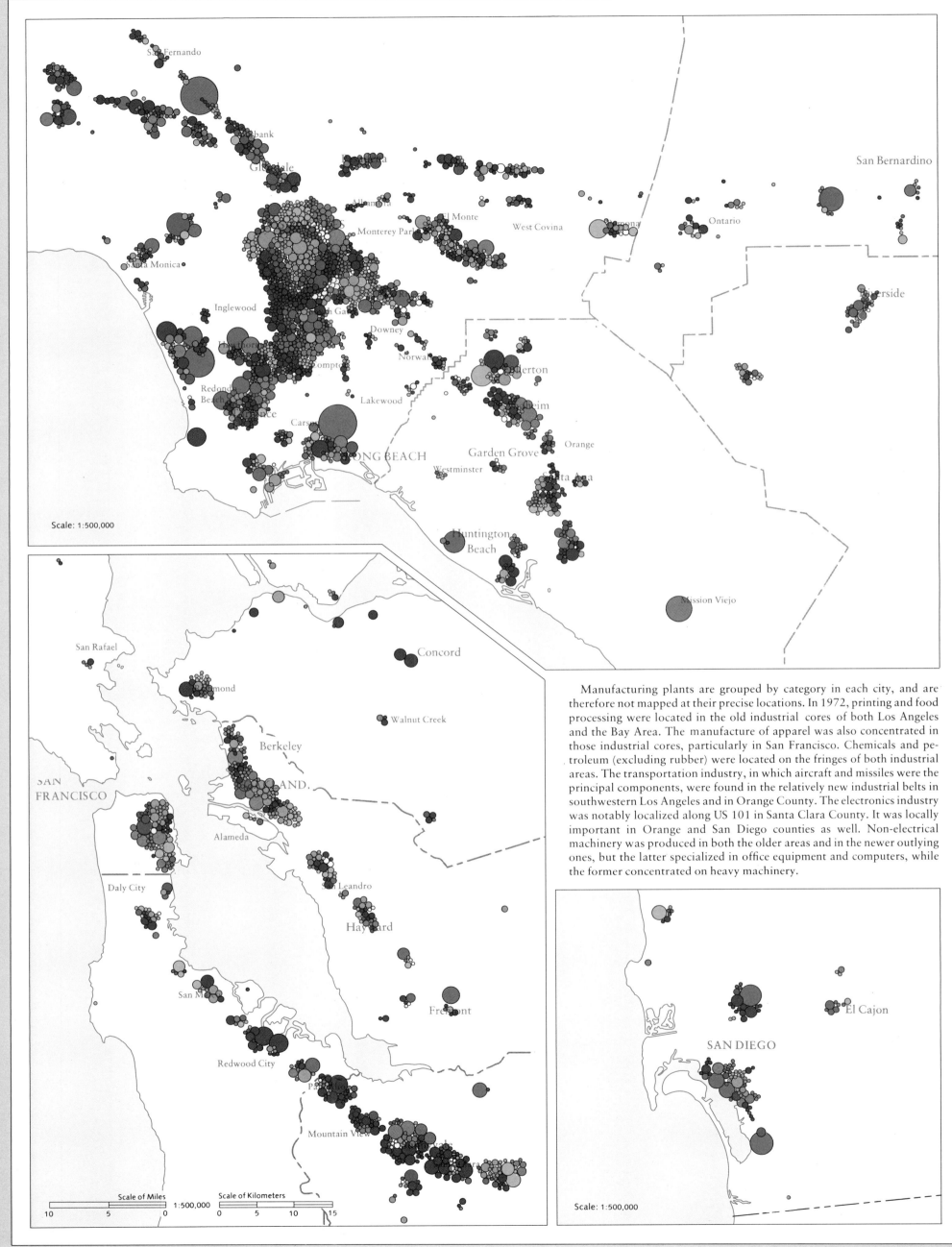

Scale: 1:500,000

Manufacturing plants are grouped by category in each city, and are therefore not mapped at their precise locations. In 1972, printing and food processing were located in the old industrial cores of both Los Angeles and the Bay Area. The manufacture of apparel was also concentrated in those industrial cores, particularly in San Francisco. Chemicals and petroleum (excluding rubber) were located on the fringes of both industrial areas. The transportation industry, in which aircraft and missiles were the principal components, were found in the relatively new industrial belts in southwestern Los Angeles and in Orange County. The electronics industry was notably localized along US 101 in Santa Clara County. It was locally important in Orange and San Diego counties as well. Non-electrical machinery was produced in both the older areas and in the newer outlying ones, but the latter specialized in office equipment and computers, while the former concentrated on heavy machinery.

Scale of Miles   Scale of Kilometers
10   5   0   1:500,000   0   5   10   15

Scale: 1:500,000

MANUFACTURING PLANTS

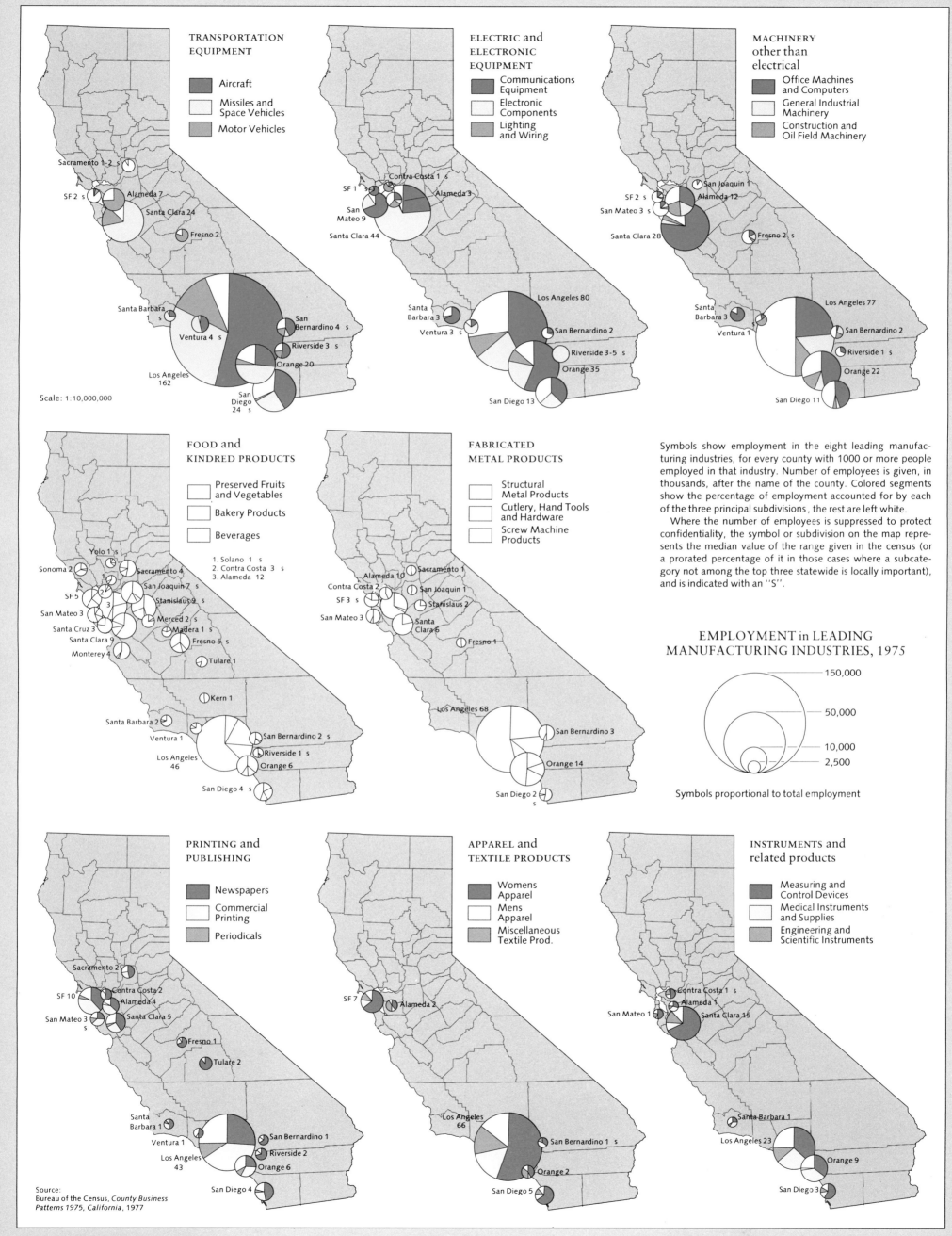

76

TRANSPORTATION EQUIPMENT

- Aircraft
- Missiles and Space Vehicles
- Motor Vehicles

Sacramento 1-2 s
SF 2 s
Alameda 7
Santa Clara 24
Fresno 2
Santa Barbara 1 s
Ventura 4 s
San Bernardino 4 s
Riverside 3 s
Orange 20
Los Angeles 162
San Diego 24 s

Scale: 1:10,000,000

ELECTRIC and ELECTRONIC EQUIPMENT

- Communications Equipment
- Electronic Components
- Lighting and Wiring

Contra Costa 1 s
SF 1 s
San Mateo 9
Alameda 3
Santa Clara 44
Santa Barbara 3
Ventura 3 s
Los Angeles 80
San Bernardino 2
Riverside 3-5 s
Orange 35
San Diego 13

MACHINERY other than electrical

- Office Machines and Computers
- General Industrial Machinery
- Construction and Oil Field Machinery

San Joaquin 1
SF 2 s
Alameda 12
San Mateo 3 s
Santa Clara 28
Fresno 2 s
Santa Barbara 3
Ventura 1
Los Angeles 77
San Bernardino 2
Riverside 1 s
Orange 22
San Diego 11

FOOD and KINDRED PRODUCTS

- Preserved Fruits and Vegetables
- Bakery Products
- Beverages

1. Solano 1 s
2. Contra Costa 3 s
3. Alameda 12

Yolo 1 s
Sonoma 2
Sacramento 4
San Joaquin 7 s
Stanislaus 9 s
SF 5
San Mateo 3
Santa Cruz 3
Merced 2 s
Madera 1 s
Santa Clara 9
Fresno 5 s
Monterey 4
Tulare 1
Kern 1
Santa Barbara 2
Ventura 1
San Bernardino 2 s
Riverside 1 s
Orange 6
Los Angeles 46
San Diego 4 s

FABRICATED METAL PRODUCTS

- Structural Metal Products
- Cutlery, Hand Tools and Hardware
- Screw Machine Products

Alameda 10
Sacramento 1
Contra Costa 2
San Joaquin 1
SF 3
Stanislaus 2
San Mateo 3
Santa Clara 6
Fresno 1
Los Angeles 68
San Bernardino 3
Orange 14
San Diego 2 s

Symbols show employment in the eight leading manufacturing industries, for every county with 1000 or more people employed in that industry. Number of employees is given, in thousands, after the name of the county. Colored segments show the percentage of employment accounted for by each of the three principal subdivisions, the rest are left white.

Where the number of employees is suppressed to protect confidentiality, the symbol or subdivision on the map represents the median value of the range given in the census (or a prorated percentage of it in those cases where a subcategory not among the top three statewide is locally important), and is indicated with an "S".

EMPLOYMENT in LEADING MANUFACTURING INDUSTRIES, 1975

150,000
50,000
10,000
2,500

Symbols proportional to total employment

PRINTING and PUBLISHING

- Newspapers
- Commercial Printing
- Periodicals

Sacramento 2
SF 10
Contra Costa 2
Alameda 4
San Mateo 3 s
Santa Clara 5
Fresno 1
Tulare 2
Santa Barbara 1
Ventura 1
San Bernardino 1
Riverside 2
Los Angeles 43
Orange 6
San Diego 4

APPAREL and TEXTILE PRODUCTS

- Womens Apparel
- Mens Apparel
- Miscellaneous Textile Prod.

SF 7
Alameda 2
Los Angeles 66
San Bernardino 1 s
Orange 2
San Diego 5

INSTRUMENTS and related products

- Measuring and Control Devices
- Medical Instruments and Supplies
- Engineering and Scientific Instruments

Contra Costa 1 s
Alameda 1
San Mateo 1
Santa Clara 15
Santa Barbara 1
Los Angeles 23
Orange 9
San Diego 3

Source:
Bureau of the Census, *County Business Patterns 1975, California*, 1977

PRINCIPAL INDUSTRIES

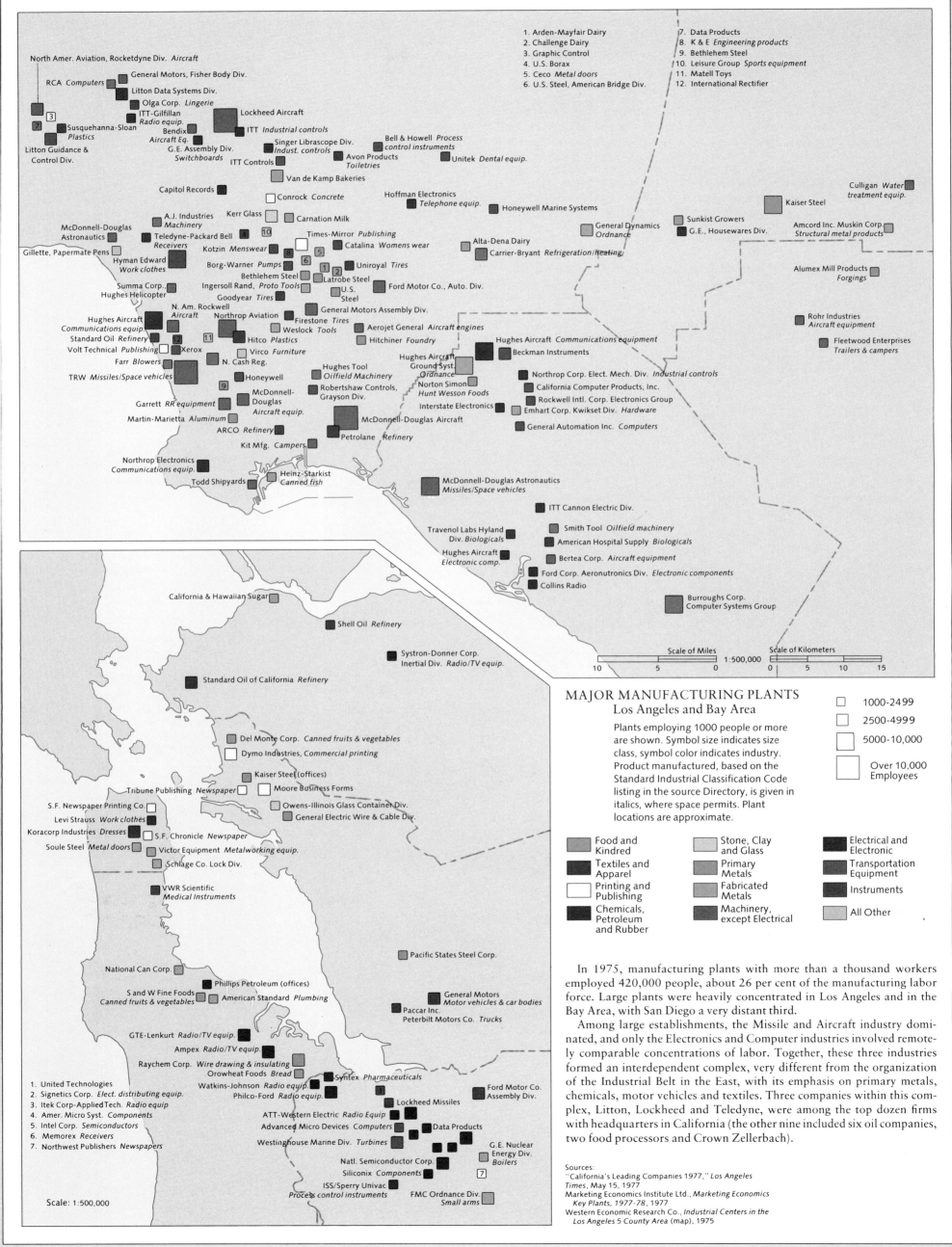

1. Arden-Mayfair Dairy
2. Challenge Dairy
3. Graphic Control
4. U.S. Borax
5. Ceco *Metal doors*
6. U.S. Steel, American Bridge Div.
7. Data Products
8. K & E *Engineering products*
9. Bethlehem Steel
10. Leisure Group *Sports equipment*
11. Matell Toys
12. International Rectifier

North Amer. Aviation, Rocketdyne Div. *Aircraft*
RCA *Computers*
General Motors, Fisher Body Div.
Litton Data Systems Div.
Olga Corp. *Lingerie*
ITT-Gilfillan *Radio equip.*
Susquehanna-Sloan *Plastics*
Bendix *Aircraft Eq.*
Litton Guidance & Control Div.
G.E. Assembly Div. *Switchboards*
ITT Controls
Lockheed Aircraft
ITT *Industrial controls*
Singer Librascope Div. *Indust. controls*
Avon Products *Toiletries*
Bell & Howell *Process control instruments*
Unitek *Dental equip.*

Capitol Records
Conrock *Concrete*
Van de Kamp Bakeries
Hoffman Electronics *Telephone equip.*
Honeywell Marine Systems
General Dynamics *Ordnance*
Sunkist Growers
G.E., Housewares Div.
Kaiser Steel
Culligan *Water treatment equip.*
Amcord Inc. Muskin Corp. *Structural metal products*

McDonnell-Douglas Astronautics
A.J. Industries *Machinery*
Teledyne-Packard Bell *Receivers*
Kerr Glass
Carnation Milk
Times-Mirror *Publishing*
Catalina *Womens wear*
Alta-Dena Dairy
Carrier-Bryant *Refrigeration/heating*
Gillette, Papermate Pens
Kotzin *Menswear*
Alumex Mill Products *Forgings*
Hyman Edward *Work clothes*
Borg-Warner *Pumps*
Uniroyal *Tires*
Bethlehem Steel
Latrobe Steel
U.S. Steel
Ford Motor Co., Auto. Div.
Summa Corp., Hughes Helicopter
Ingersoll Rand, *Proto Tools*
Goodyear *Tires*
N. Am. Rockwell *Aircraft*
General Motors Assembly Div.
Rohr Industries *Aircraft equipment*
Hughes Aircraft *Communications equip.*
Northrop Aviation
Firestone *Tires*
Weslock *Tools*
Aerojet General *Aircraft engines*
Hughes Aircraft *Communications equipment*
Fleetwood Enterprises *Trailers & campers*
Standard Oil *Refinery*
Hitco *Plastics*
Hitchiner *Foundry*
Hughes Aircraft *Ground Syst. Ordnance*
Beckman Instruments
Volt Technical *Publishing*
Xerox
Virco *Furniture*
Norton Simon *Hunt Wesson Foods*
Northrop Corp. Elect. Mech. Div. *Industrial controls*
Farr *Blowers*
N. Cash Reg.
Hughes Tool *Oilfield Machinery*
California Computer Products, Inc.
TRW *Missiles/Space vehicles*
Honeywell
Robertshaw Controls, Grayson Div.
Rockwell Intl. Corp. Electronics Group
Garrett *RR equipment*
McDonnell-Douglas *Aircraft equip.*
Interstate Electronics
Emhart Corp. Kwikset Div. *Hardware*
Martin-Marietta *Aluminum*
ARCO *Refinery*
McDonnell-Douglas *Aircraft*
General Automation Inc. *Computers*
Kit Mfg. *Campers*
Petrolane *Refinery*
Northrop Electronics *Communications equip.*
Todd Shipyards
Heinz-Starkist *Canned fish*
McDonnell-Douglas Astronautics *Missiles/Space vehicles*
ITT Cannon Electric Div.
Travenol Labs Hyland Div. *Biologicals*
Smith Tool *Oilfield machinery*
American Hospital Supply *Biologicals*
Hughes Aircraft *Electronic comp.*
Bertea Corp. *Aircraft equipment*
Ford Corp. Aeronutronics Div. *Electronic components*
Collins Radio
Burroughs Corp. Computer Systems Group

California & Hawaiian Sugar
Shell Oil *Refinery*
Systron-Donner Corp. Inertial Div. *Radio/TV equip.*
Standard Oil of California *Refinery*

Del Monte Corp. *Canned fruits & vegetables*
Dymo Industries, *Commercial printing*
Kaiser Steel *(offices)*
Moore Business Forms
Tribune Publishing *Newspaper*
S.F. Newspaper Printing Co.
Owens-Illinois Glass Container Div.
Levi Strauss *Work clothes*
General Electric Wire & Cable Div.
Koracorp Industries *Dresses*
S.F. Chronicle *Newspaper*
Soule Steel *Metal doors*
Victor Equipment *Metalworking equip.*
Schlage Co. Lock Div.
VWR Scientific *Medical Instruments*
Pacific States Steel Corp.
National Can Corp.
Phillips Petroleum *(offices)*
S and W Fine Foods *Canned fruits & vegetables*
American Standard *Plumbing*
General Motors *Motor vehicles & car bodies*
Paccar Inc. Peterbilt Motors Co. *Trucks*
GTE-Lenkurt *Radio/TV equip.*
Ampex *Radio/TV equip.*
Raychem Corp. *Wire drawing & insulating*
Orowheat Foods *Bread*
Syntex *Pharmaceuticals*
Ford Motor Co. Assembly Div.
Watkins-Johnson *Radio equip.*
Philco-Ford *Radio equip.*
Lockheed Missiles
ATT-Western Electric *Radio Equip*
Advanced Micro Devices *Computers*
Data Products
Westinghouse Marine Div. *Turbines*
G.E. Nuclear Energy Div. *Boilers*
Natl. Semiconductor Corp.
Siliconix *Components*
ISS/Sperry Univac *Process control instruments*
FMC Ordnance Div. *Small arms*

1. United Technologies
2. Signetics Corp. *Elect. distributing equip.*
3. Itek Corp-AppliedTech. *Radio equip*
4. Amer. Micro Syst. *Components*
5. Intel Corp. *Semiconductors*
6. Memorex *Receivers*
7. Northwest Publishers *Newspapers*

Scale: 1:500,000

Scale of Miles   1:500,000   Scale of Kilometers
10   0   0   5   10   15

MAJOR MANUFACTURING PLANTS
Los Angeles and Bay Area

Plants employing 1000 people or more are shown. Symbol size indicates size class, symbol color indicates industry. Product manufactured, based on the Standard Industrial Classification Code listing in the source Directory, is given in italics, where space permits. Plant locations are approximate.

1000-2499
2500-4999
5000-10,000
Over 10,000 Employees

Food and Kindred
Textiles and Apparel
Printing and Publishing
Chemicals, Petroleum and Rubber
Stone, Clay and Glass
Primary Metals
Fabricated Metals
Machinery, except Electrical
Electrical and Electronic
Transportation Equipment
Instruments
All Other

In 1975, manufacturing plants with more than a thousand workers employed 420,000 people, about 26 per cent of the manufacturing labor force. Large plants were heavily concentrated in Los Angeles and in the Bay Area, with San Diego a very distant third.

Among large establishments, the Missile and Aircraft industry dominated, and only the Electronics and Computer industries involved remotely comparable concentrations of labor. Together, these three industries formed an interdependent complex, very different from the organization of the Industrial Belt in the East, with its emphasis on primary metals, chemicals, motor vehicles and textiles. Three companies within this complex, Litton, Lockheed and Teledyne, were among the top dozen firms with headquarters in California (the other nine included six oil companies, two food processors and Crown Zellerbach).

Sources:
"California's Leading Companies 1977," *Los Angeles Times*, May 15, 1977
Marketing Economics Institute Ltd., *Marketing Economics Key Plants, 1977-78*, 1977
Western Economic Research Co., *Industrial Centers in the Los Angeles 5 County Area* (map), 1975

INDUSTRIAL LOCATION

Dunn & Bradstreet listed 2,950 million dollar corporations in California: the cities of Los Angeles and San Francisco contained the headquarters of over 850; another 46 cities in those metropolitan areas had more than 10; and eleven other cities had more than 10.

In 1977, the top ten industrials (listed in *California's Leading Companies*) had sales or revenues ranging from $145 million to $20.18 billion. Sixty-three were headquartered in Los Angeles and Orange Counties, 32 were in the Bay Area, and one each was in San Diego, Chula Vista, Riverside, Ventura, and Santa Barbara.

Twenty-one industrials had sales or revenues of more than a billion dollars in 1977. Seven were oil companies (Standard, Atlantic Richfield, Union, Occidental, Getty, Signal, and Reserve); five were defense-related industries (Litton, Lockheed, Teledyne, Northrop, and Hewlett Packard); three were food and drug companies (Foremost-

McKesson, Carnation, and Del Monte); two were wood processing corporations (Crown Zellerbach and The Wickes Corporation); two were consumer oriented corporations (Dart, Levi Strauss); one was an aluminum producer (Kaiser), and one was a natural resource service industry (Fluor).

Non-industrial corporations also played an important role. In 1976, California had 10 transportation companies and 8 utility corporations with revenues greater than $100 million, 4 merchandising corporations with sales greater than $500 million, and 9 banks and 14 savings and loan associations with assets exceeding one billion dollars. However, a number of industrial and non-industrial enterprises with large corporate assets do not appear on the map because their home offices are not in California: Hughes Tool in Houston, the Summa Corporation in Las Vegas, and McDonnell-Douglas in St. Louis, for example.

MILLION-DOLLAR CORPORATIONS, 1977

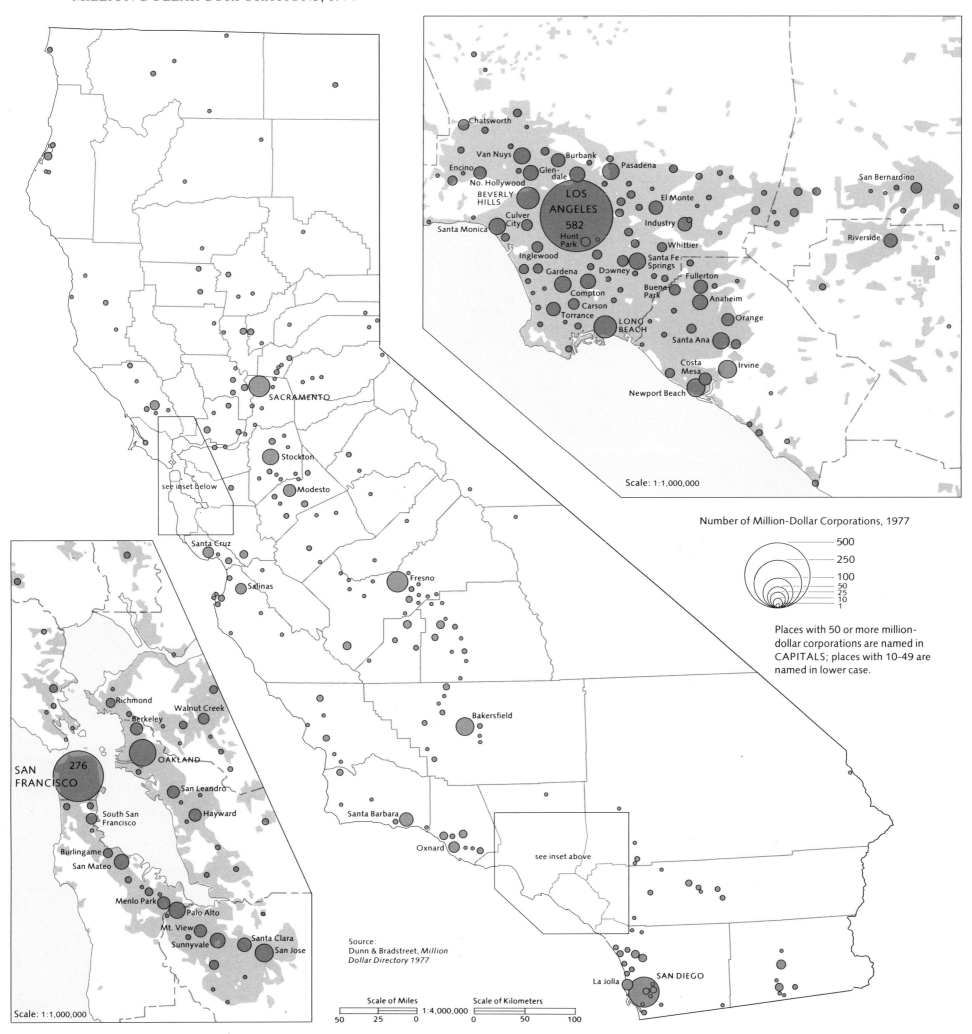

Number of Million-Dollar Corporations, 1977

Places with 50 or more million-dollar corporations are named in CAPITALS; places with 10-49 are named in lower case.

Source:
Dunn & Bradstreet, *Million Dollar Directory 1977*

MILLION-DOLLAR CORPORATIONS

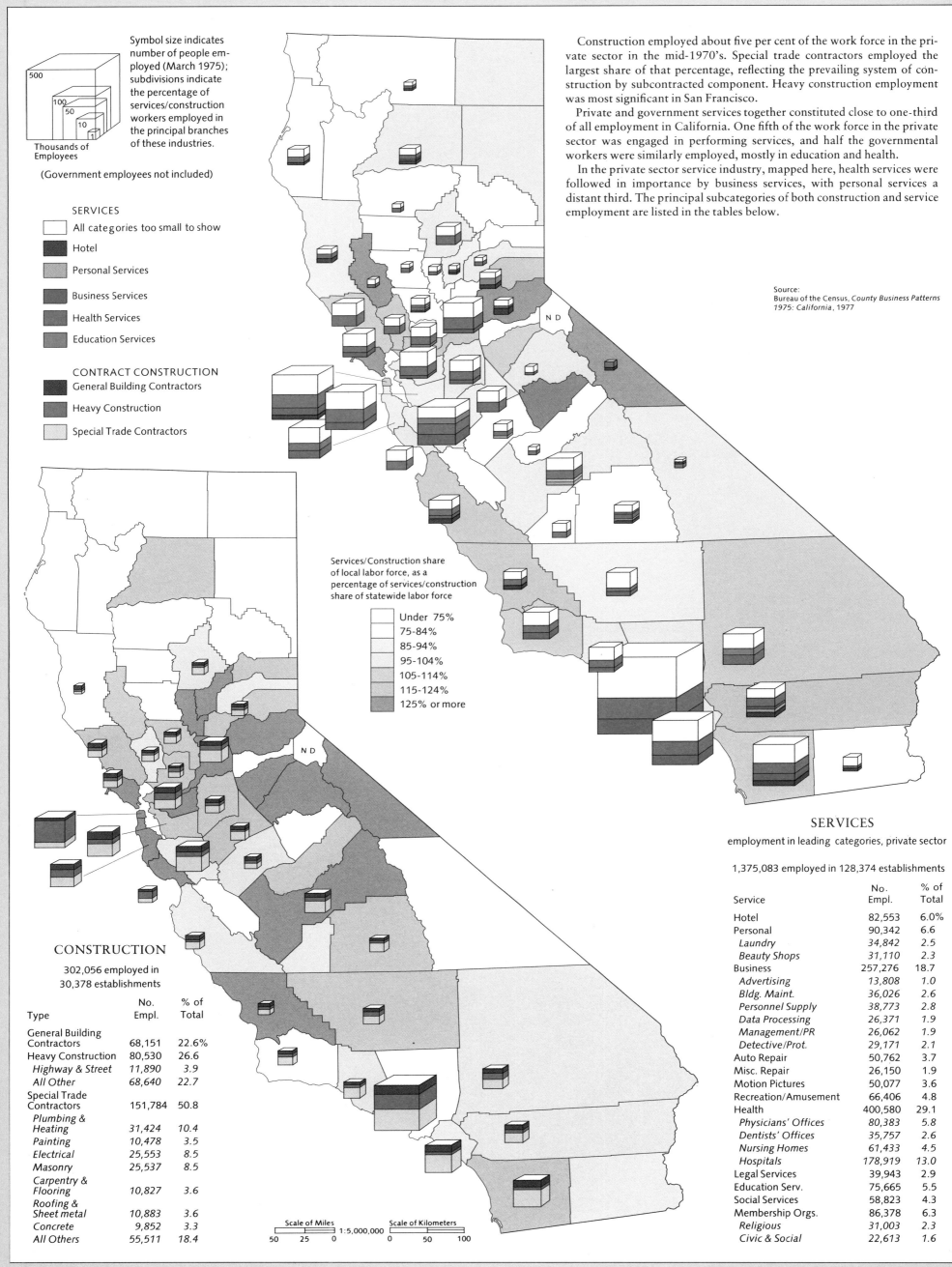

Symbol size indicates number of people employed (March 1975); subdivisions indicate the percentage of services/construction workers employed in the principal branches of these industries.

Thousands of Employees

(Government employees not included)

SERVICES
- All categories too small to show
- Hotel
- Personal Services
- Business Services
- Health Services
- Education Services

CONTRACT CONSTRUCTION
- General Building Contractors
- Heavy Construction
- Special Trade Contractors

Services/Construction share of local labor force, as a percentage of services/construction share of statewide labor force

- Under 75%
- 75-84%
- 85-94%
- 95-104%
- 105-114%
- 115-124%
- 125% or more

Construction employed about five per cent of the work force in the private sector in the mid-1970's. Special trade contractors employed the largest share of that percentage, reflecting the prevailing system of construction by subcontracted component. Heavy construction employment was most significant in San Francisco.

Private and government services together constituted close to one-third of all employment in California. One fifth of the work force in the private sector was engaged in performing services, and half the governmental workers were similarly employed, mostly in education and health.

In the private sector service industry, mapped here, health services were followed in importance by business services, with personal services a distant third. The principal subcategories of both construction and service employment are listed in the tables below.

Source:
Bureau of the Census, *County Business Patterns 1975: California*, 1977

CONSTRUCTION

302,056 employed in 30,378 establishments

Type	No. Empl.	% of Total
General Building Contractors	68,151	22.6%
Heavy Construction	80,530	26.6
Highway & Street	*11,890*	*3.9*
All Other	*68,640*	*22.7*
Special Trade Contractors	151,784	50.8
Plumbing & Heating	*31,424*	*10.4*
Painting	*10,478*	*3.5*
Electrical	*25,553*	*8.5*
Masonry	*25,537*	*8.5*
Carpentry & Flooring	*10,827*	*3.6*
Roofing & Sheet metal	*10,883*	*3.6*
Concrete	*9,852*	*3.3*
All Others	*55,511*	*18.4*

SERVICES

employment in leading categories, private sector

1,375,083 employed in 128,374 establishments

Service	No. Empl.	% of Total
Hotel	82,553	6.0%
Personal	90,342	6.6
Laundry	*34,842*	*2.5*
Beauty Shops	*31,110*	*2.3*
Business	257,276	18.7
Advertising	*13,808*	*1.0*
Bldg. Maint.	*36,026*	*2.6*
Personnel Supply	*38,773*	*2.8*
Data Processing	*26,371*	*1.9*
Management/PR	*26,062*	*1.9*
Detective/Prot.	*29,171*	*2.1*
Auto Repair	50,762	3.7
Misc. Repair	26,150	1.9
Motion Pictures	50,077	3.6
Recreation/Amusement	66,406	4.8
Health	400,580	29.1
Physicians' Offices	*80,383*	*5.8*
Dentists' Offices	*35,757*	*2.6*
Nursing Homes	*61,433*	*4.5*
Hospitals	*178,919*	*13.0*
Legal Services	39,943	2.9
Education Serv.	75,665	5.5
Social Services	58,823	4.3
Membership Orgs.	86,378	6.3
Religious	*31,003*	*2.3*
Civic & Social	*22,613*	*1.6*

Scale of Miles   Scale of Kilometers
50 25 0   1:5,000,000   0   50   100

SERVICES AND CONSTRUCTION

RETAIL CENTERS

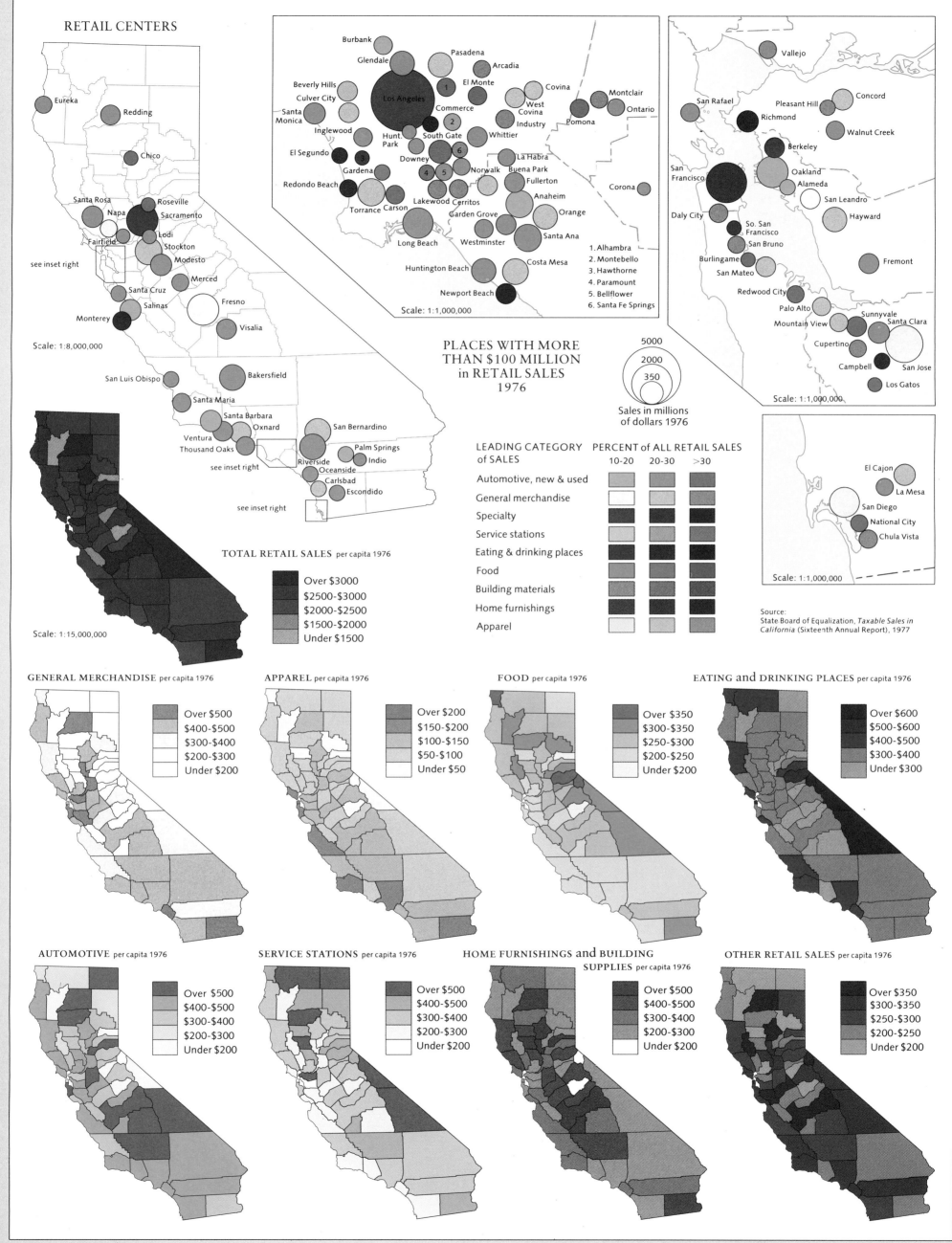

Scale: 1:8,000,000

Scale: 1:15,000,000

PLACES WITH MORE
THAN $100 MILLION
in RETAIL SALES
1976

5000
2000
350

Sales in millions
of dollars 1976

1. Alhambra
2. Montebello
3. Hawthorne
4. Paramount
5. Bellflower
6. Santa Fe Springs

Scale: 1:1,000,000

Scale: 1:1,000,000

Scale: 1:1,000,000

LEADING CATEGORY of SALES	PERCENT of ALL RETAIL SALES		
	10-20	20-30	>30
Automotive, new & used			
General merchandise			
Specialty			
Service stations			
Eating & drinking places			
Food			
Building materials			
Home furnishings			
Apparel			

Source:
State Board of Equalization, *Taxable Sales in California* (Sixteenth Annual Report), 1977

TOTAL RETAIL SALES per capita 1976

Over $3000
$2500-$3000
$2000-$2500
$1500-$2000
Under $1500

GENERAL MERCHANDISE per capita 1976

Over $500
$400-$500
$300-$400
$200-$300
Under $200

APPAREL per capita 1976

Over $200
$150-$200
$100-$150
$50-$100
Under $50

FOOD per capita 1976

Over $350
$300-$350
$250-$300
$200-$250
Under $200

EATING and DRINKING PLACES per capita 1976

Over $600
$500-$600
$400-$500
$300-$400
Under $300

AUTOMOTIVE per capita 1976

Over $500
$400-$500
$300-$400
$200-$300
Under $200

SERVICE STATIONS per capita 1976

Over $500
$400-$500
$300-$400
$200-$300
Under $200

HOME FURNISHINGS and BUILDING
SUPPLIES per capita 1976

Over $500
$400-$500
$300-$400
$200-$300
Under $200

OTHER RETAIL SALES per capita 1976

Over $350
$300-$350
$250-$300
$200-$250
Under $200

RETAIL TRADE

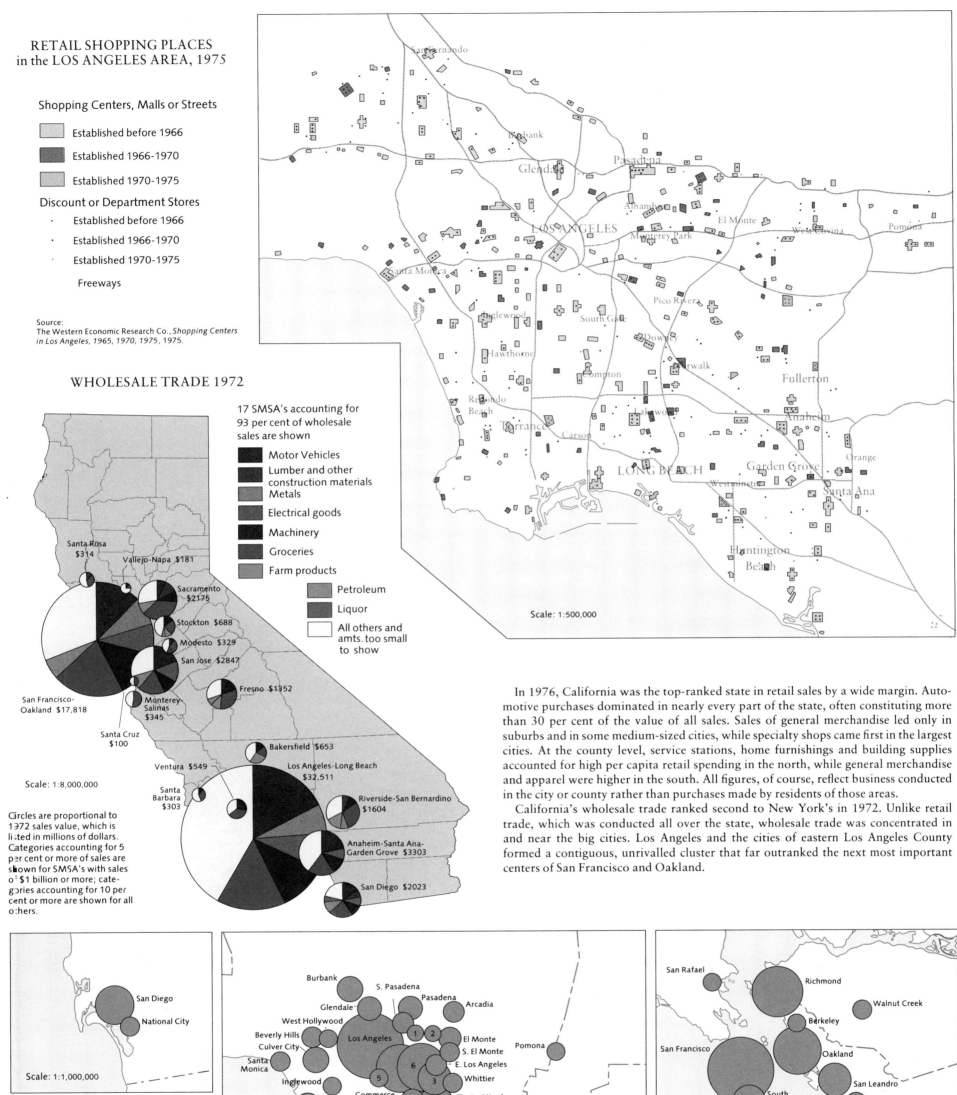

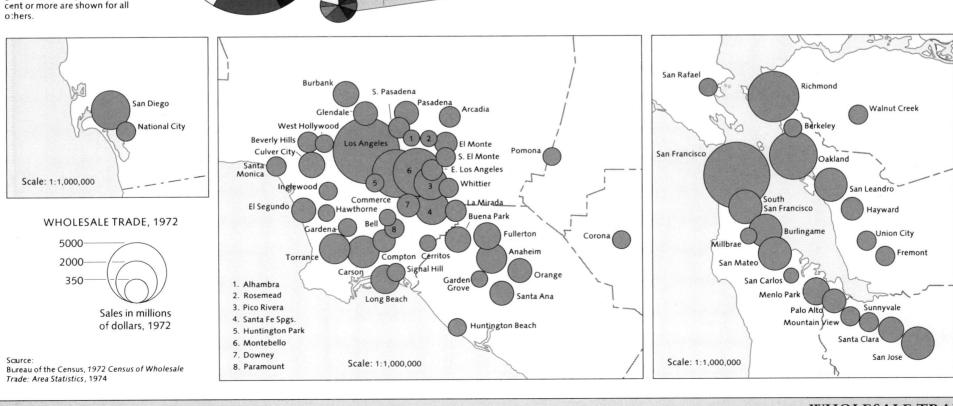

RETAIL SHOPPING PLACES
in the LOS ANGELES AREA, 1975

Shopping Centers, Malls or Streets

- Established before 1966
- Established 1966-1970
- Established 1970-1975

Discount or Department Stores

- · Established before 1966
- · Established 1966-1970
- · Established 1970-1975

Freeways

Source:
The Western Economic Research Co., *Shopping Centers
in Los Angeles, 1965, 1970, 1975, 1975.*

Scale: 1:500,000

WHOLESALE TRADE 1972

17 SMSA's accounting for
93 per cent of wholesale
sales are shown

- Motor Vehicles
- Lumber and other construction materials
- Metals
- Electrical goods
- Machinery
- Groceries
- Farm products
- Petroleum
- Liquor
- All others and amts. too small to show

Santa Rosa $314
Vallejo-Napa $181
Sacramento $2175
Stockton $688
Modesto $329
San Jose $2847
San Francisco-Oakland $17,818
Monterey-Salinas $345
Santa Cruz $100
Fresno $1352
Bakersfield $653
Ventura $549
Los Angeles-Long Beach $32,511
Santa Barbara $303
Riverside-San Bernardino $1604
Anaheim-Santa Ana-Garden Grove $3303
San Diego $2023

Scale: 1:8,000,000

Circles are proportional to
1972 sales value, which is
listed in millions of dollars.
Categories accounting for 5
per cent or more of sales are
shown for SMSA's with sales
of $1 billion or more; cate-
gories accounting for 10 per
cent or more are shown for all
others.

In 1976, California was the top-ranked state in retail sales by a wide margin. Automotive purchases dominated in nearly every part of the state, often constituting more
than 30 per cent of the value of all sales. Sales of general merchandise led only in
suburbs and in some medium-sized cities, while specialty shops came first in the largest
cities. At the county level, service stations, home furnishings and building supplies
accounted for high per capita retail spending in the north, while general merchandise
and apparel were higher in the south. All figures, of course, reflect business conducted
in the city or county rather than purchases made by residents of those areas.

California's wholesale trade ranked second to New York's in 1972. Unlike retail
trade, which was conducted all over the state, wholesale trade was concentrated in
and near the big cities. Los Angeles and the cities of eastern Los Angeles County
formed a contiguous, unrivalled cluster that far outranked the next most important
centers of San Francisco and Oakland.

San Diego
National City

Scale: 1:1,000,000

WHOLESALE TRADE, 1972

5000
2000
350

Sales in millions
of dollars, 1972

Source:
Bureau of the Census, *1972 Census of Wholesale
Trade: Area Statistics,* 1974

Burbank
S. Pasadena
Glendale
Pasadena
Arcadia
West Hollywood
Beverly Hills
Culver City
Los Angeles
El Monte
S. El Monte
E. Los Angeles
Pomona
Santa Monica
Whittier
Inglewood
Commerce
La Mirada
El Segundo
Hawthorne
Buena Park
Gardena
Bell
Fullerton
Corona
Torrance
Compton
Cerritos
Anaheim
Carson
Signal Hill
Orange
Garden Grove
Santa Ana
Long Beach
Huntington Beach

1. Alhambra
2. Rosemead
3. Pico Rivera
4. Santa Fe Spgs.
5. Huntington Park
6. Montebello
7. Downey
8. Paramount

Scale: 1:1,000,000

San Rafael
Richmond
Walnut Creek
Berkeley
San Francisco
Oakland
San Leandro
South San Francisco
Hayward
Millbrae
Burlingame
Union City
San Mateo
Fremont
San Carlos
Menlo Park
Palo Alto
Mountain View
Sunnyvale
Santa Clara
San Jose

Scale: 1:1,000,000

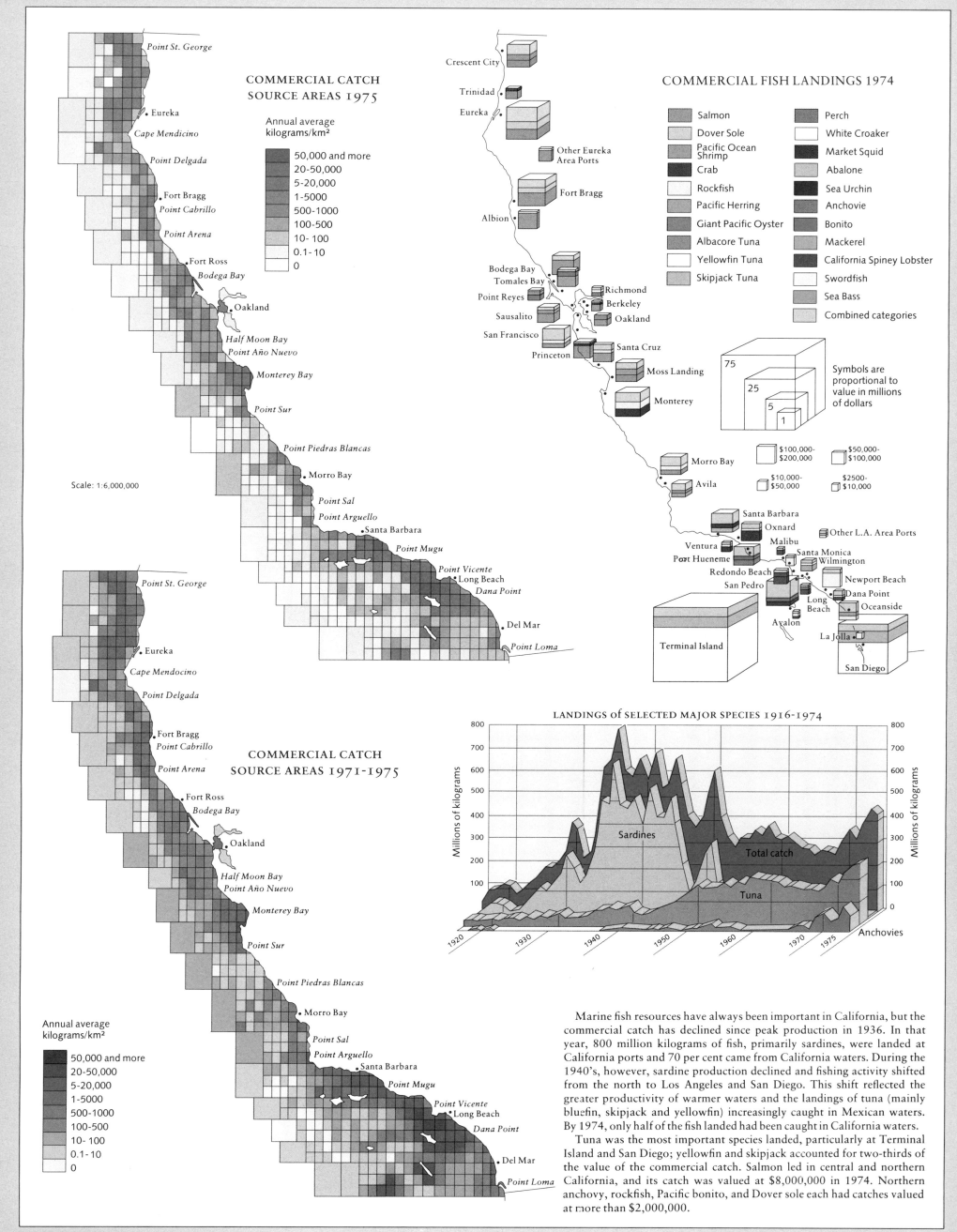

COMMERCIAL CATCH SOURCE AREAS 1975

Annual average kilograms/km²

50,000 and more
20-50,000
5-20,000
1-5000
500-1000
100-500
10-100
0.1-10
0

Scale: 1:6,000,000

COMMERCIAL FISH LANDINGS 1974

Salmon
Dover Sole
Pacific Ocean Shrimp
Crab
Rockfish
Pacific Herring
Giant Pacific Oyster
Albacore Tuna
Yellowfin Tuna
Skipjack Tuna
Perch
White Croaker
Market Squid
Abalone
Sea Urchin
Anchovie
Bonito
Mackerel
California Spiney Lobster
Swordfish
Sea Bass
Combined categories

Symbols are proportional to value in millions of dollars

$100,000-$200,000
$50,000-$100,000
$10,000-$50,000
$2500-$10,000

COMMERCIAL CATCH SOURCE AREAS 1971-1975

Annual average kilograms/km²

50,000 and more
20-50,000
5-20,000
1-5000
500-1000
100-500
10-100
0.1-10
0

LANDINGS of SELECTED MAJOR SPECIES 1916-1974

Sardines
Total catch
Tuna
Anchovies

Marine fish resources have always been important in California, but the commercial catch has declined since peak production in 1936. In that year, 800 million kilograms of fish, primarily sardines, were landed at California ports and 70 per cent came from California waters. During the 1940's, however, sardine production declined and fishing activity shifted from the north to Los Angeles and San Diego. This shift reflected the greater productivity of warmer waters and the landings of tuna (mainly bluefin, skipjack and yellowfin) increasingly caught in Mexican waters. By 1974, only half of the fish landed had been caught in California waters.

Tuna was the most important species landed, particularly at Terminal Island and San Diego; yellowfin and skipjack accounted for two-thirds of the value of the commercial catch. Salmon led in central and northern California, and its catch was valued at $8,000,000 in 1974. Northern anchovy, rockfish, Pacific bonito, and Dover sole each had catches valued at more than $2,000,000.

COMMERCIAL FISHERIES

LUMBER and PLYWOOD MILLS, 1976

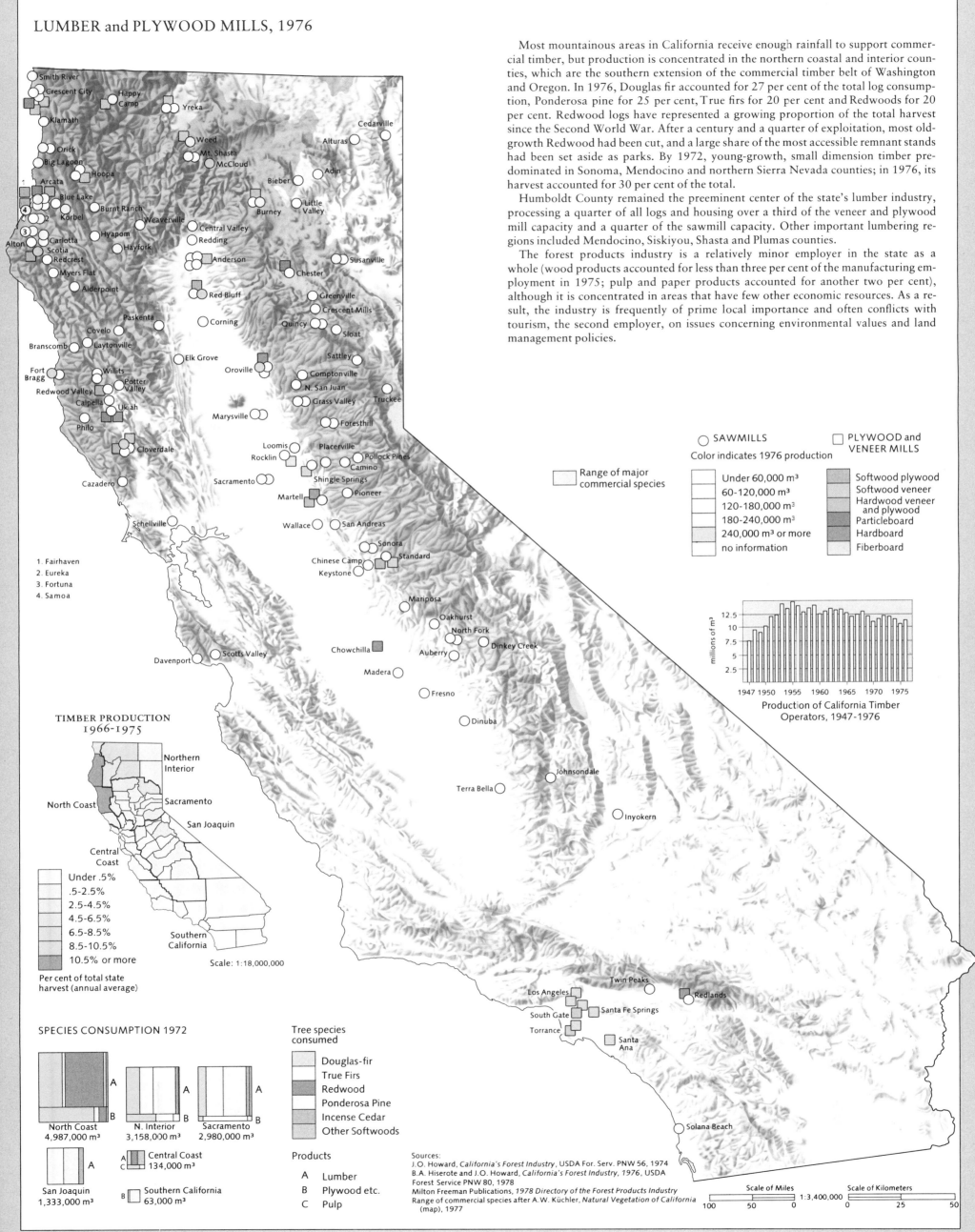

Most mountainous areas in California receive enough rainfall to support commercial timber, but production is concentrated in the northern coastal and interior counties, which are the southern extension of the commercial timber belt of Washington and Oregon. In 1976, Douglas fir accounted for 27 per cent of the total log consumption, Ponderosa pine for 25 per cent, True firs for 20 per cent and Redwoods for 20 per cent. Redwood logs have represented a growing proportion of the total harvest since the Second World War. After a century and a quarter of exploitation, most old-growth Redwood had been cut, and a large share of the most accessible remnant stands had been set aside as parks. By 1972, young-growth, small dimension timber predominated in Sonoma, Mendocino and northern Sierra Nevada counties; in 1976, its harvest accounted for 30 per cent of the total.

Humboldt County remained the preeminent center of the state's lumber industry, processing a quarter of all logs and housing over a third of the veneer and plywood mill capacity and a quarter of the sawmill capacity. Other important lumbering regions included Mendocino, Siskiyou, Shasta and Plumas counties.

The forest products industry is a relatively minor employer in the state as a whole (wood products accounted for less than three per cent of the manufacturing employment in 1975; pulp and paper products accounted for another two per cent), although it is concentrated in areas that have few other economic resources. As a result, the industry is frequently of prime local importance and often conflicts with tourism, the second employer, on issues concerning environmental values and land management policies.

1. Fairhaven
2. Eureka
3. Fortuna
4. Samoa

○ SAWMILLS
Color indicates 1976 production

□ PLYWOOD and VENEER MILLS

Under 60,000 m³
60-120,000 m³
120-180,000 m³
180-240,000 m³
240,000 m³ or more
no information

Softwood plywood
Softwood veneer
Hardwood veneer and plywood
Particleboard
Hardboard
Fiberboard

□ Range of major commercial species

Production of California Timber Operators, 1947-1976

TIMBER PRODUCTION 1966-1975

Northern Interior
North Coast
Sacramento
Central Coast
San Joaquin
Southern California

Under .5%
.5-2.5%
2.5-4.5%
4.5-6.5%
6.5-8.5%
8.5-10.5%
10.5% or more

Per cent of total state harvest (annual average)

Scale: 1:18,000,000

SPECIES CONSUMPTION 1972

North Coast 4,987,000 m³
N. Interior 3,158,000 m³
Sacramento 2,980,000 m³
Central Coast 134,000 m³
San Joaquin 1,333,000 m³
Southern California 63,000 m³

Tree species consumed
Douglas-fir
True Firs
Redwood
Ponderosa Pine
Incense Cedar
Other Softwoods

Products
A Lumber
B Plywood etc.
C Pulp

Sources:
J.O. Howard, *California's Forest Industry*, USDA For. Serv. PNW 56, 1974
B.A. Hiserote and J.O. Howard, *California's Forest Industry, 1976*, USDA Forest Service PNW 80, 1978
Milton Freeman Publications, *1978 Directory of the Forest Products Industry*
Range of commercial species after A.W. Küchler, *Natural Vegetation of California* (map), 1977

Scale of Miles   Scale of Kilometers
100   50   0   1:3,400,000   0   25   50

FOREST PRODUCTS

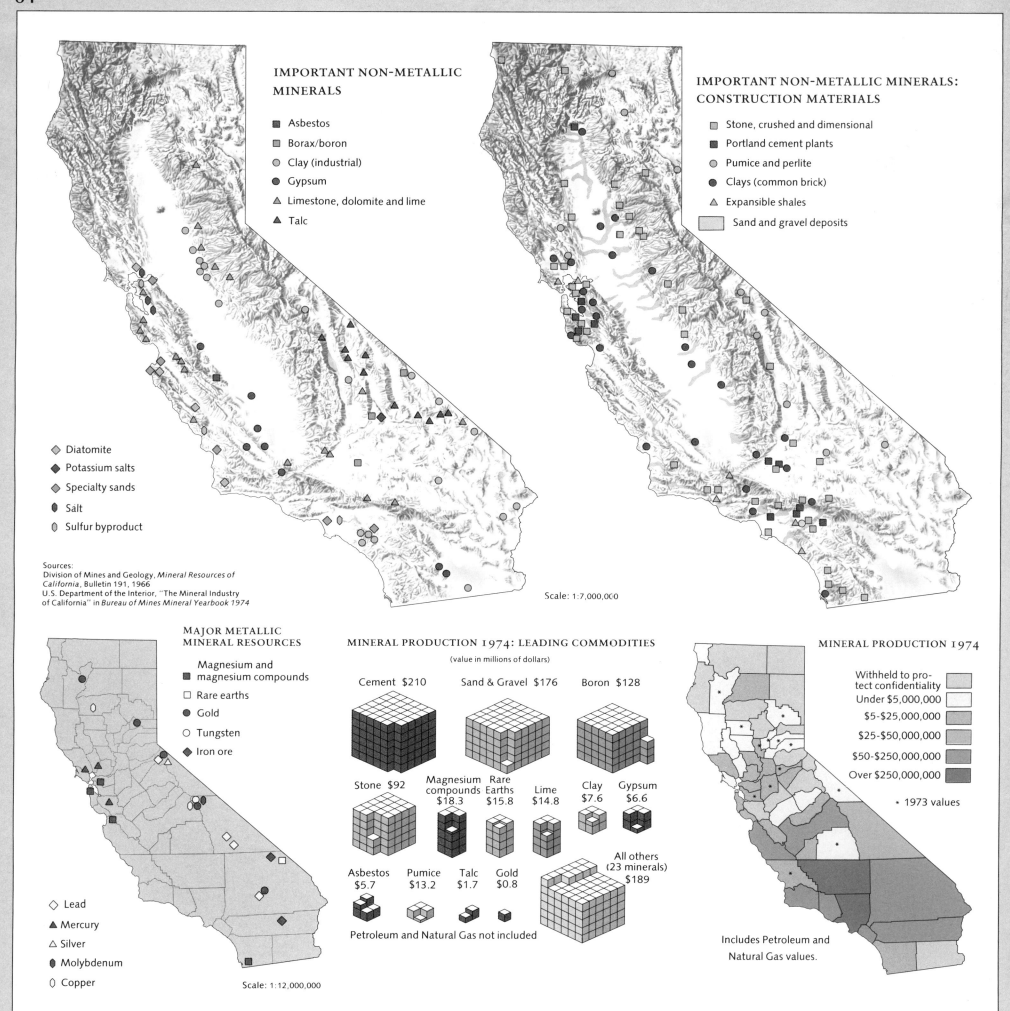

IMPORTANT NON-METALLIC
MINERALS

- ■ Asbestos
- ▫ Borax/boron
- ○ Clay (industrial)
- ● Gypsum
- ▲ Limestone, dolomite and lime
- ▲ Talc

- ◇ Diatomite
- ◆ Potassium salts
- ◇ Specialty sands
- Salt
- Sulfur byproduct

Sources:
Division of Mines and Geology, *Mineral Resources of California*, Bulletin 191, 1966
U.S. Department of the Interior, "The Mineral Industry of California" in *Bureau of Mines Mineral Yearbook 1974*

IMPORTANT NON-METALLIC MINERALS:
CONSTRUCTION MATERIALS

- ▫ Stone, crushed and dimensional
- ■ Portland cement plants
- ○ Pumice and perlite
- ● Clays (common brick)
- ▲ Expansible shales
- ▫ Sand and gravel deposits

Scale: 1:7,000,000

MAJOR METALLIC
MINERAL RESOURCES

- ■ Magnesium and magnesium compounds
- ▫ Rare earths
- ● Gold
- ○ Tungsten
- ◆ Iron ore

- ◇ Lead
- ▲ Mercury
- △ Silver
- ● Molybdenum
- ○ Copper

Scale: 1:12,000,000

MINERAL PRODUCTION 1974: LEADING COMMODITIES

(value in millions of dollars)

Cement $210   Sand & Gravel $176   Boron $128

Stone $92   Magnesium compounds $18.3   Rare Earths $15.8   Lime $14.8   Clay $7.6   Gypsum $6.6

Asbestos $5.7   Pumice $13.2   Talc $1.7   Gold $0.8   All others (23 minerals) $189

Petroleum and Natural Gas not included

MINERAL PRODUCTION 1974

- Withheld to protect confidentiality
- Under $5,000,000
- $5-$25,000,000
- $25-$50,000,000
- $50-$250,000,000
- Over $250,000,000

* 1973 values

Includes Petroleum and
Natural Gas values.

Precious metals—gold and silver—were the basis of California's mineral industry until the twentieth century, when the mineral fuels—gas and oil—took their place. Aside from fuels, non-metallic commodities, particularly those associated with construction, were the most important minerals in 1974. Portland cement, which draws heavily on limestone deposits, was the leading product by value, followed by sand and gravel. California was the second leading producer of these construction materials in the U.S., and its reserves of aggregate were considered adequate until the end of the century.

Boron compounds were the principal non-metallic resource not destined for construction. Most came from U.S. Borax and Chemical Corporation's Kern County operation and Kerr-McGee's Trona plant in San Bernardino County. California supplied all of the U.S. and most of the western world's requirements for boron and borax, and can probably do so for another 100 years. Stone, the fourth mineral commodity in value, was used principally for structural stone and aggregate. Magnesium compounds, used in the production of refractory brick and cement, were recovered from sea water in Monterey, San Mateo, San Diego and Alameda counties. Other important

non-metallic minerals included clay, gypsum, diatomite, asbestos, pumice, talc, salt, barite and sulfur. California led the U.S. production of both crude and calcined gypsum for plaster, wallboard and soil conditioners.

Iron ore led the list of metallic compounds. Most of the state's production came from the Kaiser mine at Eagle Mountain where immediate reserves totaled more than 100,000,000 metric tons. In 1974, over 3.5 million tons of ore were produced for the Kaiser steelworks at Fontana. The rare earth metals included fifteen elements widely used in industry; almost all of the U.S. output came from the Mountain Pass mine, in San Bernardino County, of the Molybdenum Corporation of America. Tungsten production in the state accounted for more than two-thirds of the U.S. output; almost all of it came from the Pine Creek mine of Union Carbide Corporation in Inyo County.

Remaining metallic minerals were not nearly as important. Molybdenum and mercury production were declining. Gold, silver, copper, lead and zinc were produced almost entirely as by-products of other mining endeavors. Soaring gold prices during the 1970s, however, had reawakened interest in mining this precious metal.

MINING AND MINERALS

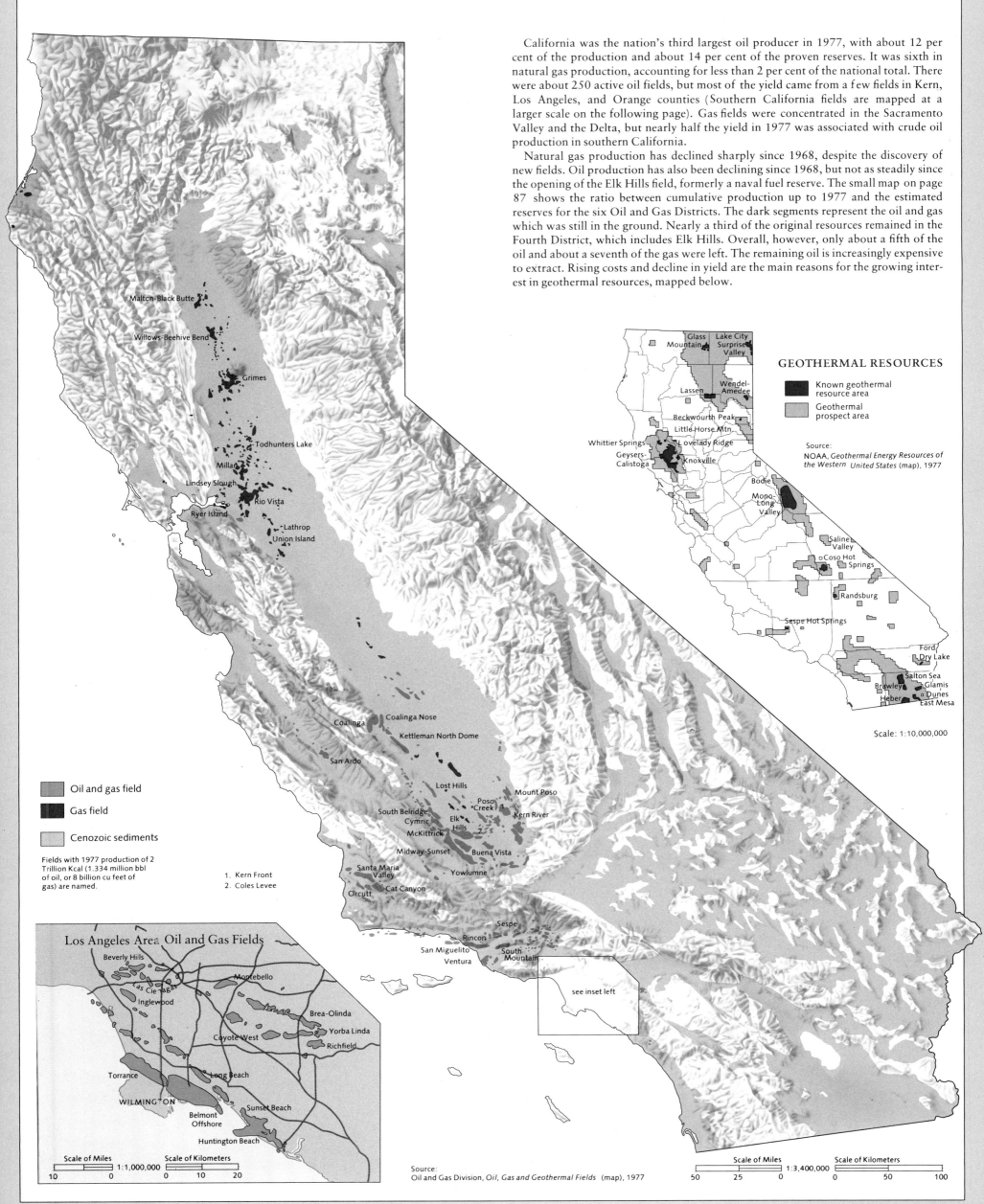

OIL and GAS FIELDS

California was the nation's third largest oil producer in 1977, with about 12 per cent of the production and about 14 per cent of the proven reserves. It was sixth in natural gas production, accounting for less than 2 per cent of the national total. There were about 250 active oil fields, but most of the yield came from a few fields in Kern, Los Angeles, and Orange counties (Southern California fields are mapped at a larger scale on the following page). Gas fields were concentrated in the Sacramento Valley and the Delta, but nearly half the yield in 1977 was associated with crude oil production in southern California.

Natural gas production has declined sharply since 1968, despite the discovery of new fields. Oil production has also been declining since 1968, but not as steadily since the opening of the Elk Hills field, formerly a naval fuel reserve. The small map on page 87 shows the ratio between cumulative production up to 1977 and the estimated reserves for the six Oil and Gas Districts. The dark segments represent the oil and gas which was still in the ground. Nearly a third of the original resources remained in the Fourth District, which includes Elk Hills. Overall, however, only about a fifth of the oil and about a seventh of the gas were left. The remaining oil is increasingly expensive to extract. Rising costs and decline in yield are the main reasons for the growing interest in geothermal resources, mapped below.

GEOTHERMAL RESOURCES

Known geothermal resource area

Geothermal prospect area

Source:
NOAA, *Geothermal Energy Resources of the Western United States* (map), 1977

Scale: 1:10,000,000

Glass Mountain, Lake City, Surprise Valley, Wendel-Amedee, Lassen, Beckwourth Peak, Little Horse Mtn, Whittier Springs, Lovelady Ridge, Geysers-Calistoga, Knoxville, Bodie, Mono-Long Valley, Saline Valley, Coso Hot Springs, Randsburg, Sespe Hot Springs, Ford Dry Lake, Salton Sea, Brawley, Glamis, Dunes, Heber, East Mesa

Oil and gas field

Gas field

Cenozoic sediments

Fields with 1977 production of 2 Trillion Kcal (1.334 million bbl of oil, or 8 billion cu feet of gas) are named.

1. Kern Front
2. Coles Levee

Malton-Black Butte, Willows-Beehive Bend, Grimes, Todhunters Lake, Millar, Lindsey Slough, Rio Vista, Ryer Island, Lathrop, Union Island, Coalinga Nose, Coalinga, Kettleman North Dome, San Ardo, Lost Hills, Mount Poso, South Belridge, Poso Creek, Cymric, Elk Hills, Kern River, McKittrick, Midway-Sunset, Buena Vista, Santa Maria Valley, Yowlumne, Orcutt, Cat Canyon, Sespe, Rincon, San Miguelito, Ventura, South Mountain

see inset left

Los Angeles Area Oil and Gas Fields

Beverly Hills, Montebello, Las Cienegas, Inglewood, Brea-Olinda, Yorba Linda, Coyote West, Richfield, Torrance, Long Beach, WILMINGTON, Sunset Beach, Belmont Offshore, Huntington Beach

Scale of Miles / Scale of Kilometers
1:1,000,000
10 — 0 — 10 — 20

Source:
Oil and Gas Division, *Oil, Gas and Geothermal Fields* (map), 1977

Scale of Miles / Scale of Kilometers
1:3,400,000
50 — 25 — 0 — 50 — 100

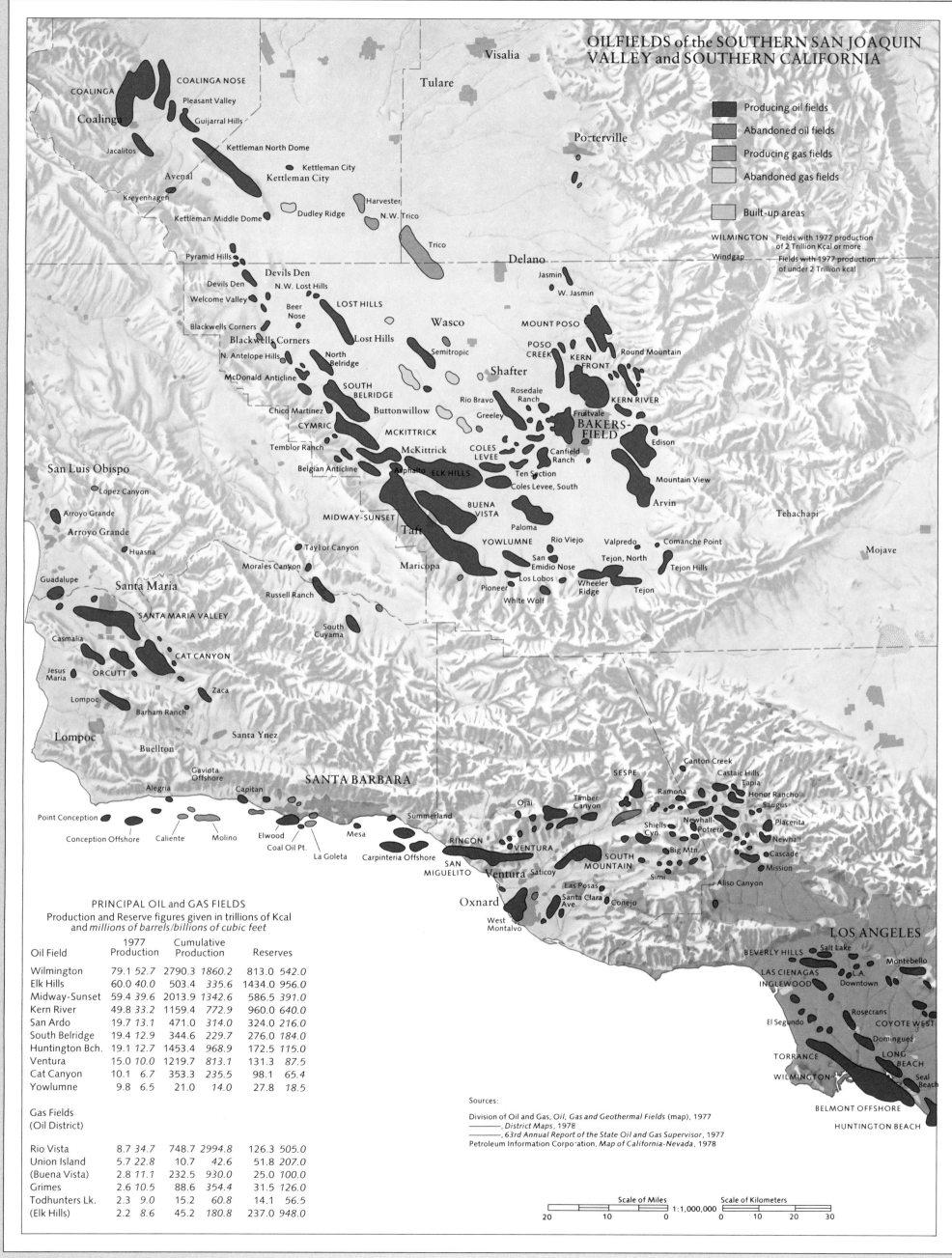

OILFIELDS of the SOUTHERN SAN JOAQUIN VALLEY and SOUTHERN CALIFORNIA

Legend:
- Producing oil fields
- Abandoned oil fields
- Producing gas fields
- Abandoned gas fields
- Built-up areas

WILMINGTON — Fields with 1977 production of 2 Trillion Kcal or more
Windgap — Fields with 1977 production of under 2 Trillion kcal

PRINCIPAL OIL and GAS FIELDS
Production and Reserve figures given in trillions of Kcal
and *millions of barrels/billions of cubic feet*

Oil Field	1977 Production		Cumulative Production		Reserves	
Wilmington	79.1	*52.7*	2790.3	*1860.2*	813.0	*542.0*
Elk Hills	60.0	*40.0*	503.4	*335.6*	1434.0	*956.0*
Midway-Sunset	59.4	*39.6*	2013.9	*1342.6*	586.5	*391.0*
Kern River	49.8	*33.2*	1159.4	*772.9*	960.0	*640.0*
San Ardo	19.7	*13.1*	471.0	*314.0*	324.0	*216.0*
South Belridge	19.4	*12.9*	344.6	*229.7*	276.0	*184.0*
Huntington Bch.	19.1	*12.7*	1453.4	*968.9*	172.5	*115.0*
Ventura	15.0	*10.0*	1219.7	*813.1*	131.3	*87.5*
Cat Canyon	10.1	*6.7*	353.3	*235.5*	98.1	*65.4*
Yowlumne	9.8	*6.5*	21.0	*14.0*	27.8	*18.5*

Gas Fields
(Oil District)

Field	1977 Production		Cumulative Production		Reserves	
Rio Vista	8.7	*34.7*	748.7	*2994.8*	126.3	*505.0*
Union Island	5.7	*22.8*	10.7	*42.6*	51.8	*207.0*
(Buena Vista)	2.8	*11.1*	232.5	*930.0*	25.0	*100.0*
Grimes	2.6	*10.5*	88.6	*354.4*	31.5	*126.0*
Todhunters Lk.	2.3	*9.0*	15.2	*60.8*	14.1	*56.5*
(Elk Hills)	2.2	*8.6*	45.2	*180.8*	237.0	*948.0*

Sources:
Division of Oil and Gas, *Oil, Gas and Geothermal Fields* (map), 1977
————, *District Maps*, 1978
————, *63rd Annual Report of the State Oil and Gas Supervisor*, 1977
Petroleum Information Corporation, *Map of California-Nevada*, 1978

Scale of Miles   Scale of Kilometers
1:1,000,000

SOUTHERN CALIFORNIA OIL FIELDS

87

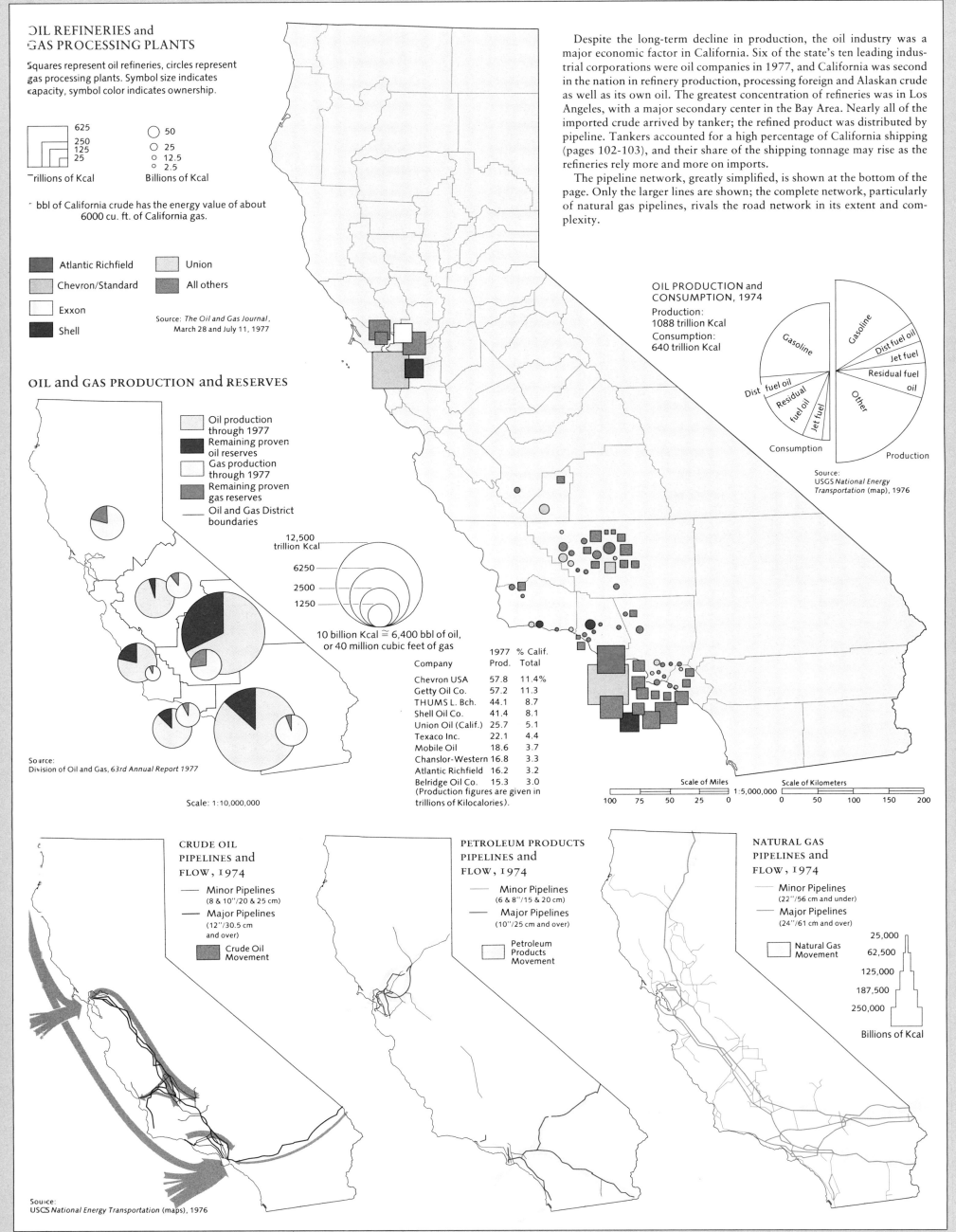

OIL REFINERIES and GAS PROCESSING PLANTS

Squares represent oil refineries, circles represent gas processing plants. Symbol size indicates capacity, symbol color indicates ownership.

625
250
125
25
Trillions of Kcal

50
25
12.5
2.5
Billions of Kcal

1 bbl of California crude has the energy value of about 6000 cu. ft. of California gas.

Atlantic Richfield
Chevron/Standard
Exxon
Shell
Union
All others

Source: *The Oil and Gas Journal,* March 28 and July 11, 1977

OIL and GAS PRODUCTION and RESERVES

Oil production through 1977
Remaining proven oil reserves
Gas production through 1977
Remaining proven gas reserves
Oil and Gas District boundaries

12,500 trillion Kcal
6250
2500
1250

10 billion Kcal ≅ 6,400 bbl of oil, or 40 million cubic feet of gas.

Company	1977 Prod.	% Calif. Total
Chevron USA	57.8	11.4%
Getty Oil Co.	57.2	11.3
THUMS L. Bch.	44.1	8.7
Shell Oil Co.	41.4	8.1
Union Oil (Calif.)	25.7	5.1
Texaco Inc.	22.1	4.4
Mobile Oil	18.6	3.7
Chanslor-Western	16.8	3.3
Atlantic Richfield	16.2	3.2
Belridge Oil Co.	15.3	3.0

(Production figures are given in trillions of Kilocalories).

Source: Division of Oil and Gas, 63rd Annual Report 1977

Scale: 1:10,000,000

Despite the long-term decline in production, the oil industry was a major economic factor in California. Six of the state's ten leading industrial corporations were oil companies in 1977, and California was second in the nation in refinery production, processing foreign and Alaskan crude as well as its own oil. The greatest concentration of refineries was in Los Angeles, with a major secondary center in the Bay Area. Nearly all of the imported crude arrived by tanker; the refined product was distributed by pipeline. Tankers accounted for a high percentage of California shipping (pages 102-103), and their share of the shipping tonnage may rise as the refineries rely more and more on imports.

The pipeline network, greatly simplified, is shown at the bottom of the page. Only the larger lines are shown; the complete network, particularly of natural gas pipelines, rivals the road network in its extent and complexity.

OIL PRODUCTION and CONSUMPTION, 1974

Production: 1088 trillion Kcal
Consumption: 640 trillion Kcal

Source: USGS *National Energy Transportation* (map), 1976

Scale of Miles   Scale of Kilometers
1:5,000,000
100 75 50 25 0   0 50 100 150 200

CRUDE OIL PIPELINES and FLOW, 1974

— Minor Pipelines (8 & 10"/20 & 25 cm)
— Major Pipelines (12"/30.5 cm and over)
Crude Oil Movement

Source: USGS *National Energy Transportation* (maps), 1976

PETROLEUM PRODUCTS PIPELINES and FLOW, 1974

— Minor Pipelines (6 & 8"/15 & 20 cm)
— Major Pipelines (10"/25 cm and over)
Petroleum Products Movement

NATURAL GAS PIPELINES and FLOW, 1974

— Minor Pipelines (22"/56 cm and under)
— Major Pipelines (24"/61 cm and over)
Natural Gas Movement

25,000
62,500
125,000
187,500
250,000
Billions of Kcal

PIPELINES AND REFINERIES

ELECTRICAL POWER PLANTS, 1976

The map at the left shows the plant capacity and ownership of the 250 electric power generating plants operating in California in the mid-1970's. The smaller map indicates the type of power used to generate electricity. Nearly two-thirds of the generating capacity was owned by Pacific Gas and Electric and by Southern California Edison. Most of the remaining operations were run by a variety of public agencies.

About 70 per cent of the power plants were hydroelectric; clustered along the Sacramento, Pit, Feather and American Rivers, with smaller concentrations on the San Joaquin and Kings rivers. Hydroelectric plants accounted for only about a quarter of the installed capacity, and much hydroelectric power was imported from plants on the Colorado and Columbia rivers.

Fossil fuel plants predominated along the coast. They involved only a quarter of all the plants, but nearly 70 per cent of the power capacity. The largest fossil fuel plants, such as Pittsburg or Alamitos, had generating capacities of about 2000 MW; by contrast, the largest hydroelectric plant (Hyatt, on the Feather River) had less than 650 MW of capacity.

Three nuclear plants operating in 1976 accounted for about four per cent of the state's capacity. The addition of the Diablo Canyon plant, which is scheduled to go on line in 1979, will more than double California's nuclear capacity. Geothermal power is produced only at The Geysers, in northeastern Sonoma County, and accounted for less than two per cent of the state total.

PLANT OWNERSHIP and CAPACITY

- Pacific Gas and Electric
- San Diego Gas and Electric
- Southern California Edison
- Other private utilities:
  California Pacific
  Pacific Power and Light
  Sierra Pacific
- U.S. Bureau of Reclamation
- Calif. Dept. of Water Resources
- Los Angeles Dept. of Water and Power
- Sacramento Municipal Utility Dist.
- San Francisco Water and Power Bureau
- Other publicly owned utilities dist.

Symbol size is proportional to installed capacity in megawatts; symbol color indicates ownership.

2000 / 1000 / 250 / 10

Installed capacity of under 10 megawatts

Sources:
State Energy Commission, *California Energy Trends and Choices, Vol. 7: Power Plant Siting*, 1977, Biennial Report of the State Energy Commission
U.S. Dept. of Energy, *Interconnected Transmission Systems* (map), E742-208-11, 1978
Bureau of Reclamation, *Lower Colorado Region Interconnected Power Systems* (map), 743-300-4, 1977

POWER SOURCE

- Hydroelectric
- Fossil Fuel
- Nuclear
- Geothermal

Scale: 1:8,000,000

Source:
State Energy Commission, *California Energy Trends and Choices, Vol. I: Plant Siting*, 1977, Report of the State Energy Commission

Scale: 1:3,400,000

POWER GENERATION

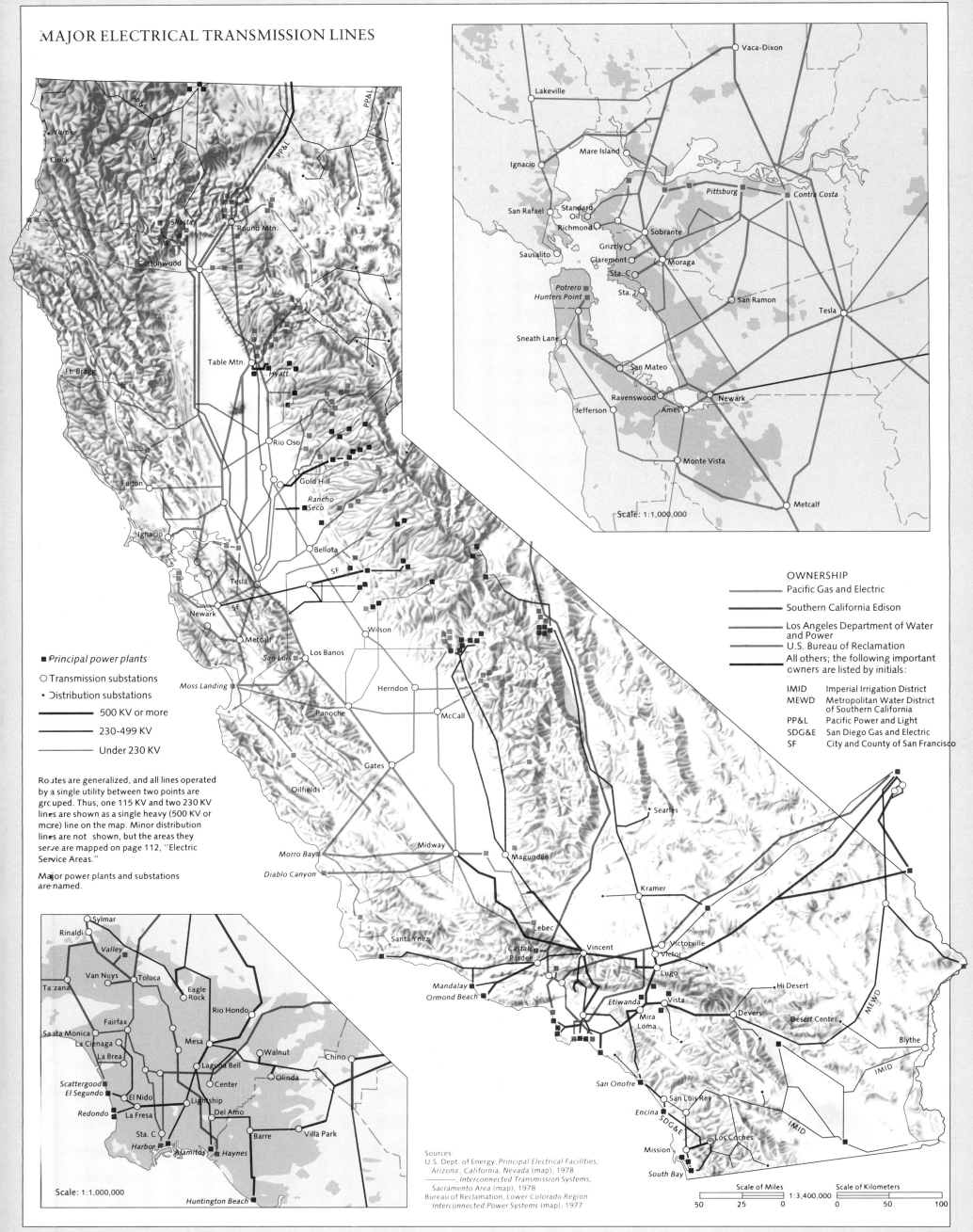

MAJOR ELECTRICAL TRANSMISSION LINES

Scale: 1:1,000,000

■ Principal power plants
○ Transmission substations
· Distribution substations

_____ 500 KV or more
_____ 230-499 KV
_____ Under 230 KV

Routes are generalized, and all lines operated by a single utility between two points are grouped. Thus, one 115 KV and two 230 KV lines are shown as a single heavy (500 KV or more) line on the map. Minor distribution lines are not shown, but the areas they serve are mapped on page 112, "Electric Service Areas."

Major power plants and substations are named.

OWNERSHIP
_____ Pacific Gas and Electric
_____ Southern California Edison
_____ Los Angeles Department of Water and Power
_____ U.S. Bureau of Reclamation
_____ All others; the following important owners are listed by initials:

IMID   Imperial Irrigation District
MEWD   Metropolitan Water District of Southern California
PP&L   Pacific Power and Light
SDG&E   San Diego Gas and Electric
SF   City and County of San Francisco

Scale: 1:1,000,000

Sources:
U.S. Dept. of Energy, *Principal Electrical Facilities, Arizona, California, Nevada* (map), 1978
_____, *Interconnected Transmission Systems, Sacramento Area* (map), 1978
Bureau of Reclamation, *Lower Colorado Region Interconnected Power Systems* (map), 1977

Scale of Miles   Scale of Kilometers
50 25   1:3,400,000   0   50   100

POWER TRANSMISSION

STATE and NATIONAL PARKS, RECREATION AREAS, and WILDERNESS AREAS

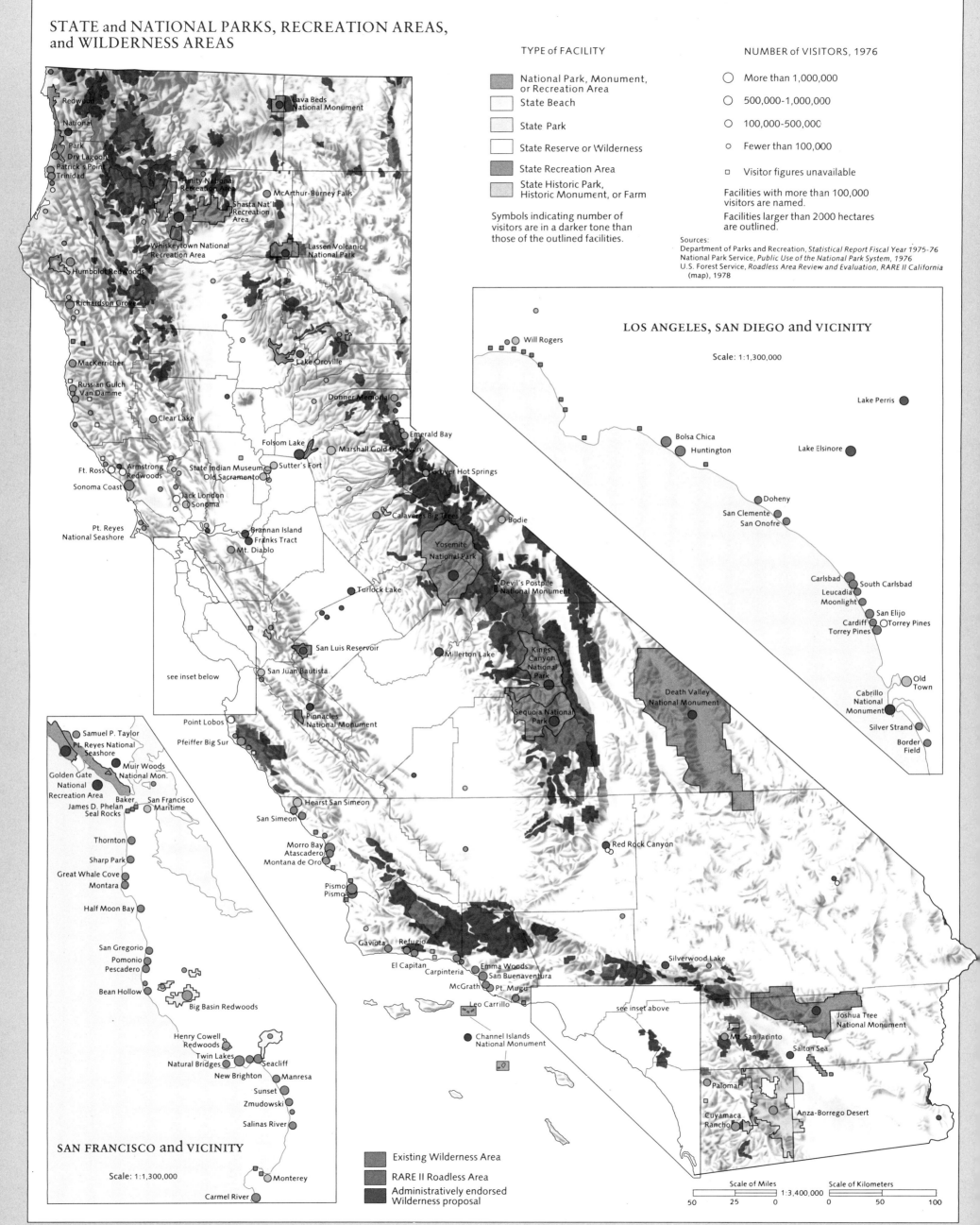

TYPE of FACILITY

- National Park, Monument, or Recreation Area
- State Beach
- State Park
- State Reserve or Wilderness
- State Recreation Area
- State Historic Park, Historic Monument, or Farm

Symbols indicating number of visitors are in a darker tone than those of the outlined facilities.

NUMBER of VISITORS, 1976

- ◯ More than 1,000,000
- ◯ 500,000-1,000,000
- ◯ 100,000-500,000
- ◦ Fewer than 100,000
- ▫ Visitor figures unavailable

Facilities with more than 100,000 visitors are named.

Facilities larger than 2000 hectares are outlined.

Sources:
Department of Parks and Recreation, *Statistical Report Fiscal Year 1975-76*
National Park Service, *Public Use of the National Park System*, 1976
U.S. Forest Service, *Roadless Area Review and Evaluation, RARE II California* (map), 1978

LOS ANGELES, SAN DIEGO and VICINITY

Scale: 1:1,300,000

Will Rogers
Lake Perris
Bolsa Chica
Huntington
Lake Elsinore
Doheny
San Clemente
San Onofre
Carlsbad
South Carlsbad
Leucadia
Moonlight
San Elijo
Cardiff
Torrey Pines
Torrey Pines
Old Town
Cabrillo National Monument
Silver Strand
Border Field
Death Valley National Monument

Redwood National Park
Dry Lagoon
Patrick's Point
Trinidad
Lava Beds National Monument
Trinity National Recreation Area
McArthur-Burney Falls
Shasta Nat'l Recreation Area
Whiskeytown National Recreation Area
Lassen Volcanic National Park
Humboldt Redwoods
Richardson Grove
MacKerricher
Russian Gulch
Van Damme
Clear Lake
Lake Oroville
Donner Memorial
Emerald Bay
Folsom Lake
Marshall Gold Discovery
Ft. Ross
Armstrong Redwoods
State Indian Museum
Old Sacramento
Sutter's Fort
Grover Hot Springs
Sonoma Coast
Jack London
Sonoma
Calaveras Big Trees
Bodie
Pt. Reyes National Seashore
Brannan Island
Franks Tract
Mt. Diablo
Yosemite National Park
Turlock Lake
Devil's Postpile National Monument
San Luis Reservoir
Millerton Lake
Kings Canyon National Park
San Juan Bautista
see inset below
Point Lobos
Pinnacles National Monument
Sequoia National Park
Red Rock Canyon
Pfeiffer Big Sur

Samuel P. Taylor
Pt. Reyes National Seashore
Muir Woods National Mon.
Golden Gate National Recreation Area
Baker
James D. Phelan
Seal Rocks
San Francisco Maritime
Thornton
Sharp Park
Great Whale Cove
Montara
Half Moon Bay
San Gregorio
Pomonio
Pescadero
Bean Hollow
Big Basin Redwoods
Henry Cowell Redwoods
Twin Lakes
Natural Bridges
New Brighton
Seacliff
Manresa
Sunset
Zmudowski
Salinas River

Hearst San Simeon
San Simeon
Morro Bay
Atascadero
Montana de Oro
Pismo
Pismo
Gaviota
Refugio
El Capitan
Carpinteria
Emma Woods
San Buenaventura
McGrath
Pt. Mugu
Leo Carrillo
Silverwood Lake
Channel Islands National Monument
see inset above
Joshua Tree National Monument
Mt. San Jacinto
Salton Sea
Paloma
Cuyamaca Rancho
Anza-Borrego Desert

SAN FRANCISCO and VICINITY

Scale: 1:1,300,000

Monterey
Carmel River

- Existing Wilderness Area
- RARE II Roadless Area
- Administratively endorsed Wilderness proposal

Scale of Miles
50   25   0

1:3,400,000

Scale of Kilometers
0   50   100

PARKS AND WILDERNESS AREAS

RATED LODGING PLACES, 1977

AMERICAN AUTOMOBILE CLUB RATING

- Very comfortable
○ Exceptional
□ Renowned

TYPE of FACILITY

Motel, motor inn
Hotel, motor hotel
Lodge, resort complex

see inset

Scale: 1:1,600,000

Scale: 1:1,600,000

see inset

Scale: 1:8,000,000

MAJOR TOURIST ATTRACTIONS, 1978

Pioneer, mining, and railroad attractions
Amusement parks and tourist facilities
Tourist towns
Natural features
Animal reserves, marinelands, parks

INDUSTRIAL and WINERY TOURS

TYPE of INDUSTRY

- Food and flowers
· Lumber, dams, boats, cars, trailers, tools, newspapers, oil, crafts
· Winery

Scale: 1:15,000,000

Underseas Gardens
Trees of Mystery
Pygmy Forest
Sutter's Fort
Lake Tahoe
Petrified Forest
Old Sacramento
Nut Tree
Hidden Treasure Gold Mine
Locke
Railtown 1897
Marriott's Great America
Pioneer Village
Yosemite Mt.-Sugar Pine RR
Winchester Mystery House
Old Town
Scotty's Castle
Roaring Camp & Big Trees RR
Santa's Village
Monterey
Carmel
17-Mile Drive
Alabama Hills
Big Sur
Calico Ghost Town
Solvang
Santa's Village
Palm Springs
Santa Catalina Island
San Diego Wild Animal Park
Balboa Park
Sea World

National and State Parks, museums and missions are not included

ATTRACTIONS in the BAY AREA and LOS ANGELES

SAN FRANCISCO AREA
○ Fisherman's Wharf
○ Ghirardelli Square
○ Jack London Square
○ Children's Fairyland
○ Chinatown
● Sausalito
○ Marine World (Redwood City)
○ Golden Gate Park
LOS ANGELES AREA
○ Olvera Street
○ Disneyland
○ Queen Mary
○ Knott's Berry Farm
○ Movieland of the Air
○ Magic Mountain
○ Ports of Call Village
● Hollywood
○ Descanso Gardens
○ La Brea Tar Pits
○ Lion Country Safari
○ Marineland Palos Verdes
○ Busch Bird Sanctuary and Gardens
○ California Alligator Park

Source: American Automobile Association, *Tourbook, California-Nevada*, 1978

Advertised splendors are often a mere lure, but California was so overwhelmingly endowed with scenery and climate that it has been difficult to exaggerate its beauties. Fortunately, much of the scenery, except along the coast, had remained in public hands, so that the ten national parks and the nearly 200 state facilities, shown on the opposite page, were California's major recreational resource in 1978, enhanced by the immense campground provided by state and national forests. Man-made attractions were nearly as spectacular. San Francisco's city and setting, Monterey's historic buildings, Hollywood and Disneyland, San Diego County's Wild Animal Park, and the Spanish missions were merely evocative of an enormous list of tourist meccas. All of the maps on this page are a reflection of the distribution of these natural and man-made attractions.

HOTELS, MOTELS, TOURIST COURTS, and CAMPS

NUMBER of ESTABLISHMENTS 1972

RECEIPTS per capita 1972

Over $230
$170-$230
$120-$170
$80-$120
$50-$80
$30-$50
$20-$30
Under $20

Number of Establishments
Over 350
200-350
125-200
75-125
50-75
25-50
15-25
Under 15

Scale: 1:12,000,000

Scale: 1:15,000,000

AMUSEMENT and RECREATION SERVICES

NUMBER of ESTABLISHMENTS 1972

RECEIPTS per capita 1972

Over $80
$70-$80
$60-$70
$50-$60
$40-$50
$30-$40
$20-$30
Under $20

Number of Establishments
Over 1200
750-1200
500-750
250-500
100-250
50-100
25-50
Under 25

Source: *Census of Selected Service Industries*, 1972

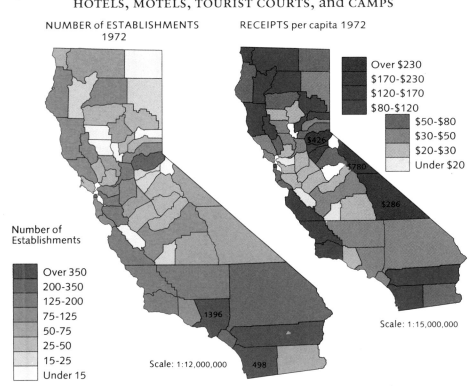
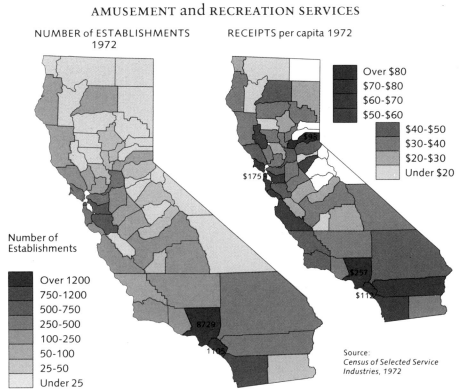
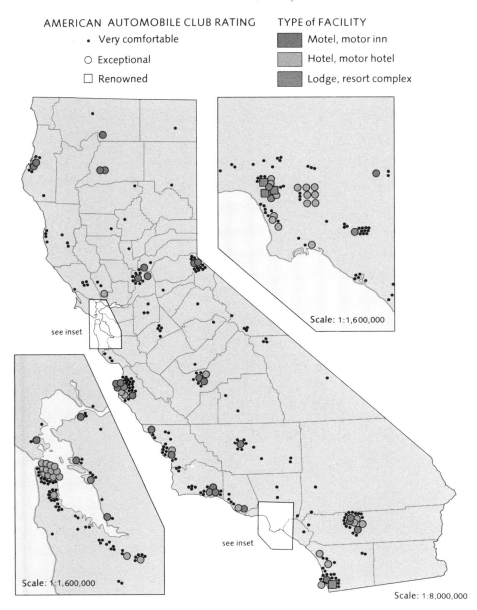

TOURISM AND RECREATION

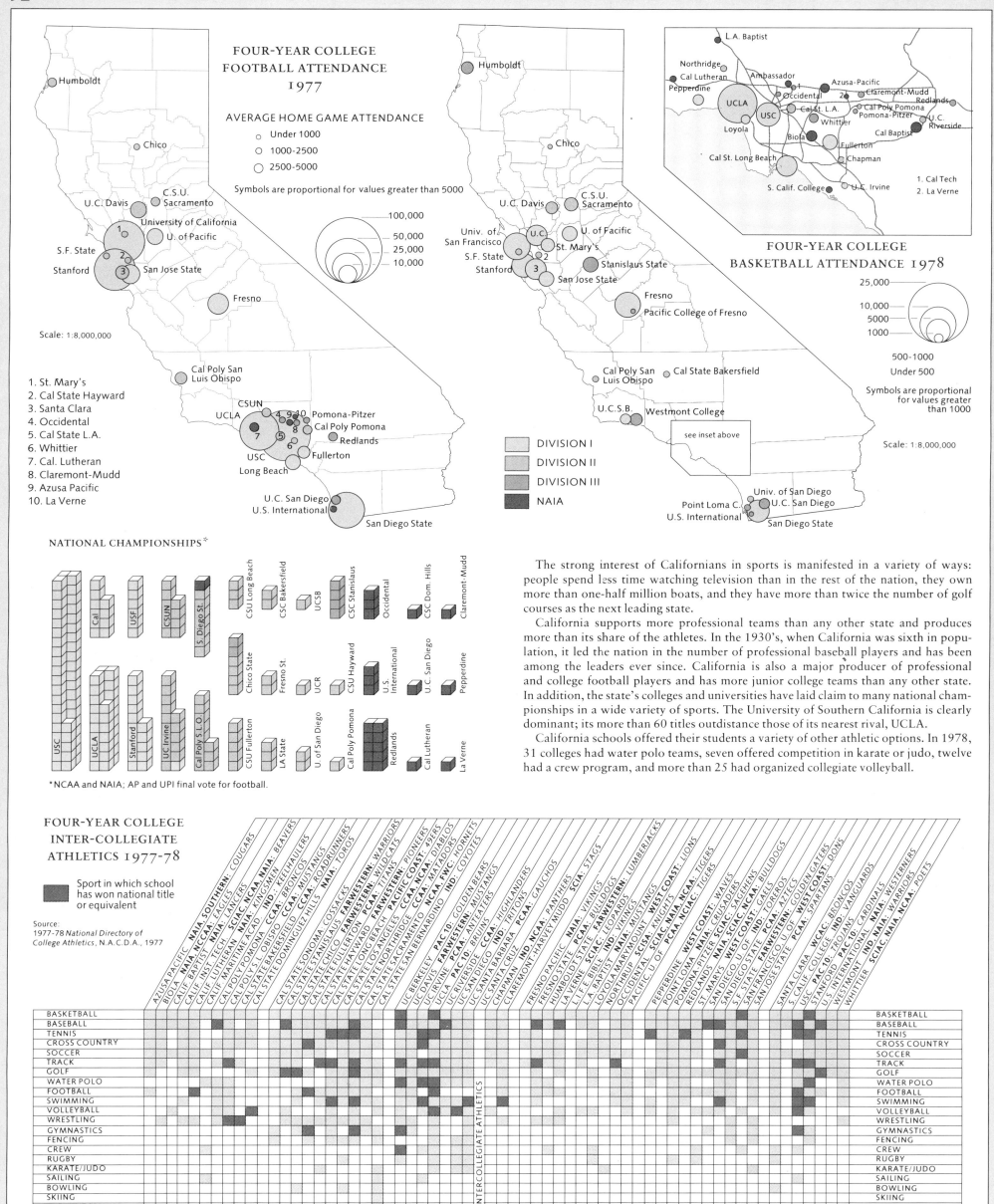

The strong interest of Californians in sports is manifested in a variety of ways: people spend less time watching television than in the rest of the nation, they own more than one-half million boats, and they have more than twice the number of golf courses as the next leading state.

California supports more professional teams than any other state and produces more than its share of the athletes. In the 1930's, when California was sixth in population, it led the nation in the number of professional baseball players and has been among the leaders ever since. California is also a major producer of professional and college football players and has more junior college teams than any other state. In addition, the state's colleges and universities have laid claim to many national championships in a wide variety of sports. The University of Southern California is clearly dominant; its more than 60 titles outdistance those of its nearest rival, UCLA.

California schools offered their students a variety of other athletic options. In 1978, 31 colleges had water polo teams, seven offered competition in karate or judo, twelve had a crew program, and more than 25 had organized collegiate volleyball.

COLLEGE ATHLETICS

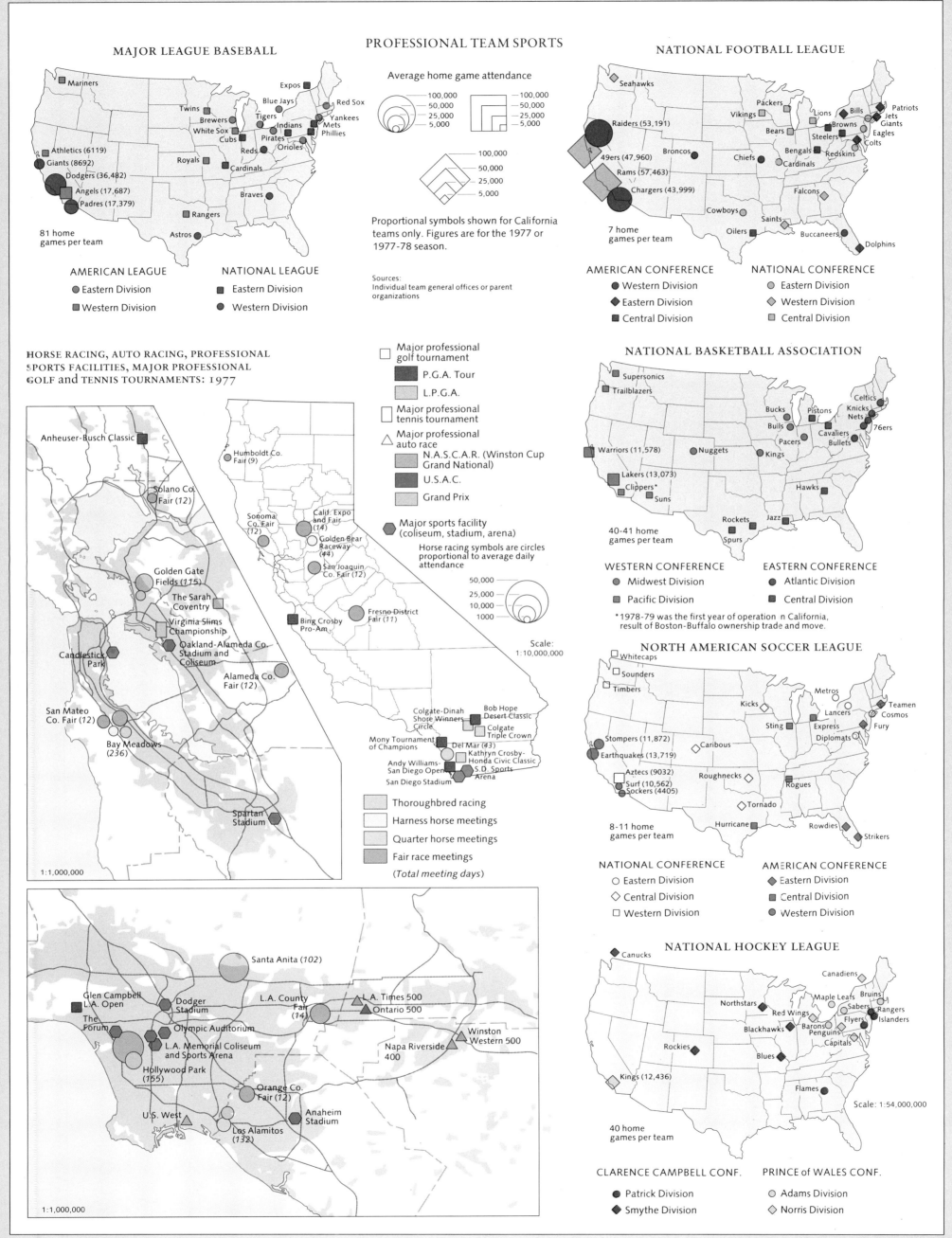

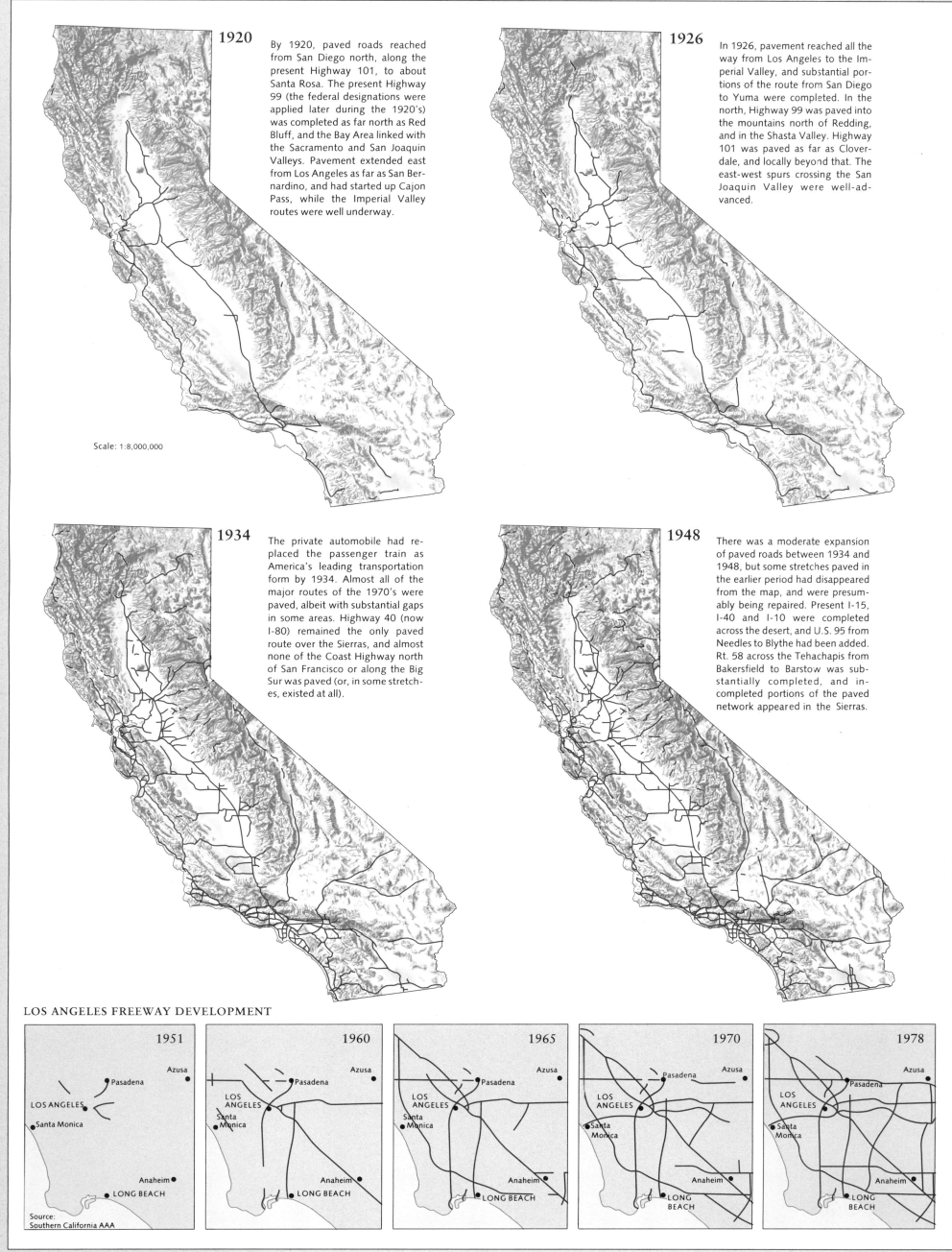

1920

By 1920, paved roads reached from San Diego north, along the present Highway 101, to about Santa Rosa. The present Highway 99 (the federal designations were applied later during the 1920's) was completed as far north as Red Bluff, and the Bay Area linked with the Sacramento and San Joaquin Valleys. Pavement extended east from Los Angeles as far as San Bernardino, and had started up Cajon Pass, while the Imperial Valley routes were well underway.

Scale: 1:8,000,000

1926

In 1926, pavement reached all the way from Los Angeles to the Imperial Valley, and substantial portions of the route from San Diego to Yuma were completed. In the north, Highway 99 was paved into the mountains north of Redding, and in the Shasta Valley. Highway 101 was paved as far as Cloverdale, and locally beyond that. The east-west spurs crossing the San Joaquin Valley were well-advanced.

1934

The private automobile had replaced the passenger train as America's leading transportation form by 1934. Almost all of the major routes of the 1970's were paved, albeit with substantial gaps in some areas. Highway 40 (now I-80) remained the only paved route over the Sierras, and almost none of the Coast Highway north of San Francisco or along the Big Sur was paved (or, in some stretches, existed at all).

1948

There was a moderate expansion of paved roads between 1934 and 1948, but some stretches paved in the earlier period had disappeared from the map, and were presumably being repaired. Present I-15, I-40 and I-10 were completed across the desert, and U.S. 95 from Needles to Blythe had been added. Rt. 58 across the Tehachapis from Bakersfield to Barstow was substantially completed, and incompleted portions of the paved network appeared in the Sierras.

LOS ANGELES FREEWAY DEVELOPMENT

1951 — Azusa, Pasadena, LOS ANGELES, Santa Monica, Anaheim, LONG BEACH
Source: Southern California AAA

1960 — Azusa, Pasadena, LOS ANGELES, Santa Monica, Anaheim, LONG BEACH

1965 — Azusa, Pasadena, LOS ANGELES, Santa Monica, Anaheim, LONG BEACH

1970 — Azusa, Pasadena, LOS ANGELES, Santa Monica, Anaheim, LONG BEACH

1978 — Azusa, Pasadena, LOS ANGELES, Santa Monica, Anaheim, LONG BEACH

HIGHWAY DEVELOPMENT: 1920-1948

The major change between the highway networks of 1958 and 1978 is the addition of Interstate 5 down the west side of the San Joaquin Valley. I-5 represents a qualitative change in the highway system: it is the first route which applies on a state scale the freeway principle, well established on a more local scale, of connecting distant important centers without regard for intervening smaller ones. At the end of the 1970's, I-5 remained incomplete between Tracy and Sacramento, but it was an important link between the Bay Area and Los Angeles. (Traffic volumes on all principal routes are shown on page 97). In addition, few unpaved segments remained anywhere in the state highway system; the gravel road had been relegated to minor routes, particularly in recreation areas. Over the Coast Range, only the Mendocino Pass route was still substantially unpaved. Incomplete stretches into the Sierras will probably remain dead-end routes, blocked by formidable mountains and increased interest in wilderness preservation.

Nearly half a million Californians were employed, in 1975, in industries directly related to the automobile. The indirect impact of the car on finance and insurance, police and government, to say nothing of the medical and legal systems, is harder to measure.

The highway network which grew with the ownership of private cars is mapped on pages 94 through 98. California's highways are arranged in roughly parallel routes, extending the length of the state and crossed by five major transcontinental east-west routes. The Central Valley route, shared by US 99 and I-5 was the most heavily travelled long-distance route in the state. The bulk of the traffic in the coastal counties followed the series of coastal and inland valleys pioneered by Portola in 1769 and later occupied by US 101. The coast highway (California 1) and US 395 were minor arteries by comparison. The most important east-west routes are I-80 and US 50, which cross the Sierra Nevada over Donner Pass and Echo Summit respectively, and the three desert routes (I-40, I-15 and I-10) leading east from the Los Angeles Basin.

1978

STATE
HIGHWAYS

Heavier lines represent four-lane roads on the 1958 map, freeways on the 1978 map.

1958

Most of the gaps in the 1948 network had been filled by 1958. Additional trans-Sierra routes were completely paved, as was much of the Coast Highway. Expansion in the northeastern and southwestern corners of the state was striking. (Rt. 20 through Clear Lake remained the most northerly fully paved route across the Coast Range, however). A four-lane network, echoing the original paved road system of 1920, included nearly all of Highway 99 as far north as Sacramento. The four-lane system was well-developed in the Los Angeles basin, extending east to Palm Springs. The freeway network, mapped on the facing page, was developing rapidly: by 1960, the Ventura, Hollywood, Santa Ana, Long Beach, and San Bernardino freeways were completed, and the Harbor freeway almost finished.

Scale of Miles
1:5,000,000
100 75 50 25 0

Scale of Kilometers
0 50 100 150 200

Source:
Department of Transportation/Highway Department, *California State Highways* (maps), for the years shown

HIGHWAY DEVELOPMENT: 1958-1978

PRINCIPAL HIGHWAY ROUTES and PASSES

HIGHWAY PROFILES

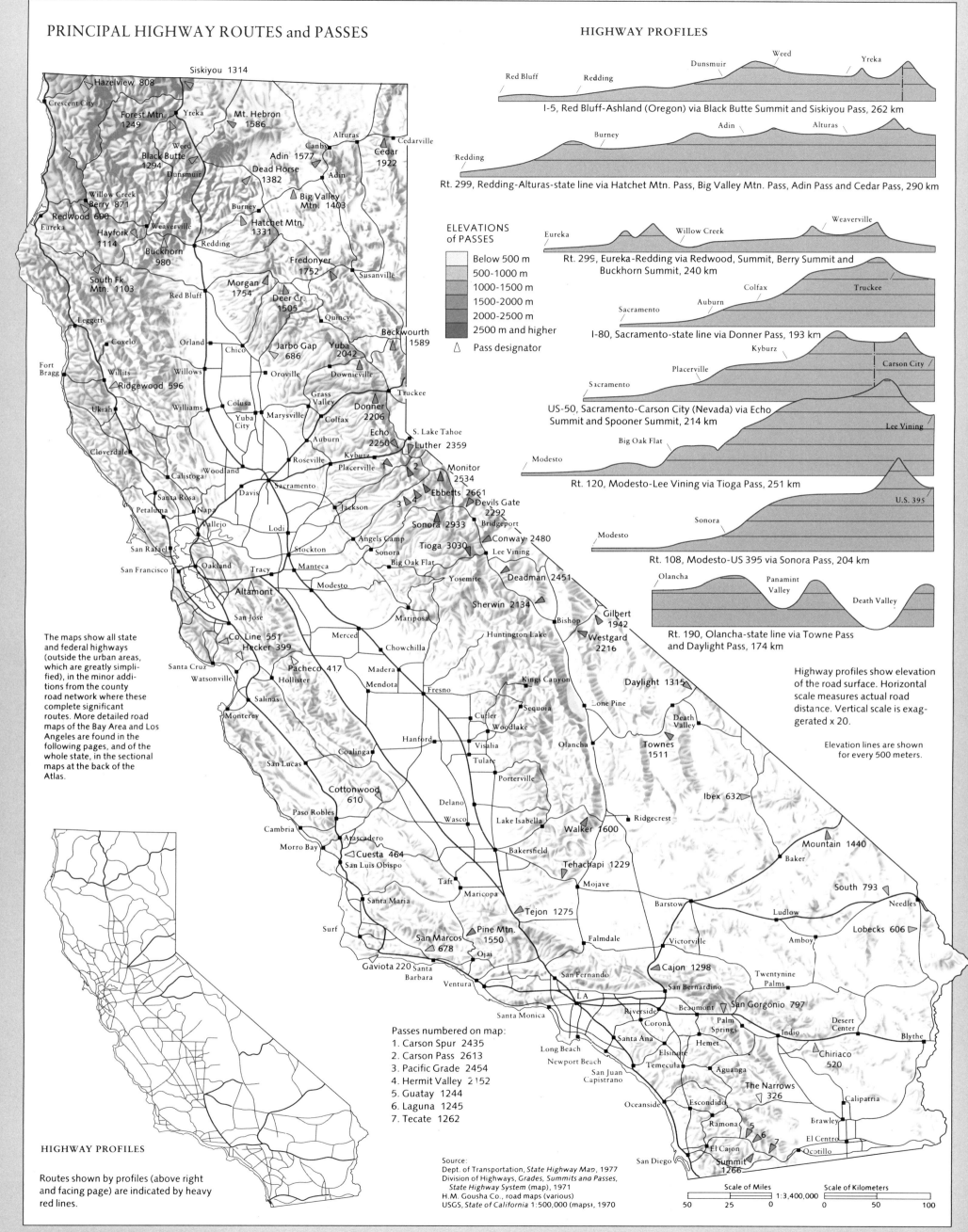

ELEVATIONS of PASSES

- Below 500 m
- 500-1000 m
- 1000-1500 m
- 1500-2000 m
- 2000-2500 m
- 2500 m and higher
- △ Pass designator

I-5, Red Bluff-Ashland (Oregon) via Black Butte Summit and Siskiyou Pass, 262 km

Rt. 299, Redding-Alturas-state line via Hatchet Mtn. Pass, Big Valley Mtn. Pass, Adin Pass and Cedar Pass, 290 km

Rt. 299, Eureka-Redding via Redwood, Summit, Berry Summit and Buckhorn Summit, 240 km

I-80, Sacramento-state line via Donner Pass, 193 km

US-50, Sacramento-Carson City (Nevada) via Echo Summit and Spooner Summit, 214 km

Rt. 120, Modesto-Lee Vining via Tioga Pass, 251 km

Rt. 108, Modesto-US 395 via Sonora Pass, 204 km

Rt. 190, Olancha-state line via Towne Pass and Daylight Pass, 174 km

Highway profiles show elevation of the road surface. Horizontal scale measures actual road distance. Vertical scale is exaggerated x 20.

Elevation lines are shown for every 500 meters.

The maps show all state and federal highways (outside the urban areas, which are greatly simplified), in the minor additions from the county road network where these complete significant routes. More detailed road maps of the Bay Area and Los Angeles are found in the following pages, and of the whole state, in the sectional maps at the back of the Atlas.

Passes numbered on map:
1. Carson Spur 2435
2. Carson Pass 2613
3. Pacific Grade 2454
4. Hermit Valley 2152
5. Guatay 1244
6. Laguna 1245
7. Tecate 1262

Source:
Dept. of Transportation, *State Highway Map*, 1977
Division of Highways, *Grades, Summits and Passes, State Highway System* (map), 1971
H.M. Gousha Co., road maps (various)
USGS, *State of California* 1:500,000 (maps), 1970

Scale of Miles   1:3,400,000   Scale of Kilometers

HIGHWAY PROFILES

Routes shown by profiles (above right and facing page) are indicated by heavy red lines.

ROUTES AND PASSES

AVERAGE DAILY TRAFFIC FLOW, 1974

California's road network reflected its physiography. In the northern two-thirds of the state, a system of north-south arterials followed the Central Valley and a series of coastal valleys. A fairly dense network of east-west highways crossed the north-south system within the Valley, but only the most important routes crossed the Coast Range or the Cascade-Sierra. This lattice merged in the south with a nearly radial network centered on Los Angeles. This southern network was shaped both by the trend of the mountains and by the absence of large settlements in the desert interior.

Of the north-south arterials, US 99 remained the most heavily travelled, at least in the San Joaquin Valley, despite the diversion of traffic onto I-5 along the western edge of the Valley. US 101, following the historic Mexican route through coastal valleys and along coastal terraces, handled an enormous volume of traffic between San Diego, Los Angeles and Santa Barbara, and in the Bay Area. Elsewhere it was less important than US 99, except for local commuter traffic. Extremely rugged terrain and distance to major urban centers made both California 1, along the coast, and US 395, east of the Sierra, more important as scenic attractions and recreational routes than as commercial arterials.

I-80, from San Francisco to Reno over Donner Pass (and ultimately to Chicago through the Wyoming Basin) was the most heavily travelled route across the state, followed by I-15 from Los Angeles and San Bernardino to Las Vegas and points east. Both routes carried an enormous volume of weekend recreational travel in addition to their more ordinary transcontinental commerce. US 50, across Echo Summit, was a much steeper route, but it carried many pleasure seekers to South Lake Tahoe and Carson City.

Source:
Dept. of Transportation, *California 1974 Average Daily Traffic on the State Highway System* (map), undated

HIGHWAY FATALITIES 1976

Transportation Districts are identified by roman numerals. Fractions indicate fatalities on the state highway system. The numerator indicates the number of people killed, the denominator gives the fatality rate, expressed as the number killed per 100 million vehicle kilometers driven. Fatality rate is also indicated by color.

Under 1
1-1.9
2-2.9
3 or more

Deaths/100 million km

Scale: 1:15,000,000

Source:
Dept. of Transportation, *1976 Accident Data on California State Highways*, 1977

2500 or less
5000
10,000
20,000
40,000
60,000
80,000
100,000

Vehicles per day (both directions)

Numbers in circles show traffic volume at busiest interchanges within cities

Rt. 58, Bakersfield-Mojave via Tehachapi Pass, 105 km

Rt. 178, Bakersfield-Rt. 14 via Walker Pass, 163 km

I-5, Bakersfield-Los Angeles via Tejon Pass, 182 km

I-8, San Diego-El Centro via Guatay, Laguna, Summit and Tecate Passes, 177 km

I-15, San Bernardino-Baker-state line via Cajon Pass and Mountain Pass, 290 km

I-10, Los Angeles-Indio-Blythe via San Gorgonio Pass and Chiriaco Summit, 365 km

Scale of Miles
Scale of Kilometers
1:3,400,000

TRAFFIC FLOW

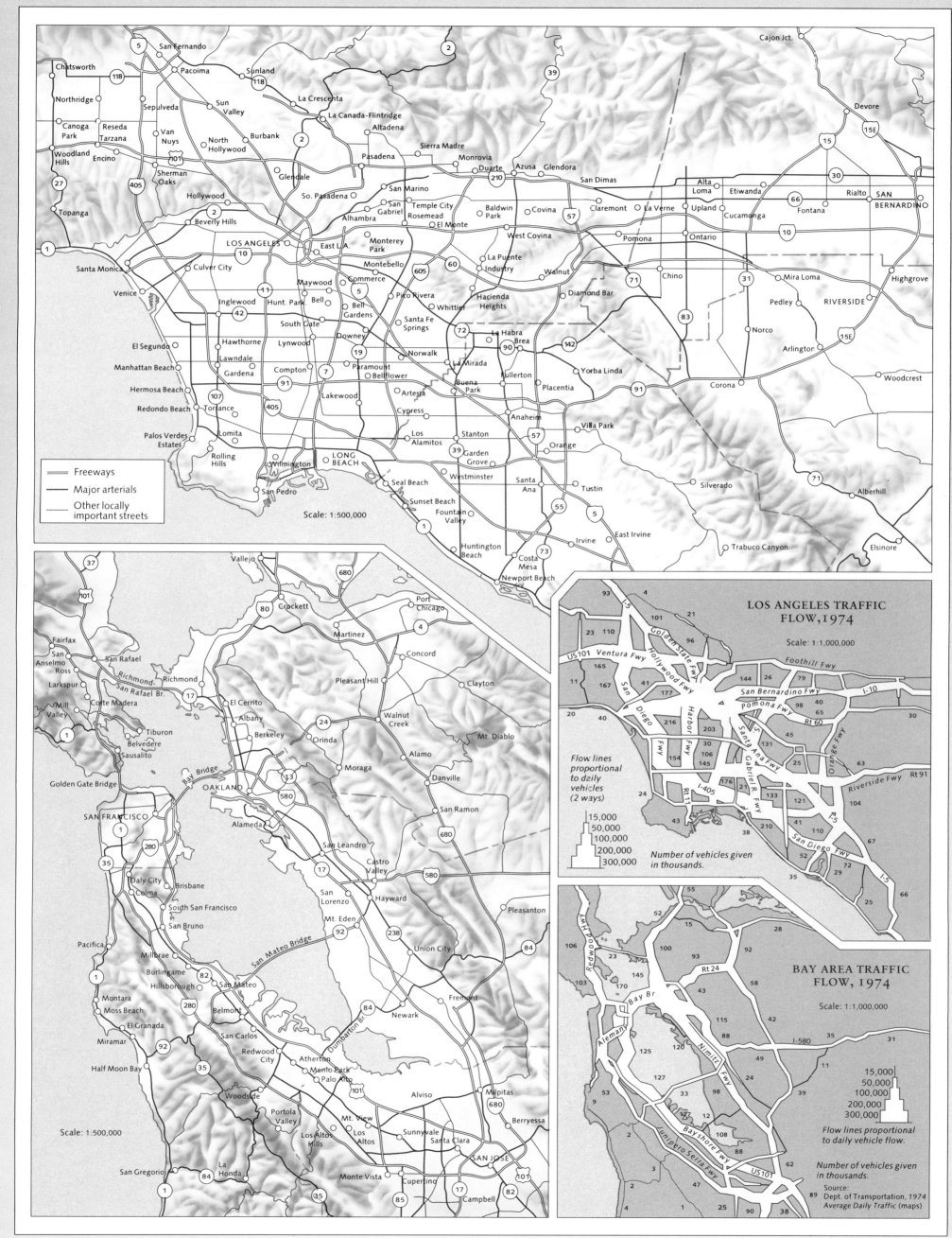

BAY AREA AND LOS ANGELES HIGHWAYS

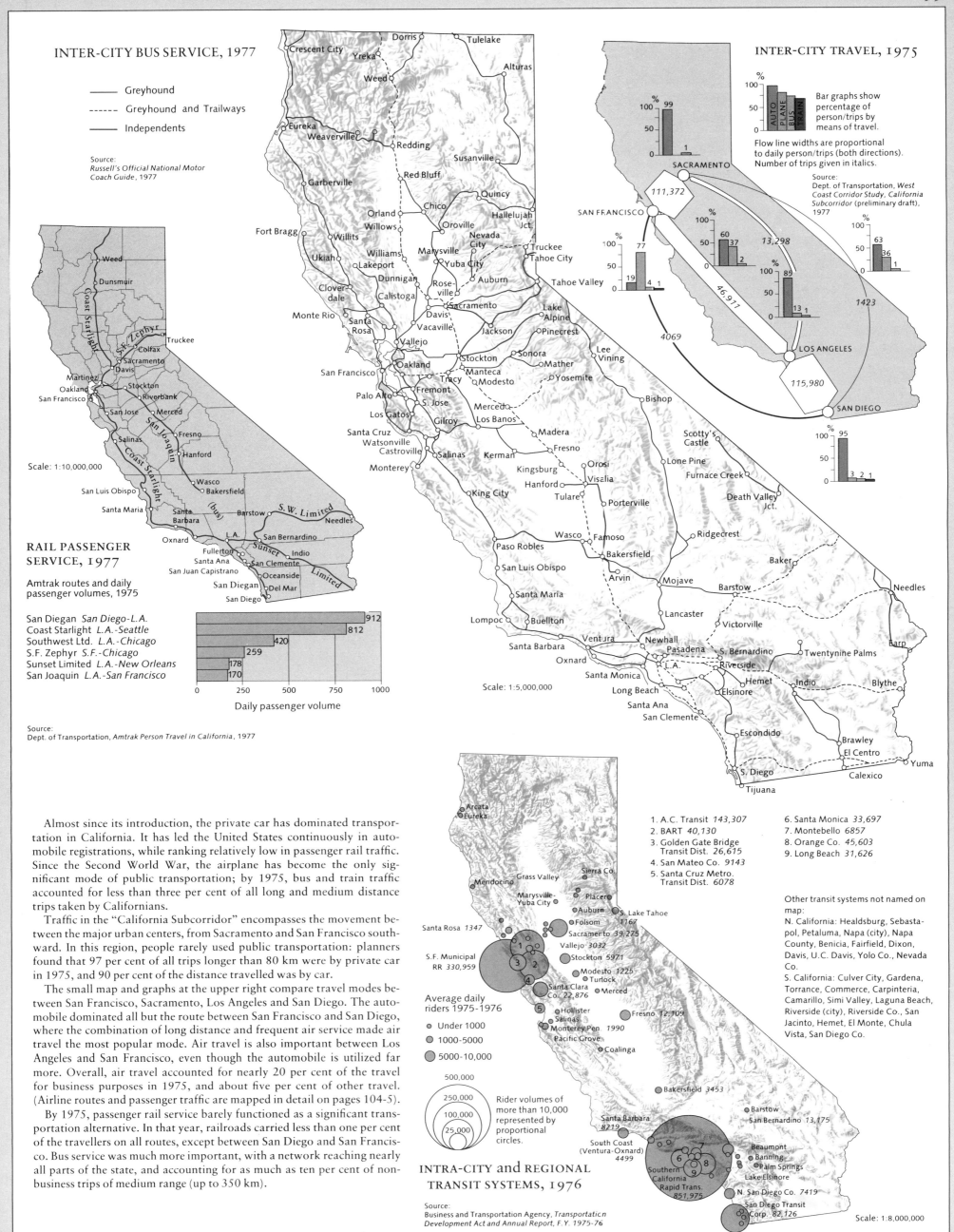

INTER-CITY BUS SERVICE, 1977

——— Greyhound

------ Greyhound and Trailways

——— Independents

Source:
Russell's Official National Motor Coach Guide, 1977

RAIL PASSENGER SERVICE, 1977

Amtrak routes and daily passenger volumes, 1975

Scale: 1:10,000,000

San Diegan *San Diego-L.A.*		912
Coast Starlight *L.A.-Seattle*		812
Southwest Ltd. *L.A.-Chicago*	420	
S.F. Zephyr *S.F.-Chicago*	259	
Sunset Limited *L.A.-New Orleans*	178	
San Joaquin *L.A.-San Francisco*	170	

0   250   500   750   1000

Daily passenger volume

Source:
Dept. of Transportation, *Amtrak Person Travel in California*, 1977

INTER-CITY TRAVEL, 1975

Bar graphs show percentage of person/trips by means of travel.

Flow line widths are proportional to daily person/trips (both directions). Number of trips given in italics.

Source:
Dept. of Transportation, *West Coast Corridor Study, California Subcorridor* (preliminary draft), 1977

111,372
13,298
46,971
4069
1423
115,980

SACRAMENTO

SAN FRANCISCO

LOS ANGELES

SAN DIEGO

AUTO PLANE BUS TRAIN

Scale: 1:5,000,000

Almost since its introduction, the private car has dominated transportation in California. It has led the United States continuously in automobile registrations, while ranking relatively low in passenger rail traffic. Since the Second World War, the airplane has become the only significant mode of public transportation; by 1975, bus and train traffic accounted for less than three per cent of all long and medium distance trips taken by Californians.

Traffic in the "California Subcorridor" encompasses the movement between the major urban centers, from Sacramento and San Francisco southward. In this region, people rarely used public transportation: planners found that 97 per cent of all trips longer than 80 km were by private car in 1975, and 90 per cent of the distance travelled was by car.

The small map and graphs at the upper right compare travel modes between San Francisco, Sacramento, Los Angeles and San Diego. The automobile dominated all but the route between San Francisco and San Diego, where the combination of long distance and frequent air service made air travel the most popular mode. Air travel is also important between Los Angeles and San Francisco, even though the automobile is utilized far more. Overall, air travel accounted for nearly 20 per cent of the travel for business purposes in 1975, and about five per cent of other travel. (Airline routes and passenger traffic are mapped in detail on pages 104-5).

By 1975, passenger rail service barely functioned as a significant transportation alternative. In that year, railroads carried less than one per cent of the travellers on all routes, except between San Diego and San Francisco. Bus service was much more important, with a network reaching nearly all parts of the state, and accounting for as much as ten per cent of non-business trips of medium range (up to 350 km).

1. A.C. Transit *143,307*
2. BART *40,130*
3. Golden Gate Bridge Transit Dist. *26,615*
4. San Mateo Co. *9143*
5. Santa Cruz Metro. Transit Dist. *6078*
6. Santa Monica *33,697*
7. Montebello *6857*
8. Orange Co. *45,603*
9. Long Beach *31,626*

Other transit systems not named on map:
N. California: Healdsburg, Sebastapol, Petaluma, Napa (city), Napa County, Benicia, Fairfield, Dixon, Davis, U.C. Davis, Yolo Co., Nevada Co.
S. California: Culver City, Gardena, Torrance, Commerce, Carpinteria, Camarillo, Simi Valley, Laguna Beach, Riverside (city), Riverside Co., San Jacinto, Hemet, El Monte, Chula Vista, San Diego Co.

Average daily riders 1975-1976
● Under 1000
● 1000-5000
● 5000-10,000

Rider volumes of more than 10,000 represented by proportional circles.

S.F. Municipal RR *330,959*
Santa Rosa *1347*
Vallejo *3032*
Stockton *5971*
Sacramento *39,275*
Modesto *1225*
Santa Clara Co. *22,876*
Monterey Pen. *1990*
Fresno *12,709*
Bakersfield *3453*
Barstow
San Bernardino *13,175*
Santa Barbara *8219*
South Coast (Ventura-Oxnard) *4499*
Southern California Rapid Trans. *851,975*
N. San Diego Co. *7419*
San Diego Transit Corp. *82,126*

INTRA-CITY and REGIONAL TRANSIT SYSTEMS, 1976

Source:
Business and Transportation Agency, *Transportation Development Act and Annual Report, F.Y. 1975-76*

Scale: 1:8,000,000

MASS TRANSIT

RAILROAD LINES OPERATING in 1977

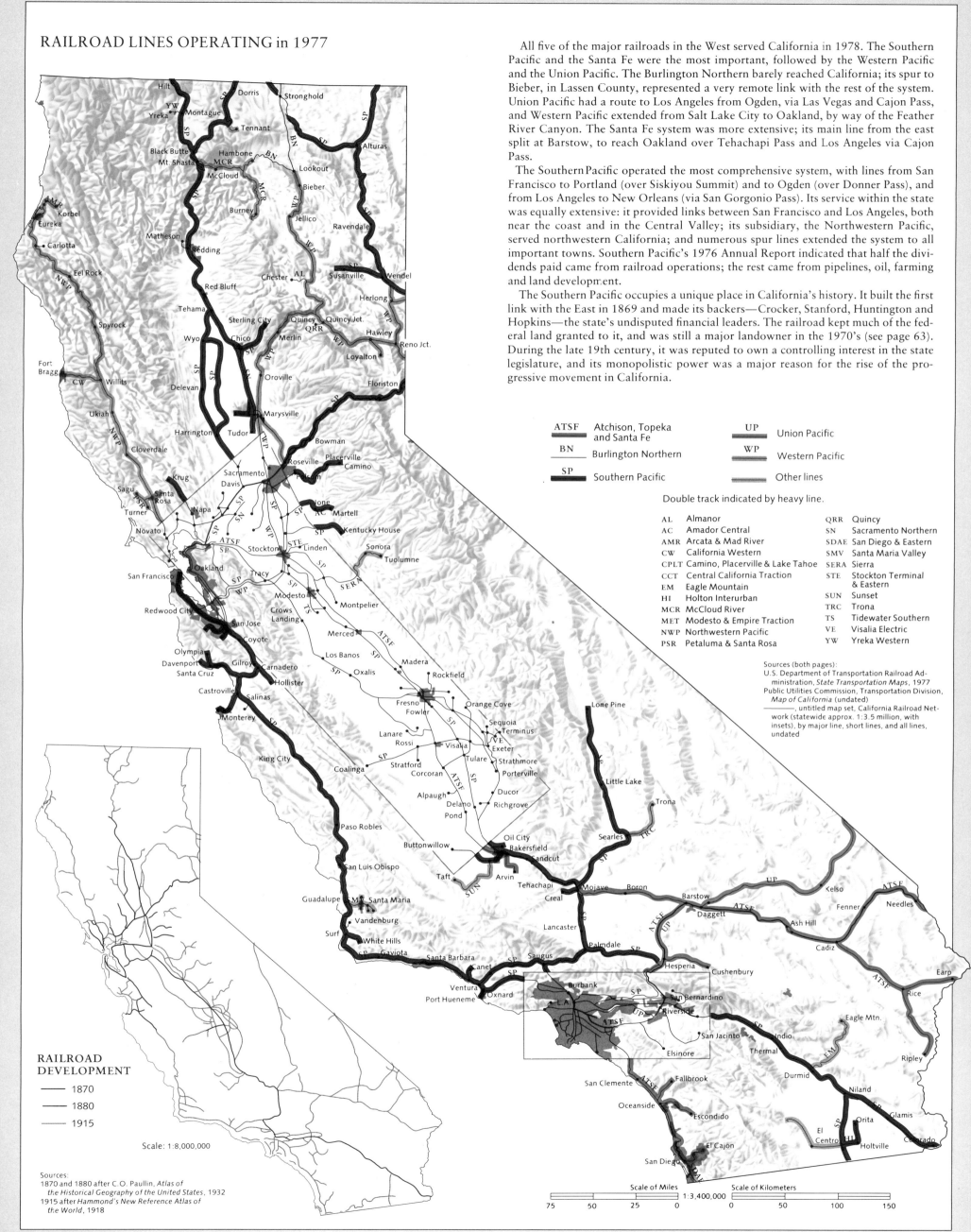

All five of the major railroads in the West served California in 1978. The Southern Pacific and the Santa Fe were the most important, followed by the Western Pacific and the Union Pacific. The Burlington Northern barely reached California; its spur to Bieber, in Lassen County, represented a very remote link with the rest of the system. Union Pacific had a route to Los Angeles from Ogden, via Las Vegas and Cajon Pass, and Western Pacific extended from Salt Lake City to Oakland, by way of the Feather River Canyon. The Santa Fe system was more extensive; its main line from the east split at Barstow, to reach Oakland over Tehachapi Pass and Los Angeles via Cajon Pass.

The Southern Pacific operated the most comprehensive system, with lines from San Francisco to Portland (over Siskiyou Summit) and to Ogden (over Donner Pass), and from Los Angeles to New Orleans (via San Gorgonio Pass). Its service within the state was equally extensive: it provided links between San Francisco and Los Angeles, both near the coast and in the Central Valley; its subsidiary, the Northwestern Pacific, served northwestern California; and numerous spur lines extended the system to all important towns. Southern Pacific's 1976 Annual Report indicated that half the dividends paid came from railroad operations; the rest came from pipelines, oil, farming and land development.

The Southern Pacific occupies a unique place in California's history. It built the first link with the East in 1869 and made its backers—Crocker, Stanford, Huntington and Hopkins—the state's undisputed financial leaders. The railroad kept much of the federal land granted to it, and was still a major landowner in the 1970's (see page 63). During the late 19th century, it was reputed to own a controlling interest in the state legislature, and its monopolistic power was a major reason for the rise of the progressive movement in California.

ATSF	Atchison, Topeka and Santa Fe	UP	Union Pacific
BN	Burlington Northern	WP	Western Pacific
SP	Southern Pacific		Other lines

Double track indicated by heavy line.

AL	Almanor	QRR	Quincy
AC	Amador Central	SN	Sacramento Northern
AMR	Arcata & Mad River	SDAE	San Diego & Eastern
CW	California Western	SMV	Santa Maria Valley
CPLT	Camino, Placerville & Lake Tahoe	SERA	Sierra
CCT	Central California Traction	STE	Stockton Terminal & Eastern
EM	Eagle Mountain	SUN	Sunset
HI	Holton Interurban	TRC	Trona
MCR	McCloud River	TS	Tidewater Southern
MET	Modesto & Empire Traction	VE	Visalia Electric
NWP	Northwestern Pacific	YW	Yreka Western
PSR	Petaluma & Santa Rosa		

Sources (both pages):
U.S. Department of Transportation Railroad Administration, *State Transportation Maps*, 1977
Public Utilities Commission, Transportation Division, *Map of California* (undated)
———, untitled map set, California Railroad Network (statewide approx. 1:3.5 million, with insets), by major line, short lines, and all lines, undated

RAILROAD DEVELOPMENT

——	1870
——	1880
——	1915

Scale: 1:8,000,000

Sources:
1870 and 1880 after C.O. Paullin, *Atlas of the Historical Geography of the United States*, 1932
1915 after *Hammond's New Reference Atlas of the World*, 1918

1:3,400,000

Scale of Miles   Scale of Kilometers

RAILROADS

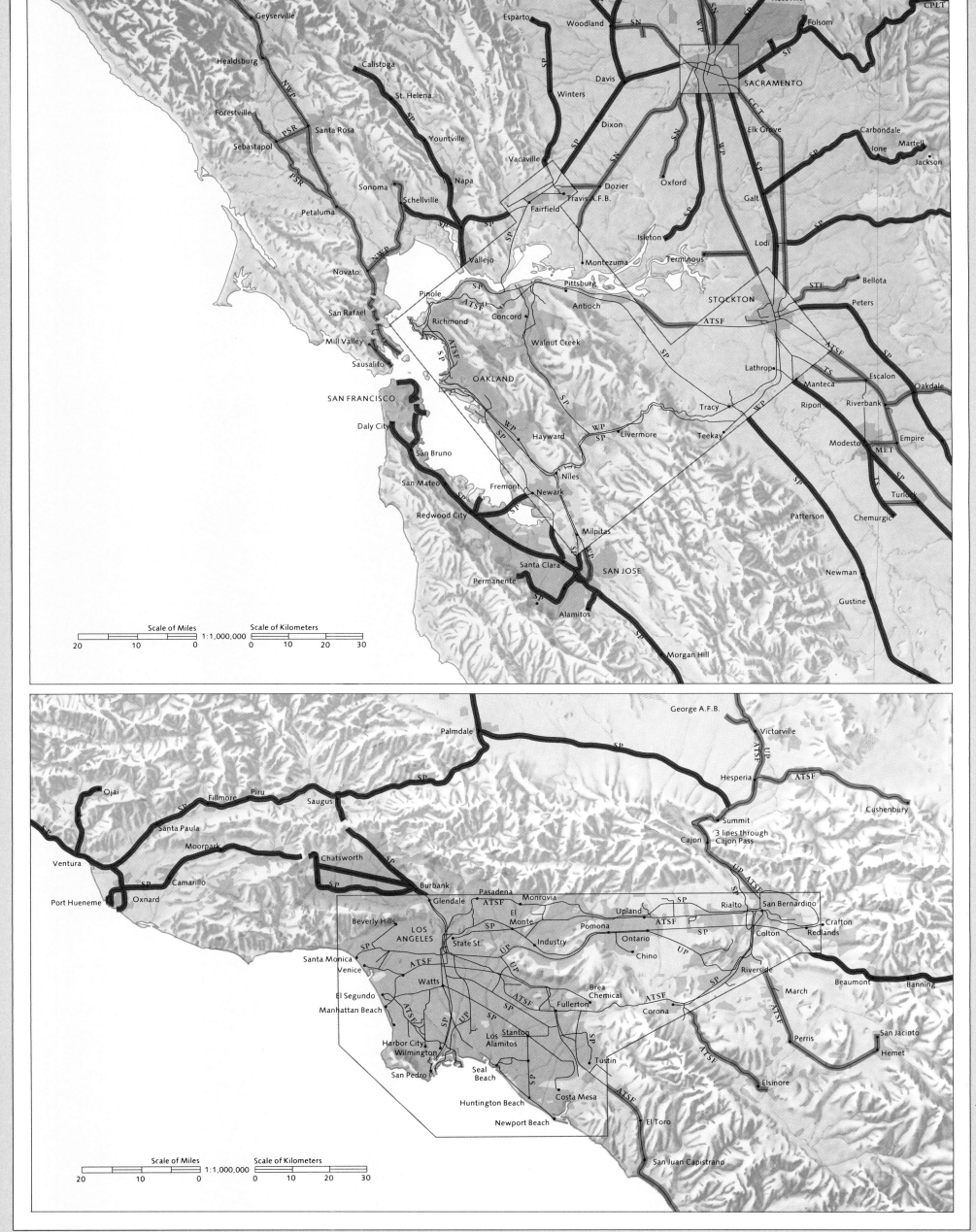

BAY AREA AND LOS ANGELES RAILROADS

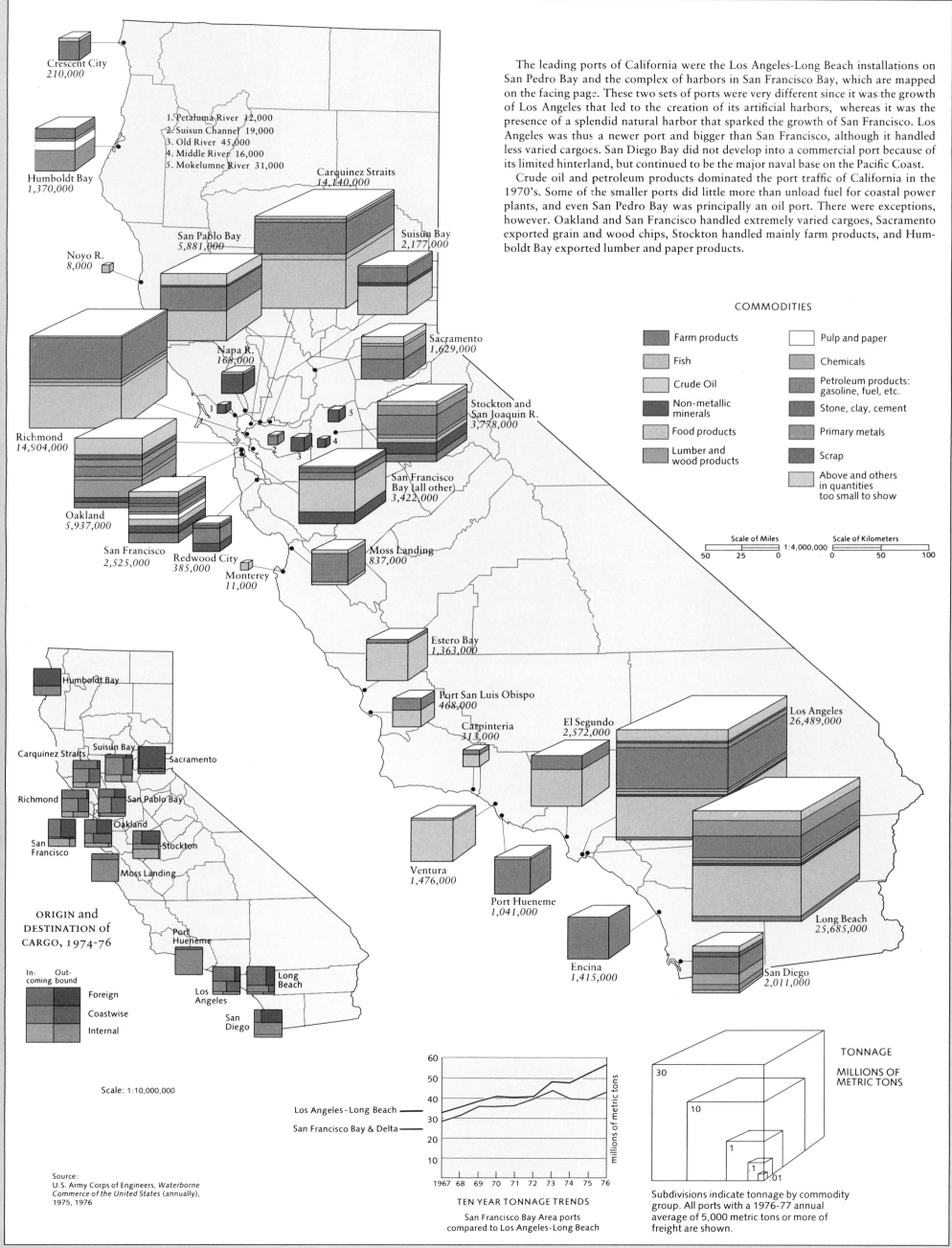

The leading ports of California were the Los Angeles-Long Beach installations on San Pedro Bay and the complex of harbors in San Francisco Bay, which are mapped on the facing page. These two sets of ports were very different since it was the growth of Los Angeles that led to the creation of its artificial harbors, whereas it was the presence of a splendid natural harbor that sparked the growth of San Francisco. Los Angeles was thus a newer port and bigger than San Francisco, although it handled less varied cargoes. San Diego Bay did not develop into a commercial port because of its limited hinterland, but continued to be the major naval base on the Pacific Coast.

Crude oil and petroleum products dominated the port traffic of California in the 1970's. Some of the smaller ports did little more than unload fuel for coastal power plants, and even San Pedro Bay was principally an oil port. There were exceptions, however. Oakland and San Francisco handled extremely varied cargoes, Sacramento exported grain and wood chips, Stockton handled mainly farm products, and Humboldt Bay exported lumber and paper products.

Crescent City 210,000

Humboldt Bay 1,370,000

1. Petaluma River 12,000
2. Suisun Channel 19,000
3. Old River 45,000
4. Middle River 16,000
5. Mokelumne River 31,000

Carquinez Straits 14,140,000

Noyo R. 8,000

San Pablo Bay 5,881,000

Suisun Bay 2,177,000

Napa R. 168,000

Sacramento 1,629,000

Richmond 14,904,000

Stockton and San Joaquin R. 3,778,000

Oakland 5,937,000

San Francisco Bay (all other) 3,422,000

San Francisco 2,525,000

Redwood City 385,000

Monterey 11,000

Moss Landing 837,000

Estero Bay 1,363,000

Port San Luis Obispo 468,000

Carpinteria 313,000

El Segundo 2,572,000

Los Angeles 26,489,000

Ventura 1,476,000

Port Hueneme 1,041,000

Long Beach 25,685,000

Encina 1,415,000

San Diego 2,011,000

COMMODITIES

Farm products

Fish

Crude Oil

Non-metallic minerals

Food products

Lumber and wood products

Pulp and paper

Chemicals

Petroleum products: gasoline, fuel, etc.

Stone, clay, cement

Primary metals

Scrap

Above and others in quantities too small to show

Scale of Miles   Scale of Kilometers
50 25 0   1:4,000,000   0   50   100

ORIGIN and DESTINATION of CARGO, 1974-76

Humboldt Bay

Carquinez Straits
Suisun Bay
Sacramento

Richmond
San Pablo Bay
Oakland
San Francisco
Stockton

Moss Landing

Port Hueneme

Los Angeles

Long Beach

San Diego

In-coming   Out-bound
Foreign
Coastwise
Internal

Scale: 1:10,000,000

Source:
U.S. Army Corps of Engineers, Waterborne Commerce of the United States (annually), 1975, 1976

TEN YEAR TONNAGE TRENDS
San Francisco Bay Area ports compared to Los Angeles-Long Beach

Los Angeles - Long Beach
San Francisco Bay & Delta

1967 68 69 70 71 72 73 74 75 76

60
50
40
30
20
10

millions of metric tons

TONNAGE

MILLIONS OF METRIC TONS

30
10
1
1
.01

Subdivisions indicate tonnage by commodity group. All ports with a 1976-77 annual average of 5,000 metric tons or more of freight are shown.

OCEAN-BORNE COMMERCE

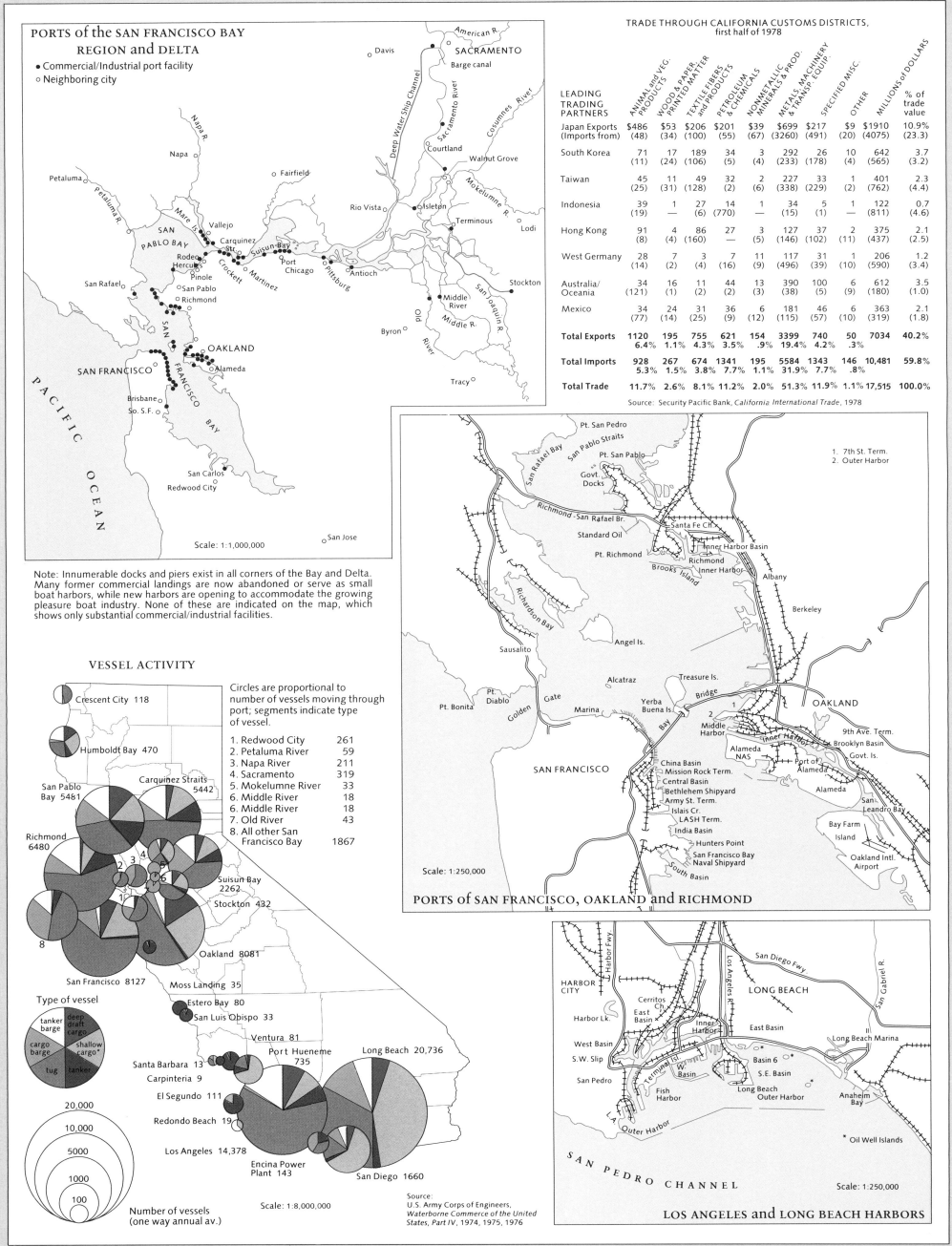

PORTS of the SAN FRANCISCO BAY REGION and DELTA

- Commercial/Industrial port facility
- Neighboring city

Note: Innumerable docks and piers exist in all corners of the Bay and Delta. Many former commercial landings are now abandoned or serve as small boat harbors, while new harbors are opening to accommodate the growing pleasure boat industry. None of these are indicated on the map, which shows only substantial commercial/industrial facilities.

Scale: 1:1,000,000

TRADE THROUGH CALIFORNIA CUSTOMS DISTRICTS, first half of 1978

LEADING TRADING PARTNERS	ANIMAL and VEG. PRODUCTS	WOOD & PAPER, PRINTED MATTER	TEXTILE FIBERS and PRODUCTS	PETROLEUM & CHEMICALS	NONMETALLIC MINERALS & PROD.	METALS, MACHINERY & TRANSP. EQUIP.	SPECIFIED MISC.	OTHER	MILLIONS of DOLLARS	% of trade value
Japan Exports (Imports from)	$486 (48)	$53 (34)	$206 (100)	$201 (55)	$39 (67)	$699 (3260)	$217 (491)	$9 (20)	$1910 (4075)	10.9% (23.3)
South Korea	71 (11)	17 (24)	189 (106)	34 (5)	3 (4)	292 (233)	26 (178)	10 (4)	642 (565)	3.7 (3.2)
Taiwan	45 (25)	11 (31)	49 (128)	32 (2)	2 (6)	227 (338)	33 (229)	1 (2)	401 (762)	2.3 (4.4)
Indonesia	39 (19)	1 —	27 (6)	14 (770)	1 —	34 (15)	5 (1)	1 —	122 (811)	0.7 (4.6)
Hong Kong	91 (8)	4 (4)	86 (160)	27 —	3 (5)	127 (146)	37 (102)	2 (11)	375 (437)	2.1 (2.5)
West Germany	28 (14)	7 (2)	3 (4)	7 (16)	11 (9)	117 (496)	31 (39)	1 (10)	206 (590)	1.2 (3.4)
Australia/ Oceania	34 (121)	16 (1)	11 (2)	44 (2)	13 (3)	390 (38)	100 (5)	6 (9)	612 (180)	3.5 (1.0)
Mexico	34 (77)	24 (14)	31 (25)	36 (9)	6 (12)	181 (115)	46 (57)	6 (10)	363 (319)	2.1 (1.8)
Total Exports	1120 6.4%	195 1.1%	755 4.3%	621 3.5%	154 .9%	3399 19.4%	740 4.2%	50 .3%	7034	40.2%
Total Imports	928 5.3%	267 1.5%	674 3.8%	1341 7.7%	195 1.1%	5584 31.9%	1343 7.7%	146 .8%	10,481	59.8%
Total Trade	11.7%	2.6%	8.1%	11.2%	2.0%	51.3%	11.9%	1.1%	17,515	100.0%

Source: Security Pacific Bank, *California International Trade*, 1978

VESSEL ACTIVITY

Circles are proportional to number of vessels moving through port; segments indicate type of vessel.

1. Redwood City — 261
2. Petaluma River — 59
3. Napa River — 211
4. Sacramento — 319
5. Mokelumne River — 33
6. Middle River — 18
6. Middle River — 18
7. Old River — 43
8. All other San Francisco Bay — 1867

Crescent City 118
Humboldt Bay 470
San Pablo Bay 5481
Carquinez Straits 5442
Richmond 6480
Suisun Bay 2262
Stockton 432
Oakland 8081
San Francisco 8127
Moss Landing 35
Estero Bay 80
San Luis Obispo 33
Ventura 81
Port Hueneme 735
Long Beach 20,736
Santa Barbara 13
Carpinteria 9
El Segundo 111
Redondo Beach 19
Los Angeles 14,378
Encina Power Plant 143
San Diego 1660

Type of vessel: tanker barge, deep draft cargo, cargo barge, shallow cargo*, tug, tanker

Number of vessels (one way annual av.)

20,000 / 10,000 / 5000 / 1000 / 100

Scale: 1:8,000,000

Source: U.S. Army Corps of Engineers, *Waterborne Commerce of the United States*, Part IV, 1974, 1975, 1976

PORTS of SAN FRANCISCO, OAKLAND and RICHMOND

Pt. San Pedro, San Pablo Straits, Pt. San Pablo, San Rafael Bay, Govt. Docks, Richmond–San Rafael Br., Standard Oil, Santa Fe Ch., Pt. Richmond, Inner Harbor Basin, Brooks Island, Richmond Inner Harbor, Albany, Richardson Bay, Berkeley, Angel Is., Sausalito, Alcatraz, Treasure Is., Pt. Diablo, Golden Gate, Marina, Yerba Buena Is., Bridge, Pt. Bonita, Bay, OAKLAND, Middle Harbor, 9th Ave. Term., Brooklyn Basin, Govt. Is., Alameda NAS, Port of Alameda, San Leandro Bay, SAN FRANCISCO, China Basin, Mission Rock Term., Central Basin, Bethlehem Shipyard, Army St. Term., Islais Cr., LASH Term., India Basin, Hunters Point, San Francisco Bay Naval Shipyard, South Basin, Alameda, Bay Farm Island, Oakland Intl. Airport

1. 7th St. Term.
2. Outer Harbor

Scale: 1:250,000

LOS ANGELES and LONG BEACH HARBORS

HARBOR CITY, Harbor Fwy., San Diego Fwy., LONG BEACH, San Gabriel R., Cerritos Ch., East Basin, Harbor Lk., Los Angeles R., Inner Harbor, East Basin, Long Beach Marina, West Basin, Basin 6, S.W. Slip, Terminal Is., W. Basin, S.E. Basin, San Pedro, Fish Harbor, Long Beach Outer Harbor, Anaheim Bay, L.A. Outer Harbor

SAN PEDRO CHANNEL

* Oil Well Islands

Scale: 1:250,000

PORTS AND HARBORS

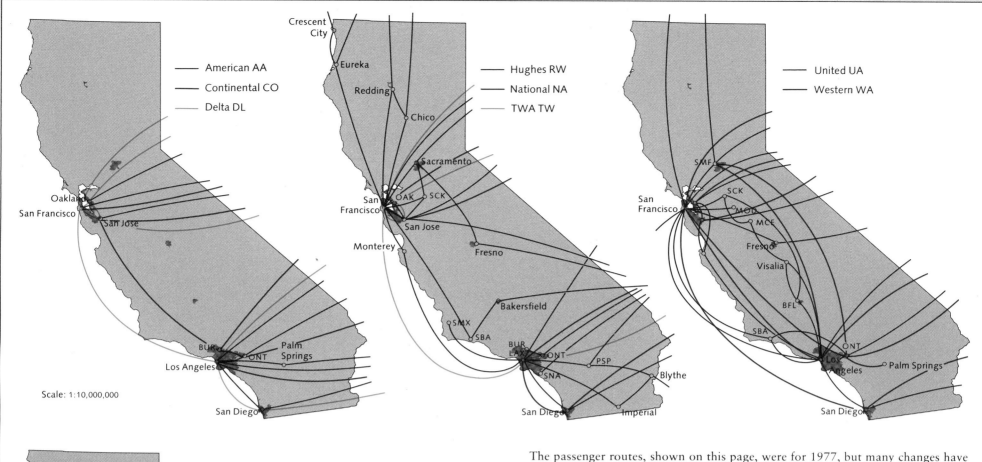

Scale: 1:10,000,000

American AA
Continental CO
Delta DL

Hughes RW
National NA
TWA TW

United UA
Western WA

Air California ACL
California Air Commuter CAC
Nor-Cal NCA
Imperial ICA

Note: Neither helicopter shuttle services nor international carriers are mapped. International service is discussed in the text.

Sources:
Public Utilities Commission, *Present and Proposed Route Structure of California Certificated Air Carriers and Routes Operated by C.A.B. Certificated Air Carriers*, 1977
————, *Intrastate Origin and Destination Report 1975-1976* (no date)
Civil Aeronautics Board, *Origin and Destination Surveys*, 1976, 1977-78 (unpublished report)
Official Airline Guide (North American and Worldwide Editions), 1978

The passenger routes, shown on this page, were for 1977, but many changes have occurred since 1978, when airlines were given increased freedom to add profitable routes and to withdraw from unprofitable ones. Thus, Air California was trying, in 1979, to end service to San Diego; United to withdraw from Merced and Visalia; and Air West to withdraw from most of the small towns it served.

LAX and SFO dominated international travel: Los Angeles had direct service to 74 cities outside North America in 1979, San Francisco had 58, and San Diego had only 19. Out of Los Angeles, 41 per cent of the flights went to Pacific and Asian cities, 34 per cent to Central and South America, and 26 per cent to Europe. The proportions were almost the same for San Francisco, whereas 90 per cent of San Diego's direct service went to Pacific and Asian cities.

PRINCIPAL INTER and INTRA-STATE ROUTES

Passenger volume (in italics) and airline share for principal carriers is for 1976 for intra-state routes, 6/77 to 6/78 for inter-state.

INTERSTATE DESTINATIONS

LA-New York
1,644,000
American 42%
TWA 29%

LA-Chicago
1,053,000
Continental 31%
American 29%

SF-New York
1,111,000
United 98%
National 1%

LA-Las Vegas
789,000
Western 73%
Hughes 20%

LA-SF (inter-state)
1,107,000
United 52%
Western 23%

LA-Honolulu
541,000
United 37%
Continental 22%

INTRA-STATE DESTINATIONS

LA-SF (intra-state)
2,022,000
PSA 55%
United 23%

LA-San Jose
620,000
PSA 100%

LA-San Diego
770,000
PSA 70%
Delta 11%

LA-Sacramento
547,000
PSA 66%
Western 34%

LA-Oakland
659,000
PSA 96%
Western 4%

Eureka Aero Industries EAI
Sierra Pacific SPA
Yosemite YAL

Pacific Southwest PSA
STOL STL
Sun Aire BSA

Apollo APL
Golden West GWA
Swift Aire SAL

AIRLINE ROUTES

GENERAL AVIATION

All airports operating under Department of Aeronautics permits are mapped at right. Private use airports are not shown. Airports with 100,000 operations per year (274 per day) are named and the number of daily operations (take-offs and landings) listed .

AIR CARRIER TRAFFIC

All airports served by P.U.C. or C.A.B. certificated airlines are mapped below. The initials after the name of each airport are its PUC/CAB designation. The initials following the colon are those of the airlines serving that airport and are listed with the route maps on the facing page.

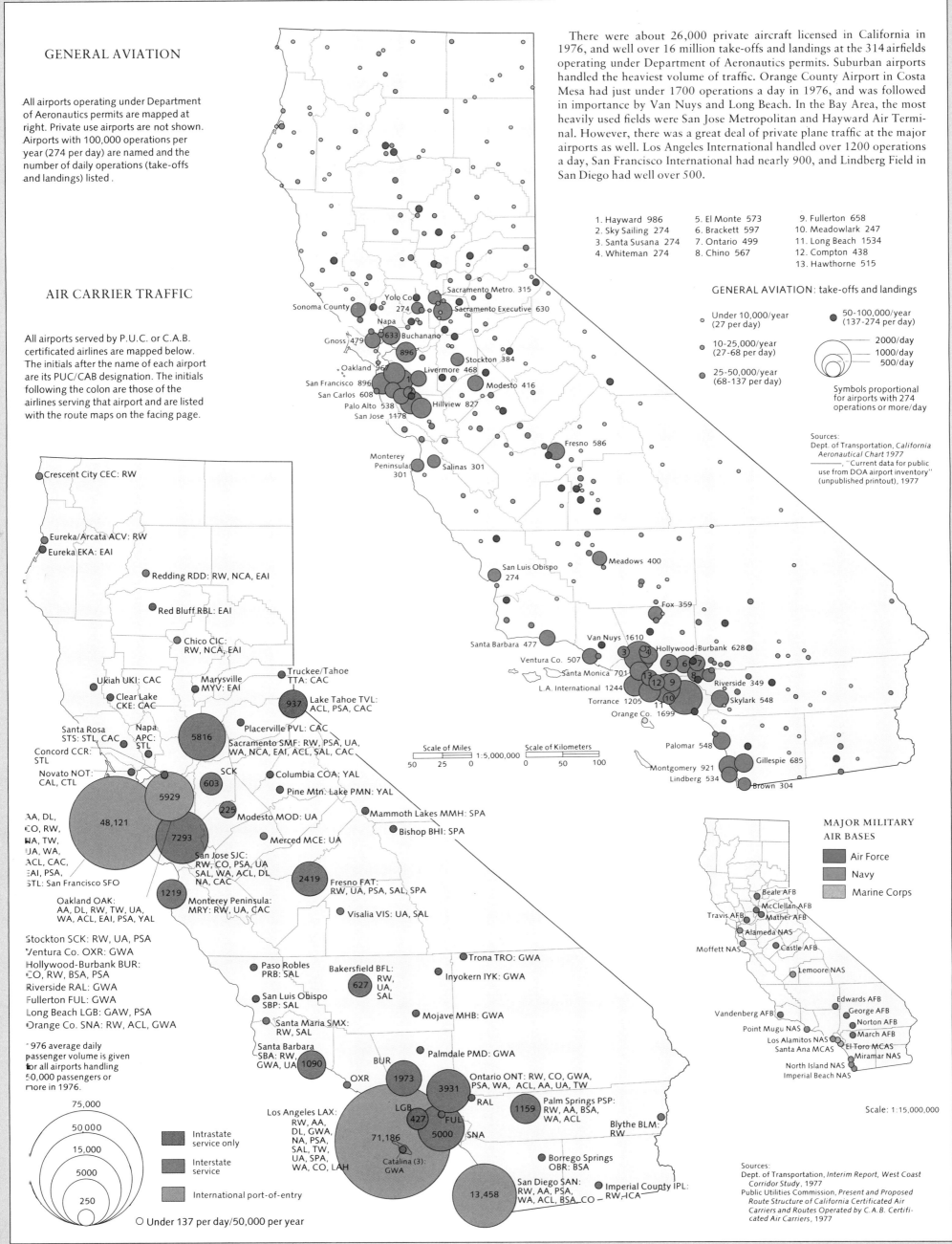

There were about 26,000 private aircraft licensed in California in 1976, and well over 16 million take-offs and landings at the 314 airfields operating under Department of Aeronautics permits. Suburban airports handled the heaviest volume of traffic. Orange County Airport in Costa Mesa had just under 1700 operations a day in 1976, and was followed in importance by Van Nuys and Long Beach. In the Bay Area, the most heavily used fields were San Jose Metropolitan and Hayward Air Terminal. However, there was a great deal of private plane traffic at the major airports as well. Los Angeles International handled over 1200 operations a day, San Francisco International had nearly 900, and Lindberg Field in San Diego had well over 500.

1. Hayward 986	5. El Monte 573	9. Fullerton 658
2. Sky Sailing 274	6. Brackett 597	10. Meadowlark 247
3. Santa Susana 274	7. Ontario 499	11. Long Beach 1534
4. Whiteman 274	8. Chino 567	12. Compton 438
		13. Hawthorne 515

GENERAL AVIATION: take-offs and landings

Under 10,000/year (27 per day)
50-100,000/year (137-274 per day)
10-25,000/year (27-68 per day)
2000/day
1000/day
500/day
25-50,000/year (68-137 per day)
Symbols proportional for airports with 274 operations or more/day

Sources:
Dept. of Transportation, *California Aeronautical Chart 1977*
——, "Current data for public use from DOA airport inventory" (unpublished printout), 1977

MAJOR MILITARY AIR BASES

Air Force
Navy
Marine Corps

Scale: 1:15,000,000

Sources:
Dept. of Transportation, *Interim Report, West Coast Corridor Study*, 1977
Public Utilities Commission, *Present and Proposed Route Structure of California Certificated Air Carriers and Routes Operated by C.A.B. Certificated Air Carriers*, 1977

976 average daily passenger volume is given for all airports handling 50,000 passengers or more in 1976.

Intrastate service only
Interstate service
International port-of-entry
Under 137 per day/50,000 per year

DAILY NEWSPAPERS, 1976

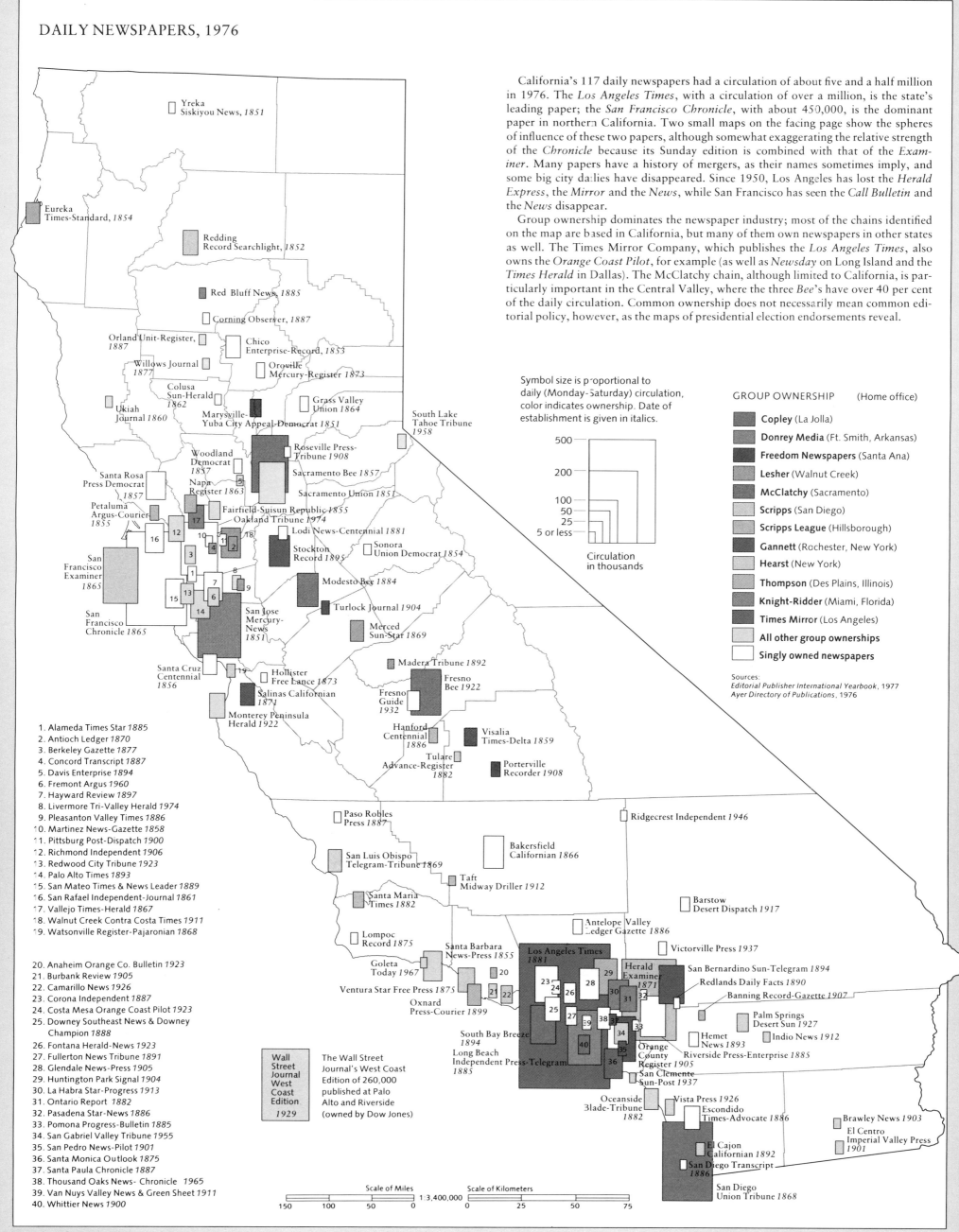

California's 117 daily newspapers had a circulation of about five and a half million in 1976. The *Los Angeles Times*, with a circulation of over a million, is the state's leading paper; the *San Francisco Chronicle*, with about 450,000, is the dominant paper in northern California. Two small maps on the facing page show the spheres of influence of these two papers, although somewhat exaggerating the relative strength of the *Chronicle* because its Sunday edition is combined with that of the *Examiner*. Many papers have a history of mergers, as their names sometimes imply, and some big city dailies have disappeared. Since 1950, Los Angeles has lost the *Herald Express*, the *Mirror* and the *News*, while San Francisco has seen the *Call Bulletin* and the *News* disappear.

Group ownership dominates the newspaper industry; most of the chains identified on the map are based in California, but many of them own newspapers in other states as well. The Times Mirror Company, which publishes the *Los Angeles Times*, also owns the *Orange Coast Pilot*, for example (as well as *Newsday* on Long Island and the *Times Herald* in Dallas). The McClatchy chain, although limited to California, is particularly important in the Central Valley, where the three *Bee*'s have over 40 per cent of the daily circulation. Common ownership does not necessarily mean common editorial policy, however, as the maps of presidential election endorsements reveal.

Symbol size is proportional to daily (Monday–Saturday) circulation, color indicates ownership. Date of establishment is given in italics.

500
200
100
50
25
5 or less

Circulation in thousands

GROUP OWNERSHIP (Home office)

- Copley (La Jolla)
- Donrey Media (Ft. Smith, Arkansas)
- Freedom Newspapers (Santa Ana)
- Lesher (Walnut Creek)
- McClatchy (Sacramento)
- Scripps (San Diego)
- Scripps League (Hillsborough)
- Gannett (Rochester, New York)
- Hearst (New York)
- Thompson (Des Plains, Illinois)
- Knight-Ridder (Miami, Florida)
- Times Mirror (Los Angeles)
- All other group ownerships
- Singly owned newspapers

Sources:
Editorial Publisher International Yearbook, 1977
Ayer Directory of Publications, 1976

Yreka
Siskiyou News, *1851*

Eureka
Times-Standard, *1854*

Redding
Record Searchlight, *1852*

Red Bluff News *1885*

Corning Observer, *1887*

Orland Unit-Register, *1887*

Chico Enterprise-Record, *1853*

Willows Journal *1877*

Oroville Mercury-Register *1873*

Colusa Sun-Herald *1862*

Grass Valley Union *1864*

Ukiah Journal *1860*

Marysville–Yuba City Appeal-Democrat *1851*

South Lake Tahoe Tribune *1958*

Woodland Democrat *1857*

Roseville Press-Tribune *1908*

Santa Rosa Press Democrat *1857*

Napa Register *1863*

Sacramento Bee *1857*

Sacramento Union *1851*

Petaluma Argus-Courier *1855*

Fairfield-Suisun Republic *1855*
Oakland Tribune *1974*

Lodi News-Centennial *1881*

San Francisco Examiner *1865*

Stockton Record *1895*

Sonora Union Democrat *1854*

San Francisco Chronicle *1865*

Modesto Bee *1884*

Turlock Journal *1904*

San Jose Mercury-News *1851*

Merced Sun-Star *1869*

Santa Cruz Centennial *1856*

Madera Tribune *1892*

Hollister Free Lance *1873*

Fresno Bee *1922*

Salinas Californian *1871*

Fresno Guide *1932*

Monterey Peninsula Herald *1922*

Hanford Centennial *1886*

Visalia Times-Delta *1859*

Tulare Advance-Register *1882*

Porterville Recorder *1908*

1. Alameda Times Star *1885*
2. Antioch Ledger *1870*
3. Berkeley Gazette *1877*
4. Concord Transcript *1887*
5. Davis Enterprise *1894*
6. Fremont Argus *1960*
7. Hayward Review *1897*
8. Livermore Tri-Valley Herald *1974*
9. Pleasanton Valley Times *1886*
10. Martinez News-Gazette *1858*
11. Pittsburg Post-Dispatch *1900*
12. Richmond Independent *1906*
13. Redwood City Tribune *1923*
14. Palo Alto Times *1893*
15. San Mateo Times & News Leader *1889*
16. San Rafael Independent-Journal *1861*
17. Vallejo Times-Herald *1867*
18. Walnut Creek Contra Costa Times *1911*
19. Watsonville Register-Pajaronian *1868*

20. Anaheim Orange Co. Bulletin *1923*
21. Burbank Review *1905*
22. Camarillo News *1926*
23. Corona Independent *1887*
24. Costa Mesa Orange Coast Pilot *1923*
25. Downey Southeast News & Downey Champion *1888*
26. Fontana Herald-News *1923*
27. Fullerton News Tribune *1891*
28. Glendale News-Press *1905*
29. Huntington Park Signal *1904*
30. La Habra Star-Progress *1913*
31. Ontario Report *1882*
32. Pasadena Star-News *1886*
33. Pomona Progress-Bulletin *1885*
34. San Gabriel Valley Tribune *1955*
35. San Pedro News-Pilot *1901*
36. Santa Monica Outlook *1875*
37. Santa Paula Chronicle *1887*
38. Thousand Oaks News-Chronicle *1965*
39. Van Nuys Valley News & Green Sheet *1911*
40. Whittier News *1900*

Paso Robles Press *1887*

Ridgecrest Independent *1946*

Bakersfield Californian *1866*

San Luis Obispo Telegram-Tribune *1869*

Taft Midway Driller *1912*

Santa Maria Times *1882*

Barstow Desert Dispatch *1917*

Lompoc Record *1875*

Antelope Valley Ledger Gazette *1886*

Victorville Press *1937*

Santa Barbara News-Press *1855*

Los Angeles Times *1881*

Herald Examiner *1871*

San Bernardino Sun-Telegram *1894*

Goleta Today *1967*

Redlands Daily Facts *1890*

Banning Record-Gazette *1907*

Ventura Star Free Press *1875*

Oxnard Press-Courier *1899*

Palm Springs Desert Sun *1927*

Hemet News *1893*

Indio News *1912*

South Bay Breeze *1894*

Orange County Register *1905*

Riverside Press-Enterprise *1885*

Long Beach Independent Press-Telegram *1885*

San Clemente Sun-Post *1937*

Wall Street Journal West Coast Edition *1929*

The Wall Street Journal's West Coast Edition of 260,000 published at Palo Alto and Riverside (owned by Dow Jones)

Oceanside Blade-Tribune *1882*

Vista Press *1926*

Escondido Times-Advocate *1886*

Brawley News *1903*

El Cajon Californian *1892*

El Centro Imperial Valley Press *1901*

San Diego Transcript *1886*

San Diego Union Tribune *1868*

Scale of Miles
150 100 50 0

1:3,400,000

Scale of Kilometers
0 25 50 75

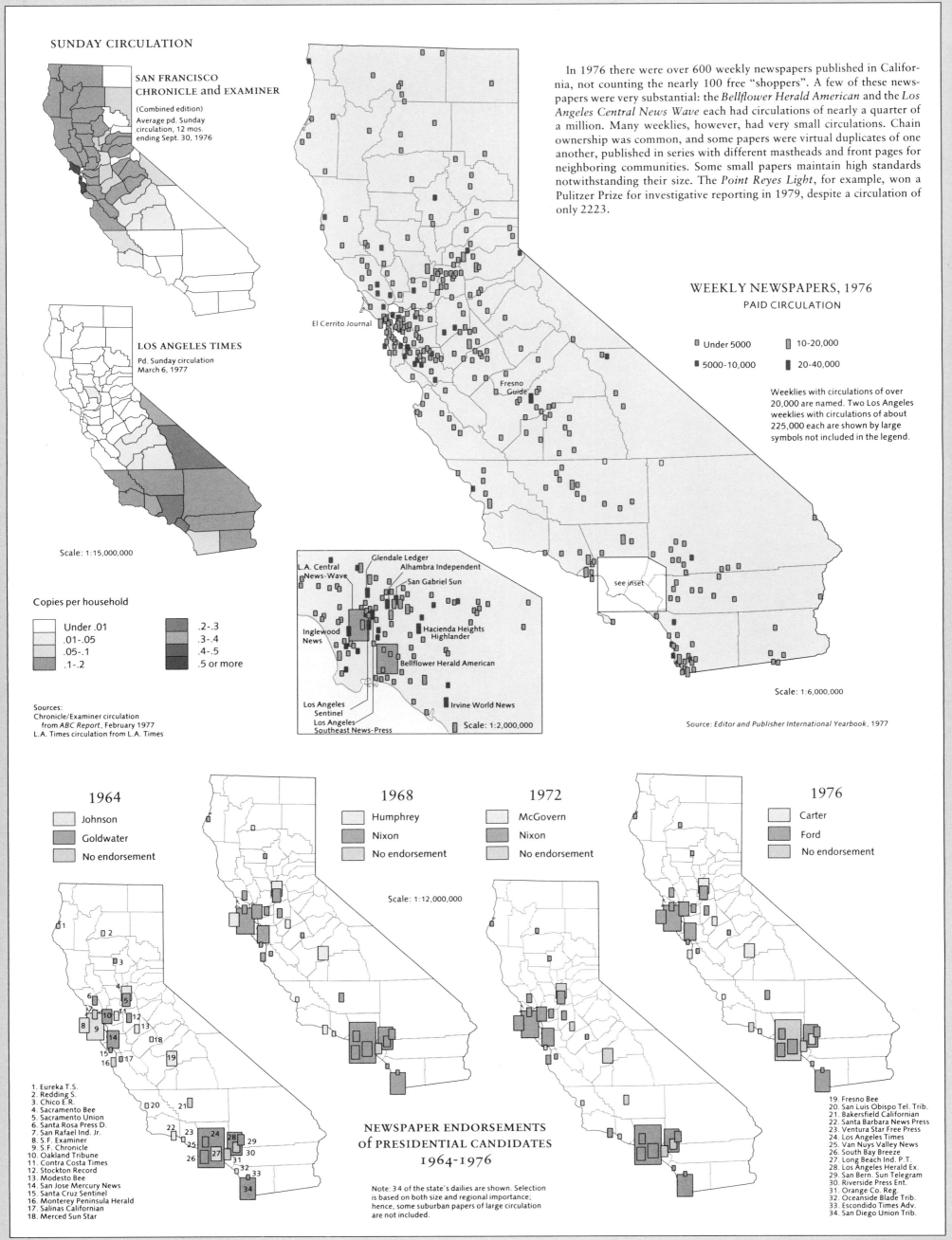

SUNDAY CIRCULATION

SAN FRANCISCO CHRONICLE and EXAMINER

(Combined edition)
Average pd. Sunday circulation, 12 mos. ending Sept. 30, 1976

LOS ANGELES TIMES

Pd. Sunday circulation March 6, 1977

Scale: 1:15,000,000

Copies per household

- Under .01
- .01-.05
- .05-.1
- .1-.2
- .2-.3
- .3-.4
- .4-.5
- .5 or more

Sources:
Chronicle/Examiner circulation from *ABC Report*, February 1977
L.A. Times circulation from L.A. Times

In 1976 there were over 600 weekly newspapers published in California, not counting the nearly 100 free "shoppers". A few of these newspapers were very substantial: the *Bellflower Herald American* and the *Los Angeles Central News Wave* each had circulations of nearly a quarter of a million. Many weeklies, however, had very small circulations. Chain ownership was common, and some papers were virtual duplicates of one another, published in series with different mastheads and front pages for neighboring communities. Some small papers maintain high standards notwithstanding their size. The *Point Reyes Light*, for example, won a Pulitzer Prize for investigative reporting in 1979, despite a circulation of only 2223.

WEEKLY NEWSPAPERS, 1976

PAID CIRCULATION

- Under 5000
- 5000-10,000
- 10-20,000
- 20-40,000

Weeklies with circulations of over 20,000 are named. Two Los Angeles weeklies with circulations of about 225,000 each are shown by large symbols not included in the legend.

El Cerrito Journal

Fresno Guide

Glendale Ledger
Alhambra Independent
L.A. Central News-Wave
San Gabriel Sun
Inglewood News
Hacienda Heights Highlander
Bellflower Herald American
Los Angeles Sentinel
Los Angeles Southeast News-Press
Irvine World News

see inset

Scale: 1:2,000,000

Scale: 1:6,000,000

Source: *Editor and Publisher International Yearbook*, 1977

NEWSPAPER ENDORSEMENTS of PRESIDENTIAL CANDIDATES 1964-1976

1964
- Johnson
- Goldwater
- No endorsement

1968
- Humphrey
- Nixon
- No endorsement

Scale: 1:12,000,000

1972
- McGovern
- Nixon
- No endorsement

1976
- Carter
- Ford
- No endorsement

1. Eureka T.S.
2. Redding S.
3. Chico E.R.
4. Sacramento Bee
5. Sacramento Union
6. Santa Rosa Press D.
7. San Rafael Ind. Jr.
8. S.F. Examiner
9. S.F. Chronicle
10. Oakland Tribune
11. Contra Costa Times
12. Stockton Record
13. Modesto Bee
14. San Jose Mercury News
15. Santa Cruz Sentinel
16. Monterey Peninsula Herald
17. Salinas Californian
18. Merced Sun Star

19. Fresno Bee
20. San Luis Obispo Tel. Trib.
21. Bakersfield Californian
22. Santa Barbara News Press
23. Ventura Star Free Press
24. Los Angeles Times
25. Van Nuys Valley News
26. South Bay Breeze
27. Long Beach Ind. P.T.
28. Los Angeles Herald Ex.
29. San Bern. Sun Telegram
30. Riverside Press Ent.
31. Orange Co. Reg.
32. Oceanside Blade Trib.
33. Escondido Times Adv.
34. San Diego Union Trib.

Note: 34 of the state's dailies are shown. Selection is based on both size and regional importance; hence, some suburban papers of large circulation are not included.

NEWSPAPERS

RADIO BROADCASTING, 1976

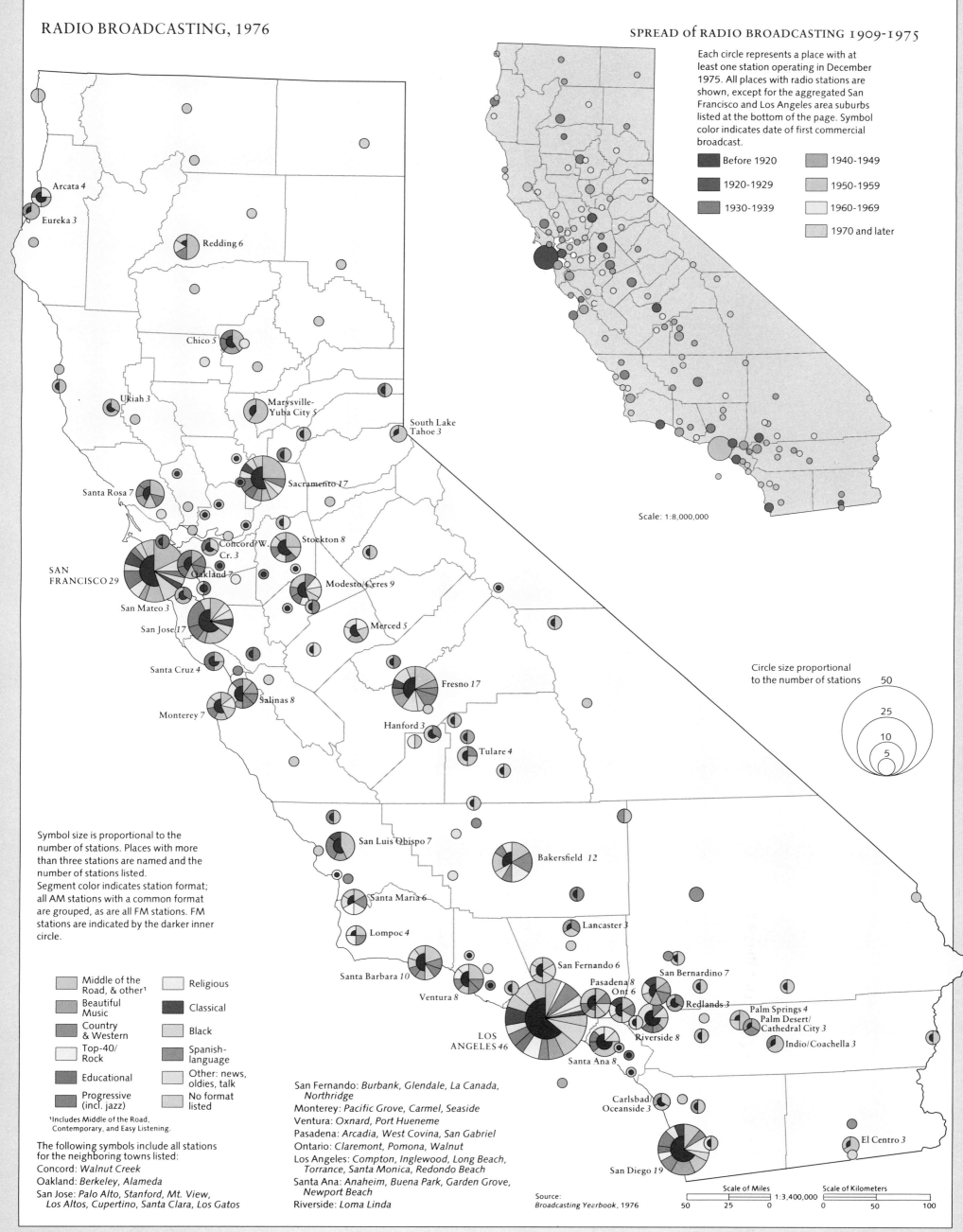

SPREAD of RADIO BROADCASTING 1909-1975

Each circle represents a place with at least one station operating in December 1975. All places with radio stations are shown, except for the aggregated San Francisco and Los Angeles area suburbs listed at the bottom of the page. Symbol color indicates date of first commercial broadcast.

■ Before 1920	▨ 1940-1949
▨ 1920-1929	▨ 1950-1959
▨ 1930-1939	▨ 1960-1969
	▨ 1970 and later

Scale: 1:8,000,000

Arcata 4
Eureka 3
Redding 6
Chico 5
Ukiah 3
Marysville-Yuba City 5
South Lake Tahoe 3
Santa Rosa 7
Sacramento 17
Concord W. Cr. 3
Stockton 8
Oakland 7
Modesto/Ceres 9
SAN FRANCISCO 29
San Mateo 3
San Jose 17
Merced 5
Santa Cruz 4
Fresno 17
Salinas 8
Monterey 7
Hanford 3
Tulare 4
San Luis Obispo 7
Bakersfield 12
Santa Maria 6
Lompoc 4
Lancaster 3
San Fernando 6
Santa Barbara 10
San Bernardino 7
Ventura 8
Pasadena 8
Ont 6
Redlands 3
Palm Springs 4
Palm Desert/Cathedral City 3
LOS ANGELES 46
Riverside 8
Indio/Coachella 3
Santa Ana 8
Carlsbad/Oceanside 3
El Centro 3
San Diego 19

Circle size proportional to the number of stations

50
25
10
5

Symbol size is proportional to the number of stations. Places with more than three stations are named and the number of stations listed.
Segment color indicates station format; all AM stations with a common format are grouped, as are all FM stations. FM stations are indicated by the darker inner circle.

▨ Middle of the Road, & other¹	▨ Religious
▨ Beautiful Music	■ Classical
▨ Country & Western	▨ Black
▨ Top-40/Rock	▨ Spanish-language
▨ Educational	▨ Other: news, oldies, talk
▨ Progressive (incl. jazz)	▨ No format listed

¹Includes Middle of the Road, Contemporary, and Easy Listening.

The following symbols include all stations for the neighboring towns listed:
Concord: *Walnut Creek*
Oakland: *Berkeley, Alameda*
San Jose: *Palo Alto, Stanford, Mt. View, Los Altos, Cupertino, Santa Clara, Los Gatos*

San Fernando: *Burbank, Glendale, La Canada, Northridge*
Monterey: *Pacific Grove, Carmel, Seaside*
Ventura: *Oxnard, Port Hueneme*
Pasadena: *Arcadia, West Covina, San Gabriel*
Ontario: *Claremont, Pomona, Walnut*
Los Angeles: *Compton, Inglewood, Long Beach, Torrance, Santa Monica, Redondo Beach*
Santa Ana: *Anaheim, Buena Park, Garden Grove, Newport Beach*
Riverside: *Loma Linda*

Source:
Broadcasting Yearbook, 1976

1:3,400,000

Scale of Miles
50   25   0   50

Scale of Kilometers
0   50   100

TELEVISION 1976

At the end of 1976, 480 radio stations were broadcasting in California: 250 FM stations (including virtually all of the 57 non-commercial stations), and 130 AM stations. The large map on the facing page shows the number of stations broadcasting from each town and indicates the station programming format. Formats represent the radio industry's best guesses on the relative importance of different audiences in different areas; Kern County's oil and cotton economy, for example, is reflected in its country and western programming. "Middle of the road,", "contemporary," and "easy listening" are designed to appeal to adults. "Beautiful music" is soothing, "country and western" is in fact Southern, "top 40/rock" is aimed at teenagers, and "progressive" plays to an older, more sophisticated audience.

The state's 56 television stations (1976) are shown on the map at left. Like radio, television ownership is regulated by the Federal Communication Commission, whose power to deny license renewal is a major concern of the owners, along with profit margins. Of the successful and profitable television stations, KNBC, KNXT, and KABC in Los Angeles are owned by the NBC, CBS, and ABC networks, respectively. In San Francisco, KPIX is owned by Westinghouse, KGO by ABC, and KRON by the Chronicle Publishing Company. Other large corporate owners of California stations include McGraw-Hill, General Electric, ChrisCraft, and Kaiser Industries. Not all authorized stations are operating, however, and some small ones have gone out of business.

Both CBS and ABC have moved their Entertainment Divisions to Los Angeles, where nearly half of the 32,000 people working in movie production (1975) were making pictures for television. These movies, and the general rise of television, have resulted in a shift of the popular image of America and its society from a setting in the green lawns and deciduous trees of the East to a firm root in Southern California.

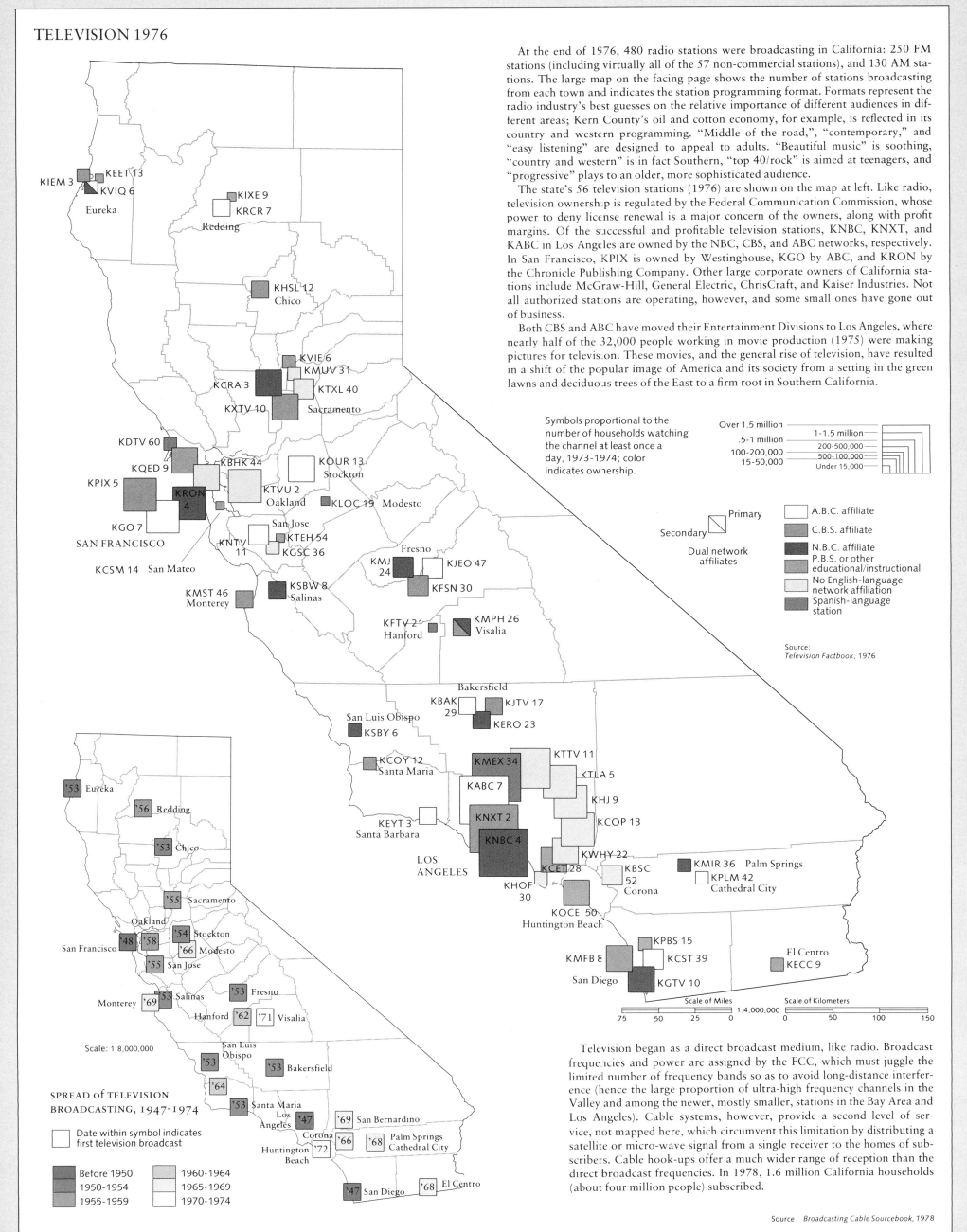

Symbols proportional to the number of households watching the channel at least once a day, 1973-1974; color indicates ownership.

Over 1.5 million
.5-1 million
100-200,000
15-50,000

1-1.5 million
200-500,000
500-100,000
Under 15,000

Primary
Secondary
Dual network affiliates

A.B.C. affiliate
C.B.S. affiliate
N.B.C. affiliate
P.B.S. or other educational/instructional
No English-language network affiliation
Spanish-language station

Source:
Television Factbook, 1976

SPREAD OF TELEVISION BROADCASTING, 1947-1974

Date within symbol indicates first television broadcast

Before 1950
1950-1954
1955-1959
1960-1964
1965-1969
1970-1974

Scale: 1:8,000,000

Scale of Miles 75 50 25 0
Scale of Kilometers 0 50 100 150
1:4,000,000

Television began as a direct broadcast medium, like radio. Broadcast frequencies and power are assigned by the FCC, which must juggle the limited number of frequency bands so as to avoid long-distance interference (hence the large proportion of ultra-high frequency channels in the Valley and among the newer, mostly smaller, stations in the Bay Area and Los Angeles). Cable systems, however, provide a second level of service, not mapped here, which circumvent this limitation by distributing a satellite or micro-wave signal from a single receiver to the homes of subscribers. Cable hook-ups offer a much wider range of reception than the direct broadcast frequencies. In 1978, 1.6 million California households (about four million people) subscribed.

Source: *Broadcasting Cable Sourcebook*, 1978

TELEVISION

ELECTRIC SERVICE AREAS
within one mile of distribution facilities

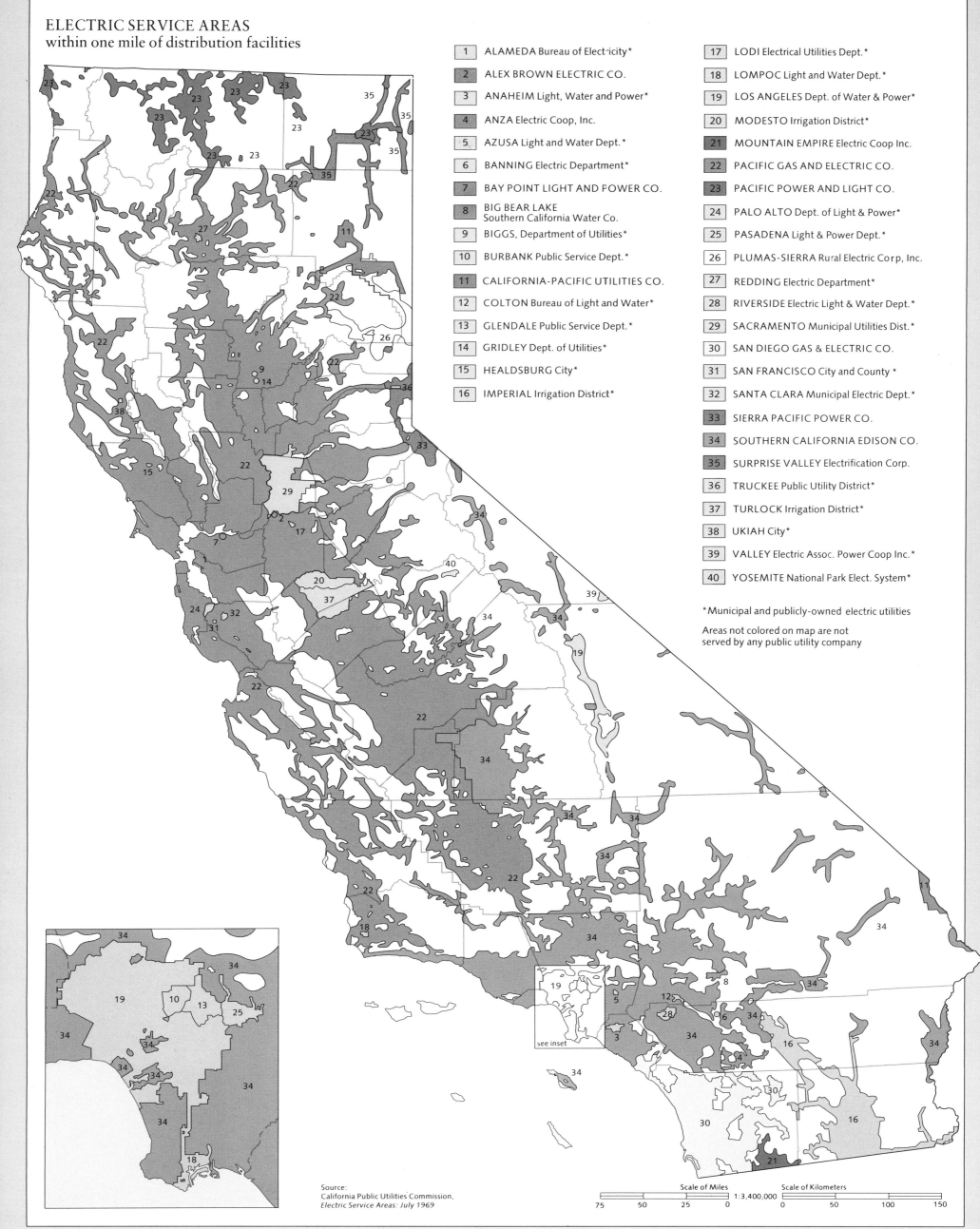

1	ALAMEDA Bureau of Electricity*
2	ALEX BROWN ELECTRIC CO.
3	ANAHEIM Light, Water and Power*
4	ANZA Electric Coop, Inc.
5	AZUSA Light and Water Dept.*
6	BANNING Electric Department*
7	BAY POINT LIGHT AND POWER CO.
8	BIG BEAR LAKE Southern California Water Co.
9	BIGGS, Department of Utilities*
10	BURBANK Public Service Dept.*
11	CALIFORNIA-PACIFIC UTILITIES CO.
12	COLTON Bureau of Light and Water*
13	GLENDALE Public Service Dept.*
14	GRIDLEY Dept. of Utilities*
15	HEALDSBURG City*
16	IMPERIAL Irrigation District*

17	LODI Electrical Utilities Dept.*
18	LOMPOC Light and Water Dept.*
19	LOS ANGELES Dept. of Water & Power*
20	MODESTO Irrigation District*
21	MOUNTAIN EMPIRE Electric Coop Inc.
22	PACIFIC GAS AND ELECTRIC CO.
23	PACIFIC POWER AND LIGHT CO.
24	PALO ALTO Dept. of Light & Power*
25	PASADENA Light & Power Dept.*
26	PLUMAS-SIERRA Rural Electric Corp, Inc.
27	REDDING Electric Department*
28	RIVERSIDE Electric Light & Water Dept.*
29	SACRAMENTO Municipal Utilities Dist.*
30	SAN DIEGO GAS & ELECTRIC CO.
31	SAN FRANCISCO City and County *
32	SANTA CLARA Municipal Electric Dept.*
33	SIERRA PACIFIC POWER CO.
34	SOUTHERN CALIFORNIA EDISON CO.
35	SURPRISE VALLEY Electrification Corp.
36	TRUCKEE Public Utility District*
37	TURLOCK Irrigation District*
38	UKIAH City*
39	VALLEY Electric Assoc. Power Coop Inc. *
40	YOSEMITE National Park Elect. System*

*Municipal and publicly-owned electric utilities

Areas not colored on map are not
served by any public utility company

Source:
California Public Utilities Commission,
Electric Service Areas: July 1969

Scale of Miles
75   50   25   0

1:3,400,000

Scale of Kilometers
0   50   100   150

UTILITY DISTRICTS

OPERATING AREAS of CALIFORNIA TELEPHONE COMPANIES

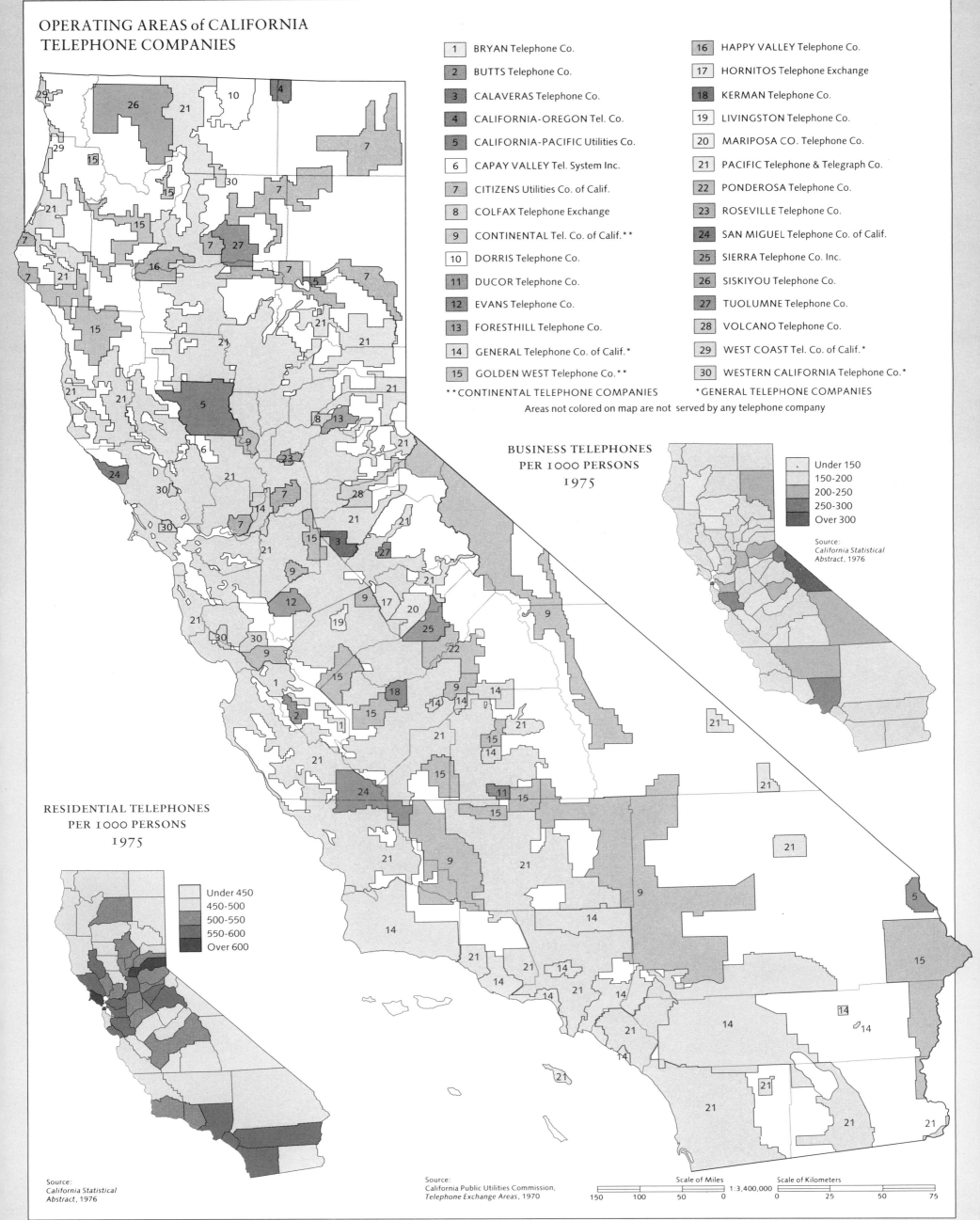

1 BRYAN Telephone Co.	16 HAPPY VALLEY Telephone Co.
2 BUTTS Telephone Co.	17 HORNITOS Telephone Exchange
3 CALAVERAS Telephone Co.	18 KERMAN Telephone Co.
4 CALIFORNIA-OREGON Tel. Co.	19 LIVINGSTON Telephone Co.
5 CALIFORNIA-PACIFIC Utilities Co.	20 MARIPOSA CO. Telephone Co.
6 CAPAY VALLEY Tel. System Inc.	21 PACIFIC Telephone & Telegraph Co.
7 CITIZENS Utilities Co. of Calif.	22 PONDEROSA Telephone Co.
8 COLFAX Telephone Exchange	23 ROSEVILLE Telephone Co.
9 CONTINENTAL Tel. Co. of Calif.**	24 SAN MIGUEL Telephone Co. of Calif.
10 DORRIS Telephone Co.	25 SIERRA Telephone Co. Inc.
11 DUCOR Telephone Co.	26 SISKIYOU Telephone Co.
12 EVANS Telephone Co.	27 TUOLUMNE Telephone Co.
13 FORESTHILL Telephone Co.	28 VOLCANO Telephone Co.
14 GENERAL Telephone Co. of Calif.*	29 WEST COAST Tel. Co. of Calif.*
15 GOLDEN WEST Telephone Co.**	30 WESTERN CALIFORNIA Telephone Co.*

**CONTINENTAL TELEPHONE COMPANIES   *GENERAL TELEPHONE COMPANIES

Areas not colored on map are not served by any telephone company

BUSINESS TELEPHONES PER 1000 PERSONS 1975

- Under 150
- 150-200
- 200-250
- 250-300
- Over 300

Source:
California Statistical
Abstract, 1976

RESIDENTIAL TELEPHONES PER 1000 PERSONS 1975

- Under 450
- 450-500
- 500-550
- 550-600
- Over 600

Source:
California Statistical
Abstract, 1976

Source:
California Public Utilities Commission,
Telephone Exchange Areas, 1970

Scale of Miles
150   100   50   0
1:3,400,000
Scale of Kilometers
0   25   50   75

THE PHYSICAL ENVIRONMENT

California's surface configuration exhibits greater variation than any other comparable area of the United States. Despite this variety, the state can be generalized into eleven physiographic regions based on form and process.

The Cascade Range in California, an otherwise low and unabrupt range, has conspicuous volcanic peaks which rise above the general surface. Mount Shasta, a stratovolcano at 4300 m, is the second highest peak in the entire chain. Lassen Peak, at 3186 m, is the most recently active volcano in the system, having erupted between 1914 and 1917.

East of the Cascades lies the Modoc Plateau, a semi-arid basaltic tableland averaging about 1300 m in elevation. These Pleistocene volcanic flows are similar in age and type to those of the Columbia Plateau, but because of extensive faulting they are structurally closer to the Basin Ranges of Nevada.

The Klamath Mountains, in northwestern California, contain several individually named "ranges", such as Siskiyou, Trinity, Marble, and Scotts Bar. All are rugged, old and highly dissected. Individual peaks range from 1800 to 2700 m above sea level, and the highest elevations are glaciated.

The Sierra Nevada, the largest and highest mountain range in the state, is a massive fault block which stretches more than 675 km from the Cascades to the Tehachapis. Drainage is almost entirely down the gently sloping western surface of the batholithic mass. On the east, the abrupt flank towers more than 3300 m above the Owens Valley; several peaks in the Mt. Whitney area exceed 4240 m above sea level. Rocks of the Sierra Nevada are primarily granitic, with remnants of paleozoic sediments and metamorphic rocks.

The Central Valley parallels the Sierra Nevada. This structural depression resulted from the tilting that created the Sierra Nevada, but the present configuration is the result of filling by debris eroded from the mountains. The northward-draining San Joaquin and the southward-flowing Sacramento join in the Delta and exit from the valley through Carquinez Strait.

The Coast Ranges extend from Eureka to Lompoc. Divided into northern and southern sections by San Francisco Bay, they comprise a system of low, roughly parallel ranges, strongly controlled by complex folding and faulting. Miocene strata predominate and drainage parallels the structure in general.

The Basin Ranges are an extension of the Great Basin, dominated by relatively short north-south fault blocks of high local relief. The ranges are separated by closed basins which comprise three-fourths of the area.

The ranges of the Mojave Desert are virtually an extension of the Basin Ranges, but they lack the distinct and parallel alighment, and are lower and more deeply eroded.

The Transverse Ranges trend east-west. The structure and rock composition of these mountains are very complex. In general, steep folds are aligned to major faults and are broken by numerous secondary fractures. All of the component ranges have intrusive granitic cores similar to those found in the Sierra Nevada.

The Peninsular Ranges, originally one mass which subsequently broke along fault lines, are a northward extension of Baja California. The mountains and their associated basins are generally aligned to the structures of the Coast Ranges and roughly parallel to the San Andreas Fault system to the east.

The Colorado Desert, a relatively flat alluvial surface, occupies a structural depression that was sealed off from the Gulf of California by the development of the Colorado River Delta. The Salton Sea was inadvertently created in 1905 and 1906 when part of the Imperial Valley, a depression lying below sea level, was flooded because of substandard irrigation engineering on the Colorado River.

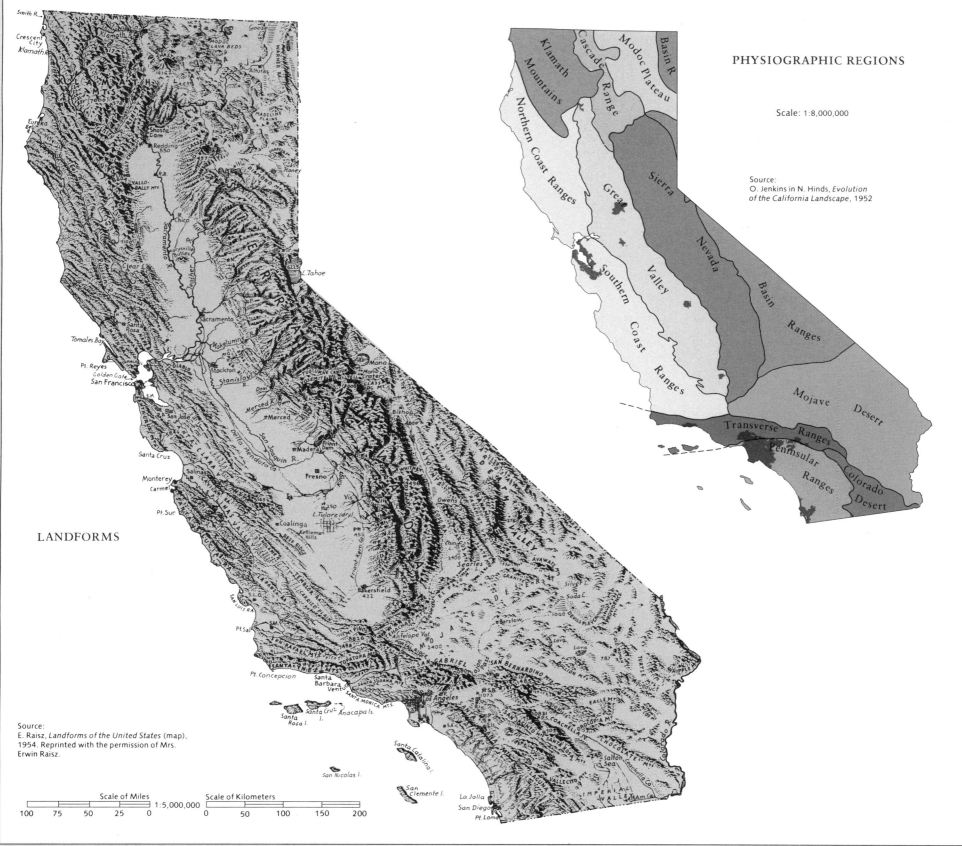

PHYSIOGRAPHIC REGIONS

Scale: 1:8,000,000

Source:
O. Jenkins in N. Hinds, *Evolution of the California Landscape*, 1952

LANDFORMS

Source:
E. Raisz, *Landforms of the United States* (map), 1954. Reprinted with the permission of Mrs. Erwin Raisz.

Scale of Miles   Scale of Kilometers
100 75 50 25 0   0   50   100   150   200
                 1:5,000,000

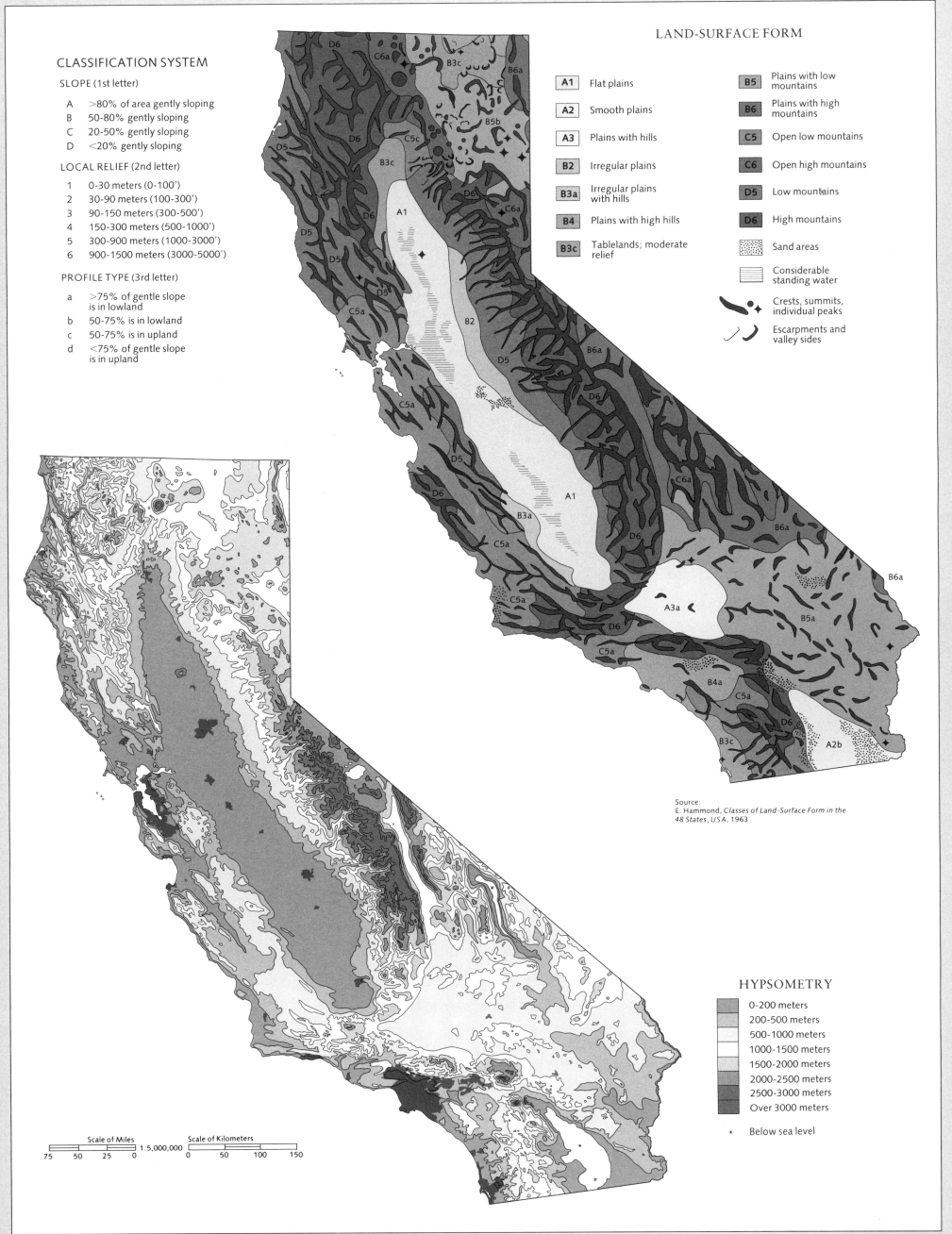

CLASSIFICATION SYSTEM

SLOPE (1st letter)

A >80% of area gently sloping
B 50-80% gently sloping
C 20-50% gently sloping
D <20% gently sloping

LOCAL RELIEF (2nd letter)

1 0-30 meters (0-100')
2 30-90 meters (100-300')
3 90-150 meters (300-500')
4 150-300 meters (500-1000')
5 300-900 meters (1000-3000')
6 900-1500 meters (3000-5000')

PROFILE TYPE (3rd letter)

a >75% of gentle slope is in lowland
b 50-75% is in lowland
c 50-75% is in upland
d <75% of gentle slope is in upland

LAND-SURFACE FORM

A1 Flat plains
A2 Smooth plains
A3 Plains with hills
B2 Irregular plains
B3a Irregular plains with hills
B4 Plains with high hills
B3c Tablelands; moderate relief
B5 Plains with low mountains
B6 Plains with high mountains
C5 Open low mountains
C6 Open high mountains
D5 Low mountains
D6 High mountains

Sand areas

Considerable standing water

Crests, summits, individual peaks

Escarpments and valley sides

Source:
E. Hammond, *Classes of Land-Surface Form in the 48 States, USA*, 1963

HYPSOMETRY

0-200 meters
200-500 meters
500-1000 meters
1000-1500 meters
1500-2000 meters
2000-2500 meters
2500-3000 meters
Over 3000 meters

* Below sea level

Scale of Miles 75 50 25 0
Scale of Kilometers 0 50 100 150
1:5,000,000

LANDFORMS

116

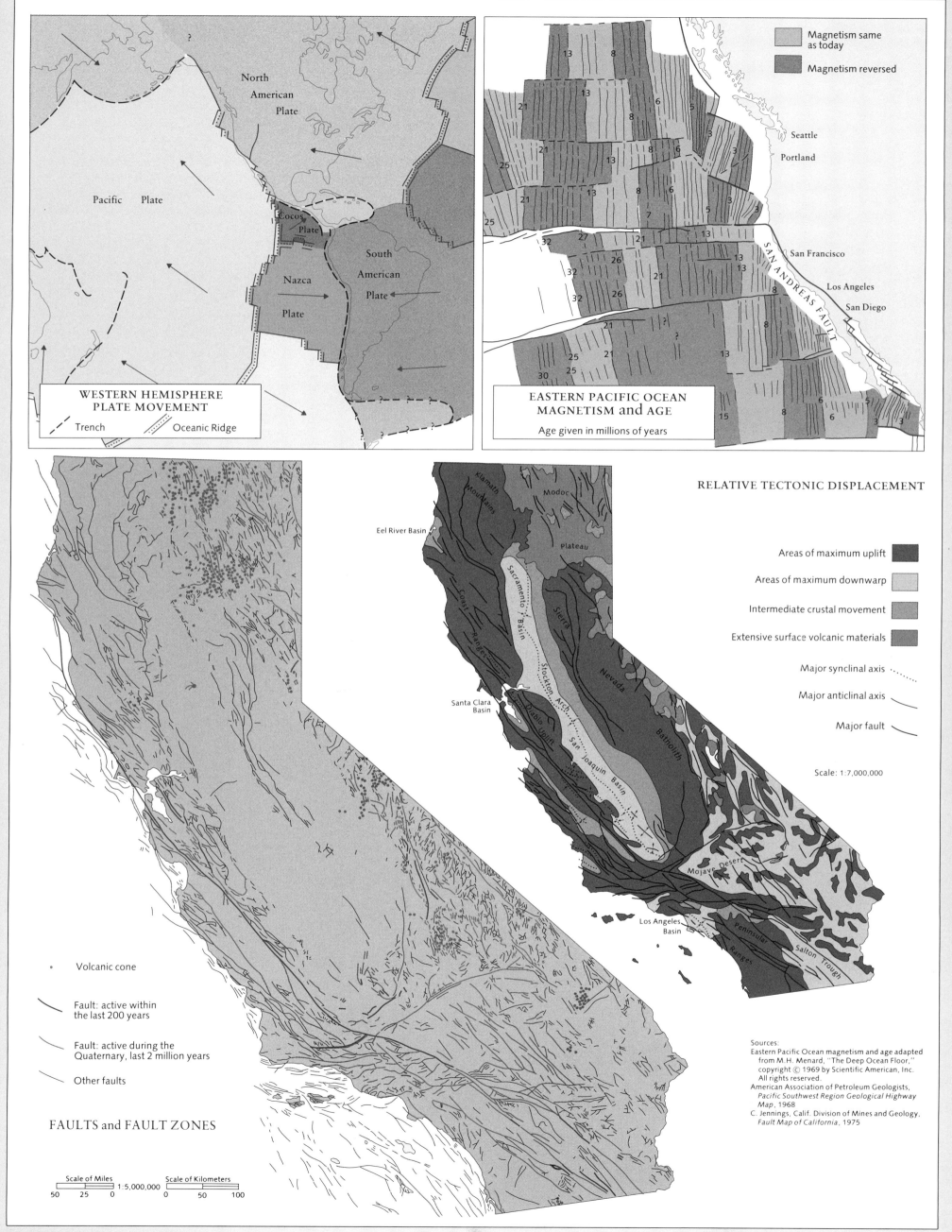

WESTERN HEMISPHERE PLATE MOVEMENT

Trench   Oceanic Ridge

EASTERN PACIFIC OCEAN MAGNETISM and AGE

Age given in millions of years

Magnetism same as today

Magnetism reversed

RELATIVE TECTONIC DISPLACEMENT

Areas of maximum uplift

Areas of maximum downwarp

Intermediate crustal movement

Extensive surface volcanic materials

Major synclinal axis

Major anticlinal axis

Major fault

Scale: 1:7,000,000

Volcanic cone

Fault: active within the last 200 years

Fault: active during the Quaternary, last 2 million years

Other faults

FAULTS and FAULT ZONES

Scale of Miles   1:5,000,000   Scale of Kilometers
50 25 0   0   50   100

Sources:
Eastern Pacific Ocean magnetism and age adapted from M.H. Menard, "The Deep Ocean Floor," copyright © 1969 by Scientific American, Inc. All rights reserved.
American Association of Petroleum Geologists, Pacific Southwest Region Geological Highway Map, 1968
C. Jennings, Calif. Division of Mines and Geology, Fault Map of California, 1975

TECTONICS

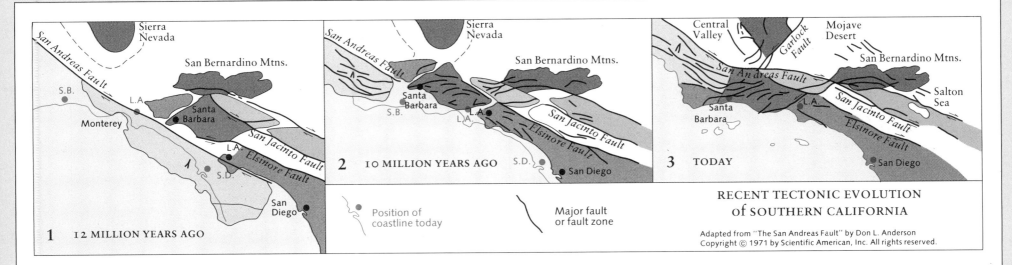

1 12 MILLION YEARS AGO

2 10 MILLION YEARS AGO

3 TODAY

Position of coastline today

Major fault or fault zone

RECENT TECTONIC EVOLUTION of SOUTHERN CALIFORNIA

Adapted from "The San Andreas Fault" by Don L. Anderson
Copyright © 1971 by Scientific American, Inc. All rights reserved.

Geology, earthquakes, and structural evolution are intimately linked to regional tectonics and the shifting of the earth's crustal plates. California lies astride the San Andreas fault, which separates the North American Plate from the Pacific Plate. The latter has been moving in a northwesterly direction at a rate of about 6 cm per year for the last million years. The compression caused by the relative movements of the two plates and the resulting secondary adjustments in smaller areas have produced the structure and arrangement of rock types shown on pages 116-119.

Crustal plates are somewhat rigid, so that the enormous forces necessary for their movement results in faults or crustal fractures, which are shown on the facing page. California's generally northwest to southeast structural alignment is evident in the folding of the Coast Ranges, the upward displacement of the Sierra Nevada, and downwarp of the Central Valley. Volcanic cones have developed in the northeast and adjacent to the Sierra Nevada due to recent volcanic activity and the extrusion of molten rock material.

The amount of movement and the intricacies of structural adjustment are illustrated in the Southern California example above. For 12 million years, the area west of the San Andreas fault has been sliding northward, moving off the mass of the San Bernardino Mountains and inching around the tip of the Sierra Nevada batholithic mass. The Transverse and Peninsular Ranges have developed as a result, the one aligned

east-west in order to avoid the Sierra, the other aligned with the San Andreas system and the general structural system. The Mojave Desert has been moved in an easterly direction because of this pinching action.

Earthquakes, movements along faults, occur when stress forces become great enough to overcome the resistance of friction between blocks. Hundreds of such sporadic movements occur every year, but most are small slippages reflecting fairly constant adjustment. Periodically, long-developing pressures are released as a single large movement, and these earthquakes wreak havoc on the state.

The frequency of earthquakes in California is about ten times higher than for the world as a whole, and the state falls into the highest seismic risk category in the nation. Three earthquakes in the state's history were equal to or greater than Richter magnitude 8: the San Francisco shock of 1906 (at 8.3), the Fort Tejon quake on January 9, 1857, and the Lone Pine quake on March 26, 1872. Three others—Point Arguello on November 4, 1927, Imperial Valley on May 18, 1940, and Arvin-Tehachapi on July 21, 1952—measured between 7 and 8.

The net result of tectonics over millions of years, displacement along faults, and the warping of many rock types of varying ages produced the geological patterns on the following pages.

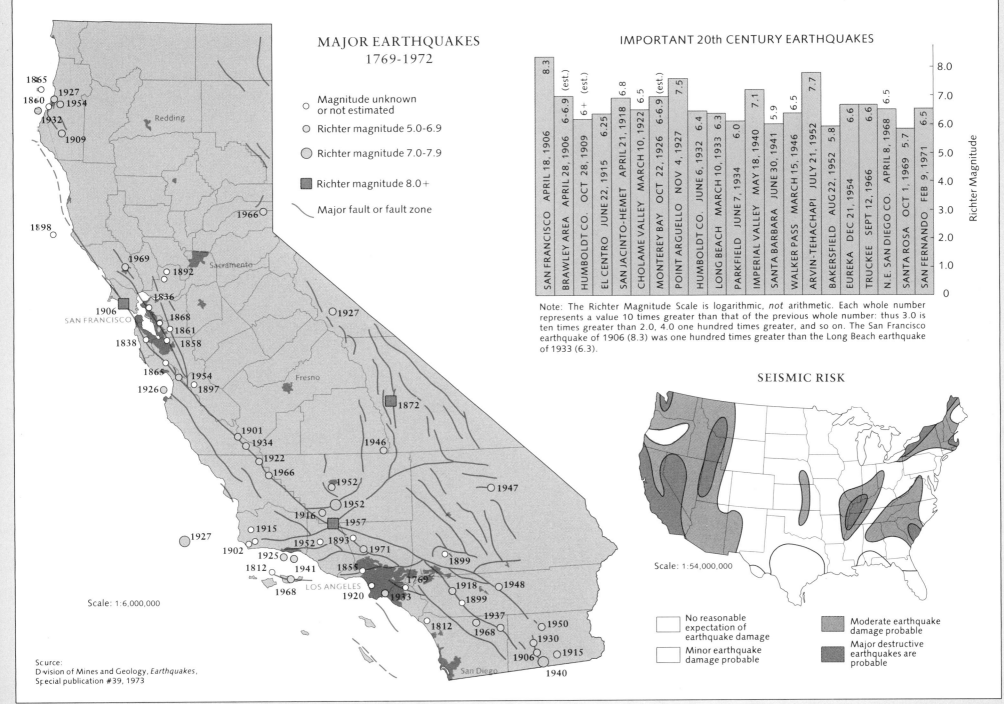

MAJOR EARTHQUAKES 1769-1972

○ Magnitude unknown or not estimated

○ Richter magnitude 5.0-6.9

◯ Richter magnitude 7.0-7.9

■ Richter magnitude 8.0+

Major fault or fault zone

Scale: 1:6,000,000

Source: Division of Mines and Geology, *Earthquakes*, Special publication #39, 1973

IMPORTANT 20th CENTURY EARTHQUAKES

Location	Date	Magnitude
SAN FRANCISCO	APRIL 18, 1906	8.3
BRAWLEY AREA	APRIL 28, 1906	6-6.9 (est.)
HUMBOLDT CO.	OCT 28, 1909	6+ (est.)
EL CENTRO	JUNE 22, 1915	6.25
SAN JACINTO-HEMET	APRIL 21, 1918	6.8
CHOLAME VALLEY	MARCH 10, 1922	6.5
MONTEREY BAY	OCT 22, 1926	6-6.9 (est.)
POINT ARGUELLO	NOV 4, 1927	7.5
HUMBOLDT CO.	JUNE 6, 1932	6.4
LONG BEACH	MARCH 10, 1933	6.3
PARKFIELD	JUNE 7, 1934	6.0
IMPERIAL VALLEY	MAY 18, 1940	7.1
SANTA BARBARA	JUNE 30, 1941	5.9
WALKER PASS	MARCH 15, 1946	6.5
ARVIN-TEHACHAPI	JULY 21, 1952	7.7
BAKERSFIELD	AUG 22, 1952	5.8
EUREKA	DEC 21, 1954	6.6
TRUCKEE	SEPT 12, 1966	6.6
N.E. SAN DIEGO CO.	APRIL 8, 1968	6.5
SANTA ROSA	OCT 1, 1969	5.7
SAN FERNANDO	FEB 9, 1971	6.5

Richter Magnitude

Note: The Richter Magnitude Scale is logarithmic, *not* arithmetic. Each whole number represents a value 10 times greater than that of the previous whole number: thus 3.0 is ten times greater than 2.0, 4.0 one hundred times greater, and so on. The San Francisco earthquake of 1906 (8.3) was one hundred times greater than the Long Beach earthquake of 1933 (6.3).

SEISMIC RISK

Scale: 1:54,000,000

☐ No reasonable expectation of earthquake damage

☐ Minor earthquake damage probable

▨ Moderate earthquake damage probable

■ Major destructive earthquakes are probable

EARTHQUAKES

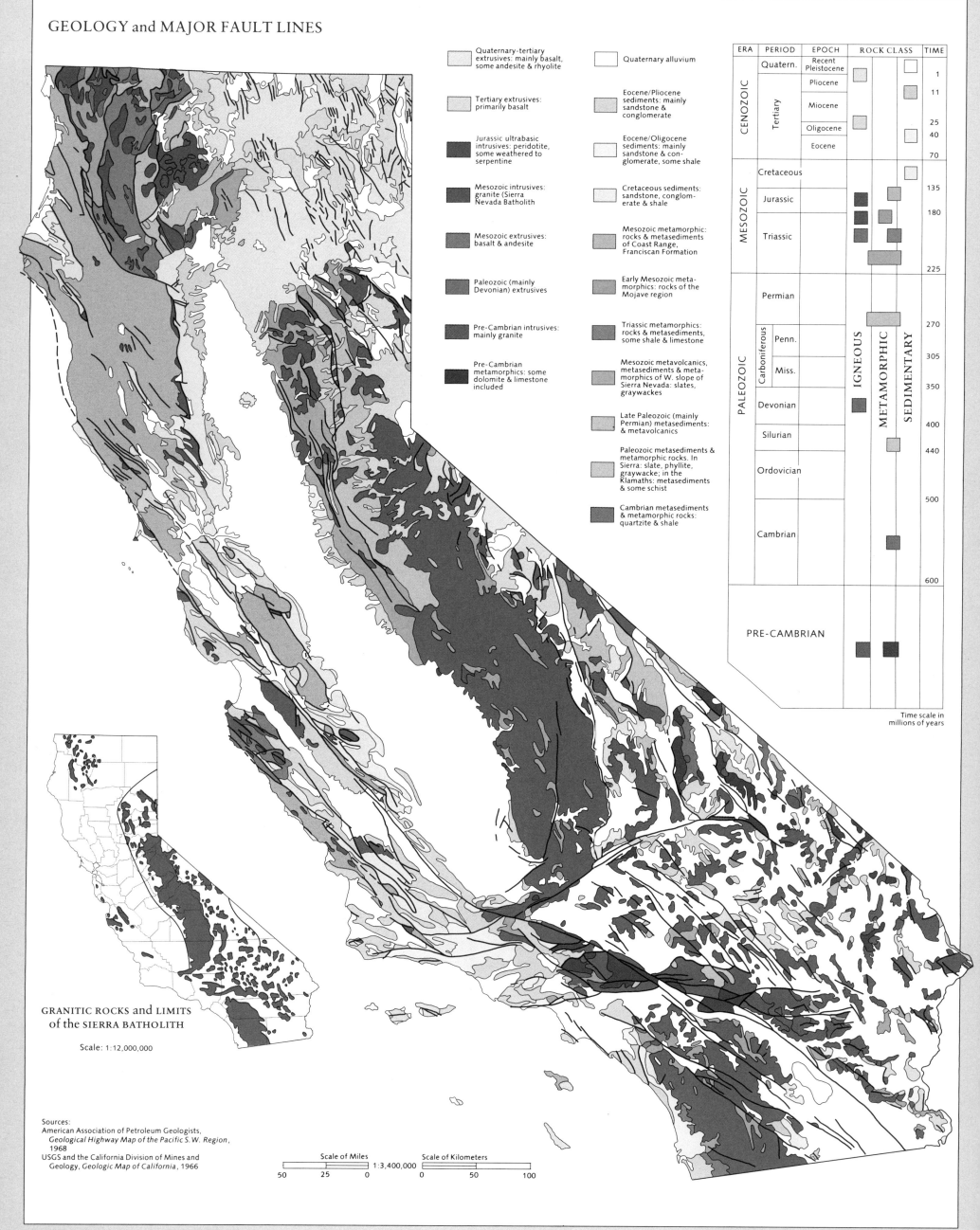

GEOLOGY and MAJOR FAULT LINES

GRANITIC ROCKS and LIMITS of the SIERRA BATHOLITH

Scale: 1:12,000,000

Sources:
American Association of Petroleum Geologists, *Geological Highway Map of the Pacific S.W. Region,* 1968
USGS and the California Division of Mines and Geology, *Geologic Map of California,* 1966

GEOLOGY

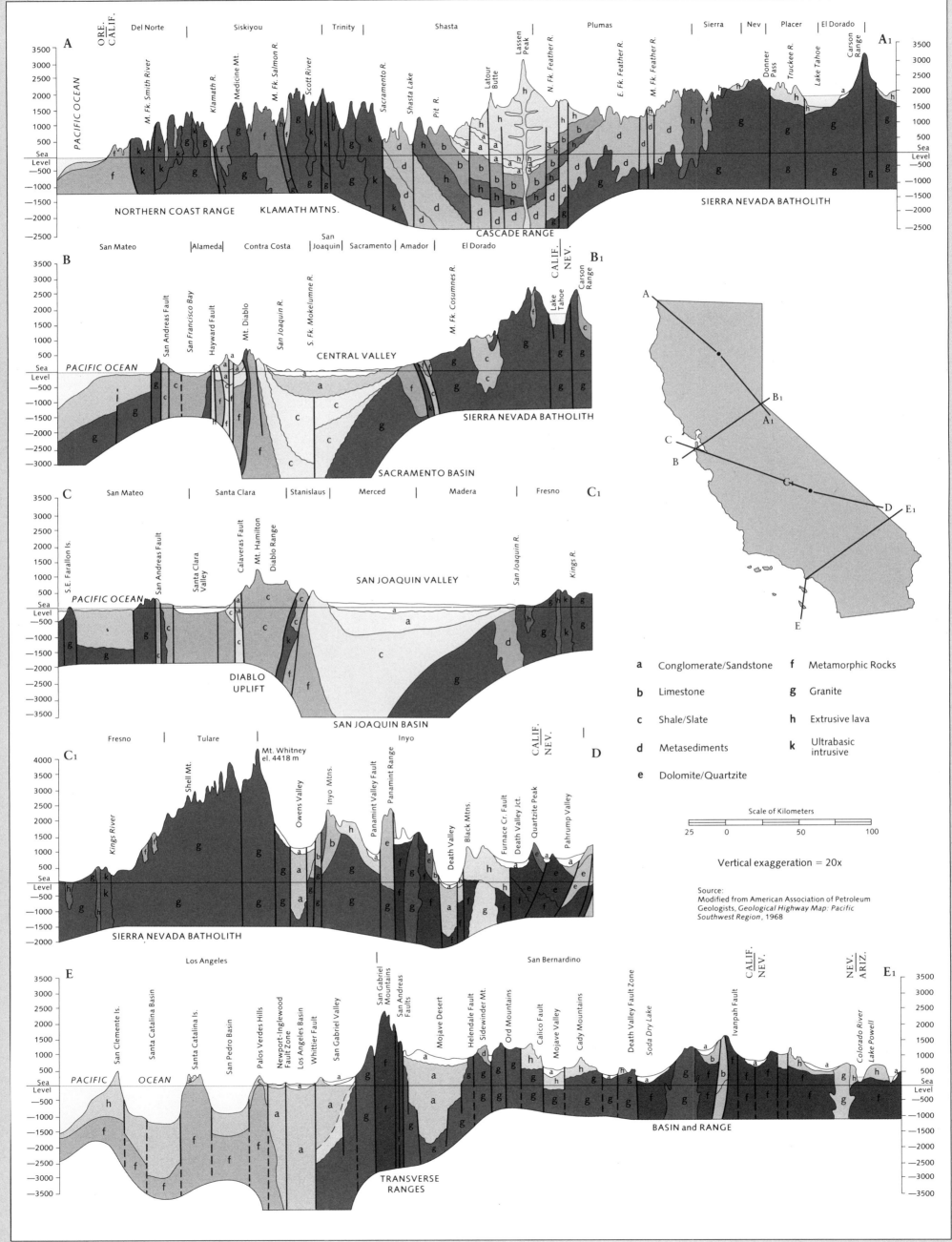

GEOLOGIC CROSS-SECTIONS

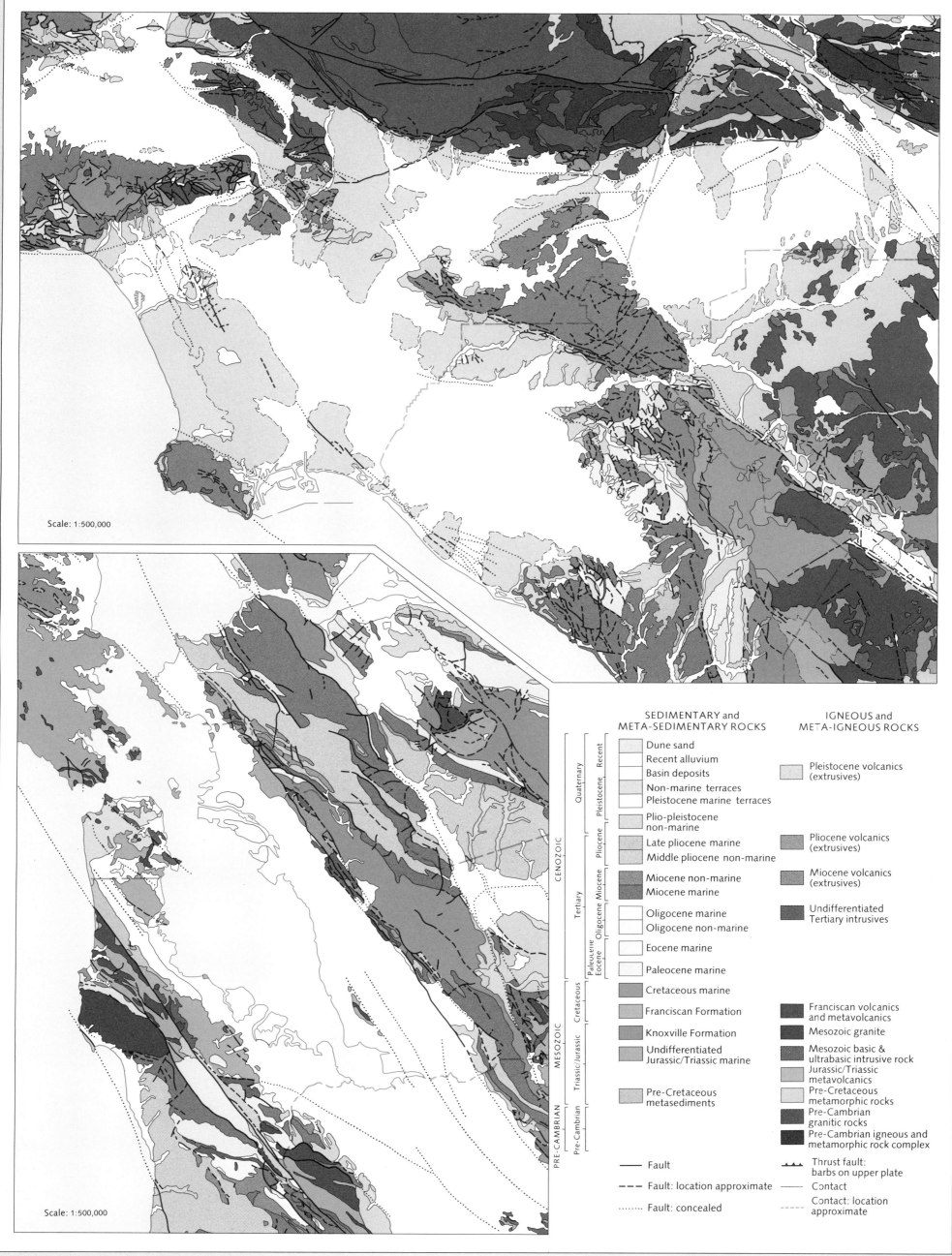

Scale: 1:500,000

Scale: 1:500,000

SEDIMENTARY and META-SEDIMENTARY ROCKS

IGNEOUS and META-IGNEOUS ROCKS

CENOZOIC

Quaternary — Recent: Dune sand, Recent alluvium, Basin deposits
Pleistocene: Non-marine terraces, Pleistocene marine terraces
Pliocene: Plio-pleistocene non-marine, Late pliocene marine, Middle pliocene non-marine

Tertiary
Miocene: Miocene non-marine, Miocene marine
Oligocene: Oligocene marine, Oligocene non-marine
Eocene: Eocene marine
Paleocene: Paleocene marine

MESOZOIC

Cretaceous: Cretaceous marine, Franciscan Formation, Knoxville Formation
Triassic/Jurassic: Undifferentiated Jurassic/Triassic marine

PRE-CAMBRIAN
Pre-Cambrian: Pre-Cretaceous metasediments

Pleistocene volcanics (extrusives)

Pliocene volcanics (extrusives)

Miocene volcanics (extrusives)

Undifferentiated Tertiary intrusives

Franciscan volcanics and metavolcanics
Mesozoic granite
Mesozoic basic & ultrabasic intrusive rock
Jurassic/Triassic metavolcanics
Pre-Cretaceous metamorphic rocks
Pre-Cambrian granitic rocks
Pre-Cambrian igneous and metamorphic rock complex

——— Fault
– – – Fault: location approximate
· · · · · Fault: concealed

▲▲▲ Thrust fault: barbs on upper plate
——— Contact
– – – Contact: location approximate

GEOLOGY: THE BAY AREA AND LOS ANGELES

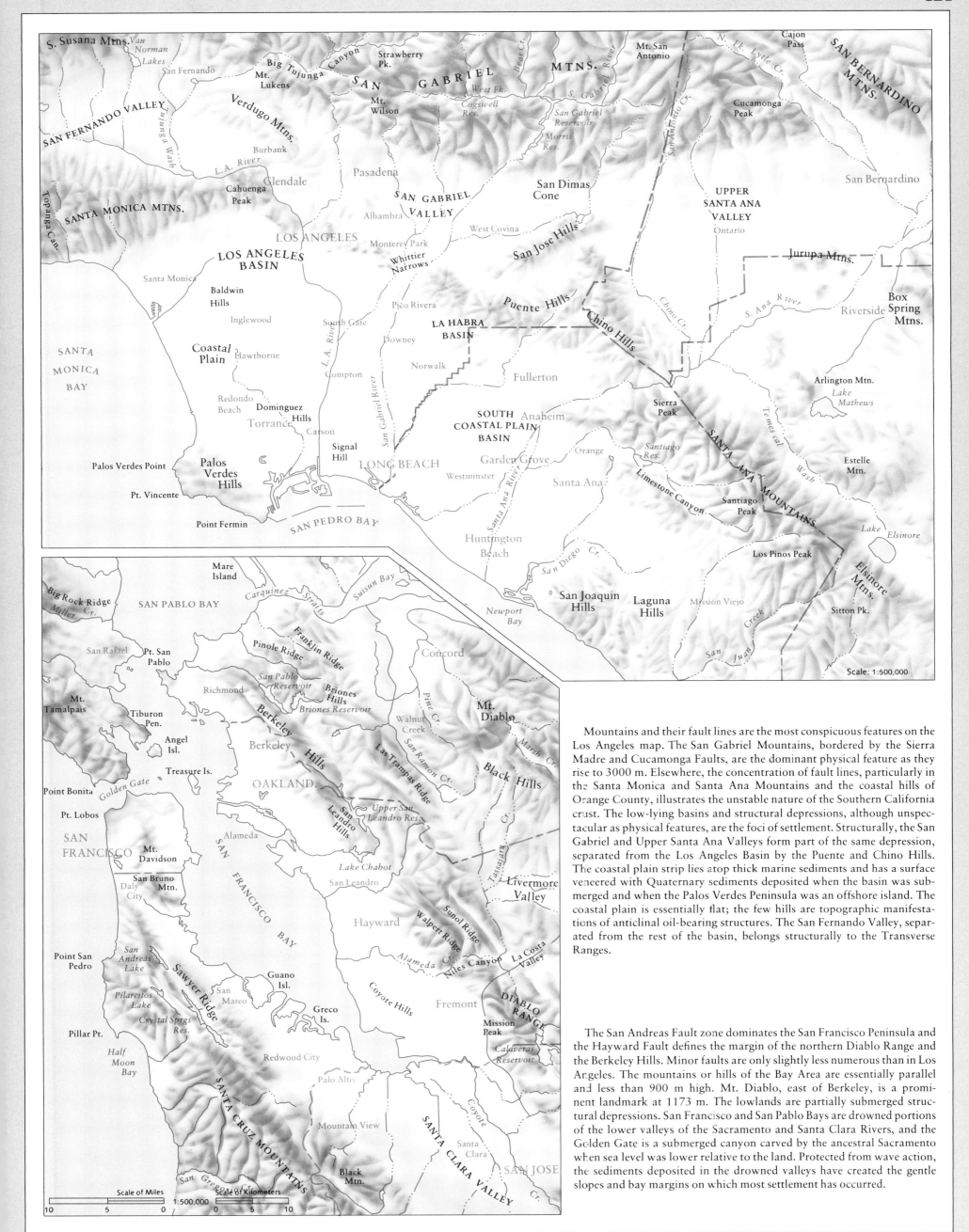

Mountains and their fault lines are the most conspicuous features on the Los Angeles map. The San Gabriel Mountains, bordered by the Sierra Madre and Cucamonga Faults, are the dominant physical feature as they rise to 3000 m. Elsewhere, the concentration of fault lines, particularly in the Santa Monica and Santa Ana Mountains and the coastal hills of Orange County, illustrates the unstable nature of the Southern California crust. The low-lying basins and structural depressions, although unspectacular as physical features, are the foci of settlement. Structurally, the San Gabriel and Upper Santa Ana Valleys form part of the same depression, separated from the Los Angeles Basin by the Puente and Chino Hills. The coastal plain strip lies atop thick marine sediments and has a surface veneered with Quaternary sediments deposited when the basin was submerged and when the Palos Verdes Peninsula was an offshore island. The coastal plain is essentially flat; the few hills are topographic manifestations of anticlinal oil-bearing structures. The San Fernando Valley, separated from the rest of the basin, belongs structurally to the Transverse Ranges.

The San Andreas Fault zone dominates the San Francisco Peninsula and the Hayward Fault defines the margin of the northern Diablo Range and the Berkeley Hills. Minor faults are only slightly less numerous than in Los Angeles. The mountains or hills of the Bay Area are essentially parallel and less than 900 m high. Mt. Diablo, east of Berkeley, is a prominent landmark at 1173 m. The lowlands are partially submerged structural depressions. San Francisco and San Pablo Bays are drowned portions of the lower valleys of the Sacramento and Santa Clara Rivers, and the Golden Gate is a submerged canyon carved by the ancestral Sacramento when sea level was lower relative to the land. Protected from wave action, the sediments deposited in the drowned valleys have created the gentle slopes and bay margins on which most settlement has occurred.

TERRAIN: THE BAY AREA AND LOS ANGELES

The Pleistocene period in California, as elsewhere, is characterized by climatic change, the growth and retreat of glaciers, and changing sea levels. The glacial sequence was best developed and most extensive in the Sierra Nevada. It included six successive glaciations: McGee, the oldest, was followed by Sherwin, Mono Basin, Tahoe, Tenaya and Tioga. The last three are subdivisions of the more general Wisconsin Advance recognized in the eastern part of the country as beginning roughly 100,000 years ago and ending within the last 10,000 years.

Climatic change, along with varying amounts of ice, resulted in the formation and disappearance of many fresh water lakes and a rising and falling sea level. Because of widespread tectonism and volcanism during the last one million years, the complexities of Pleistocene events, particularly in the coastal zone, are difficult to unravel. Less is known of glacial age California than is known of other places where crustal stability has helped to preserve the forms and relative positions of relict features.

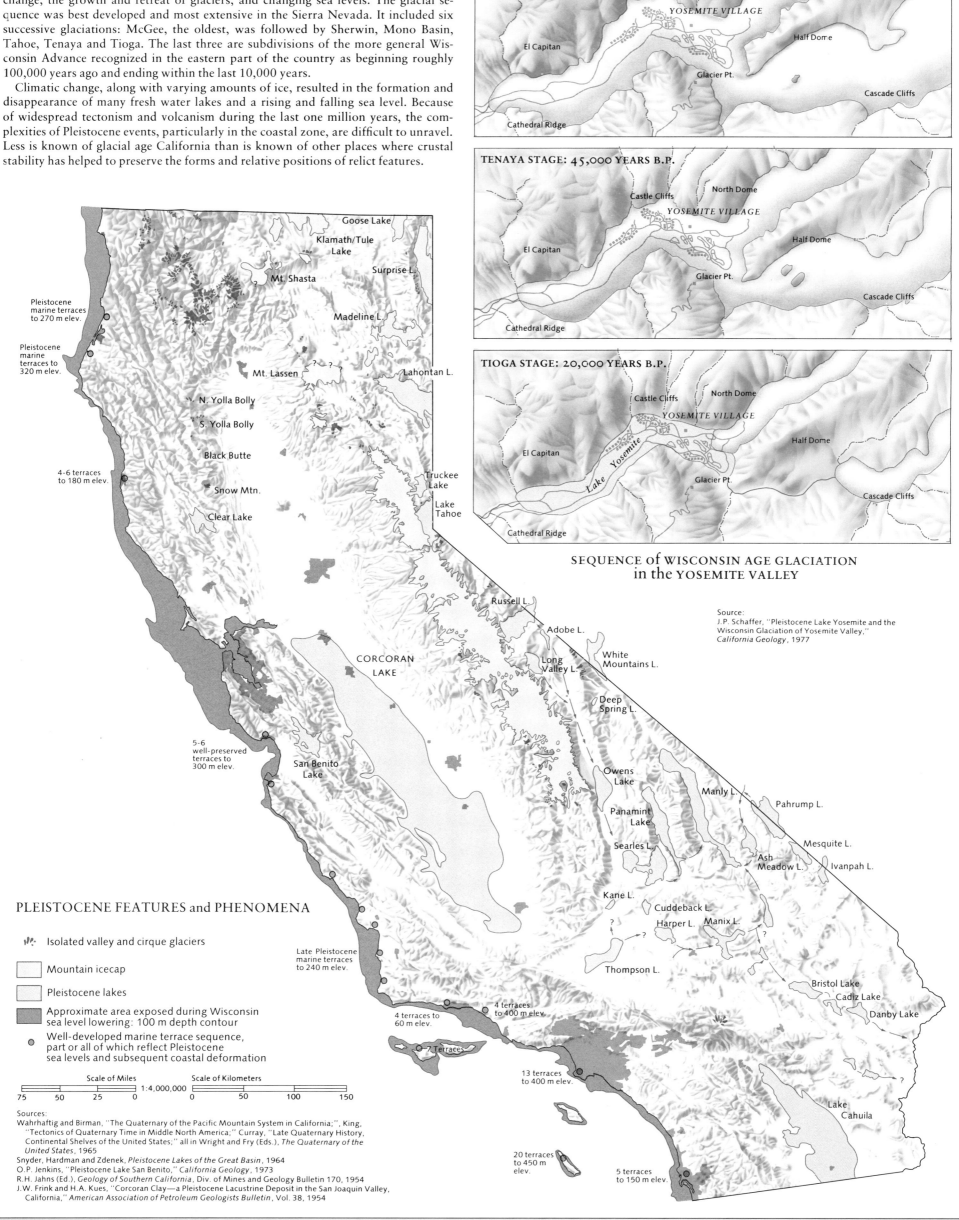

TAHOE STAGE: 70,000 YEARS B.P.

Castle Cliffs · North Dome · YOSEMITE VILLAGE · El Capitan · Half Dome · Glacier Pt. · Cascade Cliffs · Cathedral Ridge

TENAYA STAGE: 45,000 YEARS B.P.

Castle Cliffs · North Dome · YOSEMITE VILLAGE · El Capitan · Half Dome · Glacier Pt. · Cascade Cliffs · Cathedral Ridge

TIOGA STAGE: 20,000 YEARS B.P.

Castle Cliffs · North Dome · YOSEMITE VILLAGE · El Capitan · Lake Yosemite · Half Dome · Glacier Pt. · Cascade Cliffs · Cathedral Ridge

SEQUENCE of WISCONSIN AGE GLACIATION
in the YOSEMITE VALLEY

Source:
J.P. Schaffer, "Pleistocene Lake Yosemite and the Wisconsin Glaciation of Yosemite Valley," *California Geology*, 1977

Goose Lake · Klamath/Tule Lake · Surprise L. · Mt. Shasta · Madeline L. · Mt. Lassen · Lahontan L. · N. Yolla Bolly · S. Yolla Bolly · Black Butte · Snow Mtn. · Clear Lake · Truckee Lake · Lake Tahoe · Russell L. · Adobe L. · White Mountains L. · Long Valley L. · Deep Spring L. · Owens Lake · Manly L. · Pahrump L. · Panamint Lake · Searles L. · Mesquite L. · Ash Meadow L. · Ivanpah L. · Kane L. · Cuddeback L. · Harper L. · Manix L. · Thompson L. · Bristol Lake · Cadiz Lake · Danby Lake · Lake Cahuila

CORCORAN LAKE

San Benito Lake

Pleistocene marine terraces to 270 m elev.

Pleistocene marine terraces to 320 m elev.

4-6 terraces to 180 m elev.

5-6 well-preserved terraces to 300 m elev.

Late Pleistocene marine terraces to 240 m elev.

4 terraces to 60 m elev.

4 terraces to 400 m elev.

13 terraces to 400 m elev.

20 terraces to 450 m elev.

5 terraces to 150 m elev.

7 Terraces

PLEISTOCENE FEATURES and PHENOMENA

- Isolated valley and cirque glaciers
- Mountain icecap
- Pleistocene lakes
- Approximate area exposed during Wisconsin sea level lowering: 100 m depth contour
- Well-developed marine terrace sequence, part or all of which reflect Pleistocene sea levels and subsequent coastal deformation

Scale of Miles · Scale of Kilometers
75 50 25 0   1:4,000,000   50 100 150

Sources:
Wahrhaftig and Birman, "The Quaternary of the Pacific Mountain System in California;", King, "Tectonics of Quaternary Time in Middle North America;" Curray, "Late Quaternary History, Continental Shelves of the United States;" all in Wright and Fry (Eds.), *The Quaternary of the United States*, 1965
Snyder, Hardman and Zdenek, *Pleistocene Lakes of the Great Basin*, 1964
O.P. Jenkins, "Pleistocene Lake San Benito," *California Geology*, 1973
R.H. Jahns (Ed.), *Geology of Southern California*, Div. of Mines and Geology Bulletin 170, 1954
J.W. Frink and H.A. Kues, "Corcoran Clay—a Pleistocene Lacustrine Deposit in the San Joaquin Valley, California," *American Association of Petroleum Geologists Bulletin*, Vol. 38, 1954

PLEISTOCENE ENVIRONMENTS

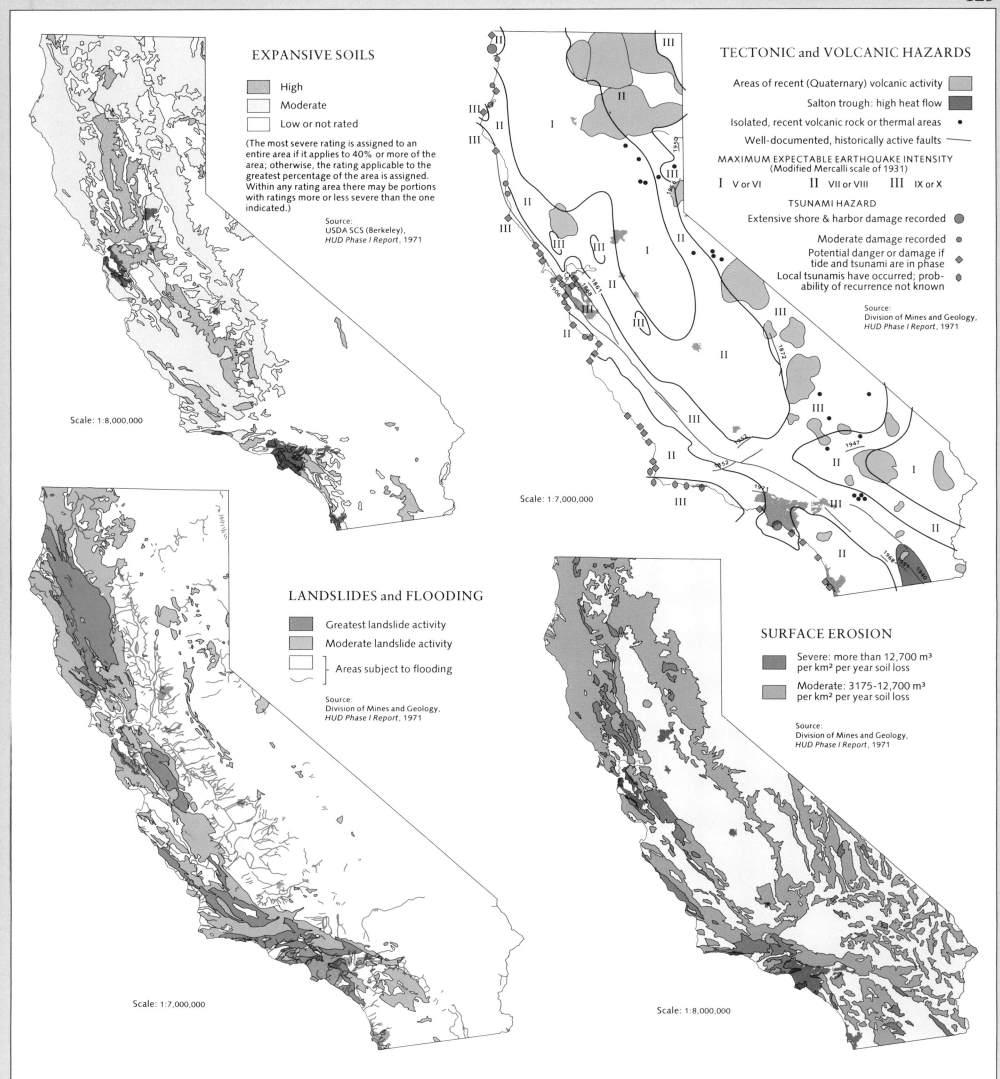

EXPANSIVE SOILS

High

Moderate

Low or not rated

(The most severe rating is assigned to an entire area if it applies to 40% or more of the area; otherwise, the rating applicable to the greatest percentage of the area is assigned. Within any rating area there may be portions with ratings more or less severe than the one indicated.)

Source:
USDA SCS (Berkeley),
HUD Phase I Report, 1971

Scale: 1:8,000,000

TECTONIC and VOLCANIC HAZARDS

Areas of recent (Quaternary) volcanic activity

Salton trough: high heat flow

Isolated, recent volcanic rock or thermal areas

Well-documented, historically active faults

MAXIMUM EXPECTABLE EARTHQUAKE INTENSITY
(Modified Mercalli scale of 1931)

I V or VI   II VII or VIII   III IX or X

TSUNAMI HAZARD

Extensive shore & harbor damage recorded

Moderate damage recorded

Potential danger or damage if tide and tsunami are in phase

Local tsunamis have occurred; probability of recurrence not known

Source:
Division of Mines and Geology,
HUD Phase I Report, 1971

Scale: 1:7,000,000

LANDSLIDES and FLOODING

Greatest landslide activity

Moderate landslide activity

Areas subject to flooding

Source:
Division of Mines and Geology,
HUD Phase I Report, 1971

Scale: 1:7,000,000

SURFACE EROSION

Severe: more than 12,700 m³ per km² per year soil loss

Moderate: 3175-12,700 m³ per km² per year soil loss

Source:
Division of Mines and Geology,
HUD Phase I Report, 1971

Scale: 1:8,000,000

Four potential natural hazards, whose severity ranges from mild to catastrophic, are mapped on this page. Among these, expansive soils, whose compositions include swelling clays of the illite and montmorillonite groups, can absorb water. When they do, they expand and often damage human structures. They also lose their internal strength on absorbing water, and are likely to deform or slide.

Landslides and floods usually result from the kind of heavy precipitation which reduces soil strength and promotes mass movement. Winter torrents in particular erode adjacent slopes severely, and often trigger slides on built-up residential slopes in Southern California. In addition, wild fires or construction of buildings and roads alters surface form, removes binding vegetation, and promotes landsliding, surface runoff, and flooding.

Earthquakes are clearly perceived as a hazard by Californians, but two other tec-

tonic hazards, volcanic eruptions and tsunamis, are less recognized. The possibilities of volcanic eruptions are limited to the least populated areas of the state, but tsunamis, or tidal waves, pose a threat to populous coastal zones. They are caused by underwater earthquakes in the Pacific Basin, and normally do little damage. On March 27, 1967, however, the Alaska Earthquake generated a tsunami that killed eight people and caused $11,000,000 in damages at Crescent City, on the northern coast.

Surface erosion often causes major damage by decreasing the productivity of the soil and its water retention capacity. The transport of eroded materials does further damage: silt in streams damages the habitat for fish and increases flood potential by clogging drains and canals, for example. Almost all surface erosion is accelerated by human activities that disturb vegetation and soil surface, although the quantities of soil lost also depend on slope and soil type.

NATURAL HAZARDS

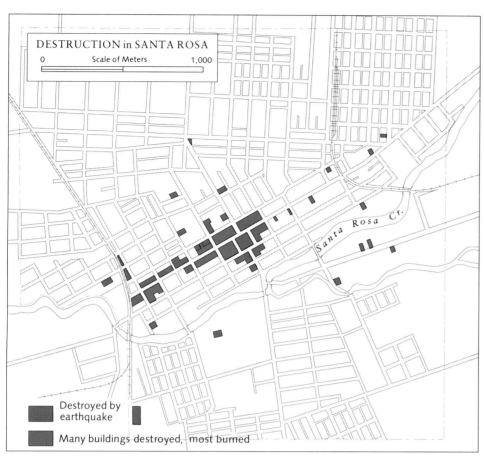

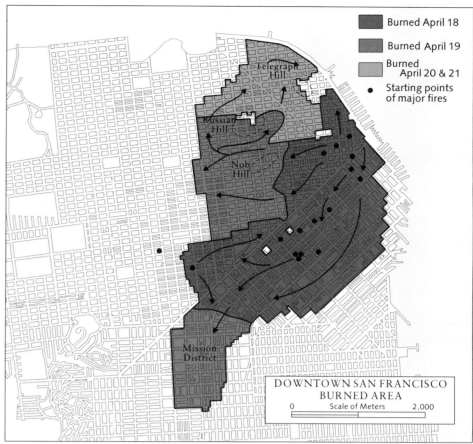

On the morning of April 18, 1906, northern California experienced the worst earthquake in the state's history. Massive displacement along the San Andreas Fault shook the earth for more than a minute, registered 8.3 on the Richter Scale, and caused destructive movement along a zone about 50 km wide and more than 400 km long. Estimates of the damage reached one billion dollars and 700 lives.

San Francisco was the hardest hit; property losses were estimated at $520,000,000, and some 450 persons died. Many of San Francisco's buildings were severely damaged by the quake itself, but 80 per cent of the losses resulted from fires that broke out and swept the city in the aftermath of the shock. Ruptured gas lines accounted for many of the more than fifty reported fires. Most of them were quickly extinguished, but more than fifteen assumed major proportions. Broken water mains became a major problem for the fire fighters, who were reduced to dynamiting buildings in order to create fire breaks. The use of explosives did little to check the spread of the flames, and in fact poorly placed charges often helped spread the conflagration. Within 24 hours, the fire had burned a large area south of Market Street and destroyed the homes of 100,000 people. When the last flames had been put out, two days later, the entire business district and three-fifths of the town's residences were in ruin. In all, 490 blocks, or more than 1130 hectares, were burned, and 250,000 San Franciscans were homeless.

Extensive damage was reported elsewhere. North of San Francisco, the city of Santa Rosa was nearly destroyed, and 75 people died. Even though the fault was 30 km away, the destruction was intense and widespread. Most of the brick buildings in the business district crumbled with the initial jolt, and the fires that followed burned downtown and adjacent areas. The damage, it was later determined, resulted from low quality building materials and poor design standards used in the construction of many of the structures. Other communities along the northern line of the fault also suffered. Much of Fort Bragg burned, and towns such as Tomales, Sebastopol and Point Reyes were considerably damaged. Even places as far north as Eureka were badly shaken.

The situation was no better south of San Francisco. Much of Stanford University was ruined. At Agnew State Hospital, north of San Jose, 100 people died when the main structure collapsed. In San Jose itself, the earthquake left nineteen people dead and 8000 homeless.

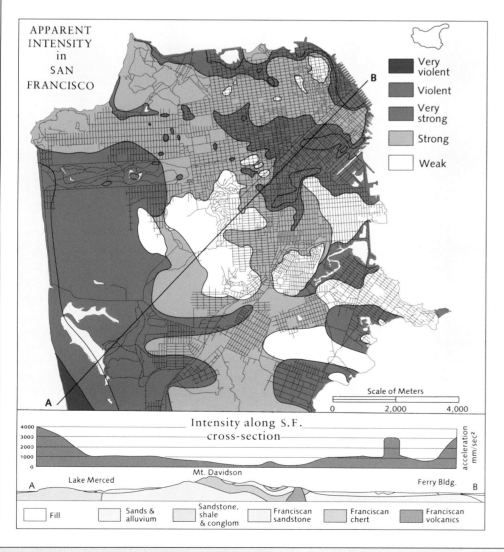

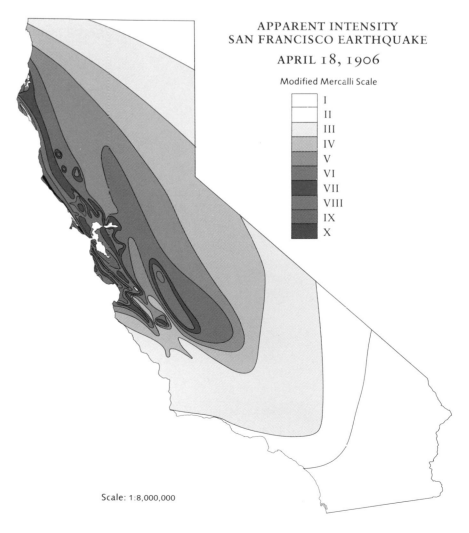

THE SAN FRANCISCO EARTHQUAKE

Among the many catastrophes that have struck California, four have been selected to illustrate the range of disasters that have affected the state.

California has suffered many destructive fires, but few have burned over wider areas than the Marble-Cone Fire of August, 1977. The fire, caused by lightning strikes on August 1, burned continuously for 21 days and spread over almost 72,000 ha (about 180,000 acres), mainly in the Monterey District of the Los Padres National Forest. Several factors contributed to the magnitude of the burn. In January, 1974, an unusual snowstorm broke many limbs and compressed the brush. Two successive seasons of drought in 1976 and 1977 transformed this underbrush into a powder keg. Once the lightning struck and the blaze ignited, the situation was further complicated by inaccessibility, steep slopes, many simultaneous fires and the lateness in the fire season. By the time the fire had been put out, $11,900,000 had been spent on firefighting and losses were estimated at $350,000,000.

Earthquakes have always been a spectre of California living and a significant number of disastrous tremors have occurred since statehood. The shock that rocked the San Fernando Valley in February of 1971 is one of the recent major seismic events. The earthquake had a Richter magnitude of 6.5, resulted in 64 deaths and caused an estimated $511,000,000 in damage. But damage could have been much worse: the early hour of the shock, at six a.m., prevented loss of life from reaching higher and the dam on Lower Van Norman Lake did not completely fail. Secondary ramifications of the quake included the near dam failure, which resulted in the

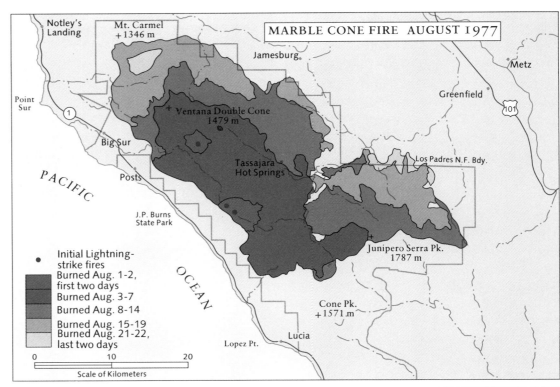

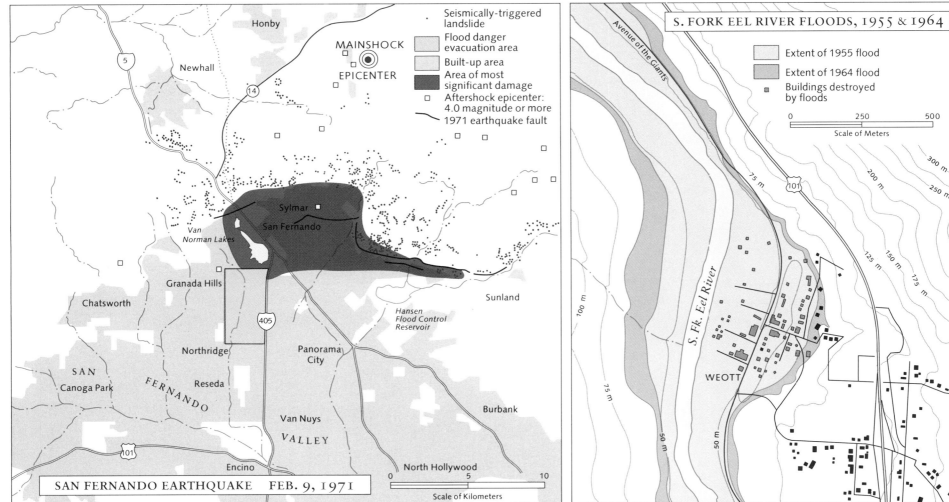

evacuation of a large section of the Valley, and more than a thousand landslides triggered by the ground motion.

Disastrous floods occurred along many rivers in northern California in 1955 and 1964. Conditions in 1964 along the South Fork of the Eel River in Humboldt County are representative. At Weott, a community about three kilometers above the mouth of the South Fork, water was about twenty meters above normal river level and about nine meters above the Avenue of the Giants during the December 1964 flood. Nineteen persons lost their lives in the Eel River Basin and almost all the buildings at Weott were destroyed.

The Saint Francis Dam failure resulted from an error in engineering. The dam, 56 m high in San Francisquito Canyon, north of Saugus, had side foundations anchored in schist and conglomerate that was not competent. Just before midnight, on March 12, 1928, the west side foundations gave way, the dam collapsed and a huge wall of water moved downstream. This man-made flash flood killed approximately 420 people and devastated the entire Santa Clara River Valley before it finally reached the ocean near Ventura some five and a half hours later.

Sources:
Maps and reports provided by Los Padres National Forest, King City
The San Fernando, Calif. Earthquake of Feb. 9, 1971, USGS Professional Paper 733, 1971
San Fernando, Calif. Earthquake of 9 February 1971. Division of Mines and Geology Bulletin 196, G. Oakeshott, ed. 1975
C.F. Outland, *Man-Made Disaster: the Story of the St. Francis Dam*, 1963
U.S. Army Corps of Engineers, *Flood Plain Information: S. Fork Eel River, Weott to Myers Flat, Humboldt Co., California*, 1968

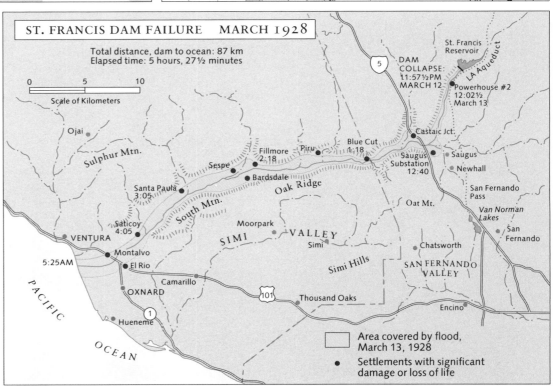

CATASTROPHES

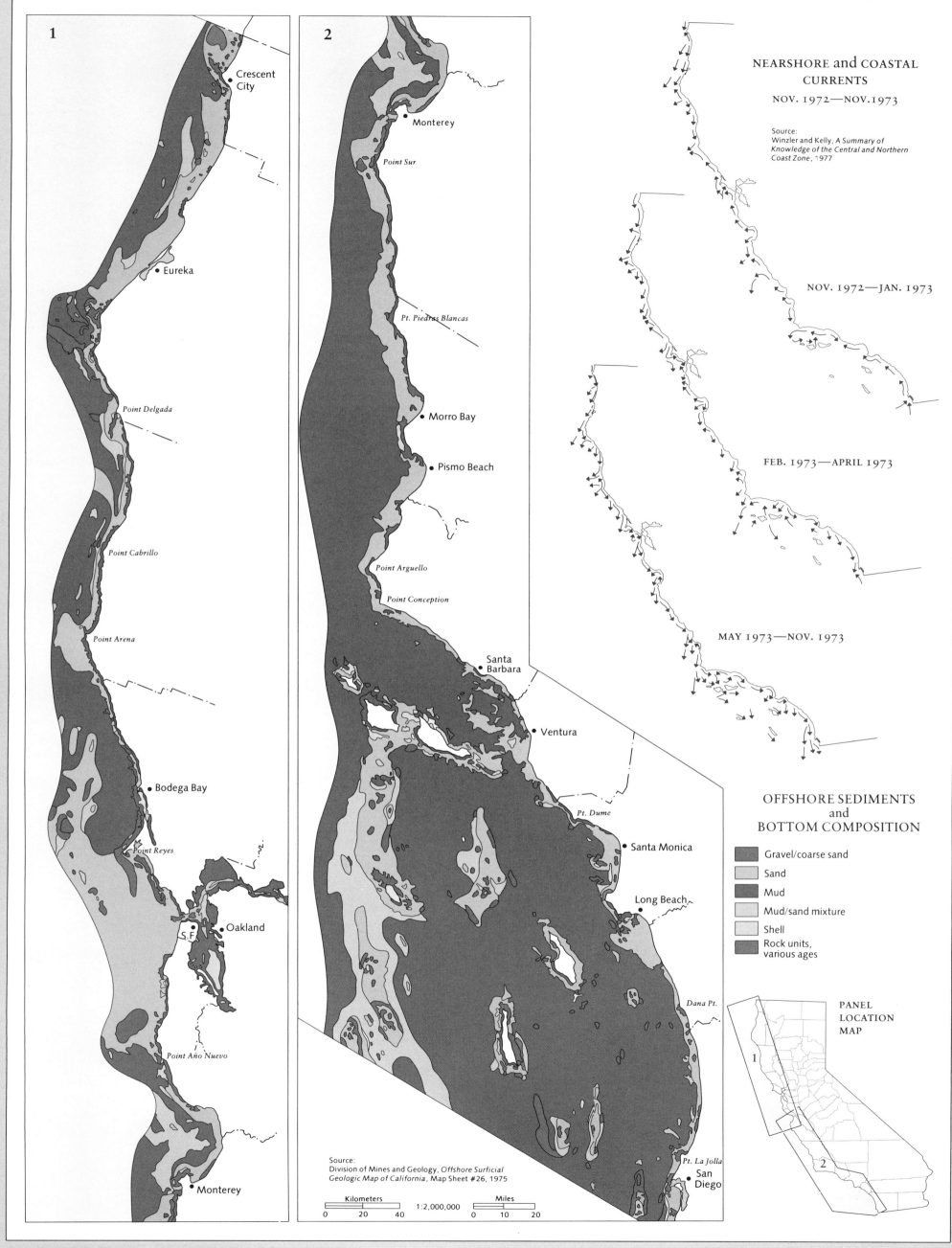

1

2

Crescent City

Monterey

Point Sur

Eureka

Pt. Piedras Blancas

Point Delgada

Morro Bay

Pismo Beach

Point Cabrillo

Point Arguello

Point Conception

Point Arena

Santa Barbara

Ventura

Bodega Bay

Pt. Dume

Santa Monica

Point Reyes

Long Beach

S.F. Oakland

Dana Pt.

Point Año Nuevo

Pt. La Jolla
San Diego

Monterey

Source:
Division of Mines and Geology, Offshore Surficial
Geologic Map of California, Map Sheet #26, 1975

Kilometers   Miles
0   20   40   1:2,000,000   0   10   20

NEARSHORE and COASTAL CURRENTS
NOV. 1972—NOV. 1973

Source:
Winzler and Kelly, A Summary of
Knowledge of the Central and Northern
Coast Zone, 1977

NOV. 1972—JAN. 1973

FEB. 1973—APRIL 1973

MAY 1973—NOV. 1973

OFFSHORE SEDIMENTS and BOTTOM COMPOSITION

- Gravel/coarse sand
- Sand
- Mud
- Mud/sand mixture
- Shell
- Rock units, various ages

PANEL LOCATION MAP

1

2

OFFSHORE SEDIMENTS AND CURRENTS

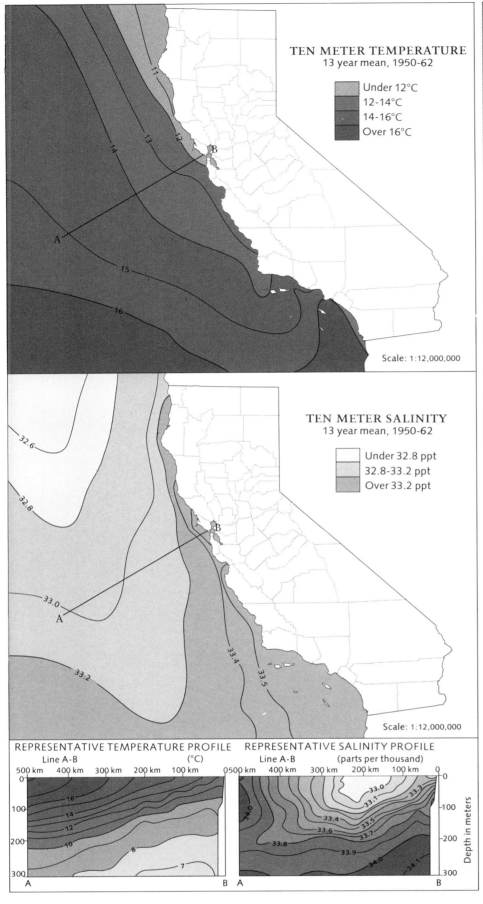

TEN METER TEMPERATURE
13 year mean, 1950-62

- Under 12°C
- 12-14°C
- 14-16°C
- Over 16°C

Scale: 1:12,000,000

TEN METER SALINITY
13 year mean, 1950-62

- Under 32.8 ppt
- 32.8-33.2 ppt
- Over 33.2 ppt

Scale: 1:12,000,000

REPRESENTATIVE TEMPERATURE PROFILE
Line A-B (°C)

500 km 400 km 300 km 200 km 100 km

REPRESENTATIVE SALINITY PROFILE
Line A-B (parts per thousand)

500 km 400 km 300 km 200 km 100 km

Depth in meters

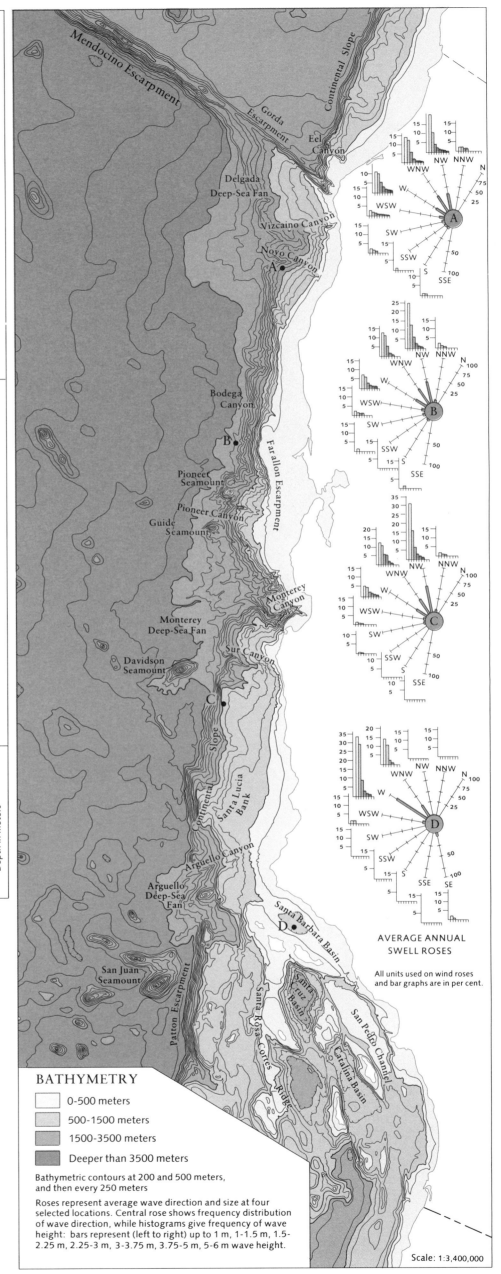

AVERAGE ANNUAL SWELL ROSES

All units used on wind roses and bar graphs are in per cent.

BATHYMETRY

- 0-500 meters
- 500-1500 meters
- 1500-3500 meters
- Deeper than 3500 meters

Bathymetric contours at 200 and 500 meters, and then every 250 meters

Roses represent average wave direction and size at four selected locations. Central rose shows frequency distribution of wave direction, while histograms give frequency of wave height: bars represent (left to right) up to 1 m, 1-1.5 m, 1.5-2.25 m, 2.25-3 m, 3-3.75 m, 3.75-5 m, 5-6 m wave height.

Scale: 1:3,400,000

California's coastal configuration and oceanic environment is extremely diverse. The San Andreas Fault determines the configuration of the continental shelf north of San Francisco as well as the undersea mountain range called the Mendocino Escarpment. The continental shelf is narrow here, unlike southern California, where the same tectonic forces have created a broader shelf with islands and submarine mountain ranges separated by basins. North of Point Concepcion, submarine canyons and deep-sea fans caused by violent turbidity currents punctuate the shelf; southward, seamounts or submerged mountains are numerous.

A complex set of currents shifts the shore sediments and debris. The dominant coastal current, the California Current, comes from the north, lowering temperatures and salinity values. In the nearshore area, water moves in response to the coastal configuration and to weather conditions. The overall pattern of movement is again to the south, but some areas have northward or offshore flows for part of the year. Storms and wave direction also vary the patterns of movement, as seen on the average swell roses above.

The nearshore pattern of circulation moves most of the coastal debris and creates the patterns of bottom and offshore sediments shown on page 126. Debris removed from areas of active erosion leaves exposed rock units and headlands; sand is shifted along the coast and deposited where current velocity or wave energy diminishes. Lighter particles are transported seaward into deeper waters, blanketing the basins and the shelf margin.

OCEANOGRAPHY

SOIL ORDERS

Soils are mapped here at two levels of generalization. General patterns for the whole state are shown by using the *Seventh Approximation* of the U.S. Department of Agriculture classification system. Only the major division of soils, into *orders*, is shown. Tehama, Madera and San Diego counties, shown on the facing page, were selected to illustrate the variety of soils and physical regions in the state. The older, more familiar place-associated classification based on names of soils series is used on these more detailed maps.

In general, California's soils and the soil orders correspond to the physiographic regions (see page 114) because landform and geomorphic processes strongly influence soil formation. In the Central Valley, in other major river valleys and in flat or gently sloping basins, alluvial soils develop on the river deposits. As a rule, these are the most productive soils for agriculture, although poor drainage or the presence of alkali may be a drawback. Alluvial soils are generally deep, but lack the distinctive horizons that develop from the transfer of material from one layer to another by long-term weathering.

Mountainous areas such as the Sierra Nevada, Klamath Mountains and Coast Ranges contain a variety of residual soils (developed in place as the bedrock weathers). Their character differs from north to south and with elevation, depending on slope and climate. In general, however, high precipitation and low slope angle produce deeper and better soils. The thinnest and most poorly developed soils are found on the east face of the Sierra Nevada and in the Transverse and Peninsular Ranges, where sparse vegetation has accelerated erosion on steep slopes.

In the desert, light colored alluvial soils of low organic content are found in areas of low relief; irrigation can make some of them highly productive. At higher elevations, soils are very thin or non-existent.

SOIL ORDERS Seventh Approximation

- Alfisols predominate
- Aridosols predominate
- Entisols predominate
- Histosols predominate
- Inceptisols predominate
- Mollisols predominate
- Ultisols predominate
- Vertisols predominate
- Badlands, dunes, granite and lava rockland: no appreciable soil development

Sources:
USDA Soil Conservation Service, *Classification of Soil Series of the United States*, 1977
————, *Soil Association Maps*, 1976

EXPLANATION OF MAJOR SOIL ORDERS FOUND IN CALIFORNIA

ALFISOLS: Developed under forest cover, characterized by downward leaching of clay particles

ARIDOSOLS: Light-colored soils of dry regions

ENTISOLS: Lack genetic horizons, generally developed on or of transported materials

HISTOSOLS: Developed in deposits of organic material

INCEPTISOLS: Represent early stages of soil formation; incomplete or poorly developed horizon structure

MOLLISOLS: Dark surface color, generally developed under grass cover

ULTISOLS: Similar to Alfisols, but bases have been more completely depleted

VERTISOLS: Dominated by expansive clays

Scale of Miles   Scale of Kilometers
75 50 25 0   1:3,400,000   0 50 100 150

SOILS

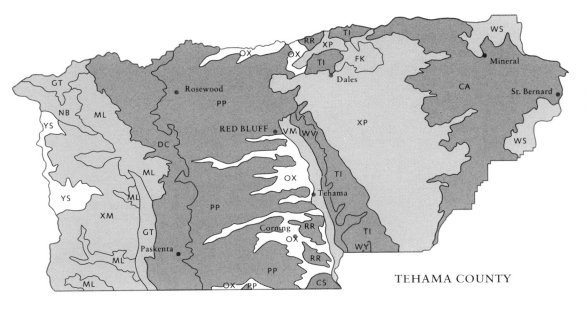

TEHAMA COUNTY

SOIL ASSOCIATIONS
Selected Counties

AR	ARLINGTON-RAMONA-PLACENTIA: moderately well-drained, deep, sandy soils (alluvial fans)
AS	AHWANNEE-AUBERRY-SIERRA: well-drained, moderately deep, coarse sandy loams (granite rock)
BT	BLASINGAME-TRIMMER-LAS POSAS: well-drained, moderately deep, stony loams (acid igneous rock)
CA	COHASSET-AIKEN-McCARTHY: well-drained, deep to moderately deep, stony loam (volcanic plateau)
CC	CHESTERTON-CARLSBAD-MARINA: Moderately well-drained, fine sandy loams (low coastal ridges)
CF	COARSEGOLD-FRIANT-SAN ANDREAS: well-drained, moderately deep, loam and clay loam (basic igneous rock)
DC	DIBBLE-CONTRA COSTA-SEHORN: moderately drained, moderately deep, clay loams (sandstone and shale)
FE	FRESNO-EL PECO: imperfectly drained, moderately deep, fine sandy loam (older alluvium)
FV	FALLBROOK-VISTA-BONSALL: well-drained, moderately deep, sandy loams (granodiorite rock)
HO	ANTIOCH-OLIVENHAIN: moderately well-drained, sandy and cobbly loam (marine sediments)

HS	HOLLAND-SHAVER-CHAWANAKEE: well-drained, moderately deep, sandy loam (granite rock)
LD	LAS FLORES-DIABLO-ANTIOCH: moderately well-drained, loamy fine sands (marine sandstones)
NS	NEWVILLE-SOPER-POSITAS: moderately well-drained, sandy loam & gravelly loam (coastal terraces)
OJ	OPHIR-JAMES CANYON-COOLBRITH: well-drained, coarse sands & sandy loams (alluvial fans & basins)
PP	POSITAS-PERKINS-HILLGATE: well-drained, moderately deep, clay loams and gravelly loams (terraces)
RO	REDDING-OLIVENHAIN-RED BLUFF: well-drained, moderately deep, gravelly loam over hardpan (marine terrace)
RR	REDDING-RED BLUFF-CORNING: well-drained, shallow, gravelly loams over claypan (old terrace alluvium)
SX	SAN JOAQUIN-EXETER-COMETA: well-drained, moderately deep, sandy loam over hardpan (old alluvium)
TI	TUSCAN-IGO: well-drained, shallow, cobbly and gravelly, clay loam over hardpan (older terraces)
WV	WYMAN-VINA-ELDER: well-drained, deep, silt loams and fine sandy loam (older channel alluvium)
CM	COACHELLA-MECCA-INDIO: well-drained, deep, coarse sandy loam (granitic alluvium)
CV	CIENABA-VISTA-FALLBROOK: excessively-drained, shallow, coarse, sandy loam (granite rock)
GV	GAVIOTA-VALLECITOS: well-drained, shallow, fine sandy loam (marine sandstone)
HG	HANFORD-GREENFIELD-TUJUNGA: well-drained, deep, sandy loam, occasional hardpan (recent alluvium)
IT	INDIO-THERMAL-GLENBAR: well-drained, very deep, silt loams (alluvium)
MO	MARINA-OCEANO-GAREY: well- to excessively-drained, deep, loamy coarse sands (old berm ridges)
OX	ORLAND-CORTINA-RIVERWASH: well-drained, deep, gravelly silt loams (recent alluvium)
RM	ROSITAS-GILMAN-MELOLAND: somewhat excessively-drained, very deep, loamy coarse sands (alluvium)
TC	TOIYABE-CORBETT-ROCKLAND: well-drained, shallow, rocky and coarse sandy loam (granite rock)
TP	GLENBAR-PLAYAS: poorly-drained, deep, silt and clay (alluvium and lacustrine deposits)

TS	TUJUNGA-SOBODA-RIVERWASH: excessively-drained, very deep sands (granitic alluvium)
XR	CARRIGO-RIVERWASH: excessively-drained, very deep, very gravelly sands (granitic alluvium)
YS	YOLLABOLLY-ROCKLAND-KINKLE: excessively-drained, shallow, gravelly-rocky loam (schist)
AE	AUBURN-EXCHEQUER-SAN MIGUEL: well-drained, shallow to very shallow, silt loams (metabasic volcanics)
DD	MEELS-TALLAC-DINKEY: well-drained, shallow, gravelly-sandy loam (granite rock)
FK	FORWARD-KIDD-LAVA ROCKLAND: well-drained, shallow, sandy loams (rhyolite turf flows)
GT	GOULDING-TOOMES-INKS: excessively drained, shallow, gravelly loams (serpentine intrusives)
HA	HORNITOS-AMADOR: well-drained, shallow, gravelly-sandy loam (sandstone and conglomerate rock)
ML	MAYMEN-LOS GATOS-ROCKLAND: excessively-drained, very shallow, gravelly loams (sedimentary and metamorphic rock uplands)

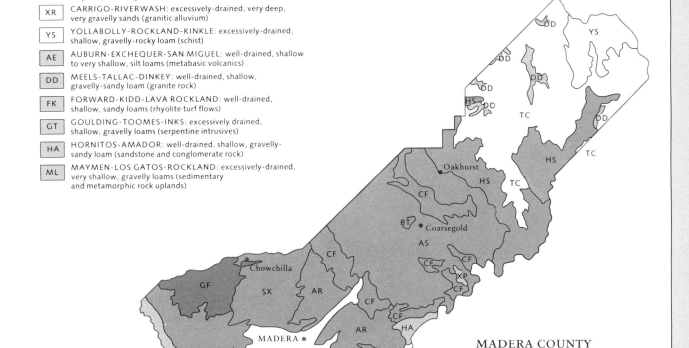

MADERA COUNTY

Scale of Miles   Scale of Kilometers   1:1,000,000

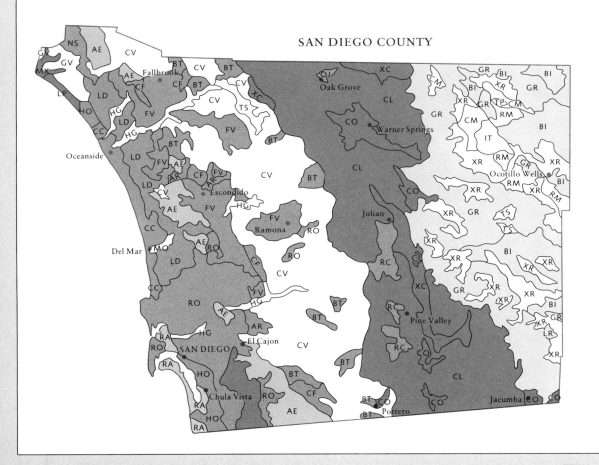

SAN DIEGO COUNTY

NB	NEUNS-BOOMER-SITES: well-drained, moderately deep to shallow, gravelly sandy loam & stony loam (serpentine)
RA	REYES-ALVISO-TIDAL FLATS: imperfectly drained, deep, fine sands and salts (tidal flats, coastal littoral)
TT	TEMPLE-TULARE-ROSSI: imperfectly drained, deep, clay and clay loams (recent alluvium)
VM	VALDEZ-MERRITT-COLUMBIA: well-drained, deep, silt loam (gravelly near river) (flood plain alluvium)
WS	WINDY-ROCKLAND-MEISS: well-drained, moderately deep, gravelly sandy loam (volcanic flows)
XM	SHEETIRON-MASTERSON-KINKEL: well-drained, shallow, gravelly loams (metamorphic rock)
XP	TOOMES-PENTZ-PARDEE: well-drained, very shallow, very rocky loams (volcanic flows)
CL	CROUCH-LA POSTA-SHEEPHEAD: well-drained, moderately deep, coarse sandy loam (acid igneous rock & schist)
CO	CALPINE-MOTTSVILLE-CAVE ROCK: well-drained, very deep, coarse sandy loams (granite alluvium)
GF	GRANGEVILLE-FOSTER: imperfectly-drained, deep, slightly alkaline, fine sandy loam (alluvial fans)
LP	LIVERMORE-PLEASANTON: well-drained, moderately deep clays (soft fine sediments)
MX	MOCHO-SORRENTO-SALINAS: well-drained, deep, clay loams (alluvium)
XC	SHEEPHEAD-CRAFTON: well-drained, shallow, fine sandy loams (schist and gneiss)
CS	CLEAR LAKE-SACRAMENTO-WILLOWS: well-drained, deep, silt and silty clay loam (recent floodplain)
BI	BADLANDS: essentially barren areas, underlain by sedimentary rock material; deeply dissected
GR	GRANITIC ROCKLAND: essentially barren areas underlain by granitic rock
LR	LAVA ROCKLAND: essentially barren areas underlain by various types of volcanic rock

Source:
USDA Soil Conservation Service, 1976

SOILS

The general circulation of the atmosphere is illustrated by two seasonal maps for winter and summer. In winter, low pressure centers develop in the Gulf of Alaska and move southeastward onto the continent. The Pacific High is weak and centered south of California, so that frontal precipitation can penetrate as far south as San Diego, even though the frequency of the storms decreases rapidly from north to south. Occasionally a blocking high develops on land, and continental conditions replace the more normal penetration of marine air. Three simplified daily weather maps illustrate the consequences of these conditions. A frontal storm hit California on January 2, 1977, and the result was a typically rainy winter day. Windflow aloft was westerly, skies were completely overcast, and rain fell over most of California. Temperatures under the overcast were mild, particularly at night. An equally typical winter day, but without rain or clouds, occurred on February 21, 1976. High pressure, northeast of California, had temporarily blocked the Pacific air flow. Skies were clear and daytime temperatures were about the same as if it had rained, but the minima were 5° colder than under an overcast. The third winter map, for January 2, 1976, represents the rare occasion on which a continental high dominated the circulation, and winds blew into California from the cold land surfaces of Idaho and Montana. Minimum temperatures were well below freezing, and even coastal stations experienced sub-zero weather.

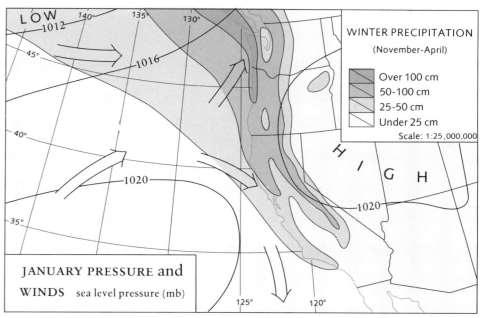

WINTER PRECIPITATION
(November-April)

- Over 100 cm
- 50-100 cm
- 25-50 cm
- Under 25 cm

Scale: 1:25,000,000

JANUARY PRESSURE and WINDS   sea level pressure (mb)

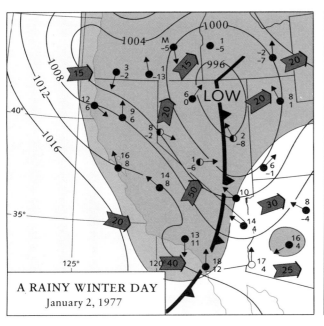

A RAINY WINTER DAY
January 2, 1977

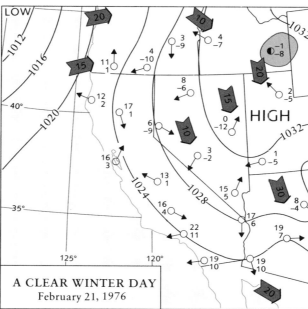

A CLEAR WINTER DAY
February 21, 1976

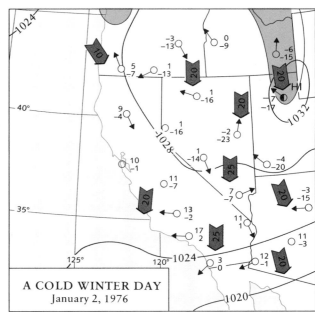

A COLD WINTER DAY
January 2, 1976

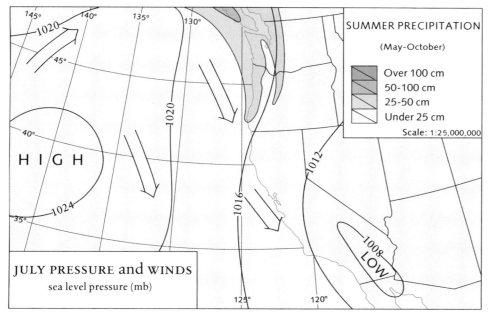

SUMMER PRECIPITATION
(May-October)

- Over 100 cm
- 50-100 cm
- 25-50 cm
- Under 25 cm

Scale: 1:25,000,000

JULY PRESSURE and WINDS
sea level pressure (mb)

The summer situation is dominated by the Pacific High, which is much stronger and further north than in winter. It forces the infrequent frontal storms northward and replaces the winter air masses by stable air formed over the Pacific High itself. Furthermore, the pressure pattern causes northwesterly flow along the coast, which in turn results in a southward-flowing cold current. The coldness of this water is intensified by upwelling due to off-shore deflection of the surface layers. Stable air masses from the north-central Pacific are further stabilized as they cross the cold coastal zone. There is little rain, but the cold water makes the moisture in the air condense, often forming a stratus deck. As in winter, continental conditions replace the dominant maritime inflow whenever high pressure covers the continent northeast of California. The dominant weather situation is illustrated by an average summer day, on August 24, 1976. The coast was overcast and had slightly lower maxima and somewhat higher minima than under clear skies. Inland temperatures, particularly during the day, were much higher. On June 26, 1976, the normal flow of air broke down, and surface winds from the north brought very hot weather, even to the coast. Only Eureka remained inside the domain of maritime air.

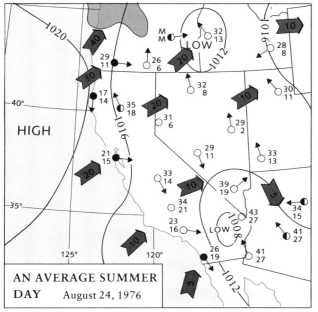

AN AVERAGE SUMMER DAY   August 24, 1976

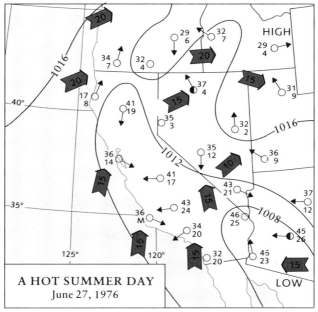

A HOT SUMMER DAY
June 27, 1976

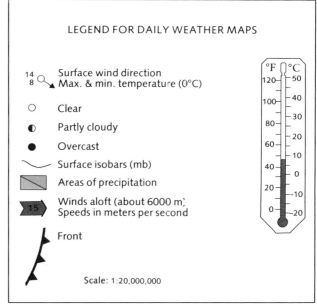

LEGEND FOR DAILY WEATHER MAPS

14 Surface wind direction
8   Max. & min. temperature (0°C)

○ Clear
◑ Partly cloudy
● Overcast

⌒ Surface isobars (mb)

▨ Areas of precipitation

⬅15 Winds aloft (about 6000 m)
     Speeds in meters per second

◣ Front

Scale: 1:20,000,000

WEATHER PATTERNS

MEAN DAILY INSOLATION

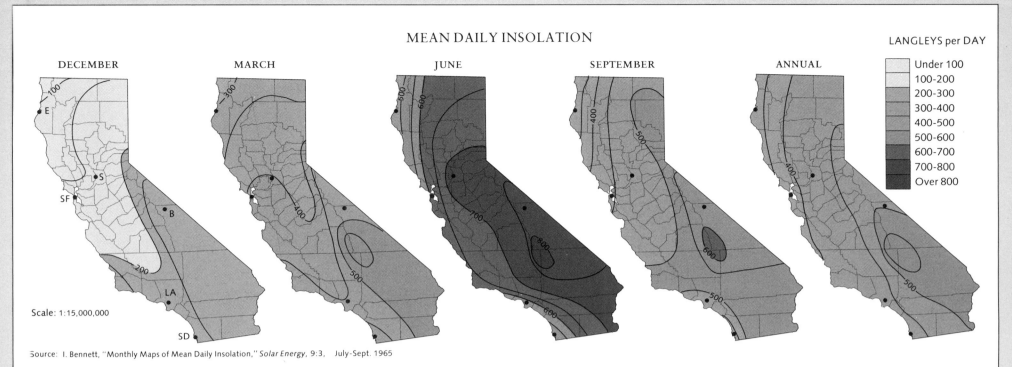

DECEMBER   MARCH   JUNE   SEPTEMBER   ANNUAL

LANGLEYS per DAY

Under 100
100-200
200-300
300-400
400-500
500-600
600-700
700-800
Over 800

Scale: 1:15,000,000

Source: I. Bennett, "Monthly Maps of Mean Daily Insolation," *Solar Energy*, 9:3, July-Sept. 1965

All climatic phenomena depend ultimately on the sun for their source of energy. The five maps above show the seasonal changes in this incoming energy. In December, insolation ranges from less than 100 ly/day along the foggy northwest coast to over 250 ly/day in the cloudless skies of the southeast (a langley is one gram calorie per cm²). By March, insolation doubles over much of California. Low values are still found in the north and along the coast, with an additional tongue of low radiation over the Sierra Nevada. As in all seasons, the highest values are found in the southeast. In June, the range of insolation is greater, with inland gradients from 500 ly on the cloudy coast to more than 800 ly in the Mojave Desert. September takes on the same aspect as March, although there is more insolation. The annual values, as could be expected, resemble those of March and September.

The five maps below show a similar phenomenon: the average number of hours of sunshine, as a percentage of the total number of hours during which the sun is up. December has the least sunshine, ranging from less than 30 per cent of the possible amounts in the far northwest to more than 80 per cent in the southeast. In June, even though the coast is cloudy, the sun shines at least 50 per cent of the time, and toward the southeast the figure rises to 90 per cent. The agricultural potential of the Central Valley depends, in part, on its high rates of sunshine during the summer.

The six graphs at the left represent the processes whereby the surplus of radiation, which exists over most of California, is disposed of, so that the ground can retain its average temperature from year to year. Some of the surplus is used to evaporate water (green on the graphs), some is used to heat the air directly (blue on the graphs) and a little is used to heat the subsoil (but that part is returned to the surface in winter). The major differences from place to place is in the total surplus called "net radiation" (the top line on the graphs), and the division of that surplus between evaporation and atmospheric warming. Eureka and Bishop represent two extremes in California. At Eureka a large part of the moderate surplus is used to evaporate water from the wet ground. At Bishop, the ground is dry and most of the large surplus must be transferred directly to the atmosphere, thus raising air temperatures.

ANNUAL REGIMES of the DISPOSITION of NET RADIATION

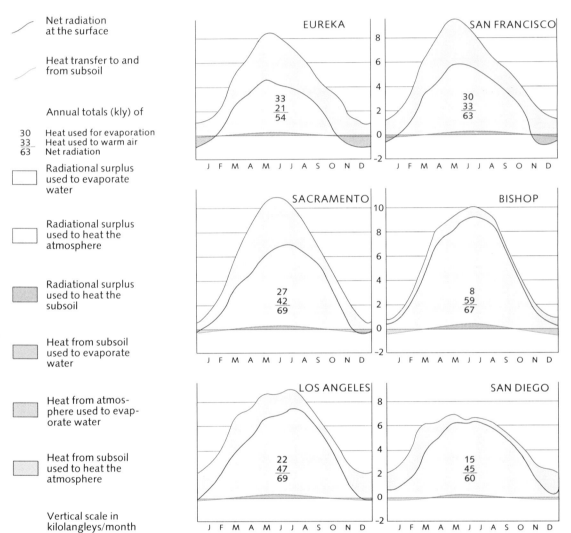

Net radiation at the surface

Heat transfer to and from subsoil

Annual totals (kly) of

30 Heat used for evaporation
33 Heat used to warm air
63 Net radiation

Radiational surplus used to evaporate water

Radiational surplus used to heat the atmosphere

Radiational surplus used to heat the subsoil

Heat from subsoil used to evaporate water

Heat from atmosphere used to evaporate water

Heat from subsoil used to heat the atmosphere

Vertical scale in kilolangleys/month

MEAN PERCENTAGE of POSSIBLE SUNSHINE

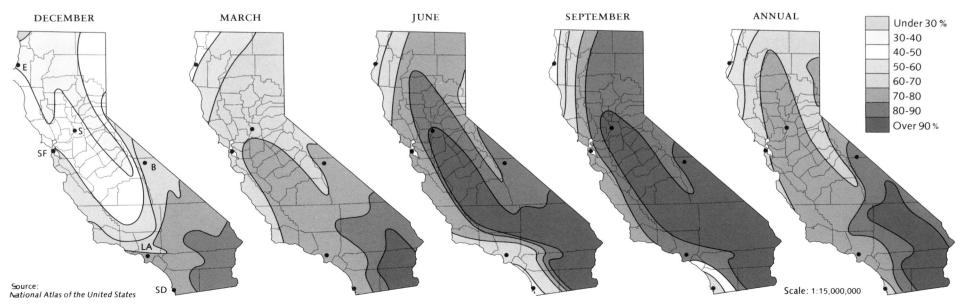

DECEMBER   MARCH   JUNE   SEPTEMBER   ANNUAL

Under 30 %
30-40
40-50
50-60
60-70
70-80
80-90
Over 90 %

Source: National Atlas of the United States

Scale: 1:15,000,000

SOLAR RADIATION

Three principal factors affect temperature—latitude, as a gross index of the distribution of radiation, elevation, and distance from the moderating effect of water—but elevation is the most important in California. The average temperature of the coldest month is shown below. The outline of the Sierra Nevada is clearly evident, and other ranges are indicated almost as well. North-south differences are not conspicuous although they amount to about 6°C, along the coast from Oregon to Mexico, and two to three times that much inland. The coldest time of the year is nearly the same everywhere. A few places in the Central Valley experience their minima before January 1 and some, in coastal southern California, have their minima after January 15; but for most areas the minima occur soon after the solstice, during the first ten days of January.

Summer temperature is affected mainly by distance from the cold coastal waters and by elevation. Latitudinal gradients are relatively small, despite a north-south range similar to that in winter. The two pockets of heat at the northern and southern extremities of the Central Valley show that the distance from water (by way of Carquinez Strait) is more important than the influence of latitude. The dates of the maxima vary from early July until late September, although nine-tenths of the state experiences a normal continental maximum in July. Along the coast, however, the combination of delayed maxima in the water itself, and the presence of fog in early summer retards the maxima until late in the year. The September maximum in San Francisco is an outstanding example.

The difference between summer and winter patterns gives the annual range of temperature. The effects of elevation disappear, but the alignment of mountain ranges is still evident. By obstructing the inland penetration of air, the coastal chains create a temperature gradient that is essentially coastal-inland. The annual temperature range hardly changes from north to south, but inland from the coast it increases by more than 25°C in 100 km. From San Francisco northward, the coast has annual ranges of temperature of about 5°C, practically unmatched in similar latitudes elsewhere.

On the facing page, two maps illustrate extremes of temperature. The number of days on which the temperature drops below freezing is strongly related to elevation and maritime influences. Places with less than 30 days of freeze are in the low deserts of the southeast, in the Central Valley, and along the coast. The map showing the number of days with temperatures above 32°C (90°F) is quite different. The moderating oceanic influences do not reach the Central Valley as easily in summer; and the coastal zone has temperature affinities with the high mountains and not the low desert. The map of the freeze-free season shows a favored coastal belt of more than 330 frost-free days that is narrow and limited to Southern California. Agriculturally disadvantaged areas, with less than 180 days of growing season, are limited to the Sierra Nevada and to a large part of inland northern California.

ANNUAL RANGE of TEMPERATURE

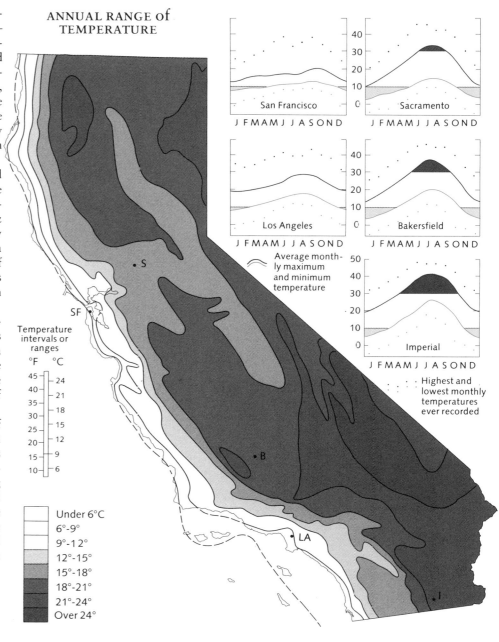

Temperature intervals or ranges

°F	°C
45	24
40	21
35	18
30	15
25	12
20	9
15	
10	6

Average monthly maximum and minimum temperature

Highest and lowest monthly temperatures ever recorded

Under 6°C
6°-9°
9°-12°
12°-15°
15°-18°
18°-21°
21°-24°
Over 24°

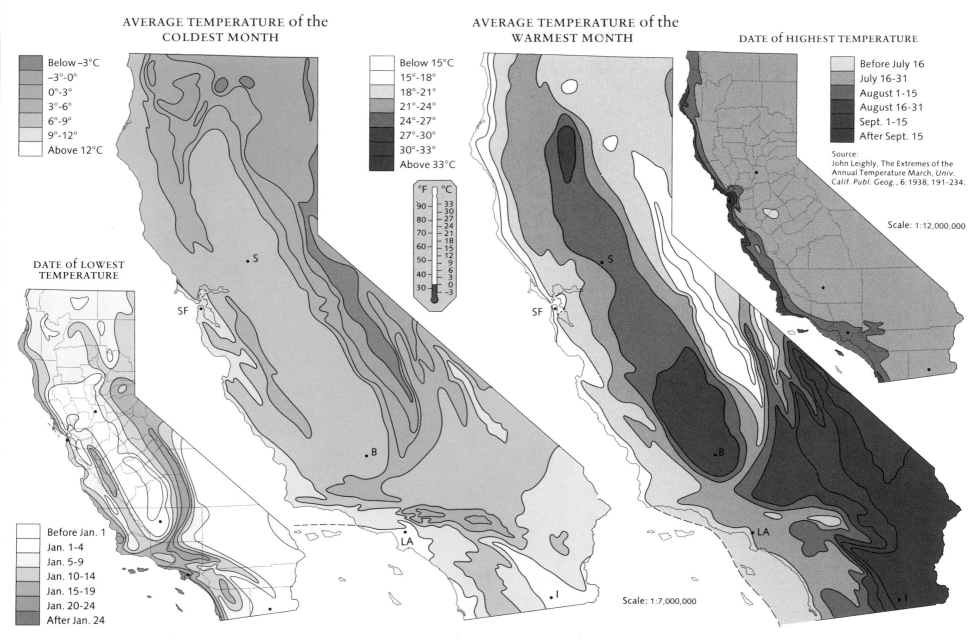

AVERAGE TEMPERATURE of the COLDEST MONTH

Below –3°C
–3°-0°
0°-3°
3°-6°
6°-9°
9°-12°
Above 12°C

AVERAGE TEMPERATURE of the WARMEST MONTH

Below 15°C
15°-18°
18°-21°
21°-24°
24°-27°
27°-30°
30°-33°
Above 33°C

°F	°C
90	33
	30
80	27
	24
70	21
	18
60	15
	12
50	9
	6
40	3
30	0
	–3

DATE of HIGHEST TEMPERATURE

Before July 16
July 16-31
August 1-15
August 16-31
Sept. 1-15
After Sept. 15

Source:
John Leighly, The Extremes of the Annual Temperature March, *Univ. Calif. Publ. Geog.*, 6:1938, 191-234.

Scale: 1:12,000,000

DATE of LOWEST TEMPERATURE

Before Jan. 1
Jan. 1-4
Jan. 5-9
Jan. 10-14
Jan. 15-19
Jan. 20-24
After Jan. 24

Scale: 1:7,000,000

TEMPERATURE

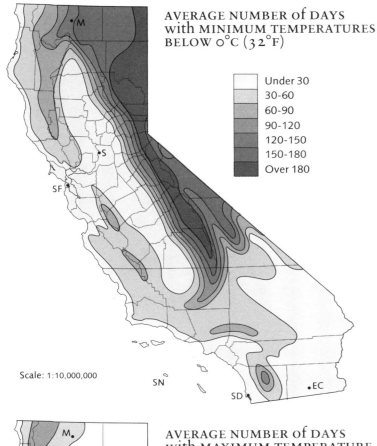

AVERAGE NUMBER of DAYS
with MINIMUM TEMPERATURES
BELOW 0°C (32°F)

Under 30
30-60
60-90
90-120
120-150
150-180
Over 180

Scale: 1:10,000,000

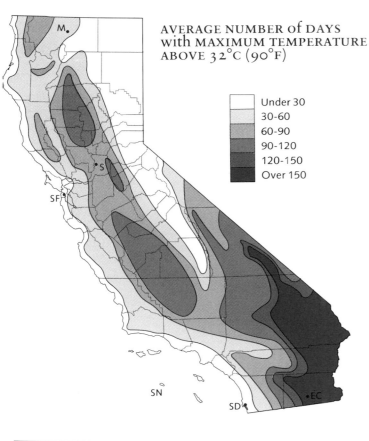

AVERAGE NUMBER of DAYS
with MAXIMUM TEMPERATURE
ABOVE 32°C (90°F)

Under 30
30-60
60-90
90-120
120-150
Over 150

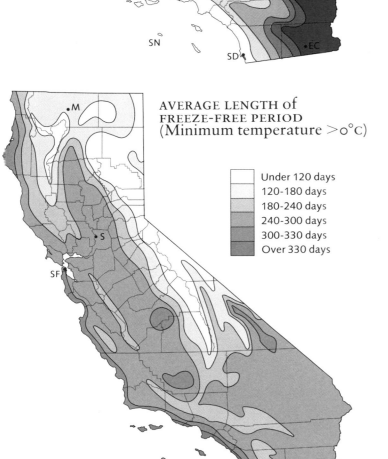

AVERAGE LENGTH of
FREEZE-FREE PERIOD
(Minimum temperature >0°C)

Under 120 days
120-180 days
180-240 days
240-300 days
300-330 days
Over 330 days

Ten-year and thirty-year running means of temperature are shown for the period of record at San Francisco's City Weather Bureau Office. (A ten-year running mean beginning in 1912, for example, is computed by taking the average for the ten-year period 1912-21, then for 1913-22, and so forth). The stability of the thirty-year means is noteworthy: there is a slight warming of less than half a degree in September, beginning in the 1900's, and in January, beginning in the 1930's. It is hard to say whether this small rise is the result of a general increase in the temperature of the atmosphere or whether it is due to the development of an urban heat island. The ten-year means are more erratic but reveal a sharp decrease in temperature beginning in the early 1940's with a return to previous temperatures ten years later.

The daily and annual marches of temperature are combined in a single graph for six stations. The horizontal axis runs from January 1 to January 1 and the vertical axis from midnight to midnight. The annual march of temperature at any given hour is read along the horizontal line representing that hour; the daily march in any month is read along the vertical line representing the middle of that month. The more vertical the general trend of the isolines, the more significant the annual range as compared to diurnal variations. Nearly circular lines, like those for San Francisco, San Nicolas Island or San Diego, indicate a highly oceanic climate where the difference between night and day temperatures is as important as that between summer and winter. A pronounced vertical trend and crowding of isolines are characteristic of continental climates such as those of Montague, Sacramento and El Centro.

TEN and THIRTY-YEAR RUNNING MEANS of JANUARY and
SEPTEMBER TEMPERATURES at SAN FRANCISCO CITY W.B.

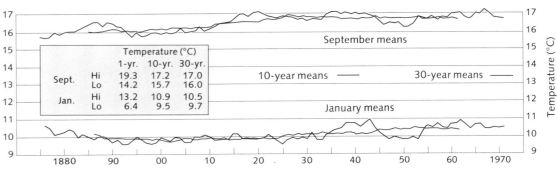

SELECTED EXAMPLES of ANNUAL and DIURNAL TEMPERATURE REGIMES

HOURLY TEMPERATURES for
EACH MONTH of the YEAR

Annual regimes for each hour of the day are shown along the horizontal axis.

Diurnal regimes for each month are shown along the vertical axis.

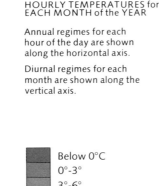

Below 0°C
0°-3°
3°-6°
6°-9°
9°-12°
12°-15°
15°-18°
18°-21°
21°-24°
24°-27°
27°-30°
30°-33°
33°-36°
36°-39°
Above 39° C

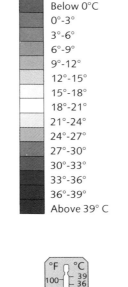

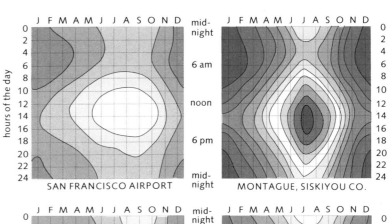

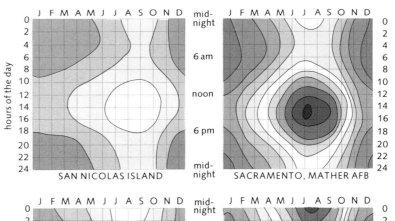

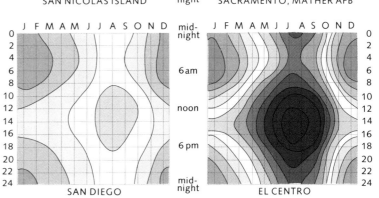

TEMPERATURE

AVERAGE ANNUAL PRECIPITATION

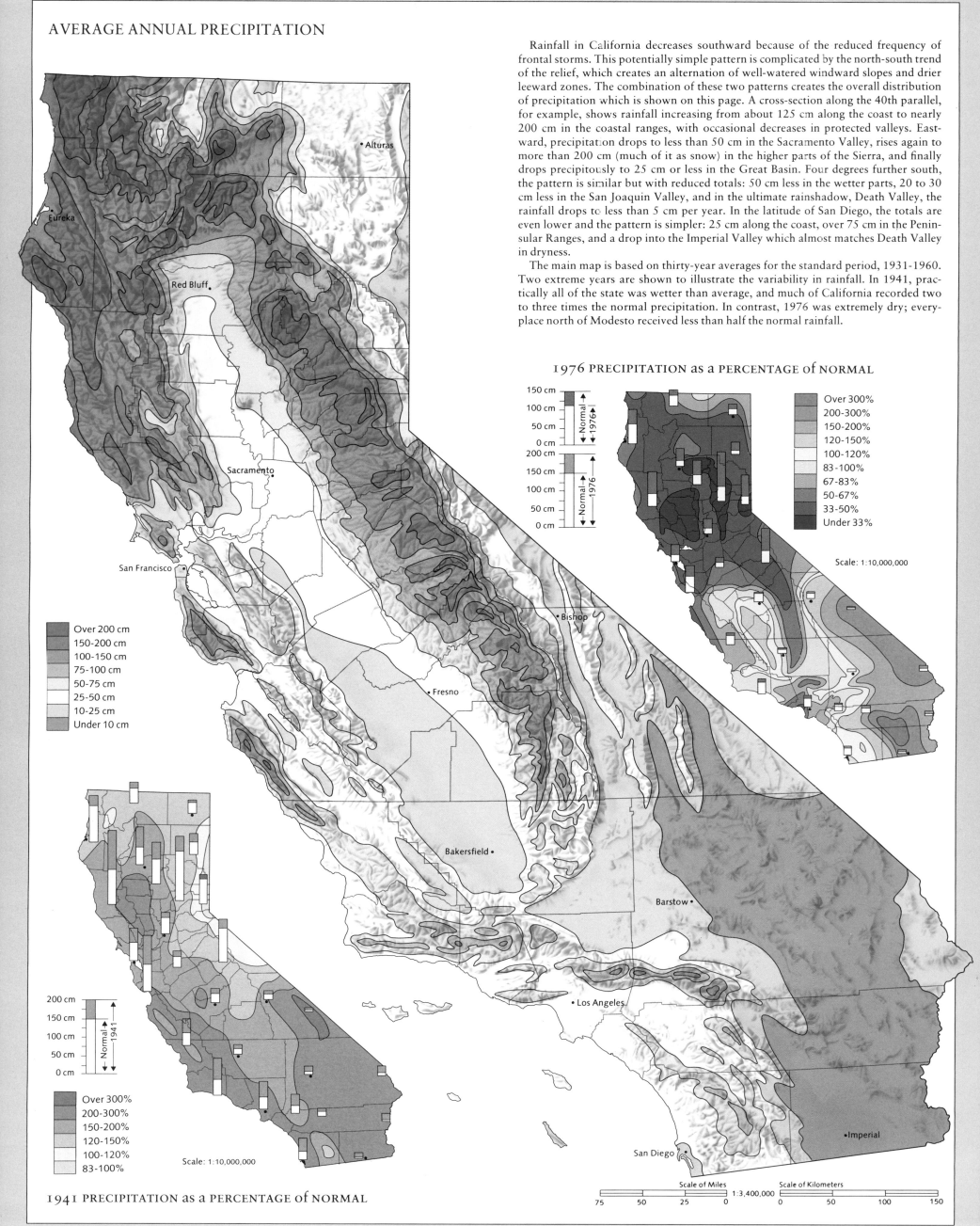

Rainfall in California decreases southward because of the reduced frequency of frontal storms. This potentially simple pattern is complicated by the north-south trend of the relief, which creates an alternation of well-watered windward slopes and drier leeward zones. The combination of these two patterns creates the overall distribution of precipitation which is shown on this page. A cross-section along the 40th parallel, for example, shows rainfall increasing from about 125 cm along the coast to nearly 200 cm in the coastal ranges, with occasional decreases in protected valleys. Eastward, precipitation drops to less than 50 cm in the Sacramento Valley, rises again to more than 200 cm (much of it as snow) in the higher parts of the Sierra, and finally drops precipitously to 25 cm or less in the Great Basin. Four degrees further south, the pattern is similar but with reduced totals: 50 cm less in the wetter parts, 20 to 30 cm less in the San Joaquin Valley, and in the ultimate rainshadow, Death Valley, the rainfall drops to less than 5 cm per year. In the latitude of San Diego, the totals are even lower and the pattern is simpler: 25 cm along the coast, over 75 cm in the Peninsular Ranges, and a drop into the Imperial Valley which almost matches Death Valley in dryness.

The main map is based on thirty-year averages for the standard period, 1931-1960. Two extreme years are shown to illustrate the variability in rainfall. In 1941, practically all of the state was wetter than average, and much of California recorded two to three times the normal precipitation. In contrast, 1976 was extremely dry; everyplace north of Modesto received less than half the normal rainfall.

1976 PRECIPITATION as a PERCENTAGE of NORMAL

Over 300%
200-300%
150-200%
120-150%
100-120%
83-100%
67-83%
50-67%
33-50%
Under 33%

Scale: 1:10,000,000

Over 200 cm
150-200 cm
100-150 cm
75-100 cm
50-75 cm
25-50 cm
10-25 cm
Under 10 cm

Scale: 1:10,000,000

Over 300%
200-300%
150-200%
120-150%
100-120%
83-100%

1941 PRECIPITATION as a PERCENTAGE of NORMAL

Scale of Miles
75   50   25   0

1:3,400,000

Scale of Kilometers
0   50   100   150

PRECIPITATION

135

LONG-TERM TRENDS of PRECIPITATION

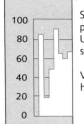

Seasonal (July 1-June 30) precipitation for duration of U.S. Weather Bureau record at six stations.

Vertical scale in centimeters; horizontal scale in years

Thirty-year running means: each dot represents the mean for thirty seasons. For example, a dot at 1920 represents the average precipitation for the period 1905-6 to 1934-35, inclusive.

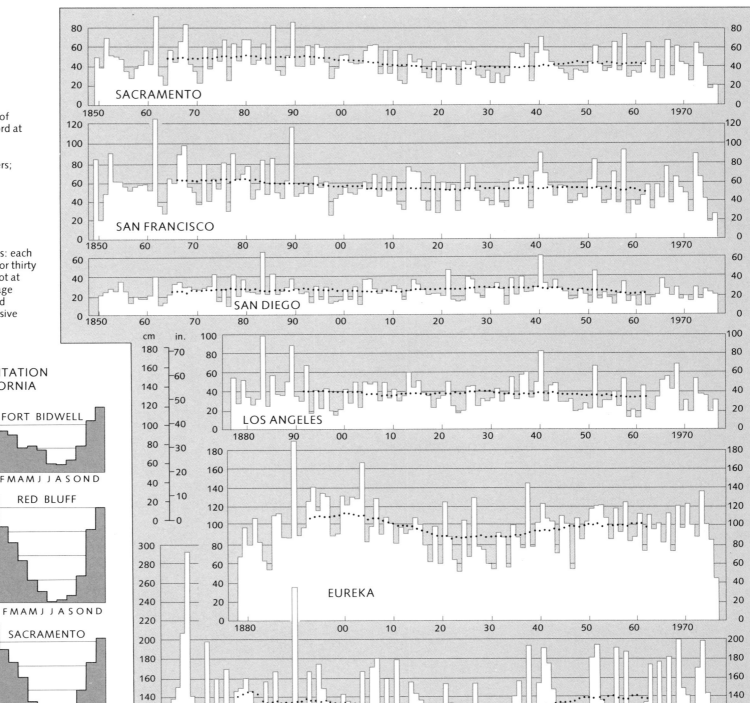

SACRAMENTO
SAN FRANCISCO
SAN DIEGO
LOS ANGELES
EUREKA
NEVADA CITY

EXAMPLES of PRECIPITATION REGIMES in CALIFORNIA

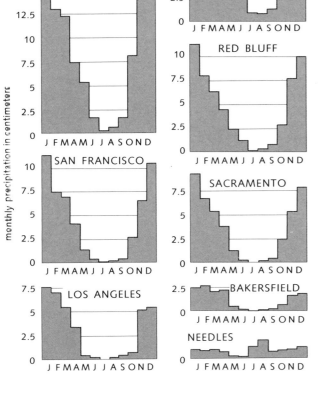

EUREKA · FORT BIDWELL · RED BLUFF · SAN FRANCISCO · SACRAMENTO · LOS ANGELES · BAKERSFIELD · NEEDLES

monthly precipitation in centimeters

J F M A M J J A S O N D

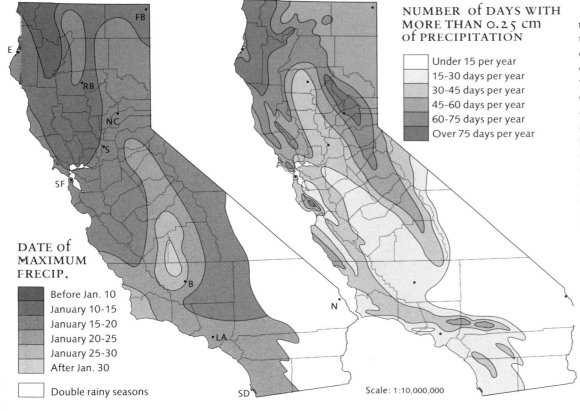

NUMBER of DAYS WITH MORE THAN 0.25 cm of PRECIPITATION

- Under 15 per year
- 15-30 days per year
- 30-45 days per year
- 45-60 days per year
- 60-75 days per year
- Over 75 days per year

DATE of MAXIMUM PRECIP.

- Before Jan. 10
- January 10-15
- January 15-20
- January 20-25
- January 25-30
- After Jan. 30
- Double rainy seasons

Scale: 1:10,000,000

The six graphs above illustrate the year-to-year variability in precipitation at selected stations. Because the general trend is difficult to see, thirty-year running means have been superimposed in the form of black dots, each of which represents the average precipitation at the mid-point of every thirty-year period. These means smooth out the season-to-season variability, but they also show how changeable rainfall averages can be, even when taken over long periods. At Nevada City, for example, there is a difference of 30 cm between the highest value (for the period 1865-95) and the lowest value (for the period 1907-37). The difference at drier places such as Los Angeles is smaller, but proportionally almost as large, amounting to 7 cm. There is an overall trend which is reflected at every station: an early maximum, around the turn of the century, is followed by a decline until the late 1920's in southern California and the late 1930's in the north, whereupon the averages rise again until the 1940's in the south and the 1960's in the north. The dry years in the late 1970's are evident in the downward turn of the running means, but the latest means shown (for 1947-77) are not as low as earlier minima, except in southern California.

The precipitation regimes illustrated above all show a characteristic Mediterranean curve with pronounced winter maxima and summer drought, even though the total rainfall varies considerably. Only Needles, in the Mojave Desert, has a different regime involving a small convectional maximum in late summer. The date of the maximum precipitation tends to be later as one goes southward in the state.

Source: *Climatic Summary of the U.S.*, U.S. Weather Bureau, various editions.

PRECIPITATION

AVERAGE ANNUAL WATER DEFICIT

Under 20 cm
20-40 cm
40-60 cm
60-80 cm
80-100 cm
100-120 cm
Over 120 cm

Scale: 1:7,000,000

AVERAGE ANNUAL WATER SURPLUS

No surplus
Under 20 cm
20-40 cm
40-60 cm
60-80 cm
80-100 cm
100-120 cm
Over 120 cm

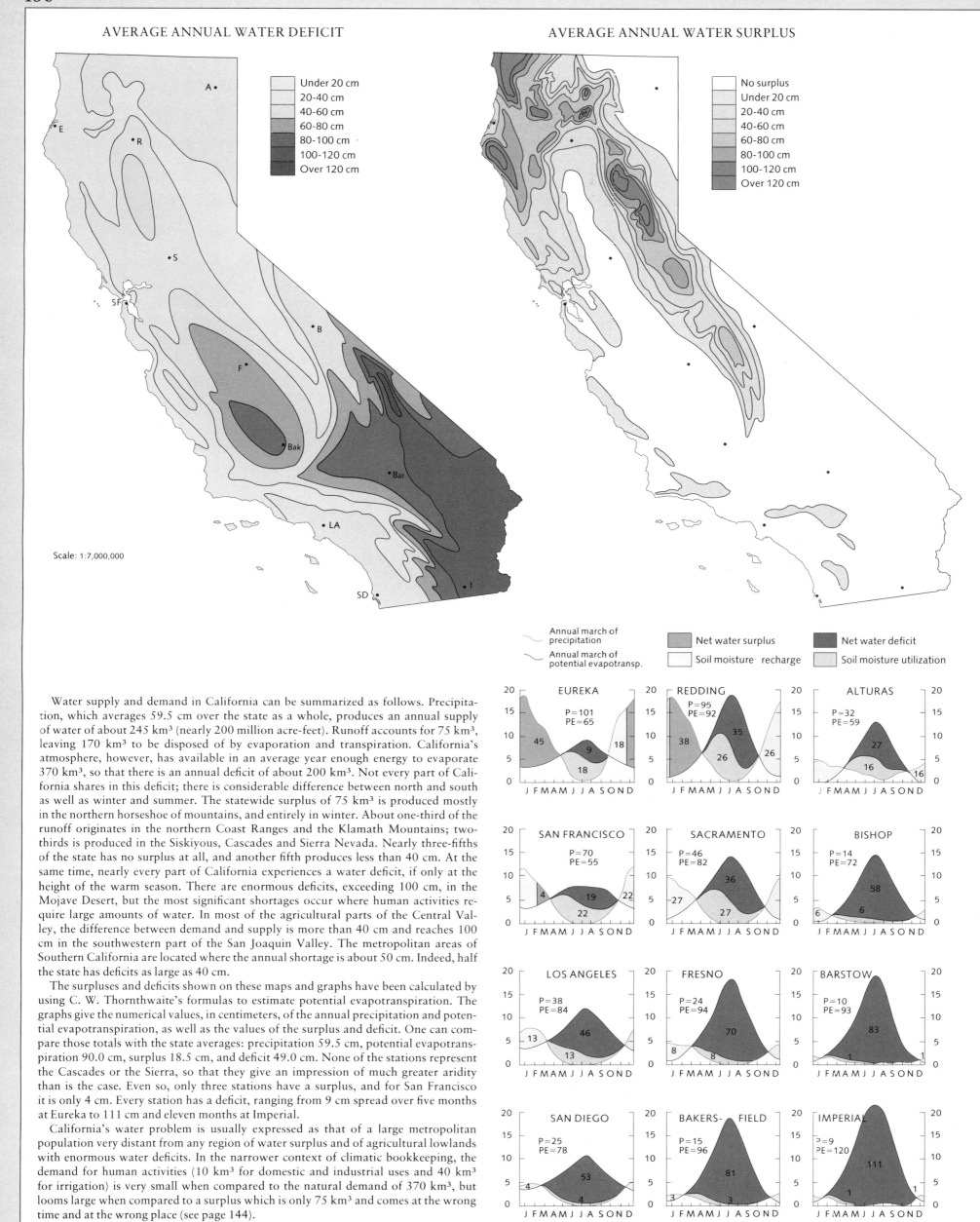

Annual march of precipitation
Annual march of potential evapotransp.
Net water surplus
Net water deficit
Soil moisture recharge
Soil moisture utilization

WATER-BALANCE DIAGRAMS at SELECTED STATIONS

Source: C.W. Thornthwaite Assoc., *Average Climatic Water Balance Data of the Continents, Part VII, 'United States', 1964*

Water supply and demand in California can be summarized as follows. Precipitation, which averages 59.5 cm over the state as a whole, produces an annual supply of water of about 245 km³ (nearly 200 million acre-feet). Runoff accounts for 75 km³, leaving 170 km³ to be disposed of by evaporation and transpiration. California's atmosphere, however, has available in an average year enough energy to evaporate 370 km³, so that there is an annual deficit of about 200 km³. Not every part of California shares in this deficit; there is considerable difference between north and south as well as winter and summer. The statewide surplus of 75 km³ is produced mostly in the northern horseshoe of mountains, and entirely in winter. About one-third of the runoff originates in the northern Coast Ranges and the Klamath Mountains; two-thirds is produced in the Siskiyous, Cascades and Sierra Nevada. Nearly three-fifths of the state has no surplus at all, and another fifth produces less than 40 cm. At the same time, nearly every part of California experiences a water deficit, if only at the height of the warm season. There are enormous deficits, exceeding 100 cm, in the Mojave Desert, but the most significant shortages occur where human activities require large amounts of water. In most of the agricultural parts of the Central Valley, the difference between demand and supply is more than 40 cm and reaches 100 cm in the southwestern part of the San Joaquin Valley. The metropolitan areas of Southern California are located where the annual shortage is about 50 cm. Indeed, half the state has deficits as large as 40 cm.

The surpluses and deficits shown on these maps and graphs have been calculated by using C. W. Thornthwaite's formulas to estimate potential evapotranspiration. The graphs give the numerical values, in centimeters, of the annual precipitation and potential evapotranspiration, as well as the values of the surplus and deficit. One can compare those totals with the state averages: precipitation 59.5 cm, potential evapotranspiration 90.0 cm, surplus 18.5 cm, and deficit 49.0 cm. None of the stations represent the Cascades or the Sierra, so that they give an impression of much greater aridity than is the case. Even so, only three stations have a surplus, and for San Francisco it is only 4 cm. Every station has a deficit, ranging from 9 cm spread over five months at Eureka to 111 cm and eleven months at Imperial.

California's water problem is usually expressed as that of a large metropolitan population very distant from any region of water surplus and of agricultural lowlands with enormous water deficits. In the narrower context of climatic bookkeeping, the demand for human activities (10 km³ for domestic and industrial uses and 40 km³ for irrigation) is very small when compared to the natural demand of 370 km³, but looms large when compared to a surplus which is only 75 km³ and comes at the wrong time and at the wrong place (see page 144).

WATER BALANCE

In order to describe the variety of California's climates, which are as diverse as that of southern Ireland and the northern Sahara, a system of classification is needed that groups relatively similar regions while highlighting the important contrasts. The Köppen classification, shown below, divides California into zones based on the relationship of rainfall to potential evaporatoin, on temperature, and on the seasonal variation of drought. The state has four major climatic zones which are subdivided into eleven categories.

The desert climates, where water need is far in excess of supply, cover the southeastern part of the state, east of the Sierra and Peninsular ranges. This region, cut off from the moisture of Pacific air masses, receives very little rain. The summer convectional rain, slight as it is, has to come all the way from the Gulf of Mexico. Winter temperatures are mild and range from 3°C to 12°C, and summer is very hot, with July averages that range from 25°C in the higher parts of the desert to almost 40°C in Death Valley. Potential evapotranspiration is correspondingly high, over 100 cm, and the region is one of enormous water deficits. It is also a region of sunshine, so that agriculture is prosperous where irrigation is practicable, and recreation is becoming increasingly important. There is a second desert region in the southwestern part of the San Joaquin Valley. Here agriculture is even more significant than in the deserts east of the mountains, but the San Joaquin has not attracted either retired persons or tourists. Major world-wide analogs of this climate are in the Sahara and in the Australian Desert.

Semi-arid or steppe climates are not extensive in California except in the San Joaquin Valley, where there are very hot steppes similar to the semi-arid fringes of the Mojave. Cooler versions occur in a narrow coastal strip south of Los Angeles, where summer fogs and daytime penetration of marine air make for moderate summers (21°C at San Diego in August) with little evapotranspiration and very mild winters, with temperatures above 12°C. This is the climate of pleasant winters, sunny summers, and very little rain which has attracted so many Easterners and Midwesterners.

Most of California has Mediterranean climates; that is, a dry summer but a winter with a surplus of moisture. The inland variety, in the Central Valley, is very similar to the more arid climates of the Valley and the Mojave. The summers are particularly hot and cloudless. The coastal Mediterranean climates are much cooler in summer and the marine fog which penetrates inland makes the coast very oceanic, with little difference in temperature between the mild winters and cool summers. From Santa Barbara to Crescent City, January averages scarcely change from 11°C to 10°C, and the variation is not much greater in August when the corresponding temperatures are 19°C and 14°C. A large part of the Coast Ranges and Sierra foothills have an intermediate climate between the hot Valley and the cool coast. These three kinds of Mediterranean climates are found in similar coastal, intermediate, and inland environments in the Mediterranean Basin, in Central Chile, and in southwestern Africa and Australia.

Finally, there are the microthermal climates, the colder highland areas of California where the coldest month is below freezing. Most of the Sierra above 2000 m, the Modoc Plateau, and the higher parts of the Trinity and Klamath Mountains belong to this climatic province of short, cool summers and relatively rigorous winters. Most of California's water originates in snowmelt and runoff from these mountain areas.

CLIMATIC REGIONS of CALIFORNIA and THEIR WORLD-WIDE ANALOGS

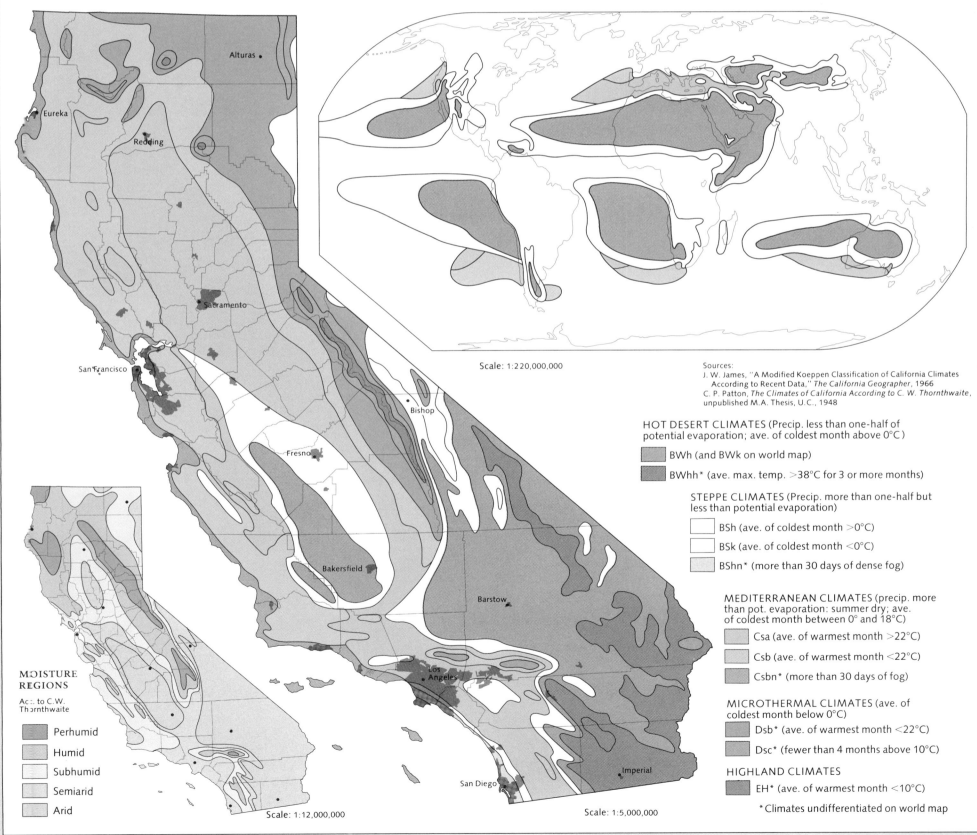

Scale: 1:220,000,000

Sources:
J. W. James, "A Modified Koeppen Classification of California Climates According to Recent Data," *The California Geographer*, 1966
C. P. Patton, *The Climates of California According to C. W. Thornthwaite*, unpublished M.A. Thesis, U.C., 1948

HOT DESERT CLIMATES (Precip. less than one-half of potential evaporation; ave. of coldest month above 0°C)

- BWh (and BWk on world map)
- BWhh* (ave. max. temp. >38°C for 3 or more months)

STEPPE CLIMATES (Precip. more than one-half but less than potential evaporation)

- BSh (ave. of coldest month >0°C)
- BSk (ave. of coldest month <0°C)
- BShn* (more than 30 days of dense fog)

MEDITERRANEAN CLIMATES (precip. more than pot. evaporation: summer dry; ave. of coldest month between 0° and 18°C)

- Csa (ave. of warmest month >22°C)
- Csb (ave. of warmest month <22°C)
- Csbn* (more than 30 days of fog)

MICROTHERMAL CLIMATES (ave. of coldest month below 0°C)

- Dsb* (ave. of warmest month <22°C)
- Dsc* (fewer than 4 months above 10°C)

HIGHLAND CLIMATES

- EH* (ave. of warmest month <10°C)

*Climates undifferentiated on world map

MOISTURE REGIONS

Acc. to C.W. Thornthwaite

- Perhumid
- Humid
- Subhumid
- Semiarid
- Arid

Scale: 1:12,000,000

Scale: 1:5,000,000

CLIMATIC REGIONS

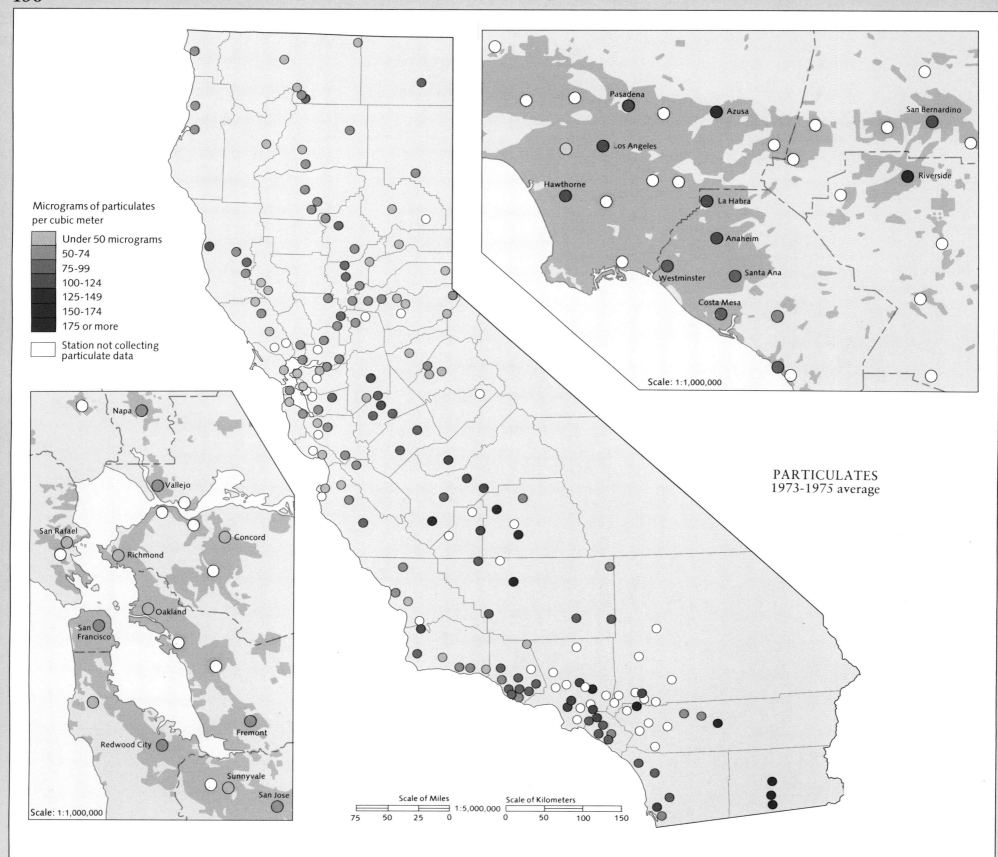

Micrograms of particulates
per cubic meter

Under 50 micrograms
50-74
75-99
100-124
125-149
150-174
175 or more

Station not collecting
particulate data

PARTICULATES
1973-1975 average

Scale: 1:1,000,000

Scale of Miles   Scale of Kilometers
75 50 25 0   1:5,000,000   0 50 100 150

Despite legislative controls that have decreased the level of air pollution since 1965, Californians continue to be preoccupied by problems of air quality. All of the major pollutants are present: particulates, carbon monoxide, oxides of nitrogen, sulfur dioxide, hydrocarbons and oxidants. Sources of industrial contamination have been controlled for the most part, but vehicular traffic continues to be a serious problem despite the imposition of stringent standards that have lowered emission per vehicle.

Particulate matter found in the atmosphere includes soot, ash, smoke and especially dust. Particulates have obvious effects on visibility, but they can also contribute to respiratory ailments, and asbestos dust is known to be carcinogenic.

By weight, carbon monoxide is the most important pollutant. The primary source is the automobile, which accounts for 90 per cent of all such pollution. Its distribution therefore resembles the road network. Dangerous concentrations, greater than 100 parts per million, have been measured in heavy traffic. Industrial processes, solid waste disposal and fires are other sources of carbon monoxide.

Nitric oxide is another byproduct of the internal combustion engine. It is converted to nitrogen dioxide in the atmosphere and becomes a primary reactant in photochemical smog formation. Nitrogen dioxide is highly toxic and respiratory irritation often results from exposure even to "normal" levels of concentration.

Sulfur dioxide is derived from burning coal or oil, and from certain operations in the chemical industry. It reacts with oxygen and water in the air to form sulfuric acid, which can be extremely irritating, even in small doses. Sulfur dioxide levels have been decreasing in California, but fuels with low sulfur content are becoming harder to obtain.

Hydrocarbons are another major form of pollution for which the car is partly responsible. They are also a byproduct of petroleum refining and the evaporation of solvents. Hydrocarbons react with nitrogen dioxide in the atmosphere to create photochemical oxidants which are California's worst pollutants. The incidence of oxidants in the air has been decreasing since its maximum in the mid-1960's, but photochemical oxidants remain the primary pollution problem in California. In the Livermore Valley and around San Jose, for example, oxidant standards were exceeded on as many as 30 days in 1975.

The factors that affect the distribution of pollutants once they have been put into the air are the same as those that control local air movement. Almost all of the features that aggravate air pollution are found in the Los Angeles Basin. The general movement of air is onshore; therefore dispersion cannot take place seaward, except at night, and even then the polluted air is often swept back on land during the day. Landward, the mountains effectively block the passage of all but the strongest winds. Upward, the air is trapped by the presence of temperature inversions in summer. As a result, the summer air overlying the Basin is often stagnant and accumulating pollutants create smog.

Topography is equally important in the San Francisco Bay Area. Here, the Golden Gate acts as a one-way valve, and dispersion is possible only northward through Carquinez Strait or southward into the Santa Clara Valley. When there is a strong inversion, as is commonly the case in summer, the Bay air becomes as stagnant as in Los Angeles, with similar results, particularly in the Santa Clara Valley.

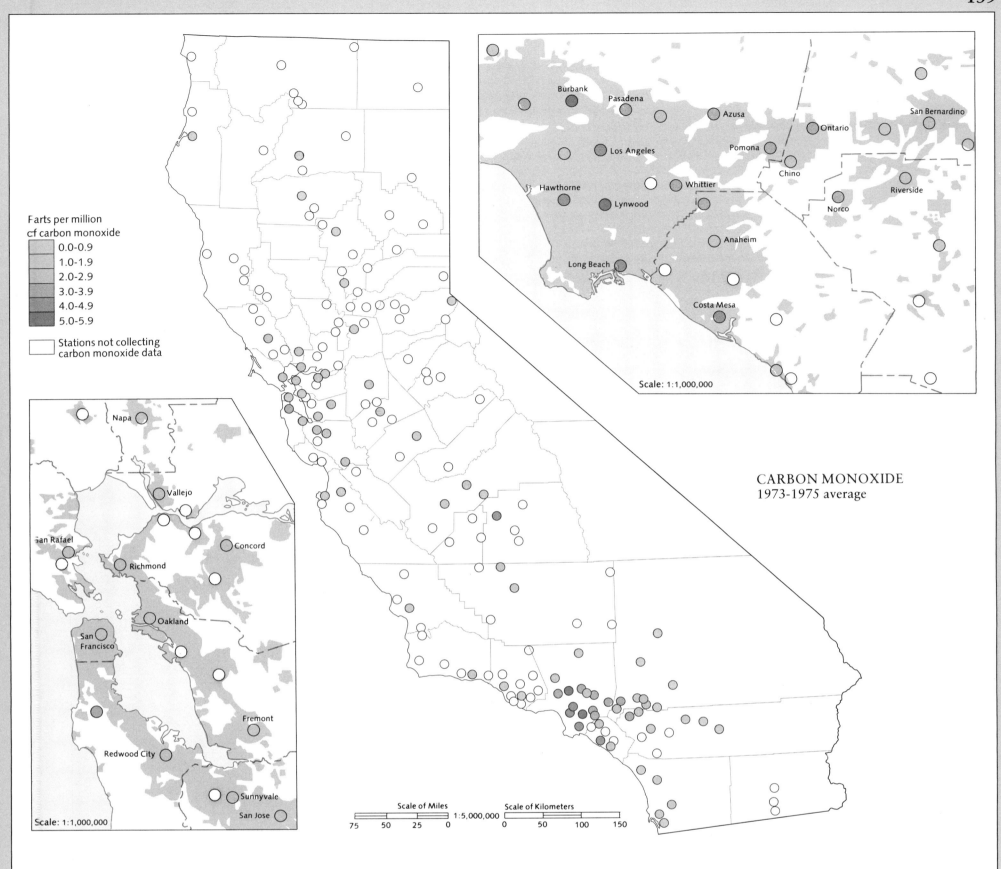

Farts per million
cf carbon monoxide

- 0.0-0.9
- 1.0-1.9
- 2.0-2.9
- 3.0-3.9
- 4.0-4.9
- 5.0-5.9

Stations not collecting carbon monoxide data

CARBON MONOXIDE
1973-1975 average

Scale: 1:1,000,000

Scale: 1:1,000,000

Scale of Miles
75 50 25 0
1:5,000,000
Scale of Kilometers
0   50   100   150

AIR BASINS	OXIDANT ppm	CARBON MONOXIDE ppm		NITROGEN DIOXIDE ppm		SULPHUR DIOXIDE ppm			PARTICULATE (µg/m³)	
	1 hour	1 hour	8 hour	1 hour	Annual	1 hour	24 hour	Annual	24 hour	Ann. mean
POLLUTION STANDARD	**0.08***	**35***	**9***	**0.25**	**.05***	**.50**	**.04**	**.03***	**100**	**60**
NORTHEAST PLATEAU	—	—	—	—	—	—	—	—	259	67
NORTH COAST	—	15	6	—	—	—	—	—	445	96
SACRAMENTO VALLEY	0.19	20	11	0.20	.025	—	—	—	263	69
LAKE COUNTY	—	—	—	—	—	—	—	—	60	21
MOUNTAIN COUNTIES	—	—	—	—	—	—	—	—	344	42
LAKE TAHOE	0.09	11	5	0.17	.016	.01	.000	.000	142	51
SAN FRANCISCO BAY AREA	0.23	31	16	0.28	.040	.23	.058	.008	201	69
SAN JOAQUIN VALLEY	0.19	32	2	0.19	.032	.06	.020	.007	640	142
GREAT BASIN VALLEYS	—	—	—	—	—	—	—	—	—	—
NORTH CENTRAL COAST	0.11	15	6	0.13	.019	—	—	—	161	53
SOUTH CENTRAL COAST	0.25	22	14	0.21	.032	.04	.016	.000	258	89
SOUTHEAST DESERT	0.27	17	10	0.30	.029	.04	.027	.006	1358	220
SOUTH COAST	0.39	41	3	0.67	.082	.27	.064	.025	467	149
SAN DIEGO	0.28	19	13	0.46	.041	.07	.021	.006	430	85

POLLUTANT CONCENTRATIONS

*National standard

Source: California Air Resources Board, 1976

MAXIMUM POLLUTANT CONCENTRATIONS 1975
by California Air Basins

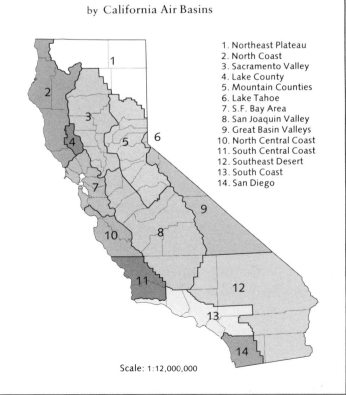

1. Northeast Plateau
2. North Coast
3. Sacramento Valley
4. Lake County
5. Mountain Counties
6. Lake Tahoe
7. S.F. Bay Area
8. San Joaquin Valley
9. Great Basin Valleys
10. North Central Coast
11. South Central Coast
12. Southeast Desert
13. South Coast
14. San Diego

Scale: 1:12,000,000

AIR POLLUTION

140

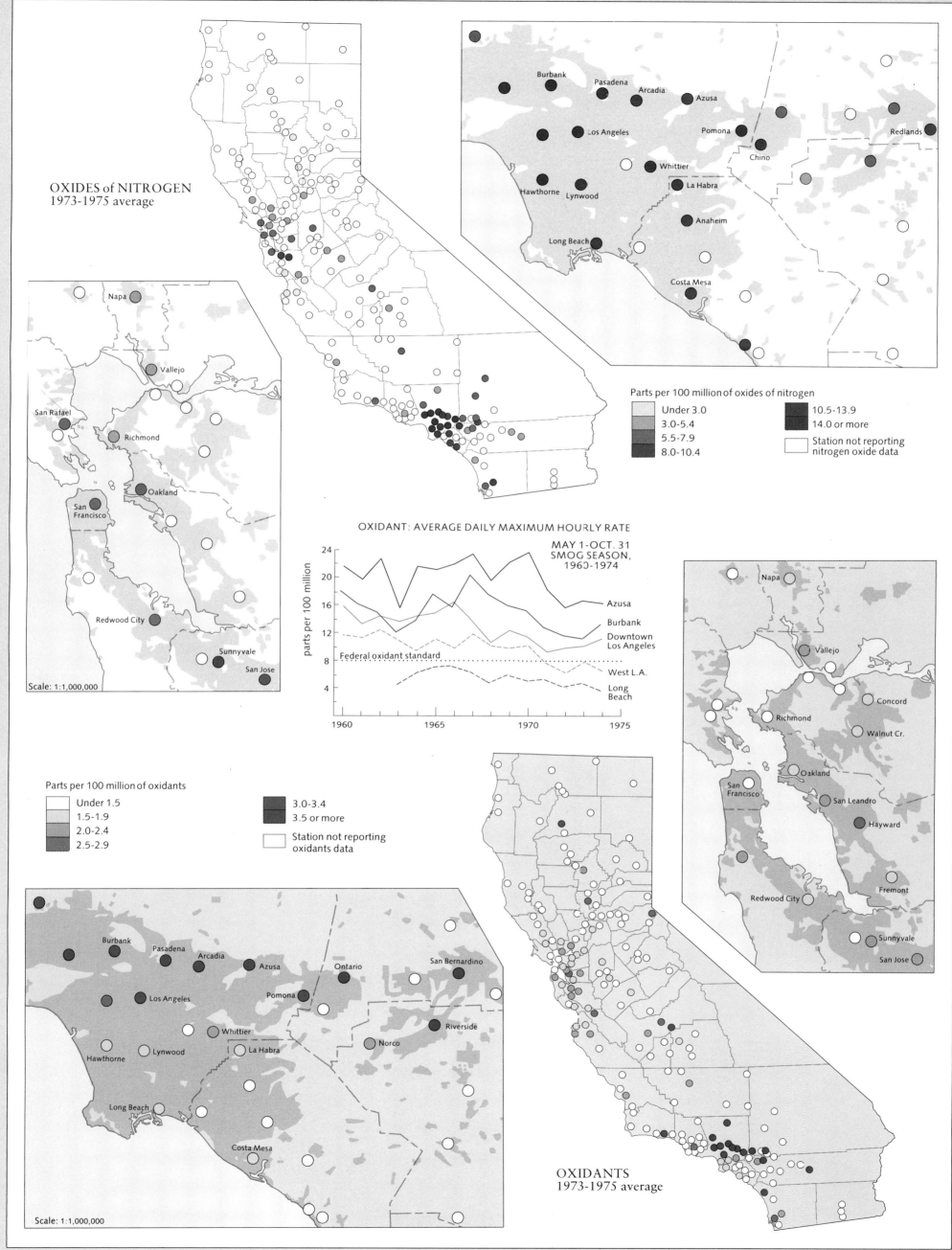

OXIDES of NITROGEN
1973-1975 average

Parts per 100 million of oxides of nitrogen
Under 3.0
3.0-5.4
5.5-7.9
8.0-10.4
10.5-13.9
14.0 or more
Station not reporting
nitrogen oxide data

Scale: 1:1,000,000

OXIDANT: AVERAGE DAILY MAXIMUM HOURLY RATE
MAY 1-OCT. 31
SMOG SEASON,
1960-1974

Azusa
Burbank
Downtown
Los Angeles
Federal oxidant standard
West L.A.
Long
Beach

Parts per 100 million of oxidants
Under 1.5
1.5-1.9
2.0-2.4
2.5-2.9
3.0-3.4
3.5 or more
Station not reporting
oxidants data

OXIDANTS
1973-1975 average

Scale: 1:1,000,000

AIR POLLUTION

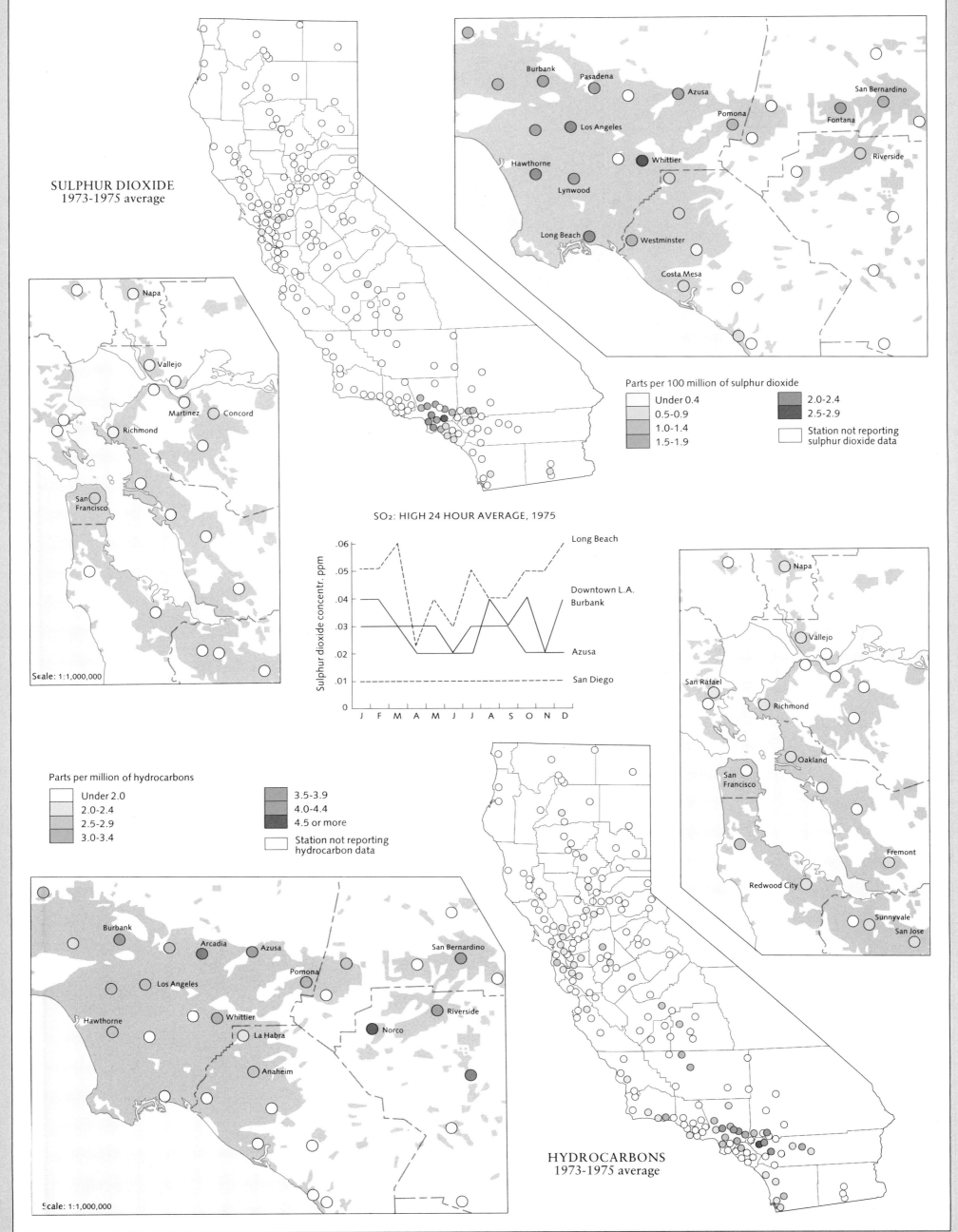

SULPHUR DIOXIDE
1973-1975 average

Scale: 1:1,000,000

Parts per 100 million of sulphur dioxide

Under 0.4
0.5-0.9
1.0-1.4
1.5-1.9
2.0-2.4
2.5-2.9
Station not reporting
sulphur dioxide data

Napa
Vallejo
Martinez   Concord
Richmond
San
Francisco

Burbank   Pasadena   Azusa   San Bernardino
Los Angeles   Pomona   Fontana
Hawthorne   Whittier   Riverside
Lynwood
Long Beach   Westminster
Costa Mesa

SO₂: HIGH 24 HOUR AVERAGE, 1975

Long Beach

Downtown L.A.
Burbank

Azusa

San Diego

J F M A M J J A S O N D

Parts per million of hydrocarbons

Under 2.0
2.0-2.4
2.5-2.9
3.0-3.4
3.5-3.9
4.0-4.4
4.5 or more
Station not reporting
hydrocarbon data

Napa
Vallejo
San Rafael
Richmond
Oakland
San
Francisco
Fremont
Redwood City
Sunnyvale
San Jose

Burbank   Arcadia   Azusa   San Bernardino
Los Angeles   Pomona   Riverside
Hawthorne   Whittier   Norco
La Habra
Anaheim

Scale: 1:1,000,000

HYDROCARBONS
1973-1975 average

AIR POLLUTION

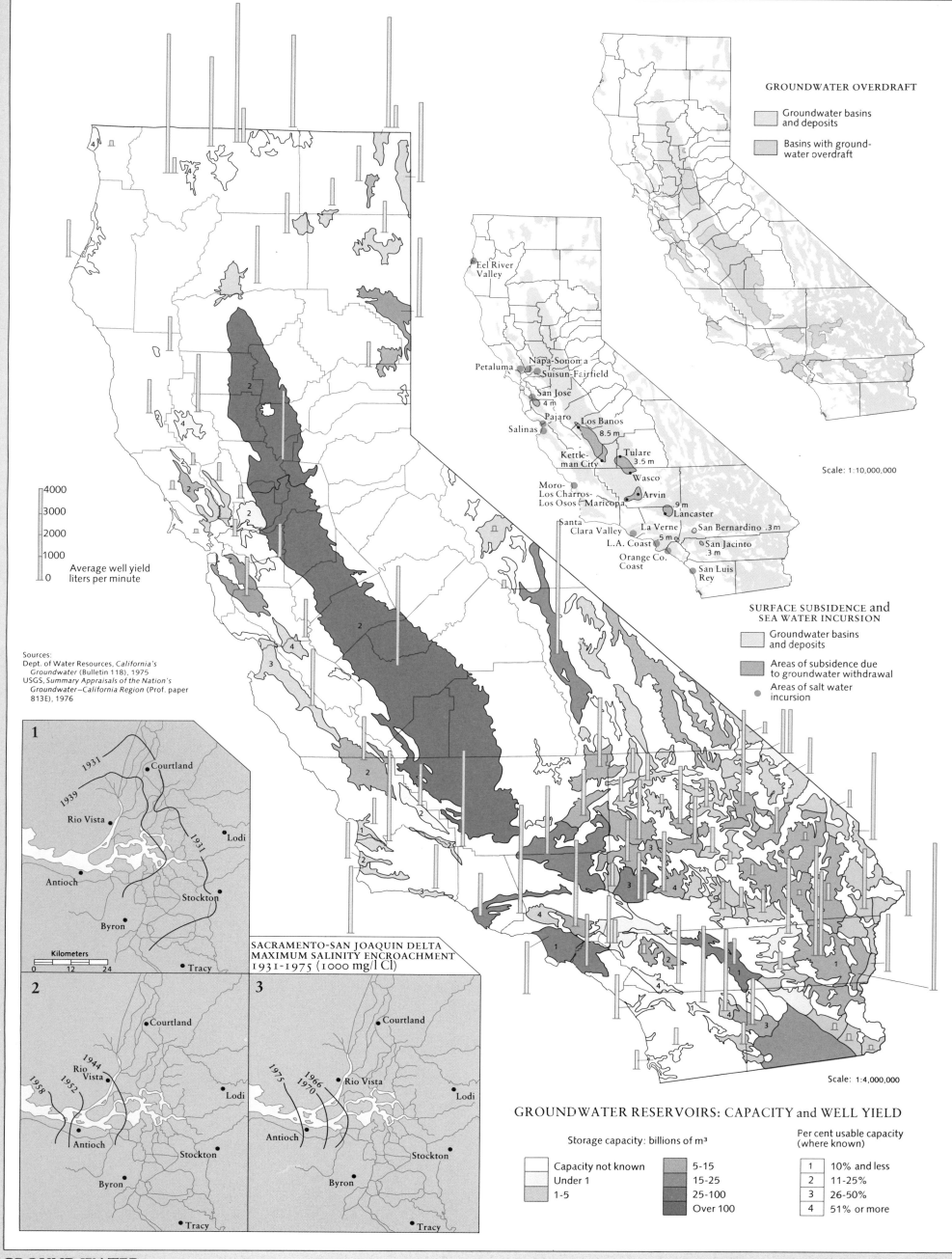

GROUNDWATER OVERDRAFT

Groundwater basins and deposits

Basins with ground-water overdraft

Eel River Valley

Petaluma
Napa-Sonoma
Suisun-Fairfield
San Jose
4 m
Pajaro
Salinas
Los Banos
8.5 m
Kettle-man City
Tulare
3.5 m
Wasco
Moro-Los Charros-Los Osos
Maricopa
Arvin
9 m
Santa Clara Valley
Lancaster
La Verne
5 m
L.A. Coast
Orange Co. Coast
San Bernardino .3 m
San Jacinto
3 m
San Luis Rey

Scale: 1:10,000,000

SURFACE SUBSIDENCE and SEA WATER INCURSION

Groundwater basins and deposits

Areas of subsidence due to groundwater withdrawal

Areas of salt water incursion

4000
3000
2000
1000
0

Average well yield liters per minute

Sources:
Dept. of Water Resources, *California's Groundwater* (Bulletin 118), 1975
USGS, *Summary Appraisals of the Nation's Groundwater–California Region* (Prof. paper 813E), 1976

1
1931
1939
1931
Courtland
Rio Vista
Lodi
Antioch
1931
Stockton
Byron
Kilometers
0 12 24
Tracy

SACRAMENTO-SAN JOAQUIN DELTA MAXIMUM SALINITY ENCROACHMENT 1931-1975 (1000 mg/l Cl)

2
1944
Rio Vista
1958
1952
Courtland
Lodi
Antioch
Stockton
Byron
Tracy

3
1975
1966
1970
Rio Vista
Courtland
Lodi
Antioch
Stockton
Byron
Tracy

Scale: 1:4,000,000

GROUNDWATER RESERVOIRS: CAPACITY and WELL YIELD

Storage capacity: billions of m³	Per cent usable capacity (where known)
Capacity not known	5-15
Under 1	15-25
1-5	25-100
	Over 100

1	10% and less
2	11-25%
3	26-50%
4	51% or more

GROUND WATER

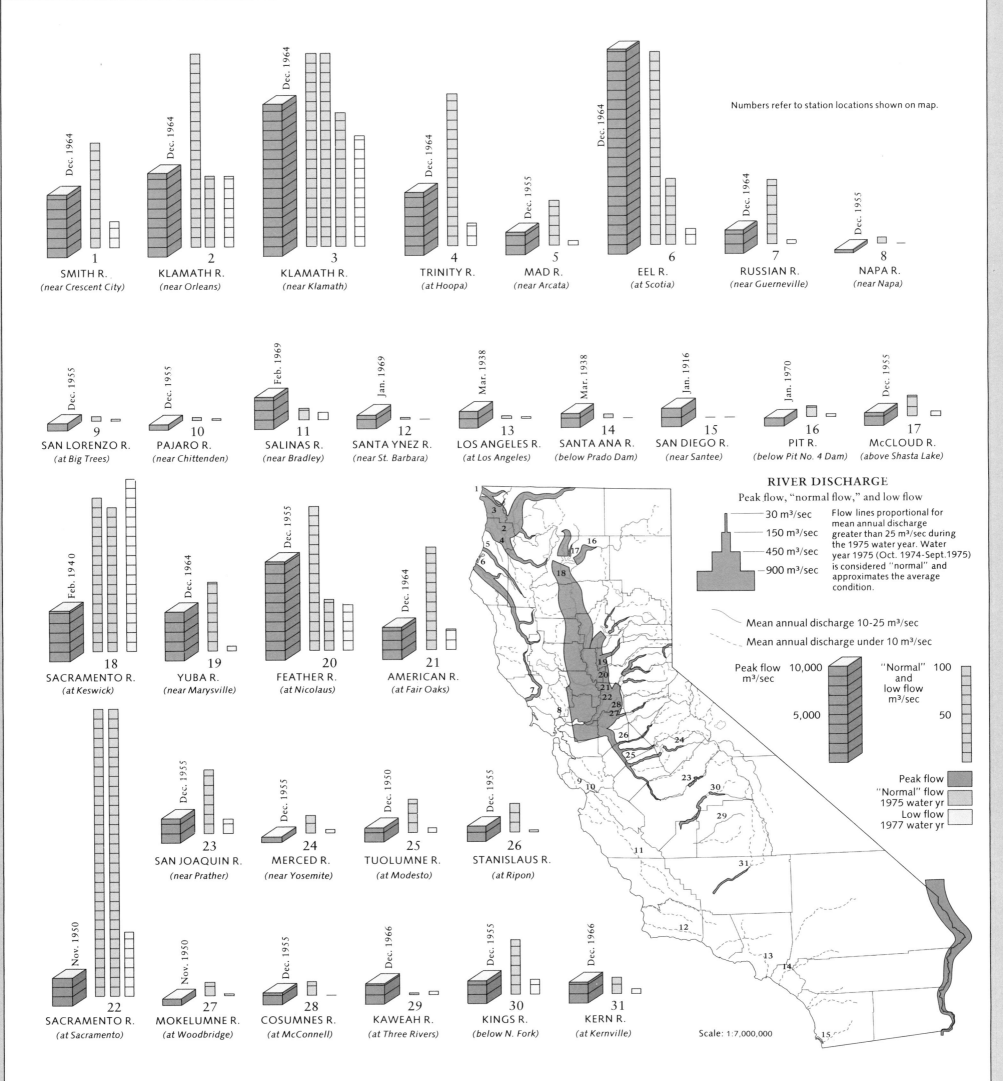

Numbers refer to station locations shown on map.

1 SMITH R. *(near Crescent City)* — Dec. 1964

2 KLAMATH R. *(near Orleans)* — Dec. 1964

3 KLAMATH R. *(near Klamath)* — Dec. 1964

4 TRINITY R. *(at Hoopa)* — Dec. 1964

5 MAD R. *(near Arcata)* — Dec. 1955

6 EEL R. *(at Scotia)* — Dec. 1964

7 RUSSIAN R. *(near Guerneville)* — Dec. 1964

8 NAPA R. *(near Napa)* — Dec. 1955

9 SAN LORENZO R. *(at Big Trees)* — Dec. 1955

10 PAJARO R. *(near Chittenden)* — Dec. 1955

11 SALINAS R. *(near Bradley)* — Feb. 1969

12 SANTA YNEZ R. *(near St. Barbara)* — Jan. 1969

13 LOS ANGELES R. *(at Los Angeles)* — Mar. 1938

14 SANTA ANA R. *(below Prado Dam)* — Mar. 1938

15 SAN DIEGO R. *(near Santee)* — Jan. 1916

16 PIT R. *(below Pit No. 4 Dam)* — Jan. 1970

17 McCLOUD R. *(above Shasta Lake)* — Dec. 1955

18 SACRAMENTO R. *(at Keswick)* — Feb. 1940

19 YUBA R. *(near Marysville)* — Dec. 1964

20 FEATHER R. *(at Nicolaus)* — Dec. 1955

21 AMERICAN R. *(at Fair Oaks)* — Dec. 1964

22 SACRAMENTO R. *(at Sacramento)* — Nov. 1950

23 SAN JOAQUIN R. *(near Prather)* — Dec. 1955

24 MERCED R. *(near Yosemite)* — Dec. 1955

25 TUOLUMNE R. *(at Modesto)* — Dec. 1950

26 STANISLAUS R. *(at Ripon)* — Dec. 1955

27 MOKELUMNE R. *(at Woodbridge)* — Nov. 1950

28 COSUMNES R. *(at McConnell)* — Dec. 1955

29 KAWEAH R. *(at Three Rivers)* — Dec. 1966

30 KINGS R. *(below N. Fork)* — Dec. 1955

31 KERN R. *(at Kernville)* — Dec. 1966

RIVER DISCHARGE
Peak flow, "normal flow," and low flow

- 30 m³/sec
- 150 m³/sec
- 450 m³/sec
- 900 m³/sec

Flow lines proportional for mean annual discharge greater than 25 m³/sec during the 1975 water year. Water year 1975 (Oct. 1974-Sept.1975) is considered "normal" and approximates the average condition.

Mean annual discharge 10-25 m³/sec

Mean annual discharge under 10 m³/sec

Peak flow m³/sec — 10,000 — 5,000

"Normal" and low flow m³/sec — 100 — 50

Peak flow

"Normal" flow 1975 water yr

Low flow 1977 water yr

Scale: 1:7,000,000

Stream discharge closely reflects precipitation. All rivers with significant flow are found in the wetter northern part of the state, whereas the Colorado River is the only significant fresh water supply in the arid southern part of the state. The map showing river discharge in 1974-75, a "normal" water year, illustrates the concentration of runoff in a few streams, notably the Sacramento and Klamath Rivers.

As seen in the bar graphs, large differences in flow exist not only between regions but also between seasonal peaks and troughs. Precipitation is concentrated in winter and peak flow occurs then, frequently turning normally dry arroyos such as the Mojave or San Diego into raging torrents. For practical purposes, this water comes at the wrong time and in the wrong place, inspiring efforts on the part of local, state, and federal agencies to manage and distribute water resources.

Water storage problems have continued despite governmental action and new storage facilities. In December of 1964, for instance, a single cyclonic storm dropped more than 40 cm of rain on the Eel and Klamath River Basins in less than 24 hours, marking the highest peak discharge and overbank flow on record in the northern part of the state. Similar floods have occurred elsewhere, as in 1913 in the Los Angeles area and in 1916 in San Diego. Although the volumes were not comparable to the 1964 flood, the ratio between mean discharge and peak flow were greater in the south because runoff was not appreciably slowed by soil or vegetation. In contrast, the severe drought affecting northern California in the 1976-77 water year left already low reservoirs with sub-normal supplies of water.

Source:
USGS Water Resource Data for California, 1976.

STREAMFLOW

California's drainage pattern and stream character are strongly linked to its geological structure and climate. Most of the surface flow originates in the mountainous areas of the north and northwest, and the streams ultimately flow into San Francisco Bay or directly into the Pacific Ocean. This drainage pattern provides northern California with scenic rivers and ample recreational facilities, but poses problems for southern California.

In the southern part of the state, water quality has been impaired because of the large population, irrigated agriculture, and low volumes of flow for dilution. Varied household and industrial wastes, agricultural chemicals, and sediment from erosion have found their way into streams despite attempts to monitor and control these contaminants.

The greater problem has been transporting the water from the north to the agricultural and residential concentrations of the south. In 1913, the Los Angeles Aqueduct

was completed, delivering water from the Owens Valley to the San Fernando Valley. For a time, it met the needs of the growing city of Los Angeles and transformed the San Fernando Valley into one of the nation's richest agricultural areas. With rapid growth in both the Los Angeles Basin and the Bay Area, however, new water projects were undertaken. The Mokelumne Aqueduct began delivering water to San Francisco in 1929. Other projects followed, including the Hetch Hetchy Aqueduct in 1932 and the Colorado River Aqueduct in 1941.

The California Water Project, run by the state, and the Central Valley Project, under federal auspices, are recent designs for distributing water from the north to the San Joaquin Valley, the Bay Area, and southern California. Many dams have been built and the California Aqueduct, 650 kilometers long, has already been constructed from the San Joaquin Valley to Lake Perris near San Bernardino. Additional features, including the controversial Peripheral Canal in the Sacramento Delta, remain to be built.

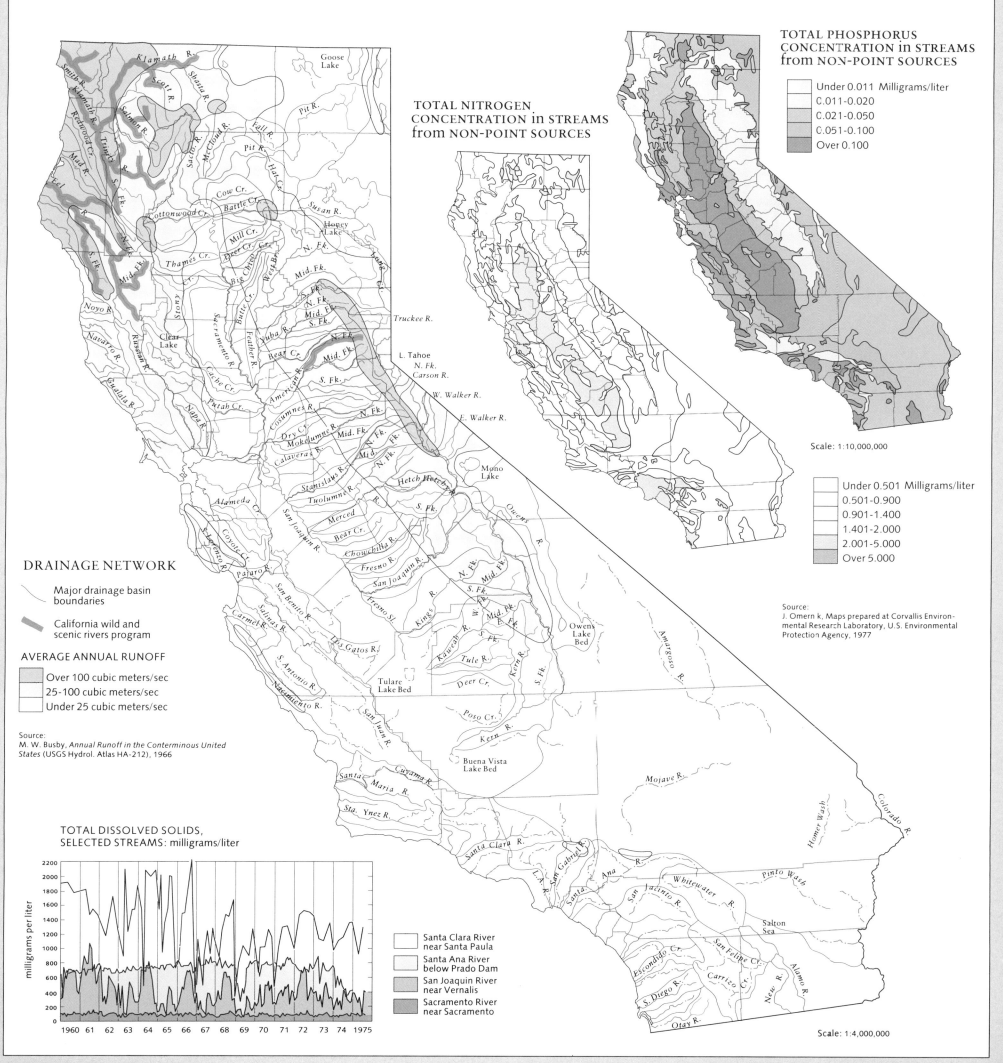

DRAINAGE NETWORK

Major drainage basin boundaries

California wild and scenic rivers program

AVERAGE ANNUAL RUNOFF

Over 100 cubic meters/sec
25-100 cubic meters/sec
Under 25 cubic meters/sec

Source:
M. W. Busby, *Annual Runoff in the Conterminous United States* (USGS Hydrol. Atlas HA-212), 1966

TOTAL NITROGEN CONCENTRATION in STREAMS from NON-POINT SOURCES

TOTAL PHOSPHORUS CONCENTRATION in STREAMS from NON-POINT SOURCES

Under 0.011 Milligrams/liter
0.011-0.020
0.021-0.050
0.051-0.100
Over 0.100

Scale: 1:10,000,000

Under 0.501 Milligrams/liter
0.501-0.900
0.901-1.400
1.401-2.000
2.001-5.000
Over 5.000

Source:
J. Omernk, Maps prepared at Corvallis Environmental Research Laboratory, U.S. Environmental Protection Agency, 1977

TOTAL DISSOLVED SOLIDS, SELECTED STREAMS: milligrams/liter

Santa Clara River near Santa Paula
Santa Ana River below Prado Dam
San Joaquin River near Vernalis
Sacramento River near Sacramento

Scale: 1:4,000,000

SURFACE WATER

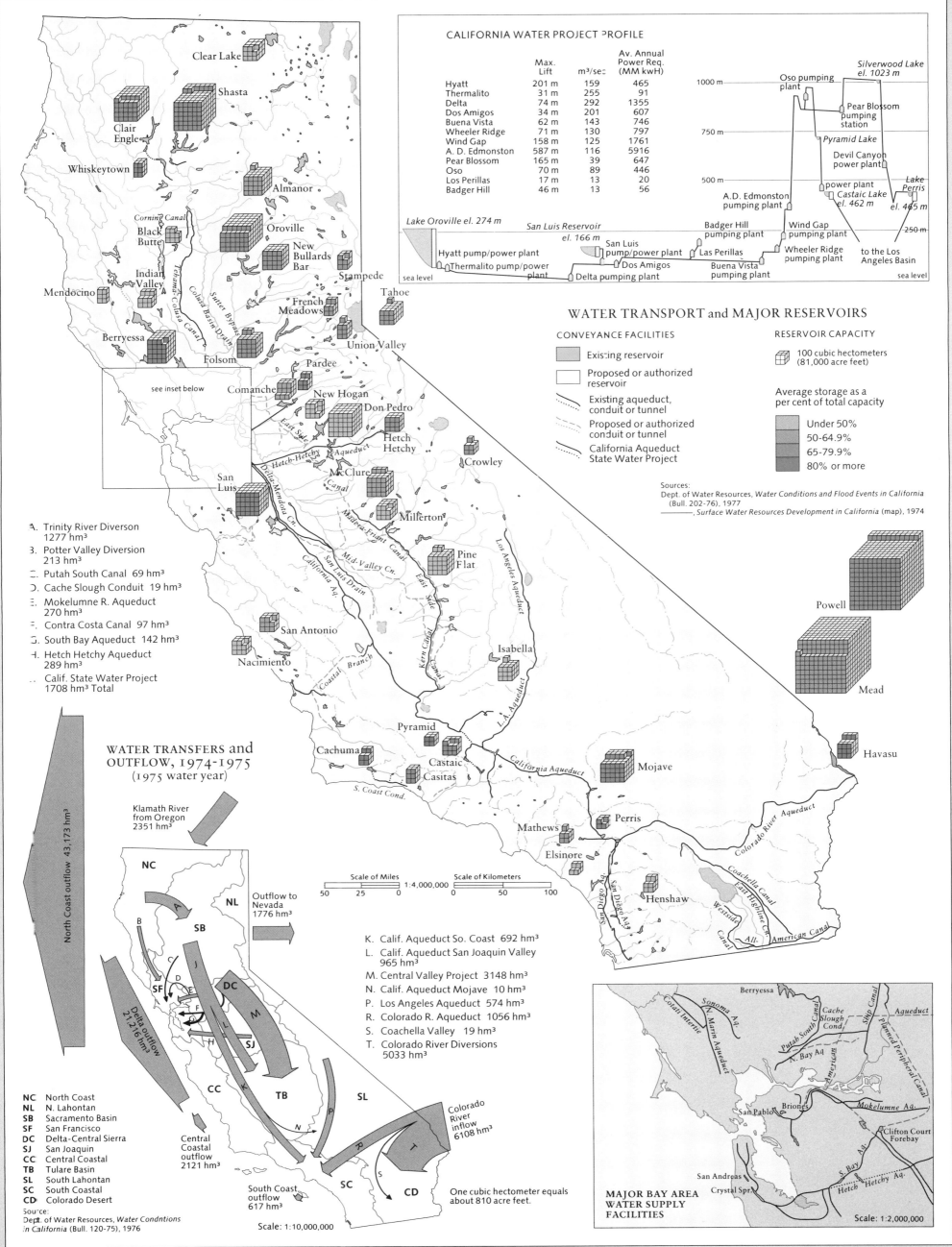

CALIFORNIA WATER PROJECT PROFILE

	Max. Lift	m³/sec	Av. Annual Power Req. (MM kWH)
Hyatt	201 m	159	465
Thermalito	31 m	255	91
Delta	74 m	292	1355
Dos Amigos	34 m	201	607
Buena Vista	62 m	143	746
Wheeler Ridge	71 m	130	797
Wind Gap	158 m	125	1761
A. D. Edmonston	587 m	116	5916
Pear Blossom	165 m	39	647
Oso	70 m	89	446
Los Perillas	17 m	13	20
Badger Hill	46 m	13	56

WATER TRANSPORT and MAJOR RESERVOIRS

CONVEYANCE FACILITIES

Existing reservoir

Proposed or authorized reservoir

Existing aqueduct, conduit or tunnel

Proposed or authorized conduit or tunnel

California Aqueduct State Water Project

RESERVOIR CAPACITY

100 cubic hectometers (81,000 acre feet)

Average storage as a per cent of total capacity

Under 50%
50-64.9%
65-79.9%
80% or more

Sources:
Dept. of Water Resources, *Water Conditions and Flood Events in California* (Bull. 202-76), 1977
————, *Surface Water Resources Development in California* (map), 1974

A. Trinity River Diversion 1277 hm³
B. Potter Valley Diversion 213 hm³
C. Putah South Canal 69 hm³
D. Cache Slough Conduit 19 hm³
E. Mokelumne R. Aqueduct 270 hm³
F. Contra Costa Canal 97 hm³
G. South Bay Aqueduct 142 hm³
H. Hetch Hetchy Aqueduct 289 hm³
J. Calif. State Water Project 1708 hm³ Total

WATER TRANSFERS and OUTFLOW, 1974-1975
(1975 water year)

North Coast outflow 43,173 hm³

Klamath River from Oregon 2351 hm³

Outflow to Nevada 1776 hm³

Delta outflow 21,216 hm³

K. Calif. Aqueduct So. Coast 692 hm³
L. Calif. Aqueduct San Joaquin Valley 965 hm³
M. Central Valley Project 3148 hm³
N. Calif. Aqueduct Mojave 10 hm³
P. Los Angeles Aqueduct 574 hm³
R. Colorado R. Aqueduct 1056 hm³
S. Coachella Valley 19 hm³
T. Colorado River Diversions 5033 hm³

Central Coastal outflow 2121 hm³

Colorado River inflow 6108 hm³

South Coast outflow 617 hm³

One cubic hectometer equals about 810 acre feet.

NC North Coast
NL N. Lahontan
SB Sacramento Basin
SF San Francisco
DC Delta-Central Sierra
SJ San Joaquin
CC Central Coastal
TB Tulare Basin
SL South Lahontan
SC South Coastal
CD Colorado Desert

Source:
Dept. of Water Resources, *Water Conditions in California* (Bull. 120-75), 1976

Scale: 1:10,000,000

1:4,000,000

MAJOR BAY AREA WATER SUPPLY FACILITIES

Scale: 1:2,000,000

SURFACE WATER

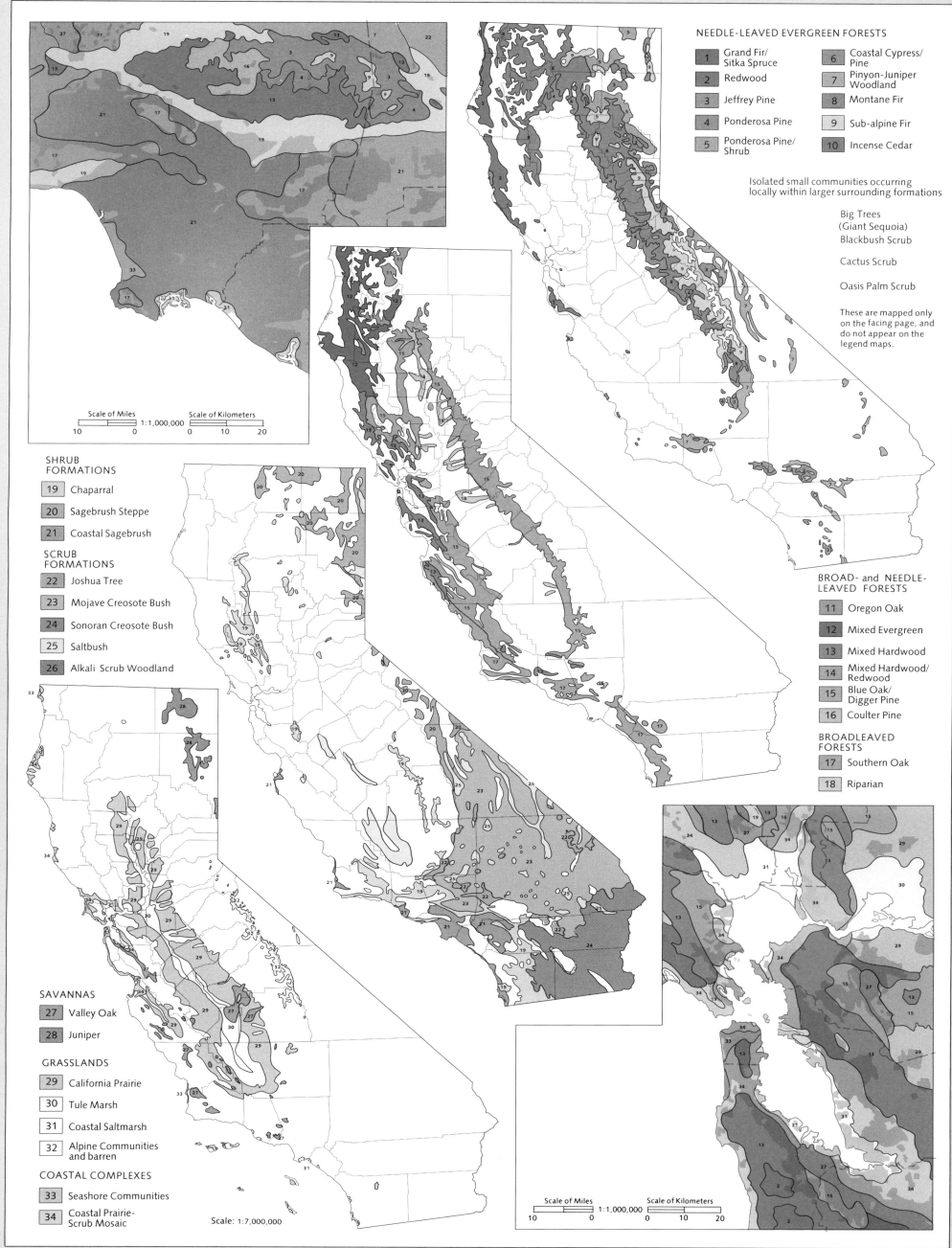

NATURAL VEGETATION

NEEDLE-LEAVED EVERGREEN FORESTS

1 Grand Fir/ Sitka Spruce
2 Redwood
3 Jeffrey Pine
4 Ponderosa Pine
5 Ponderosa Pine/ Shrub
6 Coastal Cypress/ Pine
7 Pinyon-Juniper Woodland
8 Montane Fir
9 Sub-alpine Fir
10 Incense Cedar

Isolated small communities occurring locally within larger surrounding formations

Big Trees (Giant Sequoia)
Blackbush Scrub
Cactus Scrub
Oasis Palm Scrub

These are mapped only on the facing page, and do not appear on the legend maps.

BROAD- and NEEDLE-LEAVED FORESTS

11 Oregon Oak
12 Mixed Evergreen
13 Mixed Hardwood
14 Mixed Hardwood/ Redwood
15 Blue Oak/ Digger Pine
16 Coulter Pine

BROADLEAVED FORESTS

17 Southern Oak
18 Riparian

SHRUB FORMATIONS

19 Chaparral
20 Sagebrush Steppe
21 Coastal Sagebrush

SCRUB FORMATIONS

22 Joshua Tree
23 Mojave Creosote Bush
24 Sonoran Creosote Bush
25 Saltbush
26 Alkali Scrub Woodland

SAVANNAS

27 Valley Oak
28 Juniper

GRASSLANDS

29 California Prairie
30 Tule Marsh
31 Coastal Saltmarsh
32 Alpine Communities and barren

COASTAL COMPLEXES

33 Seashore Communities
34 Coastal Prairie- Scrub Mosaic

Scale: 1:7,000,000

Scale of Miles 1:1,000,000 Scale of Kilometers

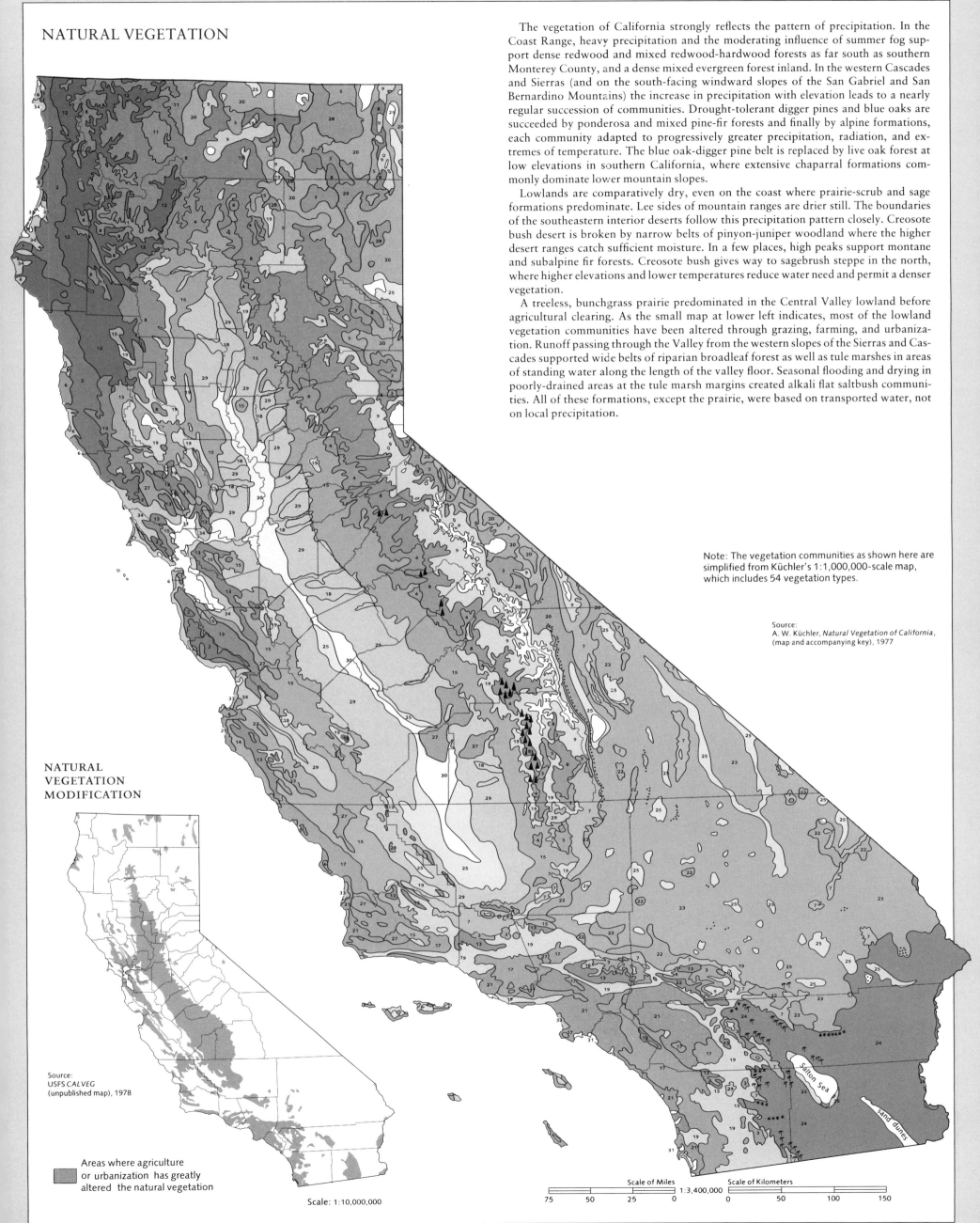

NATURAL VEGETATION

The vegetation of California strongly reflects the pattern of precipitation. In the Coast Range, heavy precipitation and the moderating influence of summer fog support dense redwood and mixed redwood-hardwood forests as far south as southern Monterey County, and a dense mixed evergreen forest inland. In the western Cascades and Sierras (and on the south-facing windward slopes of the San Gabriel and San Bernardino Mountains) the increase in precipitation with elevation leads to a nearly regular succession of communities. Drought-tolerant digger pines and blue oaks are succeeded by ponderosa and mixed pine-fir forests and finally by alpine formations, each community adapted to progressively greater precipitation, radiation, and extremes of temperature. The blue oak-digger pine belt is replaced by live oak forest at low elevations in southern California, where extensive chaparral formations commonly dominate lower mountain slopes.

Lowlands are comparatively dry, even on the coast where prairie-scrub and sage formations predominate. Lee sides of mountain ranges are drier still. The boundaries of the southeastern interior deserts follow this precipitation pattern closely. Creosote bush desert is broken by narrow belts of pinyon-juniper woodland where the higher desert ranges catch sufficient moisture. In a few places, high peaks support montane and subalpine fir forests. Creosote bush gives way to sagebrush steppe in the north, where higher elevations and lower temperatures reduce water need and permit a denser vegetation.

A treeless, bunchgrass prairie predominated in the Central Valley lowland before agricultural clearing. As the small map at lower left indicates, most of the lowland vegetation communities have been altered through grazing, farming, and urbanization. Runoff passing through the Valley from the western slopes of the Sierras and Cascades supported wide belts of riparian broadleaf forest as well as tule marshes in areas of standing water along the length of the valley floor. Seasonal flooding and drying in poorly-drained areas at the tule marsh margins created alkali flat saltbush communities. All of these formations, except the prairie, were based on transported water, not on local precipitation.

Note: The vegetation communities as shown here are simplified from Küchler's 1:1,000,000-scale map, which includes 54 vegetation types.

Source:
A. W. Küchler, *Natural Vegetation of California*, (map and accompanying key), 1977

NATURAL VEGETATION MODIFICATION

Source:
USFS *CALVEG*
(unpublished map), 1978

Areas where agriculture or urbanization has greatly altered the natural vegetation

Scale: 1:10,000,000

Scale of Miles 1:3,400,000 Scale of Kilometers

NATURAL VEGETATION

The six profiles illustrated on the facing page are sideviews, along the six transects shown at lower left, of the state vegetation map on page 147. They reflect the strong influence of relief and elevation on plant community distributions and the influence of diminishing precipitation from north to south. The first transect crosses the state from Trinity Head to the Modoc Plateau. Redwoods succeed coastal pine and cypress and are in turn followed by mixed evergreens and Oregon oak along the Trinity River. Montane fir and mixed hardwoods alternate across the Klamath Mountains and into the western Cascades. The much drier Modoc Plateau is characterized by Sagebrush steppe, Jeffrey pine, and Juniper savanna.

The second transect passes inland through a series of progressively drier hill communities alternating with Valley Oak savannas of the Petaluma and Napa Valleys. Heavy runoff from the southern Cascades and northern Sierra is reflected in the tule marshes and riparian forest of the Sacramento Valley, and in the montane fir forests of the Sierra above the dry foothills. Alpine barrens of Pyramid Peak are succeeded by Jeffrey pines at Lake Tahoe.

The third transect passes through the coastal scrub of the Pajaro Valley (now largely cleared for farming), the Valley oak savannas of the upper Santa Clara Valley, and across Pacheco Peak to the saltbush alkali flats near Los Banos. A wide prairie belt is succeeded by the Blue oaks and Digger pines of the foothills and by Ponderosa pine in the lower Sierra. Alpine barrens are encountered on Sierra peaks and on White Mountain Peak. The fourth transect (San Simeon to Death Valley) is similar, but southern oak forest appears on the coast, and the sagebrush of the northern transects gives way to creosote bush.

The fifth transect crosses the coastal sage of the Santa Ana Basin, then passes through a rapid succession of communities on the steep windward slopes of the San Bernardino Mountains. Subalpine fir gives way to Jeffrey pine, to pinyon or juniper, and finally to creosote bush on the dry northeastern slope, and creosote bush yields to saltbush and to barren salt flats at Bristol Lake. The Old Woman Mountains support a pinyon-juniper woodland. Along the sixth transect, the low Cuyamaca Mountains intercept enough rain to support a narrow belt of Jeffrey pine, and their runoff supplies springs for the oases at their eastern margins. The Sonoran creosote bush of the Imperial Valley (now cleared for farming in the valley bottom) and low Chocolate Mountains yields to an alkali scrub woodland along the Colorado River.

Profiles of the natural vegetation communities along the six transects shown here are illustrated on the facing page.

Source:
A. W. Küchler, *Natural Vegetation of California* (map and accompanying key), 1977

PROFILES INDEX MAP

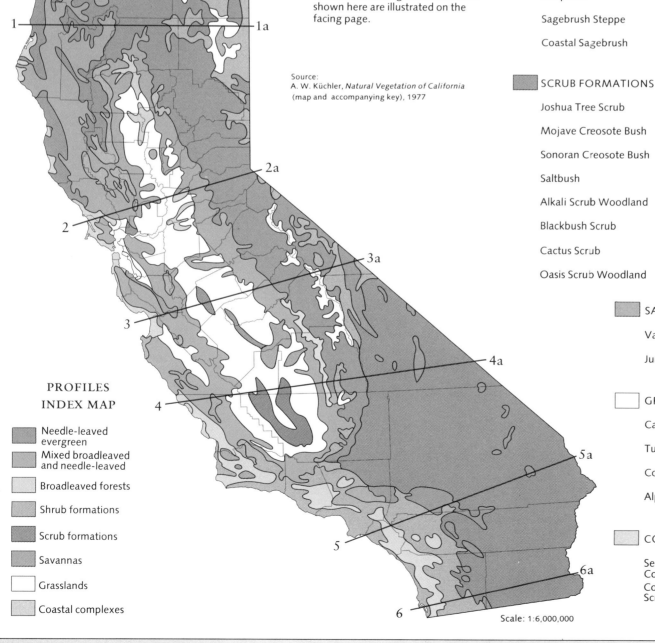

- Needle-leaved evergreen
- Mixed broadleaved and needle-leaved
- Broadleaved forests
- Shrub formations
- Scrub formations
- Savannas
- Grasslands
- Coastal complexes

Scale: 1:6,000,000

STRUCTURE and CHARACTERISTICS of VEGETATION FORMATIONS

NEEDLE-LEAVED EVERGREEN FORESTS

Grand Fir/ Sitka Spruce	Very tall & dense, with very little undergrowth. Along the coast in Humboldt and Del Norte counties.
Redwood	Very tall & dense, with broadleaved understory increasing eastward. Coast Ranges, Mont. Co. north.
Jeffrey Pine	Tall & moderately open in north (E. side Sierras, Modoc Plateau). Open & lower in Transv. & Pen. Ranges.
Ponderosa Pine	Tall & open in western Cascades & Transverse Ranges; denser in the western slopes of the Sierra.
Ponderosa Pine/ Shrub	Moderately open forest, with antelope bush (*Purshia tridentata*) shrub layer; mostly east of Cascades.
Coastal Cypress/ Pine	Low to medium tall; various species locally dominant in small areas (see pp. 150-151).
Pinyon-Juniper	Low, open groves of pinyon and juniper together, with shrub story; southeastern California.
Montane Fir	Tall in north, lower in south and east: dominants vary among regions, include true firs, pines, Douglas-fir.
Subalpine Fir	Height & density decrease with elevation; open shrub layer associated; to timberline & as krumholz beyond.
Incense Cedar	Open, low to medium tall; species widespread (see p. 151) but as dominant community only S.E. San Benito.
Sequoia (Big Trees)	Towering open groves dominating pine & fir forests in which they occur; about 70 sites, western Sierra.

MIXED BROADLEAVED and NEEDLE-LEAVED FORESTS

Oregon Oak	Medium tall broad-leaved deciduous forest, with shrub story and interspersed conifers; Northwest.
Mixed Evergreen	Dense broad-leaved forest (madrone, tanoak, canyon live oak), with Douglas-fir; N. Coast Ranges & Klamaths.
Mixed Hardwood	Lower than Mixed Evergreen; many of the same species, also chaparral; Central & Southern Coast Ranges.
Mixed Hardwood/ Redwood	Like the Mixed Hardwood forest, but with redwood along streambeds; Coast Ranges S. of Monterey Bay.
Blue Oak/ Digger Pine	Medium tall, dense to open (grading into savanna) in hot arid Sierra & Coast Range foothills.
Coulter Pine	Low open groves, with some broad-leaved evergreen & deciduous trees, Western San Gabriel Mountains.

BROADLEAVED FOREST

| Southern Oak | Low, dense to open forest dominated by coast live oak, in Peninsular, Transverse & Southern Coast Ranges. |
| Riparian | Medium tall to tall broad-leaved deciduous forest, dominated by cottonwood, with box elder, alder, sycamore, etc. |

SHRUB FORMATIONS

Chaparral	Dense, often impenetrable low shrub communities (chamise, manzanita, ceonothus), in mountains at low elevations.
Sagebrush Steppe	Low, open shrub formation dominated by basin sagebrush and wheatgrass, in Northeastern California.
Coastal Sagebrush	Low, dense shrub formations dominated by California sagebrush, white sage, blacksage; Central & Southern Coast.

SCRUB FORMATIONS

Joshua Tree Scrub	Low, dense broad-leaved shrub community, with much taller Joshua trees widely scattered; mostly in the Mojave Desert.
Mojave Creosote Bush	Very open formation dominated by creosote bush, often very evenly spaced; mostly Mojave Desert.
Sonoran Creosote Bush	Very open, dominated by creosote bush & bursage, with palo verde/ smoketree/ironwood woodland in washes.
Saltbush	Open stands of low shrubs, dominated by saltbush, in saline areas of E. Calif. & the San Joaquin Valley.
Alkali Scrub Woodland	Dense groves of low trees dom. by tamarisk & iodine bush, with cottonwoods & willows, Colo. R. & Salton S.
Blackbush Scrub	Dense to open shrub community, dominated by blackbush (*Coleogyne*); east side of the Sierra Nevada
Cactus Scrub	Low, open stands of cacti (jumping cholla & other *Opuntia* spp), N. & W. margins of Colorado Desert.
Oasis Scrub Woodland	Dense woodlands, dom. by Fan Palm but incl. cottonwoods & willows, in desert canyons & springs.

SAVANNA FORMATIONS

| Valley Oak | Widely spaced valley oaks with grassland groundcover. |
| Juniper | Bunchgrass community with scattered low, shrubby California junipers. |

GRASSLAND FORMATIONS

California Prairie	Treeless bunchgrass/forbs, now incl. many introduced grasses.
Tule Marsh	Tall, dense stands of tule and cattail; greatly reduced outside Delta.
Coastal Saltmarsh	Perennial grasses & succulents, above mean high water level.
Alpine Communities	Grassy turf, bunchgrass & cushion plants on drier sites; above timberline.

COASTAL

| Seashore Communities | Grasses & succulents on beaches, shrubs on stabilized dunes. |
| Coastal Prairie- Scrub Mosaic | Dense grassland with coyote brush near the coast. |

VEGETATION PROFILES

TRINIDAD HEAD-TRINITY ALPS-MODOC PLATEAU

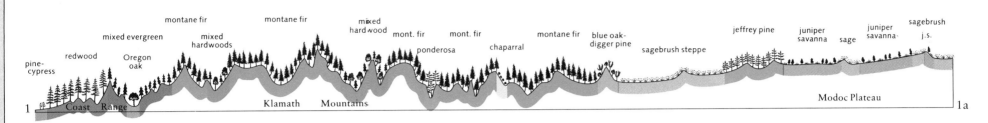

TOMALES BAY-COASTAL VALLEYS-CENTRAL VALLEY-SIERRA NEVADA

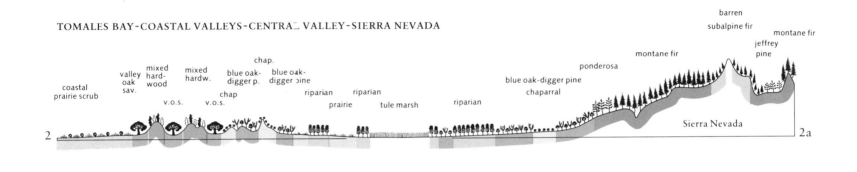

PAJARO VALLEY-GABILAN RANGE-SAN JOAQUIN VALLEY-SIERRA NEVADA-OWENS VALLEY-WHITE MOUNTAINS

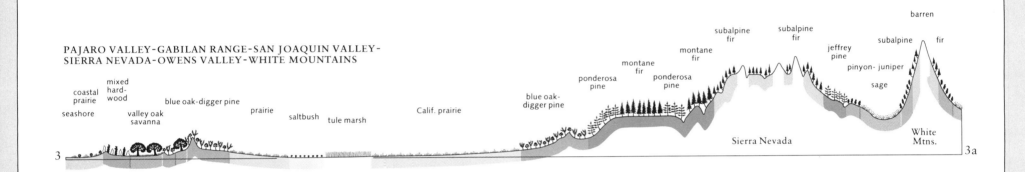

SAN SIMEON-SALINAS VALLEY-SAN JOAQUIN VALLEY-SIERRA NEVADA-OWENS VALLEY-DEATH VALLEY

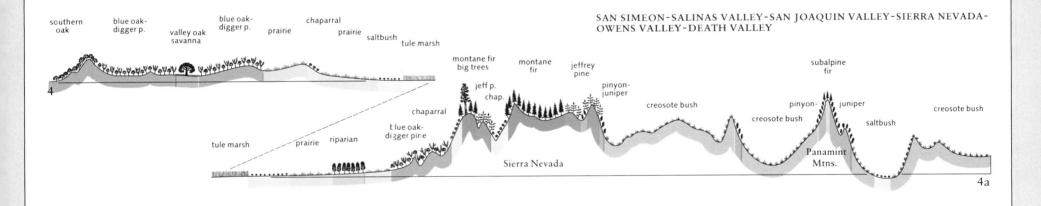

SAN PEDRO BAY-SAN BERNARDINO MOUNTAINS-OLD WOMAN MOUNTAINS-COLORADO RIVER

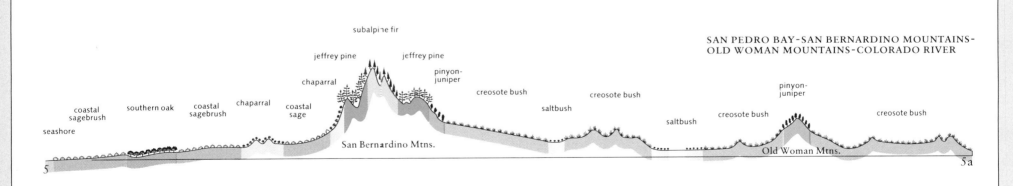

POINT LOMA-CUYAMACA MOUNTAINS-IMPERIAL VALLEY-COLORADO RIVER

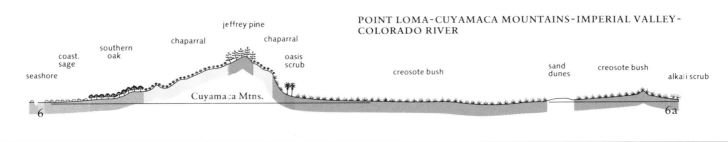

Scale: 1:1,500,000

VEGETATION PROFILES

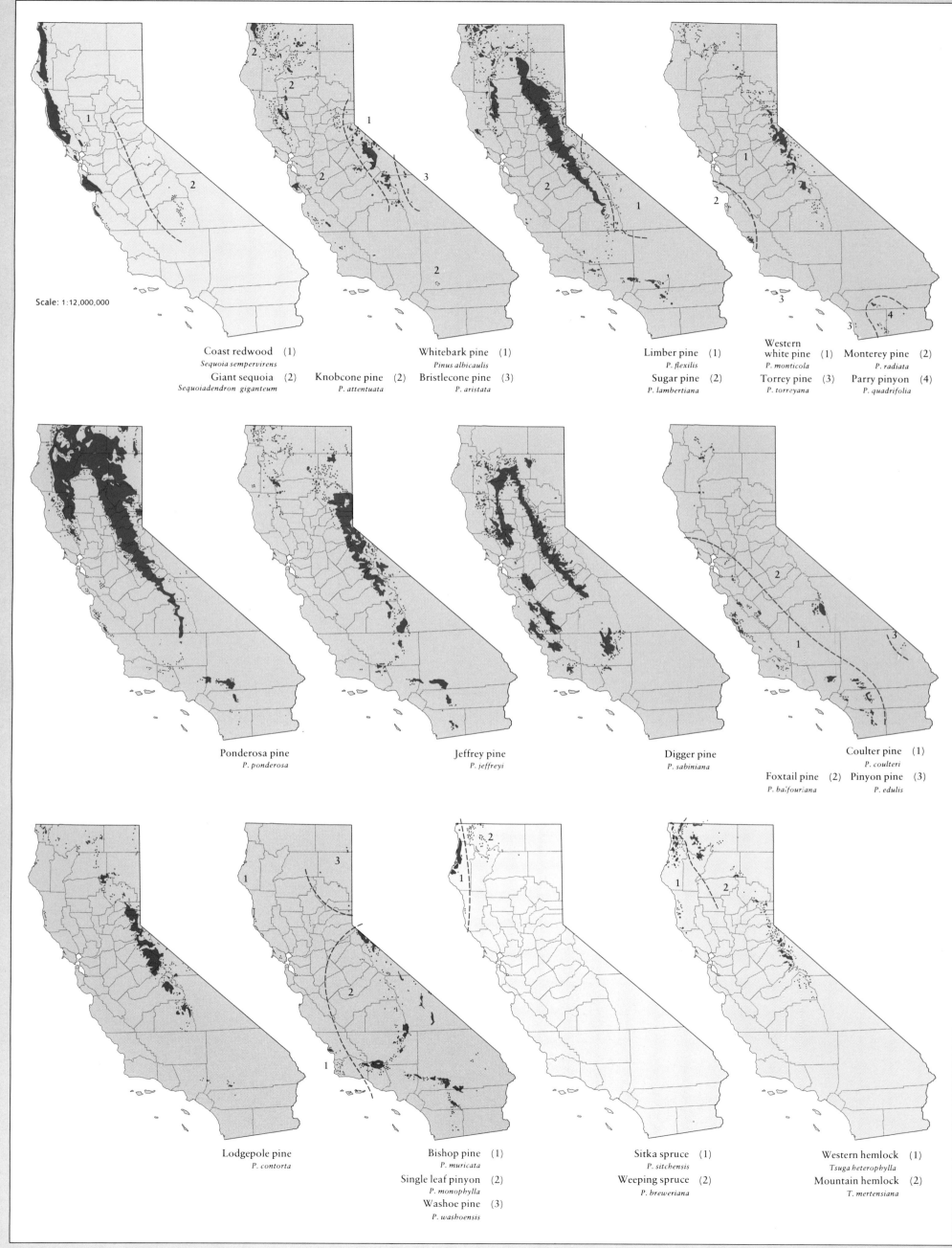

Scale: 1:12,000,000

Coast redwood (1)
Sequoia sempervirens

Giant sequoia (2)
Sequoiadendron giganteum

Whitebark pine (1)
Pinus albicaulis

Knobcone pine (2)
P. attentuata

Bristlecone pine (3)
P. aristata

Limber pine (1)
P. flexilis

Sugar pine (2)
P. lambertiana

Western
white pine (1)
P. monticola

Torrey pine (3)
P. torreyana

Monterey pine (2)
P. radiata

Parry pinyon (4)
P. quadrifolia

Ponderosa pine
P. ponderosa

Jeffrey pine
P. jeffreyi

Digger pine
P. sabiniana

Coulter pine (1)
P. coulteri

Foxtail pine (2)
P. balfouriana

Pinyon pine (3)
P. edulis

Lodgepole pine
P. contorta

Bishop pine (1)
P. muricata

Single leaf pinyon (2)
P. monophylla

Washoe pine (3)
P. washoensis

Sitka spruce (1)
P. sitchensis

Weeping spruce (2)
P. breweriana

Western hemlock (1)
Tsuga heterophylla

Mountain hemlock (2)
T. mertensiana

TREES

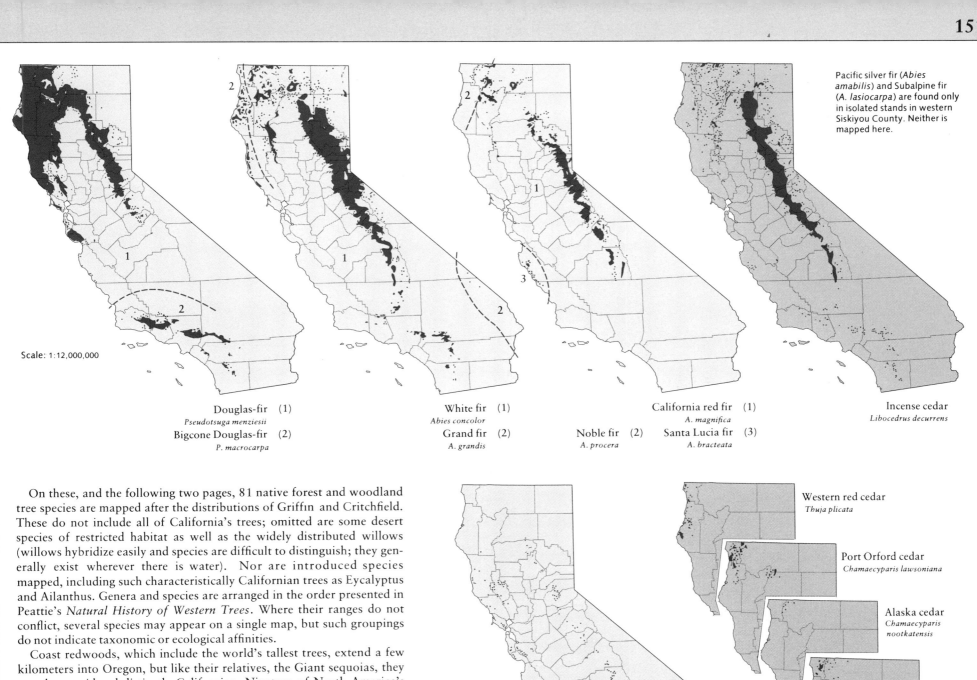

Scale: 1:12,000,000

Douglas-fir (1)
Pseudotsuga menziesii
Bigcone Douglas-fir (2)
P. macrocarpa

White fir (1)
Abies concolor
Grand fir (2)
A. grandis

California red fir (1)
A. magnifica
Noble fir (2)
A. procera
Santa Lucia fir (3)
A. bracteata

Incense cedar
Libocedrus decurrens

Pacific silver fir (*Abies amabilis*) and Subalpine fir (*A. lasiocarpa*) are found only in isolated stands in western Siskiyou County. Neither is mapped here.

On these, and the following two pages, 81 native forest and woodland tree species are mapped after the distributions of Griffin and Critchfield. These do not include all of California's trees; omitted are some desert species of restricted habitat as well as the widely distributed willows (willows hybridize easily and species are difficult to distinguish; they generally exist wherever there is water). Nor are introduced species mapped, including such characteristically Californian trees as Eycalyptus and Ailanthus. Genera and species are arranged in the order presented in Peattie's *Natural History of Western Trees*. Where their ranges do not conflict, several species may appear on a single map, but such groupings do not indicate taxonomic or ecological affinities.

Coast redwoods, which include the world's tallest trees, extend a few kilometers into Oregon, but like their relatives, the Giant sequoias, they may be considered distinctly Californian. Nineteen of North America's 59 pine species are found in the state; three of them (Monterey, Torrey and Digger) are found only in California. Bristlecone pine, the world's oldest living organism, is found at high elevations in the White Mountains. Big-cone Douglas-fir is probably restricted to California. Eight of the state's ten cypresses are found only in California; Baker cypress extends a short distance into Oregon and Tecate cypress is found well into Baja California.

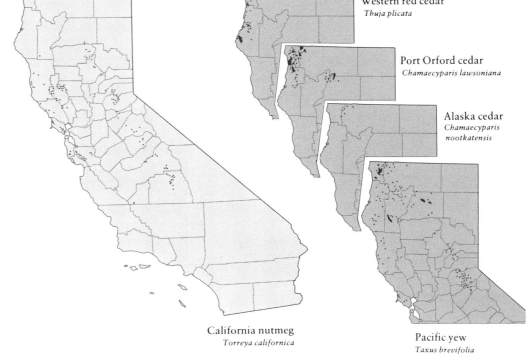

California nutmeg
Torreya californica

Western red cedar
Thuja plicata

Port Orford cedar
Chamaecyparis lawsoniana

Alaska cedar
Chamaecyparis nootkatensis

Pacific yew
Taxus brevifolia

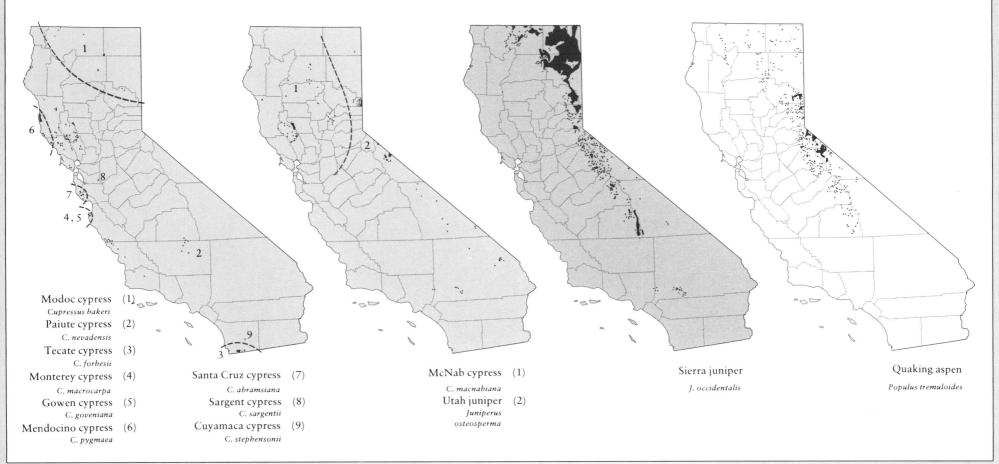

Modoc cypress (1)
Cupressus bakeri
Paiute cypress (2)
C. nevadensis
Tecate cypress (3)
C. forbesii
Monterey cypress (4)
C. macrocarpa
Gowen cypress (5)
C. goveniana
Mendocino cypress (6)
C. pygmaea

Santa Cruz cypress (7)
C. abramsiana
Sargent cypress (8)
C. sargentii
Cuyamaca cypress (9)
C. stephensonii

McNab cypress (1)
C. macnabiana
Utah juniper (2)
Juniperus osteosperma

Sierra juniper
J. occidentalis

Quaking aspen
Populus tremuloides

TREES

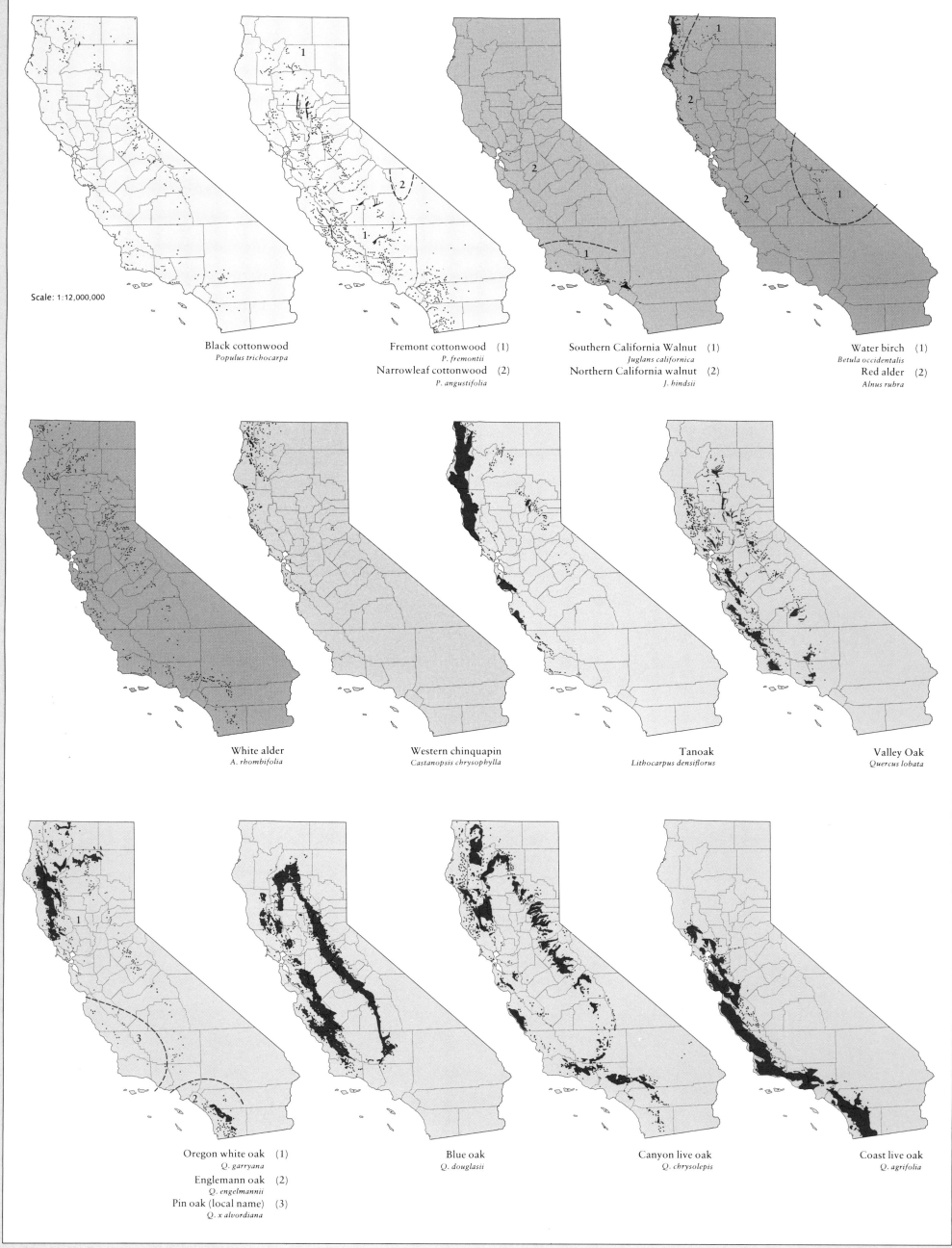

Scale: 1:12,000,000

Black cottonwood
Populus trichocarpa

Fremont cottonwood (1)
P. fremontii
Narrowleaf cottonwood (2)
P. angustifolia

Southern California Walnut (1)
Juglans californica
Northern California walnut (2)
J. hindsii

Water birch (1)
Betula occidentalis
Red alder (2)
Alnus rubra

White alder
A. rhombifolia

Western chinquapin
Castanopsis chrysophylla

Tanoak
Lithocarpus densiflorus

Valley Oak
Quercus lobata

Oregon white oak (1)
Q. garryana
Englemann oak (2)
Q. engelmannii
Pin oak (local name) (3)
Q. x alvordiana

Blue oak
Q. douglasii

Canyon live oak
Q. chrysolepis

Coast live oak
Q. agrifolia

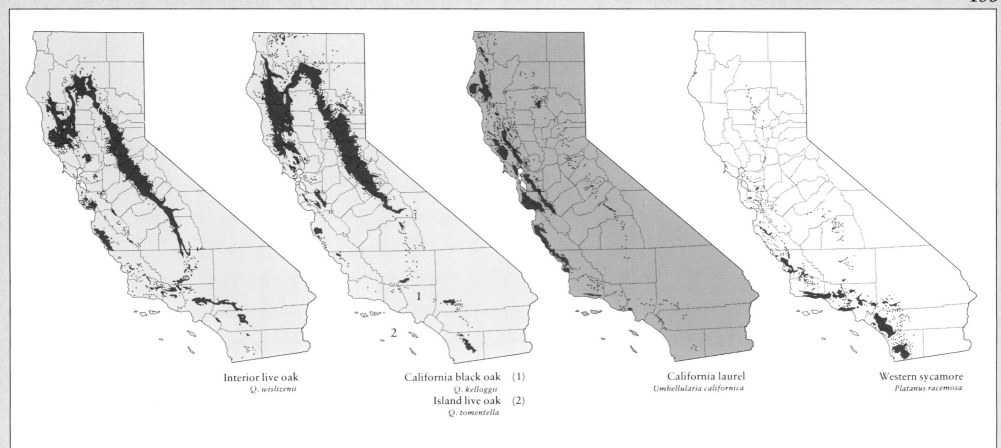

Interior live oak
Q. wislizenii

California black oak (1)
Q. kelloggii
Island live oak (2)
Q. tomentella

California laurel
Umbellularia californica

Western sycamore
Platanus racemosa

Fifteen oak species are found in California, including several shrubby varieties not mapped here. Of the nine shown, valley oak and the hybrid "Alvordiana" are restricted to California. California black oak extends into Oregon, and the live oaks extend into Baja California. The walnuts, the California buckeye and the box elder subspecies are strictly Californian. California laurel extends well into Oregon. The other species shown on this and the facing page are widespread in the West.

The maps on these two pages and the preceding three pages are based on Griffin and Critchfield (see below), which in turn is based on the maps and field notes of the Vegetation Type Map surveys of 1928-1940, on the Soil-Vegetation Surveys in progress since the late 1940's, and on supplementary data from the Forest Service and other agencies. Only confirmed, surveyed stands are mapped here. "Probable ranges," extrapolated for some species in Griffin and Critchfield, are not shown. The distributions are therefore conservative, with many species ranging beyond the limits mapped.

Source:
J.R. Griffin and W.D. Critchfield, *The Distribution of Forest Trees in California*, USDA Forest Service Res. Paper PSW 82, 1972

Scale: 1:12,000,000

Big leaf maple
Acer macrophyllum

California box elder
Acer negundo

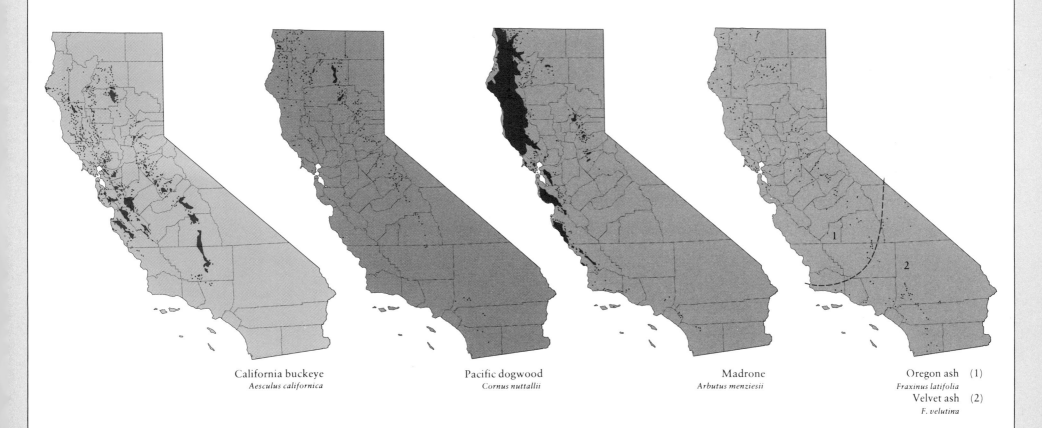

California buckeye
Aesculus californica

Pacific dogwood
Cornus nuttallii

Madrone
Arbutus menziesii

Oregon ash (1)
Fraxinus latifolia
Velvet ash (2)
F. velutina

TREES

154

BIRDS BREEDING ALONG the COAST

Fork-tailed Storm Petrel .... *Humboldt & Del Norte Co. islets*
Leach's Storm Petrel ..... *Farallones, Humboldt & Del Norte Cos.*
Ashy Storm Petrel .... *Farallones, Southern Calif. islands*
Brown Pelican .... *Point Lobos, Southern Calif. islands*
Double-crested Cormorant .... *Farallones & s. int. lakes*
Brandt's Cormorant .... *Length of coast, excl. salt water*
Pelagic Cormorant .... *Length of coast, esp. Pt. Loma*
Great Blue Heron .... *Western Calif., Salton Sea/Colo. R.*
Great Egret .... *Length of coast in lagoons & salt marshes*
Black-crowned Night Heron .... *salt and freshwater marshes*
American Bittern .... *Western California marshes*
Pintail .... *Fresh & saltwater marshes, ponds, lakes, bays*
Green-winged Teal .... *Fresh & saltwater marshes, lakes, bays*
Bald Eagle .... *Coast, large lakes & rivers, N. Calif.*
Marsh Hawk .... *Fresh and saltwater marshes, length of state*
Peregrine Falcon .... *Coast & offshore islands; rare*
Clapper Rail .... *Saltwater marshes, Marin Co. south*
Virginia Rail .... *Fresh & saltwater marshes, length of state*
Black Rail .... *Saltwater marshes, Morro Bay south*

BIRDS BREEDING in FORESTS WOODLANDS, and CHAPARRAL

California Condor .... *Very locally in Ventura Co. Mtns.*
Goshawk .... *Forests at higher elevations, esp. n. third*
Sharp-shinned Hawk .... *Open woodland, n. half of state*
Cooper's Hawk .... *Riparian & open woodland, length of state*
Red-tailed Hawk .... *Open woodland with cliffs, tall trees*
Swainson's Hawk .... *C. Valley, coastal woodlands s. to S.L.O.*
Golden Eagle .... *Open woodland with cliffs & trees*
American Kestrel .... *Open woodlands, length of state*
Red-shouldered Hawk .... *Dense riparian woodland*
Blue Grouse .... *Dense forests at higher elevations*
Ruffed Grouse .... *Dense streamside forests, locally in n.w.*
California Quail .... *Chapparal, riparian thickets*
Mountain Quail .... *Mountain chaparral and forest margins*
Turkey .... *Locally, Mendocino-Sta. Barbara, also Riverside*
Band-tailed Pigeon .... *Pine & oak woodlands, west of mtns.*
Mourning Dove .... *Oak woodland, also open country & cities*
Ground Dove .... *Riparian woodlands, thickets of S.E. deserts*
Yellow-billed Cuckoo .... *Riparian woodlands, Cent. Valley*
Screech Owl ...... *Woodland, forest & open country, lower elev.*
Flammulated Owl .... *Ponderosa pine & mixed forests*
Great Horned Owl .... *Mixed forest, riparian, also desert*
Pygmy Owl .... *Woodland & mixed forest, conif. for. margins*
Spotted Owl .... *Dense conif. for. in n.w., Sierras, s. mtns.*
Great Gray Owl .... *Dense conif. for., cent. & northern Sierra*
Long-eared Owl .... *Riparian woodlands & live oak groves*
Saw-whet Owl .... *Forests of Cascades, Sierras, So. Calif.*
Poor-will .... *Chaparral, pinyon-juniper, also desert*
Common Nighthawk ...... *Conif. for. of Cascades, Sierra, S. Bern.*
Vaux's Swift .... *Douglas-fir & redwood forests of n. coast*
Black Swift .... *Cliffs & canyons with nearby waterfalls*
Black-chinned Hummingbird .... *Woodland margins, n. to S.F.*
Anna's Hummingbird .... *Chaparral, Sac. Valley & S.F. south*
Rufous Hummingbird ...... *Coast redwood & Douglas-fir forests*
Allen's Hummingbird .... *Coastal chaparral S. Barb. north*
Calliope Hummingbird ..... *High montane forests, length of state*
Common Flicker .... *Open woodland; also in open country*
Pileated Woodpecker .... *Northern & central conif. forests*
Acorn Woodpecker ..... *Oak & mixed woodland, Marin Co. south*
Lewis' Woodpecker ..... *Oak & mixed woodland, Kern Co. north*
Red-naped Sapsucker ..... *Riparian woodlands of Modoc plateau*
Red-breasted Sapsucker .... *Montane coniferous forests*
Williamson's Sapsucker .... *Montane & subalpine con. forests*
Hairy Woodpecker .... *Montane & mixed forests, length of state*
Downy Woodpecker .... *Riparian woodlands except e. & s.e.*
Ladder-backed Woodpecker .... *Pinyon-juniper, also desert*
Nuttall's Woodpecker .... *Oak woodlands n. to about 40°N*
White-headed Woodpecker .... *Montane pine & fir forests*
Black-backed Three-toed Woodpecker .... *Lodgepole pine for.*
Ash-throated Flycatcher .... *Chap. & woodland, desert edge*
Willow Flycatcher .... *Riparian woodlands at low elevations*
Hammond's Flycatcher .... *Red fir-Lodgepole pine forests*
Dusky Flycatcher .... *Mtn. chaparral with scattered conifers*
Gray Flycatcher .... *Pinyon-juniper, sage, Modoc-Inyo Cos.*
Western Flycatcher .... *Dense for. w. of Sierra; Warner Mts.*
Western Wood Pewee .... *Mixed forest and open woodland*
Olive-sided Flycatcher .... *Mont. & subalpine conif. forest*
Violet-green Swallow .... *Open & mixed forest & woodland*
Tree Swallow .... *Any forest with woodpecker holes*
Purple Martin .... *Woodland & for. to 2000 m, w. of desert*
Gray Jay .... *Northern conif. forests, s. to Mendocino Co.*
Steller's Jay .... *Montane & coastal coniferous forests*
Scrub Jay .... *Mixed woodlands & chaparral, w. of deserts*
Yellow-billed Magpie .... *Open woodland, central Valley*
Pinyon Jay .... *Pinyon-juniper woodlands of eastern Calif.*
Clark's Nutcracker .... *Upper subalpine for., length of state*
Black-capped Chickadee .... *Riparian willows, N.W. Calif.*
Mountain Chickadee .... *Montane and subalpine forests*
Chestnut-backed Chickadee .... *Primarily coastal forests*
Plain Titmouse .... *Oak and pinyon-juniper woodlands*
Bushtit .... *Chaparral, oak, pinyon-juniper woodland*
White-breasted Nuthatch .... *All but humid northwest forests*
Red-breasted Nuthatch .... *Montane & subalpine conif. for.*
Pygmy Nuthatch .... *Coastal & montane pine forests*
Brown Creeper .... *Coastal, montane & subalpine conif. for.*
Wrentit ...... *Coastal & lowland chaparral w. of mountains*
House Wren .... *Thickets, chaparral, woodland margins*
Winter Wren .... *Dense conif. for. on coast, w. Sierra*
Bewick's Wren .... *Woodland thickets and chaparral*
California Thrasher .... *Lowland chaparral, rip. thickets*
American Robin .... *Forests & woodlands, mostly n. half*
Varied Thrush .... *Dense coastal for., Humboldt & Del Norte*
Hermit Thrush .... *Montane, subalpine & coast. conif. for.*

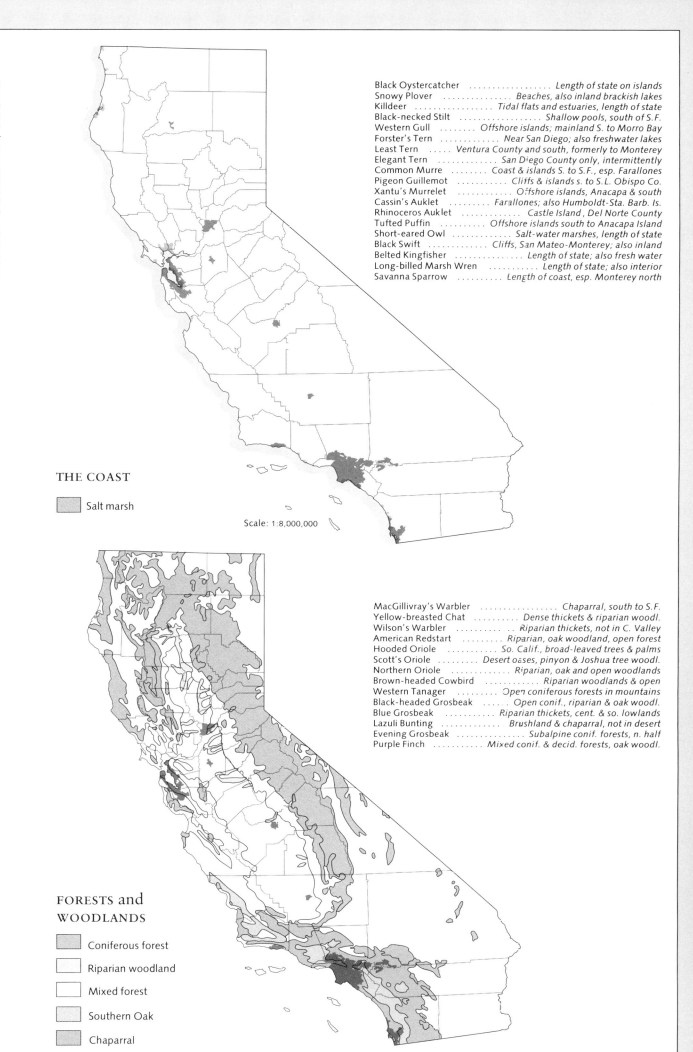

THE COAST

Salt marsh

Scale: 1:8,000,000

Black Oystercatcher .... *Length of state on islands*
Snowy Plover .... *Beaches, also inland brackish lakes*
Killdeer .... *Tidal flats and estuaries, length of state*
Black-necked Stilt .... *Shallow pools, south of S.F.*
Western Gull .... *Offshore islands; mainland S. to Morro Bay*
Forster's Tern .... *Near San Diego; also freshwater lakes*
Least Tern ..... *Ventura County and south, formerly to Monterey*
Elegant Tern .... *San Diego County only, intermittently*
Common Murre ...... *Coast & islands S. to S.F., esp. Farallones*
Pigeon Guillemot .... *Cliffs & islands s. to S.L. Obispo Co.*
Xantu's Murrelet .... *Offshore islands, Anacapa & south*
Cassin's Auklet .... *Farallones; also Humboldt-Sta. Barb. Is.*
Rhinoceros Auklet .... *Castle Island, Del Norte County*
Tufted Puffin .... *Offshore islands south to Anacapa Island*
Short-eared Owl .... *Salt-water marshes, length of state*
Black Swift .... *Cliffs, San Mateo-Monterey; also inland*
Belted Kingfisher .... *Length of state; also fresh water*
Long-billed Marsh Wren .... *Length of state; also interior*
Savanna Sparrow .... *Length of coast, esp. Monterey north*

FORESTS and WOODLANDS

Coniferous forest

Riparian woodland

Mixed forest

Southern Oak

Chaparral

MacGillivray's Warbler .... *Chaparral, south to S.F.*
Yellow-breasted Chat .... *Dense thickets & riparian woodl.*
Wilson's Warbler .... *Riparian thickets, not in C. Valley*
American Redstart .... *Riparian, oak woodland, open forest*
Hooded Oriole .... *So. Calif., broad-leaved trees & palms*
Scott's Oriole ...... *Desert oases, pinyon & Joshua tree woodl.*
Northern Oriole .... *Riparian, oak and open woodlands*
Brown-headed Cowbird .... *Riparian woodlands & open*
Western Tanager .... *Open coniferous forests in mountains*
Black-headed Grosbeak ..... *Open conif., riparian & oak woodl.*
Blue Grosbeak .... *Riparian thickets, cent. & so. lowlands*
Lazuli Bunting .... *Brushland & chaparral, not in desert*
Evening Grosbeak .... *Subalpine conif. forests, n. half*
Purple Finch .... *Mixed conif. & decid. forests, oak woodl.*

Swainson's Thrush .... *Riparian woodland thickets*
Western Bluebird .... *Open forests, edge of rip. woodlands*
Mountain Bluebird .... *Subalpine coniferous forests*
Townsend's Solitaire .... *Montane and subalpine forests*
Blue-gray Gnatcatcher .... *Chaparral of interior foothills*
Golden-crowned Kinglet .... *Coastal, montane, subalpine for.*
Ruby-crowned Kinglet ...... *Montane & subalpine conif. forests*
Cedar Waxwing ...... *Coniferous forests, Humboldt & Del Norte*
Phainopepla ...... *Oak woodlands with mistletoe, n. to Shasta*
Loggerhead Shrike .... *Pinyon-juniper woodlands (also open)*
Hutton's Vireo .... *Live oak woodlands, length of state*
Bell's Vireo .... *Dense riparian thickets n. to Tehama Co.*
Gray Vireo .... *Chaparral of S. Bern. & n. desert mtns.*
Solitary Vireo .... *Oak & mixed woodlands not in n.w.*
Warbling Vireo .... *Riparian woodlands west of deserts*
Orange-crowned Vireo .... *Live oaks, chaparral, riparian*
Nashville Warbler .... *Deciduous oaks & maples, mont. for.*
Yellow Warbler .... *Lowland & foothill riparian woodlands*
Yellow-rumped Warbler .... *Montane & subalpine forests*
Black-throated Gray Warbler ...... *Oak, mixed, & pinyon-jun.*
Hermit Warbler .... *Coniferous forests, length of state*

Cassin's Finch .... *Subalpine forests, length of state*
House Finch .... *Woodlands, chaparral, and open country*
Pine Grosbeak .... *Subalpine forests of northern Sierras*
Gray-crowned Rosy Finch .... *High Sierras, White Mtn., Shasta*
Pine Siskin .... *Coniferous montane & subalpine forests*
American Goldfinch .... *Riparian woodland & open, W. Calif.*
Lesser Goldfinch ...... *Riparian Woodland and open forest*
Lawrence's Goldfinch .... *Riparian & oak woodl., open for.*
Red Grossbill .... *Coniferous forest, esp. with pines*
Green-tailed Towhee ...... *Mountain chaparral, length of state*
Rufous-sided Towhee .... *Chaparral and riparian thickets*
Brown Towhee .... *Chaparral & thickets, cent. & west. Cal.*
Rufous-crowned Sparrow .... *Open chaparral, Sonoma south*
Dark-eyed Junco .... *Mtns., Coast Range, s. to S.L. Obispo*
Grey-headed Junco .... *Clark Mts. (San Bern. Co.), Inyo Mts.*
Chirping Sparrow .... *Length of state west of deserts*
Black-chinned Sparrow .... *Chaparral, Great Basin sagebrush*
White-crowned Sparrow .... *Chap. & thickets, s. to Sta. Barb.*
Fox Sparrow .... *Chaparral, riparian, & open mixed forest*
Lincoln's Sparrow .... *Meadows in subalpine forests*
Song Sparrow .... *Riparian and marsh-edge thickets*

BIRDS

BIRDS BREEDING ALONG RIVERS, LAKES and MARSHES

Common Loon .... *Larger lakes of the Modoc Plateau*
Eared Grebe .... *Interior lakes east of Sierra Nevada*
Western Grebe .... *Mostly in large northern lakes*
Pied-billed Grebe .... *Small marshy lakes, length of state*
Double-crested Cormorant ... *Large inland lakes, Colo. R.*
Great Blue Heron .... *W. marshes, and Colo. R., Salton Sea*
Green Heron .... *Lowlands of western and southern Calif.*
Great Egret .... *Margins of large lakes and rivers*
Snowy Egret .... *Salton Sea, San Joaquin Valley*
Black-crowned Night Heron .... *Fresh & saltwater marshes*
Least Bittern ...... *San Joaq. V. s. to Salton Sea & Colo. R.*
American Bittern ...... *West of Sierras, and in southern Cal.*
White-faced Ibis ...... *San Joaquin Valley, s. end Salton Sea*
Fulvous Tree Duck .... *Mostly south end of Salton Sea*
Mallard .... *Length of state, most wild birds in north*
Gadwall .... *Sacramento and San Joaquin Valleyw*
Pintail .... *Length of state, extremely abundant in north*
Green-winged Teal .... *Length of state (small numbers)*
Blue-winged Teal .... *Northeast; most abundant in north*
Cinnamon Teal .... *Length of state except in humid n.w.*
Northern Shoveler .... *Central Valley and northeast*
Wood Duck .... *Locally in Central Valley & coastal valleys*
Redhead .... *Northern refuges and Central Valley*
Red-necked Duck .... *Northern Sierra Nevada lakes & ponds*
Barrow's Goldeneye .... *Small northern mountain lakes*
Bufflehead .... *Lakes of Northeast, northern Sierras*
Ruddy Duck .... *Length of state, esp. interior lakes*
Hooded Merganser .... *Locally in Lassen County*
Common Merganser .... *Northern Calif. except Northeast*
Bald Eagle .... *A few large northern lakes and rivers*
Marsh Hawk .... *Marshes and wet meadows, length of state*
Osprey .... *Large northern lakes and rivers*
Virginia Clapper Rail .... *Salton Sea and Colo. R. marshes*
Virginia Rail ...... *Fresh-water marshes & salt marsh margins*
Sora .... *Fresh-water marshes, length of state*
Yellow Rail .... *Marshes & marshy meadows. Mono Co.*
Common Gallinule .... *Marshes, mid-Sacramento Valley south*
American Coot .... *Marshes & marsh-bordered lakes & streams*
Snowy Plover .... *Inland brackish lakes, also coastal beaches*
Killdeer .... *Lakes, irrigated fields, and meadows*
Common Snipe .... *Northern & N.E. marshes & wet meadows*
Spotted Sandpiper .... *Rocky shorelines in n. mountains*

Willet .... *Wet meadows in Modoc, Lassen & Plumas Cos.*
American Avocet .... *Alkaline & fresh-water lakes & ponds*
Black-necked Stilt .... *Sloughs & ponds north to San Fran.*
Wilson's Phalarope .... *N.E., Shasta Valley, San Joaq. V.*
California Gull .... *Northeastern plateau region*
Ring-billed Gull .... *A few lakes in northeastern Calif.*
Gull-billed Tern .... *South end of the Salton Sea*
Forster's Tern .... *N.E. Lakes, San Diego, Central Valley*
Caspian Tern .... *Freshwater marshes, length of state*
Black Tern .... *Lakes & marshes, N.E. s. through Central V.*
Short-eared Owl .... *Fresh & salt marshes, farmlands*
Black Swift ...... *Cliffs and canyons with nearby waterfalls*
Belted Kingfisher .... *Length of state west of deserts*
Black Phoebe .... *l. of state west of mtns., near water*
Dipper .... *Fast-flowing perennial streams, esp. in N.*
Long-billed Marsh Wren .... *Cattail, tule, bulrush marshes*
Common Yellowthroat .... *Stream/pond-bank thickets, S.F. south*
Yellow-headed Blackbird .... *Tule, cattail, bulrush marshes*
Red-winged Blackbird .... *Marsh and farmland margins*
Tri-colored Blackbird .... *Marshes, Modoc plateau, Sonoma s.*
Song Sparrow .... *Stream/pond-bank thickets, lower elev.*

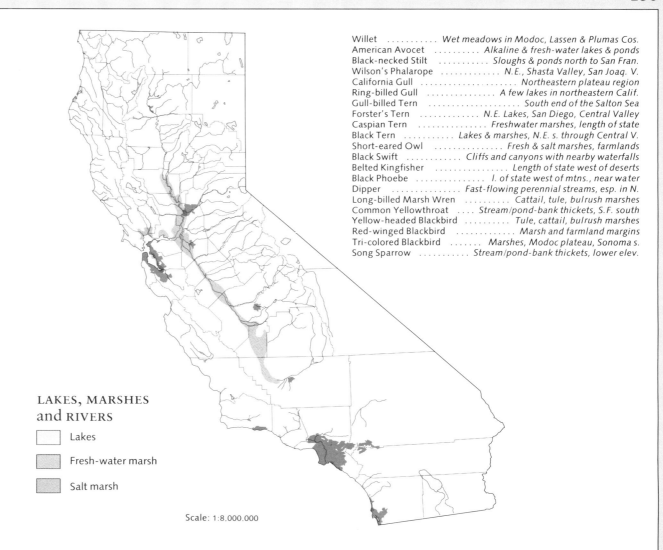

LAKES, MARSHES and RIVERS

- Lakes
- Fresh-water marsh
- Salt marsh

Scale: 1:8.000.000

Note: Maps are based on Küchler's *Natural Vegetation of California*; see page 147 for more detailed map. Character of natural vegetation has been greatly altered in farmland and built-up areas; marshlands in particular are much more restricted.

BIRDS BREEDING in OPEN COUNTRY:
grasslands, savannas, farmlands, deserts, and cities

Cattle Egret .... *Cattle pastures, esp. in Imperial Valley*
Turkey Vulture .... *Margins of open country, length of state*
White-tailed Kite .... *Farmlands, west of mtns. & deserts*
Red-tailed Hawk .... *Among cliffs, tall trees, l. of state*
Swainson's Hawk .... *Great Basin, locally in Cent. Valley*
Golden Eagle .... *Cliffs and tall trees; scarce in S.E.*
Marsh Hawk .... *Grasslands & desert sinks, also marshes*
Prairie Falcon .... *Cliff faces & rocks, except in humid N.W.*
American Kestrel .... *Length of state below timberline*
Sage Grouse .... *N.E. sage flats, south to Mono County*
Gambel's Quail .... *Mojave & Colo. deserts, near water*
Ring-necked Pheasant .... *Farmlands, length of state*
Chukkar .... *Desert and dry valley margins, l. of state*
Gray Partridge .... *Eastern Lassen and Modoc Counties*
Sandhill Crane .... *Near lakes and marshes, in Northeast*
Long-billed Curlew .... *N.E. grasslands with lakes & marshes*
Rock Dove .... *Cities, towns and farms, length of state*
White-winged Dove .... *Southeastern desert areas*
Mourning Dove .... *Cities, farms, grasslands, desert*
Spotted Dove .... *Cities, Ventura Co. south, esp. L.A.*
Ringed Turtle Dove .... *Los Angeles downtown parks*
Inca Dove .... *Parker Dam on the Colorado River*
Roadrunner .... *Chaparral margins, esp. Southern Calif.*
Barn Owl .... *Trees, barns, bridges etc. near open country*
Screech Owl .... *Length of state except N.E. & most of S.E.*
Great Horned Owl .... *Deserts; also woodland, l. of state*
Elf Owl .... *Few oases in Northern Colorado River desert*
Burrowing Owl .... *Length of state, incl. large islands*
Short-eared Owl .... *Length of state, also in marshlands*
Poor-will .... *Brushy desert, also in chaparral, woodlands*
Lesser Nighthawk .... *S.E. deserts, dry southern valleys*
White-throated Swift .... *Cliffs & rocks in arid regions*
Costa's Hummingbird .... *S.E. deserts, dry valleys*
Common Flicker .... *Length of state except S.E. deserts*
Gila Woodpecker .... *Colo R., Imperial Valley, locally*
Ladder-backed Woodpecker .... *Deserts, also pinyon-juniper*
Western Kingbird .... *Length of state, except S.E. deserts*
Cassin's Kingbird .... *Int. valleys W. of deserts, esp. S.W.*
Wied's Crested Flycatcher ..... *Oases & desert rip. woodlands*
Ash-throated Flycatcher .... *High desert, also pinyon-jun.*
Say's Phoebe .... *East of Sierra, dry interior valleys*
Vermillion Flycatcher .... *Desert rip. woodlands & oases*
Horned Lark .... *Grasslands, ploughed fields exc. N.W.*
Black-billed Magpie .... *E. of mtns. south to Inyo Co.*
Common Raven .... *Cliff faces, in open country, l. of state*
Common Crow .... *Farmlands, esp. Central & coastal valleys*
Verdin .... *Southeastern deserts in shrubs & small trees*
Cactus Wren .... *S.E. deserts and dry hills N. to Ventura*
Mockingbird .... *Lowlands N. to head of Central Valley*
Bendire's Thrasher .... *Near Cima, San Bernardino Co.*

Le Conte's Thrasher .... *S.E. deserts, arid San Joaquin V.*
Crissal Thrasher .... *Dense desert scrub, esp. Mesquite*
Sage Thrasher .... *Great Basin south to N. Mojave desert*
American Robin .... *Length of state, mostly N. half*
Black-tailed Gnatcatcher .... *Desert, dry valleys of So. Cal.*
Loggerhead Shrike ...... *Length of state except N.W., high Mtns.*
Starling .... *Cities, farmlands; not in N.W. or S.E. deserts*
Lucy's Warbler .... *Mesquite thickets of Colo. & Amargosa Rs.*
House Sparrow .... *Length of state around human settlement*
Western Meadowlark ..... *Meadows & grasslands, length of state*
Hooded Oriole .... *S. cities & farms, in palms, broadl. trees*
Scott's Oriole .... *Desert woodlands north to Inyo County*
Brewer's Blackbird .... *Cities, parks, farmlands, l. of state*
Great-tailed Grackle .... *Imperial & lower Colo. R. Valley*
Brown-headed Cowbird ..... *Except in high Mtns. & humid N.W.*
Summer Tanager .... *Lower Colo. R. Valley, Morongo Valley*

House Finch .... *Length of state; also woodland, chaparral*
Cardinal .... *Parker Dam; locally in Los Angeles County*
American Goldfinch .... *West of Cascades, Sierras, deserts*
Lesser Goldfinch .... *Savannas, also open forest & woodlands*
Abert's Towhee .... *Lower Colo., Imperial & Coachella Valleys*
Savanna Sparrow ...... *Grasslands & meadows, also salt marshes*
Grasshopper Sparrow .... *Grasslands, Tehama Co. south*
Vesper Sparrow ...... *Basin & Range desert, High Sierra meadows*
Lark Sparrow .... *Lowlands & foothills W. of Sierras, Cascades*
Black-throated Sparrow .... *Great Basin and southern deserts*
Sage Sparrow .... *Desert sage, also arid mountain chaparral*
Brewer's Sparrow .... *Open stands of Great Basin sagebrush*

Source:
A. Small, *The Birds of California*, 1974

525 bird species have been documented in California, including 277 species which regularly nest in the state. The lists on this and the facing page include only the breeding species. Birds are grouped by generalized habitat type, with additional information on breeding habitat and range as space permits. Birds breeding in a wide range of habitats may appear on more than one list. Conversely, a few birds whose breeding habitats (cliff faces and earthen banks) embrace all the categories shown are excluded for reasons of space: the Bank Swallow, Rough-winged Swallow, Cliff Swallow, Canyon Wren and Rock Wren. All information on these pages is adapted from Arnold Small's *The Birds of California*, which includes much more complete information about all California species, and photographs of a great many of them.

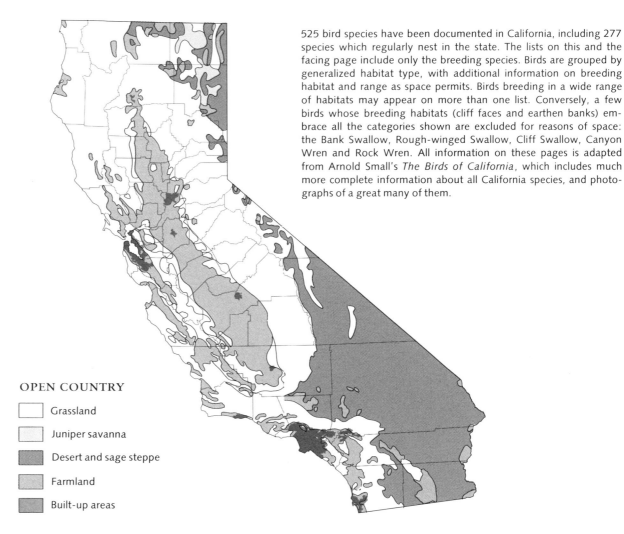

OPEN COUNTRY

- Grassland
- Juniper savanna
- Desert and sage steppe
- Farmland
- Built-up areas

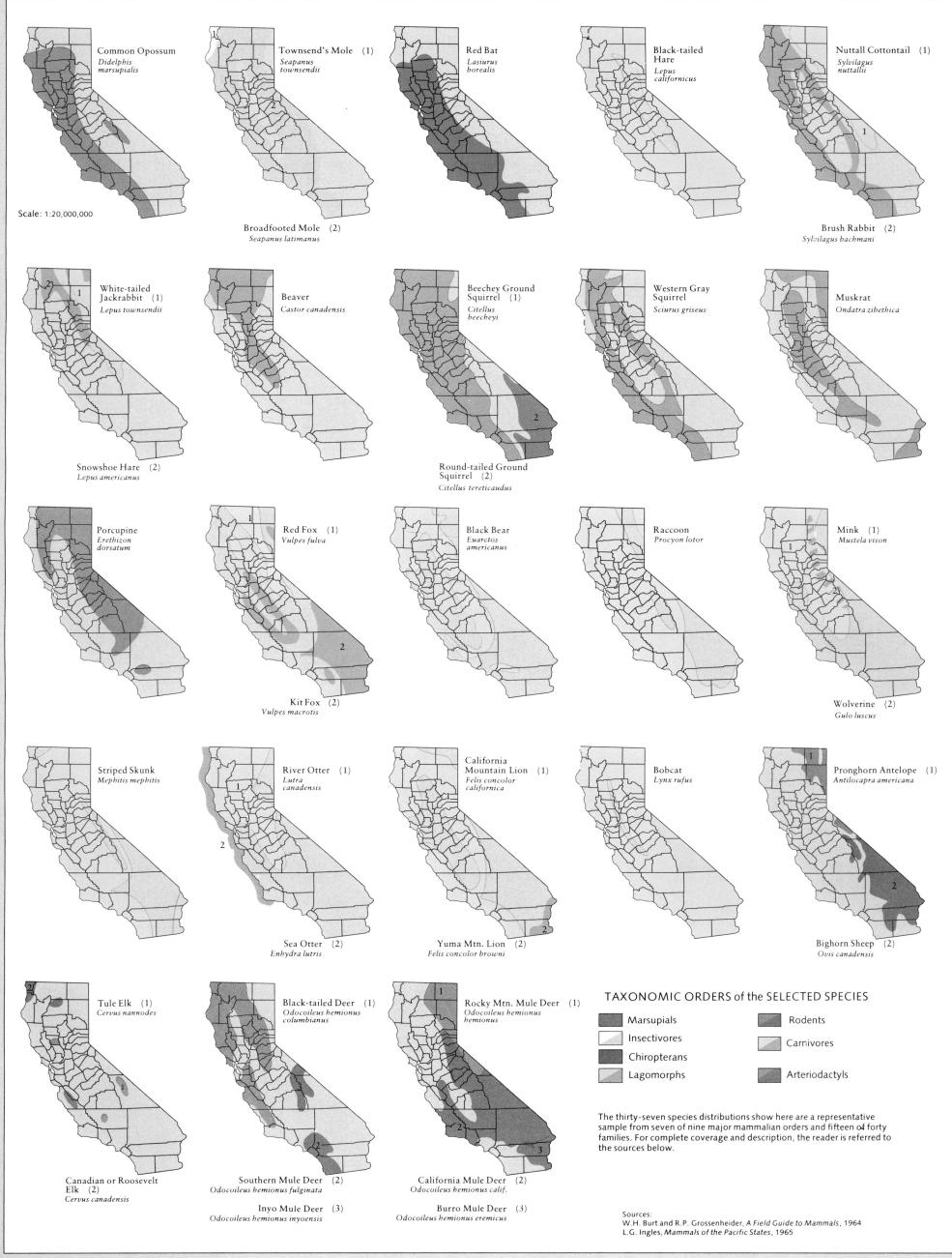

Common Opossum
Didelphis marsupialis

Scale: 1:20,000,000

Townsend's Mole (1)
Seapanus townsendii

Broadfooted Mole (2)
Seapanus latimanus

Red Bat
Lasiurus borealis

Black-tailed Hare
Lepus californicus

Nuttall Cottontail (1)
Sylvilagus nuttallii

Brush Rabbit (2)
Sylvilagus bachmani

White-tailed Jackrabbit (1)
Lepus townsendii

Snowshoe Hare (2)
Lepus americanus

Beaver
Castor canadensis

Beechey Ground Squirrel (1)
Citellus beecheyi

Round-tailed Ground Squirrel (2)
Citellus tereticaudus

Western Gray Squirrel
Sciurus griseus

Muskrat
Ondatra zibethica

Porcupine
Erethizon dorsatum

Red Fox (1)
Vulpes fulva

Kit Fox (2)
Vulpes macrotis

Black Bear
Euarctos americanus

Raccoon
Procyon lotor

Mink (1)
Mustela vison

Wolverine (2)
Gulo luscus

Striped Skunk
Mephitis mephitis

River Otter (1)
Lutra canadensis

Sea Otter (2)
Enhydra lutris

California Mountain Lion (1)
Felis concolor californica

Yuma Mtn. Lion (2)
Felis concolor browni

Bobcat
Lynx rufus

Pronghorn Antelope (1)
Antilocapra americana

Bighorn Sheep (2)
Ovis canadensis

Tule Elk (1)
Cervus nannodes

Canadian or Roosevelt Elk (2)
Cervus canadensis

Black-tailed Deer (1)
Odocoileus hemionus columbianus

Southern Mule Deer (2)
Odocoileus hemionus fulginata

Inyo Mule Deer (3)
Odocoileus hemionus inyoensis

Rocky Mtn. Mule Deer (1)
Odocoileus hemionus hemionus

California Mule Deer (2)
Odocoileus hemionus calif.

Burro Mule Deer (3)
Odocoileus hemionus eremicus

TAXONOMIC ORDERS of the SELECTED SPECIES

Marsupials

Insectivores

Chiropterans

Lagomorphs

Rodents

Carnivores

Arteriodactyls

The thirty-seven species distributions show here are a representative sample from seven of nine major mammalian orders and fifteen of forty families. For complete coverage and description, the reader is referred to the sources below.

Sources:
W.H. Burt and R.P. Grossenheider, *A Field Guide to Mammals*, 1964
L.G. Ingles, *Mammals of the Pacific States*, 1965

SELECTED MAMMALS

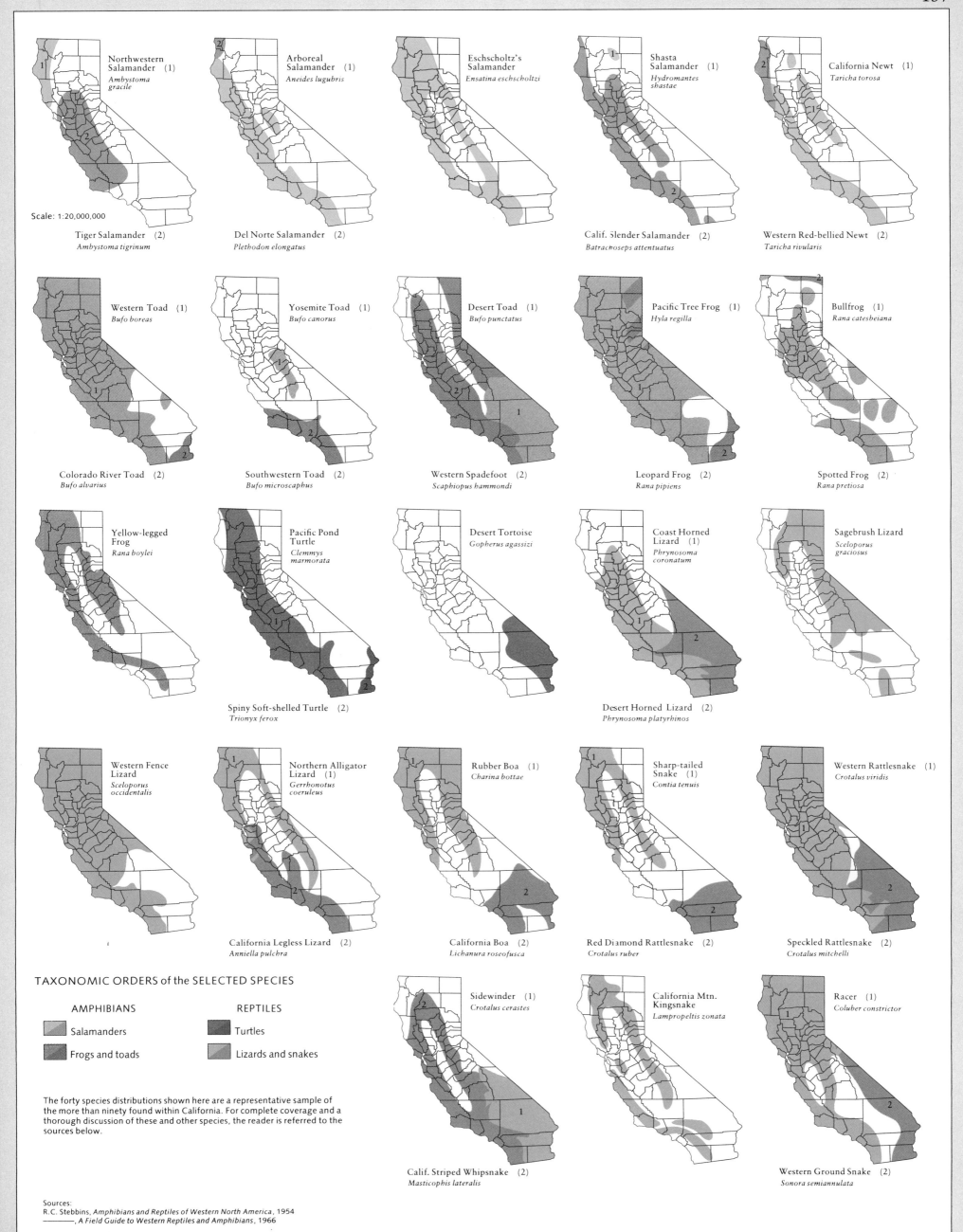

Scale: 1:20,000,000

Northwestern Salamander (1)
Ambystoma gracile

Arboreal Salamander (1)
Aneides lugubris

Eschscholtz's Salamander (1)
Ensatina eschscholtzi

Shasta Salamander (1)
Hydromantes shastae

California Newt (1)
Taricha torosa

Tiger Salamander (2)
Ambystoma tigrinum

Del Norte Salamander (2)
Plethodon elongatus

Calif. Slender Salamander (2)
Batrachoseps attentuatus

Western Red-bellied Newt (2)
Taricha rivularis

Western Toad (1)
Bufo boreas

Yosemite Toad (1)
Bufo canorus

Desert Toad (1)
Bufo punctatus

Pacific Tree Frog (1)
Hyla regilla

Bullfrog (1)
Rana catesbeiana

Colorado River Toad (2)
Bufo alvarius

Southwestern Toad (2)
Bufo microscaphus

Western Spadefoot (2)
Scaphiopus hammondi

Leopard Frog (2)
Rana pipiens

Spotted Frog (2)
Rana pretiosa

Yellow-legged Frog
Rana boylei

Pacific Pond Turtle
Clemmys marmorata

Desert Tortoise
Gopherus agassizi

Coast Horned Lizard (1)
Phrynosoma coronatum

Sagebrush Lizard
Sceloporus graciosus

Spiny Soft-shelled Turtle (2)
Trionyx ferox

Desert Horned Lizard (2)
Phrynosoma platyrhinos

Western Fence Lizard
Sceloporus occidentalis

Northern Alligator Lizard (1)
Gerrhonotus coeruleus

Rubber Boa (1)
Charina bottae

Sharp-tailed Snake (1)
Contia tenuis

Western Rattlesnake (1)
Crotalus viridis

California Legless Lizard (2)
Anniella pulchra

California Boa (2)
Lichanura roseofusca

Red Diamond Rattlesnake (2)
Crotalus ruber

Speckled Rattlesnake (2)
Crotalus mitchelli

TAXONOMIC ORDERS of the SELECTED SPECIES

AMPHIBIANS
Salamanders
Frogs and toads

REPTILES
Turtles
Lizards and snakes

The forty species distributions shown here are a representative sample of the more than ninety found within California. For complete coverage and a thorough discussion of these and other species, the reader is referred to the sources below.

Sidewinder (1)
Crotalus cerastes

California Mtn. Kingsnake
Lampropeltis zonata

Racer (1)
Coluber constrictor

Calif. Striped Whipsnake (2)
Masticophis lateralis

Western Ground Snake (2)
Sonora semiannulata

Sources:
R.C. Stebbins, *Amphibians and Reptiles of Western North America*, 1954
————, *A Field Guide to Western Reptiles and Amphibians*, 1966

SELECTED REPTILES AND AMPHIBIANS

REFERENCE

AREA and POPULATION of COUNTIES, POPULATION OF MAJOR CITIES

PLACE	POPULATION[a] 1970	POPULATION[a] 1978	AREA[b] km²	AREA[b] mi²
ALAMEDA	1,073,184	1,105,800	2,138	825
Oakland	361,561	327,800		
Fremont	100,869	120,600		
Berkeley	116,716	112,100		
Hayward	93,058	97,900		
Alameda	70,968	75,600		
San Leandro	68,698	69,400		
ALPINE	484	930	1,882	727
AMADOR	11,821	17,100	1,557	601
Jackson	1,924	2,670		
BUTTE	101,969	130,100	4,312	1,665
Chico	19,580	25,250		
CALAVERAS	13,585	17,550	2,684	1,036
Angels	1,710	2,340		
COLUSA	12,430	13,000	2,994	1,156
Colusa	3,842	4,160		
CONTRA COSTA	558,389	611,700	2,067	798
Concord	85,164	99,500		
Richmond	79,043	69,600		
Walnut Creek	39,844	50,100		
DEL NORTE	14,580	16,750	2,598	1,003
Crescent City	2,586	2,660		
EL DORADO	43,833	70,600	4,674	1,805
FRESNO	43,833	70,600	4,674	1,805
South Lake Tahoe	12,921	20,600		
FRESNO	413,053	473,000	15,535	5,998
Fresno	165,972	194,800		
GLENN	17,521	20,300	3,416	1,319
Willows	4,085	4,710		
HUMBOLDT	99,692	107,500	9,323	3,600
Eureka	24,337	24,500		
IMPERIAL	74,492	88,900	11,907	4,597
El Centro	19,272	23,400		
INYO	15,571	18,000	26,153	10,098
Bishop	3,498	3,390		
KERN	329,162	363,800	21,161	8,170
Bakersfield	69,515	86,100		
KINGS	64,610	70,900	3,718	1,436
Hanford	15,179	18,900		
LAKE	19,548	29,150	3,436	1,327
Lakeport	3,005	3,580		
LASSEN	14,960	19,300	12,148	4,690
Susanville	6,608	6,800		
LOS ANGELES	7,032,075	7,079,200	10,565	4,079
Los Angeles	2,816,061	2,787,900		
Long Beach	358,633	344,200		
Glendale	132,752	134,100		
Torrance	134,584	128,700		
Pasadena	113,327	106,900		
Santa Monica	88,289	90,900		
Inglewood	89,985	89,600		
Downey	88,445	86,700		
Burbank	88,871	85,600		
Pomona	87,374	85,500		
Norwalk	91,827	85,100		
Lakewood	82,973	81,200		
Carson	71,150	78,200		
Compton	78,611	74,800		
West Covina	68,034	73,600		
Whittier	72,863	69,900		
El Monte	69,837	67,900		
Redondo Beach	56,075	63,300		
Alhambra	62,125	61,500		
South Gate	56,909	60,100		
Hawthorne	53,304	55,700		
Bellflower	51,454	51,800		
Monterey Park	49,166	51,400		
Pico Rivera	54,170	51,100		
MADERA	41,519	51,400	5,561	2,147
Madera	16,044	18,750		
MARIN	206,038	226,500	1,523	588
San Rafael	38,977	45,500		
MARIPOSA	6,015	9,350	3,798	1,460
MENDOCINO	51,101	60,500	9,093	3,510
Ukiah	10,095	12,000		
MERCED	104,629	123,600	5,200	2,008
Merced	22,670	32,800		
MODOC	7,469	8,950	11,242	4,340
Alturas	2,799	2,990		
MONO	4,106	7,625	8,037	3,103
MONTEREY	250,071	272,000	8,609	3,324
Salinas	58,896	76,400		
NAPA	79,140	92,900	2,064	797
Napa	35,978	48,650		
NEVADA	26,346	41,100	2,570	992
Grass Valley	5,149	6,200		
ORANGE	1,420,386	1,808,200	2,033	785
Anaheim	166,701	204,800		
Santa Ana	156,601	183,900		
Huntington Beach	115,960	162,000		
Garden Grove	122,524	117,800		
Fullerton	85,826	98,500		
Orange	77,374	84,600		
Costa Mesa	72,660	78,500		
Westminster	59,865	69,300		
Newport Beach	49,422	64,300		
Buena Park	63,646	62,800		
Fountain Valley	31,828	54,100		
PLACER	77,306	102,900	3,902	1,506
Roseville	17,895	22,150		
PLUMAS	11,707	15,550	6,782	2,618
Portola	1,625	1,680		
RIVERSIDE	459,074	590,200	18,759	7,243
Riverside	140,089	155,800		
SACRAMENTO	631,498	724,600	2,630	1,015
Sacramento	254,413	261,500		
SAN BENITO	18,226	21,750	3,618	1,397
Hollister	7,663	9,750		
SAN BERNARDINO	684,072	756,800	52,225	20,164
San Bernardino	104,251	105,400		
Ontario	64,118	70,600		
SAN DIEGO	1,357,854	1,694,800	11,087	4,281
San Diego	696,769	797,400		
Chula Vista	67,901	79,700		
El Cajon	52,273	67,800		
Oceanside	40,494	66,200		
Escondido	36,792	57,100		
SAN FRANCISCO	715,674	666,500	236	91
San Francisco	715,674	666,500		
SAN JOAQUIN	290,208	310,700	3,720	1,436
Stockton	107,644	127,300		
SAN LUIS OBISPO	105,690	138,700	8,615	3,326
San Luis Obispo	28,036	34,100		
SAN MATEO	556,234	586,300	1,375	531
San Mateo	78,991	79,400		
Daly City	66,922	73,700		
Redwood City	55,686	55,000		
SANTA BARBARA	264,324	288,100	7,109	2,745
Santa Barbara	70,215	73,800		
SANTA CLARA	1,064,714	1,222,800	3,408	1,316
San Jose	445,779	587,700		
Sunnyvale	95,408	106,400		
Santa Clara	87,717	84,600		
Mountain View	51,092	56,000		
Palo Alto	55,966	54,600		
SANTA CRUZ	123,790	170,900	1,139	440
Santa Cruz	32,076	39,300		
SHASTA	77,640	103,400	9,972	3,850
Redding	16,659	40,050		
SIERRA	2,365	3,020	2,483	959
Loyalton	945	920		
SISKIYOU	33,225	37,400	16,364	6,318
Yreka	5,394	5,400		
SOLANO	169,941	203,900	2,259	872
Vallejo	66,733	70,300		
Fairfield	44,146	54,400		
SONOMA	204,885	267,800	4,138	1,598
Santa Rosa	50,006	73,500		
STANISLAUS	194,506	241,700	3,952	1,521
Modesto	61,712	94,500		
SUTTER	41,935	49,150	1,572	607
Yuba City	13,986	16,850		
TEHAMA	29,517	35,450	7,708	2,976
Red Bluff	7,676	8,925		
TRINITY	7,615	10,900	8,346	3,223
TULARE	188,322	219,100	12,548	4,845
Visalia	27,268	41,050		
TUOLUMNE	22,169	28,650	5,938	2,293
Sonora	3,100	3,490		
VENTURA	376,430	474,700	4,827	1,864
Oxnard	71,225	96,400		
Simi Valley	56,464	73,600		
San Buenaventura	57,788	68,200		
Thousand Oaks	36,334	64,800		
YOLO	91,788	106,100	2,678	1,034
Davis	23,488	35,650		
YUBA	44,736	46,700	1,655	639
Marysville	9,353	9,350		
CALIFORNIA	19,953,134	22,075,000	411,013	158,693

[a] U.S. Census values for April 1, 1970; State of California, Population Research Unit, estimates for January 1, 1978. All incorporated cities with more than 50,000 inhabitants are listed, and at least one incorporated city for each county.

[b] Area includes land and water. The state total includes 5491 km² of water surface. The six counties with more than 200 km² of area under water are Imperial (812 km²), Modoc (643 km²), Lassen (371 km²), Alameda (239 km²), El Dorado (235 km²) and Placer (214 km²).

CROPS in which CALIFORNIA LEADS the NATION

CROP and SHARE of U.S. PRODUCTION (%)	
Alfalfa seed	33.5
Almonds	99.9
Apricots	98.0
Artichokes	98.4
Asparagus	50.3
Avocadoes	82.3
Beans, lima	48.2
Broccoli	94.4
Brussels sprouts	74.3
Carrots	54.0
Cauliflower	76.2
Celery	66.2
Dates	99.4
Figs	99.5
Garlic	85.7
Grapes	90.5
Ladino clover seed	100.0
Lemons	75.7
Lettuce	73.2
Melons, cantaloupes	63.8
Melons, honeydew	79.3
Nectarines	98.2
Olives	99.9
Onions	34.7
Peaches	64.7
Pears	39.3
Persimmons	92.0
Pomegranates	99.9
Safflower	89.8
Spinach	52.3
Strawberries	70.1
Sugarbeets	29.0
Tomatoes	79.9
Walnuts	99.4

California is the nation's second producer of barley, snap beans, cotton, cucumbers, oranges, rice and tangerines.

ELEVATION of SELECTED MOUNTAIN PEAKS

The peaks are listed from north to south within each range, except in the Transverse Ranges, where they are given from west to east.

RANGE and MOUNTAIN	COUNTY	ELEVATION (meters)
KLAMATH MOUNTAINS		
Condrey Mountain	*Siskiyou*	*2168*
Preston Peak	*Siskiyou*	*2228*
King's Castle	*Siskiyou*	*2257*
China Mountain	*Siskiyou*	*2604*
Mount Eddy	*Siskiyou-Trinity*	*2759*
Russian Peak	*Siskiyou*	*2498*
Castle Crags	*Siskiyou-Trinity*	*2174*
Thompson Peak	*Trinity*	*2744*
Mount Hilton	*Trinity*	*2732*
Shasta Bally	*Shasta*	*1893*
Bully Choop Mountain	*Shasta-Trinity*	*2126*
N. Yolla Bolly Mt.	*Tehama-Trinity*	*2397*
S. Yolla Bolly Mt.	*Tehama*	*2466*
CASCADE RANGE		
Mount Hoffman	*Siskiyou*	*2412*
Mount Shasta	*Siskiyou*	*4317*
Burney Mountain	*Shasta*	*2397*
Crater Peak	*Shasta*	*2645*
Red Cinder	*Shasta*	*2552*
Lassen Peak	*Shasta*	*3187*
MODOC PLATEAU AND WARNER RANGE		
Mount Vida	*Modoc*	*2507*
Warren Peak	*Modoc*	*2960*
Eagle Peak	*Modoc*	*3015*
Hat Mountain	*Lassen*	*2663*
Observation Peak	*Lassen*	*2427*
Fredonyer Peak	*Lassen*	*2421*
NORTH COAST RANGES		
Hupa Mountain	*Humboldt*	*1248*
Board Camp Mountain	*Humboldt*	*1581*
Mount Lassic	*Humboldt*	*1790*
Leach Lake Mountain	*Mendocino*	*2023*
Sanhedrin Mountain	*Mendocino*	*1882*
Snow Mountain	*Colusa-Lake*	*2151*
Mount Konocti	*Lake*	*1310*
Mount Saint Helena	*Lake-Napa-Sonoma*	*1324*
Berryessa Peak	*Napa-Yolo*	*932*
Mount Tamalpais	*Marin*	*794*

LOCATION and CAPACITY of MAJOR RESERVOIRS

HYDROLOGIC BASIN RESERVOIR CAPACITY

HYDROLOGIC BASIN and STREAM	RESERVOIR	CAPACITY hm³
NORTH COAST BASIN		
Klamath River	*Upper Klamath*	*720*
Klamath River	*Clear Lake*	*650*
Trinity River	*Clair Engle*	*3,020*
SACRAMENTO BASIN		
Sacramento River	*Shasta*	*5,610*
N. Fork Feather River	*Lake Almanor*	*1,020*
Feather River	*Oroville*	*4,370*
North Yuba River	*New Bullards Bar*	*1,190*
American River	*Folsom*	*1,250*
Cache Creek	*Clear Lake*	*518*
Putah Creek	*Lake Berryessa*	*1,970*
SAN JOAQUIN BASIN		
Mokelumne River	*Camanche*	*533*
Tuolumne River	*Hetch Hetchy*	*444*
Tuolumne River	*Don Pedro*	*2,500*
Merced River	*Lake McClure*	*1,270*
San Joaquin River	*Millerton Lake*	*643*
San Luis Creek	*San Luis*	*2,520*
Kings River	*Pine Flat*	*1,230*
Kern River	*Isabella*	*703*
LAHONTAN BASIN		
Truckee River	*Lake Tahoe*	*919*
COLORADO RIVER BASIN		
Colorado River	*Lake Powell*	*30,800*
Colorado River	*Lake Mead*	*32,200*
Colorado River	*Lake Mohave*	*2,230*
Colorado River	*Lake Havasu*	*764*

FEDERAL LAND OWNERSHIP in CALIFORNIA

DEPARTMENT and AGENCY	AREA km²	SHARE OF STATE (%)
DEPARTMENT OF THE INTERIOR	84,915	20.7
Bureau of Land Management	*63,070*	*15.3*
National Park Service	*17,054*	*4.1*
Bureau of Reclamation	*4,521*	*1.1*
Other	*270*	–
DEPARTMENT OF AGRICULTURE	81,235	19.8
Forest Service	*81,233*	*19.8*
Other	*2*	–
DEPARTMENT OF DEFENSE	16,172	3.9
Navy	*9,737*	*2.4*
Army	*4,088*	*1.0*
Air Force	*1,910*	*0.5*
Corps of Civil Engineers	*437*	*0.1*
OTHER	77	–
ALL FEDERAL LAND	182,400	44.4

PHYSICAL FEATURES

ELEVATION of SELECTED MOUNTAIN PEAKS

RANGE and MOUNTAIN	COUNTY	ELEVATION (meters)	RANGE and MOUNTAIN	COUNTY	ELEVATION (meters)
SIERRA NEVADA			Mount Kaweah	Tulare	4207
Thompson Peak	Lassen-Plumas	2376	Mount Langley	Inyo-Tulare	4275
Mount Ingalls	Plumas	2552	Olancha Peak	Inyo-Tulare	3695
Dixie Mountain	Plumas	2537	Round Mountain	Inyo-Tulare	3013
Sierra Buttes	Sierra	2617	Sawtooth Peak	Inyo-Tulare	2429
Castle Peak	Nevada	2775	Double Mountain	Kern	2433
Granite Chief	Placer	2745	**SUTTER BUTTES**		
Freel Peak	Alpine-El Dorado	3317	Summit	Sutter	650
Pyramid Peak	El Dorado	3043	**SOUTH COAST RANGES**		
Highland Peak	Alpine	3333	Mount Diablo	Contra Costa	1173
Leavitt Peak	Mono-Tuolumne	3527	Mount Hamilton	Santa Clara	1284
Tower Peak	Mono-Tuolumne	3583	Loma Prieta	Santa Clara	1155
Matterhorn Peak	Mono-Tuolumne	3738	Fremont Peak	Monterey-San Benito	967
Mount Dana	Mono-Tuolumne	3979	San Benito Mountain	San Benito	1597
Half Dome	Mariposa	2695	Mount Carmel	Monterey	1346
Mount Lyell	Mad-Mono-Tuol	3997	Junipero Serra Peak	Monterey	1787
Mount Starr King	Mariposa	2771	Cone Peak	Monterey	1571
Minaret Summit	Madera-Mono	2797	**TRANSVERSE RANGES**		
Red Slate Mountain	Fresno-Mono	4012	Santa Ynez Peak	Santa Barbara	1310
Mount Morgan	Inyo	4190	San Rafael Mountain	Santa Barbara	2101
Mount Humphreys	Fresno-Inyo	4263	Cuyama Peak	Santa Barbara	1791
Mount Darwin	Fresno-Inyo	4215	Pine Mountain	Ventura	2289
North Palisade	Fresno-Inyo	4341	Mount Pinos	Kern-Ventura	2692
Mount Pinchot	Fresno	4113	Mount Wilson	Los Angeles	1740
Mount Clarence King	Fresno	3933	Mount San Antonio	L.A.-San Bernardino	3068
Mount Bradley	Inyo-Tulare	4050	Mount Baldy	San Bernardino	2700
Mount Brewer	Tulare	4136	Sugarloaf Mountain	San Bernardino	3033
Mount Williamson	Inyo	4382	San Gorgonio Mountain	San Bernardino	3506
Mount Whitney	Inyo-Tulare	4418	**PENINSULAR RANGES**		
			Mount San Jacinto	Riverside	3293
			Santiago Peak	Orange-Riverside	1733
			Toro Peak	Riverside	2657
			Palomar Mountain	San Diego	1871
			Volcan Mountain	San Diego	1743
			Cuyamaca Peak	San Diego	1985
			Monument Peak	San Diego	1911
			BASIN AND RANGE		
			Glass Mountain	Mono	3390
			White Mountain Peak	Mono	4342
			Waucoba Mountain	Inyo	3390
			Mount Inyo	Inyo	3385
			New York Butte	Inyo	3252
			Telescope Peak	Inyo	3368
			Dante's View	Inyo	1669
			Funeral Peak	Inyo	1946
			Maturango Peak	Inyo	2706
			Argus Peak	Inyo	2000

COUNTIES

Scale 1:8,000,000

Scale of Miles 1:3,400,000 Scale of Kilometers

SCALE and DATE of TOPOGRAPHIC MAPS

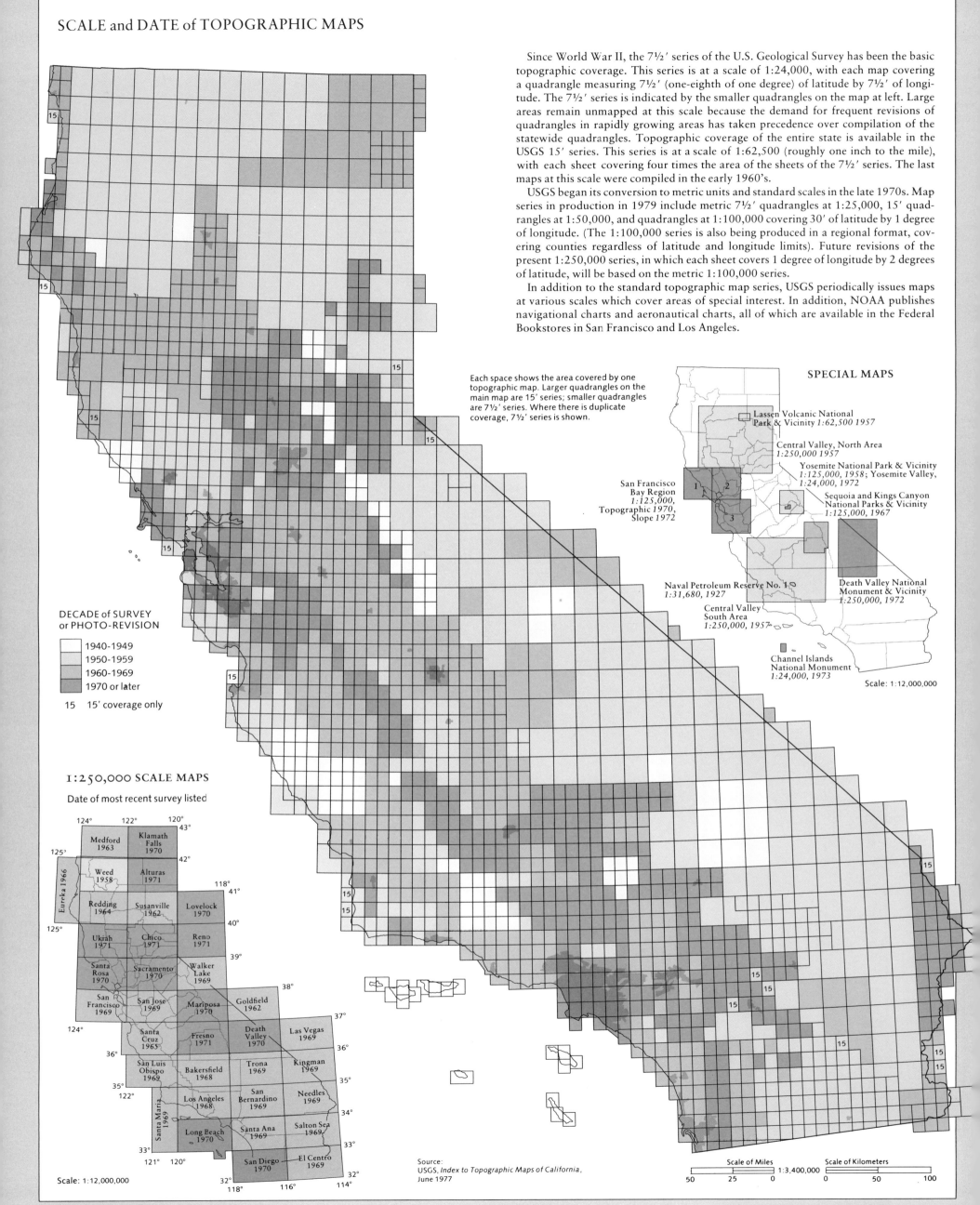

Since World War II, the 7½' series of the U.S. Geological Survey has been the basic topographic coverage. This series is at a scale of 1:24,000, with each map covering a quadrangle measuring 7½' (one-eighth of one degree) of latitude by 7½' of longitude. The 7½' series is indicated by the smaller quadrangles on the map at left. Large areas remain unmapped at this scale because the demand for frequent revisions of quadrangles in rapidly growing areas has taken precedence over compilation of the statewide quadrangles. Topographic coverage of the entire state is available in the USGS 15' series. This series is at a scale of 1:62,500 (roughly one inch to the mile), with each sheet covering four times the area of the sheets of the 7½' series. The last maps at this scale were compiled in the early 1960's.

USGS began its conversion to metric units and standard scales in the late 1970s. Map series in production in 1979 include metric 7½' quadrangles at 1:25,000, 15' quadrangles at 1:50,000, and quadrangles at 1:100,000 covering 30' of latitude by 1 degree of longitude. (The 1:100,000 series is also being produced in a regional format, covering counties regardless of latitude and longitude limits). Future revisions of the present 1:250,000 series, in which each sheet covers 1 degree of longitude by 2 degrees of latitude, will be based on the metric 1:100,000 series.

In addition to the standard topographic map series, USGS periodically issues maps at various scales which cover areas of special interest. In addition, NOAA publishes navigational charts and aeronautical charts, all of which are available in the Federal Bookstores in San Francisco and Los Angeles.

Each space shows the area covered by one topographic map. Larger quadrangles on the main map are 15' series; smaller quadrangles are 7½' series. Where there is duplicate coverage, 7½' series is shown.

SPECIAL MAPS

Lassen Volcanic National Park & Vicinity *1:62,500 1957*

Central Valley, North Area *1:250,000 1957*

Yosemite National Park & Vicinity *1:125,000, 1958*; Yosemite Valley, *1:24,000, 1972*

San Francisco Bay Region *1:125,000, Topographic 1970, Slope 1972*

Sequoia and Kings Canyon National Parks & Vicinity *1:125,000, 1967*

Naval Petroleum Reserve No. 1 *1:31,680, 1927*

Death Valley National Monument & Vicinity *1:250,000, 1972*

Central Valley South Area *1:250,000, 1957*

Channel Islands National Monument *1:24,000, 1973*

Scale: 1:12,000,000

DECADE of SURVEY or PHOTO-REVISION

- 1940-1949
- 1950-1959
- 1960-1969
- 1970 or later

15 15' coverage only

1:250,000 SCALE MAPS

Date of most recent survey listed

Medford 1963	Klamath Falls 1970	
Weed 1958	Alturas 1971	
Redding 1964	Susanville 1962	Lovelock 1970
Ukiah 1971	Chico 1971	Reno 1971
Santa Rosa 1970	Sacramento 1970	Walker Lake 1969
San Francisco 1969	San Jose 1969	Mariposa 1970	Goldfield 1962
Santa Cruz 1965	Fresno 1971	Death Valley 1970	Las Vegas 1969
San Luis Obispo 1969	Bakersfield 1968	Trona 1969	Kingman 1969
Santa Maria 1969	Los Angeles 1968	San Bernardino 1969	Needles 1969
Long Beach 1970	Santa Ana 1969	Salton Sea 1969	
San Diego 1970	El Centro 1969	

Eureka 1966

Scale: 1:12,000,000

Source:
USGS, *Index to Topographic Maps of California*, June 1977

Scale of Miles   1:3,400,000   Scale of Kilometers
50 25 0   0   50   100

TOPOGRAPHIC MAP COVERAGE

CONVERSIONS USED in the ATLAS

LENGTH

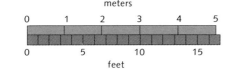

millimeters 1:1

MILLIMETERS

inches

mm x 0.0393701 = inches; inches x 25.4 = mm
100 millimeters = about 4 inches

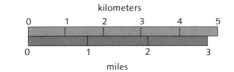

meters

METERS

feet

m x 3.28084 = feet; feet x 0.3048 = m
100 meters = about 109 yards

kilometers

KILOMETERS

miles

km x 0.621371 = miles; miles x 1.609344 = km
10 kilometers = about 6 miles

ENERGY

KILOWATT HOURS

Kwh x 3413.61 = BTUs; BTU x 0.000292945 = Kwh

KILOCALORIES

Kcal x 3.96828 = BTUs; BTU x 0.2520 = Kcal

AREA

HECTARES

(1 hectare = 100 m x 100 m)
ha x 2.4710 5 = acres; acres x 0.404686 = ha
10 hectares = about 25 acres

SQUARE KILOMETERS

(1 km² = 1000 m x 1000 m)
km² x 0.386102 = square miles; square miles x 2.59 = km²
10 square kilometers = about 4 square miles

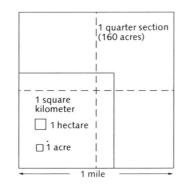

1 square mile = 640 acres (1 section),
= about 260 hectares
1/2 mile x 1/2 mile = 160 acres (1 quarter section),
= about 65 hectares

MASS

METRIC TONS

1 metric ton = 1000 kg
1 kilogram = 2.2046 lbs

metric tons x 0.984208 = long tons
long ton = 2,240 lbs
long tons x 1.01605 = metric tons

metric tons x 1.102311 = short tons
1 short ton = 2000 lbs
short tons x 0.907184 = metric tons

VOLUME

CUBIC METERS

m³ x 35.3147 = cubic feet; cubic feet x 0.0283168 = m³
1 cubic meter = about 35 cubic feet

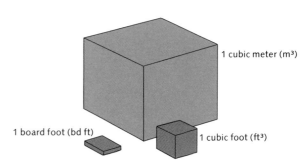

m³ x 423.776 = board feet; board feet x 0.0023597 = m³
1 cubic meter = about 424 board feet

CUBIC HECTOMETERS

hm³ x 810.713 = acre feet; acre feet x 0.00123348 = hm³
1 cubic hectometer = about 810 acre feet

TEMPERATURE

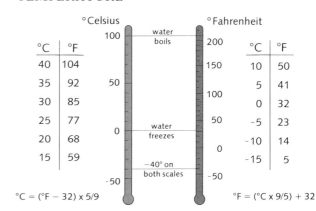

°C = (°F − 32) x 5/9   °F = (°C x 9/5) + 32

AREA

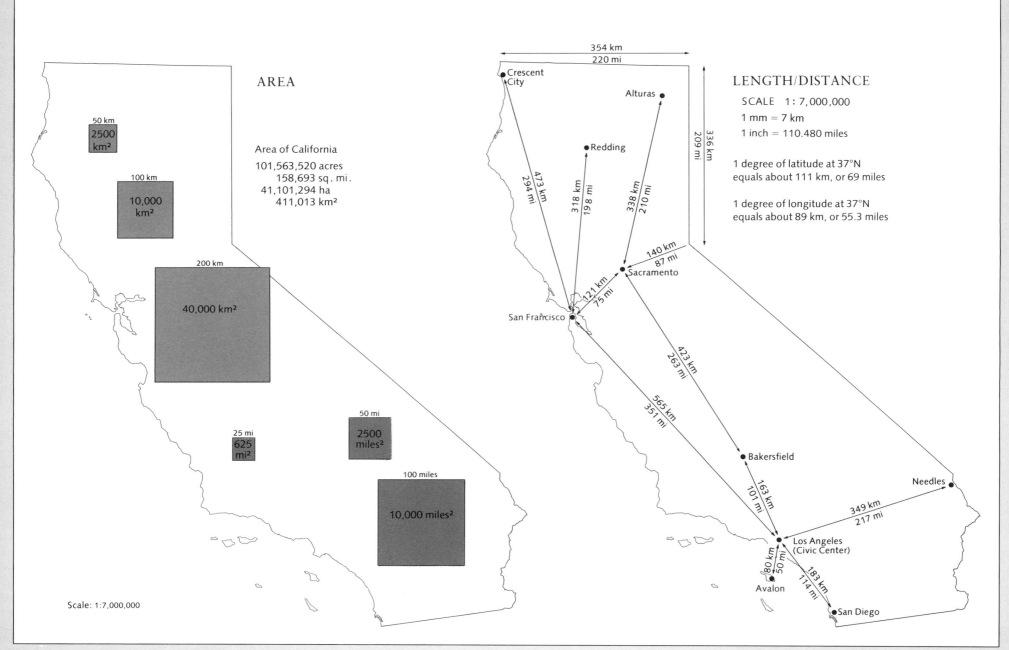

Area of California
101,563,520 acres
158,693 sq. mi.
41,101,294 ha
411,013 km²

LENGTH/DISTANCE

SCALE   1 : 7,000,000
1 mm = 7 km
1 inch = 110.480 miles

1 degree of latitude at 37°N
equals about 111 km, or 69 miles

1 degree of longitude at 37°N
equals about 89 km, or 55.3 miles

Scale: 1:7,000,000

METRIC CONVERSION

164

NORTHERN CALIFORNIA

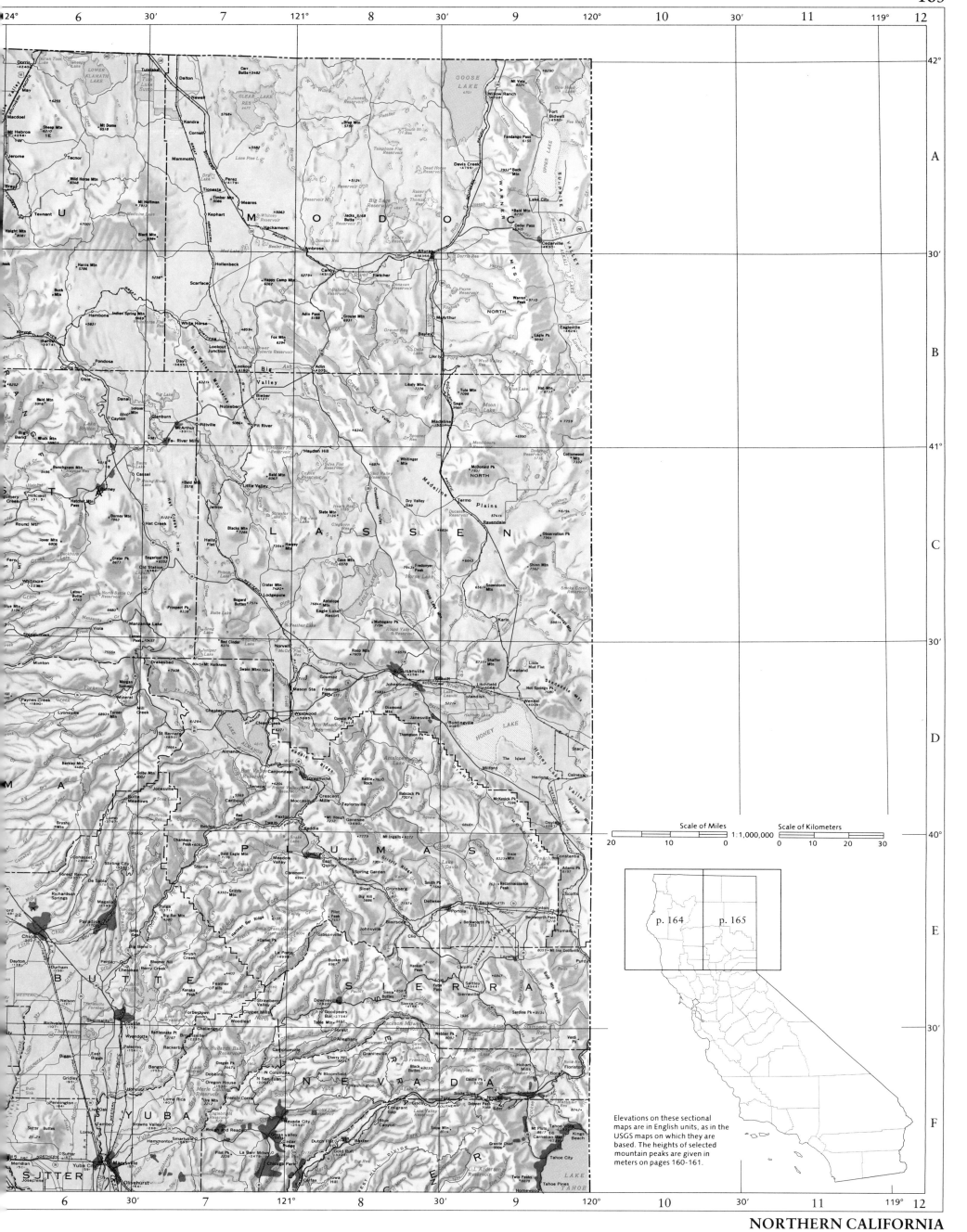

Scale of Miles
Scale of Kilometers
1:1,000,000

20   10   0   0   10   20   30

p. 164   p. 165

Elevations on these sectional
maps are in English units, as in the
USGS maps on which they are
based. The heights of selected
mountain peaks are given in
meters on pages 160-161.

NORTHERN CALIFORNIA

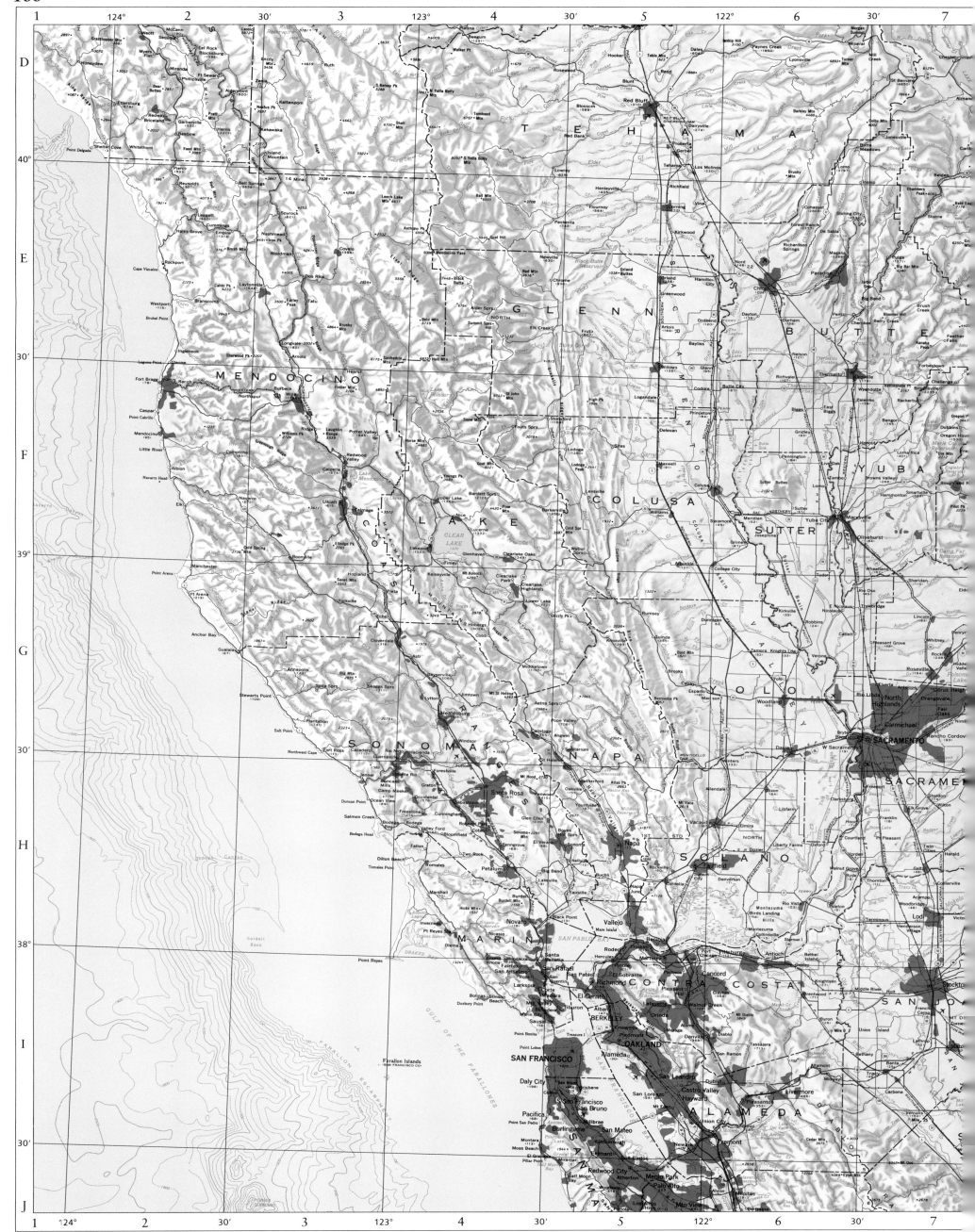

NORTH CENTRAL CALIFORNIA

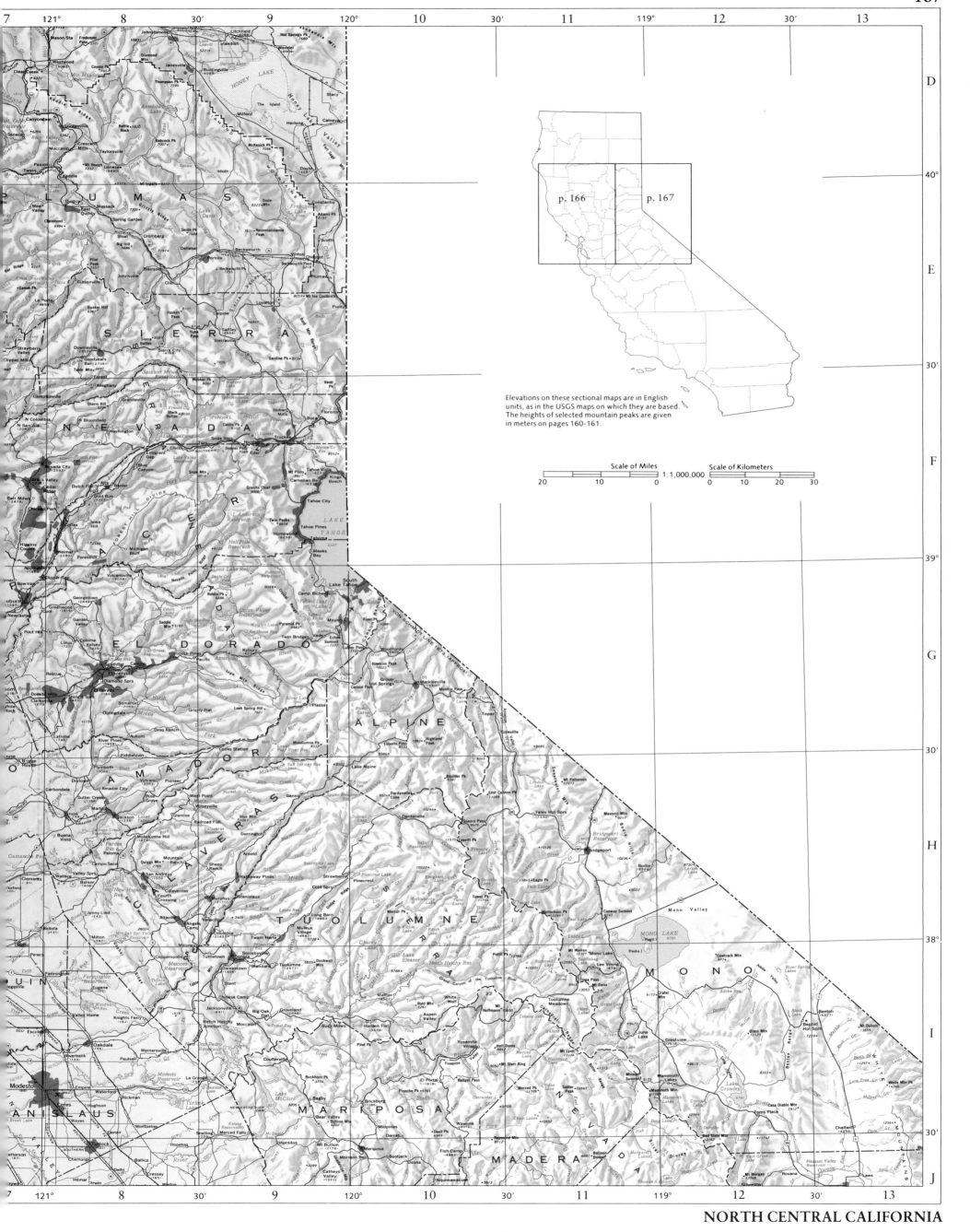

Elevations on these sectional maps are in English units, as in the USGS maps on which they are based. The heights of selected mountain peaks are given in meters on pages 160-161.

p. 166   p. 167

Scale of Miles   1:1,000,000   Scale of Kilometers

NORTH CENTRAL CALIFORNIA

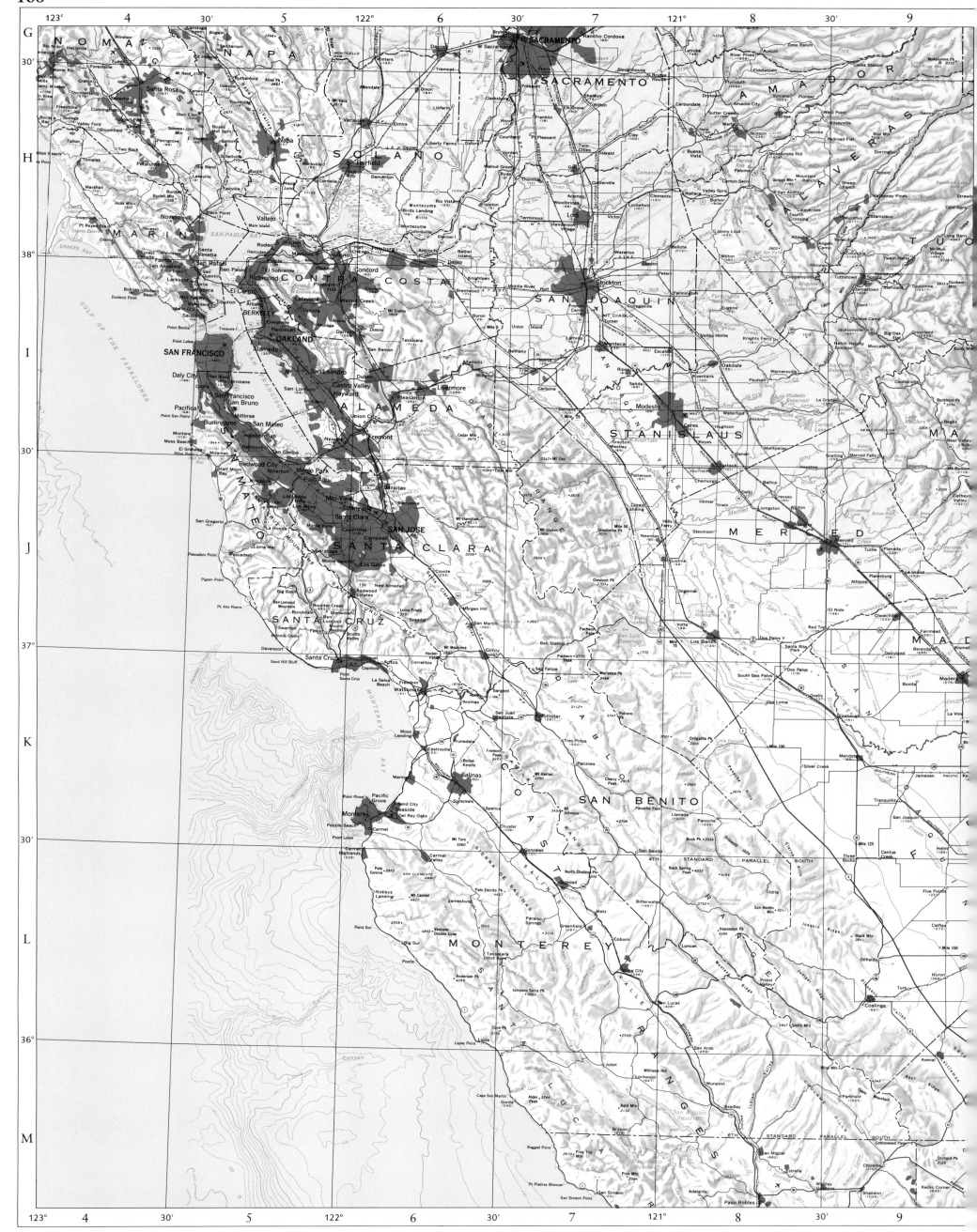

CENTRAL CALIFORNIA

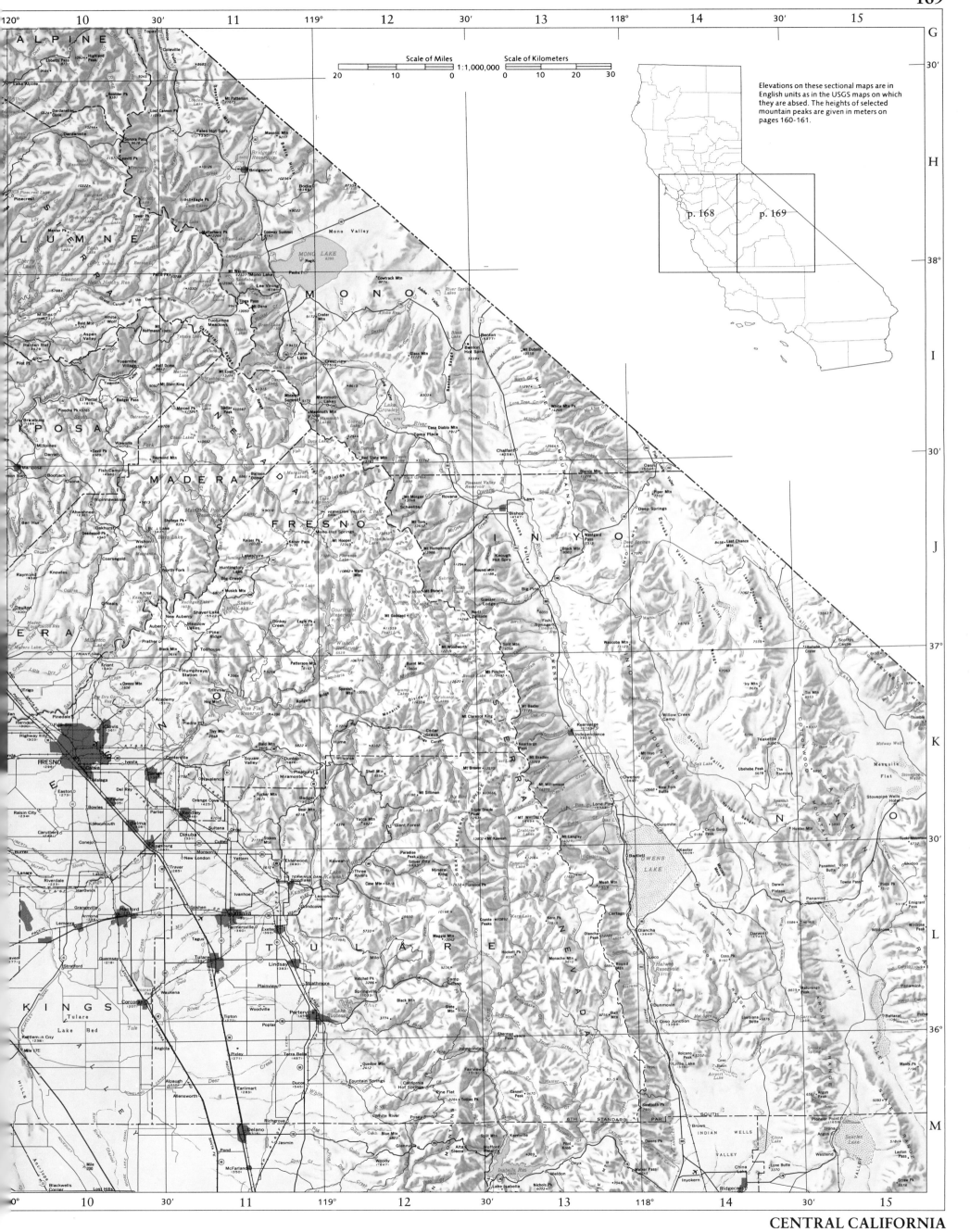

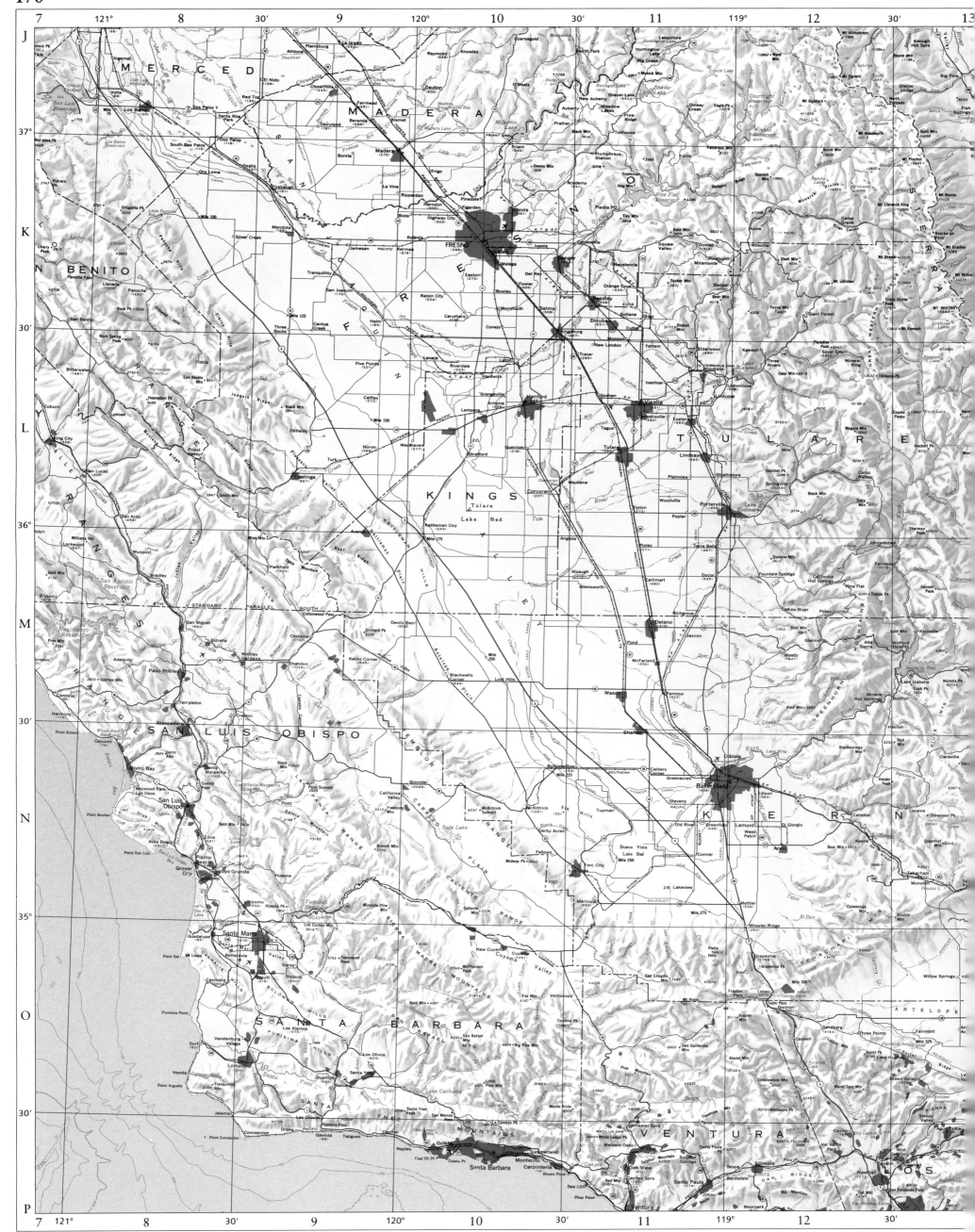

SOUTH CENTRAL CALIFORNIA

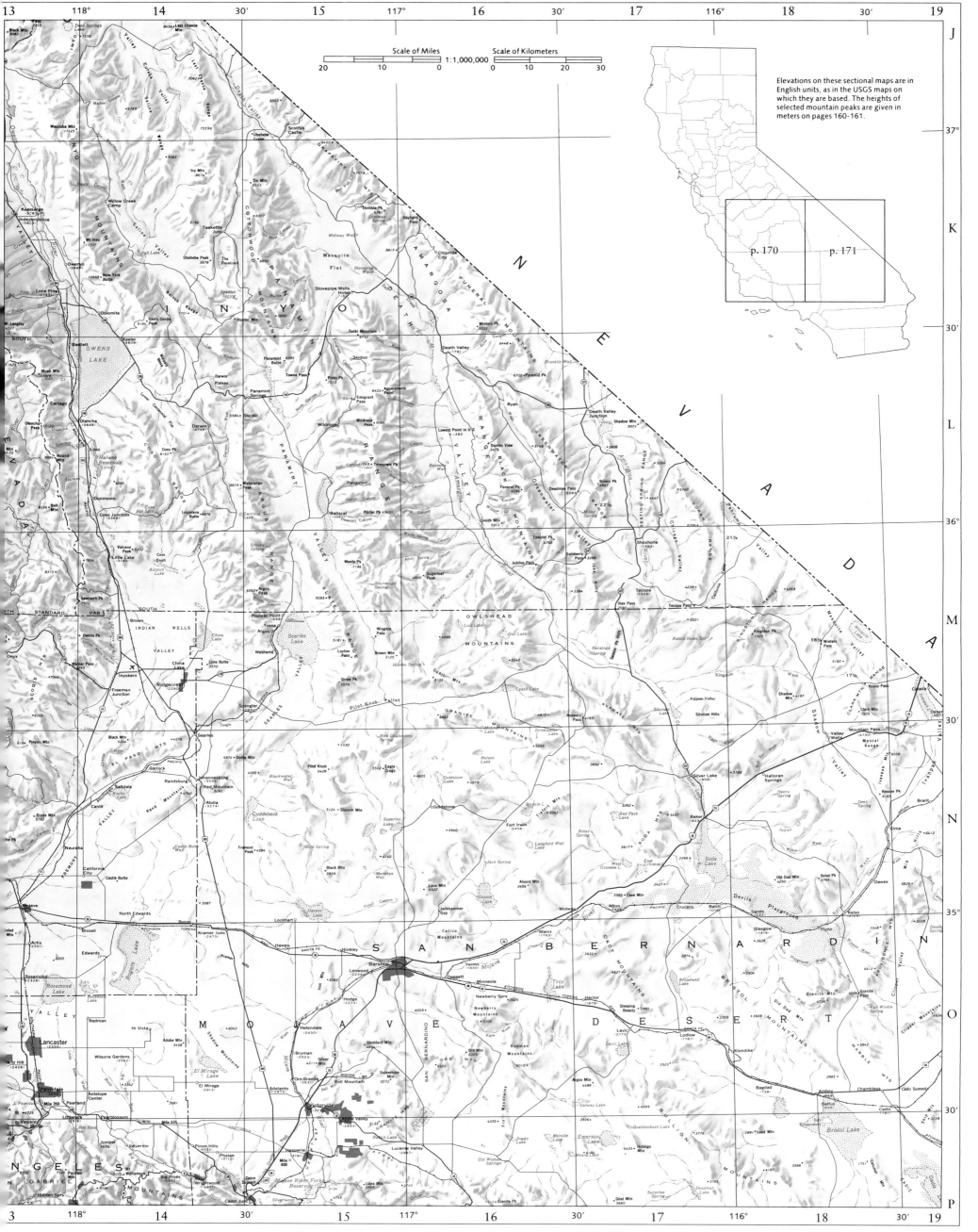

p. 172   p. 173

Scale of Miles		1:1,000,000	Scale of Kilometers	
20	10	0	0	10 20 30

SOUTHERN CALIFORNIA

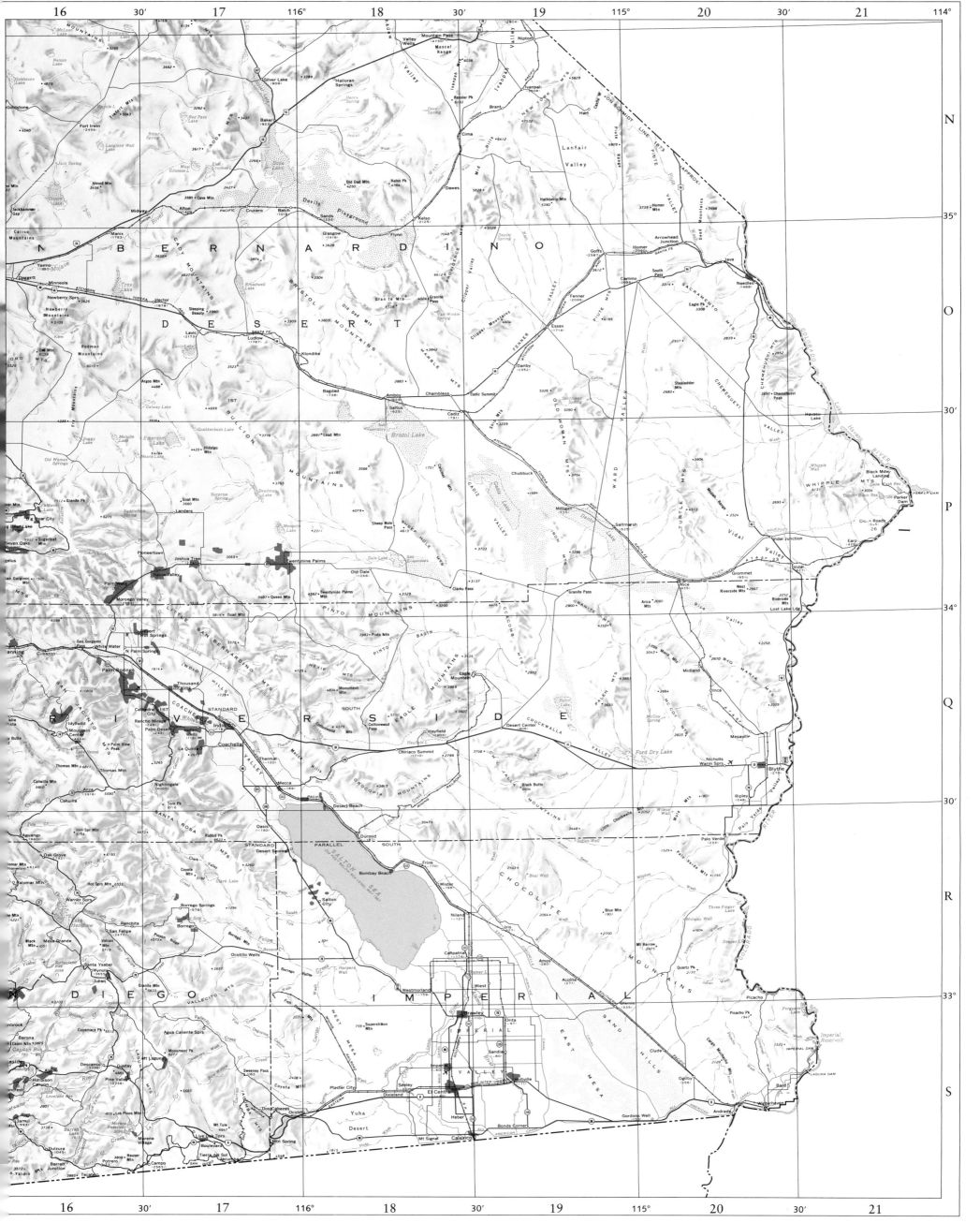

GAZETTEER

The gazetteer includes 3,063 place names. This selection is a very small sample of the total: a complete geographical gazetteer for California would include at least a hundred thousand entries before getting down to the street name level. Names listed here include all the settlement names shown on the USGS 1:500,000 sheets (1970 edition), and most of the more important physical features. Some towns and unincorporated areas not shown on the 1:500,000 map are included, and noted by asterisk.

Each entry is followed by the name of the county in which it is located (in italics), by its population or its elevation if available, and finally by the grid coordinates which locate the feature on the reference maps in the preceding section of the atlas. Elevations are in meters above mean sea level. Populations are from the Department of Transportation's 1976 City and Place Name Listing, which is based on various sources and includes figures from 1970, 1973, and 1976; *except*, all cities for which the Department of Finance Population Research Unit prepares estimates have that agency's January 1978 population estimates listed and noted.

CONVENTIONS

Rivers: grid location is for the river mouth.

Features on county lines, or overlapping into two counties: both listed, as: Marin/Sonoma.

Features, such as mountain ranges, extending into more than two counties: principal county listed, as: Sonoma+

Features extending into more than one grid area: principal grid area listed, as: I5+

Names which do not appear on the reference maps: entry followed by asterisk, as: **West Modesto***

Population listings from the Department of Finance 1978 estimate: distinguished by superscript, as:

Los Angeles *Los Angeles* pop. 2,787,900[1] P13

A

Abbotts Lagoon *Marin* H4
Academy *Fresno* K10
Acampo *San Joaquin* pop. 310 ....H7
Acolita *Imperial* R19
Actis *Kern* O13
Acton *Los Angeles* pop. 500 ....P13
Adelaida *San Luis Obispo* M8
Adelanto *San Bernardino* pop. 2,160[1] O15
Adin *Modoc* pop. 500 ....B8
Adobe Canyon *Kern* M12
Afton *San Bernardino* N17
Ager *Siskiyou* A5
Agoura *Los Angeles* pop. 500 ....P12
Agua Caliente Canyon *Santa Barbara* O10
Agua Caliente Springs *San Diego* S17
Agua Dulce *Los Angeles* pop. 200 ....P13
Aguanga *Riverside* pop. 50 ....Q16
Ahwahnee *Madera* pop. 503 ....J10
Airport Lake *Inyo* M14
Alameda *Alameda* pop. 75,600[1] I5
Alameda County pop. 1,105,800[1] ....I6+
Alameda River *Alameda* I5
Alamo *Contra Costa* pop. 1,000 ....I5
Alamo River *Imperial* R18
Albany *Alameda* pop. 15,250[1] I5
Alberhill *Riverside* pop. 230 ....Q15
Albion *Mendocino* pop. 398 ....F2
Albion River *Mendocino* F2
Alderpoint *Humboldt* pop. 200 ....D2
Alhambra *Los Angeles* pop. 61,500[1] P13

Alisal* *Monterey* pop. 20,746 ....K6
Alisal Slough *Monterey* K6
Aliso Canyon *Los Angeles* P13
Aliso Canyon *Santa Barbara* O10
Aliso Canyon *Ventura* P11
Alleghany *Sierra* pop. 120 ....F8
Allendale *Solano* H6
Allensworth *Tulare* pop. 172 ....M11
Almanor *Plumas* pop. 453 ....D7
Alondra Park* *Los Angeles* pop. 12,193 ....Q13
Alpaugh *Tulare* pop. 737 ....M11
Alpine *San Diego* pop. 3,704 ....S16
Alpine County pop. 930[1] ....G10+
Alta *Placer* p. 250 ....F8
Alta Loma *San Bernardino* pop. 1,000 ....P14
Alta Sierra *Kern* pop. 40 ....M12
Altadena *Los Angeles* pop. 42,380 ....P13
Altamont *Alameda* I6
Altaville *Calaveras* pop. 1,000 ....H8
Alton *Humboldt* pop. 275 ....C1
Alturas *Modoc* pop. 2,990[1] B8
Alviso *Santa Clara* J6
Amador City *Amador* pop. 160[1] H8
Amador County pop. 17,100[1] ....H8+
Amargosa Range *Inyo* L16
Amargosa River *Inyo* L16
Amboy *San Bernardino* pop. 200 ....O18
Ambrose *Modoc* A8
American River *Sacramento* G7
American River (Middle Fork) *El Dorado/Placer* G7

American River (North Fork) *Placer* G7
American River (Silver Fork) *El Dorado* G9
American River (South Fork) *El Dorado* G7
Amos *Imperial* R19
Anacapa Island *Ventura* P11
Anaheim *Orange* pop. 204,800[1] Q14
Anchor Bay *Mendocino* G2
Anderson *Shasta* pop. 6,400[1] D5
Anderson Lake *Santa Clara* el. 190 m J6
Andrade *Imperial* pop. 20 ....S20
Angel Island *Marin* I5
Angels Camp *Calaveras* pop. 2,340[1] H8
Angiola *Tulare* pop. 44 ....M11
Angwin *Napa* pop. 3,300 ....G5
Annapolis *Sonoma* pop. 100 ....G3
Antelope *Sacramento* G7
Antelope Center *Los Angeles* O14
Antelope Lake *Plumas* D8
Antelope Plain *Kern* M10
Antelope Valley *Los Angeles* O13
Antioch *Contra Costa* pop. 36,650[1] H6
Anvil Spring Canyon *Inyo* M16
Anza *Riverside* pop. 50 ....Q16
Apache Canyon *Ventura* O11
Apple Valley *San Bernardino* pop. 6,702 ....P15
Applegate *Placer* pop. 600 ....G8
Aptos *Santa Cruz* pop. 8,704 ....K6
Araz Wash *Imperial* S20
Arbuckle *Colusa* pop. 1,037 ....F5
Arcadia *Los Angeles* pop. 47,050[1] P13
Arcata *Humboldt* pop. 12,700[1] C1
Arcata Bay *Humboldt* C1
Arden Town* *Sacramento* pop. 82,492 ....G7
Argus *San Bernardino* M15
Argus Peak *Inyo* el. 2,000 m M15
Argus Range *Inyo* M15
Arlington* *Riverside* Q15
Armona *Kings* pop. 1,500 ....L10
Arnold *Calaveras* pop. 600 ....H9
Arnold *Mendocino* E3
Aromas *Monterey* pop. 300 ....K6
Arrowhead Junction *San Bernardino* O20
Arroyo de la Cruz *San Luis Obispo* M7
Arroyo Dos Picachos *San Benito* K7
Arroyo Grande *San Luis Obispo* N8
Arroyo Grande *San Luis Obispo* pop. 10,200[1] N8
Arroyo Hondo *Fresno* L8
Arroyo Hondo *Santa Clara* J6
Arroyo Mocho *Alameda* I6
Arroyo Salada *Imperial* R17
Arroyo Seco *Monterey* L7
Arroyo Valle *Alameda/Santa Clara* J6
Artesia *Los Angeles* pop. 15,150[1] Q13
Artois *Glenn* pop. 200 ....E5
Arvin *Kern* pop. 6,175[1] N12
Aspen Valley *Tuolumne* I10
Asti *Sonoma* pop. 30 ....G4
Atascadero *San Luis Obispo* pop. 11,350 ....N8
Atherton *San Mateo* pop. 7,850[1] J5
Athlone *Merced* J9
Atolia *San Bernardino* N14
Atwater *Merced* pop. 15,200[1] J8
Auberry *Fresno* pop. 515 ....J11
Auburn *Placer* pop. 7,150[1] G7
Auburn Ravine *Sutter* G6
Aukum *El Dorado* pop. 10 ....G8
Avalon *Los Angeles* pop. 1,720[1] R13
Avawatz Mountains *San Bernardino* M17
Avenal *Kings* pop. 3,100 ....L9
Avila Beach *San Luis Obispo* pop. 420 ....N8
Azusa *Los Angeles* pop. 25,500[1] P14

B

Bagby *Mariposa* I9
Bagdad *San Bernardino* O18
Badger *Tulare* pop. 140 ....K11
Baker *San Bernardino* pop. 570 ....N17
Bakersfield *Kern* pop. 88,100[1] N11
Balch *San Bernardino* N17
Bald Eagle Mountain *Plumas* el. 2,187 m E7
Baldwin Park *Los Angeles* pop. 44,550[1] P14
Ballarat *Inyo* pop. 3 ....L15

C

Camp San Luis Obispo*, U.S. Army Installation
(Inactive) San Luis Obispo N8
Campbell Santa Clara pop. 25,300[1] J6
Campo San Diego pop. 1,102 ......S17
Campo Seco Calaveras pop. 75 ......H8
Camptonville Yuba pop. 550 ......F7
Canby Modoc pop. 450 ......B8
Canoga Park Los Angeles pop. 89,325 ......P12
Cantil Kern pop. 20 ......N14
Cantua Creek Fresno pop. 350 ......L9
Canyondam Plumas pop. 110 ......D7
Capay Yolo pop. 90 ......G5
Cape Mendocino Humboldt D1
Cape San Martin Monterey M7
Capetown Humboldt pop. 10 ......D1
Capistrano Beach Orange pop. 4,149 ......R14
Capitan Santa Barbara P9
Capitola Santa Cruz pop. 8,575[1] K6
Caples Lake Alpine el. 2,376 m G9
Carbona San Joaquin pop. 290 ......I7
Carbondale Amador pop. 26 ......H7
Cardiff-by-the-Sea San Diego pop. 5,724 ......R15
Caribou Plumas pop. 56 ......D7
Carlotta Humboldt pop. 345 ......C1
Carlsbad San Diego pop. 27,150[1] R15
Carmel Monterey pop. 4,750[1] K6
Carmel Bay Monterey K6
Carmel Highlands Monterey L6
Carmel River Monterey K6
Carmel Valley Monterey pop. 3,079 ......L6
Carmel Woods* Monterey pop. 1,208 ......K6
Carmichael Sacramento pop. 37,625 ......G7
Carnelian Bay Placer pop. 259 ......F9
Carpinteria Santa Barbara pop. 10,050[1] P10
Carr Butte Modoc el. 1,670 m A7
Carrizo Plain San Luis Obispo N10
Carrizo Wash Imperial R18
Carrville Trinity B4
Carson* Los Angeles pop. 78,200[1] Q13
Carson River (East Fork) Alpine G10
Carson River (West Fork) Alpine G10
Cartago Inyo pop. 75 ......L13
Caruthers Fresno pop. 938 ......K10
Cascade Range Siskiyou+ ......B5+
Casitas Springs Ventura pop. 1,113 ......P11
Casmalia Santa Barbara pop. 156 ......O8
Caspar Mendocino pop. 578 ......F2
Cassel Shasta pop. 10 ......C6
Castaic Los Angeles pop. 600 ......P12
Castaic Lake Los Angeles O12
Castella Shasta pop. 275 ......B5
Castle Air Force Base* Merced J8
Castro Canyon Santa Barbara O10
Castro Valley Alameda pop. 46,700 ......I5
Castroville Monterey pop. 4,090 ......K6
Caswell Los Angeles O12
Cathedral City Riverside pop. 3,640 ......Q17
Catheys Valley Mariposa pop. 323 ......J9
Catlett Sutter G6
Cayton Shasta B6
Cayucos San Luis Obispo pop. 1,930 ......N8
Cazadero Sonoma pop. 300 ......G3
Cecilville Siskiyou pop. 90 ......B3
Cedar Grove Fresno pop. 10 ......K12
Cedar Ridge Nevada pop. 333 ......F7
Cedar Wash San Bernardino N18
Cedarville Modoc pop. 800 ......A9
Centerville Shasta C5
Centerville Fresno pop. 660 ......K11
Central Valley Shasta pop. 2,361 ......C5
Ceres Stanislaus pop. 10,500[1] I8
Cerritos* Los Angeles pop. 48,700[1] Q13
Cerro Alto San Luis Obispo el. 800 m N8
Cerro Gordo Peak Inyo el. 2,799 m K14
Chalfant Mono pop. 100 ......I13
Challenge Yuba pop. 550 ......F7
Chambless San Bernardino O18
Chanchelulla Peak Trinity el. 1,950 m D4
Chatsworth Los Angeles pop. 47,119 ......P12
Cheli Air Force Station* (Inactive) Los Angeles Q13
Chemehuevi Valley San Bernardino P20
Chemehuevi Wash San Bernardino P21
Chemurgic Stanislaus J8
Cherokee Butte E6
Cherry Lake Tuolumne el. 1,433 m H10
Cherry Valley Riverside pop. 3,165 ......Q16

Chester Plumas pop. 1,618 ......D7
Chicago Park Nevada pop. 336 ......F8
Chico Butte pop. 25,250[1] E6
Chidago Canyon Mono I13
Chilcoot Plumas pop. 54 ......E9
China Lake San Bernardino M14
China Lake Kern pop. 11,000 ......M14
China Peak Trinity el. 1,647 m C3
Chinese Camp Tuolumne pop. 150 ......I9
Chino San Bernardino pop. 36,100[1] P14
Chiriaco Summit Riverside pop. 10 ......Q18
Chloride City Inyo K16
Chocolate Mountains Imperial R19
Chocolate Mountains Gunnery Range*, U.S. Naval
Installation Imperial R19
Cholame San Luis Obispo pop. 15 ......M9
Cholame Hills Monterey M8
Chowchilla Madera pop. 4,620[1] J9
Chowchilla Canal Madera J9
Chowchilla River Merced J8
Chowchilla River (East Fork) Madera J10
Chowchilla River (Middle Fork) Madera J10
Chowchilla River (West Fork) Madera J10
Chrome Glenn E4
Chualar Monterey pop. 441 ......K6
Chubbuck San Bernardino P19
Chuckwalla Mountains Riverside Q19
Chuckwalla Valley Riverside Q19
Chula Vista San Diego pop. 79,700[1] S15
Cima San Bernardino pop. 20 ......N18
Cisco Placer pop. 30 ......F8
Citrus Heights Sacramento pop. 21,760 ......G7
City Terrace* Los Angeles pop. 7,000 ......P13
Clair Engle Lake Trinity el. 722 m C4
Claraville Kern N13
Claremont Los Angeles pop. 27,150[1] P14
Clark Mountain San Bernardino el. 2,417 m M18
Clarksburg Yolo pop. 575 ......H6
Clarksville El Dorado G7
Clavey River Tuolumne I9
Clay Sacramento pop. 50 ......H7
Clayton Contra Costa pop. 3,310[1] I6
Clear Creek Lassen pop. 400 ......D7
Clear Lake Lake el. 404 m F4
Clear Lake Reservoir Modoc el. 1,365 m A7
Clearlake Highlands Lake pop. 2,836 ......G4
Clearlake Oaks Lake pop. 1,000 ......F4
Clearlake Park Lake pop. 800 ......G4
Clements San Joaquin pop. 160 ......H7
Cleone Mendocino pop. 570 ......F2
Clio Plumas pop. 20 ......E8
Clipper Gap Placer pop. 300 ......G7
Clipper Mills Butte pop. 245 ......E7
Cloverdale Shasta D5
Cloverdale Sonoma pop. 3,750[1] G3
Clovis Fresno pop. 27,500[1] K10
Clyde Imperial pop. 850 ......S20
Coachella Riverside pop. 8,650[1] Q17
Coachella Valley Riverside Q17
Coalinga Fresno pop. 6,375[1] L9
Coarsegold Madera pop. 150 ......J10
Coast Ranges Mendocino+ ......E3+
Cobb Lake pop. 300 ......G4
Coburn Monterey L7
Codora Glenn pop. 200 ......F5
Cohasset Butte pop. 445 ......E6
Cold Spring Mountain Colusa/Lake el. 1,093 m F5
Cold Spring Mountain Mendocino el. 834 m F2
Cold Springs Tuolumne pop. 100 ......H9
Coleville Mono G10
Colfax Placer pop. 770[1] F8
College City Colusa pop. 300 ......F5
Collegeville San Joaquin pop. 290 ......I7
Collierville San Joaquin pop. 700 ......H7
Collinsville Solano pop. 60 ......H6
Colma San Mateo pop. 500[1] I5
Coloma El Dorado pop. 300 ......G8
Colorado River San Bernardino+ ......P21+
Colton San Bernardino pop. 19,300[1] P15
Columbia Tuolumne pop. 350 ......H9
Colusa Colusa pop. 4,160[1] F5
Colusa Basin Drainage Canal Yolo G6
Colusa County pop. 13,000[1] ......F5+
Colusa Trough Colusa F5
Commerce Los Angeles pop. 10,100[1] P13
Comptche Mendocino pop. 227 ......F2

Compton Los Angeles pop. 74,800[1] Q13
Concepcion Santa Barbara P9
Concord Contra Costa pop. 95,500[1] I5
Condrey Mountain Siskiyou el. 2,168 m A4
Conejo Fresno pop. 30 ......K10
Conner Kern N11
Constantia Lassen E9
Contra Costa County pop. 613,400[1] ......I6+
Cooks Station Amador G7
Cool El Dorado pop. 50 ......G7
Copco Siskiyou pop. 70 ......A5
Copperopolis Calaveras pop. 150 ......I8
Corcoran Kings pop. 5,775[1] L10
Corcoran Reservoir Kings L10
Cordelia Solano pop. 150 ......H5
Corn Springs Wash Riverside Q19
Cornell Los Angeles pop. 250 ......P12
Cornell Modoc A7
Corning Tehama pop. 4,420[1] E5
Corning Canal Tehama E5
Corona Riverside pop. 37,000[1] Q14
Corona Del Mar* Orange pop. 1,000 ......Q14
Coronado San Diego pop. 21,600[1] S15
Corral Hollow Alameda/San Joaquin I6
Corralitos Santa Cruz pop. 600 ......K6
Corte Madera Marin pop. 8,125[1] I4
Coso Hot Springs Inyo L14
Coso Junction Inyo pop. 10 ......L14
Coso Peak Inyo el. 2,443 m L14
Coso Range Inyo L14
Costa Mesa Orange pop. 78,500[1] Q14
Cosumnes River Sacramento H7
Cosumnes River (Middle Fork) El Dorado G8
Cosumnes River (North Fork) El Dorado G8
Cosumnes River (South Fork) Amador/El Dorado G8
Cotati Sonoma pop. 2,840[1] H4
Cottage Grove Siskiyou A2
Cottonwood Shasta pop. 1,288 ......D5
Cottonwood Canyon Inyo K15
Cottonwood Mountains Inyo K15
Cottonwood Wash San Bernardino O18
Cougar Siskiyou A5
Coulterville Mariposa pop. 129 ......I9
Courtland Sacramento pop. 400 ......H6
Courtright Reservoir Fresno el. 2,490 m J12
Covelo Mendocino pop. 1,000 ......E3
Covina Los Angeles pop. 33,050[1] P14
Covington Mill Trinity pop. 35 ......C4
Cow Head Lake Modoc A9
Cowtrack Mountain Mono el. 2,705 m I12
Coyote Santa Clara J6
Coyote Lake San Bernardino N16
Coyote Wash Imperial S18
Cranmore Sutter G6
Crannell Humboldt pop. 500 ......B1
Crater Mountain Lassen el. 2,262 m C7
Crescent City Del Norte pop. 2,660[1] A1
Crescent Mills Plumas pop. 201 ......D8
Cressey Merced pop. 697 ......J8
Crestline San Bernardino pop. 1,000 ......P15
Creston San Luis Obispo pop. 60 ......M8
Crestview Mono pop. 50 ......I12
Crockett Contra Costa pop. 1,000 ......H5
Cromberg Plumas pop. 44 ......E8
Cross Roads San Bernardino P21
Crows Landing Stanislaus pop. 460 ......J7
Crucero San Bernardino N17
Crystal Springs Reservoir San Mateo I5
Cucamonga San Bernardino pop. 39,900[1] P14
Cudahy* Los Angeles pop. 16,950[1] Q13
Cuddeback Lake San Bernardino N15
Cuddy Canyon Kern/Ventura O12
Cuesta Pass San Luis Obispo N8
Culver City Los Angeles pop. 38,500[1] P13
Cummings Mendocino pop. 80 ......E2
Cunningham Sonoma pop. 150 ......H4
Cupertino Santa Clara pop. 23,150[1] J5
Curtis Siskiyou B6
Cutler Tulare pop. 2,699 ......K11
Cutten* Humboldt pop. 2,228 ......C1
Cuyama Santa Barbara pop. 156 ......O10
Cuyama River San Luis Obispo/Santa Barbara N9
Cuyama Valley San Luis Obispo/Santa Barbara O10
Cuyamaca Peak San Diego el. 1,985 m S16
Cypress Orange pop. 40,450[1] Q13

D

Daggett *San Bernardino* pop. 1,000 O16
Dairyland *Madera* J9
Dairyville *Tehama* pop. 160 D5
Dale Lake *San Bernardino* P18
Dales *Tehama* pop. 40 D5
Dalton *Modoc* A7
Daly City *San Mateo* pop. 73,700[1] I5
Dana *Shasta* pop. 60 B6
Dana Point *Orange* R14
Dana Point *Orange* pop. 4,745 R14
Danby *San Bernardino* O19
Danby Lake *San Bernardino* P19
Danville *Contra Costa* pop. 1,000 I6
Dardanelle *Tuolumne* pop. 5 H10
Darrah *Mariposa* I10
Darwin *Inyo* pop. 40 L14
Darwin Wash *Inyo* L14
Daulton *Madera* pop. 2 J10
Davenport *Santa Cruz* pop. 200 J5
Davis *Yolo* pop. 35,650[1] G6
Davis Creek *Modoc* pop. 50 A9
Dawes *San Bernardino* N18
Day *Modoc* pop. 25 B7
Dayton *Butte* pop. 105 E6
De Luz *San Diego* R15
De Sabla *Butte* pop. 110 E6
Deadwood *Trinity* C4
Death Valley *Inyo* el. -86 L16
Death Valley Junction *Inyo* pop. 75 L17
Death Valley Wash *Inyo* K15
Dedrick *Trinity* C3
Deep Canyon *Riverside* Q17
Deep Springs *Inyo* pop. 40 J14
Deep Springs Lake *Inyo* J13
Deep Water Ship Channel *Solano/Yolo* H6
Deetz *Siskiyou* B5
Del Dios *San Diego* R15
Del Loma *Trinity* pop. 30 C3
Del Mar *San Diego* pop. 5,175[1] S15
Del Monte Park* *Monterey* pop. 3,629 K6
Del Norte County pop. 17,100[1] A2+
Del Paso Heights* *Sacramento* G7
Del Rey *Fresno* pop. 905 K10
Del Rey Oaks *Monterey* pop. 1,570[1] K6
Del Rosa* *San Bernardino* pop. 1,000 P15
Delano *Kern* pop. 15,650[1] M11
Delevan *Colusa* pop. 65 F5
Delhi *Merced* pop. 2,063 J8
Delleker *Plumas* E8
Delta *Shasta* C5
Denair *Stanislaus* pop. 1,128 I8
Denny *Trinity* pop. 50 C3
Denverton *Solano* pop. 10 H6
Derby Acres *Kern* pop. 300 N10
Descanso *San Diego* pop. 532 S16
Desert *San Bernardino* M19
Desert Beach *Riverside* Q18
Desert Center *Riverside* pop. 125 Q19
Desert Hot Springs *Riverside* pop. 4,210[1] Q17
Desert Shores *Imperial* pop. 370 R17
Desert View Highland* *Los Angeles* pop. 2,172 O13
Devils Canyon *Los Angeles* P14
Devils Den *Kern* pop. 60 M10
Devils Playground *San Bernardino* N18
Devils Playground Wash *San Bernardino* O18
Devore *San Bernardino* pop. 500 P15
Di Giorgio *Kern* pop. 220 N12
Diablo *Contra Costa* pop. 800 I6
Diablo Range *Santa Clara* + J7+
Diamond Bar *Los Angeles* pop. 12,234 Q14
Diamond Mountains *Lassen/Plumas* D9
Diamond Springs *El Dorado* pop. 900 G8
Dillon Beach *Marin* pop. 440 H4
Dinkey Creek *Fresno* pop. 420 J11
Dinsmores *Humboldt* pop. 100 D2
Dinuba *Tulare* pop. 9,600[1] K11
Dixie Mountain *Plumas* el. 2,537 m E9
Dixieland *Imperial* pop. 65 S18
Dixon *Solano* pop. 6,025[1] H6
Dobbins *Yuba* pop. 500 F7
Dolomite *Inyo* K14
Dominguez* *Los Angeles* pop. 5,980 Q13
Donner Pass *Nevada/Placer* el. 2,160 m F9
Dorrington *Calaveras* pop. 75 H9
Dorris *Siskiyou* pop. 820[1] A6
Dos Cabezas *San Diego* S17
Dos Palos *Merced* pop. 2,930[1] K8
Dos Palos Wye *Merced* pop. 298 J8
Dos Rios *Mendocino* pop. 100 E3
Douglas City *Trinity* pop. 60 C4
Downey *Los Angeles* pop. 86,700[1] Q13
Downie River *Sierra* E8
Downieville *Sierra* pop. 400 E8
Doyle *Lassen* pop. 175 D9
Dozier *Solano* pop. 5 H6
Drake *Santa Barbara* P9
Drakes Bay *Marin* H4
Drakes Estero *Marin* H4
Drakesbad *Plumas* D7
Dry Bone Canyon *Inyo* K15
Dry Canyon *Ventura* O11
Drytown *Amador* pop. 114 H8
Duarte *Los Angeles* pop. 14,800[1] P14
Dublin *Alameda* pop. 13,641 I6
Ducor *Tulare* pop. 271 M11
Duguynos Canyon *San Diego* S17
Dulzura *San Diego* pop. 492 S16
Duncan Canyon *Placer* F8
Duncans Mills *Sonoma* pop. 85 H3
Dunlap *Fresno* pop. 180 K11
Dunmovin *Inyo* pop. 15 L14
Dunnigan *Yolo* pop. 251 G6
Dunsmuir *Siskiyou* pop. 2,240[1] B5
Durham *Butte* pop. 1,010 E6
Durmid *Riverside* Q18
Dutch Flat *Placer* pop. 310 F8
Dwinnell Reservoir *Siskiyou* el. 851 m A5

E

Eagle Crags *San Bernardino* el. 1,680 m N15
Eagle Lake *Lassen* C8
Eagle Lake Resort *Lassen* C8
Eagle Mountain *Riverside* pop. 3,500 Q19
Eagle Mountains *Riverside* Q18
Eagle Peak *Modoc* el. 3,015 m B9
Eagleville *Modoc* pop. 200 B9
Earlimart *Tulare* pop. 3,124 M11
Earp *San Bernardino* pop. 50 P21
East Biggs *Butte* F6
East Highlands *San Bernardino* pop. 970 P15
East Irvine *Orange* Q14
East Los Angeles* *Los Angeles* pop. 105,033 P13
East Mesa *Imperial* S19
East Nicolaus *Sutter* pop. 275 G6
East Park Reservoir *Colusa* el. 365 m F4
East Quincy *Plumas* E8
East Walker River *Mono* H11
East Whittier* *Los Angeles* Q13
Easton *Fresno* pop. 1,065 K10
Ebbetts Pass *Alpine* el. 2,661 m G10
Echo *Mendocino* G3
Echo Canyon *Inyo* L16
Echo Lake *El Dorado* G9
Echo Summit *El Dorado* el. 2,248 m G9
Eder *Placer* F9
Edgemont *Riverside* pop. 1,000 Q15
Edgewood *Siskiyou* pop. 300 B5
Edison *Kern* pop. 1,000 N12
Edna *San Luis Obispo* pop. 54 N8
Edwards Air Force Base* *Kern* O14
Eel River *Humboldt* C1
Eel River (Middle Fork) *Mendocino* E3
Eel River (North Fork) *Mendocino* E3
Eel River (South Fork) *Humboldt* D2
Eel Rock *Humboldt* pop. 50 D2
El Cajon *San Diego* pop. 67,800[1] S16
El Capitan Reservoir *San Diego* el. 229 m S16
El Centro *Imperial* pop. 23,400[1] S18
El Cerrito *Contra Costa* pop. 22,450[1] I5
El Dorado *El Dorado* pop. 550 G8
El Dorado County pop. 75,000[1] G8+
El Dorado Hills *El Dorado* pop. 2,000 G7
El Encanto Heights* *Santa Barbara* pop. 6,225 P10
El Granada *San Mateo* pop. 2,700 I5
El Mirage *San Bernardino* O14
El Mirage Lake *San Bernardino* O14
El Monte *Los Angeles* pop. 67,900[1] P13
El Nido *Merced* pop. 102 J9
El Paso Mountains *Kern* N14
El Portal *Mariposa* pop. 469 I10
El Rio *Ventura* pop. 6,173 P11
El Segundo *Los Angeles* pop. 15,150[1] Q13
El Sobrante *Contra Costa* pop. 1,000 I5
El Toro *Orange* pop. 9,654 Q14
El Verano *Sonoma* pop. 1,753 H5
Elders Corner *Placer* pop. 525 G7
Elderwood *Tulare* pop. 247 L11
Elizabeth Lake Canyon *Los Angeles* O12
Elk *Mendocino* pop. 250 F2
Elk Bayou *Tulare* L11
Elk Creek *Glenn* pop. 300 E4
Elk Grove *Sacramento* pop. 3,721 H7
Elk River *Humboldt* C1
Elk River (North Fork) *Humboldt* C1
Elk River (South Fork) *Humboldt* C1
Elkhorn Slough *Monterey* K6
Elmira *Solano* pop. 200 H6
Elsinore *Riverside* pop. 5,550[1] Q15
Elverta *Sacramento* pop. 600 G7
Emerald Bay* *Orange* pop. 400 Q14
Emerson Lake *San Bernardino* P17
Emeryville *Alameda* pop. 4,490[1] I5
Emigrant Canyon *Inyo* L15
Emigrant Gap *Placer* pop. 50 F8
Empire *Stanislaus* pop. 2,016 I8
Encanto* *San Diego* S15
Encenitas *San Diego* pop. 5,375 R15
Encino *Los Angeles* pop. 62,043 P12
Enterprise *Shasta* pop. 11,486 C5
Erickson *Siskiyou* A5
Escalon *San Joaquin* pop. 2,750[1] I8
Escondido *San Diego* pop. 57,100[1] R15
Esparto *Yolo* pop. 1,023 G5
Essex *San Bernardino* pop. 100 O19
Estero Bay *San Luis Obispo* N8
Estrella *San Luis Obispo* pop. 21 M8
Estrella River *San Luis Obispo* M8
Etiwanda *San Bernardino* pop. 1,000 P14
Etna *Siskiyou* pop. 720[1] B4
Etsel Ridge *Mendocino* el. 1,693 m E3
Ettersburg *Humboldt* pop. 12 D2
Eugene *Stanislaus* pop. 30 I8
Eureka *Humboldt* pop. 24,500[1] C1
Eureka Valley *Inyo* J14
Exeter *Tulare* pop. 5,175[1] L11

F

Fair Oaks *Sacramento* pop. 11,256 G7
Fairfax *Marin* pop. 7,800[1] I4
Fairfield *Solano* pop. 54,400[1] H5
Fairmead *Madera* pop. 347 J9
Fairmont *Los Angeles* O13
Fairview *Tulare* pop. 40 M13
Fairville *Sonoma* H5
Fales Hot Springs *Mono* pop. 5 H11
Falk *Humboldt* C1
Fall River *Shasta* B7
Fall River Mills *Shasta* pop. 600 B7
Fallbrook *San Diego* pop. 6,945 R15
Fallen Leaf Lake *El Dorado* el. 1,944 m G9
Fallon *Marin* pop. 10 H4
Famoso *Kern* pop. 10 M11
Fandango Pass *Modoc* el. 1,876 m A9
Farallon Islands *San Francisco* I4
Farmersville *Tulare* pop. 4,620[1] L11
Farmington *San Joaquin* pop. 180 I8
Fawnskin *San Bernardino* pop. 590 P16
Feather Falls *Butte* pop. 350 E7
Feather River *Sutter* G6
Feather River (Middle Fork) *Butte* E7
Feather River (North Fork) *Butte* E7
Fellows *Kern* pop. 500 N10
Felton *Santa Cruz* pop. 2,062 J5
Fenner *San Bernardino* pop. 25 O19
Fenner Valley *San Bernardino* O19
Ferguson Lake *Imperial* S21
Fern *Shasta* C6

DAGGETT — FERN

Photographer Rick Furniss

The Trans

Designed by Lawrence Allen
Color Separations by Ron Mugar Photography
Printed by Graphic Arts Center
Bound by Lincoln and Allen
Printed in the United States of America

Alaska Pipeline
The Beginning

Volume I

Written and Produced by:
LAWRENCE J. ALLEN

Contributing Writer:
J. MALCOLM CAMPBELL

Copyright 1975 — Scribe Publishing Corp.
Library of Congress Card Number 75-7650
International Book Standard Number 0-915748-00-2

First Edition — Third Printing

Scribe Publishing Corporation
Seattle, Washington

Photographer James Drummond

April 29, 1975 marked the first anniversary of work on history's most remarkable construction project, the 798 mile trans Alaska pipeline system. The new pipeline will bring oil across some of the most rugged and beautiful terrain in the world, and ultimately will have very little impact on Alaska geography. Upon completion, the line will occupy only 12 square miles of the state's 586,000 square miles. The true impact will be upon the state's economy and the lifestyles of her people, although at the time of this publication there is really no way to predict exactly what that impact will be. Alaska is undergoing many social and economic changes, some of which are not directly related to the trans Alaska pipeline but it has been estimated that annual state revenues from the pipeline alone will be approximately three times the present total state budget.

A visitor to Alaska immediately senses the gusto of pipeline activity. Airlines' schedules are tight as planes fill with businessmen from the "Lower 48" states. In Fairbanks or Anchorage an airport cab driver will ask the phase of the pipeline on which you are involved, and upon asking him (or her) how long he has lived in Alaska the answer is usually "just a few months".

A respectable hotel room for one is about $36.00. A meager hamburger — $3.00. There is talk in Fairbanks of a one bedroom apartment — if you can find such — renting for $1200 per month. Twenty degrees below zero is no deterrent to short skirted ladies of the night in their attempt to cash in on those fat pipeline payrolls. Vacations for hard working pipeline workers include such exciting places as Las Vegas, Hawaii and Morocco.

This truly great Alaska project poses not only tremendous physical problems but the greatest environmental challenge ever faced by man. With Alaska's vast resources comes a requirement to protect her delicate beauty. Alyeska Pipeline Service Company is devoting itself entirely to building a pipeline which will disturb this environment as little as possible.

The 798 mile pipeline is being built for one major purpose — to make the 9.6 billion barrel oil reserves at Prudhoe Bay, on Alaska's north coast, available to U.S. consumers. Initially 1.2 million barrels (fifty million four hundred thousand gallons) of oil a day will be transported through the line from Prudhoe Bay to Valdez for shipment by tanker to U.S. ports. At capacity the line will transport two million barrels a day.

The project, which is the largest privately funded construction project in the history of mankind, is being built by the Alyeska Pipeline Service Company, which is formed by eight oil companies: the Amerada Hess Corporation, ARCO Pipe Line Company, Schio Pipe Line Company, Exxon Pipeline Company, Mobil Alaska Pipeline Company, Phillips Petroleum Company, Union Alaska Pipeline Company, and B P Pipelines Inc.

At a cost of six billion dollars, the pipeline system is being built in two phases. The first phase, scheduled for completion in mid-1977, includes completion of a new all-weather highway from the Yukon River to Prudhoe Bay, construction of a 48-inch steel pipeline from Prudhoe Bay to Valdez, building of eight pump stations, and development of oil storage for approximately 10 million barrels of oil, and tanker facilities at Valdez. The final phase includes an additional four pump stations, more oil storage, and additional tanker facilities at Valdez.

The pipeline route starts in the Arctic desert at Prudhoe Bay on the North Slope of Alaska. The pipeline then climbs 4,800 feet over Dietrich Pass in the Brooks Range, crosses the Yukon River, climbs 3,300 feet over the Alaska range and then over Thompson Pass in the Chugach Mountains before reaching the ice-free port of Valdez. Temperatures along the route range from the 90's in the summer to 80 degrees below zero in the daylong darkness of the Arctic winter.

Planning for the pipeline began in 1968 after the discovery of oil at Prudhoe Bay. Several years of legislative, environmental and court hearings were conducted in Alaska and Washington D.C. During these years, pipeline scientists and engineers carried out detailed and extensive environmental and design studies on all phases of the system. Also during this period every foot of the pipeline corridor was checked for environmental features, including animal movement zones, mineral licks, nesting areas, archeological sites, fish spawning streams and animal dens.

In November, 1973, President Nixon signed measures authorizing construction. Federal and state permits were issued shortly thereafter. Construction on the pipeline system began with work on the pipeline road, north of the Yukon River, in April, 1974.

Since the project began, accomplishments have been enormous. Only through these can one truly describe what an immense project the trans Alaska pipeline really is. For instance safeguarding the environment by: completely realigning a road and changing the site of a construction camp simply to avoid peregrine falcon nests more than a mile away; or deferring road construction until a band of Dall sheep had completed lambing.

Or the detail of flying nearly 10 million gallons of fuel north of the Yukon to support construction activities.

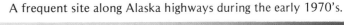

A frequent site along Alaska highways during the early 1970's.

Or the building of an ice bridge across the Yukon and a snow and ice road north in the middle of winter.

Or struggling constantly to erect enough camps to house thousands of construction workers.

And one must remember that much of this effort was accomplished with men working around the clock in temperatures as low as minus 68 degrees in winds with a chill factor reaching minus 115 degrees.

Or the multitude of new engineering accomplishments; floods that brought shortages of supplies; steel shortages in the United States forcing purchases in foreign countries; inflation and climbing interest rates that made it difficult to obtain commitments; and extensive documentation required by the government before contractors could proceed.

Throughout the following pages the publishers present for your permanent library Volume I of the photographic documentation of the trans-Alaska pipeline.

HISTORY OF ALASKA

A book about the 798 mile trans Alaska pipeline would be incomplete without also telling the history of Alaska and her people.

Alaska was discovered in 1741 by Russian explorers, led by Vitus Bering, a Dane and fleet captain in the Russian Navy. Bering discovered and named St. Lawrence Island. But the first men to step foot on Alaska came long before Vitus Bering.

Thousands of years ago an Asiatic people moved from Siberia, out across the Kamchatka Peninsula, toward Alaska. Sea charts in

Stage from White Horse arriving in Dawson, Yukon Territory.

Courtesy of University of Alaska Archives — Charles Bunnell Collection

the Bering Strait indicate that if the present water level were to drop approximately 100 feet one could walk to Russia. During the last Ice Age, called the Wisconsin glaciation, water was absorbed into mountains of ice to such an extent that the sea diminished almost three hundred feet in depth. This glaciation appears to have occurred on at least three different occasions when the land bridge emerged only to disappear again as the earth warmed.

Archeological findings on the North American continent lead scientists to speculate that the first peoples migrated from Asia over 40,000 years ago. Another crossing took place about 25,000 years ago and produced the ancestors of all Indians in North and South America. During the last land bridge nearly 12,000 years ago, the ancestors of the Eskimos crossed over, moving along Alaska's coast south toward the Anchorage area and north through Canada, then to Greenland, arriving about 2,500 B.C.

It has been proven scientifically that although the Wisconsin glaciation went as far south as St. Louis, Missouri, covering most of the United States, there was an ice-free corridor along the southwest North American continent. It is then speculated, with the help of archeological finds, that a migration took place which was the source of Indians throughout the Americas.

Oddly enough, this speculation has shown that the Alaskan Indians, instead of having come immediately from Asia, are in all likelihood a northern migration.

The Alaskan Natives of today are descendants of those first tribes, and amount to about 55,000 or one sixth of the state's population. They are the Eskimos of the far north and the western coast; the Athabascan Indians of the Interior; the Tlingit, Haida, and

Seismic unit on North Slope.

Tsimshian Indians of the Southeast; and the Aleuts of the Aleutian Islands and the Alaska Peninsula.

During the 17th and 18th centuries the French and their English successors had been making their way westward across the Atlantic. Upon reaching the Rocky Mountains they were held in check for over 100 years, but before the middle of the 19th century they had established themselves upon rivers tributary to the Pacific Ocean and Bering Sea.

The Russian stay on the North American continent lasted 126 years. The legacy of that period of history is today negligible, consisting of place names; a weakening strain of Slavic blood chiefly among the Aleuts; and a few little attended Russian and Greek Orthodox churches, among which is St. Michaels cathedral at Sitka, which was destroyed by fire in 1966 along with one-fifth of Sitka's business district. Now being restored, they will soon again house a valuable collection of icons and artifacts depicting Alaska's Russian American history.

The fur traders in discovering the wealth of martin, mink and otter among the islands of the Inside Passage, had earned themselves recognition as pioneers of civilization in the far west.

Ships captained by world-renown explorers began to sail the waterways of Russian America during the late 1700's. Russia's dominion was being pressed from both the south and the east by fur traders showing allegiance to another imperialism, Great Britain. In 1825 Russia and Britain signed a convention defining their boundaries in northwestern America and agreeing that neither should trespass on the other's domain. This convention was soon outwitted by the greater power in fur trade, the Hudson's Bay

Russian Orthodox Church and Russian trading store, Sitka, Alaska.

Courtesy University of Alaska Archives — Charles Bunnell Collection

Company. As in Russian America where the Russian-American Company was the agent and instrument of the Czar as well as a company dealing principally in furs, so was the Hudson's Bay Company officially designated the ruling power in the charter granted in 1670 by King Charles II of England. The Hudson's Bay Company was far more powerful than its Russian rival, and also 129 years older. The "Company" had established its forts not only from the Atlantic to the Pacific, but from the northern Arctic Ocean to the lower Sacramento and Columbia Rivers. During the 1860's the Russian-American company was doing poorly and the war with Britain in the Crimea had made the Russians fearful that if new hostilities arose they may not be able to hold their American colony.

A friendship existed between Russia and the United States which led to the withdrawal of Russia's American holdings. On March 29, 1867, Secretary of State William H. Seward and Baron Edouard Stoeckel, Russian Minister to the United States, completed the draft of a Treaty of Cession of Russian America to the United States at a purchase price of $7,200,000 (about 2 cents per acre). The next morning at 4 a.m., the treaty was signed during a special session of the Senate. It was Senator Charles Sumner who proposed that, under its new sovereignty, its name be "Alaska" (the Great Land). On October 18, 1867, the double-eagle ensign of Imperial Russia was lowered and the Stars and Stripes of the United States raised in its place over beautiful Sitka Harbor, first capital of the Alaska territory.

The *New York World* reported, "Russia has sold us a sucked orange." The *New York Daily News* of July 16, 1868, commented, "We wish Russia would consent to receive back the territory as a

Painting by Emmanuel Leutze "Treaty of Cession" from left to right: Chief Clerk Chew, William H. Seward, William Hunter, Waldemar Bodisco, Edouard de Stoeckl, Senator Charles Sumner, Frederick W. Seward.

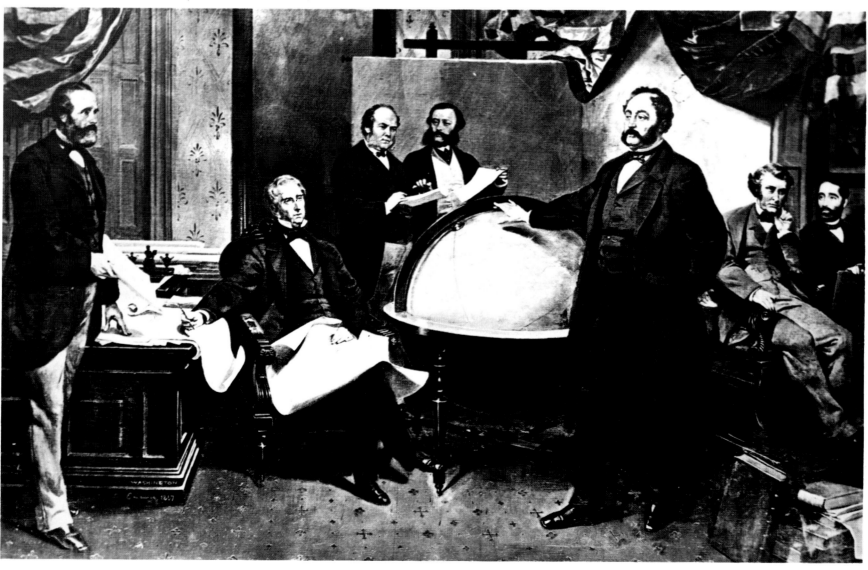

free gift from this Republic. We should deem it a very fortunate riddance." Others coined names for the Great Land such as "Seward's Ice Box", "Seward's Folly", and "Walrussia".

The first big "break" for Alaska came in the "Klondike". For thirty years after the Treaty of Cession, Alaska had been stumbling with obstacles placed before it through a general lack of interest from the United States.

"the Government of the United States, since the acquisition of this territory, instead of lighting the torch of freedom and keeping it brightly burning on these far-off shores, has by restriction — which is often worse than actual oppression — so retarded the growth and impeded the development of its material resources as to make the memory of the Russian autocratic regime appear a blessed thing by comparison with that which has come to it under our free institutions."

Henry E. Haydon
September 3, 1890

Midsummer 1897 brought the ship "Portland" back from St. Michaels, at the mouth of the Yukon, with "a ton of gold" aboard. The "rush" was on. Some sixty thousand headed north to Alaska. There were two principal routes. One was by boat from Seattle up the Inside Passage to Lynn Canal and then to the Klondike through either of two trails: the Chilkoot from Dyea, or the White Pass from Skagua (Skagway). The second route was across the Gulf of Alaska and through the Bering Sea to St. Michaels and then up the Yukon. Both routes were long, difficult and costly. Some never made it all the way and others perished. Of those who did

Prospecting in the Interior of Alaska

Courtesy of University of Alaska Archives — Charles Bunnell Collection

reach the Klondike some became rich and others even richer by supplying goods and services to the miners.

Overnight Skagway became a city of 20,000. In a mere six years the Klondike gave $100,000,000 in gold. The feverish, rough gold camps of Alaska made Seattle and Portland boom. Thousands gathered on the docks to watch the incredible spectacle of millions of dollars in gold unloaded. A new optimism spread throughout the world about Alaska's wealth; not just of gold, but silver, copper, platinum, coal, furs and timber.

It was now time for Congress to take a first hand look at Alaska. A Senate sub-committee reported that since cession Alaska had yielded the national treasury one million dollars above all the expenses of the federal government. The nation had gained a wealth of $52,000,000 in furs, $50,000,000 in fisheries, and $31,000,000 in gold.

In 1912 Alaska was granted territorial status. The new territory experienced other developments, but gold and salmon remained the main elements of its economy. After a long battle for statehood, on June 30, 1958, Congress approved legislation making Alaska the 49th state.

Most of the original 100,000 sourdoughs who came to Alaska to seek their fortunes are gone. However, there are still plenty of prospectors around and many active claims. At least $758 million in gold was taken out of Alaska and geologists report there is that much left.

The newest Alaska rush is for oil. Recoverable oil reserves on the North Slope have been estimated in a wide range from 10 billion to 30 billion barrels or more. For thousands of Alaskans — and certainly rural native Alaskans — poverty has been an accepted

Interior Alaska Indians

Courtesy of University of Alaska Archives — Charles Bunnell Collection

fact of life. During territorial days, particularly until the second world war, Alaska was a remote and somewhat neglected ward of the federal government. Financial strains imposed by statehood have prevented Alaska herself from correcting this situation. This should change when oil from Prudhoe Bay starts to flow. State revenues from North Slope production will amount to hundreds of millions of dollars annually, compared to a total state budget in 1969/70 of $168.8 million. In addition, the Native Claims Settlement Act will inject over $1 billion into the state's economy within this decade.

With careful planning and a judicial use of oil revenues, Alaska should have money for stable, long-term development and also be able to conserve the features of its unique environment. This is particularly so since development of an oil field like Prudhoe Bay creates the least possible environmental disturbance, particularly when compared to certain other resource industries. Alaska will have the money necessary to upgrade many of her critical problems of housing, education, medical care, and employment. She will have time to plan for the wise use of all her resources, including the safeguarding of the wilderness for the enjoyment of all.

The opportunities in Alaska have always challenged men's spirits. Those who have accepted this challenge hold the pioneer spirit of a young America, and are leading Alaska to the doorstep of the greatest economic development in the United States today.

HISTORY OF PETROLEUM

Petroleum, often called black gold, is a literal treasure chest of chemicals. The word "petroleum" is a derivative of two latin

Prospecting for oil in Katalla, Alaska. This is the Cudahy Company's oil outfit on the shores of Bering Lake.

Courtesy of University of Alaska — Barrett Willoughby Collection

words: petro - rock and oleum - oil. Containing hundreds of valuable chemicals, it is the earth's greatest source of energy providing needed products such as gasoline, heating oil and jet fuel plus the vast array of amazing new scientific products continually being developed.

Petroleum products are turning African deserts into useful fields and helping trees and grass to grow in areas that formerly were shifting sands. Sand dunes, when sprayed with an oil product whose coating prevents the grains of sand from being tossed about by the wind, retains water from occasional rains. Through this process, an area in North Africa turned tiny seedlings into eucalyptus trees six feet tall in one year.

The birth of the oil industry came on a Sunday afternoon, the 27th of August, 1859. In a small town in Western Pennsylvania, Titusville, Edwin L. Drake got a drill sixty-nine and a half feet into the ground and struck oil.

Edwin Drake was not the first man to bore a hole in the ground for the promise of oil, but his persistence after many failures made him an outstanding pioneer. Also his strike came at a time when America was in urgent need of fuel and lubricants — products that could be derived from oil.

Immediately after Drake's strike at Titusville, Pennsylvania, oil derricks dotted the landscapes of Ohio, West Virginia, and Kentucky. With this sudden increase in supply, the price of oil tumbled from $20.00 a barrel in 1859 to 10 cents a barrel in 1861. By the end of the 19th century, a dozen states were producing oil, and Pennsylvania surrendered leadership to Ohio — then California — then Oklahoma — then to Texas.

Good Friday Earthquake, 1964 in Anchorage, Alaska.

Courtesy of University of Alaska Archives — Alaska Air National Guard Photo

Industrial America grew rapidly during the 19th century and with new factories came new machinery. Castor oil served as one of the most common lubricants and oil from the castor bean was becoming scarce and expensive. In addition, sperm whales could not be harpooned fast enough to satisfy the growing lamp market.

Samuel M. Kier, "the Father of Modern Refining", separated the "rock oil" from the brine and began selling it as a medicine for burns, bruises, head colds, and a dozen other ailments. Kier experimented with crude oil to see if he could extract an illuminant from it that could replace whale oil. He heated the oil until it gave off vapors, and then brought them back into a liquid form by cooling.

In the early years of petroleum, transporting oil was as difficult as getting it out of the ground. There was no extensive network of railroads, trucks, and highways. Oil was first contained in barrels and moved by wagons, ships, barges and trains. The 42 gallon barrel still remains as the common unit for measuring oil.

Earliest barrels were made of wood and often leaked or split apart when bumped too hard as endless wagon trains carried them over the rough roads of Pennsylvania. Oil was also shipped in flat bottomed boats down creeks to the Allegheny, the main river of Pennsylvania. This was accomplished by impounding water behind a series of low dams and then let loose to form a flood tide that swept the vessels on their way.

In 1865, Samuel Van Syckel built the first successful oil pipeline, a two inch line connecting the Pennsylvania oil fields at Pithole with a railroad terminal five miles away. The first major pipeline was an engineering marvel of the day — and extended 110 miles across the Allegheny Mountains in Central Pennsylvania.

First commercial flight of Noel Wien

Courtesy of University of Alaska Archives — Noel Wien Collection

During an 1836 to 1839 coastal survey, Thomas Simpson, an explorer of the Hudson's Bay Company, observed deposits of oil along the Canadian Arctic shore. Simpson, who was the first traveler to reach Point Barrow from the east, could not have foreseen the effect of the presence of oil in the development of the north. In 1886 Ensign W.L. Howard, a member of the U.S. Navy's exploration expedition, made an extensive exploration of the North Slope. From the head of the Colville River he crossed the range to the Chipp River, tracing it to its mouth, then came back along the coast to Point Barrow. He brought back with him an oddity of nature, a specimen of oil he found near the upper Colville River.

A more recent discoverer was William Vanvalin, a teacher with the U.S. Bureau of Education assigned to the Arctic village of Wainwright. In 1914 Vanvalin hitched up his reindeer and made a 550 mile trip to investigate a report of an oil lake. Upon reaching the site he stated, "The sight that filled my eyes was most gratifying indeed. Two living springs of what appears like engine oil with their black beds winding over and down the hill."

Vanvalin was quite excited over what he saw and did not waste time staking his claim, which included the hill from which the oil oozed and the lake into which the springs drained. The lake acted as a death trap for fowl and animals careless enough to mistake the oil for water allowing Vanvalin to assume it may contain prehistoric fossils. Vanvalin put out his stakes and raised a sign naming his place the "Arctic Rim Mineral Oil Claim". He

North Slope pier and dock

then prepared to return the next summer and erect a house to comply with mining regulations of the day requiring a claim occupant to do at least $200 in location work to hold title.

At the same time Vanvalin was investigating his Smith Bay oil lake, E. deK. Leffingwell, a member of the U.S. Geological Survey, reported oil seepage about 50 miles southeast of Point Barrow. Alfred H. Brooks was the head of the Alaska Division of the U.S. Geological Survey, and was also known as the outstanding authority on the region. Brooks called upon the Arctic pioneer, Charles D. Brower, known as "King of the Arctic" to provide him with a sample of the seepage.

Brooks received other vague reports about seepages along the North Slope, however the region had not been surveyed and only a few of the sites located.

In 1921, two oil companies, Standard Oil of California and General Petroleum, examined seepages near Point Barrow and were encouraged by their findings. In August of 1922 these two companies received permission to drill on their Cold Bay claims from the Department of the Interior. However, they were not ready for the gamble of North Slope oil.

Alfred Brooks optimistic attitude of oil potential for the North Slope brought about a topographic and geologic survey of the area. In June of 1922 he told a group in Seattle, "I have every confidence in the world that oil will be found in Alaska, and probabilities are that there are extensive areas in the territory." This assessment of Brooks probably had much to do with the action of the federal government in creating Naval Petroleum Reserve No. 4 by Executive Order on February 27, 1923.

Arco Exxon installation at Prudhoe Bay.

"Whereas there are large seepages of petroleum along the Arctic coast of Alaska and conditions favorable to the occurrence of valuable petroleum fields on the Arctic coast;

and

Whereas the present laws designed to promote development seem imperfectly applicable in the region because of its distance, difficulties, and large expense of development:

and

Whereas the future supply of oil for the Navy is at all times a matter of national concern:

Now, therefore . . .

And President Warren G. Harding went on to designate the specific area to be set aside. The reserve comprised 35,000 square miles, extending from Icy Cape in the west to the Colville River on the east and bounded by the Arctic Ocean on the north and the Endicott Range on the south.

Secretary of Navy Fall had considered the transportation problem and stated: "In case further exploration should show the land worth developing, it would be necessary to erect huge storage tanks on the land to hold the oil until vessels could take it away during the three or four months in which the sea in that region is free from ice, or pipe it several hundred miles to Fort Hamlin on the Yukon, or to Fairbanks, on the Alaska Railway."

THE SPRING BREAK UP APRIL 30TH 1907 FAIRBANKS ALASKA.

The Navy then asked the Geological Survey to undertake a topographic and geologic survey of the entire area to determine the oil reserves. The Geologic Survey completed its work five years after starting in 1923, but timing was not right for an oil rush.

After the commencement of World War II, the Navy decided to make more extensive explorations throughout the North Slope.

From 1946 through 1953, the Brooks Range and foothills were covered by geologic mapping and seismic surveys. Also 36 wildcats and 44 core holes were drilled. The information gathered over this period revived the interest of the oil industry and they began to conduct their own explorations along the North Slope. The great Arctic oil boom was on.

The North Slope was opened for leasing in 1958 and at least ten dry holes were drilled before oil was discovered. In 1966 Atlantic Richfield, relying primarily on aircraft, moved more than five million pounds of equipment to the North Slope to begin preparations for drilling Susie Unit No. 1. Drilled to a depth of 13,500 feet, the well proved unsuccessful. The total cost of the dry hole was about $4.5 million, dramatizing the high risk nature of oil exploration.

The drilling rig was then moved 60 miles north of Susie to drill Prudhoe Bay State No. 1 on real estate leased by Atlantic Richfield, the operator, and Humble Oil and Refining Company. The Prudhoe Bay well was a major oil and gas find. Another rig was moved to a location seven miles southeast on the same geologic structure and drilling began on Sag River State No. 1 in 1968. This Sag River well confirmed a major discovery, which has been described as the largest in North America in 40 years.

The spring break up, April 30, 1907, Fairbanks.

Courtesy of University of Alaska Archives — Charles Bunnell Collection

Photographer R. Furniss

Two views of the North Slope. *Left:* Unloading a barge during the brief, ice-free summer. *Below:* "Break-up" begins.

Below: Sunset at Prudhoe Bay. "Sunset" at winter could be at high noon, and in summer at midnight.
Right: Arctic poppies on North Slope with drill rig in the background. These fragile flowers exist for only a few weeks during the brief arctic summer.

Photography B.P. Alaska — Maro Queen

Photography B.P. Alaska — Art Woleben

Photographer Rick Furniss

Photographer Jimmy Bedford

Left: Caribou grazing near permanent structures at North Slope. The caribou show little concern for man's presence, and have displayed no fear of crossing runways and other manmade obstacles. Permanent buildings on the North Slope are constructed on pilings to eliminate heat transfer and thawing of the permafrost. The space beneath the building prevents frequently blowing snow from accumulating in heavy drifts.

Below left: Barges frozen in ice at Prudhoe Bay. The barges are left year-around and are used as docking facilities during the four to six week summer period when the Beaufort Sea is accessible for marine traffic. *Below:* Sunrise over the Brooks Range. The North Slope lies between these mountains and the Arctic Ocean. These American Alps are the first of three major mountain ranges which the pipeline must cross.

Photographer Rick Furniss

Below: Living conditions within the permanent operations sites are comfortable and complete. Swimming pool is also the fire fighting reservoir. Trees are the only ones on the North Slope. *Right:* Exposed skin freezes quickly and is a constant danger in the Arctic winter.

Ellis Herwig

Dennis Cowals

Dennis Cowals

Ellis Herwig

Photography — B.P. Alaska

Below: North Slope drill rig operators. Because temperatures often reach 60 degrees below zero, working areas must be enclosed and heated. In these conditions men can work comfortably for their entire shifts in regular clothing.

Photography B.P. Alaska — Dennis Cowals

Below: Workers on the North Slope must wear extensive protective clothing to protect themselves from the frigid winter climate. *Right:* Airlines make daily flights to the North Slope in spite of weather conditions.

Photography B.P. Alaska

Photography B.P. Alaska

The Enco Gloucester performed anchorage tests in Valdez Harbor and Prince William Sound. The tanker Manhattan, fitted out as an ice-breaker, reached Prudhoe Bay via the Northwest Passage. However its progress was so slow and expensive as to eliminate the direct shipment consideration.

Photographer Bill Gasaway

ENVIRONMENTAL STUDIES

NATIVE ARTS AND CRAFTS

Upon conception of the trans Alaska pipeline, Alyeska began a series of ecological studies in the Arctic and subarctic. Alyeska wanted to know exactly what the pipeline would do to the environment and, in turn, what the environment would do to the pipeline. Environmental problems are of two kinds — those which concern the disturbance of fish, wildlife, and other environmental resources, and those which could affect the integrity of the pipeline and could therefore conceivably cause oil spills (e.g., permafrost, erosion, possible seismic action, and river scour).

The amount of technical preplanning and the extent of environmental studies undertaken in preparation for the project were unprecedented. Personnel performed research in the fields of biology, botany, zoology, geology, seismology, archeology, marine biology and oceanography. Much of the research has never been done before and will continue throughout this decade.

During the construction of a project of this magnitude, the environment is going to be disturbed. However, our decade marks the beginning of a new awareness, and a turning point when quality of life has become more than just a phrase, and a truly sincere concern. The peoples of the world have begun to recognize that we are just a small part of a large ecosystem and our actions can have both positive and disastrous effects on that system. The ecological challenge is to assure that construction disturbance will not result in anything past temporary scarring. The stipulations of the Bureau of Land Management cover a wide range of environmental factors including air, water, thermal pollution, permafrost protection, aesthetics, wildlife and fisheries protection, revegetation, and preservation of archeological findings, to mention a few.

Alaskan archeologists, with the assistance of the Bureau of Land Management, had a field day. During 1969 the Bureau of Land Management published a 50 page book of stipulations to be imposed on Alyeska Pipeline Service Company. Section L states that all archeological, paleontological or historical sites are to be investigated and protective measures taken. This Antiquities Act gave the archeologist authority to suspend operations or to re-route sections of the pipeline or its adjoining roads where necessary to excavate or preserve sites.

Alyeska Pipeline Service Company executed a contract with the University of Alaska to do the archeological work. The Arctic Institute of North America and the Bureau of Land Management also supplied archeological and anthropological consultants.

During a period of three summer seasons the entire 800-mile route of the proposed pipeline was examined. Archeologists worked with pipeline crews from the main Alyeska camps. John P. Cook, chairman of the Department of Anthropology at the University of Alaska, stated he was impressed by the cooperation between Alyeska Pipeline Service Company and the archeological crews. Crews were dropped off by Alyeska helicopters at one point along the pipeline in the morning and picked up in the evening for transportation back to the main camp. Areas impossible to cover on foot were surveyed from low-flying helicopters.

Reports indicate that about 189 sites were tested or excavated, and of those about 90 would have been affected by pipeline construction. More than 8500 catalogue entries were made — some from sites as much as 13,000 years old.

Beyond the archeological evidence recovered, the project set an important precedent in archeology. In the past, federal, state, and commercial construction and exploitation have destroyed many valuable archeology sites. Alyeska Pipeline Service Company spent a total of $227,000 on the archeological search, surveys, and excavations.

Very little detailed information was known about the types, characteristics, and location of the permafrost underlying the pipeline route. Permafrost is any material which has been frozen for two or more consecutive years. About 80% of the line will pass through permafrost area. The oil development area of the North Slope is a flat arctic plain, underlain with continuous permafrost, dotted with thousands of ponds and lakes and numerous streams and rivers. Although the tundra layer is frozen at the surface during winter, it becomes a soggy, impossible quagmire during the summer. A delicate relationship exists between the tundra and the underlying permafrost. A disruption or break in the insulating cover of the tundra, allowing ice-rich permafrost to thaw, could lead to erosion. Where erosion occurs, surface scars are slow to heal because of the very slow rate of growth of arctic vegetation. In certain areas the pipe, which will be heated to approximately 145°, is to be placed in the frozen material. As a result of the warm pipe a thaw bulb develops, which after a year may spread out to 20 or 30 feet in diameter. A 600-foot experimental pipe was installed at Fairbanks for test purposes, and actually simulates operating conditions under various ice and soil conditions. Through testing the rate of thaw is shown to be predictable.

The melting of permafrost can have a wide range of effects on soil performance. Low-ice content permafrost, such as exists in many well drained areas may be thawed with little or no harm to the pipe or the environment. Conversely, permafrost of high-ice content could present serious problems on thawing, some of which are differential soil settlement, loss of slope stability, potential for soil liquefication and erosion. In areas such as these the pipe will not be buried, but constructed on elevated supports.

In an effort to determine the best route, Alyeska Pipeline Service Company initiated the most extensive soil study program ever undertaken for a construction project. The entire route was surveyed and high and low aerial pictures obtained. In addition, remote sensing techniques were utilized including airborne thermal scanners, airborne ground probe radar and airborne side lock radar. These operations were followed with field exploration and drilling operations which have resulted in thousands of individual soil analyses.

No heat is intentionally introduced into the system since the oil leaves the well at about 175°F. Cooling the oil to below freezing temperatures to prevent melting of permafrost is considered unpractical. Cooling methods to satisfactorily handle the volume of throughput have not been developed. Cooling would also result in the deposition of 1,400 tons per day of wax, some of which would be deposited along the walls of the pipe resulting in the need for frequent scraping. There could also be the danger of crude oil solidifying in the pipeline should pumping stop, which would make it difficult to restart. In addition, the frictional flow of the thick viscous oil would generate heat and raise the temperature. These basic factors resulted in the decision to transport warm oil.

Four earthquake fault systems, which have shown movement in recent geologic times, occur within the vicinity of the pipeline. One of these, the Denali Fault, is actually known to intersect the route. Special above ground construction techniques will be employed at this point which will enable the line to withstand a horizontal movement and a vertical displacement exceeding that anticipated by the most severe earthquake.

An earthquake fault is a fracture in the earth. When the earth moves or shifts on either side of a fracture, waves of energy are released which cause the crust of the earth to tremble and quake, hence the name for this phenomenon: earthquake. For purposes of pipeline design, engineers have considered an "active" fault as one ". . . having potential for displacement at the ground surface during the design life of the line (30 years)"

The pipeline is being built to withstand the most severe earthquake ever recorded anywhere along the route. The pipeline has been designed to operate without interruption during a quake of half the ground motion of the most severe quake, and to shut down — without failing — at the most severe levels. At Valdez, the terminal facilities are being built on bedrock, well above the level of potential tsunami (seismically generated sea waves). All the facilities are out of reach of these waves except the fixed and floating berths which are designed to resist forces resulting from a 12-foot wave when a ship is in berth and a 20-foot wave without a vessel alongside. Also all of the storage tanks will be surrounded by dikes to contain any spilled oil.

Statistical possibility is low that there will be movement along the Denali Fault during the life of the pipeline. However, in the event of movement, the pipeline across the fault is being built to withstand 20 feet of lateral movement and five feet of vertical displacement. If the line should break, a spill would be limited by valves and design to 5,000 barrels of oil.

The pipe is 48 inches in diameter and has been supplied in thicknesses of .452 inches and .562 inches, in three grades. Different grades are used in different locations depending on the pressure and stress in each section. The pipe also has a special coating and a cathodic protection system to prevent bacteriological, chemical or electrolytic corrosion.

During tests at the University of California at Berkeley a pipe section was subjected to an axial force of 2.52 million pounds and a lateral deflection force of 459,000 pounds before wrinkling. Tests that simulate the worst conceivable conditions have assured the pipe's hardness, shear strength, bendability, ductility, weldability and tensile strength.

One significant result of the tests at Berkeley is the high degree of ductility demonstrated by the pipe. The deformation required to cause a crack is very large. Deflection before failure was observed to be between 7.5 feet and 12.5 feet of differential settlement over a 100-foot span. Another significant result of the Berkeley tests is that there has been no detectable effect of a large wrinkle on the ability of the pipe to withstand internal pressure. In addition, once the pipe is in place it will undergo a period of additional intensive testing. It has been shown that in the event of a sudden upward or downward force the line would crimp rather than part or rupture.

A specially instrumented pipeline "pig" has been developed which will be able to detect any deflection or out-of-roundness. This "pig" will be able to determine deflection changes of about one inch over a distance of 87 feet and ovality changes of 1/4 of an inch. The "pig" will be run through the pipeline at regular intervals and detect critical problems long before a wrinkle could develop.

In areas of active earthquake activity, a seismic monitoring system will be installed. Seismic monitoring includes geodetic nets, monument alignment, creep meters and strong motion seismographic monitors. These monitoring systems will be able to determine the rate of fault creep and initiate shutdown of the pipeline at designated levels of seismic shock. One of the greatest risks from earthquakes results from landslides and potential liquefication of soils; therefore, data from soil investigations have been utilized to carefully select the route, thus avoiding difficult soil areas and terrain.

Vegetative cover provides one of the most important elements for prevention of erosion. A program for revegetation of disturbed areas was initiated by the Institute of Arctic Biology and the Alaska Agricultural Experiment Station.

Forty different plant species were tested at twenty sites along the pipeline right-of-way. The tests using different levels of fertilization were tested in various soil conditions under both alpine and high permafrost conditions. Data from this research has been used to develop a revegetation system employing various grass mixes, which are capable of rapidly restoring vegetative cover. These grasses will hold the soil and provide biotic insulation until the natural vegetation grows back in five to seven years. Depending upon conditions, other erosion control techniques will be employed. These will include mulches, benches, diversion barriers and riprap.

During various studies the State, Bureau of Land Management and Alyeska have identified the major animals encountered and their distribution. The two which are of particular concern are the Dall sheep and caribou. The Dall sheep are of particular interest because the pipeline traverses one of their lambing and lick areas in the vicinity of the Atigun Valley. Accordingly, construction has been arranged so that any activity in the area will exert a minimal effect upon their normal reproductive activities.

About 450,000 caribou are known to graze during the summer on the North Slope. Studies have shown that with the exception of the Nelchina herd, caribou generally migrate parallel to the pipeline.

Above ground sections of the line are short enough so caribou can move around them. However, in critical areas the pipe is being buried below ground or installed high enough so the animals can pass beneath it.

Through research it has been found that in about thirteen areas construction passes through waterfowl nesting areas. One of the areas of highest concentration is on the North Slope where studies have indicated 18 to 20 nesting pair may occur per square mile. Surveys have also shown a low density of nesting pairs along most of the pipeline route south to Valdez. Construction schedules are arranged to avoid these high density breeding areas.

Concern over the transportation of crude oil from Port Valdez to West Coast ports has focused on potential hazards to marine ecosystems in the Port Valdez-Prince William Sound area of Alaska. Alyeska requested that Battelle Pacific Northwest Laboratories conduct acute and chronic bioassays to delineate possible hazards to the indigenous biota resulting from the discharge. Main objectives of this study were to: determine acute and chronic toxicity levels of simulated treated ballast on the biota; and to measure the degree of hydrocarbon accumulation within tissues of selected organisms.

Chronic and acute bioassays were conducted in a mobile laboratory at Valdez using simulated treated ballast. The simulated ballast and treatment operations were designed per Alyeska (or ASPC) instructions to reproduce the actual operations of the port facility. Oil content, aging, chemical flocculation and air flotation used in the simulation procedure were as proposed by Alyeska (or APSC) in the actual operations.

NATIVE ARTS AND CRAFTS

Authentic examples of Alaskan arts and crafts are not common examples of household items as too much time and care is put into each creation to expect wide availability. Each item is made as it was generations ago, with the same materials, patience, attention to detail, and skill. At the same time, new techniques are being experimented with by creative individuals who use their cultural heritage as a point of departure for artistic growth and development. In Anchorage, ANAC (Alaska Native Arts and Crafts Co-op) represents Native Alaskan artisans and craftsmen from more than a hundred villages and towns and offers only authentic, handmade native arts and crafts.

The "Silver Hand Label Program" is sponsored by the State of Alaska's Department of Economic Development. Labels are made available to Alaska Natives so that they may market their work through various outlets and still receive proper recognition.

Native Arts and Crafts copy and photography provided through the courtesy of the Alaska Native Arts and Crafts Co-op in Anchorage, Alaska.

IVORY

Alaskan ivory comes from the walrus that inhabit the Arctic Ocean and Bering Sea areas. Walrus herds generally migrate north in the spring, and at that time the villages along the coast harvest the animal for a variety of uses. Although the walrus provides the main meat supply for many villages the year around, it is a renewable resource, in the same sense that cattle are, and the impact of the Alaskan Native on the walrus herds is far below the herd growth level. The walrus is in no danger of becoming extinct.

The ivory tusk of the walrus protrudes downward from the upper jaw, extending as much as three feet. The tusk has three layers: an inner core of light tan, dark tan and white; a second layer of soft white; and an outer shell that, when properly worked, can be polished to a brilliant sheen. The ivory is found in three basic forms, identifiable by coloration. New ivory, or that which has been recently harvested, is the gleaming white color described above, while old ivory, like that commonly found along beaches, is usually tan or brown from exposure to the elements. Fossilized ivory, the third basic form, is often very dark from having been buried in the permafrost for many years.

BASKETS

The most notable aspect of Alaskan Native basketry is its reluctance to change from a utilitarian to a strictly decorative concept. Art and beauty, to the Alaskan cultures, are intricately interwoven with history, tradition and survival needs. The usefulness of an item, from the native point of view, is as inherently beautiful as the mere eye appeal.

Each of the five major Alaskan cultures has its own distinctive style of basketry. These baskets were designed for carrying fish or water, or for other utilitarian uses. Dryness is the chief enemy of these kinds of materials, and grass objects should be handled often to allow natural skin oils to penetrate and preserve.

WOOD

The Tlingit culture of Southeastern Alaska is highly developed and elaborate, involving a system of dual clans, each with a series of sub-clans. The Eagle and the Wolf clans are the two major divisions, and these are subdivided into the Bear, the Frog, the Whale, and other species of sea and land animal life. The Haida culture is divided into four major clans. The positive qualities of the animal chosen to represent the clan are assigned to the clan, and the image of the animal commonly appears, often in very stylized form, on the totemic designs and other carvings of clan craftsmen.

The totemic designs produced by this culture are meant both to transmit information and serve as decoration for villages and homes. Elaborate stories are conveyed in subtle fashion in the careful carvings, and the stories and symbols are reproduced and passed down through the generations in the form of miniature totem poles, masks, plaques, and other ceremonial objects.

SKIN

The durability and practicality of skin and fur garments has been proven over the years under some of the harshest climatic conditions imaginable. Temperatures of forty and fifty degrees below zero are not unusual along the Arctic coast, and the native hunter and fisherman has had to rely heavily on the strength and insulating qualities of his clothing.

Although there have been certain style changes, along with the introduction of non-skin liner materials to supplement the skin or fur, skin sewing remains today basically what it has been since the earliest presence of native cultures in Alaska. The hair seal is still the most abundant source of raw material for the craftsman, and protection from the elements is still the controlling idea behind the craft.

While seal hide is the most common substance used for skin garments, the manufacture of skin clothing is by no means restricted to seal hides. Moose, caribou and reindeer skins are also used, and, to a lesser extent, so are muskrat, wolverine, badger, fox, beaver, and mink skins. Thread used for sewing the skin has traditionally been sinew, an animal fiber drawn from muscle tissue, but modern synthetic materials like nylon and dental floss are often substituted because of their greater strength.

BONE

The artistic use of bone is another example of the waste-not ingenuity of the Alaskan Native. The gigantic rib bones of the whale are used for making drying racks and skin boats. The vertabrae of the same animal can be used to form intriguing mask designs, and the disks that separate the vertabrae are sometimes used as the bases for ivory carvings.

The bones of smaller animals are also used in many ways. The antlers, jawbone and hooves of the caribou can be made into cribbage boards, sleds, or even jewelry, and odd shaped pieces of bone, like the walrus skull, can form the base for a bird rookery.

STONE

New ideas and much originality are displayed in soapstone carvings by young native craftsmen, including variations on traditional cultural themes. This innovation reflects not so much a departure from traditional values, as it does the growth and dynamics of a viable culture in a changing environment.

Although many varieties of soapstone can be found across Alaska, little or none that is quarried in the state is suitable to the style of carvings crafted. The stone must be imported from quarries outside the state, adding to the craftsman's expense. Also, the size of the carvings has been limited by the small blocks of stone usually received. Recently, as larger pieces have come into the hands of the artist, larger and more detailed carvings have become available.

The hallmark of authentic native soapstone carving is a careful attention to detail and the integration of additional materials into the carving. Wood and ivory are at times used to enhance the completed image.

GRAPHICS

The problems involved in producing graphics in "bush" areas are considerable. Because of a chronic lack of space for an adequate studio environment, along with the problem of inks and paints being ruined by freezing while stored at home, much of the native graphics work is done while the artist is in school or studying in an urban area. These conditions create a scarcity, and in order to have these graphics available to a broad audience, commercial presses are sometimes used to reproduce them. This is especially true in the case of greeting cards.

Photographer James Drummond

Department of Interior hearings. In August, 1969, the Department of Interior held the first public hearings on the pipeline project in Fairbanks. Here issues were raised which were to grow into the five year controversy which preceded the issuance of a permit by the United States Government.

The contractors have undertaken an unprecedented program of protecting the environment. Some of the rules: no guns in camps; no hunting or fishing within five miles of the pipeline corridor; littering is cause for dismissal — so is feeding the wildlife; vehicles may be driven only on roads or predesignated trails; no disruption of lambing, spawning, and nesting seasons.

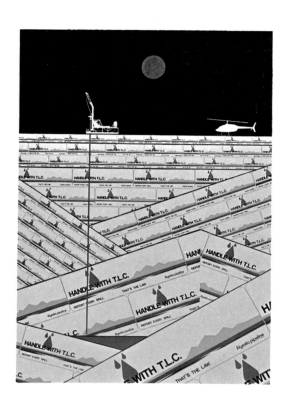

You feel insignificant out here

...you're not!

Please, do not disturb the animals. They were here first.

Alyeska pipeline
SERVICE COMPANY

Hot pipe tests. Near Fairbanks, where temperatures reach 40° below zero, tests were undertaken to obtain information about heat transfer and permafrost, and to test insulation, valves and other engineering assumptions.

Below: University of Alaska revegetation research. In a contract with Alyeska the University of Alaska conducted research to define fast-growing perennials and annual grasses with which to reseed disturbed areas after construction. These grasses will hold the soil and provide biotic insulation until the natural vegetation grows back in five to seven years. Much of the research has been basic research — research that has never before been done and will continue throughout the seventies. *Right:* Surveying the pipeline route.

University of Alaska teams carefully sift through all potential archeological sites along the pipeline corridor. Significant new information has been found about the history of Indians and the first occupants of Alaska. The University, under contract with Alyeska Pipeline Service Company, will spend the next several years analysing and evaluating material and information obtained from these digs.

Photograph Courtesy of Battelle Pacific Northwest Laboratories

Above: Oceanographic laboratory. This mobile lab was used in research conducted for nearly a year at Valdez. The Battelle Institute was one of several contractors applying marine research under contract with Alyeska Pipeline Service Company. *Right:* Marine research. Among the many questions to be answered about the suitability of Valdez Harbor were questions about marine life, tidal and current action, ocean floor compositions and weather cycles.

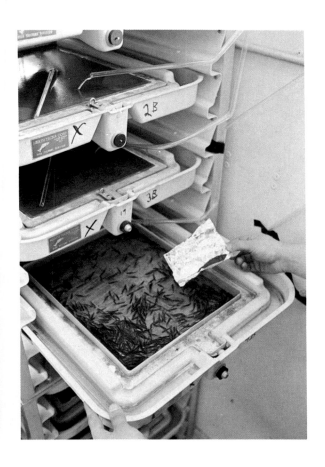

Below: Prince William Sound is the closest ice-free year around port, 800 miles away from Prudhoe Bay. Valdez Harbor, well protected from winds and heavy seas, offers a nearly ideal location for port facilities. *Right:* Valdez terminal models.

Photographer Barbara Winkley

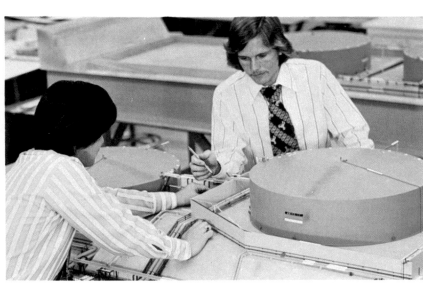 

Below: Eskimo hunters paddle unimak toward walrus pod in the Bering Sea. *Right:* Seal hunter.

Photographer Rick Furniss

Photographer Rick Furniss

Below: Eskimo women cutting up whale meat. In some Eskimo villages life continues without change to basic subsistence living. Culture intrusions have not eliminated all the "old ways". *Right:* Eskimo woman preparing salmon for drying. The trans Alaska pipeline will undoubtedly affect the culture of native Alaskans. Many natives who have followed a subsistence style of living and whose roots are in primitive cultures will face abrupt changes of life style. As the state experiences explosive economic growth, native corporations received $44 million in contracts with Alyeska during the first year alone and Alyeska committed 3500 other job opportunities to Alaska Natives. State and federal agencies monitor the project to insure minority — especially native — participation.

Photographer Rick Furniss

Photographer Barbara Winkley

Below: Eskimo dancers at Savoonga, St. Lawrence Island. *Right:* Caribou. The animal which received the most controversial attention was the caribou. The pipeline route encounters migrating patterns of two major caribou herds. The route runs parallel in one case and crosses a known migratory path only once. This animal is the source for subsistence living by some native Alaskans, even today.

Photographer Rick Furniss

Photographer Bill Gasaway

Below: A serene firelight evening sky in Southwest Alaska. *Right:* Caribou carcasses are tied together in a raft and floated down stream to native villages.

Photographer Barbara Winkley

Photographer Bill Gasaway

Willow Ptarmigan

Photographer G. C. Kelley

Horned Owl

Dall Ram   *Photographer G. C. Kelley*

Photographer G. C. Kelley

Arctic Ground Squirrel

Tidal Bowl page 76 and 77 by Barbara Winkley

Photographer David Brown

Left: Aurora Borealis. These are strings or columns of lights appearing at night visible throughout Alaska. Said to be of electrical origin, their spectacular beauty can best be seen from Arctic areas. The Aurora Australis is a similar luminous phenomenon in the southern hemisphere, and the only other aurora to be seen. *Below:* Autumn colors of the high country looking toward Mt. McKinley.

Photographer Bill Gasaway

THE MANAGEMENT CONTRACTORS

The Bechtel Corporation, with world headquarters in San Francisco, was founded in the late 1890's and has grown to include divisions in virtually every type of construction. One of the largest construction companies in the world, its experience includes the Churchill Falls hydro-electric complex in Labrador, the Fos Sur Mer steel and industrial complex in France, and the multinational Trans-Alpine pipeline which extends from the Adriatic coast near Trieste through the Alps to West Germany. Bechtel is the leading constructor of pipelines in the world, with experience in deserts, mountains and underwater in Africa, Europe, North and South America and the Far East. The company uniquely qualified as Construction Management Contractor — Pipeline and Roads.

The terminal and pump stations are the responsibility of Fluor, Alaska Inc., selected by Alyeska as Construction Management Contractor — Terminal and Pump Stations. Fluor also acts as general contractor for the port facility. Fluor is a company whose experience in the oil industry is unique. Approximately 60 years old, the giant has functioned in both the construction and operation of processing plants for petroleum and other base products around the world. Its oil drilling operations have taken the company onto platforms and drill-ships in the Gulf of Mexico, the Mediterranean, the Mid-East and Indonesia and the Far East. Fluor has worked in radioactive waste solidification (conversion from liquid) and coal gasification, and claims from its broad experience a respect and understanding for the environment and for adverse working conditions. Added to these credentials is the fact that the company had previous experience in Alaska, an important asset in competing for the Management contract.

THE LEGAL ISSUES

After their preliminary feasibility study in 1968, Arco, Humble (now Exxon) and British Petroleum announced plans for constructing a 48-inch pipeline nearly 800 miles from Prudhoe Bay to Valdez, and in June of 1969 they filed for permit with the Bureau of Land Management in Anchorage. Public hearings were held by the Interior Department in Fairbanks, followed by the release of draft stipulations to protect the environment. The oil companies, anticipating issuance of the permit, had already ordered the pipe at a cost of $100 million.

In December of the same year Congress enacted the National Environmental Protection Act. About four months later suits were filed in U.S. District Court seeking injunctions against the issuance of construction permits. Basically, the suits were issues of land title ownership, or native claims and environmental protection. Both points required legislative action to reach resolution. The Congress ultimately solved the issue of native claims by enactment of the Native Claims Settlement Act, which provides for payment of 962.5 million to Alaska Natives and the award to them of some 40 million acres of land.

The issues of the environmentalists were settled less directly. The major points of the initial suit concerned application of the National Environmental Protection Act. The courts found ultimately in favor of Interior but the plaintiffs added a new feature to their complaint, that feature being the width limitation set forth in the Mineral Leasing Act of 1920. It was this point on which the permit was stopped until Congress modified the Act in 1973. Again, the trans Alaska pipeline differed from other pipeline projects; permits had been issued for similar easements for more than twenty years.

THE INTERVAL

Between the confirmation of oil in July of 1968 and the beginning of construction in April, 1974, the trans Alaska pipeline concept became one of the most controversial and hotly debated issues of modern industry and resource development.

The climate of the country and the world changed, not just in the areas of energy and environmental awareness but in other equally abrupt ways. Unforeseeable at the time of first filing for federal permits were the rapid increase of inflation rates, citizen and grass roots involvement in issues, a world shortage in some basic construction materials and equipment, new requirements for industry, and changes in traditional international trade agreements. All of these had their effects on the developmental process and each required heavy investments of time and dollars. Absolute commitments to proceed could not be reached until all considerations were accounted for — and the issues changed as rapidly as they were resolved. As preparations and issues continued, cost projections escalated. From the original estimate of $900 million, the projected cost at the beginning of construction was $4.5 billion, an increase of 500%. The cost increases, now estimated at $5.982 billion, reflect engineering and design changes as well as inflation and unprecedented labor costs. Since the project is to be built by private capital for an expected profit return, the principal companies of Alyeska were constantly faced with the question of reasonable return on investment. The delay caused two certain results: a better pipeline system, and a much higher cost.

Clearly, the trans Alaska pipeline is better designed and more studied than any other construction project in history. The research and design phases utilized a record 1,500 man years in environmental studies, environmentally sound construction and operation methods — many of which are innovative, technical descriptions and reviews. Final design is engineered to a level referred to as "aerospace redundancy", implying state-of-the-art technology (highest known engineering perfection) and backup systems for all critical systems. Route selection, for example, was accomplished only after many studies of physical and environmental viability and of market accommodation. The question of how to get the oil out of the Arctic was necessarily tied to the question of where to take it.

Issues fell to engineers for technological answers, to governmental agencies to protect state and national interests, to the courts for settlements of disputes under existing laws, and to state and national legislatures to develop new laws. Others had no natural forum and were included in all the arenas. As late as 1973, the House Interior and Insular Affairs committee was still taking testimony on the persistent question of an alternative trans-Canada route.

ROUTE SELECTION

The final pipeline route and sites for pump stations and terminal were selected after careful studies of eight possible routes and four possible terminal locations.

The start of the line at Prudhoe Bay was fixed by the location of the North Slope oil fields. The four possible terminal locations were south central Alaska ports at Whittier, Seward, shores of Cook Inlet and Valdez.

Valdez was finally chosen because it permitted construction of the shortest possible route and offered an excellent port. A port at Valdez would be ice-free throughout the year and well protected from the open sea. A further advantage was that sufficient land is available for construction of a tank farm on bedrock, and sufficient elevation to permit the loading of ships by gravity flow.

Upon selecting Valdez as the southern terminal, the route was further defined by the selection of major mountain and river crossings. Dietrich Pass was chosen in place of Anaktuvuk Pass in the Brooks Range largely because of soil conditions and route length, although Dietrich Pass is higher than Anaktuvuk.

The Yukon river crossing had to be made along the short stretch of Rampart Canyon where the river is narrowest. Alyeska Pipeline Service Company is sharing the cost of a highway bridge across the Yukon with the State of Alaska, and using it as a crossing structure for the pipeline.

Because ice-rich permafrost is such a difficult material to work in, the ideal route would have as little ice-rich material as possible. Ice-rich soil can cause serious problems if thawed by the warm oil passing through the pipeline. If the soil is not ice-rich, and therefore thaw stable, it doesn't matter if it is thawed.

A detailed soil exploration program was started in 1970. Holes were first drilled from Valdez to Prudhoe Bay on an average of a half-mile apart to examine land forms and to verify information obtained from aerial photography. This soil exploration program cost as much as $10,000 a hole. Alyeska, often with the assistance of helicopters to protect the terrain, drilled in excess of 3,000 holes and took 30,000 core samples.

A geologist with the drilling crew logged every hole and recorded the type of soil and its condition. These cores were then kept frozen and laboratory tested in either Fairbanks, Alaska or Oakland, California.

Two categories of tests were conducted. First an index test for moisture content, plasticity liquid limit, grain size and distribution density, specific gravity, etc. The second tests were for strength, consolidation and thaw strain, which is an indication of the amount of soil settlement when permafrost thaws.

In addition to geological testing, environmental, archeological and ecological features were identified and researched as outlined earlier in this volume. Efforts were also made to minimize the length of the line, maximize buried construction in stable soils, reduce extensive grading and side hill construction, and bypass population centers.

THE ROAD NORTH OF THE ARCTIC CIRCLE

Construction of the pipeline required construction of America's first all-season highway to be built across the Arctic Circle. Construction of the Yukon-Prudhoe Bay road got underway on April 29, 1974.

Four contractors working on eight road segments pressed both north and south building the road as rapidly as possible. The 28 foot wide gravel road was laid out so as to disturb terrain features as little as possible. On stable subgrade soil the road has a three foot gravel base; on less stable soil the base is from five to six feet thick.

Bridges with steel pilings, and decked with timbers, spanned distances of 90 feet or more over 20 major creek and river crossings. The bridges have a maximum length of 420 feet, a clear roadway width of 24 feet and were built in 30 and 60-foot span lengths. The steel piles have a minimum bearing capacity of 30 tons. Openings beneath the bridges were designed to provide a four foot minimum clearance above the level of a so-called 50-year flood (the highest water expected during that period of time). In some cases ice fins were installed to protect the bridges from ice flows and debris during high water. These fins absorb the impact of floating ice and debris by diverting it away from piers and pilings. Numbers were enormous, both in the air and on the ground. Trucks hauled over 31 million cubic yards of gravel and another million cubic yards of rock while airplanes hauled 160,000 tons of supplies and material and over 8.6 million gallons of fuel. More than 60 aircraft — both helicopters and fixed wing transports — flew more than 127,000 flights, or about 700 a day, to remote airports.

Construction camps kept daily letters on their efforts, challenging nearby camps to surpass them and bragging and boasting about their progress. With competition running high and work loads sizably increased, the initial overlay on the road was completed September 29, 1974, only 154 days after starting. It was finished to State of Alaska secondary standards in mid-November.

PIPELINE DESIGN

The pipeline, which will extend from Prudhoe Bay to Valdez, is being built in three modes, depending on environmental, terrain and soil conditions. The temperature of the oil at Prudhoe Bay will be as high as 180° as it comes out of the ground. By the time the oil is received at the pipeline from producers on the North Slope, the temperature will have dropped somewhat, but will still remain at about 130° to 145°F. Due to hydraulic friction, the oil will remain warm as it passes through the line. Because the pipeline will traverse arctic and subarctic regions in which permafrost is prevalent, differential settlement and other soil stability features resulting from thawing by the warm oil are significant design considerations. The effect of heat on soils, particularly with respect to permafrost, will determine the mode of installing the pipe along the route.

Note: Construction modes are illustrated on pages 100 and 101.

CONVENTIONAL BURIAL

In stable soil conditions, the pipe will be buried in a conventional manner, which is the typical method employed in laying thousands of miles of pipeline in the United States. Conventional burial is being used in areas where soil is either bedrock, thaw-stable sand and gravel or thawed soil; or where the results of a detailed field exploration program and analysis demonstrate that soil settlement or instability resulting from thawing would not cause unacceptable disruption of the terrain.

About 409 miles of the pipeline is being installed conventionally. Burial depths will range from 18 inches minimum (in rock) to occasional depths greater than 12 feet, depending on pipe loading, bends, terrain and soil properties at each location.

ABOVE GROUND

In areas of the pipeline route where melting of the permafrost might cause excessive deformation of the pipe or create difficult soil stability conditions, the line is being installed above the ground.

About 382 miles of the pipeline is being installed in this manner.

In the above ground mode the pipe is covered with four inches of resin-impregnated fibrous glass insulation, jacketed with galvanized steel. The pipe is then mounted on support platforms, 50 to 70 feet apart.

The oil pipe is clamped in a saddle assembly and placed on a crossbeam installed between two vertical support members placed into the ground. So that thawing will not occur around the platform supports, a special thermal device will be installed as required inside many of them to keep the ground frozen. These thermal devices consist of metal tubes filled with a refrigerant which evaporates and condenses, thereby chilling the ground, whenever the ground temperature exceeds the temperature of the air. The devices are non-mechanical and self-operating.

The frozen soil below the pipeline, is in some instances, is overlain with gravel pads containing a layer of plastic foam insulation.

SPECIAL BURIED CONSTRUCTION

For several short sections where soil conditions are unsuitable for either the conventional or above ground construction modes, a special burial technique is being used. The pipe is being buried and then frozen into the ground. This method is being employed in seven places, some of them crossings for caribou and other animals. In the special burial mode the pipe is insulated with three inches of polyurethane foam and covered with a resin-reinforced fiber-glass jacket. Refrigerated brine will be pumped through pipes buried beneath the pipeline to keep the ground frozen. These refrigeration units are powered by electric motors.

EXPANSION

The above ground pipe is expanded by the movement of the warm oil. Because of this expansion the pipe is being secured in a saddle assembly and mounted on a sliding shoe which can slide on the crossbeam (See illustration on page 100). As the line expands, the pipe will be able to slide across the beam. As it contracts, the pipe will be free to slide back.

For stabilization the pipe will also be anchored in position on special platforms at the end of each zigzag configuration (every 800 to 1800 feet).

At the Denali Fault, special long-width support beams are being installed to permit still more movement. The pipeline at the fault line is being built to withstand a fault displacement of up to 20 feet sideways and five feet vertically.

CONCLUSION

As the pipeline project finishes its first actual construction season the need for the oil it will carry continues to increase. The United States consumption of oil and oil products is at a rate of approximately 17 million barrels per day (17 MBD). By 1980, when the trans Alaska pipeline should reach full capacity, the U.S. demand is projected to be 23 MBD. Excluding the Prudhoe Bay oil, U.S. production is projected to be 10 MBD, leaving a shortfall of 13 MBD, which will probably be imported. Three major problems with this are: 1. the high and unpredictable cost of foreign oil 2. the unreliability, as the country has already experienced, of foreign sources 3. a crushing deficit to U.S. balance of payments. The instability of the U.S. dollar in world markets during 1973 and 1974 was caused primarily by a balance of payments deficit which, in total, is less than the above projections would create in oil purchases alone. It appears that, in fact, the United States could not pay for that large amount of imported oil.

In 1975 plans for the distribution of Prudhoe Bay oil are that it will all be brought by tanker from Valdez to ports in Washington and California. Continuing projections of supply and demand in 1980 show that the West Coast of the United States will require 3 MBD and produce 1 MBD (This production figure excludes re-opening of off-shore California operations). The shortfall of 2 MBD will be totally met by Alaska production. Since the import of this quantity would be a relatively assured fact, the North Slope oil will simply displace imports and add a few significant advantages. Foreign vessels and crews will be replaced by U.S. tankers and crews. The balance of payments benefits, figured at $10 a barrel, will equal about $2 billion annually (more, as the price of oil goes up). Tanker traffic in ports will be reduced because of the large sizes planned for the Alaska trade.

The law requires that all oil transported through the pipeline be shipped only to domestic ports. None of the crude, then, will be exported to foreign countries with only one possible exception: the President of the United States must declare export to be in the national interest and that declaration must be ratified by the Congress; should both those conditions be met exportation would be legal.

"Proved reserves at the North Slope are conservatively estimated at 9.6 billion barrels." That is the careful statement of oil companies regarding our northern resources. However, it only begins to touch on the matter. Naval Petroleum Reserve No. 4, known as Pet 4, is a field which is also on the Arctic Coastal Plain. This plain includes a 1500 mile long sedimentary belt, of which Prudhoe Bay and Pet 4 are part; parts equaling only about 150 miles. Pet 4 has not had quite the technological attention of Prudhoe Bay, but estimates are that its reserves are at least 10 billion barrels of crude and perhaps 40 billion. The latter figure would double the proven reserves of the United States. Prudhoe Bay itself has been only partially explored and most experts agree that the total recoverable resources there will turn out to be four to ten times the generally accepted 10 billion barrel figure.

Clearly, the trans Alaska pipeline is only the beginning.

Pipe testing. The 48″ steel pipe, manufactured in Japan, was subjected to rigid specifications testing in the factory. Pipe was ordered from Japan in 1969, with the expectation of immediate federal permits, for delivery by the end of 1971. This timetable could not be met by interested U.S. manufacturers, none of whom submitted bids.

Below: Valdez. The year-around population of this beautiful town was, in 1973, 1100. At the peak of construction activities the population will reach approximately 4,000. Most of the construction workers will be housed at the terminal facility located across the bay from the town. *Right:* Valdez pipe yard. Located just outside the town of Valdez, pipe has been stored here since 1971. Nearly all the southern half of the pipeline was coated and stacked here during the four year waiting period.

Left: Alyeska developed new techniques for welding by machine and by hand in cold weather. A welder-manned machine known as "Snoopy" is used to x-ray welds from inside the pipe. Snoopy can carry a man in an air-conditioned atmosphere and pull a trailer behind it. Technical papers presented by Alyeska engineers have been significant contributions to pipe-line technology. *Below:* Surfcoating: A special coating developed by 3M Company was applied to the pipe at a cost of $25 million. This epoxy coating protects the pipe against corrosion. The coating was done while the pipe was in storage as a matter of convenience. It was easier to do the job there than in the field.

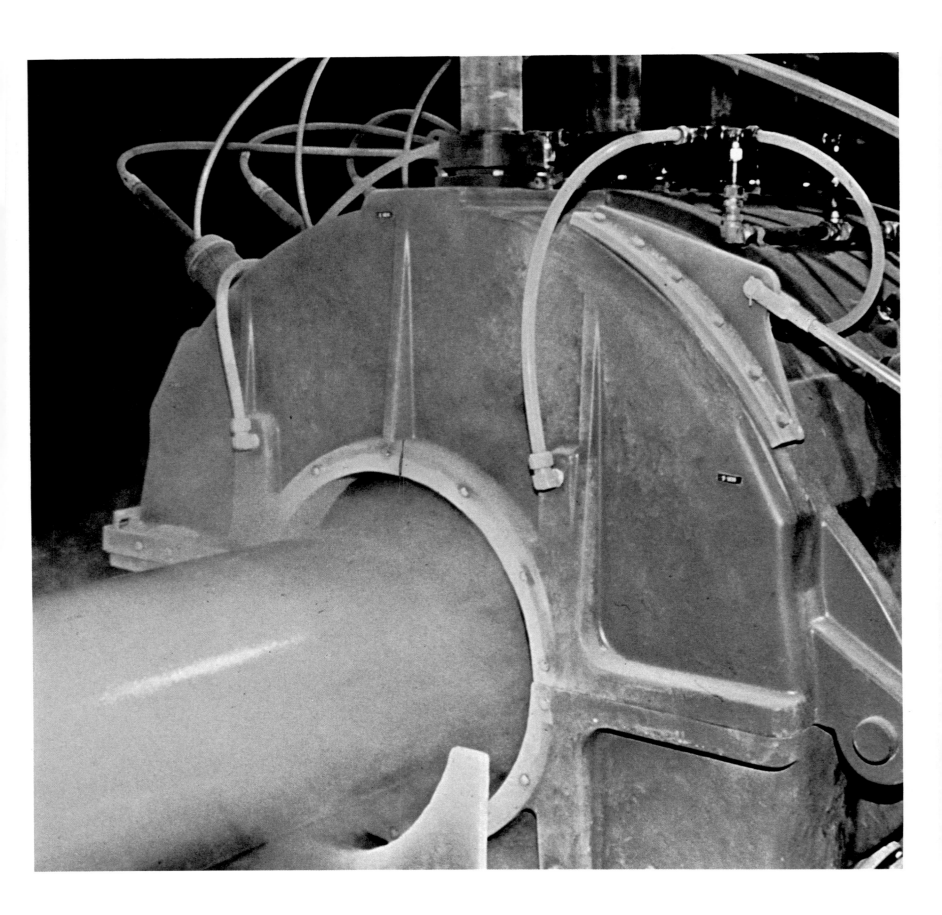

Below: An Alyeska specialist works on computer programming for maintaining accounting continuity between Alyeska and the two management contractors, Bechtel and Fluor. Additional computer services requirements were met by outside contractors with aerospace experience. *Right:* At the beginning of construction, engineering for the pipeline system was approximately 88% complete. Different from most pipeline projects which are largely engineered in work, government requirements and the unique character of the Alaskan environment dictated that nearly all engineering be done in advance.

Engineered to "aerospace redundancy", designers expended more than 1500 man years studying, testing, and designing environmentally acceptable methods of construction. Federal review of the project cost more than $9 million and resulted in a nine volume environmental impact statement, the largest ever filed.

Construction Modes

Conventional Burial

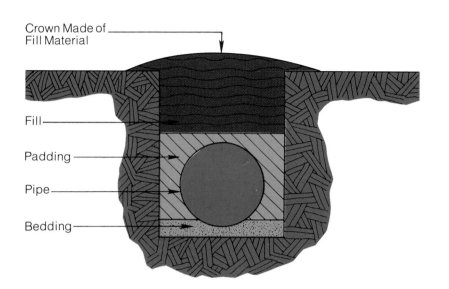

Crown Made of Fill Material

Fill

Padding

Pipe

Bedding

Special Buried

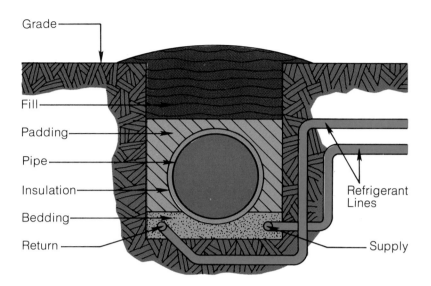

Grade

Fill

Padding

Pipe

Insulation

Bedding

Return

Refrigerant Lines

Supply

Conventional Elevated

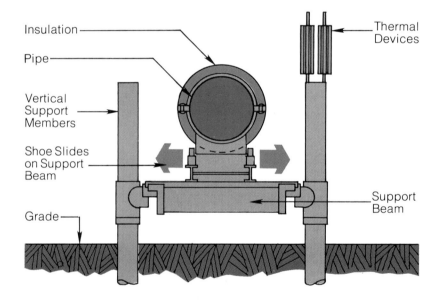

Insulation

Pipe

Vertical Support Members

Shoe Slides on Support Beam

Grade

Thermal Devices

Support Beam

Anchor Support

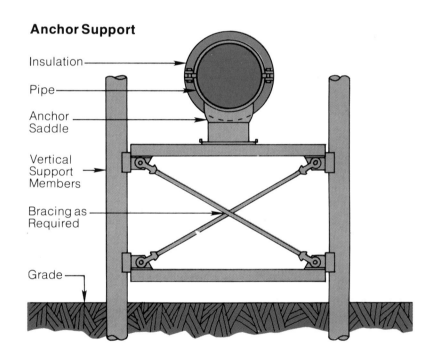

Insulation

Pipe

Anchor Saddle

Vertical Support Members

Bracing as Required

Grade

Typical Zigzag Configuration

Support Spacing 50' to 70'

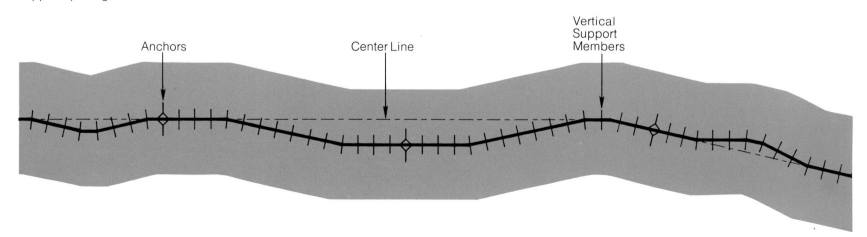

Anchors

Center Line

Vertical Support Members

Port Valdez

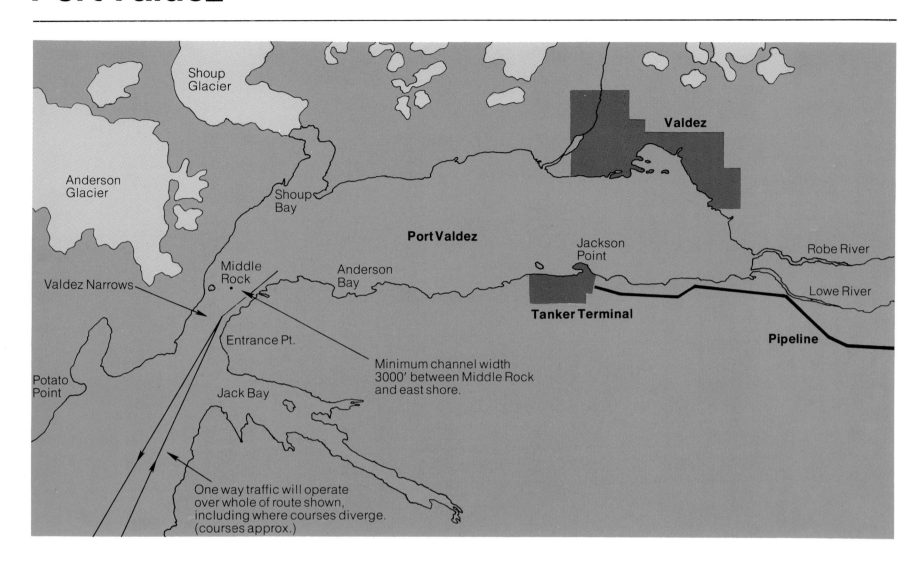

Shoup Glacier

Anderson Glacier

Shoup Bay

Valdez

Port Valdez

Jackson Point

Robe River

Valdez Narrows

Middle Rock

Anderson Bay

Lowe River

Tanker Terminal

Entrance Pt.

Potato Point

Minimum channel width 3000' between Middle Rock and east shore.

Pipeline

Jack Bay

One way traffic will operate over whole of route shown, including where courses diverge. (courses approx.)

Prince William Sound

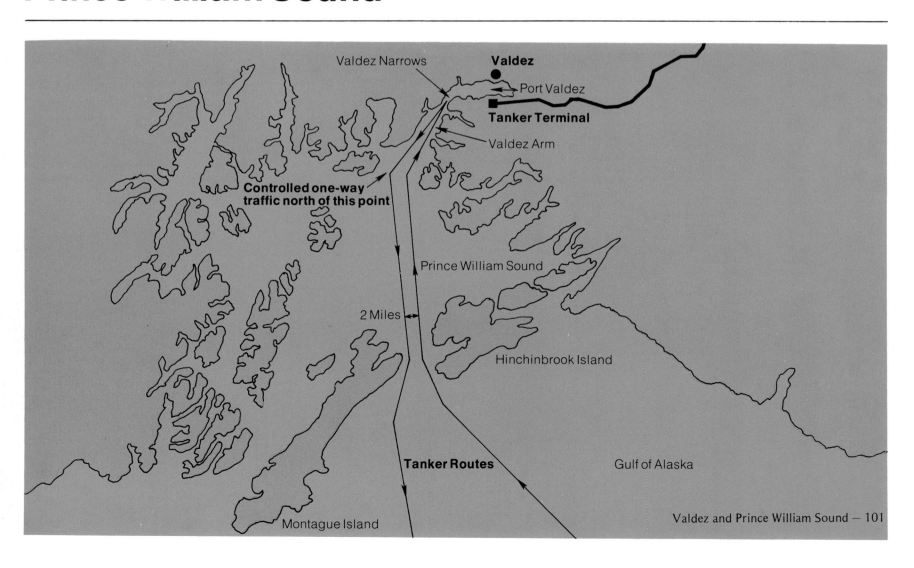

Valdez Narrows

Valdez

Port Valdez

Tanker Terminal

Valdez Arm

Controlled one-way traffic north of this point

Prince William Sound

2 Miles

Hinchinbrook Island

Tanker Routes

Gulf of Alaska

Montague Island

The Earth Resources Technology Satellite, launched by NASA is a spacecraft designed specifically for monitoring the natural resources required by man. From its outpost 568 statute miles above planet earth, the "butterfly" shaped observatory takes electronic "EKGs" of earth's health each day.

Every day an area larger than 2.5 million square miles is photographed by the satellite. It takes the spacecraft 18 days to photograph the entire earth. The imagery is providing the most comprehensive inventory of the earth's natural resources ever taken.

The ERTS program is playing an extremely vital role in the planning and development of Alaska through providing continual monitoring of the vast and varied arctic environment.

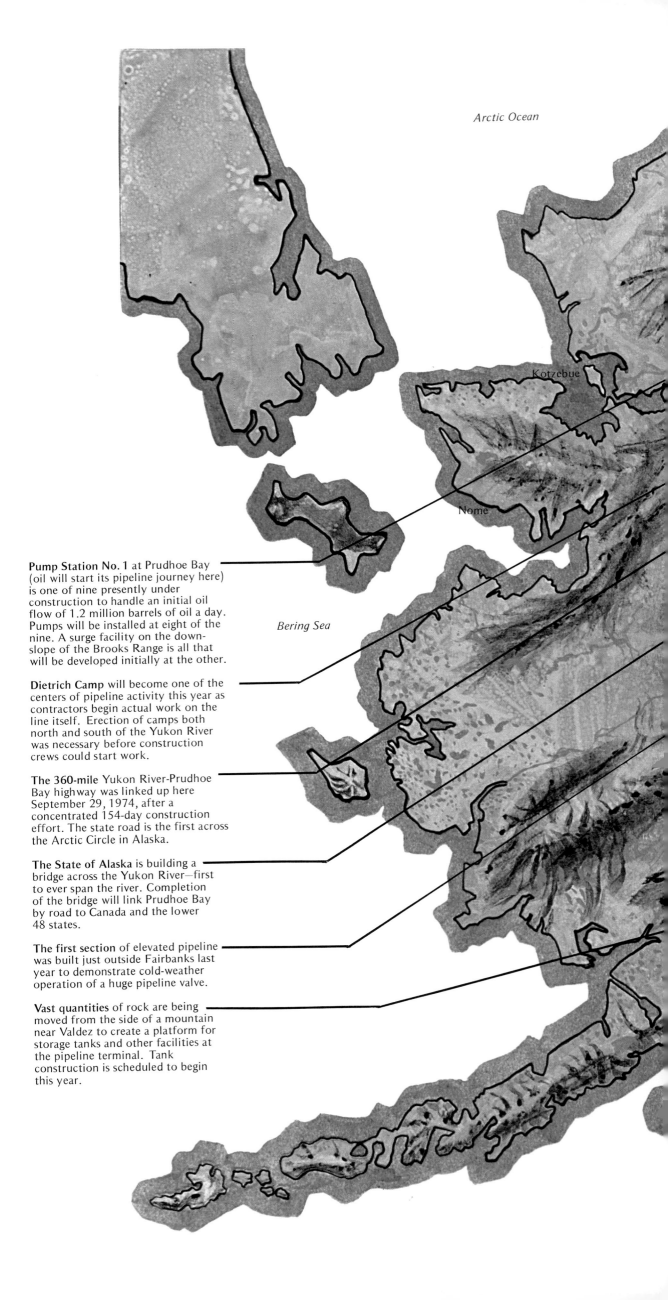

Arctic Ocean

Kotzebue

Nome

Bering Sea

Pump Station No. 1 at Prudhoe Bay (oil will start its pipeline journey here) is one of nine presently under construction to handle an initial oil flow of 1.2 million barrels of oil a day. Pumps will be installed at eight of the nine. A surge facility on the down-slope of the Brooks Range is all that will be developed initially at the other.

Dietrich Camp will become one of the centers of pipeline activity this year as contractors begin actual work on the line itself. Erection of camps both north and south of the Yukon River was necessary before construction crews could start work.

The 360-mile Yukon River-Prudhoe Bay highway was linked up here September 29, 1974, after a concentrated 154-day construction effort. The state road is the first across the Arctic Circle in Alaska.

The State of Alaska is building a bridge across the Yukon River—first to ever span the river. Completion of the bridge will link Prudhoe Bay by road to Canada and the lower 48 states.

The first section of elevated pipeline was built just outside Fairbanks last year to demonstrate cold-weather operation of a huge pipeline valve.

Vast quantities of rock are being moved from the side of a mountain near Valdez to create a platform for storage tanks and other facilities at the pipeline terminal. Tank construction is scheduled to begin this year.

Barrow

Prudhoe Bay Oil Field

North Slope

Brooks Range

Atigun Pass

Yukon Crossing

Yukon River

Fairbanks

Denali Fault

Isabel Pass

Mt. McKinley

Anchorage

Valdez

Thompson Pass

Valdez Terminal

Chugach Mountains

CANADA

Gulf of Alaska

Juneau

Alaska is a land of superlatives! In addition to being the largest state in the nation (586,412 square miles) it has 33,904 miles of saltwater coastline; 3 million lakes of more than 20 acres; 10,000 rivers and streams; four time zones, and the highest mountain peak in North America--Mt. McKinley, 20,320 feet high.

Below: Ice road construction. A bulldozer packs snow and ice to prepare a surface for truck and equipment traffic. The ice-road provided a hard surface for moving supplies and equipment without significantly disturbing the underlying fragile tundra. *Right:* During the "Winter Haul" nearly one million gallons of diesel fuel were transported to the construction camps. Approximately 500,000 gallons were flown in by aircraft; the rest was moved over the ice road.

Left: During the 83 day winter haul more than 33,000 tons of equipment and material were delivered to construction camps north of the Yukon River. Supplies included fuel, buildings, replacement parts, bridge materials and culverts, 716 pieces of construction equipment and about 2,200 tons of camp materials and supplies. *Below:* The Bell Aerospace Hovercraft was leased and delivered to the Yukon, however it was never put into use as the river froze and an ice bridge was built for trucks to drive across. The cable drawn ACT is about five times larger than the Hovercraft.

It has been said that the pipeline could not have been built without "Hercs". The Hercules aircraft, flown by Alaska International Air has been the primary method of transportation to remote sites north of the Yukon. Its tremendous payload and reliability, coupled with short takeoff and landing abilities, have made it the ideal airplane for North Slope oil development.

The main link in the supply chain to the project is maritime service. From the West Coast and as far as Japan, tow boats and container ships use major ports of Alaska for delivering everything from nuts and bolts and small hand tools, to complete buildings, trucks and 80 ton cranes. The 800 miles of 48 inch pipe was delivered on barges from Japan. Maritime transportation volume to Alaska has increased over 400% since pipeline staging began in 1969. Nearly 90% of all maritime cargo bound for Alaska originates in Washington Ports. Anchorage was considered a summer port until 1964. It is now used as a year around port inspite of the, often ice clogged, Cook Inlet.

Page 114

Ice bridge across the Yukon River. This winter daytime photograph shows the 75 foot wide, half mile long ice bridge. It was formed by spraying water from beneath the river's ice onto a narrow strip to a thickness of five feet. To insure adequate strength for supporting the heaviest trucks and equipment, spraying had to be done directly onto the ice after first removing snow from the surface. Another requirement was that temperatures be low enough to freeze the water upon contact with the ice, and yet high enough to prevent mid-air freezing. The ice was reinforced with logs and steel screens.

Page 115

Yukon River bridge. The bridge, being built by the State of Alaska, will be the first to cross the Yukon River and is in itself a major construction project. The bridge pilings must withstand the force of ice breaking up in the river and expansion factors of extreme cold. Nearly half-a-mile long, it will meet state secondary-highway specifications and be structurally capable of year-around use. Both sides of the bridge will be fitted with pipe hangers, providing for the pipeline and perhaps a future gas or crude oil line to cross the Yukon.

Below: The long wait. These trucks, part of the equipment shipped to Alaska in 1971, sat idle for more than three years awaiting construction permits. *Right:* Anaktuvuk Pass, elevation 2,300 feet, more than 100 miles north of the Arctic Circle. The winter haul road traversed this pass during the early mobilization phase of the pipeline project. The tiny village here exists without benefit of electricity or telephones. Food cache, built on stilts, protects food supply from animals. Even during the cold winter clothing is hung outside to dry.

Photographer Bill Gasaway

Five-Mile Camp. Summer and winter views of the camp, located approximately five miles north of the Yukon River. Although well below the Arctic Circle, winter temperatures here often reach 40° below zero. Summers are warm and bring temperatures of 90° and above. With the warm weather comes another problem. Alaska, a land of superlatives, claims the largest mosquitos of the North American Continent. "5-Mile" is one of 30 camps along the 800 mile pipeline route.

Left: Camp Airstrip. Alyeska built 17 airstrips for the project. Five are permanent all-weather fields and 12 will be closed after construction is finished. "Closed" means either dedicated to other use or returned to pre-construction states. *Right:* Camp food and recreation, two of the most important success ingredients for the project.

Below: Communications. Temporary microwave system provides the first north-south communications system in Alaska. It includes a mobile radio system, high frequency single sideband radios and aviation radios. The final system to these remote areas will include 41 microwave stations between Prudhoe Bay and Valdez.

Below: Earth movers. In less rocky portions of the 360 mile road, bulldozers, scrapers and dump trucks were the major participants. Working around the clock, the crews moved over 31 million cubic yards of gravel and another million cubic yards of rock. *Right:* Dietrich Pass.

Below: Diesel fuel is delivered by helicopter to remote drilling at Dietrich Pass in the Brooks Range. *Right:* In the rocky areas, blasting rough-hews the road. Here, pneumatic drills work along straight lines to prepare the holes into which dynamite will be packed.

Road Construction begins in the high passes. Air-lifted by helicopter to otherwise inaccessible sites, these drills perform the first step in carving away the rock.

Rock crushing. To avoid damaging stream beds and alluvial fans, nearly 13 percent more gravel had to be hauled almost twice as far as expected in the road construction.

The first U.S. road to cross the Arctic Circle was completed in one season and three million man-hours. Four contractors worked on eight segments, moving both north and south. Sixty airplanes and helicopters hauled 160,000 tons of materials and supplies and nine million gallons of fuel. They flew more than 127,000 flights, about 700 a day.

Below: Equipment Maintenance. Arctic and sub arctic cold create many special problems in maintaining equipment. Preventive maintenance programs are a must and include state-of-the-art methods. *Right:* Oil sample analysis. Here the oil being analyzed is not directly from a well but from a diesel engine. Engine oil samples, taken at regular intervals, are spectroscopically analyzed for foreign particles. By determining the quantity of various minerals and metals, scientists can precisely determine wear and breakdown probabilities and schedule equipment repairs before failures occur. This break-through technique, performed in the photograph by NC Machinery staff, saved thousands of hours of "down time" for equipment.

Left: Warming pipe prior to removal of interior protective coating. *Below* are three basic concepts for preheating pipe for welding. At left is an induction heating system. The other two are tynes of an electrical resistance system. The systems were evaluated by Alyeska at Prudhoe Bay in 1974.

Left: Pipe being loaded onto a truck. This eighty foot section has been welded together from two forty foot pieces. By "double-jointing" the pipe, time and field labor are saved. *Below:* A forty foot section of pipe being loaded onto a trailer. This section has been coated with concrete — used for stream crossings. Concrete weights the pipe down. All the pipe sections must be brought into place as trenching is completed. The construction of the road in 1974 was therefore a prerequisite to the pipeline construction.

A 150 foot section of pipe was erected near Fairbanks to demonstrate valve operation and construction techniques. The above-ground mode uses unique platforms which allow the pipe to move side to side during thermal expansions and contractions. The valve shown here is 28 feet high.

Tonsina River
Thursday, March 27, 1975
2:15 p.m.

Less than one year after work began on the trans
Alaska pipeline, the first section of 48-inch pipe was
lowered beneath the Tonsina River flood-plain approximately 75 miles north of Valdez.

Prior to installation, the 1900 feet of pipe was welded
together into three sections, the longest 800 feet in
length. Approximately 1600 feet was wrapped with
half-inch thick rock shield. The remaining 300 feet
laid below the active river channel was coated with
nine inches of concrete. The pipe was laid into a
ditch 1900 feet in length, and ranging in depth from
15 to 18 feet.

The Tonsina River was the first of 34 major river
crossings to be accomplished before the 798-mile
pipeline is completed.

*Scribe Publishing Corporation
wishes to acknowledge the following
contributors whose cooperation
made this book possible:*

*Alyeska Pipeline Service Company
ARCO Pipe Line Company
Alaska Airlines
Alaska Construction & Oil
Alaska Native Arts and Crafts Co-op
BP Pipelines Inc.
Barbara Sesnon
Carole Lynn Provorse
Jay Rockey Public Relations, Inc.
Kelli Allen
National Aeronautics and Space Administration
NC Machinery Company
Rainier National Bank
Sea-Land Services, Inc.
University of Alaska*